THE
LOYAL NORTH LANCASHIRE
REGIMENT

THE LOYAL NORTH LANCASHIRE REGIMENT

By
COLONEL H. C. WYLLY, C.B.

VOL. I
1741—1914

The Naval & Military Press Ltd

Published by

The Naval & Military Press Ltd
Unit 10 Ridgewood Industrial Park,
Uckfield, East Sussex,
TN22 5QE England

Tel: +44 (0) 1825 749494
Fax: +44 (0) 1825 765701

www.naval-military-press.com
www.military-genealogy.com
www.militarymaproom.com

In reprinting in facsimile from the original, any imperfections are inevitably reproduced and the quality may fall short of modern type and cartographic standards.

PREFACE

THE initiative in the preparation of the present History was taken by my predecessor, Lieut.-General Sir Gerald F. Ellison, K.C.B., K.C.M.G., and in his efforts he was ably seconded by Colonel (now Brigadier) W. P. H. Hill, C.M.G., D.S.O., then Commanding the 2nd Battalion.

The history of a Regiment of the British Army has its roots buried deep in the past. As the story grows the roots spread, and the several Battalions and Companies, as well as individuals, are found, in various places and countries, all playing separately their different parts which go to make up the whole. As a result the records and other sources of information are widely scattered, they are often difficult of access and vary considerably in value. The collection of the available material, its sifting and arrangement, and eventual preparation for publication, is consequently an undertaking which calls for a great deal of work and skill.

The Regiment is fortunate in that General Ellison was able to secure for the task the services of Colonel H. C. Wylly, C.B. Colonel Wylly has freely placed at our disposal the benefit of his knowledge and experience, which are wide in both military and literary matters, and to him, and to his able assistant, Mr. K. R. Wilson, our grateful thanks are due. And none the less on account of the circumstances in which they undertook the work: on the breakdown of a previous arrangement, Colonel Wylly stepped into the breach and began the work afresh. The present History is sufficient testimony to Colonel Wylly's qualifications for the task and our debt to him.

No one will be more ready than Colonel Wylly to acknowledge the assistance he has received from General Ellison. Not only has General Ellison read the History throughout, and advised when necessary in the distribution of draft chapters, but he has himself written the Introduction as well as the chapters dealing with the early history of the Militia and Volunteer Battalions. Brigadier W. P. H. Hill, too, has given most useful help from the beginning, and, it may be added, has been the means, at considerable sacrifice to himself on account of the misfortune already mentioned, of making possible the completion of the History. Finally, to Colonel R. E. Berkeley our thanks are due for his invaluable assistance in connection with the campaign in East Africa during 1914–1917.

To the Officers I have named, as well as to all others, both serving and retired, who have assisted in the collection and production of the material on which Colonel Wylly has worked, we owe a debt of gratitude; also again to Mr. K. R. Wilson for his ready help and practical advice, and for the excellence of the form in which this History appears.

JOHN B. WELLS,
Brigadier-General,
Colonel of The Regiment.

12th July, 1932.

INTRODUCTION

A REGIMENT is an association of men banded together for a common purpose, and that purpose—the service of King and Country and the protection of fellow-countrymen untrained to arms—is an ennobling one. Every exploit performed by it as a unit of the national forces leaves an indelible impression first on the minds, and afterwards on the spirits, of the officers and men who took part in it. This impression spreads in course of time to other members of the regiment, raising its standard of achievement and duty from within, just as the known facts of its history determine its prestige in the eyes of the world. Of those who have done much, more is expected. So it befalls that, in a regiment with a splendid past, great deeds are taken as a matter of course, for the standard by which deeds are measured is a high one and the records of bravery, endurance and self-sacrifice, set up by men who have made history by their blood and daring are not easily surpassed.

Despite the vast improvement which has taken place in the general conditions of a soldier's life to-day compared with the conditions which his comrades of even fifty years ago endured, it is none the less still true that he who embraces a military career does so at the expense of many of the good things which his fellows in civil life enjoy. A nomadic life, an uncertainty of outlook, the restraints of discipline and the continual submergence of the individual in the unit, together with the burden of responsibility which every officer—both commissioned and non-commissioned—must shoulder, all these things call for a considerable degree of self-sacrifice, even in peace-time. But when the stern ordeal of war comes, and to the minor disadvantages of peace are added physical fatigue, privation, constant exposure to discomfort, danger and even death, then the character of a soldier, as formed by nature and developed by military training, is tested to the utmost.

It is said that war brings out all that is best and all that is worst in a man. If this be true, there is little doubt, at any rate in the War of 1914–1918, when most of the manhood of Britain was flung into the retort by the Great Alchemist, that more good than evil was distilled from the aggregate. The soul of the British Army rose up from the tortured, fire-scourged mass, brighter and nobler than ever before.

And why? Because every man who joined a combatant unit of the

British Army joined a family-clan,—call it what you will,—in effect he joined a body of fellow-men who had a definite standard and a definite family history to live up to, a standard determined by the life-history and traditions of the regiment whose badge he bore. And there is no unit in the Service so devoid of history but that there are some incidents or achievements in its past life which cause those who are associated with it to say to themselves: "This and this have my Regimental forefathers done; when the time comes I must be worthy of them." It is an inspiration, leavening the whole vast family, which is bound to infect the dullest soul; and so the past trumpets to the present and the present, responding to the call, adds to its volume and flings onward to posterity the golden notes of duty and sacrifice, intensified and beautified by the sufferings and the achievements of its own generation. Every act of heroism or devotion, howsoever and whensoever performed and, maybe, unnoticed save by those just around, serves to raise the regimental tone and to embellish its traditions, and casts one more stone on to the monumental cairn from the top of which the Spirit of the Regiment speaks to the last-joined recruit.

The survey of the salient incidents of a glorious past help us dimly to understand the spirit which animated the men who sailed from England on 12th August, 1914; a spirit which impelled them to march on when their bodies were sinking from fatigue, which made them shoot true when their eyes were nigh blind from want of sleep, which induced them to hold together and close their ranks when confused by retreat and disorganized by losses and which enabled them to hold on through the mud and misery of the early days of trench warfare until the belated coming of newly-raised troops brought some slight measure of relief. "Discipline," you will say? Perhaps so, but it was the discipline founded on freely-given loyalty to their officers, their comrades and the traditions of a great regiment, rather than on the slave-driven fear of a harsh military code. The example of the men who endured unto the end for the sake of their Regiment and their Country is not lost; it will ever help to inspire succeeding generations to greater deeds and to lift to a still higher plane that strange, indefinable compound of regimental tradition, pride and idealism for which there is no English word, but which the French call *esprit de corps*.

And the men? What of the men who have passed in an endless stream through the ranks of the various battalions of The Loyal Regiment? Since 1782 the main source of that stream has been in Lancashire. On the return of the 47th Regiment from Canada in 1782, its depleted ranks were filled with men drawn from the County Palatine, and for close on one hundred years it was shown in the Army List as "The Lancashire Regiment." Till 1881 it was in fact the only Line Regiment in the Army of pure Lan-

INTRODUCTION

cashire origin. From Lancashire, too, came the sturdy Militiamen who responded to the Nation's call during the Revolutionary Wars at the end of the eighteenth century, when the Third Battalion, later to be known as the "Duke of Lancaster's Own," came into being; thence again came the Volunteers of the "Sixties" who were the progenitors of the 4th and 5th Battalions; a decade afterwards the 81st Regiment, now the 2nd Battalion, was given Lancashire as its recruiting ground; and lastly in the great conflagration of 1914, North Lancashire poured out its wealth in men and treasure to raise, fill and maintain those splendid Service Battalions which helped to make the Red Rose of Lancaster famous in three continents. Whensoever the Nation may have cried out in her extremity, never has she called to Lancashire in vain—as the graves of Lancashire men testify in hundreds of half-forgotten burial-grounds all the world over.

The sturdy patriotic spirit which has displayed itself in Lancashire in every time of crisis is the link, the invisible, indestructible link, which ever has bound, and ever should continue to bind, The Loyal Regiment to that portion of the County where it is raised. The story of its deeds should find an echo in every household and office and in every mill and workshop from the outskirts of Wigan northwards to the Cumberland border and from Bolton westwards to the sea.

The spirit of the successive generations of a regiment goes to form its soul of which the Colours are the outward and visible sign. In a unit with a long history every stitch in the Colours might be said to represent a life laid down for King and Country and the memory of the fallen is enshrined for ever in the battle-honours emblazoned upon them.

Certain incidents in the life-history of The Loyal Regiment give cause for more than ordinary pride. Two of its exploits were shared with no other regular infantry unit of the British Army and so have led to battle-honours unique to the Colours of the Loyals; others were performed at times when success was vital to the British arms, or when the results of success were particularly far-reaching.

In the first category fall the battle-honours "Defence of Kimberley" amd "Kilimanjaro." Those who remember the "black week" of December, 1899, and can recall the wave of incredulous dismay which swept over the Country as ill-tidings continued to pour in, will best appreciate the importance with which the retention of Ladysmith, Kimberley and Mafeking was regarded by the British public; an importance which suddenly became so great that the life or death of the whole Empire seemed to hang upon it. In Kimberley the only regular infantry present to stiffen the defence of the brave but untrained volunteers was a half battalion of the Loyal North Lancashire Regiment; and the vitality of the defence was increased out of all proportion by the personality of the gallant Kekewich who commanded the Loyals and was its backbone. To those at home it seemed that the Relief of Kimberley was the first flush of dawn after a long night of waiting. Its psychological effect was enormous, and went far to restore the drooping prestige of the British arms.

Fourteen years later there came a time, again under the blazing sun of the African tropics when, for many months, a battalion of the Regiment found itself the sole representative of the British Regular Army in the face of an active and enterprising foe, flushed with initial success. The long struggle to hold British East Africa until reinforcements should come and enable the offensive to be taken, is commemorated in the honour " Kilimanjaro," which stands for a long series of actions during nearly two years of ceaseless strain, at the end of which the Battalion was so worn by fatigue and wasted by disease that it had to be withdrawn from the country to recuperate. The picture which the British public has of the Great War as it was fought in East Africa is one which shows, as its chief episode, General Smuts and his South Africans sweeping through Tanganyika in a mighty drive to round up the elusive von Lettow-Vorbeck. Of the dark months of watching, waiting and misfortune, which went before there is small record. Yet the Loyal Regiment may regard with satisfaction the part which its 2nd Battalion played in sustaining the defence of the Colony in 1914-1915 and part of 1916 ; and the word " Kilimanjaro " will recall a host of forgotten actions, forays and raids in which detachments of the Regiment bore an honourable part.

In the second category there are honours, old and new, which have an epoch-making ring to their names. " Louisburg " and " Quebec " stand in the first place. Romance, pathos and glory surround the latter in a way that is hardly equalled by any other British battle since Agincourt. The romance of a great success snatched from the jaws of failure after months of weary effort ; the picturesqueness of the scene enacted that fair September morning upon the Heights of Abraham ; the pathos of the death of the gallant General Wolfe, the double glory of a tactical victory in the clash of arms and of a strategic success which, in the long run, secured the vast territories of Canada to the British Empire and settled the English-speaking race in possession of the greater part of the North American Continent ; all these are conjured up in a moment before the eye that reads the word " Quebec."

Then again " Maida." From the military point of view a peculiar interest is attached to this battle. Here in Southern Italy the infantry of Napoleon, flushed with many victories and still radiant with the glory of Austerlitz, crossed bayonets for the first time with English infantry and

INTRODUCTION

suffered defeat. It was the forerunner of many a hard battle to be fought and won a few years later by British armies in the neighbouring peninsula of Spain. It gave the first hint that the halo of invincibility which surrounded the Emperor's troops might some day be shattered.

The hardships borne and the fortitude displayed by those present at Corunna will also never be forgotten. The mention of the Peninsular War recalls at once " Tarifa," the memory of which siege is specially dear to the 1st Battalion ; " Vittoria," the battle which freed Spain from the grip of the usurper ; the blood-soaked breach of St. Sebastian ; and the grim struggles in the passes of the Pyrenees and the Battle of the Nive ; in the course of which the southern defences of France crumbled into ruin along with the Empire of Napoleon.

Then comes the campaign in Burma, followed by the war in the Crimea ; Inkerman, the " soldiers' battle," causes a thrill of pride since it brought the Regiment its first Victoria Cross. And so, after Afghanistan and South Africa, we come to the epic struggle of 1914–1918, beside which the older wars seem dwarfed, and infinitely far away.

" Mons," " Marne " and " Aisne " recall those early days of the Great War, when the tide of German invasion swept all before it until it was rolled back and checked ; " Ypres," of deathless memory, where during four years eleven out of the thirteen battalions of the Regiment present in France bore honourable part ; " The Somme," in which gigantic, bitter struggle most battalions participated ; " The Lys " with its days of crisis and anxiety ; the " Hindenburg Line " with its onward sweep to victory ; all these are epics written in blood on the soil of France and Flanders. Elsewhere in the three continents that were shrouded in the smoke of war, other battalions added to the laurels of the Regiment. The 6th (Service) Battalion gave " Suvla " to the Colours, and the same battalion is responsible for " Baghdad " ; the 12th (T.) gave " Gaza " ; while the 2nd added " Kilimanjaro," of which mention has been made. Where all battalions contributed to the honour of the Regiment with their blood and suffering, how can any, in fairness, be singled out ? If a memorial of them is wanted, look at the Colours ; look also at the list of battle-honours and learn the names of the battalions which won those precious honours for North Lancashire.

One glorious action there is, commemorated by the honour " Baghdad," which deserves a special mention. The crossing of the Diyala River in the course of the operations leading to the capture of Baghdad was an achievement of extraordinary gallantry ; it was a crucial action, securing a key position which made the capture of the city possible, and it led directly to the fall of Baghdad at a time when British prestige most needed the enhancement it duly received when the rumour flew swiftly through the bazaars of the East that the City of the Caliphs had fallen to the conquering army of Sir Stanley Maude. That one action had, in its ultimate repercussions, a far-reaching effect on the history of the war.

In the course of the Great War 357 Officers and 7,232 Other Ranks laid down their lives. Their names are enshrined in memorials far and near, and are written in the Book of Remembrance; their battlefields are inscribed on the Colours and in that longer list of battle-honours awarded; and to keep their memory green an attempt has been made in the following pages briefly to relate what they and their surviving comrades did and suffered for the sake of their King and Country, and for the honour of The Loyal Regiment.

May the rising generation, to whom the Great War is now but an episode in English history, be so taught to study the exploits of its forbears with pride and thankfulness that the achievements of The Loyal Regiment may remain for all time, not a mere tradition, but a living reality!

GERALD F. ELLISON,
Lieut.-General.

CONTENTS

THE 47TH REGIMENT

CHAPTER I

1741–1745

The British Army, 1741. The Raising of the Regiment. Colonel J. Mordaunt. The first Officers. Colonel P. Lascelles assumes command. The Rebellion of 1745. The Battle of Prestonpans. Edinburgh Castle 1

CHAPTER II

1746–1759

The Regiment sails from Ireland for Nova Scotia. War declared against France, 1756. Louisburg, 1758. The Battle of Quebec, 1759. Death of General Wolfe. Lieut.-Colonel J. Hale returns home with the despatches 13

CHAPTER III

1759–1776

In garrison at Quebec. St. Foy. Advance on Montreal. Canada becomes a British possession. Ireland. The War of American Independence. The Regiment at Boston. Battle of Bunker's Hill, 1775. Halifax. Ordered to Quebec 36

CHAPTER IV

1776–1781

The War of American Independence. Operations for the recovery of Montreal. Ticonderoga Fort. Lake Champlain. The advance to Skenesborough. The action at Stillwater. Surrender of General Burgoyne at Saratoga. Prisoners-of-war 52

CONTENTS

CHAPTER V
1781–1807

The Territorial system initiated. The "Lancashire" Regiment. Ireland. Nova Scotia. The Additional Forces Act. Cape of Good Hope. Storming of Monte Video. The attack on Buenos Ayres. General Whitelocke. India 66

CHAPTER VI
1806–1812

The 2nd Battalion: Ireland. Gibraltar. The War in the Peninsula. Battle of Barrosa. Defence of Tarifa. Siege of Cadiz. Truxillo. Colonel Skerrett. Wellington's plan of operations 81

CHAPTER VII
1813–1816

The 2nd Battalion: The Battle of Vittoria. St. Sebastian. Passage of the River Bidassoa. The Nivelle. The Battle of The Nive. Battle-honours awarded. Disbandment of the Battalion 95

CHAPTER VIII
1807–1830

India. Expeditions to the Persian Gulf. The Pindari War. The War in Burma, 1825–1826. Return home 117

CHAPTER IX
1830–1856

Ireland. Gibraltar. Malta. West Indies. The Battalion inspected by the Emperor of Russia, at Windsor. Ireland. Corfu. Malta. The Crimean War. Varna. The Landing in Kalamita Bay. The Battle of The Alma. The Battle of Inkerman. Colonel W. O'G. Haly. Pte. J. McDermond awarded the Victoria Cross. Hardships of Winter. Siege of Sebastopol. Peace signed. Malta 136

CONTENTS

CHAPTER X
1856–1881

Malta. Gibraltar. Home service. Aldershot. Colours presented. Ireland. Canada. West Indies. Ireland. Brigade Depots and Linked Battalions. Aldershot. Jersey. Ireland. Introduction of the Territorial system. The 1st Battalion, The Loyal North Lancashire Regiment 160

THE 81ST REGIMENT

CHAPTER XI
1793–1803

Previous regiments numbered " 81." The Raising of the Regiment : Major-General Albemarle Bertie. The first Officers. The West Indies. Guernsey. The Cape of Good Hope. Duelling 172

CHAPTER XII
1803–1812

Jersey. The Additional Forces Act. Malta. Sicily. The Battle of Maida : the gold medal. Colonel J. Kempt. Milazzo. Island of Ischia. Arrival in Eastern Spain 187

CHAPTER XIII
1812–1817

Operations in Eastern Spain : Alicante. Castle of Denia. Tarragona. Arrival at Biarritz. Ordered to Canada. The escape of Napoleon from Elba. Landed at Ghent. Valenciennes. Ireland . . . 203

CHAPTER XIV
1804–1809

The 2nd Battalion : Ireland. The Corunna Campaign. Death of Sir John Moore. Battle-honours awarded 217

CONTENTS

CHAPTER XV
1809–1816

The 2nd Battalion: The Walcheren Expedition. Jersey. Service in the Netherlands. Guard duty at Brussels. The Battle of Waterloo. Neuilly and Montmartre. Disbandment of the Battalion . . 233

CHAPTER XVI
1817–1856

Ireland. Nova Scotia. Colours presented. Bermudas. Ireland. Gibraltar. West Indies. Colours presented. Canada. Jersey. Ireland. First Tour of Indian service. Voyage of the "Alfred." Colours presented 245

CHAPTER XVII
1857–1858

The Indian Mutiny. Mutineers disarmed at Mian Mir. Colonel H. Renny. Amritsar and Lahore. The North-West Frontier. Operations against the Yuzafzais 258

CHAPTER XVIII
1859–1881

India. Voyage of the "Sultana." Mauritius. Aldershot. Ireland. Gibraltar. India. Operations against the Jowaki Afridis. The Second Afghan War. The Attack on Ali Masjid. Introduction of the Territorial system. The 2nd Battalion, The Loyal North Lancashire Regiment 271

THE 3RD ROYAL LANCASHIRE MILITIA

CHAPTER XIX
1797–1881

The Raising of the Regiment. The first Officers. Recruiting. Embodiments. Service in Ireland. "The Prince Regent's Own." "The Duke of Lancaster's Own." Colours presented. Colonel Lord Winmarleigh. The Crimean War, service at Gibraltar; the honour "Mediterranean." Affiliation. Two Battalions. Colours presented. Introduction of the Territorial system. The 3rd and 4th (Militia) Battalions, The Loyal North Lancashire Regiment . . . 286

CONTENTS

THE LOYAL NORTH LANCASHIRE REGIMENT
THE 1ST BATTALION

CHAPTER XX

1881–1899

Ireland. Aldershot. Gibraltar. India. The Zhob Valley. A fatal railway accident. Ceylon. South Africa. Colonel R. G. Kekewich. Formation of the Mounted Infantry Company. Political situation. Outbreak of the South African War 295

CHAPTER XXI

1899–1900

The South African War: The Defence of Kimberley. The Battles of Belmont, Graspan and Magersfontein. Kimberley relieved. The Battalion re-united 307

CHAPTER XXII

1900

The South African War: Operations in the Western Transvaal. The Volunteer Service Companies. The advance from Bloemfontein to Pretoria. Zeerust, Lichtenburg, Mafeking and Ventersdorp 324

CHAPTER XXIII

1901–1902

The South African War: Operations in the Western Transvaal. Zeerust, Mafeking, Klerksdorp, Lichtenburg, Ventersdorp. Blockhouses. Vryburg. The disaster at Tweebosch. The Volunteer Service Companies. The Mounted Infantry Company. Peace signed. Return to England 337

CHAPTER XXIV

1902–1914

Home service. The South African War Memorial unveiled. Ireland. Presentation from the Citizens of Kimberley. Tidworth. An experimental march. Strike duty. Aldershot. Colours presented. Outbreak of the Great War. Mobilization ordered 356

The 2nd Battalion

CHAPTER XXV

1881–1914

India. Home service. Jersey. Ireland. Aldershot. Malta. Outbreak of the War in South Africa. The Provisional Battalion at Shorncliffe. The Mounted Infantry School, at Malta, formed. The Mounted Infantry Company, 2nd Battalion, in South Africa, 1900–1902. Cyprus and Crete. Gibraltar. South Africa, 1904–1907. Mauritius. Colours presented: India. Outbreak of the Great War. Mobilization ordered . 366

The 3rd Battalion

CHAPTER XXVI

1881–1914

The Militia: Two Battalions. Amalgamation of Battalions, 1896. The Centenary celebrations. Field-Marshal Lord Roberts appointed honorary colonel. The South African War. Embodiment. Garrison duty at Malta. Embarkation for, and service in, South Africa. Honours awarded. The Special Reserve 376

The 4th Battalion

CHAPTER XXVII

1746–1815, 1859–1914

The Preston Volunteers. The Volunteer Movement, 1859. The 11th Lancashire R.V.C., raised. The 1st Volunteer Battalion, Loyal North Lancashire Regiment, 1883. The Volunteer Service Companies in South Africa, 1900–1902. Battle-honour awarded. The Territorial Force, 1908. The 4th Battalion. The Earl of Derby gazetted honorary colonel to both Territorial Battalions of the Regiment. Outbreak of the Great War 384

THE 5TH BATTALION

CHAPTER XXVIII

1794–1816, 1859–1914

The Bolton Volunteers. The Volunteer Movement, 1859. The 27th Lancashire R.V.C., raised. Uniform and equipment. The 14th Lancashire R.V.C., 1880. The 2nd Volunteer Battalion, Loyal North Lancashire Regiment, 1883. The Volunteer Service Companies in South Africa, 1900–1902. Battle-honour awarded. The Territorial Force, 1908. The 5th Battalion. Outbreak of the Great War . 393

INDEX 401

ILLUSTRATIONS

	TO FACE PAGE
LOUISBURG, 1758	12
QUEBEC—13TH SEPTEMBER, 1759	30
COLONEL J. HALE	34
MONTE VIDEO—3RD FEBRUARY, 1807	72
VITTORIA—21ST JUNE, 1813	100
ST. SEBASTIAN, 1813	106
BURMA, STORMING A STOCKADE—1825	130
THE COLOURS OF THE 47TH REGIMENT—1832–1858	136
INKERMAN—5TH NOVEMBER, 1854	150
THE CAMP OF THE 2ND DIVISION, CRIMEA—1855	154
LIEUT.-COLONEL R. T. FARREN	160
MAJOR-GENERAL ALBEMARLE BERTIE	174
MAIDA—4TH JULY, 1806	196
THE MAIDA TORTOISE	200
CHANGING QUARTERS—1807	216
CORUNNA—16TH JANUARY, 1809	230
LIEUT.-GENERAL SIR JAMES KEMPT, G.C.B., G.C.H.	246
THE COLOURS OF THE 81ST REGIMENT, 1854–1903	256
ALI MASJID—21ST NOVEMBER, 1878	278
KIMBERLEY—7TH OCTOBER, 1899	308
MAJOR-GENERAL R. G. KEKEWICH, C.B.	312
A BLOCKHOUSE—1901	342
MOUNTED INFANTRY—1902	354
FIELD-MARSHAL EARL ROBERTS, V.C., K.G., K.P., G.C.B., O.M., G.C.S.I., G.C.I.E., V.D.	376
THE EARL OF DERBY, K.G., G.C.B., G.C.V.O., T.D.	392

MAPS

	PAGE
THE WESTERN AND EASTERN HEMISPHERES	1
PRESTONPANS—21ST SEPTEMBER, 1745	9
THE LANDING AT LOUISBURG—8TH JUNE, 1758	19
LOUISBURG—JUNE, 1758	21
QUEBEC AND THE RIVER ST. LAWRENCE—1759	29
THE BATTLE OF QUEBEC—13TH SEPTEMBER, 1759	33
THE BATTLE OF BUNKER'S HILL—17TH JUNE, 1775	45
THE WAR OF AMERICAN INDEPENDENCE—1776–1777	55
THE ATTACK ON BUENOS AYRES—5TH JULY, 1807	77
THE PENINSULAR WAR:—	
TARIFA—1811	89
THE BATTLE OF VITTORIA—21ST JUNE, 1813	99
ST. SEBASTIAN—1813	105
THE PENINSULAR WAR—1813–1814	109
THE BATTLE OF THE NIVE—10TH DECEMBER, 1813	113
THE PERSIAN GULF—1809	119
BURMA, 1825–1826	129
THE CRIMEAN WAR:—	
THE CRIMEA—1854–1856	143
THE BATTLE OF THE ALMA—20TH SEPTEMBER, 1854	145
THE BATTLE OF INKERMAN—5TH NOVEMBER, 1854	153
SEBASTOPOL—1854–1855	157
THE BATTLE OF MAIDA—4TH JULY, 1806	195
THE WALCHEREN EXPEDITION—1809	237
ALI MASJID—21ST NOVEMBER, 1878	281
THE SOUTH AFRICAN WAR:—	
KIMBERLEY—1899	311
SOUTH AFRICA—1899–1902	331

THE BATTLE HONOURS

"Louisburg," "Quebec, 1759,"

"Maida," "Corunna," "Tarifa,"

"Vittoria," "St. Sebastian," "Nive,"

"Peninsula," "Ava,"

"Alma," "Inkerman," "Sevastopol,"

"Ali Masjid," "Afghanistan, 1878–79,"

"Defence of Kimberley," "South Africa, 1899–1902."

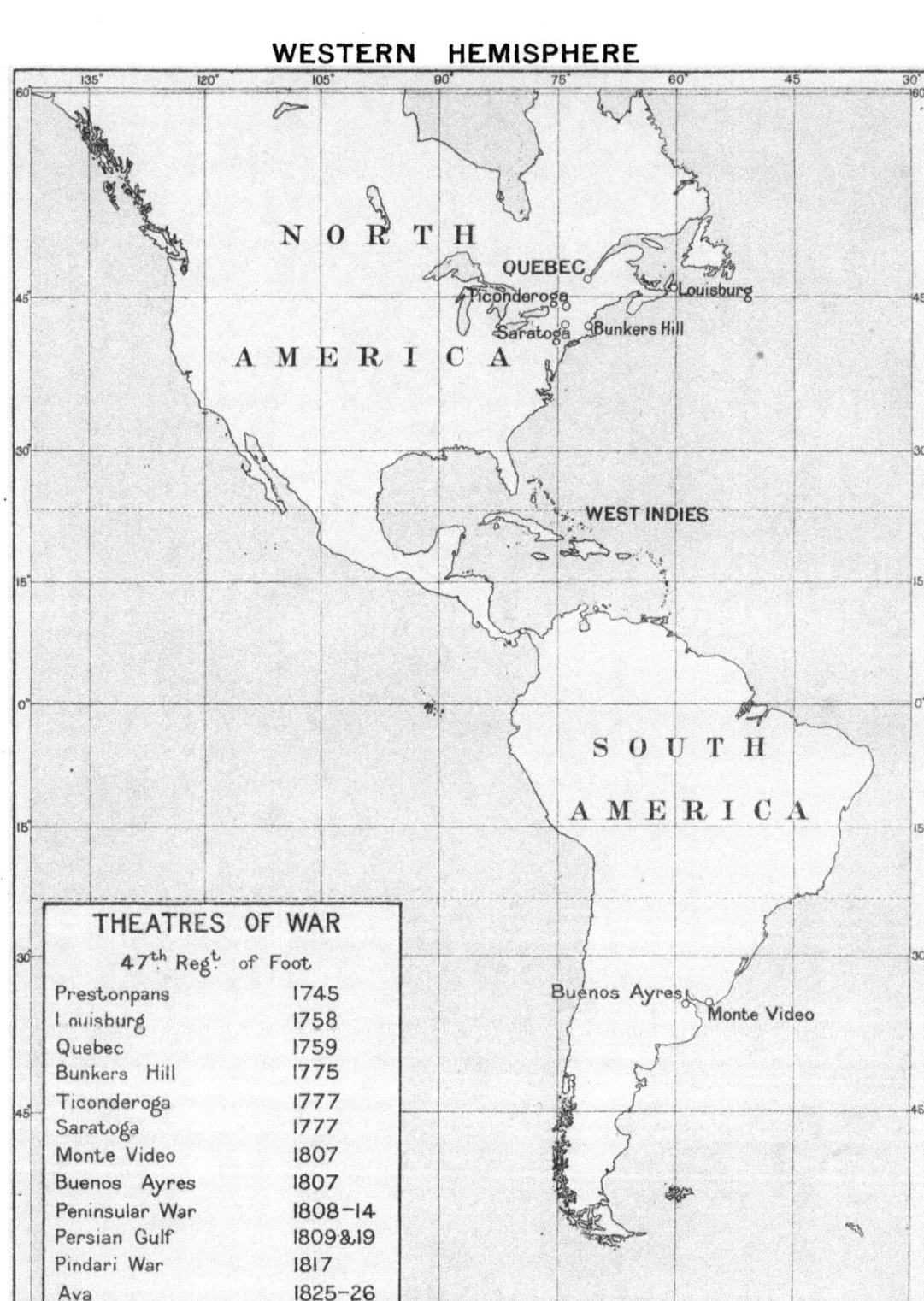

3rd Royal Lancashire Militia	Mediterranean	1855
3rd Loyal North Lanc. Rgt (Militia)	Mediterranean	1900-01
	South Africa	1901-02

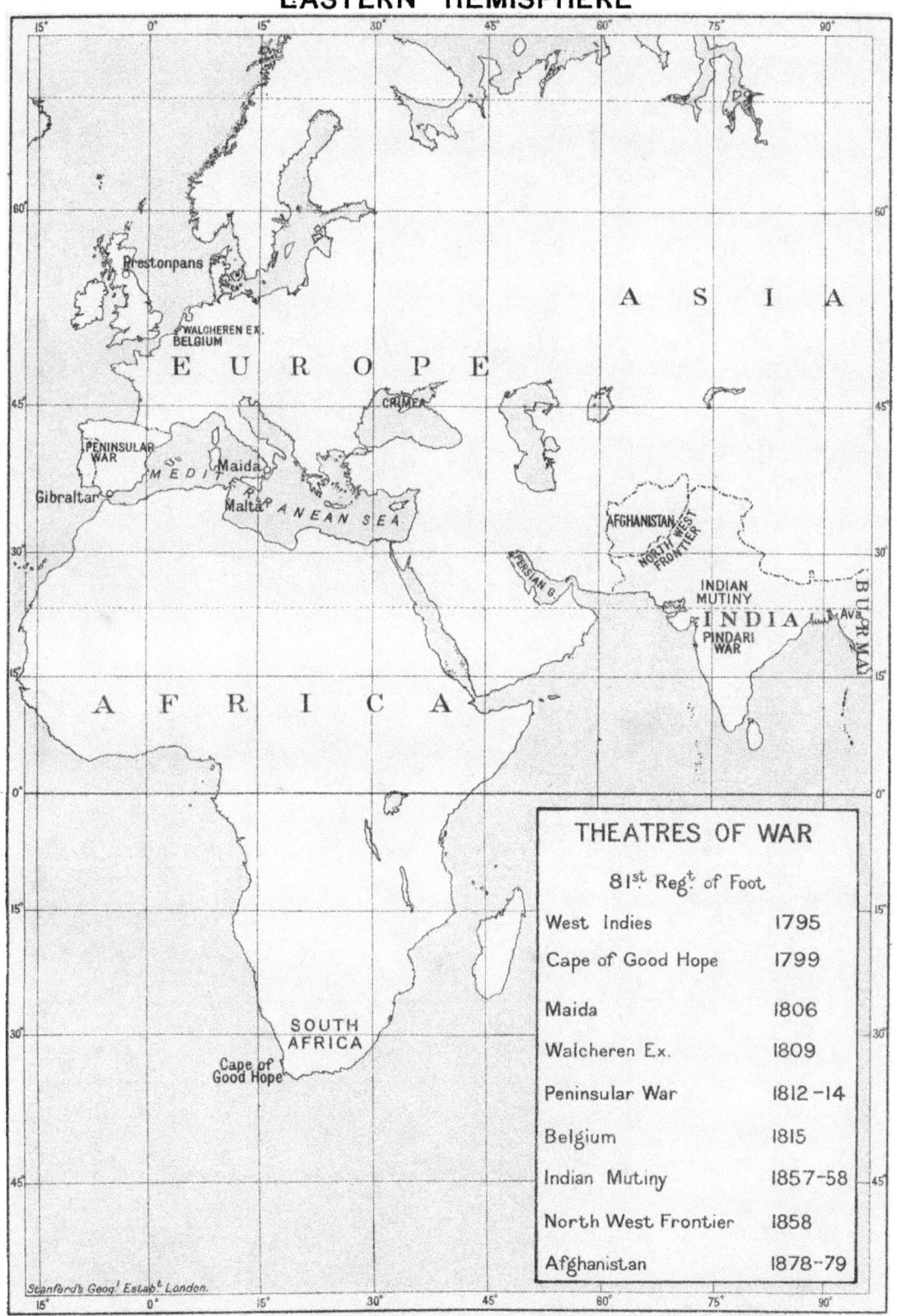

THE LOYAL NORTH LANCASHIRE REGIMENT

THE 47TH REGIMENT OF FOOT

CHAPTER I

1741–1745

THE RAISING OF THE 47TH REGIMENT, 1741
THE REBELLION OF 1745

WHEN, in the year 1739, war was declared by Great Britain against Spain, the British Army was very weak in numbers, the establishment being then fixed at no more than 18,000 men, while the Infantry battalions of the Line then in existence numbered forty-two only. The military operations, which it was now decided to enter upon, necessitated a very considerable increase in the strength of the Army, and in November, 1739, another infantry battalion and six regiments of Marines were formed, while rather more than a year later—in December, 1740—four more regiments of Marines were raised. To these numbers certain additions were hurriedly made as time went on, until by the end of 1741 the Army contained forty-three Infantry Regiments, called in each case by the name of the Colonel, but ranking in order of precedence from 1 to 43; then came the ten Regiments of Marines, numbered as Marines from 1 to 10, but also ranking among the regiments of the Army from 44 to 53; and then seven more infantry battalions with precedence from 54 to 60.

The 4th, or Colonel Wynyard's Marines, which was raised in 1739, took precedence among the Regiments of the Line as the 47th, and served in the ill-fated attack on Carthagena in 1741; it returned to England three years later and was finally disbanded with the other regiments of Marines after the Peace of Aix-la-Chapelle of 1748.

We may now consider the raising of the Regiment of Infantry, which originally numbered or ranking as the 58th, became, on the disbandment of the Marine Regiments, the 47th in order of precedence, and later in life The Lancashire Regiment, and later still, the 1st Battalion The Loyal Regiment (North Lancashire).

The order for the raising of this corps runs as follows :—

"GEORGE R.

"These are to authorize you by beat of drum or otherwise to raise volunteers in any County or part of our Kingdom of Great Britain for a Regiment of Foot under your command, which is to consist of ten companies of three sergeants, three corporals, two drummers and seventy effective private men in each company, besides commissioned officers : and all Magistrates, Justices of the Peace, Constables and others our Civil Officers whom it may concern are hereby required to be assisting unto you in providing quarters, impressing carriages and otherwise as there shall be occasion.

"Given at Our Court of St. James's this third day of January, 1741, in the fourteenth year of Our Reign.

"By His Majesty's Commands.

(sd.) "WILL. YOUNG.

"To Our Trusty and Well-beloved John Mordaunt Esq., Colonel of one of Our Regiments of Foot, or to the Officer or Officers appointed by you to raise Volunteers for Our said Regiments." *

The Colonel John Mordaunt here mentioned joined the Army on the 25th August, 1721, as ensign in the 3rd Foot Guards, became captain and lieut.-colonel a few years later, was appointed colonel to raise the above-mentioned Regiment on the 15th January, 1741, being transferred in the following March to the colonelcy of the 18th Foot. In 1745 he was promoted to brigadier-general, became successively colonel of the 12th Dragoons, 4th Dragoon Guards, and 10th Dragoons, was promoted lieut.-general in 1754, General in 1770, and was made K.B. and Governor of Berwick in the same year. He died in 1780.

General Sir John Mordaunt commanded brigades at the Battles of Falkirk, Culloden and Val, and the land forces in the Rochefort expedition of 1757.

The following appear to have been the Officers appointed to the Regiment on its being raised, with the dates of appointment :—

Colonel John Mordaunt	. . .	15th January, 1741
Lieut.-Colonel Melchier Guy Dickens		6th February, 1741
Major John Severn	. . .	21st ,, ,,

* Public Record Office, W.O. 26/19, p. 311.

Captain John Delostall	21st	January,	1741
,, William Montgomery	22nd	,,	,,
,, John Steuart	23rd	,,	,,
,, Thomas Collin	24th	,,	,,
,, Thomas Barlow	25th	,,	,,
,, George Grey	26th	,,	,,
,, Edmund Anderson	27th	,,	,,
Capt.-Lieut. Richard Corbet	28th	,,	,,
Lieut. Adam Drummond	21st	,,	,,
,, Benjamin Browne	22nd	,,	,,
,, Edward Carrick	23rd	,,	,,
,, Alexander Mackay	24th	,,	,,
,, James Johnson	25th	,,	,,
,, Edward Thompson	26th	,,	,,
,, Paul Breton	27th	,,	,,
,, Charles Dundas	28th	,,	,,
,, Robert Cony (or Conry)	29th	,,	,,
,, Bladen Swiney	30th	,,	,,
Ensign David Gordon	21st	,,	,,
,, Henry Heron	22nd	,,	,,
,, George Kelsall	23rd	,,	,,
,, John Walkinshaw	24th	,,	,,
,, William Stone	25th	,,	,,
,, Thomas Stoakes	26th	,,	,,
,, George Beaver	27th	,,	,,
,, Richard Chappell	28th	,,	,,
,, Nicholas Cox	29th	,,	,,
Chaplain Thomas Turner	15th	,,	,,
Surgeon Thomas Macarty	15th	,,	,,
Assistant Surgeon David Gordon	15th	,,	,,
,, ,, — Drummond	15th	,,	,,

The Regiment was raised in Scotland, but seems at first to have been much moved about, judging from the reports of drafts which it received or which were sent by it to other corps: thus a Warrant, dated 21st February, 1741, orders "a draft of fifty men and two drummers to be sent from Colonel Pulteney's Regiment for Colonel Mordaunt's at Birmingham." But immediately after this the Regiment was sent back to Scotland and was for many months employed on the construction of roads. Another Warrant, dated 7th April, 1742, directs a draft of ten men and three drummers to be sent to Colonel Lowther's Marines at Edinburgh.

On the 13th March, 1742, Colonel Peregrine Lascelles assumed command of the Regiment in the place of Colonel Mordaunt transferred, and remained in command for the long term of twenty years.

This officer had a long and distinguished career. Appointed ensign in Lord Lovelace's Regiment of Foot in April, 1706, he subsequently served as captain in the regiments of Colonels Lepele, Stanhope, Grant, Crosley and Kirke, and in Colonel Gore's and Colonel Churchill's Dragoons, then being appointed captain in the 1st Foot Guards in June, 1731, and captain and lieut.-colonel two years later. He was appointed Colonel of the 47th on the 13th March, 1742, became ensign-general in March, 1754, and lieut.-general in January, 1758. He served at the Battles of Almanarq, Saragossa and Villaviciosa, in the Rebellions of 1715 and 1745, and died, aged eighty-eight, on the 26th March, 1772, a tablet in St. Mary's Church, Whitby, describing him as "Bountiful to his soldiers, a Father to his officers, a Man of truth and principle, in short, an Honest Man."

The 47th—as the Regiment may now for convenience be called, although it was not so numbered until 1748, while it was not until some three years later still that corps ceased to be known by the names of their colonels—continued to be employed on road-making for some time : but when in 1745 the Jacobite Rebellion broke out, the Regiment was stationed in Edinburgh and Leith.

In this year Prince Charles Edward, the Young Pretender, having obtained some help and many promises of assistance from France, determined to make an attempt to overthrow the Hanoverian Government. He landed on the 25th July at Moidart, in Inverness-shire, and on the 19th August raised his standard at Glenfinnan, about fifteen miles from Fort William, the Western Highlands being then watched by a line of fortified posts, the chief of these being Fort William, Fort Augustus and Inverness.

At this time General Sir John Cope was commanding the Royal forces in Scotland, then numbering barely three thousand men exclusive of garrisons, and they comprised two regiments of dragoons, three and a half battalions of infantry, six weak companies of recruits, and some companies of Lord John Murray's and Lord Loudoun's Highlanders. These were much scattered and only one of the infantry battalions—that of Colonel Guise, the 6th—was an old corps. None of the others had been long raised, and in fact everything connected with the troops and the military situation was in an utterly unprepared state for active operations.

Tidings of the rising were received early in August, and this was immediately followed by the news of the capture by the insurgents of two companies which had been sent from Fort Augustus to reinforce the garrison of Fort William. The Government now made preparations in all haste; five thousand stand of arms were sent from London to the Castle at Edinburgh and that city was placed in a state of defence; while Sir John Cope had the Castle provisioned, and two companies of the 47th, each seventy strong under Brevet-Major Robertson, were stationed there in garrison. The General also issued orders for the several parties then still working on the roads to rejoin their respective corps, and made arrangements for assembling troops and storing provisions at Stirling preparatory to a march through the Highlands to the chain of forts, with the object of crushing the rebellion before it spread further.

The ovens at Leith, Stirling and Perth were kept going night and day to prepare bread and biscuit, while contracts were made for pack animals —the country being unsuited for wheeled transport. By about the 10th August the following troops were assembling at Stirling:—

> The 13th Dragoons.
> Two Companies of Lord John Murray's Highlanders.
> Five Companies of the 44th.
> Eight Companies of the 47th.
> Four $1\frac{1}{2}$-pounder Guns,

these being joined later by the 46th Regiment.

No northward movement could, however, be made until the bread and biscuit were ready, none being obtainable en route.

General Cope complained of his troops being raw and unused to taking the field, which made it difficult for him to put them in motion; and, considering that the three regular infantry regiments above-named had not yet been five years in existence, were unaccustomed to active service and had been constantly employed in road-making, the complaint can have been only too justified. On the 20th August a start was at last made, and the infantry of the force, some one thousand four hundred strong, moved from Stirling and marched by one of the newly-made military roads towards Fort Augustus, about one hundred and five miles distant. The 47th remained behind to bring on one thousand stand of arms and one hundred horse-loads of biscuit, but overtook the rest of the force at Crieff on the 21st.

On the 22nd the march was continued to Amulrie, Sir John having first, however, sent back the bulk of the spare arms to Stirling, carrying with him only some three hundred stand with which he was in hopes of arming any friendly Highlanders he might come across.

Tay Bridge, Aberfeldy, was reached on the 23rd and part of the baggage was left here; on the 24th the force was at Trinofour and at Dalnacardoch on the 25th, and here Sir John Cope learnt that the great Pass of Corriarick, over which ran the road to Fort William, ascending the pass in seventeen steep zigzags, was held by a body of Highlanders three thousand strong.

Much trouble had been experienced with the transport of the force. At Trinofour the drivers, with a hundred horses, deserted in the night, leaving their loads behind, while one hundred horse-loads had already been left at Dalnacardoch and only a few of these came in next morning. None of the promised auxiliaries had joined, while the drivers continued to carry off the horses at night despite all precautions, an easy thing to do in the rugged and difficult country in which our troops were operating.

At Dalwhinnie, which was reached on the 26th August, Sir John Cope received definite information from spies that the Corriarick Pass was occupied by the rebels and that they had twenty small field pieces in position to sweep the approaches. The way appearing to be thus wholly barred, a council-of-war was held on the 27th, and since it was clear that the Highlanders were twice the strength of General Cope's force, and that any attempt to storm the pass would certainly result in the destruction of the Royal Army, it was decided to march to Inverness where there was reason to believe many well-disposed clans would join Sir John.

A few miles north of Dalwhinnie the military road divides, one branch leading northward to Ruthven, the other to Garvamore. In order therefore to deceive the enemy, General Cope moved to within four miles of Garvamore, and then, retracing his steps, made a forced march to Ruthven, on the further bank of the Spey, crossing that river on the night of the 27th. On the following day Dalrachney was reached and Inverness on the 29th. Here only two hundred Highlanders came in to join Cope's force, and news was soon received that the rebels intended marching south, having refused to be drawn north by the movement of the Royal troops. The march north had in fact left the Lowlands open, and Prince Charles consequently took the road to Perth, entering that city on September 4th. Here he remained until the 11th, organizing his forces and then left again for Edinburgh. The Rivers Forth and Avon were crossed unopposed, the dragoons, who had been posted at the fords, retiring before him, and on the 17th the capital was occupied.

Hearing that the Prince had marched south, Sir John decided to move to Aberdeen and there embark for Leith. Leaving Inverness on the 4th he reached Aberdeen on the 11th, sailed on the 15th, and two days later landed at Dunbar where he camped to the west of the town. His artillery and stores were not, however, on shore until the 18th.

Sir John Cope now found himself in a more hopeful mood; he states that throughout their trying march the infantry had shown much spirit, while he had now been joined by the 13th and 14th Dragoons, and the Royal Army was now composed as follows :—

  13th Dragoons.
  14th Dragoons.
   6th Regiment.
  44th Regiment.
  46th Regiment.
  47th Regiment, 8 Companies, 570 All Ranks.
  Loudoun's Highlanders,

the total strength of the force being approximately 2,200.

The available artillery consisted of six $1\frac{1}{2}$-pounder galloper guns and six small mortars, but the only men to work them were two pensioners, one old man, the last survivor of the old Scottish train, and some seamen gunners.

Sir John Cope decided to march on Edinburgh at once, and on the 19th his force advanced about ten miles, encamping for the night on rising ground to the west of Haddington. Next day the march was continued along the Edinburgh road, and some officers, who had been sent forward to reconnoitre, found the insurgents marching to meet them. When this news was received, the Royalist advanced guard had reached the plain between Seaton and Preston, and, the ground being favourable for the operations of both horse and foot, General Cope took up his position facing westward, his right towards the sea and his left resting on a ditch and morass on the south.

The troops were drawn up in the following order:—

Five companies of the 44th on the right; eight companies of the 47th and two of the 6th in the centre; Murray's Highlanders on the left, with two cavalry squadrons on either flank. Two guns were placed in the centre and two on each flank of the infantry, the reserve consisting of two squadrons of Dragoons with five companies of Highlanders and a few Volunteers.

No sooner were these dispositions made than the insurgents appeared on the hill immediately above Tranent, to the south. Sir John, seeing this, changed his position so as to face the enemy, his right towards Bankton Park and his front covered by the ditch and morass, the baggage and military chest being sent to the village of Cockenzie, in rear, guarded by Loudoun's Highlanders. In the afternoon the enemy sent a party to occupy the churchyard of Tranent, but were driven out by the fire from two guns. Later on, towards sunset, another body of the enemy made a demonstration on the right of the Royal Army, causing the latter to form line facing south-west with the right towards Prestonpans; but on this body returning to their main position, Sir John resumed his former formation facing south, but rather further back from the ditch, and the whole of the rest of the afternoon was spent in marching and counter-marching.

Towards evening, advanced picquets of horse and foot were posted along the side of the morass as far east as the village of Seaton, the infantry picquets consisting of three hundred men under Captains Collier and Drummond of the 47th and Captain Blake of Murray's Regiment; the remainder of the Royal Army lay on their arms all night.

Early on the morning of the 21st September the Rebel Army moved eastward for some distance, and then turning north along a little-known path, it marched towards the sea and so gained the right flank of the Royal Army, where the rebels formed up in order of battle.

Colonel Lascelles of the 47th was on this day acting as brigadier in command of the right wing of the Royal Army, and had been round the outpost line with the field-officer of the day, when about three o'clock in the morning patrols reported that the enemy was moving north. Colonel Lascelles was at the time with Major Severn of his Regiment and he at once ordered the whole line to stand to arms, and Sir John Cope lost no time in changing front to the left to receive the enemy, the line now facing east, its right on the morass and the left towards the sea.

The outposts were at once called in and ordered to rejoin their regiments, but not being able to find them in the dark, they were formed on the right of the infantry, where they were somewhat in the way of the dragoons. Captain Collier, 47th, who had been on outpost, was ordered by the field-officer of the day to call in all his sentries and fall in with them on the right of the infantry; this he did, but Colonel Lascelles, noticing he was on the ground told off to the cavalry, directed him to move to the left. Lieutenant Cox, 47th, with the regimental quarter guard, and Captain Drummond, who had been on picquet, also joined Captain Collier's party.

It was hardly yet light when several bodies of the enemy, advancing rapidly towards the right of the line, opened fire on the escort for the guns which broke and fled, leaving Colonel Whiteford, the O.C. artillery, who kept his guns for some time in action single-handed. Colonel Whitney, commanding the 13th Dragoons, was now directed to charge the enemy in flank, but for some reason this movement was ineffective.

When the dragoons advanced, Colonel Lascelles, who was at the head of the line, dismounted and ordered some platoons to wheel towards the enemy, intending thereby to help the cavalry movement and cover the right of the infantry. The men, however, were unsteady, and though fire was opened along the line, it was badly delivered and was of small effect. The Rebels charged straight into the guns, the right of our line was open,

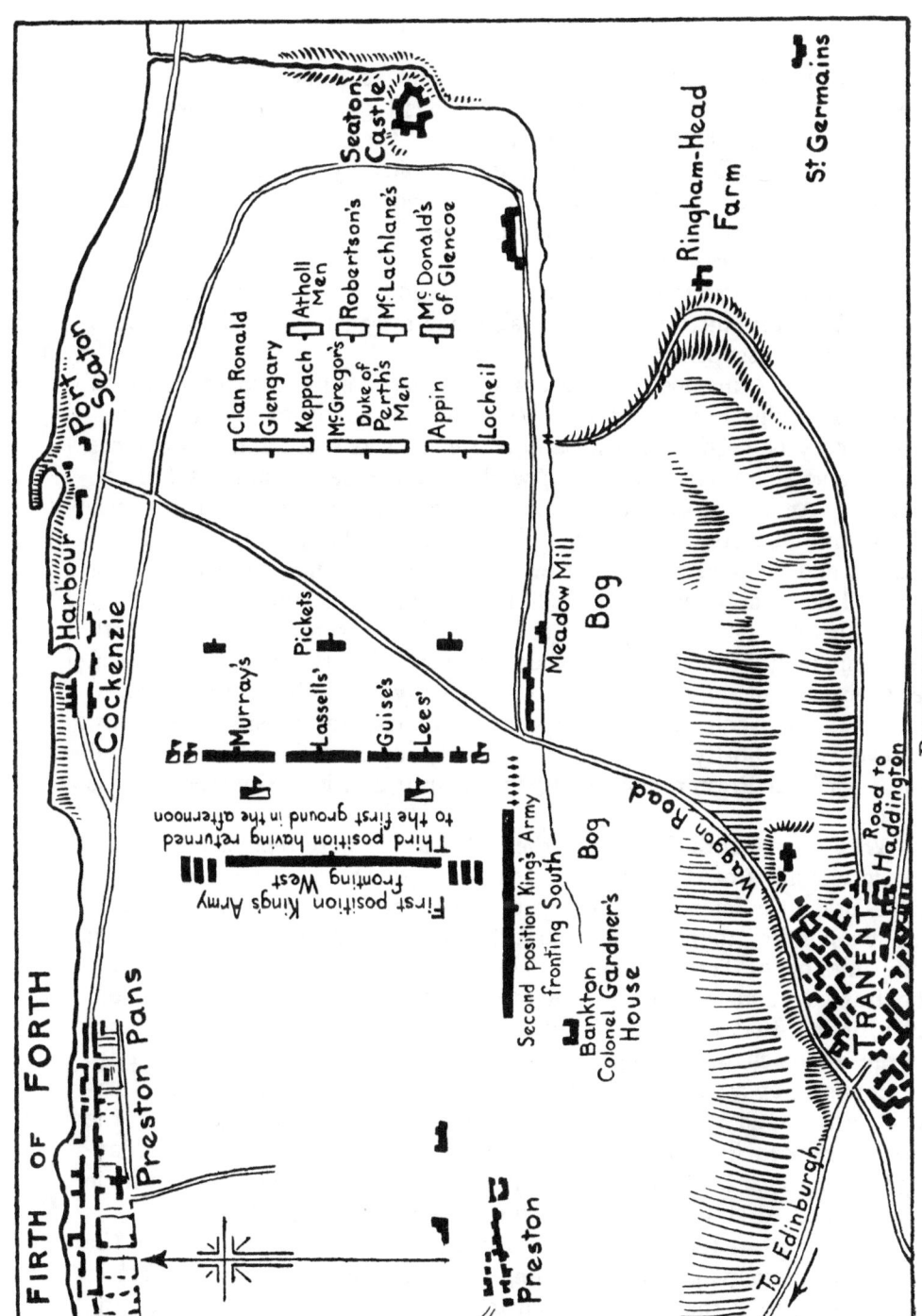

PRESTONPANS.
21st September, 1745.

and Colonel Lascelles, seeing the enemy about to attack it, ran in that direction, intending to wheel up some platoons to ward off the threatened danger. The men, however, broke, despite all the efforts of their officers, and Colonel Lascelles himself was made prisoner by an insurgent officer and his men; he was disarmed, but managed to escape and, getting a horse at Seaton, he rode off to Haddington where he met some of the dragoons and so made his way to Berwick.

The Battle of Prestonpans ended very speedily in favour of the enemy, and the Royal infantry were nearly all made prisoners, only the dragoons effecting their escape.

The Royal Army lost six officers and some five hundred other ranks killed, while nine hundred more were wounded, nearly all by the broadsword, or scythe. Of the 47th, Captain Steuart was killed and Lieutenants Swiney and Heron were wounded, while Major Severn, Captains Barlow, Forrester, Anderson, Collier and Corbet, Captain-Lieutenant Drummond, Lieutenants Johnson and Dundas, Ensigns Stone, Cox, Bell, Gordon and Goulton and Surgeon Drummond were all taken prisoner, the whole being marched off to and confined in Edinburgh and the neighbourhood.

As already stated, Sir John Cope had left two companies of the 47th Regiment in Edinburgh Castle when he marched north, and the garrison here consisted of some artillery and a company of invalids, in addition to the 47th, the whole under the command of General Preston, who was, however, very shortly afterwards temporarily superseded by Lieut.-General Guest, General Preston continuing to do duty as Lieut.-Governor of the Castle.

When on the 16th September the Rebel forces were reported as within a very few miles of the city, the 13th and 14th Dragoons were posted at Colt's Bridge to defend the passage of the River Leith, and sixty muskets and five hundred rounds of ball cartridge were issued to each of the fifteen companies of the Trained Bands. When, however, the enemy drew nearer the trained bands and other volunteers dispersed, and General Preston then, finding that the City of Edinburgh was likely to offer no resistance to the approach of the insurgents, sent Ensign Robertson of the 47th, accompanied by a party of some twenty men, with orders to spike or otherwise destroy the guns mounted on the city walls. This, however, the Provost refused to allow to be done, with the result that when, at daylight on the 17th September, the city was surprised, all the guns and some twelve hundred stand of arms fell into the hands of the Rebels.

No attempt at the capture of Edinburgh Castle was made prior to the Battle of Prestonpans, and something over a hundred men and one officer who escaped from the field managed to make their way to Edinburgh and were added to the garrison of the Castle. A council-of-war was now held and the proposal was seriously made that, by reason of the weakness of its numbers, the garrison should surrender; this suggestion was, however, stoutly opposed by General Preston, and General Guest then handed over the command temporarily to him. Although General Preston was enfeebled by age and wounds, he caused himself to be wheeled in a chair round the guards and sentries every two hours and directed fire to be opened upon any of the enemy who might show themselves.

On the night of the 3rd October some of the Clan Cameron commenced to entrench themselves on the Castle Hill, but were fired on by the guns of the Half-Moon Battery, while a party of the 47th sallied out under cover of this fire and succeeded in capturing thirty men and an officer. Early on the following morning Major Robertson and a strong party of the Regiment, with muskets slung and carrying picks and spades, proceeded to the Castle Hill and there made a trench which they occupied, and the same night fire from two hundred muskets and several field guns was kept up on the city. At the same time the heavy 32-pounders from the Castle batteries also opened fire, sweeping the High Street of the city with round shot, grape and canister. Then under cover of this heavy fire the 47th made a second sally and secured some much-needed food supplies from the neighbouring houses, which the party set on fire before they fell back. A deserted arms-foundry was also destroyed.

Many citizens were killed by the fire from the Castle batteries while endeavouring to save the burning houses.

This success by the Castle garrison so irritated Prince Charles that he ordered the entrenchment on Castle Hill to be stormed, which was done, the detachment of the 47th occupying it being driven out, and retired firing by platoons. The Prince then sent a message to old General Preston that if he again opened fire upon the city the house of a relation of his in the neighbourhood would be destroyed, but undeterred by this threat, fire was again opened from the Castle walls on the 21st October, and again some days later when Prince Charles was reviewing the Rebel Army prior to its march into England.

In Home's *History of the Rebellion*, p. 135, he tells us that " after long and anxious deliberation, Charles and his Council resolved to march into England and push the enterprise to the utmost. Hopes were still entertained of an invasion from France, of an insurrection in England, and some, the bravest and most determined, trusted in themselves; for after the Battle of Preston, the generality of the rebels entertained a wonderful opinion of the Highlanders, and held the King's troops in great contempt. Orders were given in the end of October to call in all their parties, to collect their whole force, and prepare for their march to England." Early in November Prince Charles left the capital and marched south with his army, the garrison of Edinburgh Castle being no further molested; and here in the spring of the year following, those of the Regiment, who had been taken prisoner at Prestonpans and since held in confinement, joined the companies in the Castle.

There was a good deal of feeling that General Sir John Cope had not acted throughout the early stages of the operations with sufficient enterprise and promptitude, and a Board of General Officers was ordered to assemble for the purpose of inquiring into his conduct, and that also of two of his officers, Colonels Fowke and Lascelles, immediately subordinate to him. Field-Marshal Wade was president of this Board, the other members being Lieut.-Generals Lord Cadogan, Folliot, the Duke of Richmond and Guise. The inquiry lasted five days with the result that General Cope, Colonels Fowke and Lascelles were all honourably acquitted.

The verdict in the case of Colonel Lascelles was as follows:—

"As to Colonel Lascelles, it does not appear to us that any misconduct or misbehaviour can be laid to his charge, he having plainly proved that he was at his post both before and after the action."

So ended for the 47th its first experience of active service in the field—a trying one indeed for a newly-raised regiment composed practically entirely of recruits, and led probably by officers many of whom had for years languished on half-pay; "while the young soldiers were opposed to an enemy fighting on their own ground, and whose impetuosity and dash in attack had often in the past prevailed against the best regular troops."

In the accompanying illustration, Louisburg is seen from Lighthouse Point; in the background is Gabarus Bay, where the British troops landed, with our fleet lying at anchor; on the high ground to the right of the picture, in front of the wood, is the British camp; to the left centre is Goat (Battery) Island; the City of Louisburg is in the centre and the captured French fleet is anchored in the harbour, on the right.

LOUISBURG.

1758.

CHAPTER II

1746–1759

**THE CONQUEST OF CANADA
LOUISBURG AND QUEBEC**

IN 1746 the Regiment was moved to England and was in the autumn of this year called upon to furnish a draft to complete the 30th Regiment, which in September sailed on the expedition against L'Orient: the order runs as follows:—" Warrant for drafting eighty-four men from Lascelles' Regiment to General Frampton's. Such men as have been enlisted for a time on account of the Rebellion, etc., or of such others as you shall think not able to undergo the fatigues of a sea-voyage, or are otherwise disqualified for this service," were to be drafted to Lascelles' Regiment to take the place of those sent abroad.

Again in the following year the 47th appears to have furnished a draft for a regiment serving under the East India Company.

In 1748 the Regiment was sent over to Ireland and was for some time quartered in Dublin.

" The conclusion of the Peace of Aix-la-Chapelle was followed by the usual reduction of the forces in Britain. The ten new regiments and several other corps were disbanded, leaving for the cavalry all the regiments now in the Army List down to the 14th Hussars, and in the infantry the Foot Guards and the 1st to the 49th Regiments. The strength of all corps was, of course, diminished and the British Establishment was fixed at 30,000 men, two-thirds of them for service at home and one-third for colonial garrisons. The rest of the Army, thirty-seven regiments in all, but very weak in numbers, was as usual turned over to the Irish Establishment." *

In the *Gentleman's Magazine* for October, 1748, there is a list showing all the Regiments of the Army—those remaining on the British Establishment in Colonial garrisons, on the Irish Establishment, and those to suffer disbandment, and among those on the Irish Establishment we find the name " Lascell."

The general effect of these reductions, and particularly the disbandment of the Marine Regiments raised in 1739 and 1740, and of the regiment,

---

* Fortescue, *History of the British Army*, Vol. II, p. 261.

then numbered 42nd, raised by General Oglethorpe for service in Georgia, was that those regiments which had since come into existence were all moved up in order of precedence, and Lascelles' Regiment now took its place in the Army List as the 47th.

In 1750 the Regiment sailed from Ireland for Nova Scotia and on arrival was quartered in Halifax.

Nova Scotia, called by the French "Acadia," was at this period in a very unsettled state. It had been ceded by France to England by the terms of the Treaty of Utrecht of 1713, but the Acadians were still thoroughly French in their ideas and inclinations, and the authorities in Canada and Cape Breton lost no opportunity of keeping them hostile to England. Boundary disputes and frontier troubles were of constant occurrence, and the British commanders were convinced that the frequent attacks made upon our posts by the Indians were instigated by the French. In 1749 the Home authorities sent out two thousand five hundred emigrants to form a settlement and establish a post in the Bay of Chebucto, on the south coast of Nova Scotia; this was intended as a counterpoise to the French naval and military station at Louisburg in Cape Breton, which had been restored to the French in 1748 by the Treaty of Aix-la-Chapelle. In this way the town of Halifax arose, and before the end of the year 1749 it was palisaded and defended by timbered redoubts, garrisoned by the 29th and 45th Regiments, which had lately arrived from Louisburg after its rendition. Besides Halifax, and the old capital of Annapolis Royal, there were some seven other posts held by our troops; these were Chignecto, Piziquid, Mines, Lunenburg, Dartmouth, George's Island and Fort Sackville.

At the time when the 47th landed at Halifax, Colonel Charles Lawrence of the 40th had just been appointed Lieut.-Governor of Annapolis Royal, and in August, 1750, he was ordered to proceed with a small force to Chignecto, where the French were believed to have taken up a position. Lawrence left Piziquid for Mines on the 19th August, taking with him the 47th and three hundred of the 45th, and embarked on several small ships for Chignecto; Cornwallis, the Governor of Acadia, speeding the troops on their way with the remark that he "never saw a detachment of better men." The little expeditionary force reached Chignecto in due course, and here Lawrence found that his landing would be opposed by a large body of French and Indians strongly entrenched. "Notwithstanding this opposition," we read in Murdoch's *History of Nova Scotia*, "the gallant and intrepid behaviour of the English beat them out, although the defenders are said to have outnumbered them sixfold. A schooner that led in was near being destroyed, when Lawrence, perceiving, did not wait for the entire landing of his troops, but put himself at the head of one hundred and eleven who had got on shore, marched up boldly to the entrenchment and received their fire, not a man of his offering to discharge his piece in return until they were at the foot of the entrenchment, when his men poured in their fire and the foe took to flight. On the English side there were six killed and twelve wounded."

The 47th now appears to have formed the garrison of a recently-established post known as Fort Lawrence near Beaubassin, and remained there for some considerable time; here two officers of the Regiment died—Captains Carter and Gordon.

Already in 1750 the French had commenced the construction of a strong fort at Beauséjour, erected on some rising ground less than three miles from Fort Lawrence, a marshy stream known as the Missaquash, running between the two positions; another fort called Fort Gaspereau had been placed in Baie-Verte in order further to strengthen the position, while a third had been built at the mouth of the St. John's River on the north side of the Bay of Fundy. The depredations of the Indians were carried on continually against the English settlers, many of whom were killed and scalped, and it was no secret that they were assisted by the Acadians, incited by French agents.

The Hon. Robert Monckton had been since early in 1750 the Lieut.-Colonel of the 47th, and in November, 1754, this officer was sent by Colonel Lawrence, now Lieut.-Governor of Nova Scotia, with a letter to Shirley, the Governor of Massachusetts, in which Lawrence strongly expressed the opinion that the French were planning an aggressive movement in Chignecto, to open so soon as the fortifications of Louisburg should be completely restored. Lieut.-Colonel Monckton was directed to confer with Shirley in regard to the enlistment of two thousand men for operations in the coming spring. Shirley entered whole-heartedly into the scheme and a body of two thousand men was raised and divided into two battalions.

These troops left Boston on the 23rd May, 1755, in a fleet of thirty-eight small ships, escorted by three frigates, Lieut.-Colonel Monckton sailing in H.M.S. "Lawrence," and, touching at Annapolis, where some artillery joined, the ship anchored on June 1st within five miles of Beauséjour. Here the troops were landed and encamped about Fort Lawrence, where three hundred of the 47th were added to the force. From the camp Monckton could contemplate the Fort of Beauséjour, which was a regular work, pentagonal in form, having strong earthen parapets with bomb proofs, and mounting twenty-four guns and a mortar. The commandant was Captain de Vergor, a colonial officer in the French Army, and the garrison consisted of 160 regulars with 1,200–1,400 Acadians collected from the neighbourhood.

On the morning of the 4th June the advance began, the force moving along the south bank of the Missaquash to where a bridge, recently destroyed, had crossed, called Pont-à-Buot; "for want of horses," so the journal of Colonel Monckton, "were obliged to draw the six-pounders by men." The order of march was as follows: "a captain, two subalterns and fifty Irregulars to scour the woods; then the Regulars, about two hundred and seventy rank and file; after the Regulars Captain Broome with the detachment of the Artillery, four field six-pounders, tumbrils and materials for a bridge; then followed the 2nd Battalion of Irregulars, the 1st Battalion bringing up the rear." On the further side of the stream was a blockhouse and timber breastwork, defended by four hundred Regulars, Acadians and Indians.

"These latter remained quiet and unseen until the head of the column had reached the opposite side, near the bridge, when they opened fire causing some loss, but on the guns coming into action the enemy gave way, upon which," reports Colonel Monckton, "I immediately marched over with the Regulars, followed by the two battalions, at the sight of which the enemy ran off and we took possession of the hill.

"On the first fire of the enemy, followed by the Indian cry, the troops in general were a little surprised, but afterwards behaved very well, the Regulars in particular. In this affair we had but one man killed and about twelve wounded, the shot in general flying over, or falling short, of us."

When all had crossed the river, the march was continued unopposed towards Beauséjour, on nearing which the force turned to the right and encamped among the wooded hills half a league from the fort.

Colonel Monckton spent some days in preparing his camp and reconnoitring the fort, and then on the 14th a party of Irregulars under Lieut.-Colonel Scott and some of the 47th under the command of Captain Spital, occupied a ridge where it was intended to open trenches for the investment of the place. There was some opposition and a few casualties, and Colonel Monckton remarks that "the detachment of Regulars under the command of Captain Spital behaved much to his and their credit."

The guns opened with effect at daybreak on the 16th; about midday the French commandant expressed his desire to capitulate, and between seven and eight o'clock that evening the fort was handed over, the greater part of the garrison being sent away the next day.

Fort Gaspereau, some twelve miles distant, also surrendered unconditionally and the troops then returned to their stations, the 40th, 45th and 47th Regiments apparently composing the garrison of Nova Scotia until the commencement of the preparations for the siege of Louisburg three years later.

The loss incurred by the British in the reduction of Forts Beauséjour and Gaspereau totalled no more than twenty killed and twenty wounded, and to the 47th Colonel Monckton pays the following tribute:—

"The Regulars under the command of Captains Hussey, Hale and Spital, as also the other officers and men, ever showed themselves diligent and behaved much to their credit."

Besides the above three officers of the 47th, Colonel Monckton also mentions Ensign Joseph Peach in his diary: this officer appears to have been employed during the operations against Fort Beauséjour as an acting field engineer.

In a book entitled *Selections from the Public Documents of the Province of Nova Scotia*, there are many letters and other papers which describe the work upon which the regiments remaining in the Province were now for some time engaged. After Cape Breton was ceded by France to Britain in 1713, all the French inhabitants who desired to remain in the country were required to take the oath of allegiance to King George. The French-Canadian authorities, however, did their best to prevent this being done, and employed agents to keep the people hostile to England. The priests, especially, did all they could to persuade their flocks that they were still subjects of King Louis. Matters remained, however, tolerably quiet until the war of 1745 when trouble again arose, and from 1754 onwards the above-mentioned book contains many letters from Captain Murray, 45th Regiment, who was then commanding at Fort Edward, to the north of Halifax, where three officers of the 47th—Captain Cox, Lieutenant Mercer and Ensign Peach—were also stationed. Murray's letters are to the Governor, and in these he describes all the very serious difficulties occasioned by the attitude of the French settlers.

Finally, late in 1755, the French colonists, through their deputies, flatly refused to take any but a qualified oath of allegiance, and it was thereupon decided that all the French inhabitants should be removed from Acadia and distributed among the various English colonies.

The officers of the regiments forming the garrison of the Province had to carry out this most distasteful duty, some six thousand men, women and children being removed from Nova Scotia during the autumn and winter of the year. It was not, however, until the Treaty of Paris of 1763 that France finally resigned all claim to Acadia.

On the 18th May, 1756, war was declared in London against France, and on the 22nd July the Earl of Loudoun arrived in New York to take command of all the troops in North America and conduct such operations as might be determined upon against the French possessions in these parts; at the same time Colonel Lawrence was appointed Captain-General and Commander-in-Chief, and Colonel Robert Monckton, Lieut.-Governor of Nova Scotia.

Lord Loudoun had been sent out from home with orders to reduce Louisburg and then to proceed against Quebec; and by the end of April, 1757, he had concentrated a force of six thousand three hundred men with abundant siege material at New York, where he awaited the coming of Admiral Holborne, who was escorting the ships bringing out further reinforcements. On the 13th June, Loudoun had transferred his force to Halifax, where he exercised his men in attacks upon fortified positions, and here early in June five thousand more men were landed from Cork. Knox, who arrived with these troops after a voyage of nearly eight weeks, tells us in his Journal that he found the Grenadier Companies of the 40th, 45th and 47th Regiments encamped on the hill close to the citadel.

The expeditionary force embarked on the 1st and 2nd August, preparatory to sailing for Louisburg, when it was discovered from some captured letters that twenty-two French ships-of-war had recently reached Cape Breton, the garrison of Louisburg being now increased to seven thousand men. On this Loudoun decided to abandon the enterprise for that season, and he returned to New York with some of his troops, distributing the remainder among various posts on the Acadian peninsula.

Pitt, the head of the Home Government, now became so disgusted with the delays that followed, that on the 30th December he recalled Lord Loudoun, appointing General Jeffrey Amherst to command in his stead.

On the 19th February, 1758, a powerful armament sailed from Portsmouth under Admiral Boscawen, consisting of twenty-three ships of the line, eighteen frigates and fire-ships besides numerous transports carrying eleven thousand six hundred men, and by the end of May all had arrived at Halifax. The infantry of the force detailed for the capture of Louisburg was drawn from the following regiments, viz., 1st, 15th, 17th, 22nd, 28th, 35th, 40th, 45th, 47th, 48th, 58th, the 2nd and 3rd Battalions 60th and the 63rd, and was at the outset divided into two wings each of two brigades. The 47th was in the first instance told off to the 1st Brigade, commanded by Lieut.-Colonel Burton of the 48th and containing also the 1st, 28th, and 2nd Battalion 60th, but this distribution suffered some change after arrival at Cape Breton.

The garrison of Louisburg now contained some three thousand Regulars and seven hundred Canadians, the Regulars being made up of twenty-four companies of Marines, two companies of artillery and four infantry battalions.

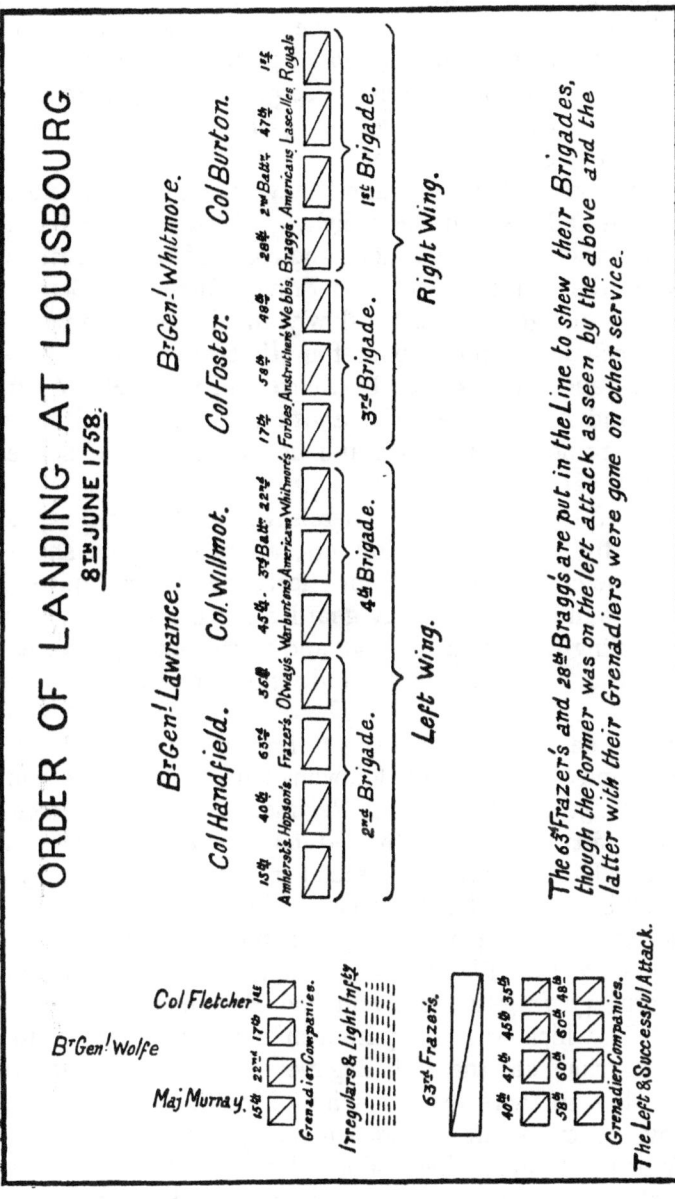

THE LANDING AT LOUISBURG.

8th June, 1758.

The 47th Regiment embarked in its transports on the 20th and 21st May, and in the *Diary of the Reduction of Louisburg* by a "Spectator," the strength of the Regiment is given as one lieut.-colonel, one major, five captains, fifteen lieutenants, nine ensigns, one adjutant, one quarter-master, one surgeon, two surgeon's mates, 38 sergeants, 18 drummers and 856 rank and file. Lieutenant Henry Dobson, 47th, was named in orders of the 15th May to act as brigade-major.

At dawn on May 29th H.M.S. "Namur" gave the signal to unmoor, and by 9 a.m. the armada was under weigh. "With varying but not unfavourable weather the fleet tacked along the coast of Nova Scotia and Cape Breton. When the weather cleared on Friday, June 2nd, Boscawen saw Louisburg and with light airs came slowly to his chosen anchorage in Gabarus Bay, which he reached about four that afternoon. He was followed that evening and the next day by the rest of the fleet. As they passed in Amherst and his men saw rise above the circumvallation the slender spires of the principal buildings, and beyond them the slenderer masts of the ships in the harbour." *

On the evening of the 2nd June Generals Amherst, Lawrence and Wolfe, accompanied by several naval officers, approached the shore in boats, looking for some convenient place for effecting a landing, but every accessible point was found to be strongly guarded; the surf was also too high to permit of putting the troops on land, and it was not until the early morning of the 8th that the force, in three divisions, rowed towards the shore.

The left division under Wolfe, which was to form the real attack, made for Freshwater Cove, and consisted of the following: first, the four Grenadier Companies of the 1st, 15th, 17th and 22nd Regiments, then a picked corps of five hundred and fifty marksmen from different regiments, then the Rangers and Frazer's Highlanders, the Grenadier Companies of the 35th, 40th, 45th, 47th, 48th, 58th and 60th following in support.

The centre division, under Lawrence—15th, 22nd, 35th, 40th, 45th and 3rd Battalion 60th—rowed for Flat Point; while the right division, under Whitmore—1st, 17th, 47th, 48th, 58th and 2nd Battalion 60th—was to make for White Point which was not quite a mile distant from the fortifications. On the previous day the 28th Regiment had been sent towards L'Orembec with orders to there make a feint of landing.

Freshwater Cove, where Wolfe intended to land, was strongly held by one thousand Frenchmen under Lieut.-Colonel de St. Julien, who was entrenched with abbatis in his front, and his men held their fire until Wolfe's party was within close range, when they poured on his boats a

* McLennan, *Louisbourg*, p. 242.

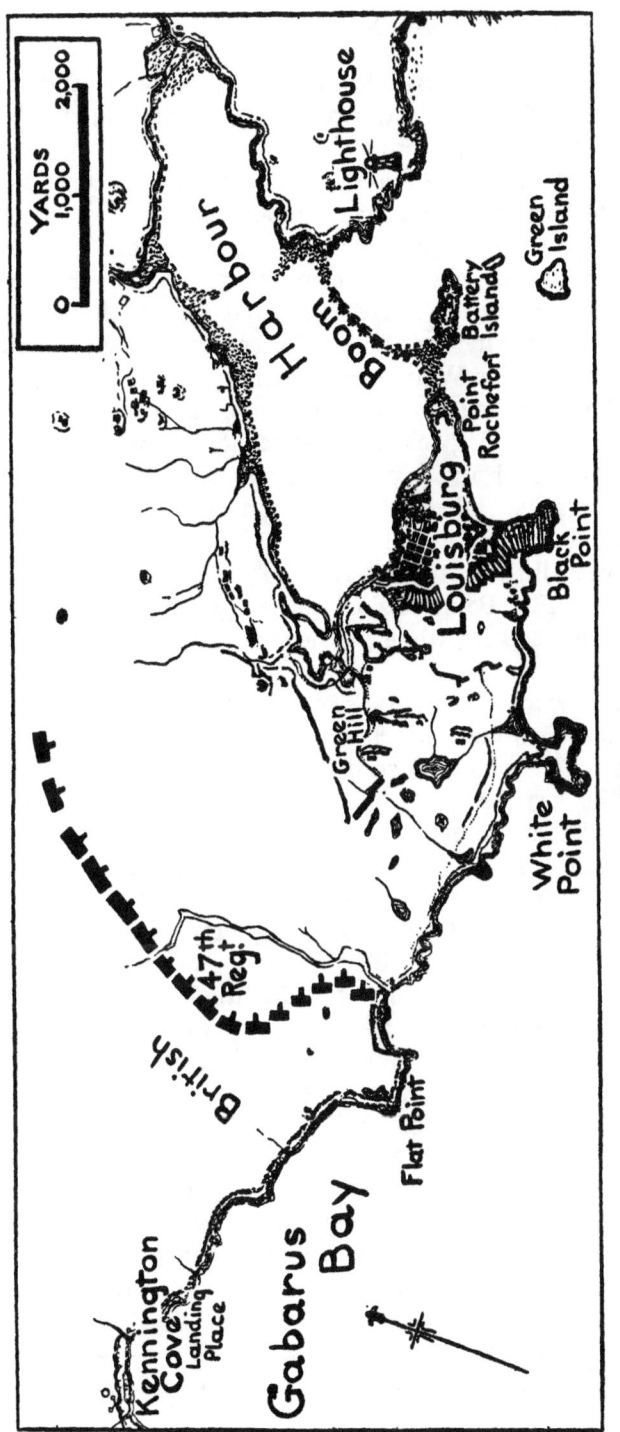

LOUISBURG.

June, 1758.

heavy discharge of grape and musketry, sinking some boats and causing loss in others. Wolfe had his flagstaff broken by a shot, and the fire and surf were such that he made a signal to retire, but on the right the attackers, mistaking the signal, made for the shore which they succeeded in gaining. On seeing this Wolfe hurried on, and was among the first to land, armed only with a cane. Some men were drowned in the surf and many boats were stove in on the rocks, but the remainder of the party struggled to land, then forming up and carrying the nearest French battery with the bayonet.

Lawrence's division now inclined to the left and also landed, followed in like manner by that under Whitmore; whereupon the enemy, fearing to be cut off from the town, fled into the woods, pursued over most difficult ground by the British. Having reached a suitable spot whence to invest the place, the troops halted and lay upon their arms for the night.

The French loss was 50 killed and 70 wounded, that of the British 109 men killed and wounded, while nearly a hundred boats were also destroyed; but nearly all the enemy's advanced guns were captured. The landing of the stores at Flat Point was only accomplished with the greatest difficulty on account of the surf, while the siege guns were not got on shore until the 18th.

The British camp, which extended for two miles, was formed in a valley along the banks of a little stream which ran into the sea east of Flat Point. Low hills, covered with wood and scrub, concealed the British position from the view of the fortress; in front of the camp redoubts were constructed, while in order to protect it from the bands of Acadians hovering about the woods, blockhouses were erected in the rear and on the left flank. The entrance to the harbour was well guarded; opposite to it on the north side stood the Grand Battery mounting forty guns, near its centre was situated Goat Island with a battery of eight guns, while at the east side of the entrance was another battery at Lighthouse Point.

After the landing there was a further rearrangement of brigades, and under date of June 8th it was ordered:—" The 3rd Brigade to be composed of the 17th, 47th, 2nd Battalion 60th and 35th Regiments; General Wolfe to have the inspection of this Brigade."

In Amherst's despatch, dated the 12th June, he states that hearing that the enemy had destroyed the Grand Battery and called in his outposts, he detached General Wolfe with four companies of Grenadiers, three companies of Rangers, one thousand two hundred other troops and some Light Infantry round the north-east harbour to the Lighthouse Point to silence the Island Battery and destroy the ships in the harbour. Wolfe was successful in capturing Lighthouse Point and all the enemy posts on that side of the harbour, the French abandoning several guns. The

Grenadier Companies employed in this operation were those of the 35th, 40th, 45th and 47th Regiments and were under the command of Lieut.-Colonel Hale, 47th.

The batteries, which Wolfe was now able to erect and man at Lighthouse Point, opened fire on the 20th, and others of our guns joined in, and on the 25th the enemy battery on Goat Island was silenced; in the meantime General Amherst had decided upon the spot, within half a mile of the ramparts, where he proposed opening his trenches, and commenced the construction of a communicating road, which called for the constant labour of a fatigue party one thousand strong, who had to work day and night under the fire of the fortress and the ships.

Wolfe continued to harass the defence; on the 1st July he drove back into the town a party of the enemy who attempted to carry off some stores; on the 9th six hundred of the garrison made a sally upon and tried to destroy an advanced post made a week or more previously, and the enemy onset fell upon the Grenadier Company of the 17th, which had an officer and several men killed; Major Murray, 45th, however, came up with two Grenadier Companies of other regiments and drove the French back with loss. On the 15th again an attack was made upon a post at the end of the north-east harbour, occupied by Captain Sutherland, 45th, but here too the enemy was repulsed.

The British lines were now gradually drawing nearer to the fortress, every day more guns were placed in position and the fire grew heavier. The condition of the besieged was becoming desperate; nearly one-fourth of the garrison was sick in hospital; no place was safe from our shot; the enemy guns were being everywhere dismounted; and the masonry of the parapets was falling about the ears of the defenders. On the 21st three big ships in the harbour were burned; on the 22nd the citadel was in flames; and on the following day the barracks in the town caught fire and were destroyed. On the 25th a naval party from our fleet rowed into the harbour, captured one of the only two remaining French ships-of-war and burned the other. Finally, on the 26th the last gun on the ramparts was silenced, and on the same day the Governor of Louisburg, the gallant Chevalier Drucour, made offers of capitulation.

Next day terms were agreed upon and three companies of Grenadiers took possession of the Dauphine Gate, when the British marched in, and the garrison laid down their arms, the troops being sent to England and the colonists to France.

The prisoners taken numbered 5,637 officers and men, and among the trophies of war were 221 cannon, 18 mortars, 15,000 stand of arms, 11 stand of Colours and quantities of ammunition and other stores.

During the siege the French lost over 1,000 men ; the British had 21 officers and 150 men killed, 30 officers and 320 men wounded—of these the 47th had 9 killed and 30 wounded.

Lieutenant Gordon, of the 40th, gives in his diary of the Siege a " Return of the Men," of the 35th, 40th, 45th and 47th, " who went as volunteers to erect the two last batteries against Louisburg with me," and the names of the men of the 47th may well be recorded here ; they were :—George Ferguson, Hugh Lacey, William Walker, William Petreap, George White, William English, Edmund Thomas, Samuel Squires, John Hardgrove, James Nugent, Thomas Boyd, John Garrison, Daniel Dickens and John Negley.

Brigadier Whitmore was appointed Governor of Louisburg and remained there with the 22nd, 28th, 40th and 45th Regiments as garrison ; on the 30th August General Amherst left Louisburg with five regiments, one of these being the 47th, and landed at Boston on the 14th September, the Regiment then moving to winter quarters in the Jerseys ; before the autumn came to an end the expeditionary force had been broken up, the troops which had composed it being distributed between Halifax, Annapolis Royal, Albany, Philadelphia, New England, the Jerseys and Fort Stanwix.

General Wolfe went home to England immediately after the fall of Louisburg, but was recalled to North America in the following spring on nomination by Pitt to command the force to be directed against Quebec.

The attack on Quebec and the overthrow of the French power in Canada were to be effected by three separate expeditionary forces, all of which were eventually to come together before Quebec. General Amherst, with the main army twelve thousand strong, was to start from Lake George, and, proceeding down the Richelieu River, occupy Montreal, then descend the St. Lawrence and join Wolfe before Quebec ; Wolfe, with another force of twelve thousand men, was to sail up the St. Lawrence from Louisburg ; and Brigadier Prideaux, with a smaller body of troops, was to reduce Fort Niagara and then, moving through Ontario and down the rapids of the St. Lawrence, endeavour to co-operate with Amherst and Wolfe.

" It was the middle of February when Wolfe sailed from England in H.M.S. ' Neptune,' the flag-ship of a fleet of twenty-one sail under Admirals Saunders, Holmes and Durell. The voyage was long and tedious, and when at last Louisburg was reached the harbour was found to be blocked with ice, so that the fleet was obliged to make for Halifax. From thence Durell was detached, too late as was presently proved, to the mouth of the St. Lawrence to intercept certain transports that were expected with supplies from France ; Holmes was sent to convoy the troops that were to sail from New York; and in May the entire armament for the reduction of Quebec was assembled at Louisburg." *

Wolfe's force was considerably weaker than had been intended; several regiments which were to have joined him from the West Indies were not forthcoming, while others of those provided from local garrisons were very much under strength; all were, however, of excellent quality. The commanders of Wolfe's three brigades were Brigadiers Monckton,† Townshend and Murray, and the 47th was in Townshend's brigade with the 28th and 2nd Battalion 60th.

The troops consisted of ten battalions of infantry, six companies of Rangers and a Corps of Light Infantry; the Grenadier Companies of the regiments remaining in garrison at Louisburg—the 22nd, 40th and 45th —were formed into a separate corps, under Major Murray, 45th, called the Louisburg Grenadiers; every man was issued with thirty-six rounds of ammunition, Lieutenant Dobson, 47th, was again detailed as brigade-major of one of the Brigades, and the 47th was ordered to furnish twenty-four men for Captain Adams' company of Light Infantry. On the 2nd June entrenching tools were issued to the troops, the 47th receiving 70 picks, 30 spades, 10 shovels and 10 billhooks. The embarkation return of the 5th June gives the following as the strength of the 47th Regiment: 36 Officers, 40 Sergeants, 603 Rank and File with 19 Men sick; and states that the Regiment embarked at Perth Amboy near New York on May 5th, sailed on the 8th and arrived at Louisburg on the 22nd. Since the reduction of Louisburg the 47th had lost four hundred and four and had recruited ninety-seven men.

The fleet sailed from Louisburg in three divisions, Townshend's Brigade in the second, but it was not until the 6th June that the last of the transports left Louisburg Harbour. On the 7th the fleet made the coast of Newfoundland, on the 20th it was off the mouth of the deep and gloomy Saguenay, on the 23rd "the Narrows" were passed, two days later the difficult passage of "the Traverse" was safely negotiated, and on the 26th the fleet anchored off the Island of New Orleans.

In the evening of this day a party of the Rangers landed and had a slight skirmish with some of the inhabitants, these giving way and abandoning the island during the night. Then early on the morning of the 27th the troops were landed in a cove under the Church of St. Lawrence and remained for some little time drawn up on the beach, then moved further to the westward and there encamped. Meanwhile Wolfe, accompanied by an escort, furnished by the Light Infantry, proceeded to a point on

* Fortescue, Vol. II, pp. 360, 361.
† Formerly 47th, but since December, 1757, Col.-Comdnt. 60th.

the west side of the island, from where the city and fortress of Quebec could plainly be seen, lying some four miles to the west on a rocky height on the north bank of the St. Lawrence. He was now for the first time able to estimate the difficulties of the enterprise to which he was committed.

Along the northern shore, from the St. Charles River to the Montmorency Falls ran a line of heights some six or seven miles in length; on these redoubts and entrenchments had been constructed, guarding and obstructing every approach from the riverside, while behind these were fourteen thousand men under the Marquis de Montcalm. In the centre of this position the little River Beaufort ran into the St. Lawrence, and near this spot were encamped five regular battalions of French infantry, and here also was Montcalm's headquarters. The rest of the troops consisted of Militia or Colonials. In Quebec itself there was a garrison of two thousand men under the Chevalier de Ramsay, and one hundred and five guns were mounted on the ramparts and in the many batteries.

On the evening after the landing the French made an attempt against the British fleet with some fire-ships, but the effort was a failure, some of the fire-ships running ashore, while others were taken in tow by the men from the ships and towed out of harm's way. On the following morning Monckton's Brigade was ferried over to the high ground at Point Lévis, opposite Quebec, which was occupied; and on the 5th July working parties broke ground to the west of Point Lévis and began the construction of batteries under fire from the city. Part of the 2nd Brigade (Townshend's) was also employed in throwing up earthworks on the western point of the Island of Orleans for the protection of our ships in the basin.

Wolfe's great wish was to come to close quarters with the enemy, and it appeared that the only way of doing this was to carry the force from the Island of Orleans across the north channel of the St. Lawrence, and establish it on the high ground east of the Montmorency River, from which position an attack on the enemy's left or rear might be carried out. With this idea Monckton was ordered to make a demonstration up the river, while several vessels of war cannonaded the entrenchments of the Chevalier de Lévis, which lay just west of the Montmorency.

In Camp Orders, dated Orleans, 7th July, it is directed that "Bragg's, Lascelles', Monckton's, the Light Infantry and Rangers, with three companies of Grenadiers, should hold themselves in readiness to march next day at 10 o'clock, taking three days' provisions and half their tents." The troops embarked accordingly on the evening of the 8th—Murray's Brigade also taking part—and landed on the morning of the 9th in front of the parish of L'Ange Gardien, a short way below the mouth of the Montmorency. They climbed the heights, and, driving off the Canadians and

Indians who opposed them, commenced to entrench themselves, holding the position against several heavy attacks.

On this date the strength of the 47th present is given as : Grenadier Company 79, Light Company 72, Battalion Companies 335.

The batteries at Point Lévis were completed by the 12th July, when they opened fire on the city, doing much damage to the buildings, and so alarming the citizens that they begged Vaudreuil, the Governor, to allow fifteen hundred Canadians to go over and silence the batteries. Permission was granted, but the venture miscarried, the attacking party being seized with a panic and hurriedly retreated, having effected nothing.

Having examined many points where attack seemed to promise success and none appearing very hopeful of result, Wolfe now formed the somewhat desperate resolve of assailing the enemy's camp in front, at a point nearly one mile west of the Falls of Montmorency, but within range of the British batteries on the east bank of that stream. Here, at the foot of the steep slope that rises from the St. Lawrence, was a strand about 200 yards wide at high water, though when the tide was out nearly half a mile of mud flats were left exposed. Defending this open space was a 4-gun redoubt near the foot of the slope, which was commanded from above, but of this the British were not at the time aware. By landing here Wolfe hoped to induce the enemy to come down in force, and that a general engagement would result, or that at the least an opportunity might be afforded for reconnoitring Montcalm's main position. On the 29th orders were accordingly issued for an attack on the 31st.

On the morning of that day three light men-of-war stood close in and opened fire on the redoubt at the foot of the slope, while more than forty guns in battery at Montmorency bombarded the left of the French entrenchments.

In many accounts the blame for the failure of this enterprise has been laid upon the thirteen companies of Grenadiers by whom it was mainly conducted, and critics have no doubt been largely influenced by the very scathing and unjust condemnation which Wolfe published in next day's orders. It should be remembered that for this attack Wolfe could muster no more than 5,000 men, drawn from the Grenadier Companies of his force, from the 15th and 60th Foot and Frazer's Highlanders, while the French were able to meet this attack in a strong position defended by from 10,000–12,000 men.

Two accounts of the action were sent home by the O.C. Louisburg Grenadiers and in these he wrote :—" On the 31st July we had a very smart action ; the ten companies of Grenadiers and my Corps were ordered to attack an entrenchment, which we did with great or rather too much heat, as the General himself says, and were repulsed after three attempts ; we had a good many killed and wounded "—actually the thirteen companies of Grenadiers had 33 officers and 400 other ranks killed and wounded, a loss which Wolfe describes in his Order of the Day as " very inconsiderable " ! Among the officers of Grenadiers wounded was Lieutenant Elphinstone, 47th, who was hit in the neck. The retirement was covered by the 15th and Highlanders, and Wolfe admits in his despatch that these two corps " did not attack in time."

Amongst the killed in this action was Sergeant Edward Botwood of the 47th, a well-known character in the Regiment, called by his comrades " Ned Botwood the Poet," who wrote the ballad " Hot Stuff," so popular among the British troops during the war.

Every possible point of attack now appeared to have been tested, and parties which had been landed in several directions laid waste the country with the object of exhausting the resources of the Colony and inducing the Militia to desert ; Montcalm, however, remained quiescent and refused to be drawn from his entrenchments. The British camps had now become unhealthy, dysentery and fever were prevalent, and the death-rate was high ; the casualties in action had also by this time amounted to 850 killed and wounded, 57 of these being officers. Meat was scarce and the troops subsisted mainly on horse-flesh.

In Knox's Journal of the campaign he describes the following as having taken place during the siege :—" Yesterday, on the north side, a party of Indians were discovered, in number between two and three hundred, by a small party of men under the command of Volunteer Cameron of the Light Company of the 47th, who is so greatly distinguished in the orders of the day. They first showed themselves, and then retired to a house at a small distance, whence they drubbed the savages very gallantly. The General, upon the alarm, flew to their assistance with the picquets, sustained by a detachment from the Line. Upon sight of these troops they took to flight over the river, dragging their killed and wounded with them to the number of fifteen or more, according to their practice."

The sequel to this appears in the Orders of the 17th August, where it states :—

" Mr. Cameron, a volunteer in the Light Infantry of General Lascelles' Regiment, having distinguished himself in a remarkable manner in the defence of a house, with only a sergeant, corporal and sixteen men of Lascelles' Regiment of Infantry, against a body of savages and Canadians, greatly superior in numbers, the General has ordered that the first vacant commission in the Army be given to Mr. Cameron, in acknowledgment of his good conduct and very gallant behaviour."

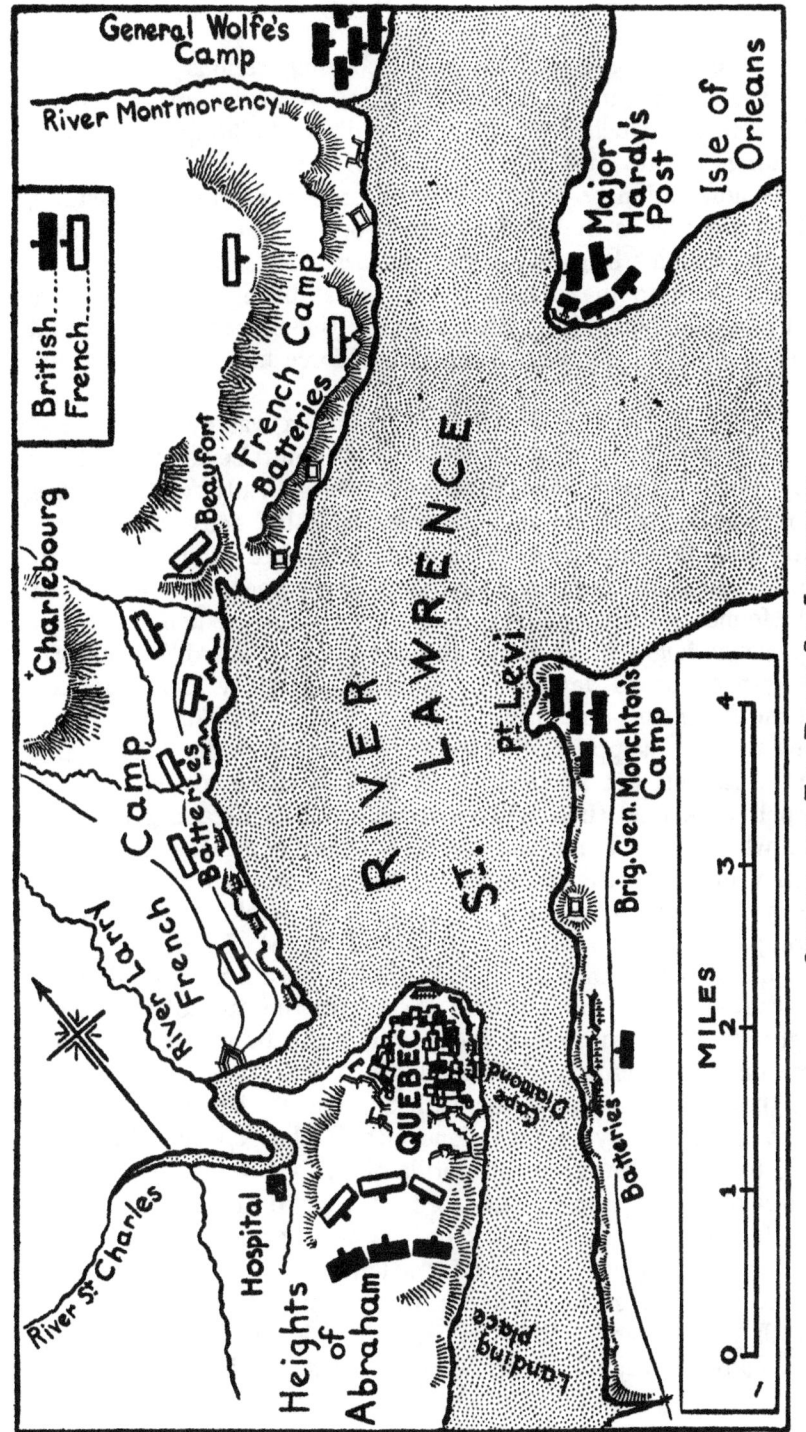

QUEBEC AND THE RIVER ST. LAWRENCE.
1759.

The distress of the besieged was now becoming serious; they were short of provisions, the Canadians were deserting in large numbers, pillage and disorder were rife, Quebec was in ruins, while all buildings which were beyond the range of our guns were crowded with sick and wounded.

Wolfe was now seriously ill, and the winter season was approaching, when the fleet must leave the St. Lawrence from fear of being ice-bound.

Having consulted his brigadiers as to the best methods for forcing an issue, it was decided to make an attempt to establish the army above Quebec on the north shore of the St. Lawrence, the effect of which would be to cut off Montcalm's sources of supply and force him to fight, or surrender.

On the 3rd September the Montmorency position was evacuated, and on the 4th all available troops were collected at Point Lévis, a flotilla of flat-bottomed boats being passed above the batteries ready for taking the regiments on board; while on the 5th a considerable body of infantry, the 47th forming part, marched some miles westward along the south bank of the St. Lawrence as far as Goreham's Cove, where they embarked in Admiral Holmes' waiting ships, making on the 7th a demonstration against Cap Rouge, eight miles above the city. The "Ward" transport, having the 47th on board, landed one hundred and sixty men, approximately half the Regiment, and all went ashore carrying blankets and camp kettles and two days' supplies, the troops sheltering in the village and church of St. Nicholas, but all ready to embark at short notice.

The French were now thoroughly alarmed, and Montcalm reinforced Bougainville who was in command about Cap Rouge, charging him to watch the movements of the British with the utmost vigilance. Meanwhile Wolfe had further reconnoitred the various possible landing-places, finally hearing of a path on the north side of the St. Lawrence which ascended the cliffs about a mile and a half from Quebec from a small cove called the Anse du Foulon, and wound thence up the face of the steep wooded heights to the open ground above, where the French had a small post of some hundred men, chiefly Canadians.

Learning that on the night of the 12th September the French would attempt to throw a convoy of provisions into Quebec on the ebb tide, Wolfe decided to send forward his own flotilla of flat-boats carrying English soldiers in place of French stores; and word was sent to Admiral Saunders, who, at nightfall, made a feint attack on the enemy position below the city, as if intending to clear the way for a landing. Wolfe, meanwhile, lay quietly near Cap Rouge, ten miles further up stream.

On the 12th Wolfe, from H.M.S. "Sutherland," issued his final orders, in which it was directed that "the first body that gets on shore is to march

QUEBEC.

13th September, 1759.

directly to the enemy and drive them from any little post they may occupy ; the officers must be careful that the succeeding bodies do not by any mistake fire on those who go before them. The battalions must form on the upper ground with expedition, and be ready to charge whatever presents itself.

"The officers and men will remember what their Country expects of them, and what a determined body of soldiers inured to war is capable of doing against five weak French battalions mingled with a disorderly peasantry."

About 9 p.m. on the 12th the troops took their places in the boats, the 47th, in the First Division, occupying boats furnished by the ships "Medway" and "Captain"; and on this day the strength of the Regiment is given as one lieut.-colonel, five captains, eight lieutenants, eight ensigns, thirty-one sergeants, two drummers and three hundred and five rank and file.

Soon after two on the morning of the 13th September the tide began to ebb, the signal was given, and the boats cast off and fell down the stream in the darkness. Twice were the leading boats challenged by French sentries on the bank, but on the reply being given that the boats contained the expected convoy, they were allowed to pass and the cove was reached. Here some of the Light Infantry landed, gained the summit of the cliff and drove off the enemy picquet, the officer here in command being wounded and taken prisoner. The remainder of the force now landed and formed up on the plain above the cliffs, the Light Infantry being sent off to silence the enemy batteries at Samos and Sillery.

On a plain of fairly level ground known as the Plains of Abraham and within a mile of the walls of Quebec, Wolfe formed his regiments in line of battle facing east in the following order : on the extreme right at the edge of the cliffs overhanging the St. Lawrence was a platoon of the 28th, and thence from right to left came the 35th, the Louisburg Grenadiers, the 28th, the 43rd and the 47th, the left of this corps being on a road running through the centre of the line towards the city and on which were placed two of our guns ; on the left of the road came the Highlanders, then the 58th and on the extreme left the Grenadier Company of the 2nd Battalion 60th. Under Wolfe, Monckton commanded the troops on the right and Murray those on the left of the road. In second line and in rear of the flanks were the 48th and 3rd Battalion 60th on the right, and the 15th and 2nd Battalion 60th on the left under Townshend.

The first line was hardly formed when a body of the enemy appeared on a ridge about 500 yards in front. This was the battalion of Guienne, apparently on its way to where it was intended to have been in support of the Cove picquet. Between six and seven o'clock parties of the enemy began to appear, and then numbers of Canadians and Indians, estimated at one thousand five hundred, established themselves in the copses and bushes opposite the British line, and in the thickets towards the valley of the St. Charles, and opened a fire which caused many casualties.

Knox of the 43rd, whose regiment was on the right of the 47th, tells us in his Journal that "what galled us most was a body of Indians and other marksmen concealed in the corn opposite our centre, inclining towards our left, but Colonel Hale, by Brigadier Monckton's orders, advanced some platoons alternately from the 47th Regiment, which, after a few rounds, obliged these skulkers to retire. We were now ordered to lie down and remained some time in this position."

It was 9 a.m. before Montcalm was able to commence forming his line of battle—the regiments of Béarn, Guienne, La Sarre, Longuedoc and Royal Roussillon and battalions of Colonial Regulars—but these as they formed up were all much galled by the fire of our two brass 6-pounders, placed on the road. Covered by the fire from their Canadian and Indian auxiliaries in the thickets and broken ground along the valley of the St. Charles, the French moved forward about ten o'clock, when on arrival within forty paces of the British line, the word was given to fire, and the volley that followed was remarkable for its precision and effect.

Knox records that "when the General formed the line of battle he ordered the regiments to load with an additional ball. The 43rd and 47th in the centre, being little affected by the oblique fire of the enemy, gave them with great calmness as remarkable a close and heavy discharge as I ever saw performed at a private field of exercise." The French afterwards described it as "un coup de canon." When the smoke cleared away, the enemy's line appeared a shattered wreck, hardly any of the two front ranks were standing, and the confused mass of wounded and disorganized men were rendered incapable of further resistance. Meanwhile the British had reloaded, and another volley was delivered, followed by independent firing. The order to charge was then given, and the line advanced, driving before it the white uniforms of France, Montcalm trying hard to rally his men.

Townshend in his despatch wrote:—"It was at this moment that each corps seemed in a manner to exert itself with a view to its own peculiar character. The Grenadiers, Bragg's and Lascelles' pressed on with their bayonets." In a letter from an officer present we are told that "our regiments that sustained the brunt of the action were Bragg's, Lascelles' and the Highlanders, the two former had not a bayonet or the latter a broadsword untinged with blood."

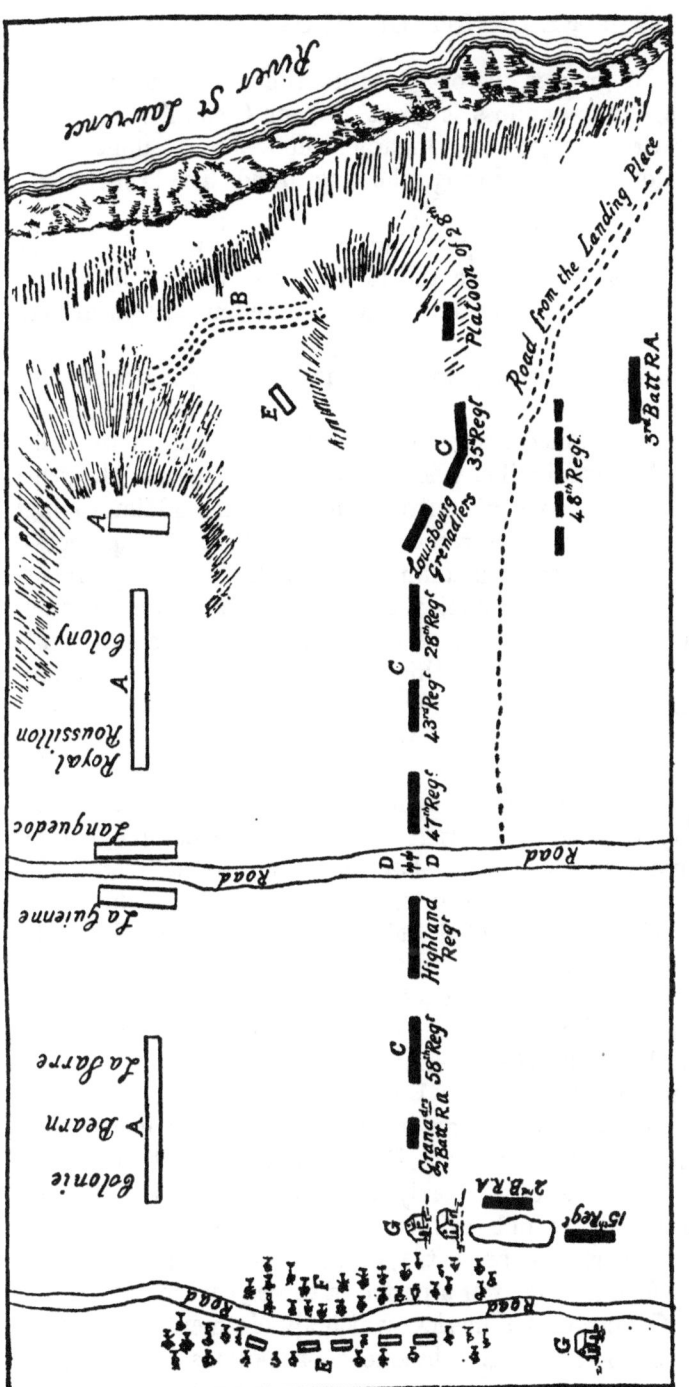

THE BATTLE OF QUEBEC.

13th September, 1759.

"A." French Army.
"B." Canadians in three Indian files endeavouring to gain our flank.
"C." English Army.
"D." Two pieces of Artillery served with grape.
"E." Canadians who "galled our flanks."
"F." Copse lined with Canadians.
"G." Houses filled with Light Infantry and Grenadiers to prevent the Canadians from gaining our flank.

"Never was there a greater victory," wrote the commander of the Louisburg Grenadiers, "but our loss is great as poor General Wolfe was killed on the right with my people, Brigadier Monckton wounded but will do well." Monckton was shot through the lungs beside his old regiment, the 47th.

The 47th and 58th did not stop pursuing until close to the St. Louis and St. Jean Gates of the City, when the former was checked by a fire of grape from the ramparts, and the latter by the cannon on two armed hulks in the river.

General Montcalm was mortally wounded as he fell back near the St. Louis Gate.

Townshend had now assumed command, reformed his battalions after the pursuit, drove back Bougainville, who was advancing against the rear of the British, and then set to work entrenching himself and improving the path up the cliff to enable the stores and guns to be brought up necessary for the siege which now seemed imminent. On the 17th September the fleet was placed in position to attack the lower town, and by the same date Townshend had sixty-one pieces of heavy and fifty-seven of light ordnance mounted in position. Everything was, however, in confusion in Quebec, and on the 18th the place surrendered and a British garrison marched in, though it was the 29th before the bulk of the force was accommodated within the walls.

According to a return given in Doughty's *Siege of Quebec and The Battle of the Plains of Abraham*, the 47th lost during the campaign two officers—Lieuts. Seymour and Matheson—two sergeants and eighteen other ranks killed, eleven officers, three sergeants, three drummers and fifty-five rank and file wounded; the wounded officers were Captains Gardner, Spital and Smelt, Lieuts. Peach, Elphinstone, Mountain, Guinet, Ewer and Henning, Ensigns Dunlop and Faunce.

At the dying request of General Wolfe, Lieut.-Colonel Hale of the 47th was sent home with the despatches describing the action.

John Hale had served with the 47th Regiment in Scotland during the Rebellion of 1745; he was promoted captain in 1752, major in 1755, lieutenant-colonel in 1758; he had also been with the Regiment throughout the whole of the campaign in North America. Shortly after his return to England he severed his connection with his old regiment; being entrusted to raise a regiment of Light Dragoons, the present 17th Lancers, of which he was appointed to the colonelcy in 1763 after a period of three years in command. In 1770 he was made Governor of Limerick, which appointment he vacated later for that of Londonderry. His subsequent promotions were major-general 1772, lieutenant-general 1777, general 1793. Born in 1728 he

COLONEL J. HALE.

received his first commission in the 47th Regiment at the age of fourteen years. He died in 1806, near Guisborough, Yorkshire, leaving a family of seventeen children. For bringing back the Quebec despatches he was awarded the sum of £500 ; ten thousand acres on Hales River, near Halifax, Nova Scotia, were also granted to him in recognition of his services during the campaign, but these lapsed to the Crown in course of time. " He was well received at Court, and being a talented officer, well acquainted with the nature of the service of cavalry, infantry and artillery, his merits procured him the favour of his Sovereign."

It was not until close upon a century and a quarter later that the Regiment was accorded any recognition of its services in the capture of Louisburg and of Quebec, for it was only on the 29th April, 1882, that the following letter was received by the then Colonel of the Regiment.

" No. 20/Gen. No./1459.
" Horse Guards, War Office, S.W.
" 29th April, 1882.

" SIR,—

" By desire of H.R.H. The Field-Marshal Commanding-in-Chief I have the honour to acquaint you that Her Majesty has been graciously pleased to command that the Victories of Louisburg and Quebec, 1759, shall be inscribed on the Colours of The North Lancashire Regiment, and the same will be recorded in the next issue of ' the Queen's Regulations and Orders for the Army ' in addition to present achievements.

" I have etc.
" G. J. WOLSELEY.
" A. G.

" General Sir W. S. R. Norcott, K.C.B.
" Colonel, 1st Battn. North Lancashire Regiment."

CHAPTER III

1759-1776

THE CONQUEST OF CANADA
HOME SERVICE IN IRELAND
THE WAR OF AMERICAN INDEPENDENCE
THE BATTLE OF BUNKER'S HILL

MONCKTON, being still disabled by his wound, went to New York, and Townshend sailed almost at once for England, where he was soon appointed to a command in the British force serving in Germany under Lord Granby. This left Brigadier Murray in command of the troops remaining in Quebec, of which city he became Governor, with Colonel Burton of the 48th Regiment as Lieut.-Governor.

The garrison was now composed of ten battalions of infantry, one company of Rangers and two of artillery, the total effective strength on the 29th October being 7,317, that of the 47th on this date being one major, two captains, fifteen lieutenants, eight ensigns, one adjutant, one chaplain, one surgeon, one surgeon's mate, one quartermaster, thirty-eight sergeants, seventeen drummers, two fifers and 538 rank and file.

After the surrender of the fortress the troops were kept very busy, filling in entrenchments, repairing the fortifications, storing provisions, cutting firewood and generally providing for the winter. The duties too were especially heavy, every day 25 officers and 930 other ranks being on guard, while many parties were employed working on the fortifications and in other fatigue duties.

Towards the end of October the enemy's light troops became troublesome and cattle were frequently raided, and in November many skirmishes took place, and demonstrations were made against the British outposts. On the 11th November Major Hussey, commanding the 47th, was ordered to hold himself in readiness for service with 721 men, besides officers, every man carrying fifty rounds and three flints for his musket, and six days' provisions. A party of these, one hundred strong, was attacked on this day outside the town, but the enemy retired, on Major Hussey and the remainder of his men turning out. On the 14th Major Hussey marched out and occupied the Church of Lorette and St. Foy, some twelve miles from Quebec, when he, in company with Colonel Walsh of the 28th Foot, attacked the French posts at Point-au-Tremble, and laid waste that part of the country.

When the winter arrived the British troops suffered greatly from the cold: there were many cases of frost-bite, the clothing issued was quite unsuited to the climate and fuel was not always obtainable. Firewood had to be cut and brought in from a distance of four miles in sleighs, each drawn by eight men: nine of these sleighs were issued to the 47th. The wood-cutting parties were protected by strong guards, and all worked with slung muskets. Living, as all did, on salt provisions with no vegetables, scurvy broke out, and before the spring of 1760 one thousand men had died and two thousand were unfit for duty. The local farmers were themselves so poorly supplied that such food as was to be bought was at famine prices, while the men's pay was not only small but irregularly forthcoming. In the beginning of March, 1760, the effective strength of the garrison had fallen to 4,800, and by the 24th April to little over 3,000; the 47th on this date had only 305 rank and file fit for duty, while 170 men were sick and 64 had died since the 18th of the previous September.

On the 23rd April the Grenadier Battalion and the 15th, 28th, 47th, 58th and 3rd Battalion 60th Regiments had been ordered to hold themselves in readiness to take the field, these being the most effective of the corps available, the General intending to encamp at St. Foy, strengthen the advanced posts and prevent any landing by the French, reports having been received that General Lévis was preparing to attack Quebec. This officer had retired to Montreal with the remains of Montcalm's army, and during the winter had got together a really formidable force, containing eight regular battalions, two Colonial battalions, 3,000 Canadians, 400 Indians and a train of artillery. The French also possessed several small war-vessels, thus having command of the St. Lawrence, since the British had no naval force with which to oppose them.

Lévis embarked his troops on April 20th, landed on the 26th and at day-break on the 27th arrived close to St. Foy; here early the following morning General Murray arrived, determined to give battle; he had at his disposal three thousand men with twenty field-guns and two howitzers. On this day the strength of the 47th Regiment was one major, two captains, eleven lieutenants, five ensigns, thirty sergeants and two hundred and sixty-four other ranks.

Murray drew up his little force on the same ground whereon Montcalm had opposed Wolfe at the Battle of Quebec. The French could be seen moving along the edge of Sillery Wood, their right forming on two block-houses not far from the Anse du Foulon, and their left on some rising ground near a house and windmill close to the St. Foy road. Murray decided upon an immediate attack before the French line was fully formed, and the British line was drawn up as follows :—

Colonel Burton was in command of the right wing composed of the 15th, 48th, 58th and 2nd Battalion 60th, its flank covered by Major Dalling's Light Infantry, while in the left wing were the 28th, 43rd, 47th and the Highlanders under Colonel Frazer, the left protected by a company of Rangers and a hundred volunteers ; the 35th and 3rd Battalion 60th formed the reserve. In the intervals between each battalion the guns were posted, and these, coming into action, by their fire compelled the French to fall back in some disorder. Murray now unwisely decided that the day was won and left his advantages of position, his guns thereby getting into low ground where they were bogged and could not be favourably employed.

The French now rallied, their main column came up and on the flanks of the opposing armies a fierce infantry fight developed. The houses on the St. Foy road became the scene of a bitter struggle, the British Light Infantry attacking them again and again, but the French, having been substantially reinforced, drove back the light troops who retired across the front of the right brigade, masking its fire. In like manner did the French right, by force of numbers, creep round the English left. Murray now flung his reserve regiments into the fight on either flank, but they did not suffice to restore the balance, while our gunfire was ineffective and ammunition too was beginning to fail. The British were gradually forced back, and Murray at last gave the order to retreat. This was carried out in an orderly manner, the French having been too seriously handled to make a really effective pursuit. The sorely-battered troops gained at last the shelter of the city walls, having left on the field all their guns and one-third of their fighting strength.

Murray's force had suffered a loss of close upon eleven hundred of all ranks, killed and wounded, while in the 47th Major Hussey, the commanding officer, and eleven non-commissioned officers and men were killed, and five officers—Lieutenants Forster, Basset, Stratford, Ewer and Ensign Uftick—and forty-seven other ranks were wounded, and Captain Archbold and Lieutenant Sherriff were wounded and taken prisoner.

As to the losses of the French in the action, estimates vary, but they were heavy enough to prevent Lévis from making any attempt at a *coup de main* against the fortress, while Murray was preparing to withstand a siege. Within twenty-four hours Murray had his men well in hand again, and men and officers alike were set to work on the defences. In a very short time one hundred and fifty guns were mounted on the ramparts and the besiegers were heavily bombarded and their casualties were many. The siege indeed made little enough progress, although the garrison consisted in the words of one who shared their labour, of "but 2,400 half-starved and scorbutic skeletons."

On May 19th a frigate appeared round the Isle d'Orléans bearing up for Quebec; she was cleared for action and no ensign floated from her masthead. Every eye in both armies was bent upon her, for if she were English, she would mean relief for the besieged, while if French her arrival portended that Lévis had gained what time he needed for the task of reducing the fortress; and so both sides watched anxiously for the frigate to declare herself. At last the Cross of St. George broke from her main halliards—she was the "Lowestoft" frigate and her coming meant salvation for the defenders.

On 15th May an advance squadron arrived and, running past the city, attacked and burnt Lévis's stores further up the river. The same night the French commander withdrew, leaving behind him forty guns, his entrenching tools and all his sick and wounded, Murray sending in pursuit some infantry battalions of which the 47th was one. The French, however, had got too good a start and Lévis made his way, practically unmolested, to Jacques Cartier.

Montreal was to be the next object of attack, and with its fall the conquest of Canada would be completed. To this end General Amherst, the Commander-in-Chief in America, had planned a combined movement, in which three forces, starting from widely-separated points, were to converge on Montreal. Amherst, with the main army, ten thousand strong, was to move from Lake Ontario down the St. Lawrence; Haviland, with three thousand four hundred Regulars and Provincials, was to make his way from Crown Point by Lake Champlain; while Murray was to advance up the river with all the troops that could be spared after providing a garrison for Quebec, followed by two battalions from Louisburg under Lord Rollo. The French made such preparations as they could to oppose the British advance, La Corne being sent to defend the rapids above Montreal, Bougainville took post at Isle-aux-Noix to oppose Haviland, while detachments at Point-au-Tremble, Jacques Cartier and Deschambault were to do all they could to delay Murray.

Murray now re-drafted his field army, forming of it five composite battalions and two grenadier battalions. Detachments, each of nine officers and 161 other ranks, were furnished by the 47th and 48th Regiments to compose the 5th Composite Battalion under Major Spital of the 47th, and the Grenadier Company of the Regiment was in the 1st Grenadier Battalion with those of the 15th, 35th, 58th and 3rd Battalion 60th. When, on July 15th,

Murray's force embarked in thirty-two vessels and moved up the river, its strength was rather over 2,500 all ranks.

The force proceeded slowly up the river, skirmishing all the way, until on August 24th it arrived at Contrecour, about twenty miles below Montreal; here it halted while parties were sent out to gain touch with Haviland, who had received on the 27th the surrender of St. John's, joining hands with Murray the same day. The combined force now advanced on Montreal, where Murray landed on the Isle St. Thérèse, while Haviland occupied Chambly on the south bank. The resistance met with at Fort Lévis, and the damage suffered by his transports in passing the rapids, had delayed for a few days the arrival of Amherst and the main army, but on September 6th these came in, landing at La Chine and camping under the walls of the city. Thus the junction of the three widely-scattered armies was accomplished, and the British had now concentrated some seventeen thousand men in the presence of the enemy.

In the French army desertion and demoralization were rife, and when on the 7th September the French commanders reviewed the situation, they found that they had only some two thousand five hundred men available for defence, and resistance appearing therefore to be hopeless, Vaudreuil, the commander, opened negotiations with Amherst. On the 8th September, 1760, the capitulation was signed and Canada passed for all time into British possession.

The detachment of the 47th serving under Murray in the Composite and Grenadier Battalions now returned to Quebec, where the headquarters of the Regiment remained until the year 1762, in June of that year its strength being given as 45 officers and 443 effective other ranks, with 37 men sick. During part of this year, and also in 1763, nine companies appear to have garrisoned Charlburgh, while one company was on detachment at Point-au-Tremble; but late in 1763 the 47th was again concentrated at Quebec, having now been ordered home after nearly thirteen years of foreign service, for peace had in February been signed with France and the long war was over.

The 47th landed at Cork on the 5th December, 1763, and served for the next ten years in Ireland—at Cork from 1763 to 1766; at Limerick in 1766; Dublin in 1767; Athlone and Carrick-on-Shannon in 1768; Limerick again in 1769 and 1770; at Charlesfort in 1771 and 1772; and in many detachments in County Cork in 1772 and 1773. In May, 1773, the 47th was concentrated at Cork preparatory to proceeding again on foreign service, and on the 18th of this month it sailed again for America, and arrived on the 28th July. The companies were now quartered as follows:—four companies at Perth Amboy, three companies at Brunswick and three at Elizabeth Town.

In the American Colonies there had for some years past been signs of ill will against the Home Government; and there had been many disputes between the Mother Country and the Colonies, often insignificant in themselves, but "rendered dangerous by hesitation and ignorance in the rulers, by persistent and dexterous agitation on the part of the subjects." As far back as 1767 the Legislature of New York had refused, in defiance of the terms of the Mutiny Act, to supply the Royal troops with quarters, while a year later the Council of Boston similarly refused accommodation for two regiments ordered thither from New York.

At the close of the war with France, the establishment of the Army had, as usual, been greatly reduced, being fixed at something over forty-five thousand men. The Army List for 1773, the year the 47th was ordered to America, shows fourteen infantry battalions as being then quartered in that country, but these were probably very weak, as the establishment for the whole of our Colonies was fixed at ten thousand men only; and while the regiments in America had to provide garrisons for New York, Halifax, Quebec, Boston, Mobile and Pensacola, they had also to find detachments for a chain of posts extending for some three hundred miles from the St. Lawrence to the Mississippi.

In 1765 the Cabinet in London had carried the Stamp Act, under which a tax was levied on the colonists in return for the protection afforded them by the presence of the Royal troops. This measure raised a great outcry throughout the American Colonies, where it was contended that there could be no taxation without representation. The unpopularity of the tax caused its repeal in 1766, but a year later it was re-imposed, when so bitter a controversial spirit was aroused that it appeared inevitable that the matter could not be settled without an appeal to arms.

Such was the situation when the 47th landed in America, 457 strong, in 1773, being quartered in the State of New Jersey; but in the autumn of the following year it was moved to Boston, where troops were being assembled to meet the menace of the continued and growing lawlessness of the colonists, and it landed there on the 23rd October.

General Gage, who some years previously had succeeded Amherst as Commander-in-Chief in America, and who was also now Governor of Massachusetts with headquarters at Boston, had early recognized the serious nature of the situation. By the beginning of 1775 he had concentrated eleven infantry regiments, of which the 47th was one, in or near Boston, and he had done his best to make the home authorities realize how desperate matters were likely to become, urging that not fewer than twenty thousand men would be needed to suppress the revolt, since some sixteen thousand armed Americans were collecting in the immediate vicinity of Boston. In consequence of his representations the Home Government acted with unusual promptitude, a regiment of cavalry and seven infantry battalions having left England for America before the middle of May, 1775, while three general officers—Howe, Burgoyne and Clinton—were also dispatched in advance, all three landing at Boston on the 25th May.

General Gage had already taken action in regard to the inimical attitude of the colonists and had seized certain small collections of warlike stores; but at last, on April 19th, occurred the collision which at once transformed a smouldering rebellion into a serious and long-enduring conflict.

The General received information that the colonists had formed a depot of munitions at Concord, a small town about twenty miles north-west of Boston, and this he determined to destroy, detailing for this service a force of some eight hundred men under command of Lieut.-Colonel Smith, 10th Foot, and composed of the Grenadier and Light Companies of the Regiments in garrison, including those of the 47th, and also some Marines. The advance guard of this force arrived at Lexington, a small village on the Boston–Concord road, about 5 a.m. on the 19th April, and here a body of Colonial Militia was discovered parading under arms on the village green. Shots were exchanged and casualties suffered on both sides, after which the colonials retired, and the British force pursued its way to Concord, six miles further on, where some stores were seized and burnt.

The alarm had now, however, been given, the whole country-side was aroused, and the Militia had received substantial reinforcements; the parties which Colonel Smith had sent out to hold the approaches to the village were driven in by sheer weight of numbers, and the British commander now decided, somewhat belatedly, that it was time to fall back. When at noon the troops began their retirement on Boston, the whole country-side had turned out under arms, and from behind every bank, rock and tree, lining the tortuous and difficult road, concealed marksmen maintained a heavy fire upon the retiring troops. Time after time did the column face about, hoping to bring the enemy into the open; the attackers were nowhere visible, and while bringing down our men by their carefully-aimed fire from concealed positions, our volley firing was conducted against no visible target. In sorry plight, short of ammunition, the soldiers hungry and weary after fourteen hours' continuous marching and fighting, the column reached Lexington once more at two o'clock in the afternoon, and was met here by a relief force composed of the remaining companies of the 4th, 23rd, 47th and Marines, and two guns, the whole under Major-General Lord Percy.

After a brief halt, the retreat was resumed, but for the remaining fifteen miles into Boston the column continued to be harassed by a heavy and sustained fire from all sides. About sunset the exhausted survivors of this expedition reached Boston, the pursuit only ceasing when the colonists came under the fire of the guns of the defences.

Colonel Smith's detachment had marched thirty miles in eighteen hours and had sustained a running fire for eighteen miles. The losses too had been heavy, for of the eighteen hundred men who had taken part in the operations from first to last, nineteen officers and two hundred and fifty other ranks had been killed and wounded; in the 47th Regiment five men were killed, while two officers—Lieutenant Donald M'Leod and Ensign Henry Baldwin—one sergeant and twenty-one rank and file were wounded.

"The effect of the skirmish at Lexington made itself felt far beyond New England. In New York, where there had been symptoms of a return to loyalty, the populace seized the magazines and two provision-ships, elected a Provincial Congress, and began to arm and organize a military force. In Philadelphia and New Jersey the same spirit was at work, and the conciliatory proposals of Lord Dartmouth, the Secretary for the Colonies, were everywhere rejected. And meanwhile New England, not content with defensive measures, resolved with great promptitude, while the British were still weak, to make a sudden attack upon the British posts on the Lakes." *

For more than a month the troops were confined to Boston, awaiting the arrival of reinforcements from England, while the colonists formed a line of investment extending from Roxbury on the right to the Mystic River on the left, strengthened by redoubts and artillery. In May several regiments arrived in Boston Harbour and were at once disembarked; and on the 16th June the order was given out that "every soldier was to be completed with sixty rounds of ammunition and three good flints and to see that his arms are put in the best order."

Fortescue tells us in his *History of the British Army* that "the object of the Americans was to drive the British from Boston, but though they had already given Gage much trouble to collect supplies, they could only dispossess him by seizing some of the hills which commanded the town. The situation of the two armies, dictated of course by the configuration of the ground, was somewhat peculiar. The Americans occupied a line of heights in a semicircle from north to south, with the curve to westward, around the inner harbour; while the British held the peninsula of Boston, which forms, roughly speaking, the southern half of the base of that semicircle. There were two eminences from which Boston could be commanded by artillery; one called Dorchester Heights to the south-eastward, the other on the peninsula of Charlestown, which forms the northern half of the base of the semicircle, called Bunker's Hill. The latter, being the

* Fortescue, Vol. III, p. 152.

nearer, was the more important of the two, and Gage, soon after the arrival of the reinforcements, resolved to occupy it."

This design came, however, to the knowledge of the Americans, and during the night of the 16th–17th June they occupied and entrenched some high ground known as Breed's Hill, on the same range of hills but nearer to Boston, and so situated that Gage could either have landed troops on the flanks or rear of the entrenchment, or have raked it by fire from a war-vessel placed on either flank. He decided, however, to turn out the force holding the line by a frontal attack.

The following order was accordingly issued at 10 a.m. on the 17th June :—" The ten Eldest Companies of Grenadiers and ten Eldest Companies of Light Infantry (exclusive of those of the Regiments lately landed), the 5th and 38th Regiments to parade at half after eleven o'clock with their arms, ammunition, blankets and provisions ordered to be cooked this morning. They will march by files to the Long Wharf. The 43rd and 52nd Regiments, with the remaining Companies of Light Infantry and Grenadiers, to parade at the same time with the same directions, and march to the North Battery. The 47th Regiment and 1st Battalion of Marines will also march as above directed to the North Battery after the rest are embarked and be ready to embark there when ordered.

" The rest of the troops will be kept in readiness to march at a moment's warning.

" One subaltern, one sergeant, one corporal, one drummer and twenty privates to be left by each corps for the security of their respective encampments."

By 1 p.m. on this day the Grenadiers, Light Infantry, the 5th, 38th, 43rd and 52nd Regiments had landed on the eastern end of the Charlestown peninsula at a spot known as Moulton's Point, and remained here under cover ; while Major-General Howe, who was in command of this attack reconnoitred the ground, and discovered that the enemy on the heights was in force and strongly posted, while some houses in Charlestown itself, which covered the right flank were occupied by sharpshooters. Another disturbing fact now came to light, that the ordnance had issued shot for 12-pounders, while the guns with Howe's troops were 6-pounders only !

On the 43rd and 52nd being disembarked the force was drawn up in three lines—the ten Light Companies on the right and the ten Grenadier Companies on their left ; in rear of these were the 5th and 38th, and in rear of these again the 43rd and 52nd. The heat this day was very great, the grass on the hill was knee-high and every man carried a kit weighing close upon 125 lb.

During the advance which now commenced, the regiments deployed,

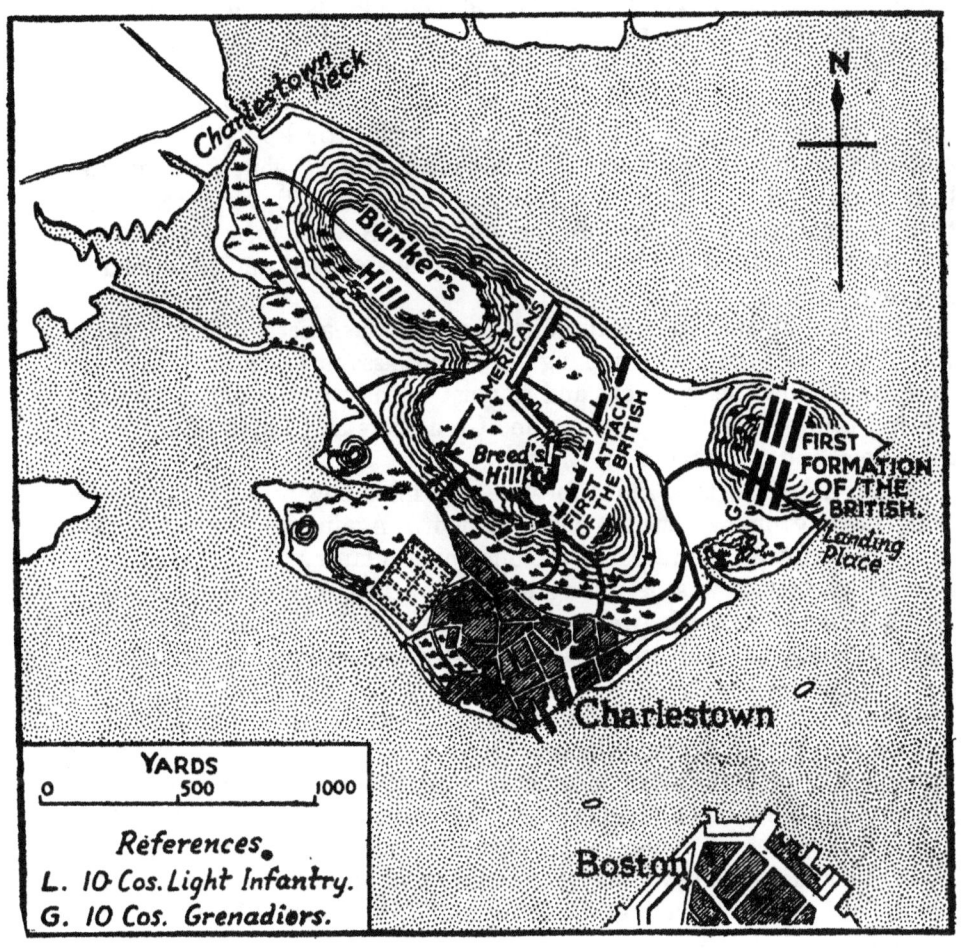

The Battle of Bunker's Hill.

17th June, 1775.

the Light Infantry Battalion moving against the extreme left of the enemy position, while the Grenadier Battalion, supported by the 5th and 52nd, attacked it in front. "Between the rebels' line and ours," wrote General Howe, "there were very high and strong fences of posts and railing, which were parallel to the enemy's works; these fences greatly impeded the attacks by the difficulty of passing them in a very hot fire, and prevented the troops rushing on with their bayonets, which would soon have decided the victory in favour of the King's troops with little loss." The British, moreover, seem to have opened fire at too great a range, while the Americans held theirs until the attack grew near and then fired with very great effect, their sharpshooters picking off the officers. Howe's men now, having suffered many casualties, fell back out of range, rallied and re-formed for a second attack.

Howe led his men on again, but the attack was a second time repulsed with heavy loss, and before making yet a third assault he ordered his troops to throw off their heavy packs and to trust to the bayonet only; now also General Clinton hurried up with some Grenadiers and Light Infantry, the 47th Foot and a battalion of Marines.

Again did the attack move forward, the guns now also advancing and firing heavily on the enemy entrenchment. Again did the rebels deal destruction among the ranks of the oncoming infantry; but the ammunition of the defence was beginning to fail, the British infantry was not to be denied and the works were carried with a rush, the defenders falling hurriedly back and suffering many casualties when crossing Charlestown Neck to the mainland.

The loss of the Americans in this action was no more than 450 killed and wounded, that of the British amounted to 1,146 killed and wounded out of 2,500 men who went into action; in the 47th two officers—Lieutenants R. Gould and C. Hilliard—one sergeant and fifteen rank and file were killed or died of wounds, while five officers, three sergeants and forty-seven other ranks were wounded; the five wounded officers were Major T. Smelt, Captains R. England, J. H. Craig and J. D. Alcock and Lieutenant P. England.

In his report on the action to General Gage, Howe wrote:—"The valour of the British officers was at no time more conspicuous than in the action; nor were the soldiers the least dismayed upon seeing the great superiority of numbers opposed to them; on the contrary, they were ardent in their wishes to get at them with their bayonets. In a word, Sir, the gallantry and conduct of the officers, as well as the bravery of the soldiers, deserve the highest praise."

Then in a General Order, dated the 19th June, General Gage, who had witnessed the whole action from some rising ground, twelve hundred yards distant, wrote :—

"The Commander-in-Chief returns his most grateful thanks to Major-General Howe for the extraordinary exertion of his military abilities on the 17th inst. He returns his thanks also to Lieut.-Colonels Nesbitt, '(47th),' Abercrombie, Gunning and Clark, Majors Butler, Williams, Bruce, Tupper, Spendlove, Smelt '(47th)' and Mitchel and the rest of the officers and soldiers, who by remarkable efforts of courage and gallantry overcame every disadvantage and drove the rebels from their redoubt and strongholds on the Heights of Charlestown and gained a complete victory."

The position captured was now entrenched and held and the ground considerably extended, but the 47th appears to have remained posted at the entrance to Charlestown.

In certain General Orders published about this time, the following refer to the 47th Regiment :—in those of the 22nd June Lieutenant Marr is appointed to act in the D.Q.M.G.'s Department until further orders ; on the 25th "the following promotions are made by the Commander-in-Chief until His Majesty's pleasure is known : 47th (Carleton's), Ensign James Poe to be Lieutenant *vice* Gould killed ; Thomas Bunbury, Volunteer, to be Ensign *vice* Poe preferred ; Ensign Henry Baldwin to be Lieutenant *vice* Hilliard killed ; Joseph Dowling, Volunteer, to be Ensign *vice* Baldwin preferred." It will be noticed that in official documents the 47th is no longer styled "Lascelles'" but "Carleton's," Major-General Guy Carleton having been appointed colonel of the Regiment under date of the 2nd April, 1772, in the place of Lieut.-General Lascelles, whose death occurred on the 26th March of that year.

On the 27th O.C. Corps were directed to send "careful sober women to the General Hospital to take care of their wounded men who are greatly suffering for want of proper attendance " ; and in the same day's orders Lieutenant John McKinnon, 47th Regiment, is appointed quartermaster to the Corps of Grenadiers.

On the 21st July the 47th returns show sixty-four sick and an effective strength of three hundred other ranks.

On the 25th July Major Smelt, 47th, was appointed to the Grenadiers.

The muster rolls signed on the 22nd September, and in which Ensign J. Rotten of the Regiment is shown as a prisoner with the Americans, give the strength of the 47th Regiment as sixteen sergeants, eighteen corporals, ten drummers, two fifers and 238 privates present and effective, while four sergeants, twelve corporals and ninety-nine privates were absent from various causes.

On the 27th September the thanks of His Majesty King George, for the gallantry in action of his troops at Bunker's Hill, were published in orders, and at the same time the order appears to have been received for the recall of General Gage. That officer does not seem to have at once proceeded home, for it was not till the 10th October that the following announcement appears in Orders :—

"The King having ordered the Commander-in-Chief to repair to Britain and that during his absence Major-General Carleton should command His Majesty's Forces in Canada and upon the Frontiers with the full powers of Commander-in-Chief, and that Major-General Howe should have the like command within the Colonies on the Atlantic Ocean from Nova Scotia to West Florida inclusive, orders are hereby given to the troops to obey the said Major-Generals accordingly."

When Gage landed in England he found that the Government was seriously taking steps to reinforce the British army in America; a regiment of cavalry and sixteen infantry battalions were under orders and some had actually sailed, while arrangements were being made for the hire of some twenty thousand foreign troops from minor German States.

As winter approached, the troops in and about Boston began to suffer greatly from hardships and privation; for months past they had been tolerably closely invested and provisions and fuel were alike scarce. The supplies sent out from home started too late in the season, and many of the supply ships experienced heavy weather and were wrecked or driven out of their course. Smallpox was rife in Howe's army; "the ill-equipped hospitals were full to overflowing; the streets were never without armless or legless men, maimed survivors of Bunker's Hill."

On the 10th November the following was published in orders :—

"His Majesty has been pleased to direct that the regiments in America (the 18th and 59th excepted) should be forthwith augmented by an addition to each of the ten companies of one sergeant, one drummer and eighteen privates, as also that two companies, each consisting of one captain, one lieutenant, one ensign, five sergeants, three corporals, two drummers and fifty-six private men should be added to each of the said regiments. In consequence of which His Majesty has been pleased to make the following appointments in the regiments under the command of the Honourable Major-General Howe :—

* * * * *

"47th. Captain Archibald Robinson, late 100th Regiment, to be Captain.

"Lieutenant Barnard George Ward, late 96th Regiment, to be Lieutenant.

"William Eyre, Gentleman, to be Ensign."

Then, finally, in orders of the 20th November, the complete establishment of these augmented regiments of twelve companies is given as one colonel, one lieut.-colonel, one major, nine captains, fourteen lieutenants, ten ensigns, one chaplain, one adjutant, one quartermaster, one surgeon, one mate, thirty-six sergeants, thirty-six corporals, twenty-four drummers, two fifers and 672 private men, including three contingent men per company.

About the 11th December all the troops appear to have been concentrated in Boston, the Charlestown position being held by a detachment of nearly two hundred officers and men, which was relieved every fortnight; and the 47th now, with the Light Infantry, six companies of Grenadiers, the 43rd, 44th, 49th, 52nd, 63rd and two battalions of Marines, came under the command of Major-General Earl Percy. On the 21st January, 1776, however, we find the 47th told off to Brigadier-General Grant's Brigade with the 4th, 40th, 49th and some Grenadier Companies.

Major-General Howe was very much in advance of his time in adopting formations more suited to the nature of the fighting likely to be experienced than was sanctioned by the very rigid drill regulations of those days; and on the 29th February he issued an order which seems to have been the very first of its kind to be given out by a commander in the field: "Regiments," so the order ran, "when formed by companies in Battalion, or when on the General Parade, are always to have their files eighteen inches distant from each other, which they will take care to practise for the future, being the order in which they are to engage the enemy."

Since June, 1775, there had been no serious fighting; Washington, who just before the Battle of Bunker's Hill had been appointed commander of the American forces, was engaged in raising and training his army, and Howe was constrained to remain inactive since even if he had defeated the Colonial troops, he was wholly deficient of the transport necessary to follow up a victory. Early in the year 1776 he decided to withdraw his army from Boston, where he was only holding his ground in expectation of the arrival from home of sufficient shipping to enable him to convey his troops to Halifax.

By the 4th March Washington had 18,000 men under his command—Howe on this date had no more than 6,646 men fit for duty—and the American General now landed his troops on Dorchester Heights, which commanded Boston from the south. Howe had intended to attack on the night of the 9th but, a very heavy snow-storm coming on, the project was abandoned, upon which Washington advanced his works to Nook's Hill, a promontory flanking the British lines on Boston Neck. From the 5th March onwards Howe's orders contain many instructions as to evacuation and embarkation, a task of very considerable magnitude, since not only the fighting men but the loyalists and their families had also to be evacuated.

In the orders of the 13th March the troops were directed to embark in two columns at different wharves, the 47th and five other regiments to embark at Hancock's Wharf under the supervision of Brigadier-General Grant; and, finally, on the 16th it was enacted that " the whole garrison to be under arms at 4 o'clock in the morning, and to be ready to embark when ordered "; and on the 17th March the fleet of three men-of-war and 160 transports set sail for Halifax, arriving there on the 2nd April.

The 47th, made, however, only a very brief stay in Halifax, for in orders of the 12th April, it is intimated that " the 47th Regiment to hold themselves in readiness for embarkation," and the Regiment actually sailed for Quebec on the 20th of the month, being apparently despatched by General Howe, without the necessary sanction from the War Office having first been obtained. He was at first directed to recall the Regiment, but this order was later cancelled. The 47th reached Quebec on the 8th May.

Rather more than a month after the 47th had left Halifax a draft seems to have arrived for the Regiment from home, for in orders dated the 20th May it is directed " the detachments of the 8th and 47th to be collected by Ensign Eyre of the 47th and to go on board the transports of the 38th Regiment until further orders."

Major-General Carleton, afterwards Lord Dorchester, was at this time Governor-General of Canada, and he found himself in sore straits to defend the Colony against the invasion of the Americans led by Montgomery and Benedict Arnold. He had at the outset but eight hundred Regular troops and five hundred of these had been thrown into St. John's, where, after a gallant defence of over seven weeks, they had been compelled to surrender early in November, 1775. Carleton, who, with a mere handful of troops had been repulsed in a desperate attempt to relieve the garrison, then evacuated Montreal and returned hurriedly to Quebec, then threatened by another American force under Arnold. Early in December Montgomery and Arnold joined forces before the capital, bringing the number of the besieging troops up to nearly twelve hundred men. Carleton had nearly as many under his command, but only sixty were Regulars, the remainder being colonials, or militia.

After a feeble attempt to bombard the city, the American commander proceeded to storm it on the 31st December—with, however, disastrous results, Montgomery being killed and Arnold wounded, while the attack was completely repulsed. Carleton was not, however, strong enough to follow up his success, and consequently the Americans remained encamped round Quebec, blockading it and retaining control of the water-way of the St. Lawrence up to the Lakes.

Carleton had appealed for reinforcements both to Halifax and to London, and the first to reach him were the 47th from Halifax and the 29th from England, both regiments arriving on the same day. Carleton then at once disembarking some of these troops, sallied out to attack the enemy, but these did not wait, raised the siege and hurriedly retired, leaving their guns and baggage behind them. Within a very few days, however, Carleton was joined by Major-General J. Burgoyne with eight more regiments from England besides a division of Brunswick troops, and by the 8th June the whole army was concentrated at Three Rivers, about thirty leagues up the River St. Lawrence.

CHAPTER IV

1776-1781

THE WAR OF AMERICAN INDEPENDENCE
SARATOGA

THE reinforcements which had now arrived in Quebec brought the strength of the army to approximately thirteen thousand men, with a large number of guns, of which sixteen were 24-pounders and ten were 12-pounders. The army was now told off into four British Brigades and a German Division, and the 47th was in the 1st Brigade commanded by their own Colonel, Nesbitt, and the Brigade contained also the 9th and 31st Regiments. In the orders of the 10th June, 1776, Lieut.-Colonel Nesbitt was given the rank of Brigadier-General, and in those of the day following Lieutenant T. Story of the 47th was appointed Brigade-Major of the 1st Brigade.

There had already been some skirmishing with the enemy, on the 8th June a brush occurring with a small force which had approached the river, and in this affair some three hundred Americans fell into our hands and surrendered to Colonel Nesbitt.

The first object of the operations now to take place was the recovery of Montreal and the reduction of the Forts of Chambly at the head of the Richelieu River and of St. John, all of which were in American hands; and to this end the flotilla pushed on up the river. An officer of artillery who formed part of the expeditionary force has recorded in his journal: "this day the army embarked, the weather being fine. The music and drums of the different regiments were continually playing and contributed to make the scene and passage extremely pleasant."

Sorel was reached on June 14th and here the 1st Brigade, the Grenadiers and Light Infantry and the 24th Foot, were landed, and the whole party marched under General Burgoyne to attack these posts. Chambly was reached four days later, and was found to have been deserted and burnt, and then, moving on towards St. John, touch was en route established with the enemy's rearguard which was hurriedly falling back. When St. John was arrived at, it was also found abandoned and in flames, so a party two hundred strong was left here in garrison, the rest of the force returning to Chambly.

The fort at Ticonderoga was now the next objective, and a reconnoitring party consisting of one company of the 47th, was sent up the Richelieu River with orders to establish itself at the Isle-aux-Noix, where more troops were to gradually assemble.

The strength of the 47th at Chambly on July 1st is given as twenty-two officers and 485 other ranks, with twelve sick, and the Regiment received forty-eight men out of a draft that arrived on the 25th of the month.

It was the 10th September before any further move forward was possible, for the gunboats, sent out from England to enable our flotilla to cope with the enemy, had arrived in sections, and much time was occupied in putting them together, and preparing and distributing the boats intended to carry the troops. In the orders of the 10th September we read that: "twenty-six boats are to be delivered to each battalion, the 9th, 21st, 31st, 47th, 53rd, and 62nd, to embark for the purpose of going in quest of the rebels."

At this time Brigadier-General Nesbitt, of the 47th, seems to have fallen sick and was sent back to Quebec, where he died on the 5th November, and Lieut.-Colonel Hamilton assumed temporary command of the 1st Brigade in his place.

The army, now under Carleton—Burgoyne marching with a western column—moved slowly across Lake Champlain, and on October 11th an action was fought with the American forces under Arnold, who had taken up a very strong position, and his ships were so roughly handled that the capture of his entire force seemed more than likely. Arnold, however, slipped away in the night, and the British did not overtake him until the 13th when he turned and covered the retreat of his main body very skilfully. The British captured seven of his ships, but he managed to land the bulk of his men near Crown Point and withdrew with them into Ticonderoga. Carleton also landed here, fifteen miles from Ticonderoga, on the 3rd November, and then decided that it was too late in the season to advance further. This decision was come to much against the advice of his officers, who considered, and with good reason, that Ticonderoga could certainly have been captured in three or four days. The result of this resolve was to delay the operations of the ensuing year and to dishearten the loyalists, of whom there was a strong body in these parts.

The troops now returned to Canadian soil and occupied cantonments for the winter, the 47th being distributed as follows: four companies at St. Laurens, four at Saint-au-Recollect, one at Longueil and one, the Grenadier Company, at Vauchere. On the death of Colonel Nesbitt, Major Nicholas Sutherland of the 21st Foot was appointed to command the

Regiment in his place. Captain L'Estrange of the 47th was drowned in the St. Lawrence during this winter.

Colonel Powell now took over command of the 1st Brigade from Lieut.-Colonel Hamilton and this Brigade then contained the 9th, 47th and 53rd Regiments.

Suggestions had been put forward to the English Ministry at home by general officers and government officials on the spot, that the best way of crushing the American Rebellion was to occupy the line of the Hudson River, so as to divide the ardent separationists of New England from the moderates of the central and southern provinces who were less inclined to complete independence. Burgoyne went home on leave during the winter of 1776-1777 and while in London drew up a scheme for the invasion of New England from Canada, whereby the line of the Hudson River would be occupied down to Albany. This was a somewhat hazardous plan of campaign, involving the passage of a comparatively small force through a wide tract of wild and hostile country : while its complete success depended largely upon the co-operation of a second British force, which was to advance up the Hudson from New York—then in British hands—and meet the other column at Albany. The Secretary of State for the Colonies—Lord George Germaine—foolishly proposed to direct this combined operation from London ; but the scheme at the very outset was doomed to disaster by his crass negligence, since Lord George drafted a despatch to General Howe at New York explaining the proposed scheme of co-operation with Burgoyne, and then omitted to send it ! The result of this extraordinary carelessness was that Burgoyne left for Canada with precise instructions to advance across country to Albany and there place himself and his troops at General Howe's disposal, while General Howe remained without any orders on the subject at all !

Burgoyne arrived back in Quebec on the 6th of May, 1777, bearing Germaine's despatches to Carleton, ordering the latter to hand over to Burgoyne the command of the projected expedition ; he was also definitely told what troops were to be released to take part in it. Carleton was, not unnaturally, very disgusted at his supersession and at the meddling minuteness of the orders sent him ; he consequently forwarded his resignation to England, and in the meantime settled down loyally to help Burgoyne in all the necessary preparations for the expedition.

The regular troops told off to Burgoyne's command numbered something over 7,200 ; the regiments in the British Division were the 9th, 20th, 21st, 24th, 47th, 53rd and 62nd, with the Grenadier and Light Companies of the 29th, 31st and 34th Regiments in addition ; these, with about 500 artillerymen, brought up the numbers of the British troops to 4,135. The

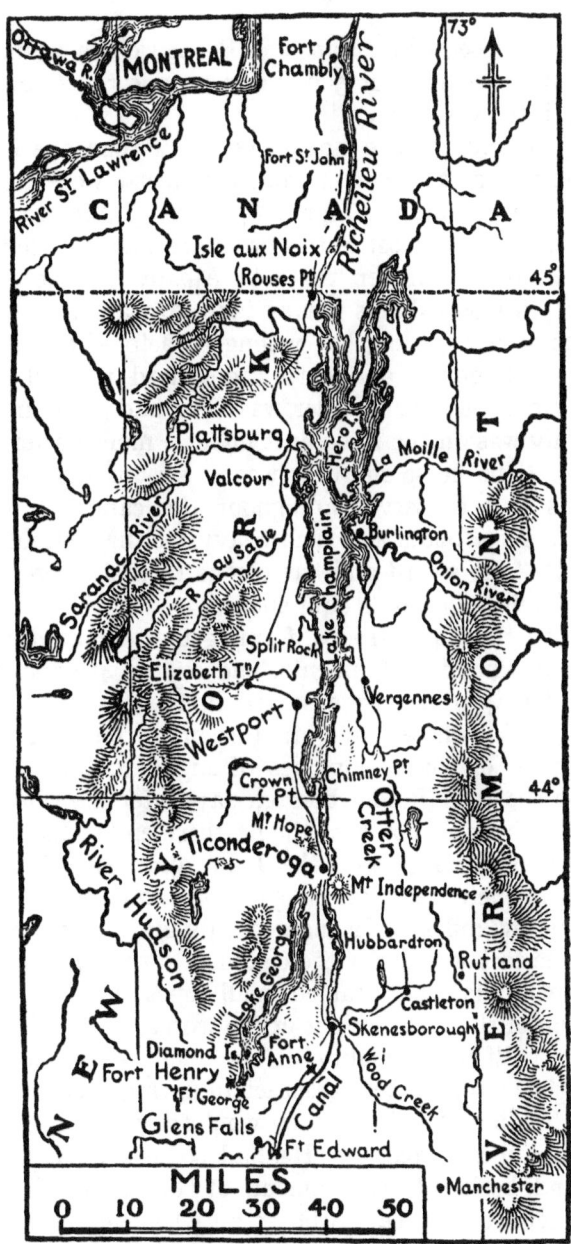

The War of American Independence.

1776–1777.

German Division, composed of Hessians and Brunswickers, numbered 3,116, while a few Canadians and about 500 Indians made the total strength of Burgoyne's army just over 7,900 all told.

When the expeditionary force started no fewer than one hundred and thirty guns, great and small, mortars and howitzers, were dragged along with the column—an enormously high proportion of guns to muskets for those days; since, however, most of this ordnance was intended to arm the forts it was hoped to capture en route to Albany, no more than some forty-five guns of various calibres got as far as Saratoga.

The Canadians were anything but willing to help, either as soldiers or as transport drivers; horses and carts were hard to find, boats were insufficient in number and the weather was very bad; but in spite of all difficulties the army was on the move just under a month after Burgoyne's arrival in Quebec. The horse shortage was so serious that a regiment of German Dragoons had to serve throughout the campaign dismounted, wearing, moreover, huge boots and such heavy kit that one of the British Officers wrote that " the sword and hat of one of them were as heavy as the whole of an English Private's equipment."

On the 3rd June the Light troops, forming the advanced corps, began to move from their winter cantonments, and on the 4th the whole army was in motion. The 47th was represented in the advance guard of the army by Captain Craig, whose name often occurs in histories of this war; and he, in command of four companies of Light Infantry, reached the Bouquet River on the 10th June, while ten days later the whole army was concentrated at Cumberland Point, at the northern end of Lake Champlain. On the 28th Headquarters crossed the Lake and reached Crown Point where two hundred men were left in garrison, and the army was here within only a very few miles of Ticonderoga, its first objective.

At this time the fort was under the command of the American General St. Clair, who seems to have entertained small hopes of his ability to defend the place by reason of the great extent of the works, the inadequacy of the garrison and the indifferent quality of the men composing it. " Had every man I had," he wrote, " been disposed of in single file on the different works and along the line of defence, they would have been scarcely within the reach of each other's voices." He had some sixteen hundred men under his command, besides three regiments of Hampshire Militia, engaged for no particular term of service, " who go off whenever they please; two regiments of Massachusetts Militia of 252 rank and file for duty; meat for seven weeks only; no teams and not a stick of wood; no cartridge paper; and the bateaux in ruins for want of pitch and tar."

Ticonderoga was in itself a strong work situated on a peninsula at the point where Lake George and the South River meet; the original fort on the west side of the river was supported by a companion work on the east bank, called Fort Independence, the two being connected by a bridge, above which an immensely strong boom blocked the river.

General Burgoyne's troops had started to surround the place, preparing to lay siege to it in due form, when Major-General Phillips, who now commanded the brigade containing the 47th, noticed that a height, known as Sugar Loaf Hill, to the south of the position and separated from it by the narrow waterway connecting Lake Champlain with Lake George, was undefended by the Americans, either because they could not spare the men to hold it or because they judged it inaccessible. General Phillips, an ex-artillery officer, at once realized that from its summit guns could command both Fort Ticonderoga and Fort Independence.

During the night the difficult task of getting the guns on to the top of the hill was successfully accomplished, and when day broke on the 4th July the Americans found their defences commanded by our artillery; the defenders at once retired, leaving all their guns and most of their stores, and, crossing to the eastern bank, they retreated towards Castleton, some thirty miles to the south-east.

General Frazer with the Light Troops, and General Riedesel with the German Division, started at once in pursuit and came up with the enemy rearguard near Hubbarton on the 7th July. The British Light troops who had outmarched the overladen Germans, at once attacked and were near being repulsed by reason of the gallant defence of the rebels and their own inexperience in bush-fighting.

The arrival of the Germans, however, on the enemy flank, forced the Americans to retreat, suffering some 324 casualties and leaving twelve guns in British hands.

The British loss totalled 183, of which the Light Company 47th claimed three killed, Captain J. H. Craig and two men were wounded, while Lieutenant P. England was taken prisoner. The strength of the 47th this day was 524 all ranks.

Having destroyed the boom and cleared the water-way and established a garrison in Ticonderoga, Burgoyne advanced to Skenesborough, where his force was concentrated on July 10th. During the advance to this place the 9th Regiment was detached against Fort Anne, which was found to be very strongly held; reinforcements were urgently called for and the two other Regiments of the Brigade—the 47th and 53rd—were immediately hurried up in support.

Meanwhile, however, the 9th had become heavily engaged, and only the arrival of some Indian auxiliaries and the approach of the two other regiments saved the situation. Finally, the garrison set fire to Fort Anne and retired southward to Fort Edward.

The next objective was now the Hudson River, and to reach this from Skenesborough, Burgoyne had the choice of two routes ; having placed garrisons in his captured posts, he might return to Ticonderoga and move by water to the southern end of Lake George whence a comparatively easy march of ten miles would bring him to the valley of the Hudson ; or he might struggle onward through wild and difficult country for more than twenty miles and finally strike the river at Fort Edward. Unfortunately, several reasons, the chief of which was the fear of the possible ill effect of anything like a retirement on the mind of the local population, induced him to adopt the latter route, and the time he lost in clearing his road and laying more than forty bridges over streams, creeks and swamps, proved in the end to be his undoing. It took him twenty days to cover a little more than twenty miles from Skenesborough to Fort Edward, where he finally arrived on July 30th.

Considering the natural difficulties of the country, and the very many obstacles of all kinds left behind by the retreating enemy, this march was of itself no mean feat, but the time thereby lost in the concentration of the British forces proved of incalculable value to the Americans.

With the view of easing the position in the matter of supplies, an expedition had been sent out from Fort Anne, where Burgoyne lay from the 25th to the 28th July, in order to effect the capture of a quantity of foodstuffs, and horses said to be collected at Bennington, a town some thirty miles to the south-east. The fate of the expedition was singularly unfortunate and ended in something of a disaster costing the British army some five hundred men, who could ill be spared at this stage of the expedition ; worse still, it further encouraged the Americans in their resistance to the invaders.

Burgoyne remained at Fort Edward until September 13th collecting provisions and throwing a bridge across the Hudson River ready for his advance. By this date he had collected thirty days' supplies for his army, together with boats and transport for the projected movement ; and finally, urged thereto by positive orders issued six months previously by a Minister three thousand miles away, he decided to set out. No word had reached him from General Howe, no modification of the original orders had come from home, so Burgoyne feared lest any further delay on his part might mean undue enemy pressure on the colleague who he hoped and believed was marching to meet him at Albany ; he advanced therefore fully conscious of the risks he ran.

Before, however, crossing the Hudson, Burgoyne had to detach nearly one thousand men to garrison Ticonderoga and other fortified posts on the Lakes, and among these went two companies of the 47th under Captain T. Aubrey, these being detailed for Diamond Island near the head of Lake George; another detachment of the 47th, commanded by Lieutenant G. Irvine, found the garrison of Fort George itself. The remainder of the Regiment appears to have been stationed on the west bank of the Hudson, some time before the rest of the army, engaged in covering the preparations for the advance. In the orders dated the 6th September, "Lieutenant P. England of the 47th Regiment is appointed to act as Fort Major at Ticonderoga, etc."

When the crossing of the river was accomplished, six companies of the 47th were ordered to camp close to the river covering the provision depots, and in the orders of the 13th September it is laid down that "the present post of the six companies of the 47th Regiment being destined to cover the depot of provisions, those companies are not to take any of the duties of the line, but will augment their own picquet to forty men, which will during the night occupy a post upon the Island and upon the point of land on the south side of Fishkill where it falls into the river . . . the 47th Regiment keeps its ground, and is to defend it to the last against any attack from the other side of the water, and the four companies that cover Headquarters are to take post in the redoubt above the bridge that leads to Headquarters."

By September 15th everything was across the Hudson and the bridge was then destroyed, the force being now definitely committed to the march down the river, the troops being glad to exchange the tangled swamps they had lately traversed for the beautiful wooded valley of the Hudson with the tolerably defined road leading to Albany but thirty miles distant.

The American General Schuyler, when he evacuated Fort Edward, fell down the river to the mouth of the Mohawk, where he was superseded by General Horatio Gates,* who advanced on the 8th September with six thousand men and took up a strong position on the Beamis Heights, near Stillwater. The position ran at right angles to the Hudson and consisted of two hills, the larger and nearer to the river being completely fortified and occupied, the smaller hill separated from the other by a ravine some 300 yards wide being unoccupied by the enemy. Arnold here was on the

---

* Entered the British Army, 1745: Ensign, 20th Foot, 27.6.1748: Captain, 24.11.1749: Captain, 45th Foot, 1.6.1750: Major, 24.4.1762: Major, 60th Foot, 27.10.1764: Retired in 1765. Served with General Braddock at the Monangahela, wounded, and with General Monckton in the West Indies. On outbreak of War of American Independence became A.G. and Commander of Northern Army. Defeated Burgoyne at Saratoga and was himself defeated by Lord Cornwallis at Camden. Died 10.4.1808.

left and slightly advanced, and the whole American force was composed of some fourteen thousand men.

Perceiving that from this hill the whole of the American camp could be commanded and the works enfiladed, Burgoyne resolved to attack in three columns, moving separately through the woods and concentrating in front of the enemy position. The left column was under General Riedesel and consisted of the 47th—in charge of the boats—the German Division, the heavy guns and the baggage, and followed the road by the river. The centre column, under Burgoyne himself, was made up of the 9th, 20th, 21st and 62nd Regiments, and was to advance through the forest, parallel to this road and about a mile from it. The right column under Frazer contained the Grenadier and Light Companies of the army and also the 24th Regiment, and was to move on the right of the two other columns, and to it was entrusted the mission of capturing and occupying the hill on the enemy's left. The centre and right columns were intended to unite before the attack was actually delivered, and the opening of the action was to be signalled to the left column by the firing of three heavy guns from the centre, for the woods were so dense that no visual signal could have been seen.

Burgoyne had roughly five thousand men at his disposal with which to attack rather over thirteen thousand in an entrenched position, so that the odds were very greatly against him.

Between one and two o'clock on the 19th September the guns gave the signal and General Riedesel, leaving the 47th at the water's edge, turned inland to join the other two brigades which had arrived punctually on the appointed ground where they deployed. The action then commenced with the capture of Freeman's Farm, a house in front of the centre. About three in the afternoon Arnold counter-attacked, attempting to turn the right flank of the centre column, but was himself out-flanked by Frazer's right brigade and driven back. Noticing, however, the serious weakness of the British centre Arnold came on again and a close and desperate action ensued. Possessing, as he did, the advantage of greatly superior numbers, Arnold launched attack after attack upon the centre brigade, and though as often repulsed at the point of the bayonet, he could always bring forward fresh troops to replace those which had fallen back broken from the front of the three regiments of regular infantry—20th, 21st and 62nd—under Burgoyne's immediate command, of which nearly fifty per cent. had already fallen. Frazer's men could give little or no help, and it was not until dusk that Riedesel, appearing suddenly on Arnold's flank, charged with the bayonet, finally forcing Arnold to retire.

So ended the wholly indecisive action of Stillwater, the British, having lost some five hundred men—one-third of their force this day employed—remaining in bivouac on the ground, while the Americans, whose loss had been about the same, fell back on their entrenched camp.

In this action Captain J. H. Craig of the 47th was again wounded, for the third time since this campaign opened.

On the 20th September the British army moved up almost to within cannon-shot of the enemy position and proceeded there to entrench, throwing up works to protect their stores and boats. Whatever proposition Burgoyne was then considering was finally decided for him on the next day, when a messenger arrived in camp from General Clinton at New York, stating that a diversion in Burgoyne's favour was about to be made up the Hudson River in the direction of Albany. Upon hearing this Burgoyne settled down behind his entrenchments to await the movements of his colleague.

Here Burgoyne remained quiescent until October 5th, by which date Clinton's operations had produced no effect on the situation, while the position of Burgoyne's force was becoming very critical; for he had many sick and wounded men on his hands, only sixteen days' rations remained, and the enemy was showing in force on every side.

On October 5th then, a council-of-war was assembled and at this it was decided that a further reconnaissance of the American position must at once be made, and it was hoped that under cover of this the foraging parties might be able to bring in some supplies, while if the reconnaissance disclosed favourable conditions for such action, the hostile position should at once be assailed. Accordingly at noon on the 7th October, Burgoyne moved out with fifteen hundred men and ten guns in the endeavour to locate and turn the enemy's left flank.

The Americans, however, did not wait to be attacked, but left their lines and assailed Burgoyne's weak and weary troops in overwhelming force, so that the British left had to be wheeled back and it was only with the greatest difficulty that the first onset was repulsed. A fresh attack was then made on the centre where a battalion of Germans gave way, while at the same time both British flanks began to be pressed back by sheer weight of numbers. Frazer was already forming the Light Infantry Battalion and hurriedly brought it into the fight; for a moment the balance was restored, but he was himself then mortally wounded by an American sharpshooter, and the opportunity was lost. The enemy was all the time being steadily reinforced and Burgoyne now realized that he must retreat to save his camp, and consequently withdrew, fighting hard, within his entrenchments, leaving behind six of his guns and all his wounded.

The Americans followed up at once and attacked the British lines;

their first assault was beaten back with heavy loss, but coming on again and again they finally broke into the position and drove a wedge between Burgoyne and the right of his line, thus isolating the German Grenadiers and Light Infantry holding the outer flank. These held on desperately to their ground until nightfall when they fell back, and the whole position became untenable. Burgoyne then withdrew to another further to the rear and nearer to the river.

As no attack was made upon him next day, Burgoyne decided to endeavour to retire on Fort Edward, and, evacuating the position on the night of October 8th, the British army fell back unmolested to Saratoga, some ten miles up the river, leaving behind, however, some five hundred sick and wounded, who had to be abandoned to the enemy.

The 47th had been sent on ahead to secure the road and the Regiment arrived at Swords House, just below Saratoga, in a blinding storm, the rest of the troops coming in about daybreak on the 9th October. Colonel Sutherland of the 47th had reconnoitred the ford across the Hudson, and he at once reported to the General that the heights just north of Fish Creek were but lightly held by the enemy and that the crossing could be forced if the army decided to march on: Burgoyne was, however, of opinion that his men were incapable of further effort and decided to halt. This delay enabled the enemy to close up and practically invest the British force.

The troops "dug themselves in," and lay for four days under a continuous cannonade, soaked to the skin, without food, and waiting for the expected help which did not materialize; and when the 14th October arrived, there was still no news from Clinton, and the limit of the army's endurance appeared to be reached, consequently Burgoyne sent out to Gates proposing terms of surrender.

Captain J. H. Craig of the 47th was one of the officers deputed to settle the subordinate terms of the Treaty preparatory to the surrender of Burgoyne's army, and there is in existence a letter of his to Colonel Wilkinson of General Gates' Staff, from which it is clear that it was at his—Craig's—instance that the word "Convention" was substituted for "Capitulation" in the original draft.

The Convention was finally signed on the 17th October, and the forces which surrendered to General Gates numbered the following:—

British Officers . . .	383	Rank and File . .	2,139
German ,, . . .	422	,, ,, ,, . .	2,022
Canadian ,, . . .	67	,, ,, ,, . .	830
Totals .	872		4,991

The American forces consisted of 1,377 officers and 7,716 men of Continental Brigades, and 747 officers and 3,382 men of Militia, a total of 13,222.

The strength of the 47th at the date of surrender was 342 rank and file, this being the total for eight companies only, since two companies and a detachment were absent holding posts on the Lakes.

The terms of the Convention were not too hard on the defeated army, " and all ranks of the victors vied with each other in showing to the vanquished that courtesy and consideration which is never denied by brave men to brave men : Gates, with a chivalrous feeling which did him honour, kept his men in camp while the British piled their arms." The British army was to march out with the honours of war, the sanctity of private property was to be respected, the officers were not to be separated from their men, and finally all were to march by easy stages to Boston, there to be provided with free passage to England on giving an undertaking not to serve again in America during the war. The American Generals kept their share of the bargain, so far as concerned the military part of the agreement, but Congress, with shameless ill-faith, evaded the agreement to return the prisoners to England under a series of pretexts, each flimsier than the last, and, ill-fed, ill-clothed and ill-treated, the remnants of the army were marched about the country for three years.

The actual recorded casualties of the 47th Regiment in the campaign previous to the surrender of Saratoga were sixteen men killed, Captain Craig and thirteen men wounded, Lieutenant England taken prisoner and twenty-two men missing.

There is in existence a state of the 47th Regiment dated Prospect Hill, 1st April, 1778, which shows 17 officers and 255 other ranks fit for duty, with 23 sick, 2 officers and 31 other ranks were prisoners, while 10 officers and 165 other ranks are shown as " on command."

Then in the *Orderly Book of Lieut.-General John Burgoyne* there is on p. 176 a document dated 13th December, 1777, described as the " Parole of Burgoyne's Officers," containing the names of one hundred and eighty-nine officers agreeing to certain limits laid down within which they are at liberty to move about : this is signed by the following officers of the 47th : fifteen in number, virtually agreeing therefore with the number shown as present in the above-quoted State. The names are :—Lieut.-Colonel N. Sutherland, Major P. Irving, Captains R. England, J. D. Alcock, and H. Marr ; Lieutenants T. Story, J. Poe, H. Baldwin, A. French, B. G. Ward, J. Rotten and T. Bunbury ; Ensign J. Percy ; Surgeon L. Dobbin and Quartermaster W. Paxton.

While the headquarters of the Battalion was bearing its part in the tragedy which terminated at Saratoga, the companies and detachments at Diamond Island and Fort George had been giving a good account of themselves. While Burgoyne's army lay before the entranched camp at Stillwater, the Americans had made a stroke at his communications and had temporarily possessed themselves of Ticonderoga, capturing some of the 53rd Regiment together with several gunboats and river craft. In these latter they then embarked and descended upon the magazines at Diamond Island and Fort George, but the defenders of these posts put up an excellent fight, recovered much of the captured material, beat off their assailants and forced them to retire in disorder over the mountains to the east of the lake.

The following is a report on this affair by Lieutenant Irvine, 47th:—

"Fort George.
"24th September, 1777.
"SIR,—

"I think it necessary to acquaint you, for the information of General Burgoyne, that the enemy, to the number of two or three hundred men, came from Skenesborough to the carrying place near Ticonderoga and there took seventeen or eighteen bateaux with gunboats. Their design was first to attack the fort, but considering they could not well accomplish it without cannon, they desisted from that scheme. They were then resolved to attack Diamond Island, which island Captain Aubrey commands. They began to attack the island with cannon about nine o'clock yesterday morning. I have the satisfaction to inform you that after a cannonading for near an hour and a half on both sides the enemy took to their retreat. There were gunboats sent in pursuit of them which occasioned the enemy to burn their gunboats and bateaux and made their escape towards Skenesborough in great confusion. We took one gunboat from them with a 12-pounder in her and a good quantity of ammunition. We have heard there was a few killed and many wounded of them. There was not a man killed or hurt during the whole action of His Majesty's troops.

"I have the honour to be, Sir,
"Your most obedient and most humble Servant,
(sd.) "GEORGE IRVINE, Lieut. 47th Regiment
"Comdg. at Fort George."

While prisoners-of-war in America, the British troops, and the 47th Regiment among them, appear to have been quartered at Prospect, at Cambridge near Boston, at Rutland, at Lancaster in Virginia, at Albemarle, Charlottesville and back to Lancaster, where, contrary to the terms of the

Convention, the officers were separated from their men, the former being now sent to New York, while the men remained in Lancaster.

In one of the articles of the Convention it was stated that the British troops would be at liberty to return home, on the undertaking not to serve again, against the Americans, during the period of hostilities; but Congress, probably reflecting that immediately our troops arrived in England, an equal number of men could be spared to take their places in America, determined to delay the return of the Saratoga troops from any port whatsoever " until a distinct and explicit ratification of the Convention should be properly notified by the Court of Great Britain to Congress," and passed a resolution to that effect, which was unquestionably a breach of the agreed terms. It seems that the only prisoners-of-war who were fortunate enough to be released were those given in exchange.

The detached companies of the 47th returned to Canada after Burgoyne's surrender at Saratoga, and in the summer of 1778 Captain Aubrey was sent by General Haldimand with other troops to establish a post on Carleton Island on Lake Ontario, remaining here for some time.

It appears to have been in the summer of 1781 that the general exchange of the officers of the Convention troops was authorized by Congress, and a large proportion of these returned to England in the autumn of that year, but the balance of the troops were held as prisoners-of-war in various places until released in 1783. The companies which had been on Carleton Island with Captain Aubrey came home in 1781, arriving in England on the 1st November, and formed the nucleus of the Regiment now to be reconstructed at Lancaster, where on disembarkation they were quartered.

It is interesting to note that during some recent excavations at Ticonderoga several old buttons and badges of the 47th Regiment were found.

CHAPTER V

1781-1807

ASSUMPTION OF THE TERRITORIAL TITLE
MONTE VIDEO AND BUENOS AYRES

DURING the years while the 47th Regiment had been held as prisoners-of-war in America, something of the nature of a crisis had arisen at home. In 1778 France had concluded a treaty with the revolted colonies and in the following year Spain had declared war against England. In June of this year a Bill was brought in to double the strength of the Militia and to empower individuals to raise corps of volunteers. At the same time many private individuals came forward offering to raise regular regiments at their own expense, and before the end of the year there had come into existence thirteen regiments of infantry for general service, three regiments of fencible infantry, two regiments of cavalry, and one hundred and fifty companies of volunteers, each with a strength of at least fifty men. Some of the English counties devoted themselves to the raising of special regiments, and thus, as Fortescue tells us, " was initiated that which is known as the Territorial System."

While the 47th Regiment lay at Lancaster, Lieut.-Colonel Irving being then in command, every effort was made to recruit up to the establishment, but the muster roll dated the 18th February, 1782, shows that many of the non-commissioned officers and men were still in Canada, with the following officers :—Captain Irvine, Captain-Lieut. Duport, Lieutenants England and Johnson, while Captain Douglas was absent from England with the expedition which in March, 1781, had sailed for India under command of General Medows.

47TH (THE LANCASHIRE) REGIMENT OF FOOT

It was while stationed at Lancaster that the connection of the 47th Regiment with the County Palatine became an accomplished fact, for on the 31st August, 1782, a Circular Letter was sent out to all Infantry Regiments from the 1st to the 70th, framed in the case of the 47th in the following words :

" His Majesty having been pleased to order that the 47th Regiment of Foot which you command shall take the County name of the 47th, or the Lancashire Regiment, and shall be looked upon as attached to that County, I am to acquaint you that it is His Majesty's further pleasure that you should in all things conform to that idea, and endeavour by all means in your power to cultivate and improve that connection so as to create a mutual attachment between the County and the Regiment which may at all times be useful towards recruiting the Regiment.

"But as the completing of the several Regiments, now generally so deficient, is in the present crisis of the most important national concern, you will on this occasion use the greatest diligence to your officers and recruiting parties, and by every suitable attention to the Gentlemen and considerable inhabitants; and as nothing can so much tend to conciliate their affections as an orderly and polite behaviour towards them, and an observance of the strictest Discipline in all your Quarters, you will give the most positive orders on that Head; and you will immediately make such a disposition of your Recruiting parties as may best answer that end." *

This letter is signed by General H. B. Conway, who was at the time Commander-in-Chief, and is addressed to Lieut.-General Sir G. Carleton, K.B., who was then Colonel of the 47th; the Circular also contains a roll of forty-two Counties or divisions of Counties, in alphabetical order, giving the different regiments affiliated to them.

There has always been a tradition in the 47th that it was intended, having been raised originally in Scotland, to call it the "Lanarkshire Regiment," and that it was owing to the similarity of name that it was instead called "the Lancashire Regiment." On the error being pointed out to the revising officer, he decided that "the name should remain as written." Some seven weeks later the following letter † was sent to each of the regiments in the above list :—

"GEORGE R.

"Whereas We have been pleased to direct that Our 47th Regiment of Foot under your command shall take the County name of the Lancashire Regiment, and to be considered as attached to that County. These are to authorize you by beat of drum or otherwise to raise so many men in the County of Lancashire in Our Kingdom of Great Britain as are or shall be wanting to recruit and fill up the respective numbers of Our said Regiment to the numbers allowed upon the Establishment. And all Magistrates, Justices of the Peace, Constables and other of our Civil Officers

* Public Record Office, W.O. 3/36, Folio 57, C.-in-C.'s Out-Letter Book.
† Public Record Office, W.O. 26/31, Folio 264.

whom it may concern, are hereby required to be assisting unto you in providing quarters, Impressing Carriages and otherwise, as there shall be occasion. And for so doing this Our Order shall be and continue in force until the 25th day of March next.

"Given at Our Court of St. James's this 11th day of October, 1782, in the twenty-second year of Our Reign."

This period in British history may well be described as "a crisis of the most important national concern," since, under the Ministry of Lord North, we had lost eight of our West Indian Islands and thirteen of our Colonies.

During, however, the sixteen years that now immediately followed, the 47th played no part in the struggle for existence in which the British Empire was now engaged, and which ended only on the field of Waterloo. This was no doubt in large measure due to the weakness of the Regiment and to the time it took to build up its numbers again, for even as late as 1789 the muster rolls show an effective strength of three hundred and thirty-three men only.

From Lancaster the 47th proceeded in 1782 to Warrington, in 1783 to Preston and Whitehaven, moving in November of this year to Ireland, where, as was then usual in the case of regiments on service in Ireland, it experienced many moves and provided a large number of detachments of varying strength. The headquarters were in the first instance at Dublin, whence in 1784 it moved to Drogheda and in the summer to Limerick, where the Regiment remained for a year. In July, 1785, the 47th was split up in detachments as follows : Ross Castle, three companies ; Tralee, two companies ; Mill Street, one company ; Castle Island, one ; Dingle, one, and Clare Castle, one. During the latter part of 1786, and during over four months of 1787, it was again quartered in Dublin, from where it was once more dispersed in the following detachments : the Cove of Cork, one company ; Cloyne, two companies ; Youghal, one company ; Dungarvan, one company ; Middleton, one, and Castle Lyons, one. In the spring of 1788 the Regiment appears to have been concentrated at Cork, and here it remained until the 24th April, 1790, when it embarked for Halifax, Nova Scotia, arriving there on the 30th May.

There is little or nothing to chronicle about the services of the Regiment during the twelve years that now followed ; in 1791 the 47th went to New Providence and to the Bahamas, and remained here until 1793 when we find it quartered in New Providence, Bermuda and Turks Island, and here it seems to have remained until ordered back to England late in 1802, when it sailed in the "Ormella," transport, under the command of Lieut.-Colonel Backhouse and arrived in Portsmouth on the 1st February, 1803. For the first few months after landing the Regiment was quartered at Gosport, moving in June to Battle in Sussex, and again in September to Colchester.

In June of this year one John Harley had joined the 47th as quartermaster on transfer, or exchange, from the 54th and he tells * a curious story about an officer who was posted to the Regiment and joined in October at Colchester; this was a Captain Maurice Farmer who at this date was only seventeen years of age and yet was one of the senior captains then serving in the British Army, "having obtained his commission while still in his cradle." He had been gazetted to a company in the 107th Foot in February, 1795—when presumably no more than nine years of age, and was brought in to the 47th—second senior captain in point of date —when in June, 1803, a Second Battalion was raised for the 47th Regiment.

When on the 16th May, 1803, England declared war against France, our superiority at sea was overwhelming, while we possessed also an unusually large Regular Army. Mr. Addington, the Prime Minister, had just introduced what was known as "the Additional Forces Act," with the object of raising an Army of Reserve of fifty thousand men, each county providing its quota, and these were to be formed into Second Battalions for fifty Regiments of the Line. One of these was the 47th and the dates of appointment of all the officers posted to the new battalion were the 9th July, 1783.

For some time the two battalions of the Regiment remained together at Colchester and then at Woodbridge in Suffolk, both moving from there in December to Liverpool, where both embarked for Dublin, arriving here in January, 1804. Within a month the 1st Battalion moved to Kilkenny and the 2nd Battalion to Clonmel, both being united again for the summer at the Curragh.

In September, 1805, the 1st Battalion proceeded from Kilkenny to Cork, where, on the 9th April, 1806, it embarked, eight hundred and three strong, for Portsmouth, but on arrival there, was transhipped to three Indiamen and sailed on the 14th May for the East Indies. Touching at the Cape of Good Hope, which in January of this year had been surrendered by the Dutch to a British force under Sir David Baird, the 47th was landed, and was then diverted by General Baird from its original destination, that officer intending the Regiment to remain in garrison at the Cape to take the place of the 71st.

Commodore Sir Home Popham had been associated with General Baird in his operations resulting in the occupation of the Cape of Good Hope,

* *The Veteran*, Vol. I, pp. 196, 197.

and some years previously the Commodore had come in contact with a Spanish colonial adventurer, one General Miranda, who was very anxious that the British Government should support a movement in the Spanish Colonies in South America for emancipation from the rule of the Mother Country. The idea of an expedition to South America was considered by Mr. Pitt in 1804, but was abandoned early in 1805, largely at the instance of Russia, who pointed out the danger to the existing alliance, which might easily result from any serious dispersion of the British naval and military forces.

Cape Town having been occupied, and his formidable squadron being left with no immediate objective, Sir Home Popham persuaded himself and also Sir David Baird, that the real object of his mission had been, not the conquest of the Cape, but the more dazzling project against the Spanish settlements on the Rio de la Plata. He then managed to "borrow" from Sir David Baird the 71st Foot, a handful of dragoons and four guns, placed under the command of Major-General Beresford, sailed on the 13th April and reached St. Helena on the 30th. Here he persuaded the Governor to let him have a small reinforcement of local troops, and finally on the 8th June he anchored off Cape Santa Maria, not far from the mouth of the Rio de la Plata.

Beresford was urgent to disembark at and attack Monte Video, about a hundred and thirty miles up the river, but Popham insisted upon making for the capital, some twenty miles further up stream. The troops were accordingly landed unopposed eight miles below the city, and after an insignificant action on the 26th June, the capital surrendered next day to Beresford, a city of seventy thousand inhabitants, rich with stores and treasure, thus passing into the hands of an invading force less than one thousand seven hundred strong. The Spaniards soon, however, recovered from their first panic, realizing the really insignificant strength of Beresford's troops: emissaries from Buenos Ayres incited the country folk to rise in arms; and in the capital an insurrection was planned under the very nose of the unsuspecting Beresford. Meanwhile Colonel Liniers, a French officer in the Spanish service, crossed over to the south side of the river from Monte Video on the 4th August at the head of a thousand regulars, and co-operating with the militia and armed inhabitants of Buenos Ayres, attacked the small British garrison, which on the 12th August was forced to surrender.

When Sir David Baird heard at Cape Town of the initial success at Buenos Ayres, he dispatched the 38th and 47th Regiments under Lieut.-Colonel Backhouse, of the latter regiment, to reinforce Beresford. These troops sailed from the Cape on the 29th August—the embarking strength of the 47th being 770 all ranks—and arrived in the Rio de la Plata on the 12th October, where Lieut.-Colonel Backhouse was greeted with the news of Beresford's surrender, and found himself stranded in a hostile country, without any orders from his superiors, instructions from the Government, or any sort of information as to the plan of campaign.

The fleet now sailed up to Monte Video, which it was proposed to attack, but this idea had to be abandoned as the water was too shallow to allow of the ships approaching sufficiently near to the shore to cover the landing of the troops. The force then proceeded to Maldonado, a small seaport some seventy miles east of Monte Video, which was considered a suitable place to occupy until the arrival of reinforcements, which were known to be on their way from England; after some skirmishing, a safe anchorage was secured for the squadron and the troops then occupied Maldonado as a fortified base, and settled down here for some three months.

The expected reinforcements—some four thousand men under Brigadier-General Sir Samuel Auchmuty—arrived on the 5th January, 1807, off the mouth of the Rio de la Plata, to find the small garrison of Maldonado in woeful plight; it was very short of stores, in imminent peril of famine and constantly harassed by the enemy's mounted men, of whose tactics General Auchmuty said that "they ride up, dismount, fire over the backs of their horses, mount and gallop off."

The troops were now brigaded, the 47th being in the 2nd Infantry Brigade under Brigadier-General Lumley, with one company of the 71st, a Light Infantry Battalion composed of the Light Companies of various regiments, and a force of seven hundred seamen and Marines.

On the 13th January Auchmuty evacuated Maldonado and on the 18th he disembarked in a small bay about nine miles below Monte Video. On the 19th the advance towards the town commenced, the troops being attacked en route by a body of irregular horse, but these were easily repulsed, and by the evening of this day the British occupied a commanding position near the walls but out of range of the Spanish guns.

The town of Monte Video stood upon a rocky promontory protected on three sides by the sea, and divided from the suburbs on the mainland by a narrow valley from three to four hundred yards wide. On the east, or landward side, of the town ran a continuous line of comparatively recently constructed fortifications, a mile and a quarter long, mounting sixty-four guns; in the centre of this line was a strong, square citadel, covered by a ditch and a ravelin and flanked by two demi-bastions; while the walls were further strengthened by two more demi-bastions about three hundred yards north and south of the citadel. There were two entrances to the town—the North Gate, situated between the citadel and the northern demi-bastion, and the South Gate near the water and covered by two batteries besides those already mentioned. The batteries on the river-face of the town mounted some fifty more guns, and were so well sited and so strong that an attack from the water presented many difficulties. It is evident, therefore, that the decision to attack from the landward side was a wise one. The garrison consisted of about six thousand men, good troops though indifferently trained; while, contrary to the reports in the possession of the home authorities, the fortifications were in a thoroughly good state of repair.

The British landed a number of 24-pounders from the ships, establishing batteries against the citadel and South Gate, and on the 25th January fire was opened on these points; a breach was soon made near the South Gate and on the 2nd February this was pronounced practicable, and no reply being received to a summons sent to the Governor to surrender, orders were given for an assault to be carried out on the morning of the 3rd.

The attack opened early on the morning of the 3rd February, but the 47th was this day held in reserve with the greater part of General Lumley's brigade and had no share in the fighting; the Light Company of the Regiment took part, however, in the assault by the left column of attack as part of the Light Battalion. The stormers moved forward, exposed to a heavy fire from the walls, but the ramparts were won and the troops advanced to clear the town. For a time they were checked by the fire of guns placed at the head of the main streets, but advancing with the bayonet, the guns were taken and the streets cleared, and by daylight Monte Video was in our hands.

Our losses were heavy, for out of twelve hundred officers and men who composed the storming column, one hundred and twenty were killed and two hundred and seventy-seven were wounded, the casualties being heaviest in the Light Battalion and 38th Foot.*

After the storming of Monte Video, General Auchmuty sent detached parties of troops into the surrounding country to watch the enemy and to assist in the collection of supplies. A party of two hundred men of the 47th was sent under Colonel Backhouse to Canalon, some twenty miles north of Monte Video; another occupied St. Lucia further to the north; while the Light Battalion and three companies of the 95th proceeded by sea to Colonia—on the north bank of the river and thirty miles from Buenos Ayres—and this was occupied without opposition on the 5th March.

All these detachments were frequently attacked by the enemy. Thus,

* Major Purdon's History of the 47th gives Lieutenant Backhouse, 47th, as wounded in the assault; his name is not, however, among the casualties in Auchmuty's despatch of the 6th February, 1807.

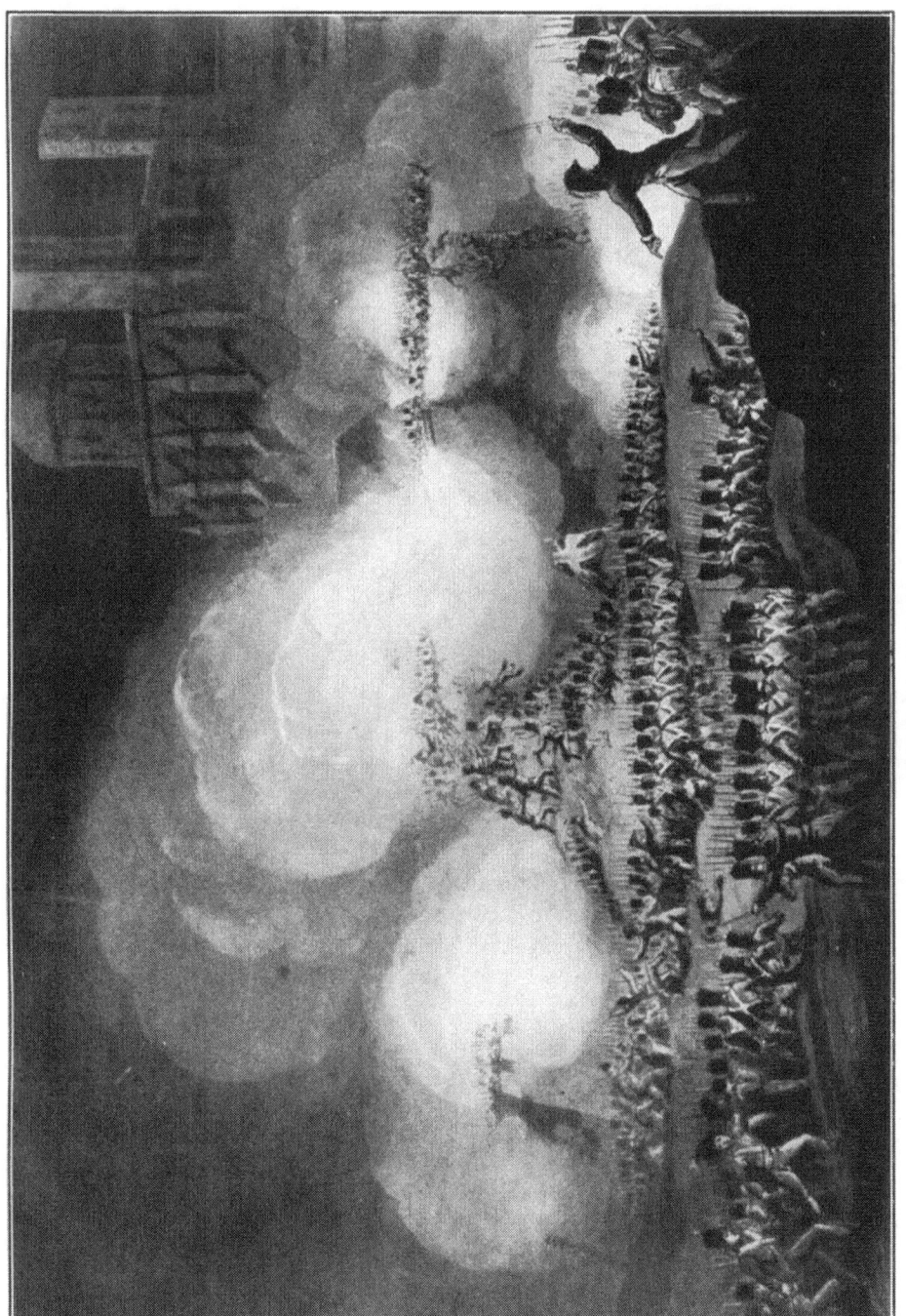

MONTE VIDEO.

3rd February, 1807.

on the 20th March the British outposts in front of Colonia were driven in about midnight, but on the garrison turning out the enemy retired after firing a few rounds. A more serious attempt was made against the place on June 6th; when two thousand of the enemy's regular troops crossed over from Buenos Ayres and encamped at St. Pedro, some fourteen miles from Colonia. Lieut.-Colonel Pack, 71st, who was now commanding here, having learnt of the projected attack, moved out early on the 7th with such troops as he had at his command, Lieutenant T. Backhouse, 47th, acting as his staff officer, and at daybreak came upon the enemy, drawn up on the far side of a small stream. The British crossed to the attack, and on arriving within eighty yards of the enemy, the Spaniards broke and fled, throwing away their arms and accoutrements and leaving a Colour, six guns and a hundred prisoners in our hands.

While these events were transpiring, the home authorities had been considering the sending forth of fresh expeditionary forces, while forwarding also reinforcements to those already engaged in warlike operations.

When the original reinforcements were sent to South America under Sir Samuel Auchmuty, the Minister also decided to despatch a force for the conquest of the western coast of South America. For this purpose, at the end of October, 1806, a body of some four thousand three hundred men was embarked under Brigadier-General Robert Craufurd, with surely the most remarkable orders ever issued to any commander of an expeditionary force. Craufurd was to capture the seaports and fortresses and effect the reduction of the Province of Chili, having done which he was "to establish an uninterrupted communication with General Beresford," in Buenos Ayres—"by a chain of posts or in any other adequate manner"! A chain of posts, that is, strung out across the Andes and over the thousand miles of enemy country separating Craufurd and Auchmuty!

Craufurd eventually sailed with his troops in November, 1806, and on arrival at the Cape of Good Hope in March, 1807, he was met by instructions to proceed to the Rio de la Plata; the home authorities had also now decided that the combined forces of Auchmuty and Craufurd should be placed under an officer of superior rank, and Lieut.-General Whitelocke had been selected for the command, and he arrived in the Rio de la Plata on the 9th May.

General Whitelocke was accompanied by some 1,630 reinforcements, but those under Craufurd did not reach Monte Video until the 14th June, by which time the bulk of the troops had been upwards of nine months on board ship, and it was nearly the end of June before the advanced portion of the force left Colonia en route to Buenos Ayres.

On June 12th a force was sent out from Monte Video to support Lieut.-Colonel Backhouse, who was at Canalon with two hundred men, and who was there invested by a body of fourteen hundred of the enemy. Colonel Backhouse had safely evacuated Canalon, when he came up with the relieving troops and the two bodies then advancing, the enemy hurriedly retired.

On the departure of General Whitelocke's force for Buenos Ayres, a garrison was left behind at Monte Video composed of detachments of the 20th and 21st Light Dragoons, one company of artillery, two companies of the 38th, one company of the 45th, the whole of the 47th, six hundred and eighty-five strong, less one company, the Light Company, the whole under Colonel Brown of the 40th. The Light Company of the 47th formed part of the Light Battalion which was in the brigade commanded by Brig.-General Craufurd; the company was apparently commanded by Captain R. G. Elrington, and Lieutenant W. Rutledge was one of the subalterns.

It is claimed in the Digest of Service that the Grenadier Company was also at Buenos Ayres, but no Grenadier Battalion as such was employed in those operations, and a careful search at the Public Record Office reveals no mention of the Grenadier Company as detached from the Regiment. Further, the Digest distinctly states that in the attack on Buenos Ayres " Lieutenant Backhouse was slightly and Lieutenants Heatley and Rutledge severely wounded." In General Whitelocke's despatch on the 10th July, 1807, however, we read first under " 47th Regiment, 1 Rank and File, killed : 1 Lieutenant, 2 Rank and File, wounded ; 1 Rank and File, missing," and further on, under " Names of Officers, wounded," we find again " 47th Regiment, Lieutenant Rutledge severely," this being the only officer of the 47th shown as wounded.

On the 28th June the transports crossed to Ensenada de Barragon, on the south bank of the river about thirty miles east of Buenos Ayres, where at dawn Craufurd's Light Brigade waded ashore, unopposed, to cover the disembarkation of the remainder of the army, which took up the whole of the rest of the day. On the 29th June, so writes one who was there, " the main body advanced from the shore, and then the chapter of surprises was opened in earnest. Between the strand and the heights lay a swamp, nowhere less than two feet deep in water, which extended for a distance of fully two miles. Gower "—Whitelocke's second-in-command—" on the previous day had found what was pointed out to him as the usual road through it, and in attempting to discover a better track had several times experienced the greatest difficulty in extricating his horse from the slough. Moreover, the foundation, not being of sand but of earth, grew steadily worse with the trampling of many feet ; and the passage was far more difficult for the rear of the column than it had been for the van. Into this sea of liquid black mud the six thousand men of the main body now plunged in a narrow column, and floundered forward, tripping over reeds and aquatic plants and reeling over the treacherous bottom as best they could." The guns stuck fast, five out of the sixteen that had been landed had to be abandoned, while much of the biscuit and rum for the supply of the army had to be left behind.

The Light Brigade marched off ahead of the main body which did not advance till the morning of the 30th, but there was still a very serious shortage of rations, even the three days' supply of cooked food ordered to be carried on the men having become uneatable through wading in the swamp: happily a flock of sheep was now rounded up and these were hurriedly slaughtered and distributed at the rate of one sheep to every twelve men; but before these could be cooked the men were again on the march and much of the meat had to be thrown away.

Though the enemy hovered upon the flanks of the column, cutting off stragglers, no organized attack was made, and on the 30th the Light Brigade reached the village of Redaction and on the evening of July 2nd arrived, hungry and exhausted, at a large enclosure known as the Coral de Miserere, the slaughter-yard of Buenos Ayres and about one mile west of the city. Here the column halted and the men, their ranks unbroken, were standing easy, when suddenly an enemy gun opened from the far end of the enclosure, the low walls of which, as also the hedges, gardens and orchards round about, were occupied by enemy musket-men who opened a heavy fire on the Light troops, while a battery also joined in.

Craufurd's Brigade—little more than nine hundred strong—was completely surprised, but Craufurd rushed to the front and led his men in a bayonet charge against the enemy, who hardly awaited the shock but fled in confusion, leaving the guns in the hands of the British. Craufurd followed in hot pursuit for three-quarters of a mile and was anxious to pursue his advantage still further, being of opinion that with the assistance of Lumley's Brigade he could capture the town then and there.

Night was, however, coming on, some of the troops had been without food all day and were dead-beat, and General Gower, who had come up during the fighting, decided to leave picquets on the ground which had been won and withdraw the main body to the Coral.

Early in the morning of the 4th July General Whitelocke came up with the rest of the army, which during the day occupied a position about the Coral. The Spaniards made many attacks upon the outposts but were driven back into the city with loss. A summons to General Liniers to surrender the town had been rejected and Whitelocke and Gower now decided upon a plan of assault; the small army of no more than five thousand six hundred men was to be formed into sixteen different detachments, of which one was to act as a reserve and one was to guard the headquarters, while the remaining fourteen were to fight their way into the city—the streets of which were known to be entrenched and swept by guns and the houses barricaded—by as many different parallel routes, secure the main buildings on the water front, re-establishing touch when they should arrive there.

The assault was fixed for the next morning—July 5th—and at 6.30 a.m. a cannon-shot from the centre gave the signal to advance. From left to right the attacking force was disposed as follows, each battalion being broken up into two wings: 38th, 87th, 5th, 36th, 88th, 95th, Light Battalion, 6th Dragoon Guards and 9th Light Dragoons, both dismounted, and 45th; the 38th, to 88th inclusive formed the Left Attack under Auchmuty and Lumley, the remainder under Craufurd the Right Attack.

The following is a description of the city about to be attacked; it was laid out in regular rectangular blocks, each about 130 yards square, its eastern face abutting on the river, and measured, roughly, about two miles from north to south by one mile from east to west. The ground sloped gently upwards from the river, so that the Coral, upon which the British army was encamped, overlooked the whole of the buildings down to the water's edge. The main buildings were all close to the shore, the fort being in the centre of these along the east front, and was a square work, flanked by small bastions and having walls about fifteen feet high; it was, however, commanded by several neighbouring houses, and its western face abutted on the Plaza Mayor. Nearly a mile to the south of the Plaza Mayor was the Plaza de Toros, placed on rising ground near the Rio de la Plata at the north-east angle of the city. At the south-east angle of the city was the Residencia.

Craufurd's Light Brigade was divided into two columns, each consisting of a wing of the Light Battalion supported by a wing of the 95th, and the Light Company of the 47th found itself with the left column under command of Lieut.-Colonel Pack; Craufurd himself led the right column. Covered by an advance party of one subaltern and thirty men, the right column moved off towards its objective—the Church of San Domingo—and made its way towards the water-front under a harassing fire that increased in intensity as the advance proceeded. In due time the church was reached, but by then the casualties were so heavy that Craufurd decided to occupy it and there hold his ground. Several attempts were made to break out in order to unite with one of the other columns, but to no purpose, and the defenders of the church were exposed to a biting

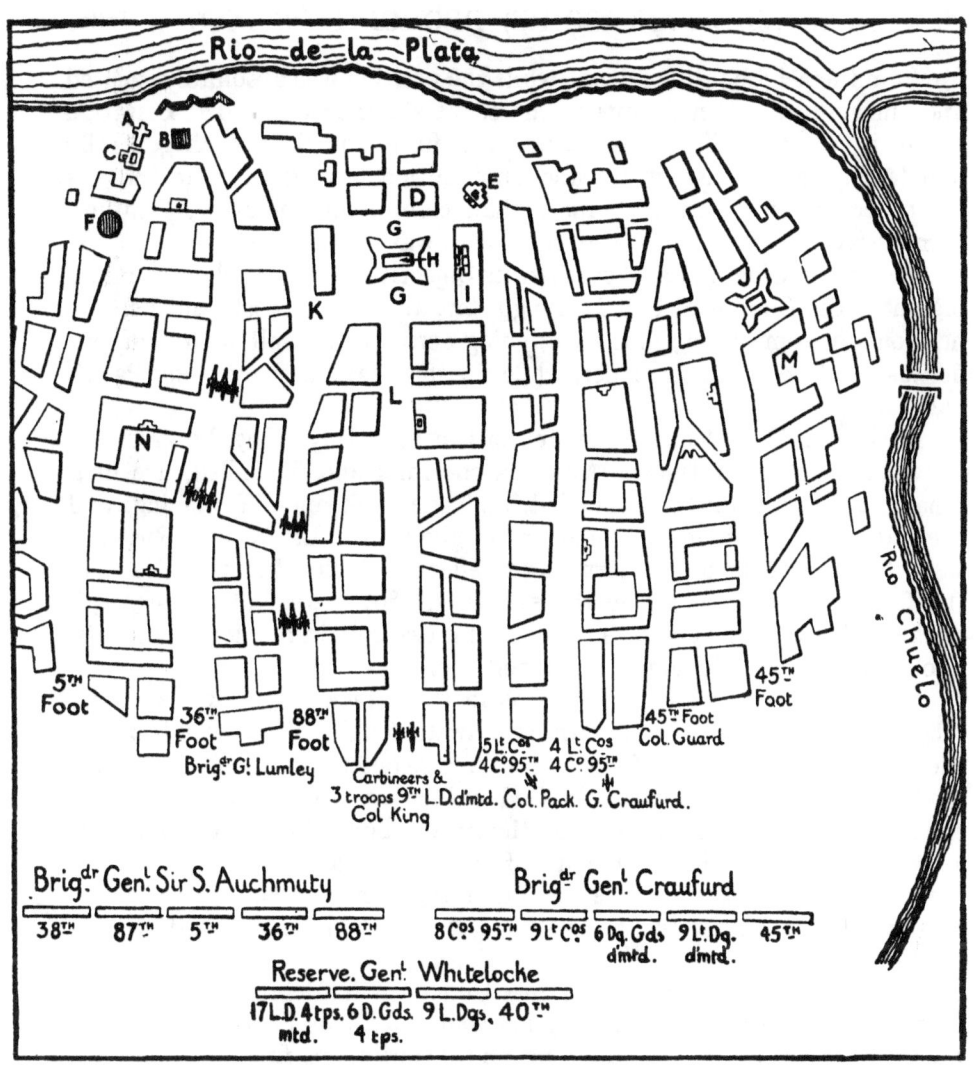

THE ATTACK ON BUENOS AYRES.

5th July, 1807.

REFERENCES.

A. St. Catalina Church.
B. Arsenal.
C. St. Catalina Convent.
D. Jesuits' College.
E. St. Domingo Convent.
F. Plaza de Toros.
G. Great Square.
H. The Fort.
I. Franciscan Church.
J. The Residencia.
K. Left wing of 88th Regt.
L. Right wing of 88th Regt.
M. Market Place.
N. Law Courts.

fire from the neighbouring houses, while the position was absolutely isolated and surrounded by an enemy estimated at six thousand. The cessation of fire in all other directions warned Craufurd that the attack generally had failed, and at last, water and ammunition having run out and the troops being exhausted with more than eight hours' fighting, Craufurd surrendered and the troops were marched away to the Fort.

Pack's left wing had also reached its objective and cleared some buildings near the Church of San Domingo, but at a heavy cost, and here he held out for some time ; but then, going across to consult with Craufurd he was involved in his surrender, while the same fate later overtook Pack's column.

In General Whitelocke's despatch of the 10th July, 1807, he gives the losses of the 47th at Buenos Ayres as one rank and file killed, one lieutenant, two rank and file wounded, and one rank and file missing, and the name of the wounded subaltern is given as "Lieutenant Rutledge severely." Then in a "Return of the effective force after the attack of the City of Buenos Ayres on the 5th July, 1807," we find the strength of the 47th Regiment given as one captain, two subalterns, four sergeants, two drummers and fifty-nine rank and file.

The fortunes of the other columns in the attack may now be briefly followed. On the left the 38th and 87th fought their way through the streets in the face of considerable resistance, captured the Plaza de Toros and successfully established themselves there ; they had captured one thousand prisoners and thirty-two guns, but had themselves lost very heavily. The 5th had suffered comparatively few casualties, but owing to the losses in the two other regiments Auchmuty could not muster more than twelve hundred bayonets when he consolidated his position.

The 36th and 88th had experienced an even harder time. The 36th pushed through the city and occupied some buildings on the river-front, where they held out all the morning under continuous fire from the guns of the Fort and from concealed marksmen on every surrounding housetop. At last Lumley, who was with the 36th, got a message through to Auchmuty asking for instructions, and received a reply advising him to concentrate at the Plaza de Toros ; and about 3 p.m. what remained of the 36th managed to make their way along the water-front and joined up with General Auchmuty. The 88th had, however, been especially unfortunate ; both columns of this regiment had met the full weight of the enemy resistance and had suffered severe losses before they got well into the town. One wing was trapped in a cul-de-sac, and, after holding out on the house-tops until two-thirds of its effectives were down, it was compelled to surrender. The other wing was unable to make its objective and, entangled in a maze of narrow streets, it was practically shot to pieces before the survivors were captured.

On the extreme right the 45th moved through the western part of the town and, with a loss of three officers and sixty-nine men killed and wounded, captured a large building on the water-front known as the Residencia, and remained here until the end of the day's fighting.

The Spanish force was estimated to have been about nine thousand regulars, militia and organized volunteers, with some six thousand irregulars operating in groups and bands. The citizens themselves, however, were really the most formidable element in the defence; for not only did they give every assistance to their troops, but also they themselves, with their negroes, and even, it is said, with their women, barricaded their houses and used all available weapons against the invaders. General Liniers proved himself to be a capable commander and certainly knew how to make the best use of what advantages he possessed.

During these proceedings General Whitelocke, from his position in the rear of the centre, did not seem to have had any very clear idea of all that was happening to his different and isolated columns; in fact, the information which reached him from time to time during the afternoon was of a reassuring character, to the effect that a number of the enemy's guns and several hundred prisoners were in our hands, only to be denied later when the truth became realized.

Towards evening the Spanish commander sent a flag of truce to General Whitelocke informing him of the full extent of the disaster which had overtaken part of the British force, and this appears to have been the first intimation Whitelocke had received of the fate of the 88th, and Light Brigade. Although he at first refused General Liniers' offer of terms, he agreed to a suspension of arms for twenty-four hours for the purpose of collecting the wounded. Later, however, having consulted with Generals Gower and Auchmuty and realizing the hopelessness of the military situation, a definite treaty was signed on the 7th July, under which the Province was to be evacuated, Monte Video being held in our possession for two months, while the troops were being withdrawn and shipped home, or to the Cape of Good Hope.

The re-embarkation of the army commenced on the 9th July and continued during the following days, the troops proceeding to Monte Video, where some of them remained for several weeks. On the 1st August, however, the 47th, having received a draft of eighty-six privates from the 45th, sailed back to the Cape of Good Hope, which it left again in October and arrived at Madras on the 29th December, 1807, to inaugurate its first tour of India service—a very prolonged one which was to endure for twenty-two years.

On the 28th January, 1808, Lieut.-General Whitelocke was tried by a court-martial on four charges, and was ordered to be cashiered "and declared totally unfit and unworthy to serve His Majesty in any military capacity whatever." Of General Whitelocke, Fortescue states that "his most objectionable characteristic seems to have been arrogant but spasmodic self-confidence, with an affectation of coarse speech and manners, which he conceived to be soldierly bluntness, but which often degenerated into mere rudeness towards some of his inferiors and familiar obscenity of manners towards others. He stooped to court the favour of the rank and file by affected use of their phrases, with the inevitable result that he earned only their thorough contempt."

Of the results of this campaign and of some of those who held high positions in the expeditionary force, an officer who served with it set down the following in his journal:—" The Army are certainly much incensed at the disgraceful termination of their labours, and speak loudly of the lofty and abusive language used by almost all the general officers during the service ; in this I can join, for I never saw so much done to make men think little of themselves at a time when they required encouragement and deserved thanks for bearing severe privations without a murmur. Not only the Generals, but the staff, who had little right to do it, used this privilege, which is certainly becoming too general in our Service. Those who judged harshly then of every trifling omission or neglect are now most severely handled in return."

The narrative of the 1st Battalion is continued in Chapter VIII.

CHAPTER VI

THE 2ND BATTALION, 47TH REGIMENT

1806–1812

THE PENINSULAR WAR
THE BATTLE OF BARROSA: THE DEFENCE OF TARIFA

WE left the 2nd Battalion of the 47th Regiment in Ireland when in April, 1806, the 1st Battalion embarked for the Cape of Good Hope. From the Curragh the Battalion had gone to Kilkenny, and it was while quartered here that Captain Harley, who was appointed paymaster in July, 1805, tells us of an unfortunate dispute between two young officers of the Battalion—Ensigns A. Wormhold and W. H. Lemon—which led to a duel whereby the former officer lost his life.

From Kilkenny the 2nd Battalion was sent to Cork and thence to Cahir, and of the Battalion's stay in Cahir Captain Harley has an extraordinary story to relate: a Mr. William Ryan had been gazetted to an ensigncy in the Regiment, and on the same day two young men arrived at the headquarters of the 2nd Battalion, both claiming the commission. The matter had to be referred to the War Office for an official decision on this rather nice point!

From Cahir the Battalion went to Belfast and early in 1806 found itself quartered at Enniskillen, with the object, so Harley states, "to complete our Regiment, to facilitate which Government promised commissions to such gentlemen as could procure a certain number of recruits." In March, 1807, the 2nd Battalion 47th moved to Omagh and in May of the same year left Ireland for England, where it was stationed at Preston. In the autumn a further move took place, this time to Chelmsford, where the Battalion appears to have been completed to establishment by volunteers from the Militia.

In October, 1809, the 2nd Battalion 47th embarked for its first tour of foreign service, proceeding to Gibraltar, which was then held by a strong force under the command of Lieut.-General Campbell. The Battalion seems to have barely arrived there when a new officer joined—"Ensign D. S."—complete with a wife and nine children.

At the time when the 2nd Battalion, 47th Regiment, arrived in the South of Spain, the Peninsular War had been more than two years in progress; the opening Battles of Rolica and Vimiera had been fought, and the Campaign of Corunna had come to its somewhat disastrous conclusion, but the victory of Talavera had done something to restore the balance in our favour.

During the greater part of 1810 Cadiz, one of the only two places outside Portugal now held by the British, was under a close blockade by the French, and the general commanding at Gibraltar decided in April of this year to send a small body of troops to Tarifa, a town lying between Gibraltar and Cadiz, and sufficiently close to the rear of the blockading lines to be something of a menace to the communications of the French. The flank companies of the 9th, 28th, 30th and 2nd/47th, were accordingly sent to Tarifa under Colonel Browne of the 28th, upon which the French commander detailed a column to attack Colonel Browne's force, which was at once reinforced by four more companies of the 2nd/47th under Captain O'Donoghue, and here this force remained until September when it was recalled to Gibraltar.

In March, 1810, Lieut.-General Sir Thomas Graham had been sent to Cadiz to take command of the British portion of the force there in garrison and which was now reinforced; and towards the end of the year the blockading army was considerably reduced in strength by reason of ten thousand men having been taken away to act elsewhere, and Graham now made preparations for an attack upon the depleted besieging force.

Bad weather, the want of the necessary shipping and the difficulty of co-ordinating plans with the Spanish commanders, all combined to delay matters, and it was well into the new year before preparations were completed.

The plan agreed upon was that a sortie of British and Spanish troops should be made from Cadiz, and that simultaneously a Spanish force from Algeciras and a single British battalion—the 28th Foot—from Tarifa should advance upon the French lines from the rear. The scheme came somehow to the knowledge of the French and something new had to be devised, and finally it was decided that the operation should take the form of a disembarkation in rear of the enemy's lines, Graham now consenting to serve under the command of the Spanish General Lapena, employing in the venture all the British troops procurable.

On the 21st February, 1811, the troops set sail from Gibraltar, disembarked at Algeciras and marched thence to Tarifa, where on the 26th the entire British contingent of something over five thousand men, with ten guns, was assembled. Graham now organized his troops in two brigades and two flank battalions, the 2nd Battalion 47th Companies being in the flank battalion, 594 strong, under Lieut.-Colonel A. Barnard, with four companies of the 3rd Battalion 95th. The 47th Companies were at a strength of eight officers and 209 other ranks, Captain Wainwright being in command of the Grenadier Company and Captain Featherstone of the Light. Ten thousand Spanish troops landed on the 27th, when the whole force moved forward.

On the 2nd March the vanguard of the Spaniards seized Casa Viega, and then Lapena, marching towards the coast, drove the French from Vejer de la Fronteria, and on the 5th reached the Barrosa Hill, an isolated height rising about one hundred and sixty feet above the plain, and from its dominating position forming the key of the isthmus.

General Graham had been promised by Lapena that the troops should make short marches in order to keep them fresh, and that they should attack the enemy united; but these promises were disregarded and there was much straggling, and the Spanish general now made for a bridge which had been thrown over the Santi Petri near its mouth, ordering Graham to follow. This he did, though he felt that the Barrosa Hill ought to be held, but he was now directed on Bermeja.

In the meantime Marshal Victor had some nine thousand of his best troops concealed in the woods about Chiclana, and with these and fourteen guns he awaited the approach of the allied force. Then, seeing the very scattered condition of the Anglo-Spanish columns—the baggage left on Barrosa Hill, one column moving by the seashore, another some considerable distance in rear, two Spanish brigades on the Bermeja and Graham marching through the woods—the French general suddenly brought his men forward. With one brigade and two selected battalions of Grenadiers, Victor gained Barrosa Hill, cut off the rear column of the Spaniards, drove the rearguard off the hill, and sent the baggage-guard in headlong flight towards the sea, pursued by the French hussars.

General Graham, now seeing the desperate situation of the Allies— Barrosa Hill, the key of the position in the enemy's hands and General Laval's division coming rapidly down on his flank—turned about, and his troops in two columns, went straight at the enemy. Colonel Barnard's flank battalion, which included the 47th Companies, together with some Portuguese, advanced in extended order and soon became warmly engaged with Laval's Tirailleurs. Barnard's men were followed by the 87th Foot and three companies of the Coldstream Guards, the 67th and 28th Regiments. As they neared Laval's main body, which was suffering much loss from the fire of our guns, Barnard's battalion and the Portuguese advanced on the left of one of the British brigades, and both sides came forward boldly to meet one another. The 87th, by a gallant charge, broke through the 8th French Regiment of Infantry, capturing their Eagle, while the 47th and 95th Companies fought the 54th French Regiment at the edge of a wood above the head of the Almarya Creek and the whole line, pushing on, completely overthrew Laval's division and his reserves.

In *Seven Years' Campaigning in the Peninsula and Netherlands*, we are told that " the panic occasioned by the charge of the 87th was followed up by the gallantry of the Guards and 47th Regiment, and Laval's division, being totally discomfited was driven helter-skelter to the wood."

The French divisions fell back fighting hard, but the victors, who had been under arms and without food for twenty-four hours, were too exhausted to make any effective pursuit, and Marshal Victor finally drew off his men, unmolested though in great disorder, to Chiclana. The Spanish commander left his allies wholly unsupported in this action, and Graham expressed himself with much righteous indignation on the subject in a letter dated the 24th March to the Right Hon. Henry Wellesley. In this he wrote : " Had the whole body of the Spanish cavalry, with the horse artillery, been rapidly sent by the sea-beach to form in the plain and to envelop the enemy's left—had the greatest part of the infantry been marched through the pine wood in our rear to turn his right, what success might not have been expected from such decisive movements ! The enemy must either have retired instantly and without occasioning any serious loss to the British division, or he would have exposed himself to absolute destruction, his cavalry greatly outnumbered, his artillery lost, his columns mixed and in confusion, a general dispersion would have been the inevitable consequence of a close pursuit. . . . The moment was lost. Within a quarter of an hour's ride of the scene of action the General "—Lapena is of course meant—" remained ignorant of what was passing and nothing was done ! "

Seeing that his colleague did not move, Graham marched his troops across the St. Petri into the Isla.

The Battle of Barrosa only lasted an hour and a half, but so obstinate had been the fighting that the British losses amounted to 1,293 officers and men killed and wounded, while the French casualties were 2,000, with two general officers, eighteen other officers and 420 other ranks taken prisoner. An Imperial Eagle—one of the five taken in action during the Peninsular War—three stand of Colours and six guns were also captured.

The 2nd Battalion, 47th Regiment, had Ensign Delacherois, one drummer and nineteen men killed, Captain Featherstone and forty-nine rank and file wounded ; it appears that Ensign Delacherois was killed while out skirmishing in front of the force. The day was warm and he was stooping to drink at a stream when he was shot dead by a French tirailleur.

Early in May, 1811, Marshal Suchet had arrived in front of Tarragona, drove the Spaniards within their works and sat down in front of the place, which was very strong but inadequately defended. Conditions within the fortress becoming serious, General Graham wrote on the 14th June to Lord Liverpool stating that the Spanish Government had caused to be represented to him " the urgency of affording some assistance to Tarragona, and that a few hundred British troops now would be of more importance than thousands at a later period " ; and that consequently he had decided to send thither Colonel Skerrett with the 2nd Battalion 47th, a detachment of the 3rd Battalion 95th and half a company of Royal Artillery.

General Graham's instructions to Colonel Skerrett are dated the same day, and in these he is ordered to embark that evening with his troops in the " Regulus " and " Metcalf," and is to put in to Gibraltar, the Governor of which was asked to make a small contribution to his force. Colonel Skerrett was especially enjoined that before landing or committing himself at Tarragona, he was to state to the Governor that he is " to have at all times free and open communication with any of H. B. M.'s ships-of-war ; and that in the event of the place being under the necessity of surrendering, he is to be at liberty to withdraw the troops under his command on board of the said ships previous to the capitulation."

Contreras, the Governor of Tarragona, was thus to be offered the aid of this small British force only on the condition that it should be allowed to escape in the event of the place falling !

Picking up some Light Companies at Gibraltar, thus making his little force 1,147 in all, Colonel Skerrett arrived off Tarragona in very rough weather on June 26th, to find that the condition of the garrison had become somewhat desperate. Some days before the French had captured the lower town, thus effectually closing the harbour to the besieged so that all landing and embarkation had to be done through the heavy surf on the open beach. Colonel Skerrett landed early on the 27th and inspected the defences in company with the commandant, the British admiral and several other officers, and found these in a very sorry condition, while the small British reinforcement could make no vital difference to the garrison ; again, if he landed his men and took part in the defence, the prospect of re-embarking them was more than doubtful, since the fire of the French squadron had driven our squadron out of gun-shot ; the sea was rough and Contreras expressed himself as very doubtful of his ability to resist any really determined assault.

Under the circumstances, and in view of his very clear orders from

General Graham, Colonel Skerrett decided against disembarkation, and agreed to join a Spanish relieving force further up the coast, sailing on the evening of the 27th. On his departure Suchet's troops at once assaulted and captured the town, nearly the whole garrison, and very many of the civilian inhabitants, being killed or captured. Meanwhile Skerrett had sailed up the coast to join hands with the relieving force, but on a French column from Tarragona appearing, the Spaniards abandoned their base and fled inland, Skerrett then sailing first to Minorca and then back to Cadiz, as Captain Harley remarks, " quite disappointed and out of temper with our fruitless expedition, and because we had no opportunity of assisting our friends and foiling the atrocious Suchet."

The 2nd Battalion 47th was now brigaded in the Isle of Leon with the 87th Foot and the 20th Portuguese, under command of Colonel Skerrett, Major Broad being in charge of the 47th ; and here the Regiment remained tolerably peacefully until October, by which time Lieut.-General Graham had left Cadiz to join the main army, Major-General Cooke assuming command in his place.

Marshal Soult, who commanded the French army in Andalusia, had made certain plans for his future operations, but he proposed first to endeavour to crush one Ballisteros, a Spanish guerrilla chief, who had for long been a thorn in the side of the French generals. Whenever hard pressed, Ballisteros had been in the habit of taking temporary refuge in Cadiz, Gibraltar or Tarifa, and, Cadiz being already under blockade, Soult determined to close Tarifa to the Spanish chief, and in October he laid siege to it with a body of troops consisting of two divisions and a covering force—approximately twelve thousand of all ranks.

At this time the garrison of Tarifa was only a small one, composed of the flank companies of the 11th, 47th and 82nd Regiments, and in view of the threatening aspect of affairs it was obviously necessary that it should be strengthened and it was arranged for reinforcements to be despatched there from Cadiz. The troops sent were the remaining eight companies of the 2nd/47th, 570 strong, the 87th, 560, one company (75 men) of the 2nd/95th, and seventy Hussars of the King's German Legion, with a field battery. These landed in Tarifa on October 14th, and brought the total strength of the British garrison up to 1,774 all ranks, the whole being under the command of Colonel Skerrett. Three days later a Spanish contingent of 1,350 all ranks also landed, when the Spanish General, Copons, as senior officer, became commandant of Tarifa.

The allied forces at once began sending out reconnoitring parties to locate the French, and on the 12th November Colonel Skerrett moved out with some of his troops to Vejer, " a town," so Harley tells us, " situated on the top of a hill in form of a sugar-loaf, close to the Santa Petri River, and about ten leagues distant from Tarifa," from which place a small French force fell back before them. However, on the following day the appearance of a much larger hostile force caused the allied troops to retire again to Tarifa. A reconnaissance was next pushed out in the direction of Algeciras with the object of joining hands with Ballisteros, who was now —November 29th—close to Gibraltar: learning, however, that Marshal Victor had left the blockading lines before Cadiz and was moving south in force, Colonel Skerrett's troops returned to Tarifa, before which the French shortly arrived, and on December 22nd siege operations proper commenced.

The town of Tarifa occupies a promontory some seventeen miles southwest of Gibraltar and sixty south-east of Cadiz. The town contained some three thousand inhabitants and was surrounded by a rampart, battlemented and flanked at intervals by square towers, but was not of sufficient strength to withstand a serious bombardment. To east and north Tarifa was commanded by hills only a few hundred yards distant; to the south it was protected by the sea; while the western face was flanked by the guns of the ships in the roadstead and by an important work on the foreshore known as the Battery of Santa Catalina. The ramparts enclosed a space roughly four hundred yards square, in the south-west corner of which the Castle abutted on the walls, and near this again, was an exceptionally strong tower, called the Tower of the Guzmans, forming the actual south-west bastion of the enceinte. The south-eastern angle was strengthened by two flanking towers, the northern of which—the Jesus Tower—covered to some extent the eastern, and far the most vulnerable, face of the town. Not only was this face commanded by an adjacent ridge, but it was further weakened by the fact that it was pierced by a mountain torrent which flowed from the hills through the town to the sea. The entry was protected by a strong tower called the Retiro, but the ravine containing the stream formed so perfect a covered way that it positively invited attack. On the north side and slightly in advance of the walls was a convent which the defenders had occupied and made into a strong work. The last important feature to be noticed was a round island, some five hundred yards from the shore, connected with the town by a causeway. This island was practically impregnable by reason of its precipitous cliffs, while the approach to it was commanded by a powerful battery, but there was on it no shelter for troops.

As soon as Colonel Skerrett's force arrived at Tarifa his Engineer officer made a careful survey of the place and foresaw that any assault would probably be made on the east side; he therefore caused the Retiro Tower to be fortified and loopholed all houses overlooking the torrent; if forced to fall back, the garrison here was to withdraw to the Castle and the Tower of the Guzmans and thence to the island. On the north side the suburb was razed and the convent made into a strong outwork. Eleven guns were mounted on the walls and outworks, and twelve guns—including 24-pounders—on the island. There were only two heavy guns—18-pounders—in the town, one was mounted on the Tower of the Guzmans and the other in the Santa Catalina Battery, covering the road to the island.

The troops had been busily occupied in the work of strengthening the defences and clearing and improving the field of fire, when on December 16th Colonel Skerrett received definite intelligence that the French were drawing near. They gradually closed in on Tarifa, and by the evening of the 19th, they had occupied the hills surrounding the town. Next day the Light Companies, supported by the picquets under Major Broad, 47th, made a sally and held the enemy in check for some time, till the latter, coming on in force, gradually pressed them back into the town, which by the evening was closely invested.

On the two following days further small sallies took place, solely to harass the enemy, and casualties were incurred on either side; but despite these activities and the fire from our gunboats in the roads, the French, on the night of the 23rd, broke ground upon the eastern ridge, as the Engineer officer had anticipated; before dawn their first and second parallels were completed and the work went steadily forward under a hot fire from the town.

The defence of the east side of the town was entrusted to the 87th; the 2nd Battalion 47th held the southern face and had also one hundred men under Captain Campbell in the convent on the north and a captain's guard of fifty men in the Castle; there was a Spanish battalion on the west front and another in the town; the Battery of Santa Catalina was held by the Light Company of the 11th; while the island was occupied by four companies of the 82nd and two hundred Spaniards. Two field-guns and a picquet were kept as a mobile reserve, while in the event of a retirement to the island becoming necessary, the 47th was to hold the Castle, covering the movement of the other troops, which completed, the 87th was to form between Santa Catalina and the causeway leading to the island and then in turn cover the retreat of the 47th from the Castle.

For some time all went well with the enemy preparations, and by dawn on the 26th the French approaches were within one hundred and fifty yards of the walls. Then on this day rain began to fall heavily and so continued during the two following days, but in spite of the wet and the ceaseless fire of the defence, the French managed to complete their batteries—one just south of the Retiro to breach the wall, and one on higher ground

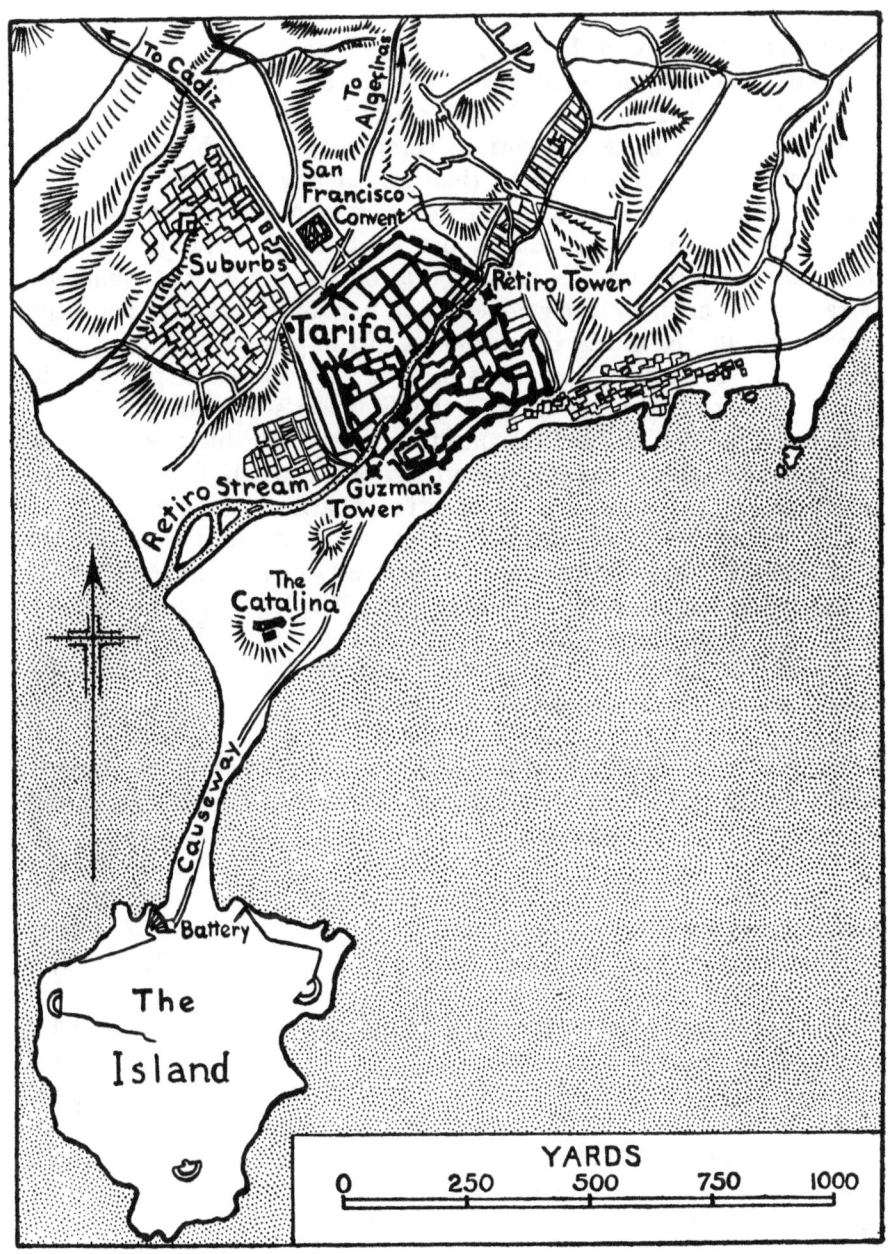

TARIFA.

1811.

in rear to silence the guns of the besieged. The French dragged their heavy guns through the rain and slush up to the battery positions and by the morning of the 29th December all were ready to open fire.

"And now there ensued a curious complication which might easily have brought disaster not only to this but to any military enterprise. The idea of holding Tarifa had originated not with Wellington nor with General Cooke, his deputy at Cadiz, but solely with General Campbell, the Governor of Gibraltar. Skerrett's brigade was under the command of Cooke, but the artillery, the engineers and part of his infantry had been lent by Campbell. Realizing the weakness of the place when the French attacked it by the regular operations of a siege, and unable, perhaps, to appreciate the subtlety of Smith's"—the Engineer's—"plan of defence, Skerrett had hesitated to take responsibility by risking his troops in the venture, and had applied to Cooke for orders. On the 24th Cooke's answer came that the brigade was to be at once re-embarked for Cadiz; and on that night Skerrett held a council-of-war wherein opinions were divided between Cooke's party, represented by Skerrett, and Campbell's party, represented by Major King" (82nd) "and Captain Smith" (R.E.). Gough of the 87th, though his regiment belonged to Cadiz, appears to have carried the decision of the council against Skerrett; and it was resolved that resistance should be continued.*

On the 29th December the fire from the French guns effected a breach in the walls just to the south of the Retiro, and by the next morning it was thirty feet wide, and the besieging general now called upon the garrison to capitulate. The demand was curtly rejected and fire was reopened, so that by sundown the gap was sixty feet in width. Rain again fell heavily and all entrenchments were awash; an assault at the moment was out of the question, but there was no doubt it would be launched so soon as the weather should clear, and the following were the dispositions made by the defence to meet it.

The 87th was stationed on the walls on either side of the breach, with two companies held in reserve; two companies of the 95th were stationed on the left of the 87th, and two of the 47th, under Captain Livesay, held the Jesus Tower,† which flanked the breach on the right of the 87th. The remaining companies of the 47th, less the garrison of the convent, were on the south front, while a battalion of Spaniards was posted in the street behind the palisades in rear of the breach.

It was not until eight o'clock on the morning of the 31st December

---

* Fortescue, Vol. VIII, p. 331.
† *Royal Military Chronicle*, Vol. IV, pp. 277–92. Colonel Skerrett's Journal tells us: "Thus they stood and cool determination sat upon their countenances."

that the French columns were seen to be advancing, thirty-two companies of grenadiers and voltigeurs, massed into four battalions and numbering some two thousand men, forming the assaulting party. The grenadiers were the actual stormers, the voltigeurs and an infantry battalion demonstrating on the right and left, while the grenadiers advanced down the hollow way formed by the bed of the torrent; these, however, moved straight on instead of making for the breach to the right. They thus came under a terrific fusillade from the 47th and 87th, many of their leaders fell killed and wounded, while the others extended, knee-deep in mud, along the ramparts and opened a feeble fire. Some reached the breach and even mounted it, but were there at once shot down, while grape from the Tower so swept the attackers that they shrank away and finally fell back.

The French dead covered all the slopes and filled the bed of the torrent, while two hundred wounded crawled under the breach. The loss of the defenders, on the other hand, was surprisingly small, only five officers and thirty-one other ranks being killed and wounded; in the 47th Lieutenant R. Hall and one man were killed, while Lieutenant G. Hill and two men were wounded; Captain O'Donoghue and Lieutenant de Burgh and a few men of the 47th were also wounded during the siege.

During the whole of the 7th January, 1812, all the troops were busily employed in levelling and destroying the enemy's works, and on the 9th Colonel Skerrett published an order extolling the bravery and good conduct of his troops in the recent operations. In this the following occurs:—

"To Major Broad, who commanded the picquets of the 47th and 87th on the 20th December, and who assisted in keeping the immense force of the enemy in check and who advanced on the enemy and repulsed them; and to Captains Livesay and Summers of the Light Companies of the 47th and 87th Regiments. To Captain Livesay and the officers and men of the Light Company of the 47th Regiment, and the remaining officers and men of his detachment, amounting to one hundred of the 47th Regiment, who in the first instance defended the east tower and flanked the right of the breach during the assault, and who with admirable coolness kept their possession under a heavy fire from the cannon and musketry, and afforded on that distinguished occasion the most essential service.

"To Captain Campbell, 47th Regiment, who, with a very small detachment, twice entered the enemy's entrenchment and brought away a great many entrenching tools and a wall-piece. Colonel Skerrett is happy to bear testimony to the zeal and bravery of Major Broad, who has offered himself on almost every occasion of public service."

Captain O'Donoghue, of the Battalion, who had officiated as A.D.C.

to Colonel Skerrett during the siege, was sent home with despatches, receiving a brevet majority for his services. Tarifa was now left in charge of the Spaniards, and before the end of January, 1812, the 2nd Battalion 47th found itself back again in Cadiz, Colonel Skerrett resuming command of his old brigade and Major Broad taking up that of the Battalion.

The siege of Cadiz went slowly on, but Wellington's victories in the north, and especially the capture of Ciudad Rodrigo and Badajoz and the success of Salamanca, led to the receipt of orders by Soult to raise the siege of Cadiz, evacuate Andalusia and retire towards Toledo; and finally, in the last week in August he drew off towards Granada.

Just prior to the raising of the siege Colonel Skerrett had been sent away to create a diversion and operate with some Spanish troops against Soult's communications, and he had reached Alcala on his way to Seville, when about September he was joined by General Cooke, who had moved out from Cadiz on the conclusion of the siege, bringing with him a large body of troops, included in which was the 2nd/47th. Cooke had evidently moved out in anticipation of orders from Wellington to join him, and these, though dated the 9th September, did not reach him at Alcala until the 28th, and in the instructions now received, Colonel Skerrett was directed to lead some four thousand five hundred men to Truxillo, while Cooke retained command of about four thousand more intended to garrison Cadiz, Tarifa and Carthagena.

Wellington's orders close as follows :—" Whenever the 2nd Battalion, 59th Regiment, shall arrive after you have carried these orders into execution, you will send to Lisbon whichever of that battalion or the 2nd Battalion, 47th Regiment, is most fit for service, retaining at Cadiz one British battalion."

The troops having been refitted for the field, Colonel Skerrett left for Truxillo on the 30th September, taking with him a detachment of the 3rd Battalion Grenadier Guards, the 47th and 87th, two companies of the 95th, the 20th Portuguese, a squadron of German Hussars and two companies of artillery; and marching by Los Santos, Villa Franca and Medellin, Truxillo was reached on the 12th October. Here he received orders to join General Hill's force at Talavera de la Regna and he duly arrived there on the 18th, his troops having covered two hundred and sixty-two miles in nineteen days.

" On arriving at Truxillo," so Captain Harley tells us, " Major Broad, of our Regiment, fell ill of a violent fever, and died in the very house in which, it is said, Pizarro had lived and died. There was an extraordinary circumstance attending his death. On his first entering this house, having tripped against a board which caused him to stumble, he exclaimed, though by no means superstitious, ' I hope that board may not make my coffin.' His loss was a very severe one for the Regiment of which he was a very valuable officer."

Soult had by this time managed to effect a junction with the Army of the Centre under King Joseph, and their united forces, amounting to sixty thousand men and eighty-four guns, were in movement to drive the Allies from the Tagus. General Hill sent notice to Wellington of the enemy's approach and drew his own forces together; he retired his left behind the Tajuna, and posted his right at Toledo, at the same time destroying the bridge at Aranjuez and securing that at Puente Largo. General Hill had now forty thousand men at his command for the defence of Madrid, nearly half of these being, however, Spaniards. Wellington, hearing of the concentration of the enemy and having failed at Burgos, ordered General Hill to abandon the line of the Tagus, evacuate Madrid, and, falling back through the Guadarama Pass, form a junction with him (Wellington) near Salamanca.

Preparations were accordingly made for retreat, the bridge of Puente Largo was mined, and the 47th and 95th of Skerrett's brigade, forming the rearguard, were ordered to defend the bridge, holding the enemy here for twenty-four hours so as to let the main body get well away. The Aranjuez-Madrid road here passed over the Puente Largo, the approach to which on the enemy's side was covered by trees and an inn, while it was commanded on the south by some high ground.

The bridge had been mined, but the charges failed to explode, and some abattis had been placed in position and a breastwork thrown up to defend the passage, when on the 30th October Soult's troops here attacked the rearguard of the 47th and 87th, covered by the French guns on the high ground, to which three Portuguese 9-pounders replied.

The enemy charged forward twice, hoping to carry the bridge, but each time fell back under the fire of the defence, and then arranged for a suspension of hostilities while they collected their wounded; when night came on the British slipped quietly and unmolested away. They had suffered some sixty casualties, nearly all of these among the 2nd Battalion 47th, Ensign Lindsay being killed and Lieutenants Vaughan and Mountain wounded. In his report on this action General Hill wrote:—" After they discovered the failure of the mine the enemy made a vigorous attempt to get possession of the bridge, but were repulsed in a very handsome manner by the 47th Regiment and a detachment of the 95th, under Colonel Skerrett, placed there by Lieut.-General Cole, who had charge of the rearguard." The weather was so misty that it was late on the 31st October before Soult realized that the whole of Hill's army had managed to get safely away, to effect its junction with Wellington at Alba de Tormes by November 8th.

Wellington had now some sixty-eight thousand Allied troops concentrated under his command, and with these he withdrew, practically unmolested, into Ciudad Rodrigo, within the walls of which fortress he had arrived by the 19th November, thus bringing to an end the campaign of 1812.

The French army fell back into a more hospitable part of the country, while the troops under Wellington moved into winter quarters in the valleys of the Douro, the Coa and the Mondego. The 2nd Battalion 47th was on the 1st December posted to the 2nd Brigade of the 5th Division, the headquarters of which was at Lamego on the Douro ; and in some villages hereabouts the Battalion passed the winter. The 2nd Brigade of the 5th Division was commanded by Major-General Pringle and contained the 4th and 47th and the 5th Provisional Battalion, this last made up of the remnants of the Second Battalions of the 30th and 44th Regiments : one weak company of the Brunswick Oels was attached to each brigade.

The winter at Lamego was uneventful, except that a very deadly type of fever broke out, which carried off from ten to twelve men daily. Much was done in the direction of reorganizing and re-equipping the troops ; a fine pontoon train was completed and carts suitable for the rough and hilly roads were requisitioned or constructed ; and the heavy iron camp kettles, which up to this time had been carried by the men, were discarded for others of a very much lighter pattern.

Early in January, 1813, the 2nd Battalion 47th appears to have had an effective strength of 447 rank and file, while there were 185 sick, and 311 wanting to complete.

Colonel Skerrett had now left the 47th, to which since 1804 he had belonged, on promotion to command a brigade in the 4th Division, and the Battalion would appear to have been temporarily commanded by Major Robert Kelly.

CHAPTER VII

THE 2ND BATTALION, 47TH REGIMENT

1813–1816

THE BATTLE OF VITTORIA. THE SIEGE OF ST. SEBASTIAN
THE BATTLE OF THE NIVE

THE plans for the Campaign of 1813 had been well considered by Wellington, and were conceived with the idea of driving the French armies out of Spain. Knowing that the enemy had strengthened his defences on the Douro, Wellington resolved to turn them by throwing his left wing across that river and move along the right bank, thereafter uniting with the Spanish army of Galicia, crossing the Esla ahead of the rest of the army, and so threatening the French right. The allied centre and right were to concentrate at Salamanca and force the passage of the Tormes, then, aided by the turning movement on the left, drive the enemy towards Burgos into Biscay. It was hoped in this way to throw the enemy back on the Pyrenees before they could organize their scattered forces for any successful resistance, and to establish a new base near the sea in Biscay, from which the French communications with France could be threatened.

When the campaign opened, the French were still uncertain as to Wellington's intentions and their armies were not suitably disposed to meet his advance. King Joseph moved his headquarters to Valladolid in March, leaving ten thousand men in Madrid; one division was behind the Tormes, three were on the Douro and Reille's cavalry was on the Esla; but the King had found it necessary to send four divisions to aid Clausel in putting down the insurrections in Biscay and Navarre, thereby seriously reducing his forces.

On the other hand, Wellington had forty-five thousand British and twenty-eight thousand Portuguese troops, all in good order and ready for the great forward movement. A large portion of the troops forming the left wing had been gradually moved towards the Lower Douro, and as early as the 2nd May a large body of cavalry passed that river near Oporto. The 5th Division crossed about the 14th, and by the 15th many of the infantry were north of the Douro, crossing between Lamego and Castello de Alba.

The 5th Division, which contained the 2nd Battalion 47th, was in the left wing of Wellington's Army under Lieut.-General Graham, and this also included the 1st, 3rd, 4th, 6th and 7th Divisions, two Portuguese brigades and three brigades of cavalry.

The route to be followed by Graham's wing lay over the Tras-os-Montes, a most difficult and rugged country to traverse, the narrow mountain roads and the deep ravines which had to be crossed making the march one of no ordinary toil. The movement began on the 13th May, on which date the divisions began to leave their winter quarters, and by the 26th the whole of Graham's army started out in three columns as follows :—*

" 1. From Braganza marched, as the northern column, Anson's light and Ponsonby's heavy dragoon brigades, preceding the 1st Infantry Division and Pack's Portuguese independent brigade. Crossing the frontier river, the Manzanas, at fords by Nuez, they were ordered to move on Tabora in four marches by the country road through Sesnande.

" 2. From Outeiro and Vimioso marched, as the central column, following D'Urban's Portuguese light horse, Bock's heavy German dragoons accompanied by the 3rd and 5th Divisions and Bradford's independent Portuguese brigade. They were directed to move by Alcanizas in four marches on Losilla, five miles south of Tabora.

" 3. From Miranda de Douro marched, as the right column, close to the river, the 4th, 6th and 7th Divisions. Having a shorter distance to cover than the other two columns, their van was to reach Carvajales on the 28th in three marches."

The cavalry at the head of Graham's three columns reached their destinations—Tabora, Losilla and Carvajales—on May 28th, the infantry on the following day; but Graham now found himself checked by the River Esla, much swollen by recent heavy rain, while every practicable ford was watched by French patrols. However, on the night of the 30th, part of the Hussar brigade and some infantry crossed, and a foothold was thus gained on the eastern bank, a pontoon bridge was laid and several divisions crossed. On the 2nd June the mounted men reached Toro, and here the whole army halted during the 3rd, while Wellington's right wing crossed the river.

On June 4th Wellington set his army in motion in four columns; on the extreme left the Spanish forces of Giron moved eastward on Beceril; in the left centre Graham, with the 1st and 5th Divisions, two Portuguese brigades and two brigades of cavalry, moved northward on Medina and

* Oman, *History of the Peninsular War*, Vol. VI, pp. 325, 326.

Palencia; in the right centre was the main column, with the Light, 3rd, 4th, 6th and 7th Divisions and three cavalry brigades; while on the right General Hill marched on Valladolid and on arrival there turned north again. On June 7th Giron was at Beceril, Graham was at Grijoto and Wellington at Palencia, while Hill was to the right rear near Duenas. On this same day the French army was holding a very strong position between the Pisuerga and Arlanzon Rivers, but dearth of supplies obliged the enemy to fall back to a position some ten miles south-east of Burgos, where it remained from the 9th to the 12th June. On this latter date Graham and his troops were at Soltresgudo.

Joseph and Marshal Jourdan, having well considered the general situation, decided that it would be well not to stand and fight a general action, so the Castle of Burgos was blown up, and the army fell back to the line of the Ebro.

"The position which Joseph had now taken up was by nature a very strong one. The river itself formed a good line of defence, while the road leading to it from Burgos passed through confined mountain gorges, one of which especially, the defile of Pancorbo, held by the French and defended by a small castle, was so narrow that a mere handful of men could have held it against a large force. To have attacked this position in front would have entailed great loss upon the Allies, and the result must have been very doubtful. Wellington, therefore, again attempted to turn it, if possible. . . . The Allied army moved forward with the object of crossing the Upper Ebro near its source about Rocomunda and Puente Arenas; and so coming down the left bank upon the position of the French near Vittoria.*

News reached the French in due course that the English cavalry had crossed the Upper Ebro at Medina del Pomar on the 16th June, but it was not yet certain whether this meant that Wellington was trying to outflank the French, or whether he was moving on Bilbao, there to establish a new base.

On the 14th Graham was at San Martin, by the 17th he had reached La Cerca and by this it was becoming abundantly clear that the Ebro position was turned. To quote Napier's matchless prose :—" And now with an eagle's sweep Wellington brought his left wing round, and pouring his numerous columns through all the deep, narrow valleys and rugged defiles, descended towards the great road of Bilbao, between Frias and Orduna. At Medina del Pomar he left the 6th Division to guard his stores and supplies; but the march of the other divisions was unmitigated. Neither the winter gullies, nor the ravines, nor the precipitous passes amongst the rocks

* Robinson, *Wellington's Campaigns*, pp. 288, 289.

retarded the march even of the artillery. Where horses could not draw, men hauled; and where the wheels would not roll, the guns were let down or lifted up with ropes. And strongly did the rough veteran infantry work their way through those wild but beautiful regions. Six days they toiled incessantly; and on the seventh, swelled by the junction of Longa's division and all the smaller bands which came trickling from the mountains, they burst like raging streams from every defile and went foaming into the basin of Vittoria."

On the 20th the Allies, having turned the Ebro, encamped along the River Bayas, halting here to concentrate before attacking Joseph and his army, disposed along the little River Zadorra, covering the town of Vittoria. Vittoria is situated in a plain some eight miles long and six broad, watered by the Zadorra which flows through it in a westerly direction. Here the armies of Portugal, the South and North were crowded together.

The French were drawn up in a series of positions covering Vittoria to the west, while observation troops were pushed out north of the Zadorra on the roads leading to Bilbao. On June 20th the Army of the South under General Gazan, twenty-six thousand strong, occupied the westernmost ridge of the plain stretching from the height above the bridge of Nanclares in the north to the village of Subijana de Alava in the south; here a brigade occupied a slightly advanced position beneath the Heights of Puebla with strong observation posts thrown out on the hill-tops. A mile and a half in rear of the right of this first line was Villatte's division on the knoll of Arinez, whereabouts a division of light cavalry was also posted. D'Erlon's Army of the Centre—ten thousand strong—occupied a parallel ridge about two miles behind Gazan, just to the west of the village of Gomecha, and was disposed north and south of the main road; two cavalry brigades were slightly in rear. The Army of Portugal, some twelve thousand in all, and under General Reille, was drawn up on the ridge running between the village of Zuazo and the town of Vittoria.

Cavalry covered the front from Margarita eastward and watched the Bilbao road, and the reserve artillery was parked in Vittoria or to the east of that town. In all, King Joseph's Army numbered 45,000 infantry, 7,000 cavalry and 150 guns.

On the 20th Wellington made a careful reconnaissance of the enemy's position and resolved to attack next day with his army of 70,000 men and 90 guns; the following were his dispositions:—the Right, under Hill, 20,000 strong, was to move across the Zadorra by Puebla de Arganzon and endeavour to gain the Heights of Puebla and force the Puebla Pass: the Right and Left Centres under Wellington, about 30,000 in all, were to march, the right centre by Subijana de Morillos to Nanclares, the left centre

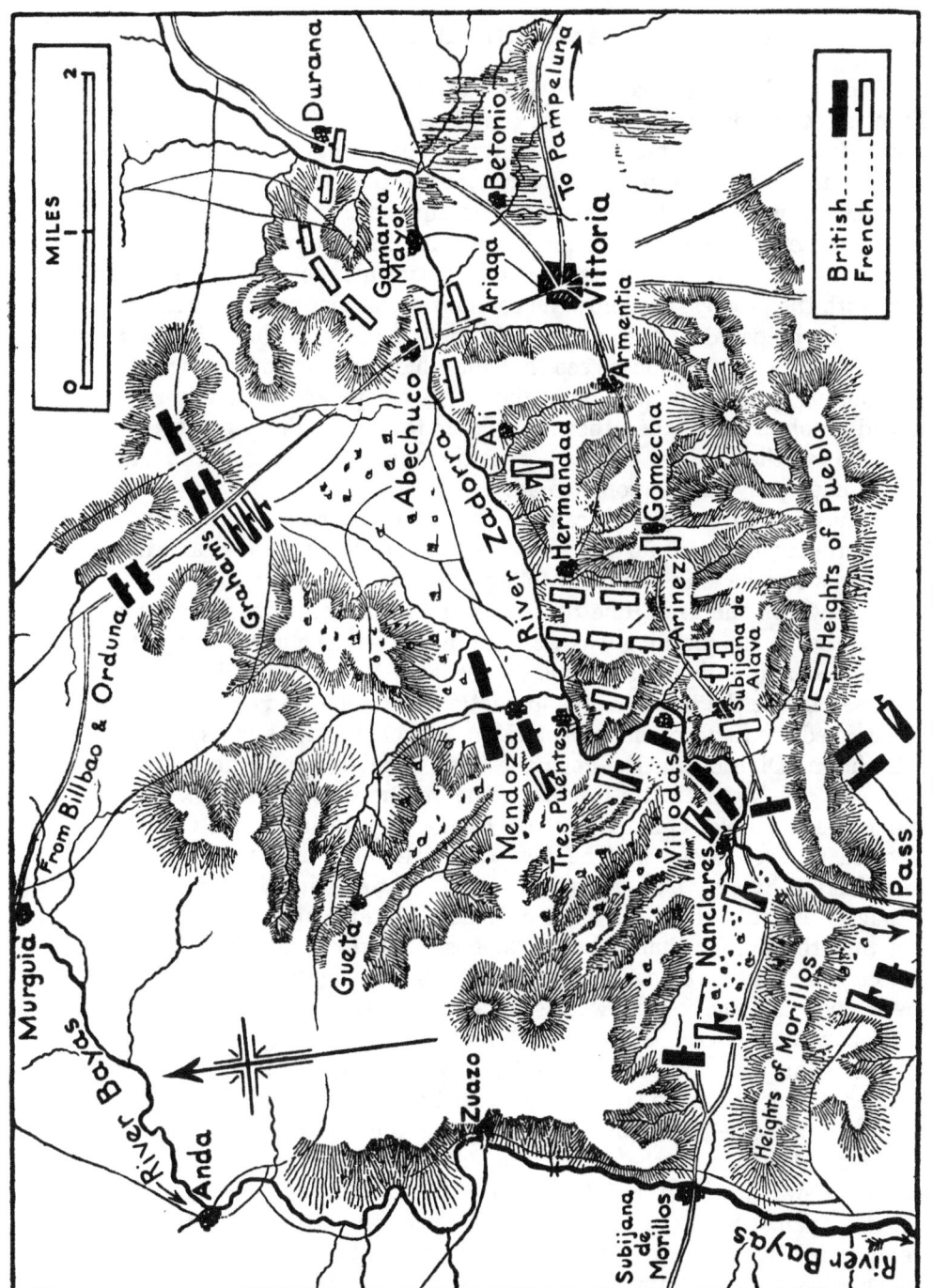

The Battle of Vittoria.
21st June, 1813.

by Anda on the River Bayas to Gueta de Ariba and thence towards the Zadorra, connecting with the right centre: the Left Column, 20,000 men under Graham, was to move from Murguia, near the Bayas, by the Bilbao road to the bridges north of Vittoria, connecting with the Left Centre Column, by which it was to regulate its advance.

"The Left Column had an important and difficult part to play in the operations. Graham was instructed to regulate his movements in accordance with the progress made by the columns on his right; and at the same time to be prepared to turn the French right and the town of Vittoria, if required to do so. Should he see that the Allied columns on his right were not gaining ground he was immediately to co-operate with them: but should he observe, on the other hand, that they were driving the French back, he was then to turn his whole attention towards cutting off the retreat of the enemy by the Bayonne road.

"Thus he had to act with caution and reserve until the certain success of the other columns, or further instructions from Wellington, clearly determined the line he was finally to follow." *

At dawn on the 21st June the Allied troops moved from their camps: the weather in the morning was wet and misty, but about nine o'clock the fog cleared and brilliant sunshine succeeded. Rough ground had to be traversed before the troops came into action, but about ten o'clock General Hill crossed the Zadorra and attacked the French on the Heights of Puebla with the 2nd Division and the Portuguese and Spaniards under his command. Presently the Right Centre Column came on the scene, the 4th Division, under General Cole, crossing by the bridge of Nanclares and the Light Division at Tres Puentes. The Left Centre Column arrived last, having been delayed by very bad ground, but Sir T. Picton, with the 3rd Division, managed to cross the river by the Mendoza bridge and a ford close by, and the 7th Division, under Lord Dalhousie, by the fords near Margarita on Gazan's right. The columns once over, the battle became general and the French left and centre were soon hard pressed.

Meanwhile General Graham had left Murguia at eight o'clock and assembled his force on the Bilbao road, where it was joined by Longa's Spaniards, four thousand strong. General Reille had four or five thousand infantry and some squadrons of cavalry on the high ground above the village of Abechuco, to the east of the Bilbao road. About eleven o'clock General Oswald, with the 5th Division, Pack's Portuguese brigade and Longa's Spaniards began to drive the French from these heights, which were carried by the Portuguese. General Oswald then advanced with the 5th Division to attack Gamarra Mayor, about a mile distant, while Longa's

* Robinson, *Wellington's Campaigns*, pp. 293, 294.

VITTORIA.

21st June, 1813.

men made themselves masters of Gamarra Menor, and later proceeded against Durana, causing the enemy division there to fall back.

The assault on Gamarra Mayor has been described by two historians of the Peninsular War. Napier writes:—" Robinson's brigade, being formed in three columns, made the attack at a running pace. At first the fire of artillery and musketry was so heavy that the British troops stopped and commenced firing also, and the three columns got intermixed, yet encouraged by their officers, and especially by the example of General Robinson, they renewed the charge, broke through the village and even crossed the bridge. One gun was captured and the passage seemed to be won, when Reille suddenly turned twelve pieces upon the village, and La Martinière, rallying his division under cover of the cannonade, retook the bridge; it was with difficulty the allied troops could even hold the village until they were reinforced. Then a second British brigade came down and the bridge was again carried; but again these new troops were driven back in the same manner as the others had been. Thus the bridge remained forbidden ground."

The following is Leith Hay's account: " Gamarra Mayor was stormed by Robinson's brigade of the 5th Division—4th, 47th and 59th, which advancing in columns of battalions, regardless of a heavy and destructive fire of artillery and musketry, pursued its steady, orderly, and not to be obstructed course without returning a shot, and at the point of the bayonet forced back the enemy, who retired in confusion with the loss of three pieces of cannon. Although in possession of the town, General Robinson was not in sufficient force to carry the bridge, on the opposite end of which the enemy had rallied. . . . Repeated and violent efforts were made to recover possession of the village, but these were rendered unavailing by the unshaken gallantry of the 5th Division. . . . In these affairs the 5th Division had nearly five hundred men either killed or wounded. The village of Abechuco was carried by the Light Battalion of the German Legion, supported by General Bradford's brigade. The enemy does not appear to have considered this point of equal importance with the possession of Gamarra Mayor, nor were similar efforts made either to maintain or to recover the bridge, which near to Abechuco also afforded means of passing the Zadorra."

It being impossible to force the passage of the river at these bridges while Reille was so strongly posted on the further bank, matters remained here in abeyance until the defenders were threatened in rear by the victorious advance of the British centre. Wellington, having driven the French from their successive positions, at length reached Vittoria, and some of his cavalry appearing in rear of Ariaga, Reille withdrew his men, who retired towards a wood on the Salvatierra–Pampeluna road; here, at Betonio, a reserve had been stationed and this helped Reille to fight his way to Metanco, on the Salvatierra road, and make good his retreat. The flight of the French was very rapid and there was great confusion and congestion on the roads.

The way being now open to Graham, his troops pressed on, Anson's cavalry crossing by the Gamarra Mayor bridge; but the French rearguard engaged our mounted troops in the woods, and this resistance and the nature of the ground favoured their escape, the pursuit finally closing as darkness fell, some two leagues from Vittoria.

The French got away in tolerable order, leaving some two thousand prisoners in our hands, but in and about the town of Vittoria there was the plunder of a kingdom in the abandoned wagons. "No estimate," says Alison, " can be formed of the amount of private plunder which was taken on the field, but it exceeded anything witnessed in modern war. Enormous spoil fell into the hands of the private soldiers, and the cloud of camp followers and sutlers who followed in their train swept the ground so completely that only a hundred thousand dollars of the whole taken was brought in to the military chest."

All order and discipline were for the time being destroyed, and the number of men who were for days and weeks absent from their Colours amounted to several thousands.

The loss of the Allies was 5,176 killed, wounded and missing, and of these 3,567 were British; the French casualties were some 7,000, including prisoners. Of the 2nd Battalion 47th two officers—Lieutenants J. Harley * and G. Hill *—two sergeants and sixteen rank and file were killed, four officers, five sergeants and eighty-three other ranks were wounded; the four wounded officers were Captains W. A. Hodges, H. Parsons and W. W. Yates and Lieutenant T. S. Shortt.

General Graham's column bivouacked on the night of the action at Zurbano, Yarraza and Metanco; next day the pursuit was continued to Salvatierra, but so rapid had been the flight of the French that nothing was this day seen of them. The 5th Division remained at Salvatierra while Wellington went on in the tracks of the enemy; but on arrival at Pampeluna, hearing that Clausel, who had come up to Vittoria the day after the battle, had fallen back on Logrono, Wellington decided to try and intercept him. Marching then on the 27th with eighteen thousand men on Tudela, he directed the 5th Division from Salvatierra, the 6th from Vittoria and a large body of cavalry to march on Logrono, to prevent the escape of Clausel on that side. The French general was, however, not to be caught

* These two officers were the one a son, the other a nephew of Captain Harley.

in the net spread for him, and made a forced march upon Saragossa and thence across the frontier into France.

Lord Wellington now decided to hold the line of the Pyrenees, but to assist in this object it was necessary that the fortresses of Pampeluna and St. Sebastian should be reduced. General Graham, with ten thousand men, was detailed to conduct the siege of the last-named fortress, and the 5th Division, with Bradford's and Wilson's Portuguese brigades, was placed under his orders. These troops, with a siege train of forty guns, arrived before St. Sebastian on the 9th July.

"St. Sebastian was a fortified stronghold situated upon a low, sandy peninsula jutting out into the Bay of Biscay. Except on the south side it is surrounded by water—the River Urumea, which is unfordable for about two hours before and after high water, forming its boundary to the east. To the north of the fortress rises the Monte Orgullo, which is washed by the sea and crowned by the castle of La Mota. Separated as it was from St. Sebastian itself by a line of defensive works, this castle could be held after the fall of the fortress which it commands. The land front to the south, stretching across the isthmus between the Urumea and the sea, consisted of a high rampart with half-bastions at either end and a lofty casemated bastion in the centre; while in advance of this was a strong hornwork; then further south was a small redoubt formed of casks and termed the Cask Redoubt. Still more to the south was the ridge of San Bartolomeo, and upon this stood the convent of that name and other buildings, which could be made defensible as outworks.

"On the eastern bank of the River Urumea, over which a bridge existed near the suburb of St. Catherine, stretched a sandy plain called the Chofre Sand Hills, at the north-east point of which rose the Monte Olia."*

The weak side of the fortress was the east, where the ramparts, low and not well flanked, were commanded by guns placed on the Chofre Sand Hills.

General Graham's plan of attack was to approach from the south and east, working up from the south against the Convent of San Bartolomeo and the hornwork, establishing main batteries on the Chofre Sand Hills, and after making a breach in the eastern rampart, endeavour to carry the place by assault on that side.

During the days that had elapsed between the Battle of Vittoria and the arrival of General Graham's troops before St. Sebastian, General Rey, the commander of the fortress, had made every effort to improve the defences; he had sent away many of the civilian inhabitants, he had mounted seventy-six heavy guns on the ramparts, the bridge over the

* Robinson, *Wellington's Campaigns*, pp. 308, 309.

River Urumea was destroyed, and his troops, reinforced from the sea, now numbered about three thousand men.

Between July 10th and 14th batteries were erected against the Convent and redoubt of San Bartolomeo, which was taken by assault on the 17th; on the 19th the French were driven from the Cask Redoubt; and on the 20th all the breaching batteries opened from the Chofre Sand Hills. Of the making of one of these breaching batteries Captain Harley tells us the following:—" Our miners had to cut through the burying ground of the Convent, and here was presented a melancholy spectacle as the soldiers proceeded in their work. Coffins and bodies appeared in every stage of decay; some recently interred and becoming decomposed, others already mouldering into clay. . . . During these scenes every heart became callous, even the coffins were broken up and made fuel of."

Heavy fire was continuously maintained on the place until the 23rd July, by which date two breaches had been made in the eastern rampart, and an assault was fixed for the night of the 24th–25th, for it was considered desirable to hasten the capture of St. Sebastian since Marshal Soult with eighty thousand men had now arrived at the foot of the mountains between the Bidassoa and St. Jean Pied du Port, announcing that it was his intention to " chase Wellington beyond the Ebro."

The assault, carried out by Hay's brigade of the 5th Division, failed with considerable loss, and Wellington then gave orders that the siege must be turned into a blockade; in the meantime took place the Battle of the Pyrenees with which this History has no concern.

By the middle of August a fresh brigade arrived from England and was sent to the 5th Division; by the 19th some heavy guns had been sent from home and by the 26th a continuous fire from these was opened from the batteries on the Chofre Sand Hills against the eastern rampart and from the heights of San Bartolomeo against the hornwork; and on the 30th August practicable breaches had been made and the guns of St. Sebastian had been almost completely silenced. Wellington now gave orders that the assault should take place at eleven o'clock on the following morning.

General Sir James Leith had recently assumed command of the 5th Division, and was given charge of the assault and the direction of the attack west of the Urumea; and Wellington now, believing that the failure of the earlier assault had dispirited the 5th Division, gave orders that volunteers from the 1st, 4th and Light Divisions should lead. General Leith would, however, have none of this and determined that the leading troops in the storm should belong to his own division, and directed that the assault should be carried out by the 5th Division, supported by Spry's Portuguese, while the volunteers and the 5th Cacadores were to cover the advance by

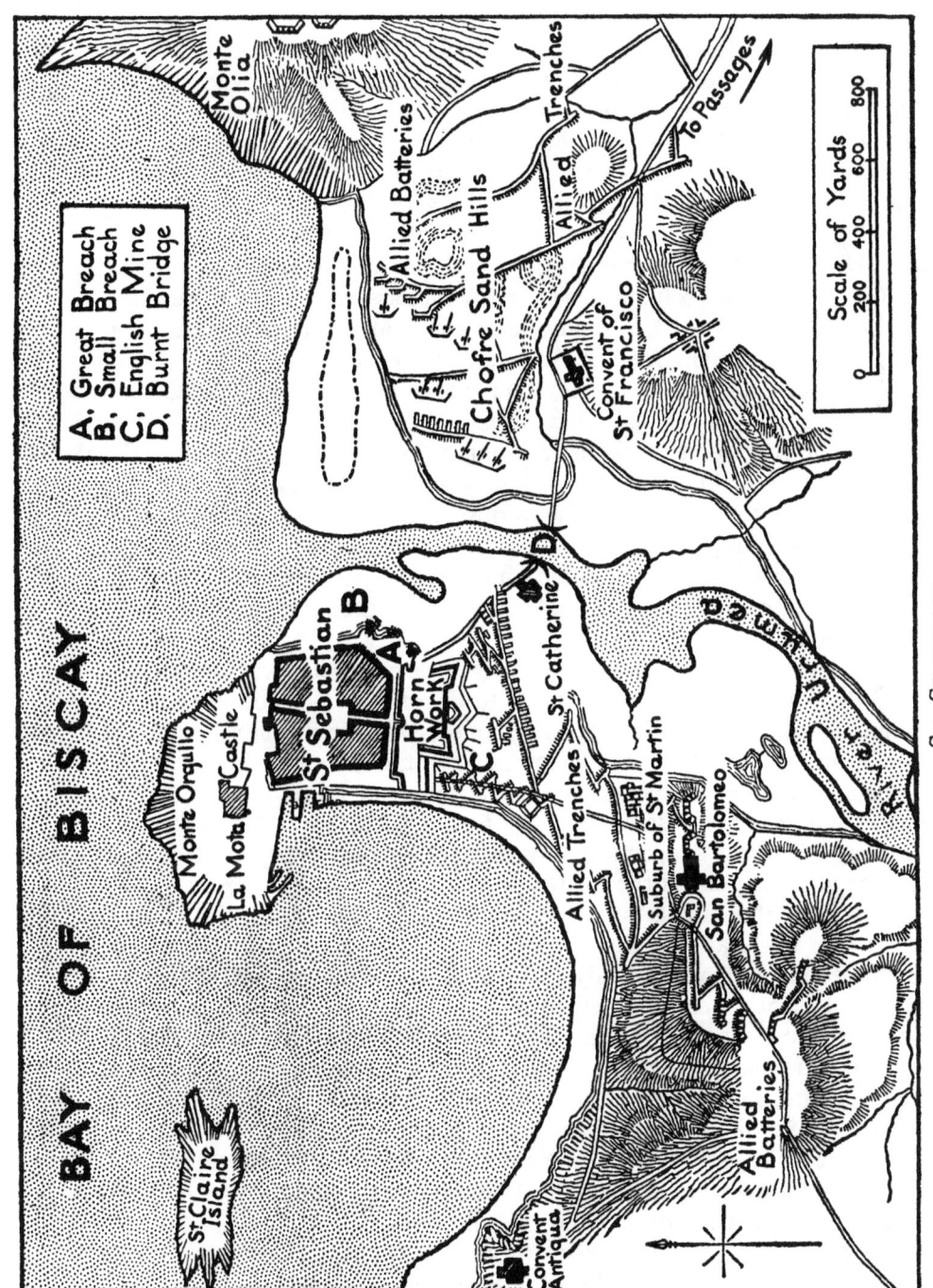

St. Sebastian.
1813.

fire from the trenches; and according to Graham's despatch of the 1st September, 1813, "the column of attack was formed of the 2nd Brigade of the 5th Division, commanded by Major-General Robinson, with an immediate support" of 950 volunteers from various corps and divisions which are named; the rest of the 5th Division was in reserve.

At eleven o'clock on the morning of the 31st August, the tide having fallen, General Robinson's Brigade—the 4th, 47th and 59th Regiments, the whole about one thousand bayonets, moved out of the trenches in front of St. Catherine in two columns; the first was to assault the great breaches, the other the bastion of St. John and the end of the high curtain. On leaving the trenches the first column had to pass over one hundred and eighty yards of open strand, strewn with rocks and sea-weed, before reaching the great breach. When half-way across the column was assailed by a heavy fire of grape and musketry and many fell. At the same time the enemy, in hopes of blocking the way with fallen masonry, exploded two mines under the covered-way of the hornwork; these, however, were fired prematurely and only some forty men at the head of the column were injured. In no way daunted, Robinson's brigade pressed on, swarmed up the breach and gained the crest under a storm of fire, but here they were at last checked.

It was now seen that from the top of the breach to the level of the town beyond there was a drop of from sixteen to thirty feet: the houses formerly standing against the wall had been removed, while immediately opposite and not forty yards distant, an entrenchment had been made and the neighbouring houses loopholed, and from these an annihilating fire was opened. Many of the assaulting party now fell, the survivors took what cover they could, the supporting column came under a heavy fire from the river-face and the guns of the Castle, and shouts of victory were raised by the French on the ramparts.

"At this crisis an expedient was resorted to which could only have been successful with very steady troops. The assaulting columns at the foot of the breach were directed to halt and lie down, while forty-seven guns played close over their heads upon the enemy's ramparts, and especially the works flanking the breach. This artillery fire was so accurate and so heavy that in a short time the portions played upon were cleared of their defenders, while the guns on them were dismounted, and in about twenty minutes a terrific explosion of numerous powder barrels and shells took place, blowing three hundred of the French into the air.

"Then the British troops again rushed forward, and after a desperate conflict succeeded in entering the works. At the same time the lesser breach was successfully stormed by the Portuguese troops, and the garrison

ST. SEBASTIAN.

1813.

now took refuge in the castle on Monte Orgullo. . . . This surrendered on September 9th."

As at Badajoz, so here, very great excesses took place after the capture of the town, and these only ended with the destruction of nearly the whole town by fire.

From first to last some 3,800 of all ranks were killed and wounded during the siege, of whom over 2,500 fell in the last four days of the operations, while of the total casualties 2,400 fell upon the British troops. In Robinson's brigade the loss during the siege amounted to 872.

Of the losses in the 2nd Battalion 47th Captain Harley wrote: "Major Robert Kelly, who commanded the 47th, accosted me about seven o'clock when he was going down to the trenches and requested I would dine with him at half-past four o'clock; humorously remarking 'provided I live so long.' He led on the Regiment, and in an hour after was killed between the trenches and the breach. Our Regiment suffered severely, out of twenty-two officers and five hundred men, we had eight officers killed and nine wounded and two hundred men killed. Among the number wounded mortally was Captain Livesay, who received a wound through the shoulder. He was an officer of long standing, having served since he had been a very young man in the 47th Regiment. . . . He fell, bravely leading the Light Company through the breach, being shot from the top of the wall by a French rifleman."

Actually the casualties in the 2nd Battalion 47th were as follows:— killed, Major R. Kelly, Captain W. A. Hodges, Lieutenants T. S. Shortt and G. Norris, Ensigns J. Bakewell, J. Campbell and T. Bennett, nine sergeants, one drummer and ninety-eight rank and file; wounded, Captains C. E. Livesay (mortally) and H. Oglander, Lieutenants T. Power, W. Kendall, W. M. K. Johnson, J. R. Nason and E. Agar, Ensigns A. Hall and S. Burke, eight sergeants, one drummer and one hundred and eighteen other ranks. Lieutenant Nason had been previously wounded on the 10th August.

The citadel was kept under a heavy bombardment until the 8th September when the commandant surrendered, and marched out with his very greatly reduced garrison.

"During the siege," so Captain Harley tells us, "the enemy sprang a mine near the breach, by which Colonel Sir R. Fletcher, of the Engineers, Captains Hodges and Shortt, of the 47th Regiment, were blown up. Lieutenant Lyne, of the 47th, bravely rushed from the trenches and went in through the breach, for which he was afterwards put under arrest by General Hay for being too forward, or rather going without leave, though it was a courageous act of the poor fellow."

The command of the Battalion now devolved temporarily upon Lieutenant Power who himself was wounded, and General Graham in his despatch on the conclusion of the siege wrote that "Lieutenant-General Sir J. Leith commends highly Captain Livesay, who succeeded to the command of the 47th Foot on Major Kelly being killed, and kept it till wounded, when the command devolved on Lieutenant Power, who ably performed the duty."

The 2nd Battalion 47th remained in the vicinity of the fortress for some three weeks, and during this time the command was assumed by Lieut.-Colonel R. Chetham, who signed the muster rolls at Ernani on the 24th September.

Wellington had only been waiting for the fall of St. Sebastian, and the now daily expected surrender of Pampeluna, to attack the French positions on the Bidassoa. Here the main enemy concentration line ran from Urrugne, close to the mouth of the river, through Olhette, Sare and Ainhoa to St. Jean Pied du Port, with well-defended posts all along the river frontier. As the month of September drew to a close, news began to come through of the serious defeats which the Napoleonic armies were suffering in Central Europe, and now Wellington decided to force an entrance on to French territory by attacking the heights on the Lower Bidassoa, which as he wrote, "command such a view of us that the sooner we get them the better." These commanding heights referred to were the Ridge of the Café Republicain, and the high ground south-east of it known as the Croix de Bouquets, the Hill of Louis XIV, the Hill of Briatou, and to the left rear the Mont du Calvaire; against these he decided to throw the 1st and 5th Divisions and the brigades of Wilson and Aylmer, some fifteen thousand men in all.

Other columns, mainly Spanish, were to cross the Bidassoa higher up, while further inland forces under Generals Hill, Picton and Colville were to operate or make demonstrations to prevent the French reinforcing the main point of attack.

All was ready by the evening of the 6th October, on which day the 1st Division was assembled about Fuenterabia and the 5th at Irun.

The morning of the 7th October was dark and stormy, when the Allies left their tents standing and descended to the river. "Those columns on the Lower Bidassoa wound like huge snakes through the level sands, and were in some places almost immersed in water before they reached the firm ground on the opposite side." The British guns opened fire on a rocket signal being made, and all the columns then commenced the passage.

"General Robinson passed the river on foot at the head of his brigade, amidst a shower of musketry and up to the middle in water; also there was much cheering and the bands played the National Anthem as the 5th Division crossed over, and were the first British troops whose Colours waved

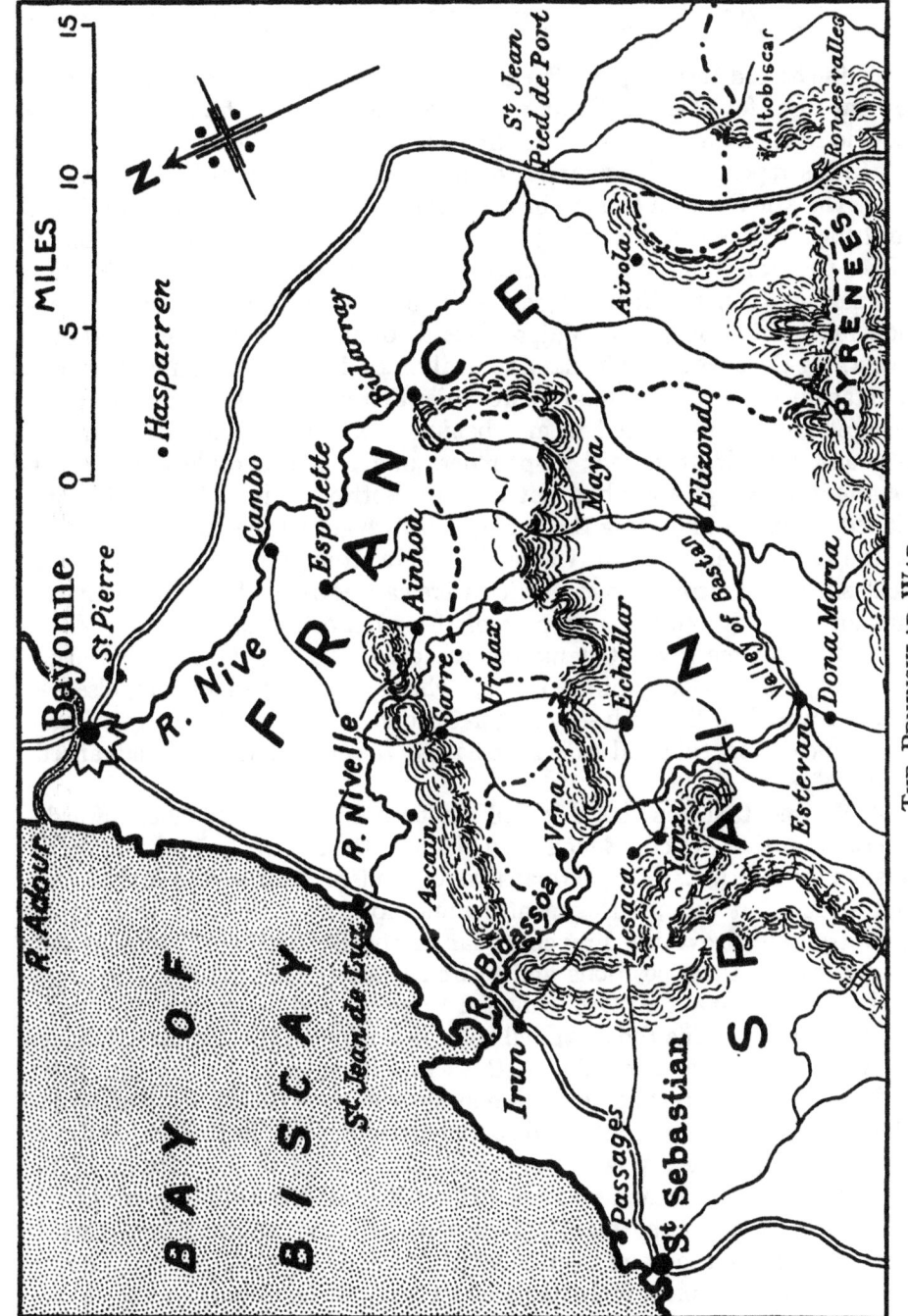

The Peninsular War.
1813-1814.

over the sacred territory of Napoleon. The enemy were completely taken by surprise, for Marshal Soult was reviewing troops in the centre of his position when the first gun was fired on the Lower Bidassoa."

In his report the Commander of the 5th Division wrote as follows :—

"The 5th Division crossed in three columns; the left column at No. 1 ford towards the sea, consisting of No. 2 Brigade, guns and cavalry under Major-General Robinson. The crossing took place at 7.30 a.m., the tide not serving sooner. Being myself with the left column, I cannot express how much I feel obliged to Major-General Robinson for his able assistance in turning the enemy's right flank several times, in one of which movements a detachment of the 47th and a Grenadier Company of the 3rd Portuguese charged the enemy posted in and behind a battery on our left near the sea, and took it with four 24-pounders and a considerable quantity of ammunition, which they had not time to destroy. The column still continued turning and driving the enemy until we got to the flank and nearly to the top of their position, where they were strongly posted behind some field works and strong hedges, which were carried by a charge of the 47th, supported by the 59th and a part of the 3rd Portuguese.

"At this time my left flank was attacked, and the flankers driven in by a very superior body of the enemy, who were most gallantly repulsed—whilst I was with the 47th—by Major-General Robinson and the 4th Regiment, and driven, till I had ordered to halt, to the ground where our advanced picquets now are.

"The resistance on this side had not been obstinate but more towards the right, at the Croix de Bouquets, which was the key of the position, there was severe fighting. The Germans were repulsed with severe loss in the first attack, but the 9th Regiment coming up carried the post with great gallantry, and drove the French as far as the Royal Road. Finally the enemy lost all their positions and retired towards Bayonne."

In this fighting the 47th had one sergeant and four men wounded. Soult, driven from the Bidassoa, fell back on the line of the Nivelle, covering his whole front with formidable earthworks, his right being about St. Jean de Luz and the left resting on the mountain known as the Pic du Mondarin. This position Wellington intended to have tried to force in the closing days of October, but a heavy fall of rain and snow caused the operations to be postponed and the attack was not delivered until the 10th November.

On this occasion the main attack was delivered against the enemy's centre with forty thousand men under Hill, while General Hope with some nineteen thousand men, including the 1st and 5th Divisions, was to make a feint attack, though a very closely pressed one, against the works of St. Jean de Luz, the object being not to force the French right, but to prevent Soult from withdrawing any of his troops from here to reinforce his centre.

Hope's columns drove in the enemy's outposts on their right early in the morning and forced the French out of the camp of Sans Culottes, advancing then to an inundation in front of Bordegain and Siborne; but these divisions had no share in the main battle, whereby the enemy were driven from their principal works, which had cost them three months' labour, with the loss of fifty-one guns, 1,400 prisoners and 2,870 killed and wounded.

On the next day the 1st and 5th Divisions forded the Nivelle above St. Jean de Luz and occupied cantonments about Bidart, remaining here in very cold and inclement weather for three weeks. There was some skirmishing at the outposts, as in the 47th casualty returns two men are shown as being taken prisoners on the 17th November, one as killed on the 20th and two more taken prisoners on the 22nd; many of those wounded at the siege of St. Sebastian appear to have later died of their wounds.

Driven from the line of the Nivelle, Soult had fallen back towards the entrenched camp at Bayonne, where he so disposed his troops that he watched the main roads to Bayonne on both sides of the Nive and the crossings of that river, having broken down the bridge near Ustarritz.

The period between the Battle of the Nivelle and the 9th December was, for the Allies, one of comparative inaction, and this was not entirely due to the extreme inclemency of the weather causing all the fords over the Nive to become impassable, but in even greater measure to the deadlock which had arisen in Wellington's relations with the Spanish authorities, and the failure of the Portuguese Government to carry out its obligations. As one result of these difficulties Wellington sent nearly the whole of the Spanish troops back into Spain.

Early in December Wellington had completed his plans to resume his forward movement, intending with a portion of his army to cross to the right bank of the River Nive and occupy the country between it and the Adour, while at the same time maintaining his position on the left bank. The idea was that Hope's corps on the left was to threaten the Lower Adour and the entrenched camp about Bayonne; Hill on the right was to effect the actual crossing of the Nive about Cambo, driving home the real attack in the direction of Bayonne along the main road from St. Jean Pied de Port; the 3rd and 6th Divisions were to support the main attack so far as possible, crossing the river near Ustarritz; while the 4th and 7th Divisions were to demonstrate on the extreme right to keep the French on this flank inactive.

The action commenced at daylight on the 9th, Hope moving by the great road from St. Jean de Luz to Bayonne. The 5th Division was on the left near the sea and in its advance crossed the valley between Bidart and Biarritz; the Light German Brigade was sent out in advance of the right of the 1st Division; while the light companies of the 5th Division covered the front of this part of the line. The 5th Division swept the whole country between Anglet and the sea as far as the banks of the Adour, and its Light Infantry occupied the Bois de Bayonne, a large pine wood covering the ground on the left of the Adour between the entrenched camp and the sea.

Hope having thus effected what was virtually an active demonstration, fell back towards his original position, the 5th Division about Bidart and the 1st near St. Jean de Luz.

Meanwhile the right had succeeded in crossing the Nive and in driving back the enemy, who retired within the shelter of their entrenched camp, and the actual passage of the river had been successfully accomplished at a comparatively small cost. On the next day, however, Soult began a series of efforts to drive Wellington back, and the actions which ensued are variously known as " the Battles of the Nive " or the " Battles before Bayonne " and endured from the 10th to the 13th December.

Early on the morning of the 10th Soult left his entrenchments and suddenly fell upon Hope's scattered command. The enemy advanced in two columns; the right, two divisions under General Reille, attacked Campbell's Portuguese brigade in advance at Anglet, drove it out of that village with heavy loss, and forced it back nearly to Bidart where it rallied on Robinson's brigade, a confused and desperate conflict taking place. The British and Portuguese held their positions until reinforced by other troops of the Division, when the enemy were repulsed. In the meantime General Clausel on the left had fallen on the Light Division at Arcangues, where the fighting was very severe until two divisions crossed the Nive in support; when Soult desisted from further attacks and the action came to an end.

In General Hay's report he wrote: "Colonel de Regan with the 3rd Portuguese made a fine charge on the Bayonne road, assisted by the 47th"; and this latter Regiment suffered many casualties this day, twelve men being killed, while Lieutenant A. Mahon, Ensign J. Ewing, five sergeants and forty-five men were wounded, and Lieutenant R. W. McDonnell, one sergeant and forty-nine men were missing.

On the 11th a reconnoitring force was sent out from Hope's corps to establish the position of the enemy, and entering the village of Pucho it was met by a superior body of troops and driven back. Soult then assaulted the ridge of Barrouilhet, the defenders of which were rather taken by surprise. There was some desperate hand-to-hand fighting, and the French

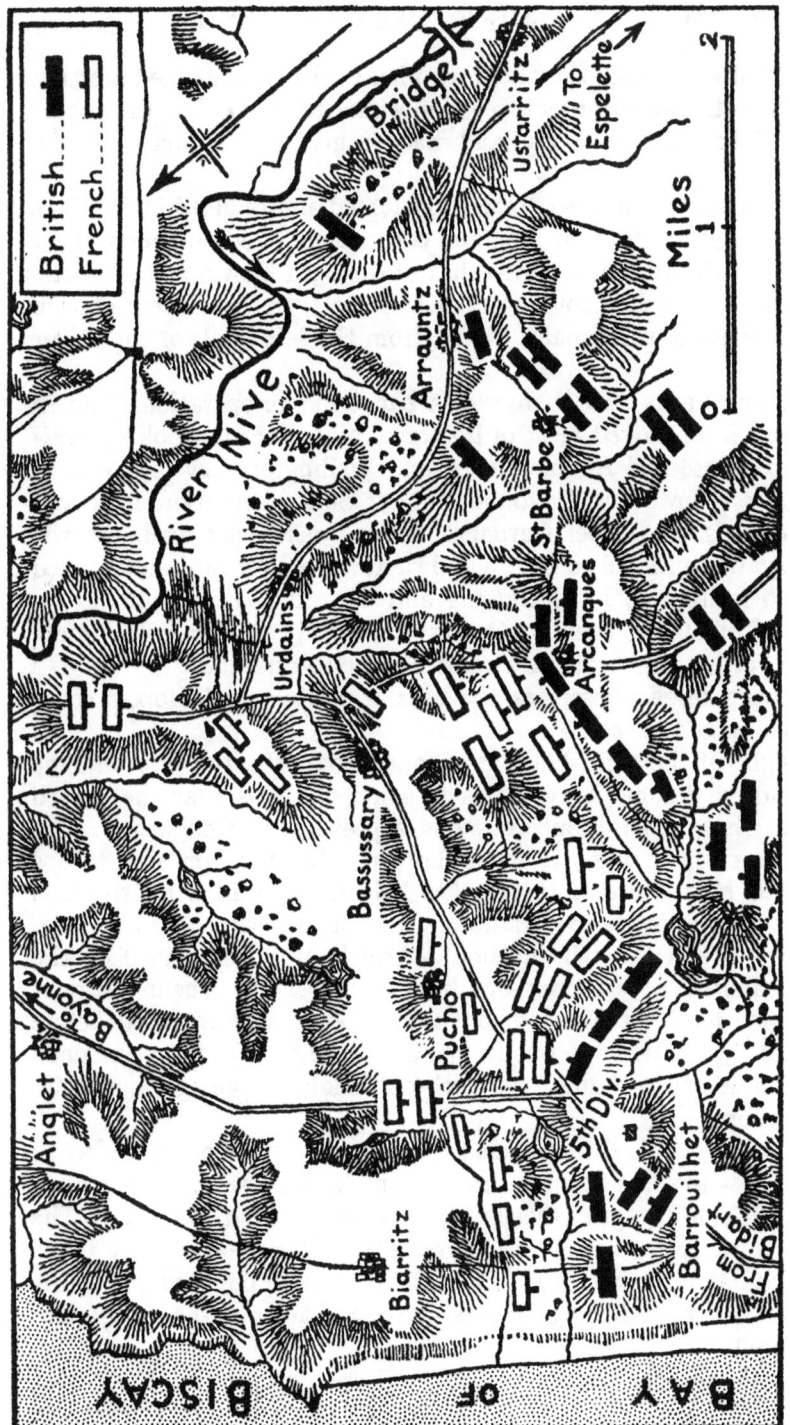

The Battle of The Nive.
10th December, 1813.

were finally repulsed, though they kept up a heavy fire on the allied position till dusk. The 47th had this day three men wounded, while General Robinson was shot through the body and had to give up command of the brigade.

The 5th Division was now so greatly exhausted and reduced in numbers that it was relieved in the front line, and consequently took no active part in the fighting of the 12th and 13th—that of the 13th known as the Battle of St. Pierre, when the rival combatants had some 5,500 casualties between them and the French were finally driven from the left bank of the River Adour.

For some few weeks now there was a pause in the operations, and in January, 1814, Soult moved most of his force to his left and took up positions on the Bidouse and Adour Rivers, and Wellington now proposed to cross the latter river below Bayonne, cut off Soult from Bordeaux and drive him towards the Upper Garonne. Operations began again on the 14th February, when the allied centre and right moved forward and obliged the French to retire across the Bidouse and Gave d'Oleron, Soult falling back first to Sauveterre, then to Orthes and finally to Toulouse, where on the 18th April, 1814, hostilities came at last to an end.

The following briefly describes the part which General Hope's corps played in attaining this end.

On the night of the 22nd February Hope moved the 1st Division, the Rocket Brigade and some heavy guns to some sandhills near the mouth of the Adour, the 5th Division occupying a position at Monguerre. The passage of the river commenced next day on rafts, the opposing troops being dispersed by the fire of the Rocket Brigade, now used for the first time. The 1st Division and Bradford's Portuguese were passed over, covered by the fire of the 5th Division, a firm footing was gained on the further bank, and the construction of a bridge was begun. The investment of Bayonne was now put in hand, but many losses were incurred before this was effected, and while it was in operation the 5th Division remained on the south side of the Adour, the 47th at Urdains, a village four miles south of Bayonne.

Siege works were raised and armed, but on the 14th April the French made an attack with three thousand men upon Hay's brigade, accompanied by a feint attack on the 5th Division posts at Anglet and Bellevue. The French were initially successful and caused much loss, General Hay being killed and General Hope wounded and made prisoner; but reinforcements arriving upon the scene, the assailants were driven back and the lost ground was re-captured.

In this sortie the 2nd Battalion 47th had one drummer and two men killed, Lieutenants J. H. de Burgh and W. Kendall and eleven rank and file wounded, while ten men were missing.

The official announcement of Napoleon's abdication reached Wellington on the 12th April, but Soult declined to enter into negotiations till the news was definitely confirmed; however, on the 18th a convention was agreed to and hostilities then ceased, peace being finally signed on May 30th.

On the 14th June the Duke of Wellington published a General Order in which he bade farewell in the following terms to the troops he had so long commanded:—

" 1. The Commander of the Forces, being on the point of returning to England, again takes the opportunity of congratulating the Army upon the recent events which have restored peace to their country and to the world.

" 2. The share which the British Army has had in producing these events, and the high character with which the Army will quit this country, must be equally satisfactory to every individual belonging to it, as they are to the Commander of the Forces; and he trusts that the troops will continue the same good conduct to the last.

" 3. The Commander of the Forces once more requests the Army to accept his thanks.

" 4. Although circumstances may alter the relations in which he has stood towards them, so much to his satisfaction, he assures them he shall never cease to feel the warmest interest in their welfare and honour; and that he will be at all times happy to be of any service to those to whose conduct, discipline and gallantry their Country is so much indebted."

For its services in the Peninsular War the 2nd Battalion, 47th Regiment, was granted the following Battle-Honours—nearly all of them after disbandment and consequently assumed by the Regiment.

"Tarifa" in a Memorandum dated 27th October, 1812.
"Peninsula"   ,,   ,,   18th April, 1815.
"Vittoria"   ,,   ,,   24th June, 1818.
"St. Sebastian" ,,   ,,   24th June, 1818.

It was not, however, until 1847, that, in a General Order dated the 1st June, the so-called "Military General Service Medal" was granted for service in the various campaigns and actions which commenced in 1793 and ended in 1814; the medal was granted to survivors only, and of the 47th Regiment nine officers and exactly one hundred non-commissioned officers and men received it.

The 2nd Battalion the 47th Regiment embarked for home on the 24th August at Bordeaux, landed at Portsmouth and marched to Chichester, where, in due course, men of the Battalion, who had been taken prisoners during the war, rejoined the Colours. Early in October the Battalion marched to Liverpool, where it arrived on the 10th and where the Regimental Depot appears to have been established.

Here on the 24th October the 2nd Battalion 47th was disbanded, most of the effective officers and men being sent out to India to join the 1st Battalion.

On the return of the Emperor Napoleon from Elba and the renewal of hostilities with France, the 2nd Battalion of the Regiment was re-formed at Chelmsford, under date of the 4th May, 1815, being finally disbanded in January of the year following when peace had been once more restored to the States of Europe.

CHAPTER VIII

1807–1830

EXPEDITIONS TO THE PERSIAN GULF
THE PINDARI WAR
THE FIRST BURMA WAR OF 1824–1826

WE left the 1st Battalion of the 47th Regiment just arrived at Madras from the Cape of Good Hope and the Buenos Ayres expedition at the end of 1807, but the stay here was only a very brief one, for early in the following year it was sent to Bombay, where it arrived on the 3rd March. The following month the 47th found itself in garrison at Surat, and at the end of the year it had the unusual experience of garrisoning two places—the Left Wing at Demaan and the Right Wing at Dieu—which formed part of the Portuguese possessions in India. As early as 1798 the Governor-General of British India had considered the desirability of occupying the Portuguese settlement with British troops, both for its protection from invasion from Mysore and also to safeguard it from the aggressions of the French. An English garrison was admitted to the settlement in September, 1799, and our troops remained here until the general peace in Europe following upon the victory of Waterloo.

The Regiment returned to Bombay in 1809 in rather a sickly state and was for some time stationed on Butcher's Island, and it was from here that a part of the 47th was now ordered on what was originally intended to be no more than a friendly mission, but later became something of the nature of a military expedition.

The Emperors of France and Russia, recently deadly enemies, had now become close allies and began to concert schemes for the invasion of India. To meet this menace the Indian Government decided to endeavour to raise barriers on the border countries against a hostile advance from the west; and to the Punjab, to Afghanistan and to Persia friendly missions were to be sent, and Colonel John Malcolm was placed in charge of that proceeding to Persia. Certain troops stationed in Bombay were told off as an escort for the Persian mission, the sending of which then seems to have been abandoned, owing to the outbreak of trouble in the Persian Gulf;

but later in the year the Bombay Government decided upon an expedition to the Gulf, mainly for the purpose of suppressing the Joasmi pirates, whose stronghold was Ras-al-Khyma to the west of the Ras-el-Jebel promontory. The naval portion consisted of two ships of His Majesty's Royal Navy and nine of the Company's cruisers. The troops, who were embarked in four transports, were the 65th Regiment, the flank companies of the 47th Regiment, a detachment of Bombay artillery, and about one thousand sepoys, the whole under the command of Colonel L. Smith, 65th Regiment.

The expeditionary force sailed from Bombay in September, but did not arrive off Muskat until the 23rd October; here a few days were spent and then, sailing on, the transports anchored before Ras-al-Khyma on the 11th November, but the water here was found to be so shallow that the larger ships could not get within two miles of the shore.

"The narrow, low peninsula on which Ras-al-Khyma stands is about three-quarters of a mile in length and a quarter of a mile broad; across the isthmus was a high wall flanked by four towers, and along the shore in front of the town were numerous batteries and entrenchments, evidently erected under European supervision. The harbour, formed by the peninsula and mainland, is about half a mile broad. The number of armed men in the place was about five thousand, but within a few days reinforcements could be sent in from the adjacent posts. Towards the outer end of the harbour the houses were so close to the beach that to land seemed impossible. After the ships of the fleet had bombarded the fort it was arranged to land troops early on the morning of the 13th November." *

While it was still dark on the 13th the 65th, the flank companies of the 47th, some marines and native troops rendezvoused alongside one of the cruisers, while two gunboats and small boats rowed towards the mouth of the harbour, and, opening fire at dawn, drew the enemy's attention in that direction. Meanwhile the main body advanced rapidly in the remaining boats, when the pirates, seeing that their fire from the towers and other buildings did not check the landing party, came down to the beach sword in hand.

When one company only had disembarked, the enemy made a desperate attack on its left, but the fire from the gunboats checked them and so gave time for the formation of the British advanced guard. This party in turn made a very successful charge and by sunrise the town was in our possession.

A gradual advance was made, the place being set on fire as our troops moved forward, the Joasmis being thus smoked out of their positions; the town and many of the enemy's vessels were burnt, and the force, somewhat over-hurriedly, re-embarked on the morning of the 14th.

* *Frontier and Overseas Expeditions*, Vol. VI, p. 246.

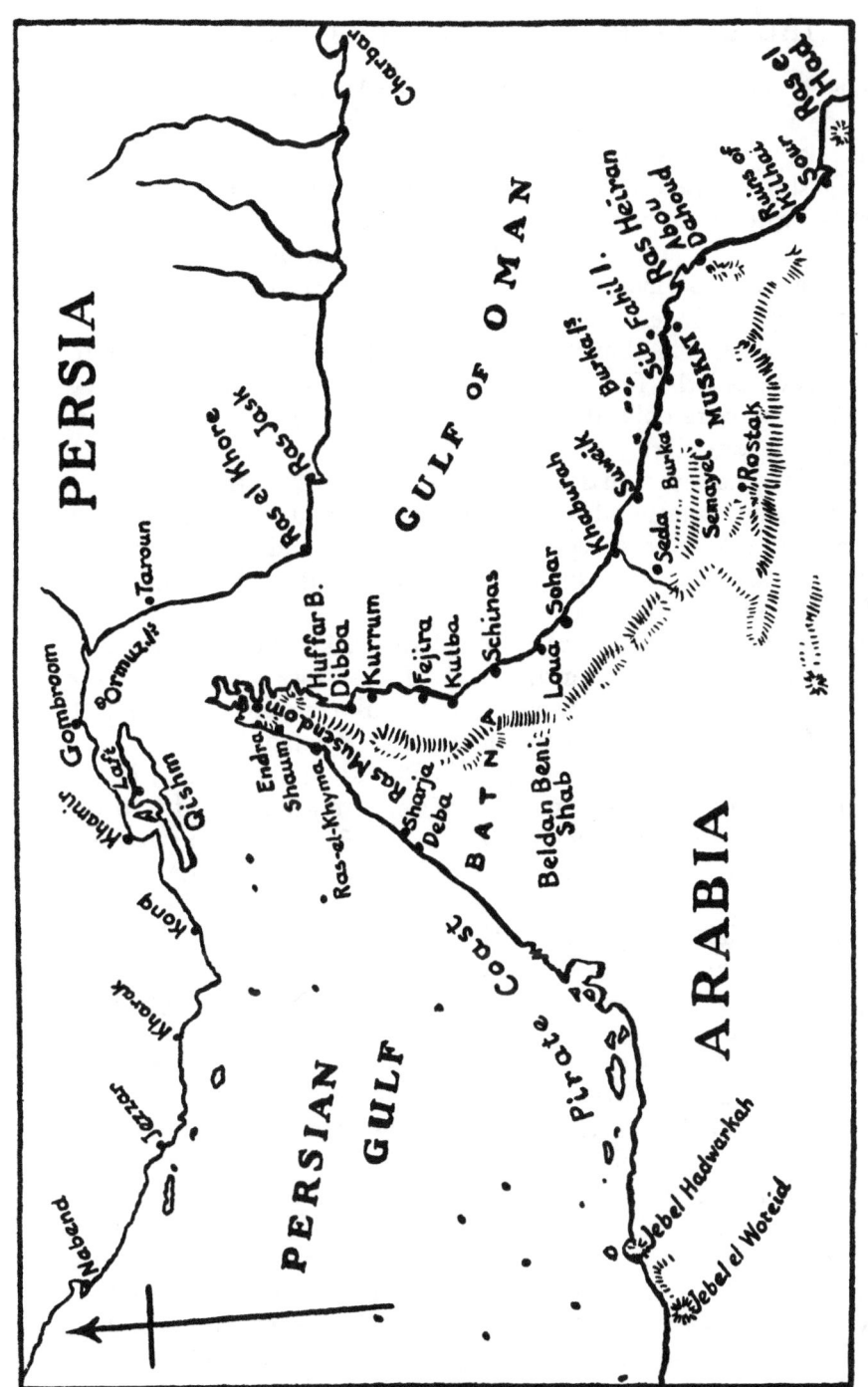

The Persian Gulf.
1809.

Portions of the force were then sent to Lingeh, a Joasmi post on the northern side of Quishm, and also to Burka about forty miles to the west of Muskat; later a strong body went on to Laft on the north side of the Island of Quishm where, on the afternoon of the 27th November, Colonel Smith landed with three hundred men, consisting of the Light Company of the 47th, half a company of the 65th, a detachment of Native Infantry and some seamen and marines, and summoned the garrison here to surrender. The summons being disregarded, the town was occupied and an attack made upon the castle. A howitzer was brought into action in order to blow in the gate, but the fire from the loopholed buildings was so heavy that the attackers were obliged to fall back and take shelter behind some sandhills until it was dark.

The gunboats, however, maintained a very hot fire, so that by sunset the castle was much shattered, and during the night it was evacuated, a party of the 47th taking possession at dawn. In this affair the British had nearly seventy casualties, and the 47th had Lieutenant S. Weld and three men killed, one sergeant and nine men wounded.

Having re-embarked, the force returned to Muskat, and it being now considered that the most important part of the work required of the expeditionary force had been completed, the flank companies of the 47th and some two hundred sepoys were sent back to Bombay.

The 47th remained in Bombay throughout 1810 and 1811, and in the cold weather of this year the flank companies were again called into the field, being required, again in company with the 65th, to form part of a small expeditionary force, which was required to act against the chief of Navanagar, a town on the south-east coast of the Gulf of Kutch in Kathiawar, who had rebelled against his overlord, the Gaikwar of Baroda. The force sailed on the 21st December and on landing at Torbandar the Light Company of the 47th joined a Light Battalion commanded by Major Warren of the 65th. Navanagar, the objective of the expedition, was reached on the 21st February, 1812, and after a certain amount of skirmishing, in which Captain W. Phelan of the 47th was killed, Navanagar surrendered, and the flank companies were back with their headquarters in Bombay by the last week in April, 1812.

On the 6th August the Regiment marched from Bombay to Poona, arriving there on the 23rd, just a month later proceeding to join a force under Colonel Montressor, and returning to Bombay at the end of December.

In April of this year Lieutenant G. F. Sadlier, of the 47th, was sent to Persia, where he was employed in the training of the Persian Infantry; he remained so employed until June, 1815, having the local rank of major, and for his services was presented with a sword by H.H. the Shah.

The Regiment remained on in Bombay until the 1st November, 1814, when it sailed for Surat, arriving there on the 7th and 8th, but the flank companies were detained in Bombay, being again required, once more in company with the 65th Regiment, to form part of a small expeditionary force proceeding to Gujerat. Embarking at Bombay on the 23rd November, the companies landed at Broach and marched by way of Baroda to Raunpore, where a strong brigade was assembling. This body of troops marched through the State of Kathiawar, crossed the Little Rann of Kutch, and, after taking the fort of Anja, occupied Bhuj, the capital. Leaving here again on the 25th January, 1815, several smaller posts were subdued, and the flank companies eventually rejoined headquarters at Surat on the 14th June.

The whole Battalion was back again in Bombay by the 25th September, but on the 17th June, 1816, it marched for Baroda, where it arrived in three divisions on the 10th, 11th and 15th August, and here it remained until it was called upon to take part in the Pindari War of 1817.

The Pindaris were in a way a military organization of all races and religions; they lived by plunder, and every year when the hot weather came to an end, it was their custom to carry out extensive and carefully organized raids, moving with remarkable rapidity and secrecy and covering the longest distances. All the Mahratta States encouraged the Pindaris and freely utilized their services in their own private quarrels. "During the season of 1816–17, the ravages of the Pindaris extended over a wider expanse of territory than had ever before been attempted. Having crossed the Narbada with ten thousand horsemen, they separated into two bands; one of which proceeded due south into the country of the Nizam and reached the banks of the Godavari. The other marched eastward and entered the Company's territory of Ganjam, where in the course of twelve days they killed and wounded nearly seven thousand persons, and carried off or destroyed property to the value of £100,000; a third party crossed the Tapti at Burhanpore and overran the dominions of the Peishwa to some distance beyond Poona."[*]

The Marquis of Hastings, the Governor-General, had made up his mind to completely root out the Pindaris, though he was by no means unmindful of the fact that in so doing he might have serious trouble with the Peishwa and also with Scindia; the proposed operations must in any case be upon a very large scale, involving the concentration of a great number of troops upon one common centre, while the theatre of the campaign "may be defined roughly as the space enclosed by the Jumna, from Allahabad to Delhi on the north, the Narbada to the south and the Aravalli mountains on the west."

[*] Burton, *The Mahratta and Pindari War*, p. 7.

The total strength of the native forces eventually arrayed against us is given by Colonel Burton as 106,000 Horse, 81,000 Foot and 589 guns; and to meet these there was assembled the largest army that had ever taken the field in India, the whole amounting to some 111,000 of all arms. This was divided into a Grand or Northern Army, and a Deccan or Southern Army; the former was mainly composed of Bengal troops and contained four divisions and two corps of observation; the Deccan or Southern Army contained five active divisions, a reserve division and a Gujerat division. The Grand or Northern Army was commanded by the Marquis of Hastings in person, the Deccan or Southern Army by Lieut.-General Sir T. Hislop.

The Gujerat Division was commanded by Major-General Sir W. G. Keir and with the Gaikwar's contingent of 2,000 Horse attached, was intended to protect Gujerat, to intercept the Pindaris should they attempt to cross the Narbada, and to co-operate with the Deccan Army in the event of hostilities with the Mahratta Powers. The 47th was in the 1st Infantry Brigade of this division with the 2nd Battalion, 7th Native Infantry, and the brigade was commanded by Lieut.-Colonel R. G. Elrington of the 47th.

The concentration of the Gujerat Division was delayed till the end of November, owing to the fact of certain disturbances breaking out at Pahlanpore in the northern districts of Gujerat, and part of the 1st Brigade was detached there under Colonel Elrington to put matters right. In these operations, which included the reduction of the hill forts of Verampore and Kurjah in Kathiawar on the 22nd and 27th October respectively, some of the 47th Companies were engaged: Captain T. Backhouse commanded the storming parties on both occasions and Ensign T. Luttrell and several non-commissioned officers and men of the 47th were wounded.

The Gujerat Division, under General Keir, was now somewhat needlessly marched about the country. It left Baroda on the 4th December, 1817, for Ujjain through a wild and wooded country, the column much harassed by the Bhils, who hung upon the rear and flanks of the force, capturing baggage and cutting off men and followers. On arrival on the 13th at Dohad, eighty miles north-east of Baroda, Keir was ordered by the Bombay Government to return at once to Baroda, fears being entertained lest the Gaikwar should join forces with the Bhonsla. The column had completed two marches on its return journey, when the commander received fresh orders giving him a certain latitude as to his procedure, and General Keir then sent part of his division back to Baroda, and with the remainder returned to Dohad, where he arrived for the second time on the 19th December.

Here General Keir was in direct communication with the headquarters of the Deccan Army, but he found orders awaiting him to advance imme-

THE PINDARI WAR

diately to Rutlam to lend the weight of his presence in the settlement of negotiations with Holkar, then in progress. He accordingly marched on again and reached Rutlam on the 24th December.

Here the Gujerat Division appears to have been detached to pursue a force under one Chitu, a noted Pindari chief, and moved off on the 31st in a northerly direction. Marching by way of Bari Sadri, Dheira, twenty miles to the north-west of Neemuch, on the 9th January, 1818, Deoda was reached and there the division halted, the men being thoroughly exhausted by long marches over difficult country. Having rested his force for twenty-four hours, "Keir, unwilling to leave the chase of Chitu, followed him westward from Deoda to Bhindar, where he arrived on the 12th and learned that Chitu had fled by way of Banswara (forty miles west of Rutlam) to the jungle on the borders of Gujerat. More than once he sent out light columns"—the Light Company of the 47th accompanied several of these— "upon false information to no purpose, and finally on the 16th he came back to Deoda, and on the 17th turned southward by way of Partabgarh for his original station at Mandasor. On his way he was cheered by a gleam of success, for on the 19th after a forced march of twenty miles with a light detachment, he succeeded in surprising a small party of Pindaris, of whom almost a hundred were cut down by the 17th Light Dragoons. This, however, was all that Keir could show for three weeks of exhausting marches, when on the 23rd he brought his column into Neemuch."

The Gujerat Division was now detailed to protect the Gujerat provinces, and to effect this mission General Keir moved to Rutlam and on the 3rd February to Badnawar, whence a few days later he marched to the vicinity of the camp of Bhima Bai, the sister of Holkar, who still maintained an attitude of defiance at the head of a portion of Holkar's army. She, however, speedily submitted and was sent to Badnawar under the escort of Colonel Elrington, who was proceeding thither on duty with a detachment.

By the end of February, 1818, the power of the Pindaris had been completely broken, and the army which had been operating in Central India was greatly reduced.

From the 22nd February to the 4th March General Keir's division was employed in the dispersion of parties of Pindaris in the vicinity of Indore, and he then marched towards Baroda where he arrived on the 7th April, when the force was at last broken up, the 47th remaining at Baroda in garrison.

While these operations had been taking place in Central India, some of the 47th appear to have formed part of a small force organized in Bombay to keep open the communications with Poona. This force was employed in the reduction of certain hill forts, and in Colonel Blacker's *History of the Mahratta War* there is, on page 460, a return giving the number of "wounded on the 13th and 14th March, 1818, belonging to the Field Force under Lieut.-Colonel Prother, at the Siege of Koaree," wherein one man of the 47th Regiment is shown as wounded. Then in the casualty returns in the possession of the Corps a Sergeant James Hayes is shown as killed on the 4th or 6th March, 1818, no doubt at the capture of one of these hill forts.

On the 2nd January, 1819, the 47th Regiment left Baroda and marched to Bombay where it arrived on the 13th, and from here at the commencement of the ensuing cold weather it was required to proceed on a second expedition to the Persian Gulf.

In this year the Bombay Government had resolved to take decisive measures for putting down piracy in the Persian Gulf, assembled in the autumn a powerful squadron and gave orders for the bringing together of a considerable body of troops. The force detailed numbered 1,645 Europeans and 1,424 Natives under the command of the same general officer, Major-General Sir W. G. Keir, under whom the 47th had served in the last campaign, and consisted of one company of artillery, the 47th and 65th Regiments, the 1st Bn. 2nd Bombay Infantry, the flank companies of the 3rd Bombay Infantry, the Marine Battalion and half a company of Pioneers.

The artillery and the two British regiments embarked on the 30th October and the rest of the troops on the following day, and on the 3rd November the transports set sail, escorted by H.M.S. "Eden," "Liverpool" and "Curlew" and by some of the East India Company's cruisers.

The rendezvous was at Quishm, where the force was assembled by the 17th November, and from here General Keir proceeded to Ras-al-Khyma to reconnoitre the place, the fleet arriving there on the 2nd December, when arrangements were made for disembarking the troops. This was completed by 4 a.m. the next day, two miles to the south-west of the place, the troops being formed across the isthmus between the town and the mainland, and the stores landed.

On the morning of the 4th all the Light Companies, five in all, marched under the command of Captain Backhouse, 47th, "to dislodge the enemy from a bank within 900 yards of the outer fort, which would serve as cover for the men and a depot for stores. The Arabs were driven with great gallantry from a date grove and over this bank, followed by the picquets, which took post at the sandbank, while the light troops skirmished in front. The enemy during these movements kept up a sharp fire of cannon and musketry and Major Molesworth, 47th Regiment, was killed at the head of the picquets. The troops maintained their position during the day, and at night effected a lodgment within 300 yards of the southernmost tower, and erected a battery for four guns with a mortar battery on the right and a trench for the protection of the covering party. On the morning of the 6th three 18-pounders opened on the fort, and with a couple of howitzers and 6-pounders nearly silenced the enemy's fire. The 'Liverpool' also opened on the town, but at too great a range to have much effect.

"The enemy sallied forth at 8 o'clock this evening along the whole front of our entrenchments, crept unperceived close up to the mortar battery, and, spearing the sentries, entered it. The party which occupied it was obliged to retire, but, reinforced, charged and drove the enemy out with considerable loss. The covering party simultaneously repelled the attack on the left." *

In the *United Service Journal* for 1829, Part I, p. 710 *et seq.*, there is an account of this expedition, and of the death of Major Molesworth we read :—

"The first line of trenches having been made by means of sandbags, an advanced battery opened on the place at the distance of 300 yards. A mortar battery to the right was served very effectively. There was a gun from one of the enemy's batteries which enfiladed the trenches while we could get none of our artillery to bear on it. It did considerable execution among the men. Major Molesworth, of the 47th, mounted the parapet of the trench to reconnoitre more minutely, and to ascertain how that formidable gun could be silenced. 'I see them loading it now,' said he, 'now, now, they are running it out. Look to yourselves, my lads.' In an instant he fell back in the trench, his head blown to atoms."

On the 8th more guns having been placed in position, a heavy fire was opened and by sunset a breach was visible, when preparations were made for storming and the troops ordered to be in the trenches at daybreak next day. The storming party consisted of the 47th and flank companies of the other regiments, under Colonel Elrington, and about one hundred seamen. On a signal being given the stormers rushed forward and gained the breach, only to find that the enemy had evacuated the place. However, sixty-two guns and eighty vessels were captured, while the casualties among the defenders amounted to close upon one thousand.

In his despatch General Keir mentioned Major Molesworth and Captain Backhouse of the 47th, writing of the former as "a gallant and zealous officer"; and the losses in the Regiment from the 4th to the 8th December are given as "killed, one major, one rank and file; wounded sixteen rank and file."

* General Keir's despatch of the 9th December.

In Field Orders of the 9th December, Lieut.-Colonel Elrington was mentioned as having "merited in a high degree the approbation of Major-General Sir W. G. Keir"; while in those of the 10th Captain Backhouse is praised for a spirited advance made by him on the 4th, and praise is also given to the Light troops under his command for preserving their positions during the day under so heavy a fire from the enemy.

The enemy now sent in their submission from all posts in the immediate neighbourhood of Ras-al-Khyma, but the chief of a place called Rams, six miles away to the north-east, abandoned his town and established himself, with some four hundred of his followers, in a hill fort known as Dhayah, at the head of a creek two miles from the sea, and here seemed inclined to hold out.

Thither part of the squadron now proceeded, having on board some guns, the 65th Regiment and the flank companies of the 2nd Bombay Infantry; but the general, finding on arrival that the place was very much stronger than it had been represented as being, sent for the flank companies of the 47th, under Captain Backhouse, and those of the 3rd Bombay Infantry.

From the 18th to the 22nd December, the troops were engaged in investing the place and in establishing breaching batteries, and on the latter date fire was opened. On the breach being pronounced practicable, the stormers prepared to move forward, when the white flag was raised and the garrison marched out and surrendered to the number of 398.

In this affair the 47th had one man killed and two men wounded, and Captain Backhouse's services were brought to notice both in Major Warren's report and in the Major-General's final despatch.

On the 26th December the force, which had been detached for the conduct of the operations above described, returned to Ras-al-Khyma and after visiting and destroying the forts at certain other places on the coast, the fleet and transports sailed on the 25th February, 1820, for Bombay, where all arrived on the 8th March and following days.

At Bombay the 47th remained during the greater part of the remainder of the year, when it marched to Poona, a station it was to occupy for close upon four uneventful years.

In the year 1824 trouble, which for some time past had been simmering in Burma, at last came to a head, and some account must now be given of its origin and consequences. British and Burman interests first clashed at the close of the previous century, when the people of Ava, having shaken off the yoke of Pegu, began to turn the eyes of conquest towards India. A few years later, however, peaceful counsels seemed likely to prevail, and the Governor-General of India concluded a treaty with the King of

Ava, from which it was hoped that good might result. In 1811, however, the King of Ava was misguided enough to lay an embargo on all British ships lying off Rangoon, an act which under ordinary circumstances would at once have resulted in a declaration of war; but the Indian Government of the day was extra-pacifically inclined and contented itself with sending a mission to the Court of Ava.

The result was what might have been expected; the Burmese imagined that the British were not only afraid but powerless, and the energies of the East India Company being at the time absorbed in trouble in Nepal in the north and in the Mahratta States in the south, a Burmese general was able, practically unhindered, to invade the country between Burma and Bengal, to conquer Assam and Manipore and to threaten Cachar. He then began to levy taxes on British trading boats and finally attacked a British military post, killing and wounding six of the garrison.

At this juncture Lord Amherst arrived in India as Governor-General; explanations were demanded, but no satisfaction being forthcoming, war was on the 5th March, 1824, declared against the King of Ava.

By this time the 47th Regiment was in Calcutta, having arrived there from Poona, on the 7th October of the preceding year.

Some little time previous to the outbreak of war, the Raja of Cachar, fearful of Burmese invasion, had begged that his country might be taken under British protection; and the Indian Government, recognizing that the possession of this district would impede a Burmese advance into Sylhet and lessen the danger to British territories, had acceded to this request and had sent troops thither from Dacca. Later in the year our troops serving on this frontier seem to have met with something of the nature of a serious rebuff, and it was probably for this reason that in October of this year the 47th was ordered to Sylhet. The Regiment had actually embarked and was on its way, when orders overtook it, countermanding the move, in consequence of a serious mutiny which had broken out at Barrackpore, curiously enough in a regiment of Bengal Infantry bearing the same number, and it returned to Calcutta, moving to Barrackpore on the 1st November.

Owing to the well-known repugnance of the Bengal soldier to cross the sea, it had been arranged to draw the bulk of the troops for the Burma Expeditionary Force from Madras, but the 47th Bengal Infantry had been warned also for service, and there at once arose a mutinous spirit among the men of this regiment, who considered that their caste was threatened were they required to proceed overseas.

There was some trouble in the regiment in October, and on the 1st November when ordered to parade, the men broke out into acts of open violence, remaining under arms that night and posting guards and picquets.

As it was considered inadvisable to make use of the other two Native regiments stationed at Barrackpore to overawe or disarm the 47th Native Infantry, the 47th Regiment was ordered to Barrackpore with the 1st Foot, a battery of artillery and the Governor-General's Bodyguard. The troops were ordered to parade and the mutinous regiment was ordered to ground arms; only one man obeyed the command, and the battery then opened fire upon the regiment, when the men broke, threw away their arms and fled. Many were arrested and tried by court-martial, the name and number of the offending corps being removed from the Army List.

The original destination of the 47th Foot was now changed and the intention of sending the Regiment to Sylhet was abandoned. The 47th then sailed on the 14th December in the transports " Lowjee, Family " and " Glenelg " for Rangoon, where it was disembarked on the 5th January, 1825.

During the months proceding the arrival of the 47th at Rangoon, certain successful operations had been conducted against the Burmese by Brig.-General Sir A. Campbell, commanding the force sent from India. Rangoon, the chief seaport of the Kingdom of Ava, was captured, the stockades at Kemmendine were taken by storm, while the towns of Martaban and Tenasserim had submitted; so that by the close of the year 1824 the whole of the Burmese coast, from Rangoon to the eastward, was subject to the British arms.

The command of the Burmese forces had now been assumed by one Bandula, who after several defeats retreated to Donubyu, where he collected a considerable force, and General Campbell had, by the first week in February, 1825, completed his arrangements for a forward movement on Prome. A large force was left in Rangoon with which communications had to be kept open, and General Campbell formed as many troops as he possessed transport for into two columns. With the one, about 2,400 strong, he decided to move by land, while the other, about 1,170 strong, was to proceed by water, and, capturing Panhlaing and Donubyu en route, was to meet the land force at Sarawa some distance further up the Irrawaddy.

Of these two columns, the first, under General Campbell in person, consisted of two troops of Bengal Horse Artillery, the Madras Pioneers, the Governor-General's Bodyguard, the 38th, 41st and 47th—the latter less 200 men—the 26th and 43rd Madras Native Infantry: the British Infantry numbered only 1,300 and the Indian no more than one thousand. This column was to move parallel to the Hlaing River, joining the Irrawaddy at the nearest and most convenient point for co-operating with the river column. This latter column contained 200 of the 47th under Brevet

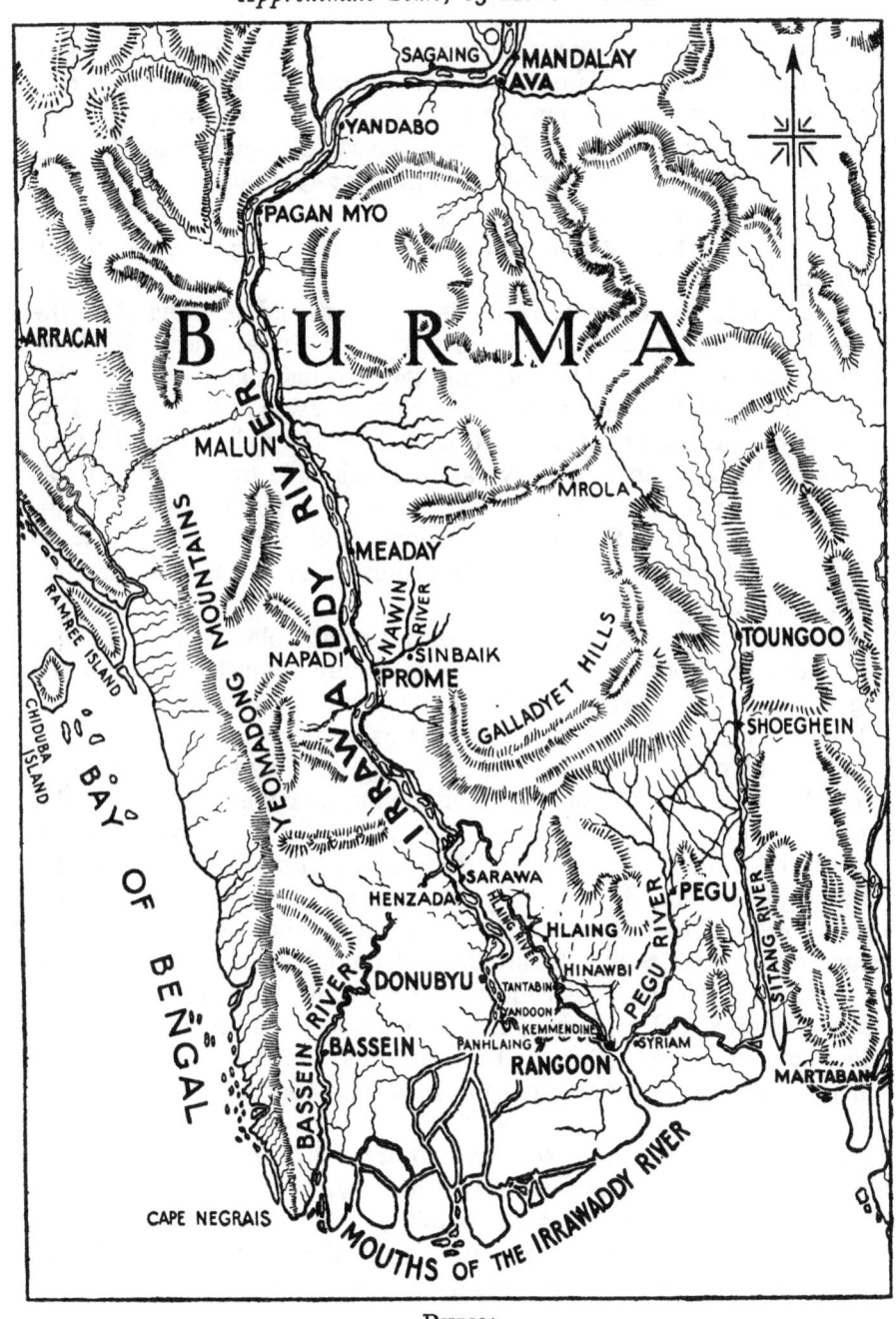

BURMA.

1825–1826.

Lieut.-Colonel J. W. O'Donoghue, the 89th Foot, the 1st Madras Europeans, 250 of the 18th Native Infantry, and some guns. Brig.-General Cotton was in command of this column, with Lieutenant H. Wainwright, 47th, as his A.D.C. and Captain G. F. Sadlier of the same Regiment as Brigade-Major. This column was accommodated in sixty-two boats.

A third and smaller column under Major Sale was to proceed against Bassein, afterwards joining headquarters at Henzada, opposite Sarawa on the Irrawaddy.

Determined to leave no obstacles in his rear, and learning that the Burmese had re-occupied the fort and pagoda at Syriam near Rangoon, the General detached Colonel Elrington, 47th, to dislodge them. Colonel Elrington moved thither on the 10th January, and was at first delayed by the necessity of repairing the bridge leading over the nullah into the fort, which had to be done under a heavy and well-directed fire. The fort was taken with a rush as was also the pagoda, and the place blown up. In this affair the 47th had Ensign J. M. Geddes and one man killed, while wounded were Captains P. Forbes (mortally) and T. Backhouse, one sergeant and eighteen rank and file.

Some of the Regiment also served with a small column under Colonel Godwin early in February in expelling the enemy from Tantabin on the Hlaing River, some twenty miles from Rangoon, but the Regiment does not appear to have sustained any loss on this occasion.

The forward movement began on the 13th February with the advance of General Campbell's column, the river column starting on the 16th and that under Major Sale a day later. The first of these columns marched through Hinawbi and Hlaing without incident and reached Sarawa on the 2nd March. Here four days were spent, and then "taking it for granted that the river force had captured Donubyu, but without making any effort to communicate with that column, General Campbell unwisely advanced twenty-six miles beyond the rendezvous to Yuadit," which was reached on the 10th March. Hearing next day of the reverse which had overtaken the river column, General Campbell retraced his steps to attack Donubyu with his whole force, but it was not until the 25th that he arrived in front of this town.

In the meantime the river column had arrived at Panhlaing, where a small garrison was dropped, on the 19th February, and, sailing on, the force came, on the 28th within sight of Donubyu, where Bandula was found to be occupying a very strong position, formidably entrenched and held by some fifteen thousand men. Bandula was called upon to surrender but refused, so on the 7th March five hundred men were landed in two columns, Lieut.-Colonel O'Donoghue, 47th, being in command of one of

BURMA—STORMING A STOCKADE.

1825.

these. Covered by the fire of two 6-pounders and some rocket-guns, the first line of stockades was captured, but the second line proved more formidable and the attack upon it was defeated with very considerable loss, some one hundred and forty of the two assaulting columns being killed and wounded; of these, three of the killed and eighteen of the wounded belonged to the 47th.

In his report of this action to General Campbell, General Cotton expresses his " strong acknowledgments to Lieut.-Colonel O'Donoghue for the gallantry and zeal displayed " in leading his column.

General Cotton now decided to make no further attack until reinforced, so re-embarked his men and guns and dropped ten miles down-stream to Yandoon.

On arrival before Donubyu General Campbell began the construction of several batteries, armed with heavy guns, the work being several times interrupted by sorties made by the Burmese. The position was on the right bank of the Irrawaddy and extended for 1,700 yards along the river and from 500–800 yards inland; it was heavily stockaded and mounted several guns, while the approach was guarded by two outworks. A heavy fire was opened on the position on the 1st April and maintained during the 2nd; one of the shells fired killed the Chief, Bandula, and his fall so disheartened the garrison that they hurriedly evacuated the place, which fell into our hands with many guns and a large amount of ammunition and grain.

The loss in the 47th Regiment from the 25th March to the 1st April amounted to three rank and file killed, Lieutenant J. Gordon and six men wounded.

On the fall of Donubyu, Sir A. Campbell marched away again, and on the 10th April was back at Sarawa, where some reinforcements joined and envoys came in professing a desire to make peace; still advancing, however, the main army occupied Prome on the 25th April without opposition. A small lightly equipped force was sent into the surrounding country under Colonel Godwin in the general direction of Toungoo to clear the country of armed bands: this party was accompanied by the flank companies of the 47th, but no serious opposition was met with and the column was back again in Prome by the 24th May, and here the army remained during June, July and August, the men tolerably comfortably hutted and supplies fairly plentiful. A state, dated the 18th August at Prome, gives the strength of the 47th as follows: field-officers, one; captains, four; subalterns, ten; surgeons, two; staff-sergeants, four; sergeants, thirty; drummers, fifteen; rank and file, 505; while five sergeants, one drummer and seventy-eight privates are shown as sick; at Rangoon there were eighty-four non-commissioned officers and men. Lieutenant E. Codd of the Regiment died at Rangoon on the 15th May and Captain H. Parsons at Prome on 16th July.

Negotiations for peace continued in progress, and late in September General Campbell had a meeting near Prome with the Burman authorities, on which occasion the Light Company of the 47th provided part of the escort; but it speedily became obvious that the war party was still in the ascendant, nothing came of the interview, and by the middle of October a large Burmese force was reported as gradually concentrating on Prome. Learning that the enemy was occupying a position at a spot some twenty miles from Prome, a small force was sent out to dislodge it, but the enemy was found to be in very much greater strength than had been expected, and the detached bodies in which the column was divided lost touch and were defeated, finally retiring on Prome, before which town the enemy now appeared to the number of 50,000–60,000.

Finding that the enemy seemed unwilling to leave the cover of the jungle, General Campbell determined to attack the Burmese position, which extended from the Napadi Hills, near the river, to the villages of Sinbaik and Sangwe, about eleven miles north-east of Prome; and leaving troops for the defence of Prome, the General moved out early on the 1st December against the enemy's left, the flotilla demonstrating against the centre of the Burmese position.

On reaching the Nawin River, the force was divided into two columns; the right, under General Cotton, marched along the left bank, attacked and drove the enemy from a strong position. The left column, which included the 47th, now came up, and on the next day, General Campbell moved on with his whole force to attack the main enemy position on the Napadi Hills.

General Campbell's column was in front, the other column being ordered to try and gain the enemy's left flank, and the opening of fire from this party was to be the signal for Campbell's men to assault. General Cotton found the jungle almost impenetrable and was unable to get up as early as expected; so the flotilla, having cannonaded the enemy's defences for some time, the 13th and 38th Foot of Campbell's column advanced under a heavy fire, while Colonel Elrington, with the 47th and the 38th Madras Infantry, moved round to the right rear and, attacking some of the flanking outworks here, created a very timely diversion. The position was captured, the Burmese being driven from stockade after stockade, and from forty to fifty guns, the whole of the Burmese war material, and all the boats and stores were captured.

In the two days' fighting the British lost one hundred and fifty-seven killed and wounded, while of the 47th Regiment three men were killed, Major T. Backhouse, Lieutenant J. Gordon, Ensign H. McNally, one sergeant and twenty-six other ranks were wounded.

On the 4th December a small force under General Cotton crossed the river and drove the left wing of the enemy from their position with heavy loss, thus completing the entire dispersal of the Burmese army.

On the 6th the advance on Ava commenced and on the 28th the force arrived in the vicinity of Malun, where Burmese envoys again came in and where at last on the 2nd January, 1826, a treaty of peace was signed, an armistice being agreed upon up to the 18th to allow of the necessary ratification.

When the armistice expired and no ratification was received from Ava, hostilities recommenced, twenty-eight guns opening at noon on the 19th January against the stockades on the further bank of the Irrawaddy, while infantry embarked in boats; the troops were disposed in several parties, the flank companies of the 47th and 87th forming with the 89th a small brigade under Colonel Blair. The brigade containing the 38th and 13th under Colonel Sale landed and assaulted the main face of the enemy's position, the other brigades effecting a landing above the place, attacked the northern works and cut in on the enemy's line of retreat.

The British now continued their advance on Ava, halting more than once on account of the receipt of peace proposals which came to nothing, while one final and decisive action had to be fought at Pagan Myo on the 9th February. But at last on the 24th February a treaty of peace was signed and ratified at Yandabo, when the First Burma War came to an end.

The 47th Regiment embarked in boats, provided under the terms of the treaty by the Burmese Government, on the 8th and arrived at Rangoon on the 26th March, there embarking in the ships " Indian," " Carron " and " McCautly " on the 29th and arriving in Calcutta on the 24th April.

In General Orders of April, 1826, the following announcement appeared: "While the Governor-General in Council enumerates with sentiments of unfeigned admiration the 1st or Royals, the 13th, 38th, 41st, 45th, 47th, 87th and 89th Regiments, the Honourable East India Company's Madras European Regiment, the Bengal and Madras European Artillery, as the European troops who have had the honour of establishing the renown of the British arms in a new and distant region, His Lordship feels that higher and more justly merited praise cannot be bestowed on these troops than that, amidst the barbarous hosts whom they have fought and conquered, they have eminently displayed the virtues and sustained the character of the British Soldier."

The thanks of both Houses of Parliament were voted to the Commanders and their troops, and in December of this year Colonels Elrington and O'Donoghue were created Companions of the Bath.

Then in the *London Gazette* of the 28th December, 1826, is the following:—

"His Majesty has been pleased to approve of the undermentioned Regiments bearing on their Colours and Appointments, in addition to any other badges or devices which may have heretofore been granted to the Regiment, the word

'AVA'

in commemoration of their services during the late Burmese War:—

* * * * *

'47th Regiment.'"

All ranks of the Regiment had, as in the case of those who served in the 2nd Battalion in the Peninsular War, to wait many a year for the issue of a Medal for the war just concluded, for it was not until the 21st March, 1851, that it was announced that Her Majesty the Queen had graciously assented to the measure proposed by the Directors of the East India Company to grant a Medal at their expense to the surviving officers and soldiers of the Crown, who had been engaged on active service in India between the years 1799 and 1826. This was known as "the India General Service Medal," and the surviving officers and men eventually received it with the clasp "Ava."

Twelve officers and one hundred and sixty-four non-commissioned officers and men of the 47th Regiment were granted this Medal and Clasp—more than a quarter of a century after they had earned it!

On the 23rd January, 1827, the Regiment left Calcutta for Berhampore, where it arrived on the 5th February, and in view of its approaching return to England, it now gave many volunteers to different corps both of Royal and Company's troops. Then on the 2nd January, 1829, the 47th returned to Calcutta, where on the 17th it embarked in the ships "James Sibbald," "Maitland" and "Caesar" for England.

On its departure from India General Lord Combermere, the Commander-in-Chief, issued an order expressing "the high sense he entertained of the uniform good conduct and excellent state of discipline of the Corps during a long series of services in the East; he alluded to the very flattering manner in which general officers had commented upon the conduct of Colonel Elrington, the officer commanding the Regiment, who had maintained the strictest discipline, without having recourse to corporal punishment, during the period of his command, which his Lordship was pleased to bring officially to the notice of General Lord Hill, Commanding-in-

Chief; also the gratification it afforded his Lordship of particularly noticing the gallantry of the Regiment in the field, when required to act, which had called forth the highest eulogiums from the general officers under whom it had served.

"General Lord Combermere was further pleased to bring Colonel Elrington to the most favourable consideration of General Lord Hill, and stated that he felt confident that wherever Colonel Elrington might be employed, Lord Hill might depend upon his unwearied exertions on behalf of His Majesty's service."

The "Caesar" reached England on the 19th July, the "Maitland" on the 18th August and the "James Sibbald" on the 18th September; each shipload of troops disembarked at Gravesend and proceeded first to Chatham and from there to the Isle of Wight, where, on the 7th October, the Regiment was concentrated, the Depot also joining.

During the year 1830 certain changes took place throughout the Army; gold lace and buttons were now to be worn by the officers, instead of silver. The Long Service and Good Conduct Medal, for the other ranks, was instituted, whereupon the award of Regimental Medals was discontinued— these medals varied in design and shape and were presented, and paid for, by the officers for individual rewards of bravery, good conduct, shooting, sobriety, etc.; inasmuch as these medals were worn by the recipients when in uniform they were recognized by the higher military authorities, but the number awarded was never very numerous. The gorget, the last survival of ancient armour, worn by officers when on duty, was abolished.

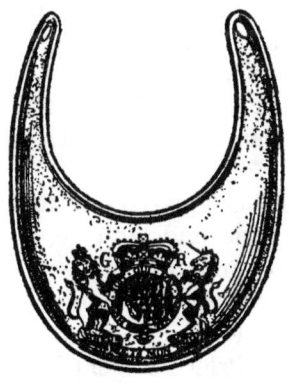

CHAPTER IX

1830–1856

HOME AND MEDITERRANEAN SERVICE
THE CRIMEAN WAR
ALMA, INKERMAN, SEBASTOPOL

THE 47th Regiment was now to experience many moves, during the next few years occupying several stations in the British Islands and in the Mediterranean for comparatively short periods.

On the 23rd and 24th February, 1830, the Regiment moved from the Isle of Wight to Portsmouth, where, on the 12th May and 4th and 22nd June of the year following, it moved to Edinburgh, and marched thence to Glasgow, where a very few months were spent. Early in January, 1832, the Regiment was sent from Glasgow to Belfast, from which place it proceeded on the 7th and 14th May in two divisions to Newry, whence many small detachments were furnished; but on the 15th June, 1833, the whole Regiment was concentrated at Londonderry. From here the 47th moved again to Mullingar, arriving there on the 26th August. This again was no more than a very temporary station, for in April, 1834, the Regiment moved again to Dublin, where this tour of Irish service came to an end, for on the 23rd September the Service Companies embarked in H.M.S. "Jupiter" for Gibraltar at a strength of twenty-three officers, thirty-one sergeants, twenty-four corporals, nine drummers, 456 privates, thirty-one women and sixty-four children. At Gibraltar the 47th arrived on the 15th October and occupied quarters in barracks in the Town Range and King's Bastion.

On the departure of the headquarters from Ireland, the four Depot companies moved first to Boyle and later to Castlebar, finally in July, 1837, being quartered at Portsmouth.

At Gibraltar the Regiment remained quietly for nearly three years, and then on the 8th and 25th February, 1837, embarked for Malta in the transports "Parmelia" and "Prince Regent," arriving on the 25th February and 10th March; during the four years of its stay in this island being quartered at Fort Ricasoli, Isola Gate, Florian and Lower Fort St. Elmo.

THE COLOURS—THE 47TH REGIMENT.
1832–1858.

On the 12th August, 1839, the establishment of the Regiment was augmented and was now to stand at one colonel, one lieut.-colonel, two majors, ten captains, twelve lieutenants, eight ensigns, one paymaster, one adjutant, one quartermaster, one surgeon, two assistant-surgeons, one sergeant-major, one quartermaster-sergeant, one armourer-sergeant, one schoolmaster-sergeant, one hospital-sergeant, one orderly room clerk, ten colour-sergeants, thirty sergeants, forty corporals, one drum-major, thirteen drummers and 760 privates.

The 47th was now ordered to the West Indies and on the 11th February, 1841, embarked in the "Abercrombie Robinson," transport, and, sailing south, arrived off the island of Barbados on the 31st March; there having been some sickness on the voyage, the Regiment was detained for some days on board, and it was the middle of April before all the companies were landed and quartered in the Brick Barracks at St. Ann's. It was while here that Colonel Elrington severed his long connection with the 47th on being promoted major-general; he had been a lieut.-colonel in the Regiment since 1813, and was succeeded in command by Major P. Dundas.

The Regiment, while quartered in the West Indies, furnished many detachments to the neighbouring islands—Demerara, Berbice, Antigua and St. Kitts, and the two companies quartered at the last-named place—the Grenadier Company and No. 7—suffered very severely from an epidemic of yellow fever, losing an officer—Major J. Gordon—and thirty-four non-commissioned officers and men, out of a total strength of one hundred and ninety. There were at this time two majors in the Regiment of the same name—both John Gordon; this one who died of yellow fever was the junior of the two.

The actual rate of mortality in the 47th during the three years it was stationed in the West Indies does not appear to have been abnormally high for those days, being only something over three per cent in 1841, nine per cent in 1842, and falling to only a little over four per cent in 1843.

At the end of 1843 the Regiment embarked for home in two divisions at an interval of some weeks, the troops of the first party, who had sailed in the "Princess Royal," disembarking at Gosport on the 3rd January, 1844, while the second party from the "Boyne" landed on the 23rd, the disembarking strength being as follows: one field officer, five captains, seven subalterns, five staff, twenty-three sergeants, nine drummers, 554 rank and file, forty-five women and ninety-one children. The Regiment was here quartered in Forton and Haslar Barracks.

In the spring of this year the Emperor Nicholas of Russia paid a visit to England, and expressed a particular wish to inspect a Line Battalion recently returned from foreign service, for, as he put it : " though your Guards are noble-looking troops, I confess I look with far more interest on the sort of soldiers who gain the victories in India and China for you."

The 47th Regiment was accordingly selected for inspection by His Imperial Majesty, and proceeded by train and march route to Windsor to attend the review by Her Majesty and the Emperor of Russia of some five thousand troops on the following day.

The Regimental Digest at this period contains many flattering letters received from those in authority by the Commanding Officer, about the appearance and conduct of the Regiment ; and on the 26th July, 1844, the Regimental Sergeant-Major was, on his discharge, made a warden of the Tower of London.

In the autumn of this year the 47th was sent to the north of England and was split up into many detachments, and in March, 1846, it proceeded to Ireland, where it remained for nearly five years. During this time Ireland was in a very disturbed state and the Regiment was constantly moved from one station to another and provided innumerable detachments, large and small. At the beginning of 1851 the Service Companies were at Buttevant, and it was here that orders were received to proceed again on foreign service ; on the 3rd January the Regiment, under command of Lieut.-Colonel Haly, proceeded by rail to Cork and there embarked in the " Java " on the 8th February for conveyance to Corfu, which was reached on the 15th March, when the headquarters and five companies disembarked and occupied quarters on the Island of Vido, the sixth company proceeding to Corfu.

The strength of the Regiment on embarkation for Corfu was twenty-two officers, thirty-one sergeants, eleven drummers, 560 rank and file, thirty-seven women and sixty-four children.

The remaining four companies of the Regiment now formed the Depot, which had been for some time with the headquarters in Ireland and now remained on in that country on the departure of the 47th on foreign service, and later, in company with the 4-company depots of the 41st and 55th Regiments, formed the Templemore Depot Battalion under the command of Colonel Townshend. On the occasion of the funeral of Field-Marshal the Duke of Wellington in November, 1852, the following officers, non-commissioned officers and men were sent to London from Ireland to represent the 47th Regiment : Captains J. H. Lowndes and W. F. A. Rooke, Lieutenant T. Roper, Sergeant J. Smith, Corporal J. Heath, Lance-Corporal H. Gill, Privates P. Burns, T. Cassidy, W. Connor, I. Court and M. Savage.

In March and April, 1853, the Regiment moved from Corfu to Malta, and on the 1st November the 47th, as also the 41st and 49th Regiments, received orders to hold themselves in readiness to embark for the West Indies; this destination was, however, very speedily changed, for by a Horse Guards letter dated the 24th February, 1854, it was stated that the 47th Regiment would form part of a force to be employed in the east of Europe, and that the strength of the corps was consequently to be augmented by one major, two captains, four subalterns, one assistant-surgeon, four sergeants, two drummers and one hundred rank and file.

This letter was followed by another dated the 6th March, directing that the three regiments above mentioned were to form one brigade, that each was to be completed to 850 rank and file, of which 200 were to be furnished from the respective depots of each corps, completed by volunteers from regiments remaining in Malta.

In compliance with the terms of the orders contained in the first letter, two of the Depot Companies of the 47th were sent out from Ireland to Malta under Major R. Farren to join headquarters, and the 47th was then made up to strength by volunteers from the 9th, 62nd, and 68th Regiments.

The nominal cause of the campaign which now resulted, and which is known as the Crimean War, was the designs of Russia upon Constantinople. The Czar of Russia had contrived by diplomatic measures of various kinds to establish a claim to a protectorate over the Christian subjects in Europe of the Sultan of Turkey, and in 1853 he had put forward demands which, if accepted, practically involved the complete disappearance of Turkey as an independent European State. Great Britain and France agreed to support Turkey against Russian aggression and declared war against Russia on the 28th March, 1853, Sardinia also joining the alliance some months later. In February, 1854, when the first British troops left England, everything seemed to point to the campaign being carried out on the Danube. In May the Russians crossed that river, opening their first parallels before the fortress of Silistria on the 19th May; consequently when the forces of England and France first arrived in Turkish waters they were initially conveyed to Varna, encamping between that place and Shumla, fully expecting to be called upon to defend these strong places by engaging the Russian Army in the field.

The British Expeditionary Force ordered to Turkey was composed of five infantry divisions, each containing two brigades and the strength of each division being about five thousand; a cavalry division of one heavy and one light cavalry brigade; three troops of horse artillery and eight field batteries.

On the 10th April the 47th Regiment, under the command of Major R. Farren—Lieut.-Colonel Haly remaining temporarily behind at Malta—embarked for Turkey in the troopship "Apollo," and, landing on the

19th at Scutari, was for the time being accommodated in the old Turkish barracks. On the 22nd Lieut.-General Sir de Lacy Evans arrived and the formation of the 2nd Division, which he was to command, was put in hand: the 1st Brigade contained the 30th, 55th and 95th Regiments and was commanded by Brigadier-General J. L. Pennefather, and the 2nd Brigade was composed of the 41st, 47th and 49th under Brigadier-General H. W. Adams. The British Crimean Army was commanded by Field-Marshal Lord Raglan, who had served throughout the Peninsular War and also at the Battle of Waterloo, where he had lost his right arm by one of the very last shots fired in that action. During recent years he had served on the Headquarter Staff as Military Secretary to the Duke of Wellington.

The establishment of the Regiment was ordered to be raised from the 10th May to the following numbers: one colonel, one lieut.-colonel, two majors, twelve captains, fourteen lieutenants, ten ensigns, one paymaster, one adjutant, one quartermaster, one surgeon, three assistant-surgeons, one sergeant-major, one quartermaster-sergeant, one paymaster sergeant, one armourer sergeant, one schoolmaster sergeant, one hospital sergeant, one orderly room clerk, twelve colour-sergeants, fifty-eight sergeants, seventy corporals, one drum major, twenty-eight drummers or fifers, and 1,330 privates.

On the 23rd May Lord Raglan returned from Varna, where he and Marshal St. Arnaud, the French Commander-in-Chief, had been holding a council-of-war with Omar Pasha, who was in command of the Turks holding the line of the Danube; and it was then decided that the allied forces should proceed to Varna to support the Turks, and orders to this end were now at once issued.

On the 16th June and two following days the troops composing the 2nd Division left Scutari, the 47th embarking on the 17th under command of Major Farren in the S.S. "Cambria" for Varna; on arrival here on the 19th the Regiment encamped on the plain outside the town. Here on the 24th Lieut.-Colonel Haly joined from Malta and took over command. "The plain round Varna for three miles," we are told, "was covered with tents. Grass, herbage and shrubs disappeared, and the fields were turned into an expanse of sand ploughed up by araba wheels and the feet of oxen, and covered with towns of canvas. There could not have been less than forty thousand men encamped around the place, including French, English, Egyptian and Turks, and the town itself was choked in every street with soldiery."

On the 30th June most of the British troops left Varna for more inland camps. The 2nd Division moved on the 3rd July to Carragoula, seven miles from Varna, remaining here for three days and then marching to Yuksukova, eight miles further, and camping here in the Devna Valley.

Here there were many cases of cholera, while malarial fever was also prevalent, but the 2nd Division does not appear to have suffered to the same degree as did the Light and 3rd Divisions.

Rumours seem at this time to have arisen that the troops of the expeditionary force were likely soon to be embarked for some point upon the Russian coast, and in the early days of August it became no secret that Sebastopol was to be the objective; all doubts were set at rest by the 23rd August when the troops of the Division marched from Yuksukova to Sombey and thence to Varna, where it arrived on the 29th, the 47th embarking two days later in the "Melbourne" at a strength of three field-officers, seven captains, fourteen subalterns, five staff-sergeants, thirty-four sergeants, fifty corporals, thirteen drummers and 682 privates.

Of the embarkation Dr. W. H. Russell, the correspondent of *The Times*, wrote as follows to his paper: "On Thursday last," this was the 31st August, "the 2nd Division embarked in excellent order. Sir de Lacy Evans, his brigadiers, Pennefather and Adams, were on board before nine o'clock. The 1st Brigade—30th, 55th and 95th Regiments—and the 2nd Brigade—41st, 47th and 49th—constitute a very fine division, which has suffered less from sickness than any other division of our army. They moved with great regularity down to the rude piers, and embarking, regiment after regiment, on board the steamers, were soon on board their respective transports."

The transports joined the rest of the armada in Baltschik Bay, but the fleet did not actually sail until the 7th September, and an officer of the 2nd Division thus states the order of sailing: "Lord Raglan is in the 'Caradoc.' Heads of divisions are in front, the Light Division taking the left, the First, Second, Third and Fourth, and then the French transports. The other ships follow the heads of their divisions, so that we may call ourselves a mass of contiguous columns, left in front."

It had been definitely arranged between the Allied Commanders that the landing should be made just to the north of Sebastopol, but at the very last moment and after the fleets had actually sailed, the proposal was made by the French that the troops should be put ashore at Kaffa, one hundred miles distant from it and on the eastern coast of the Crimean peninsula. Had this suggestion been carried out, it would have meant the temporary abandonment of the siege of the fortress. Happily the decision in the matter was left to Lord Raglan, who decided to abide by the original arrangement; he then, on the 10th, reconnoitred the western coast of the peninsula from Sebastopol to Eupatoria, and decided that the landing should be effected on a strip of open beach known as Old Fort Bay, six miles to the north of the Bulganak River.

The Crimean peninsula, which was to be the scene of operations, is nearly twice the size of Yorkshire. Near its south-west extremity, on an arm of the sea, lie the town and harbour of Sebastopol, the objective of the expedition; it is situated on the south side of the inlet and on the north side were the powerful works and some store-houses.

At nine o'clock on the morning of the 14th September the signal to disembark was made, and the landing went on throughout the day, the 1st and Light Divisions being put on shore first, and then the 2nd Division, the 47th landing about 2 p.m. Each man carried three days' rations and folded great coat, knapsacks being left behind on the transports, but were brought up to the front some twenty-four hours later.

As soon as the first three divisions were landed, they moved off, the Light Division leading and the 2nd bringing up the rear; and then, having marched some four miles, the whole bivouacked and spent the night under pouring rain. The whole of the British force was not on shore until the 18th, and at 9 a.m. on the 19th the Allied Army commenced its march on Sebastopol. The French moved on the right near the sea and the British on their left in two columns of divisions, the Light Division leading the left column, followed by the 1st and 4th, the 2nd Division being at the head of the right column with the 3rd in rear. The British cavalry covered the outer flank. Early in the afternoon the columns arrived on the banks of the Bulganak, a small and sluggish stream; this was crossed and Lord Raglan directed his troops to bivouac in two sides of a square with the river at their backs, so as to be able to deploy rapidly to front or left flank. The night, however, passed quietly, and the troops were under arms early on the 20th, but no forward movement was made till nearly 10 a.m., at which hour the British advanced over the grassy ridges on each side of the great post road from Eupatoria to Sebastopol, the 2nd Division being on the right next to the French. An hour's march brought the troops within sight of the enemy's position on the further side of the Alma, when a halt was made, and Lord Raglan, accompanied by Marshal St. Arnaud, rode forward to consider the plan of attack.

The valley through which the River Alma runs lay in front, and the ground on the further side, where the enemy had taken post, constituted a strong defensive position. From the sea almost to the village of Bourliouk, a distance of some two and a half miles, the ground is high and commanding on the south side of the Alma, and being opposite the French was naturally their objective. The space between Bourliouk and another village higher up the stream, a distance of about two miles, was the first

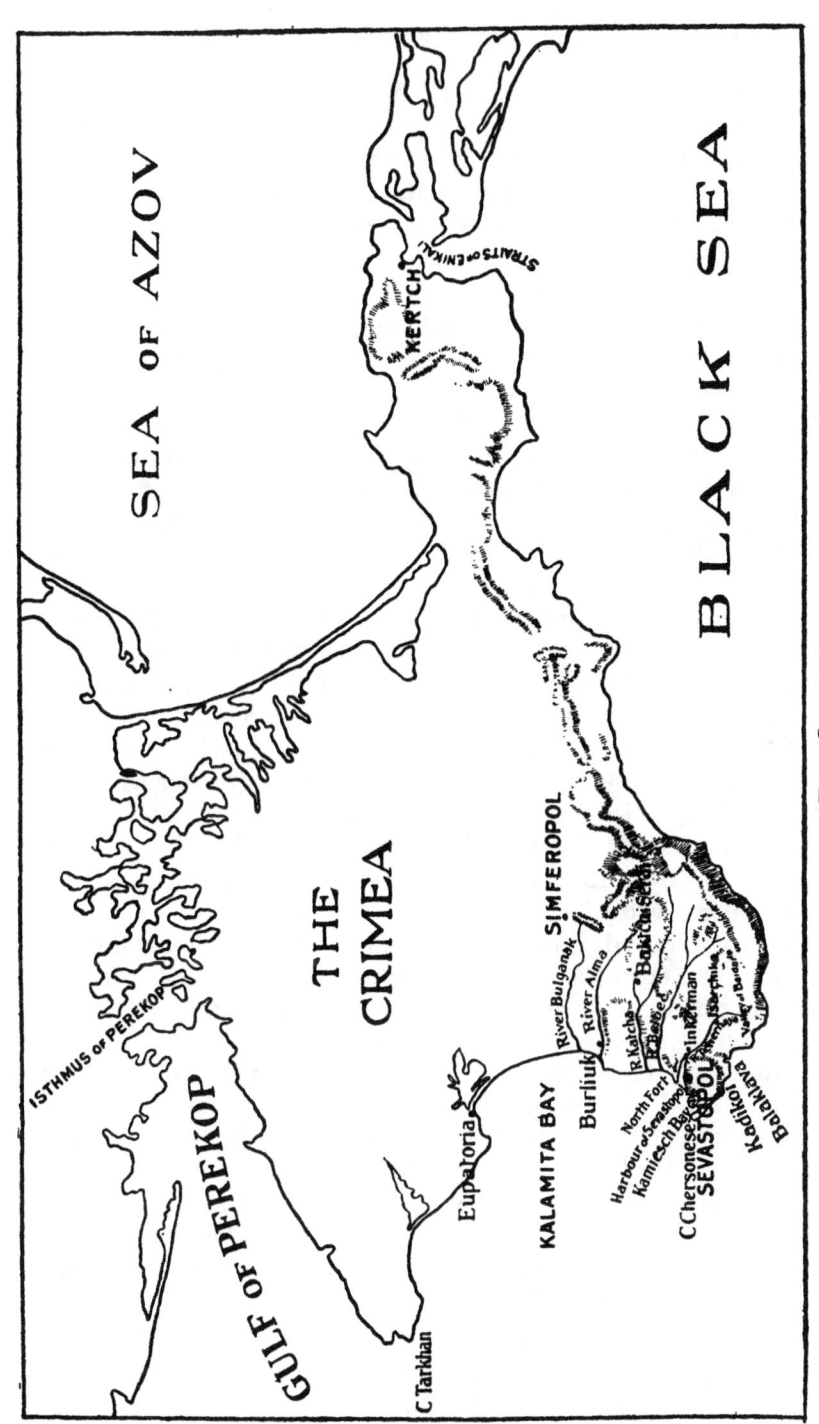

The Crimea.

1854–1856.

to be attacked by the British. Opposite here and on the Russian side of the Alma, the ascent was easy for all arms, but some way back stood the Kourgane Hill, which was strongly occupied by the Russians, while on its slopes towards the river were earthworks and heavy guns. The position also across the post road, and the Telegraph Hill to the west of it, were held in strength by the enemy.

In brief, Lord Raglan's army, of some 28,000 men and 60 guns, was confronted by 26,000 Russian and 86 guns; while 37,000 Frenchmen and 68 guns, supported by the fire of nine ships-of-war, were to oppose a Russian force of no more than 13,000 men and 36 guns. The position to be attacked by the French was everywhere steep and in many places precipitous, but it was not strong in a military sense and was undefended by any field works. On the other hand, the ground in front of the British attacks sloped gently down to the Alma, was of great natural strength and was entrenched, while all the ranges had been carefully measured and marked out.

The 2nd Division, its 1st Brigade in the front line and the 2nd in support, moved forward about 1 p.m. on the 20th, forming the extreme right of the British army, and having the 3rd French Division on its right and our Light Division on the left; and as the lines surmounted the gentle rise from the top of which the ground led down to the Alma, a historian * tells us that "those having good sight could detect on the slopes across the stream something which looked like a brown seam, and also numberless small black squares and oblongs on the green turf of the hillside. The brown seam was the Great Redoubt and the squares and oblongs were the columns of a Russian army."

The 2nd Division moved directly on the village of Bourliouk and came under the fire of the enemy's skirmishers occupying the enclosures, and the men were ordered to lie down. Suddenly the village burst into flames, having been set on fire by the Russians prior to evacuation, and the heavy guns on the Kourgane Hill opened fire and the Light and 2nd Divisions began to deploy; for this, however, there was insufficient room, the Light Division having been formed too much to the right, while the burning village so diminished the space for the deployment of the 2nd Division, that though this was in two lines, each of a brigade, its left still overlapped the Light Division right. While everything was being done to remedy this state of affairs, Lord Raglan gave the order for the advance, and Major Lysons, 23rd, who was on the staff and brought the order to the 2nd Division, has said: "I shall never forget the excited look of delight on every face when I gave the order—'the line will advance.'"

* Kinglake, *Invasion of the Crimea*, Vol. II, p. 257.

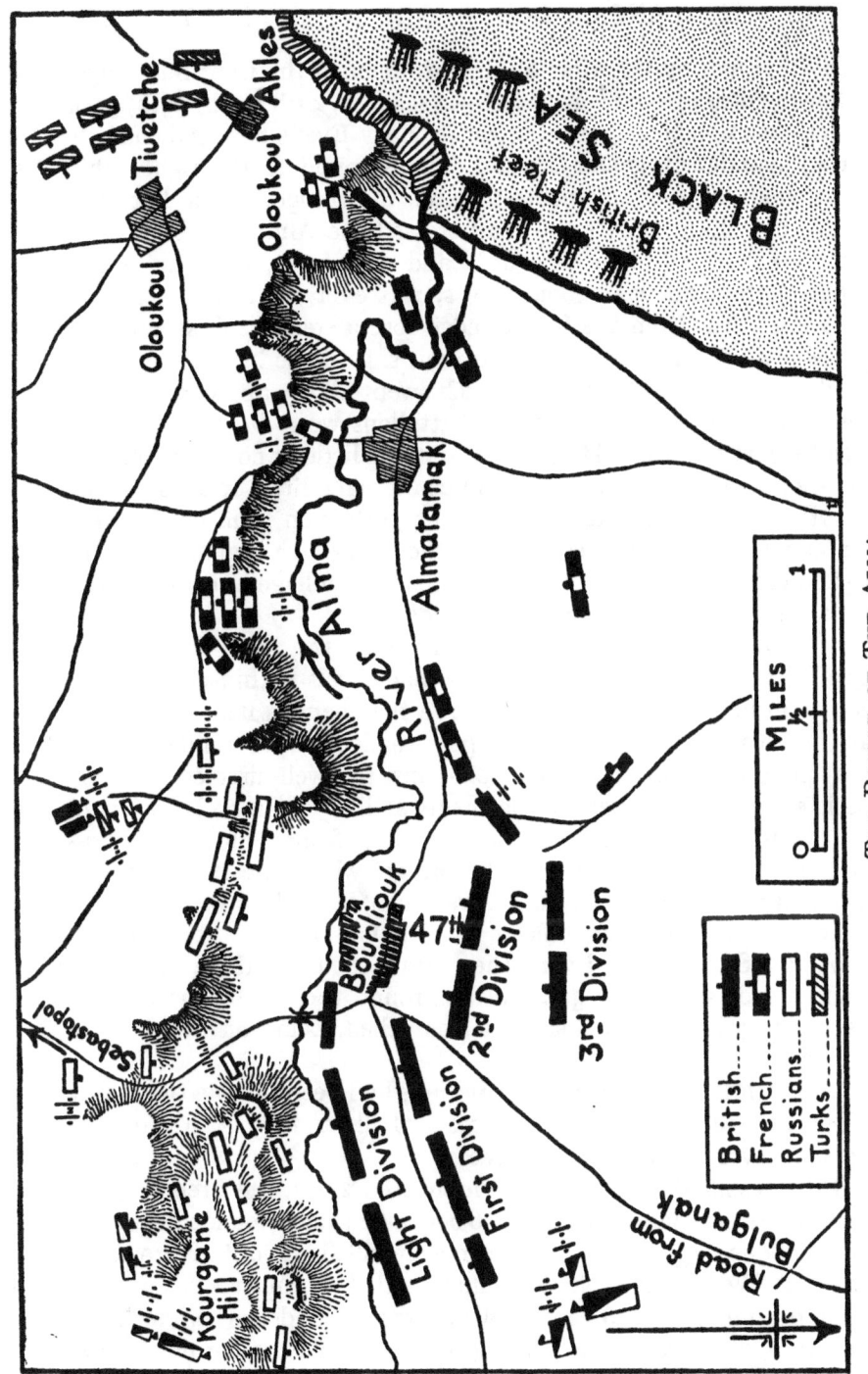

THE BATTLE OF THE ALMA.

20th September, 1854.

The Division had by this time all its battalions in the front line ranged in the following order from right to left—41st, 49th, 47th, 30th, 95th, 55th, with two batteries on the right: but Sir de Lacy Evans now detached the 41st and 49th under Brigadier-General Adams round to the right, while he led his remaining four regiments towards the bridge, to the left front and east of the village, where the road crossed the Alma. The banks of the river were covered with vineyards and enclosures, and the stream itself, while quite shallow in some places, was over six feet in depth in others. A few yards from the further edge rose a steep bank several feet in height, while a few hundred yards on their side of the bridge the enemy had placed a battery of sixteen guns which swept all the approaches, while on either side of the road six infantry battalions were disposed.

The 2nd Division, crowded together and under little or no cover, suffered from the fire here concentrated on it and could make little or no progress; but the 47th managed to obtain some slight protection from fire between the river and the burning village, while the other two regiments of the 2nd Brigade crossed at a ford to the right of the village and established themselves, precariously, on the further side.

Presently, Lord Raglan, crossing the river at the same ford as had those two battalions, made his way to a knoll well within the Russian position; from here he was able to observe the enemy's flank, and, finding that the Russian batteries on the post road could be enfiladed from this point, he ordered up two of our field-guns, the well-directed fire from which assisted in the retirement of the enemy artillery. Sir de Lacy Evans now pushed his units forward; the 47th with difficulty effected a crossing at a ford some 400 yards below the bridge, where the stream flowed in several channels, and the Regiment was then formed up in column by Captain Rooke, the mounted officers having had to pass the river at another point. Sir de Lacy Evans then established the three battalions of the 2nd Brigade and thirty guns on the ground vacated by the Russian batteries; the 47th, when a final halt was called, being on the flank of the Russian left.

In the meantime the other British divisions had been driving the enemy before them on the slopes of the Kourgane Hill, and by 3.30 p.m. the Russians were everywhere in full retreat.

The British casualties in the battle numbered 2,002, the French 1,343, and those of the Russians close upon 6,000 killed and wounded; in the 47th Regiment one sergeant and three men were killed, Major C. F. Fordyce, Lieutenants T. Wollocombe, N. G. Philips, and J. G. Maycock, four sergeants, one drummer and 56 rank and file were wounded, the loss being chiefly incurred when passing over the ground between the burning village and the river. Both Lieut.-Colonel Haly and Captain Sankey—the latter on the staff—had their horses shot under them.

The Colours were this day carried, the Queen's Colour by Ensign T. Palmer and the Regimental Colour by Ensign J. J. C. Irby, and a plunging shot passed through the Queen's Colour, killing Sergeant Lomax and Corporal Crone of the Colour party.

Lieut.-Colonel the Hon. P. E. Herbert, then A.Q.M.G. 2nd Division, brought to notice the conduct of two men of the 47th at the Alma. He stated that while lying wounded on the ground, utterly unable to move, he saw a number of men going by on the way to the rear, and feared that they were falling back without orders. He called upon them to halt and go about, but only two of those who had passed him turned back, and those two, despite a heavy fire, came over to where he was lying to explain that they were not running away, but were falling to the rear badly wounded, one being shot in the jaw and the other severely wounded in the chest by a shell. Colonel Herbert said that the fact of these two men coming back through so heavy a fire was so honourable to the Regiment to which they belonged, that it ought to be placed on record.

The advance was resumed on the 23rd September, the interval having been taken up with burying the dead and collecting the wounded, and the troops bivouacked for the night of the 24th on the wooded heights on the further bank of the Belbek River. Lord Raglan had been anxious to attack or at least invest the forts on the north side of Sebastopol, but to this the French commander would not agree, and consequently a long and hazardous march had to be undertaken with the object of passing round the fortress and establishing a new base at Balaklava on the southwest of the Crimea. The army started on this flank march at noon on the 25th, the route lying eastwards to a building known as Mackenzie's Farm, where the road from Sebastopol to Baktchi-Serai was struck. Here there was some skirmishing with the Russian rearguard, and some baggage and prisoners were captured.

The march was then resumed and the Allies, giving Sebastopol a wide berth, arrived late that evening at their bivouack on the Tchernaya River, the 47th settling down on the north bank near the Traktir bridge.

On the 26th the 2nd Division moved nearer to Balaklava, but during the attack upon and capture of this place, the Division remained in reserve on the plain of Kadikoi, ready to repel any movement upon the rear from the direction of Sebastopol. Cholera still pursued the army and on this day Orderly Room Sergeant T. Morrissey died of it.

On the 29th the Allied Armies sat down before Sebastopol, advancing to and occupying positions on the heights above it, some within range of the Russian batteries, the 2nd Division moving up to a position on the extreme right of the Allied Army. Tents were now issued and all ranks were busily engaged in bringing up and emplacing siege guns and in making gabions and fascines. On the 4th October, however, the 2nd Division moved some two and a half miles further to the right, taking up the position it was now for some months to hold on the extreme right of the besieging army, the camp being on the high ground known as Inkerman Heights, immediately behind the crest of Home Ridge, and from which three great ravines ran down to the harbour of Sebastopol. The Light and 2nd Divisions were supported by the 1st, the camp of which was rather under a mile from that of the 2nd Division.

The bombardment of the fortress by the Allied batteries and by the guns of the two fleets opened on the 17th October, the naval guns attacking the batteries on the sea-front, while the shore batteries chiefly directed their fire against a work known as the Redan and also against the Flagstaff Bastion at the head of the Dockyard Creek; this fire was very effective and was continued during the three following days. There were certain casualties among the besiegers and during the month following the Battle of the Alma the 47th had three men killed and five wounded.

On the 25th October was fought the Battle of Balaklava, generally accounted a purely cavalry action by reason of the very gallant charges of the Heavy and Light Cavalry Brigades; but detachments from certain regiments of the 2nd Division also took part and were awarded the clasp for the battle. The 47th, however, was not engaged as a regiment, though it was called out and moved up in support. The enemy remained in occupation of some of the forts and guns they had this day taken from the Turks; and it was probably with the idea of diverting the attention of the Allies from General Liprandi's movements, and with the further motive of acquainting his troops with the ground on the flank of the besiegers, over which he intended later to make a very much more serious attack, that the Russian Commander gave orders for a sortie to be made against the front of the 2nd Division on the morning of the 26th October.

The picquets this day covering the front of the 2nd Division were furnished by four companies from each of its brigades. The Russian force sent out from Sebastopol consisted of six battalions of infantry and four guns, and it advanced along the ravine and slope to attack the 2nd Division which was formed in line in advance of its camp, the 2nd Brigade on the right. Our picquets fell back after a determined stand, and when within range the enemy's guns fired over the crest behind which the Division was lying down. The Russians then moved forward in two columns, but by this time the two batteries of the 2nd Division, and also one from the

1st, had come into action, and in half an hour the enemy's guns were driven from the field. The Brigade of Guards then came up on the right, and the guns now turning their fire on the enemy columns, these began to fall back, hotly pursued by the picquets of the 2nd Division.

The 47th had this day one man killed and seven wounded.

On the news of this action reaching England the Duke of Newcastle wrote to Lord Raglan saying that he was directed to express "the Queen's gratification at the manner in which the attack, made by a numerous force of the enemy on the 26th of the month upon the 2nd Division, was repulsed by Lieut.-General Sir de Lacy Evans and the infantry under his command. The attack seems to have been well-planned and rapidly executed, and the greatest credit is due to Sir de Lacy Evans for the ability, promptitude and gallantry with which it was defeated.

"Her Majesty has received the intelligence of this gallant exploit with high approval."

The Russians had for some time past been contemplating a serious attack on the Allied positions, with the view of driving the British and French from their works and possibly back to their ships. Large reinforcements had arrived from Odessa, and by the 4th November Mentschikoff, the Russian Commander, had 115,000 men at his command. On the same date the Allies numbered 65,000, of which 16,000 were British infantry.

The most vulnerable point in the position of the besiegers was about the camp of the 2nd Division; this body of troops was, as already stated, camped across the post road on the ridge next to the valley of the Tchernaya. The ground on which the camp stood, sloped up to a crest in front, known as Home Ridge, and on the right front of this ridge a piece of ground projected some 500 yards northward, and this was called the Fore Ridge. About 1,200 yards away, west of north, was Shell Hill, near which the 47th had a picquet, and here the Russian guns were posted during the action of the 5th November. Having crossed the crest the post road descended into the Quarry Ravine, to the east of Shell Hill. On the left of the ridge was the Careenage Ravine, an offshoot of which, known as the Well Way, ended close to the left rear of the 2nd Division camp. The British position was to all intents and purposes unentrenched; there were, it is true, a few yards of trench on the crest and a wall of loose stones called the Barrier, where the road dips into the Quarry, while some 500 yards east of the Barrier a two-gun battery had recently been constructed, and afterwards dismantled, known as the Sandbag Battery.

On the day of Inkerman, Lieut.-General Sir de Lacy Evans was ill on board ship in Balaklava Harbour, and General Pennefather was in command of the 2nd Division; Sir de Lacy Evans returned to the front during the action, but did not take command.

The Russian attack was arranged as follows: General Soimonoff was to leave Sebastopol near the entrance to the Careenage Ravine with nineteen thousand infantry and thirty-eight guns, while General Pauloff, with sixteen thousand infantry and ninety-six guns, was to cross the causeway near the head of the harbour and then, moving left, was to mount the heights to the left of Soimonoff and then join hands with him. These two bodies having concentrated, General Dannenberg was to take command of the whole and conduct the attack on the 2nd Division. A Russian force near Balaklava was to demonstrate and prevent help being sent to the British right.

About 3 a.m. on the 5th November a low rumbling sound was heard in the valley of Inkerman by some of those on outpost, but it was thought to be no more than ammunition waggons on their way to the fortress. An hour later bells were heard ringing in the city, but nothing was thought of it, and indeed "no one suspected that masses of Russians were then creeping up the rugged heights over the valley of Inkerman against the undefended flank of the 2nd Division, and were bringing into position an overwhelming artillery ready to play upon their tents at the first glimpse of day."

The 2nd Division, as was its custom, stood to arms at daybreak on the 5th, the old picquets were relieved and were nearly all back in camp.

The new picquets belonging to the 2nd Division numbered 480 men, and those on the right of the post road were commanded by Lieut.-Colonel Carpenter, 41st, and those to the left of it by Lieut.-Colonel Haly, 47th. The picquet furnished by the Light Company of the 47th was posted to the left of Shell Hill, and was supported by No. 8 Company, under Captain Rooke and Ensign Palmer. The 41st had a picquet on or near Shell Hill, while on the left of the 47th a picquet of the 49th was stationed on the Mikriakoff Spur, but it was relieved before the battle opened by a picquet of the 55th. As day broke a sentry on Shell Hill saw some of the enemy advancing on him through the mist and reported it; firing opened and the picquets all found themselves suddenly attacked in force. These made a fine stand, and not only did they hold their own, but actually drove the foremost Russians back, and, when finally forced to retire, did so contesting every inch of the ground.

Lieut.-Colonel Haly of the 47th, getting far forward, called on the Light Company of his own Regiment to charge, dashed at the first body of Russians that he saw, and cut down and killed three with his sword before

INKERMAN.

5th November, 1854.
Pte. J. McDermond, V.C., saving the life of Colonel Haly.

From the Painting by Chevalier L. W. Desanges, Victoria Cross Gallery, Wantage, Berks. By kind permission.

he was himself unhorsed. He was bayoneted in the leg and must have been killed had not Captain Rowlands, 41st, and Privates Kelly and McDermond, of the Light Company of the 47th, come to his aid.

Private Kelly was killed later in the action, but Captain Rowlands and Private McDermond were awarded the Victoria Cross for their gallantry on this occasion.

The determined stand made by the picquets had given time for the 2nd Division to get under arms, and the following dispositions were made : a wing of the 30th and two companies of the 95th were sent out towards the picquets in skirmishing order; the other wing of the 30th was sent to the Barrier; a wing each of the 41st and 49th to the right front; the remainder of the 49th and a wing of the 47th to the left front with orders to watch the Careenage Ravine; while the rest of the 95th was ordered to remain for the present on Home Ridge in support of the guns; this left in reserve the few remaining companies of the 47th only.

Major Fordyce, with the Grenadier and No. 5 Company of the 47th, was now sent forward and advanced to near the point of Mikriakoff Glen, and came upon one of Soimonoff's battalions advanced through the mist to the southern side of the Glen, and here is Kinglake's * story of the encounter, which then took place :—

" Major Fordyce deployed his small force into line, pressed forward in the direction of the fire, and at length, when about eighty yards off—for the mist at this spot was not dense enough to prevent him—could see the head of the column descending the opposite ridge. The combat which followed was not an affair of close fighting, but a sample of the strife between column and line when engaged at a distance of some eighty or one hundred yards. Though already drawn out into line, the troops under Fordyce had already become yet further extended whilst making their way through tall brushwood; and notwithstanding the smallness of their comparative numbers, they now showed a much broader front than the body advancing against them in column at greater distance.

" The foremost Russians made haste to be plying their muskets, but they did our people no harm, for the force being gathered in column and firing with an inferior weapon at a range of eighty yards and from a narrow front, stood under conditions which made its energy vain. On the other hand, Fordyce's men, whilst remaining unstricken themselves, were all of them carefully file-firing from a widely extended front; and since each of them with a good rifle in his hands, and with ample space round him could shoot at his ease, they soon began to work havoc in the mass which served for their target.

* *Invasion of the Crimea*, Vol. V, pp. 147, 148.

"After enduring a few rounds the column broke in confusion, and began to fall back with all the speed that the heaviness of its formation and the nature of the ground would allow. Fordyce, moving after it at a distance of about a hundred yards, did not either cease firing or stay his pursuit till he had driven the mass before him across the opposite rib. Then being far in advance and unsupported, and having all but expended his ammunition, he came at last to a halt and caused his men to lie down close under the crest they had gained. There he kept fast his hold until other troops came to relieve him."

Another body of the enemy, pushing on, came upon a wing of the 49th, were fired into, charged and driven back, but overwhelming Russian supports now arriving on the scene, the wing of the 49th fell back in turn.

Reinforcements were now, however, beginning to reach the 2nd Division: four companies of the 88th, 290 strong, advanced on the left over the crest and deployed, but there met masses of the enemy who forced them back and captured three of our guns. Then there arrived four companies of the 77th and these, joining hands with four companies of the 47th under Major Farren, drove back the enemy, who retreated, leaving the captured guns behind them.

It was about this time that General Soimonoff, who so far had been the life and soul of the attack, was killed.

The companies of the 47th, being under fire from an enemy battery on Shell Hill, lay down north of the Well Way, and here they appear to have remained until 7.30 a.m. not actively engaged, but holding the ground while the fighting drifted further to the right, where the issue was fought out between the enemy and fresh bodies of our troops. There was heavy fighting about the Sandbag Battery, and during the next four hours victory inclined now to one side and now to the other; and it was after 1 p.m. when the last Russian battery was silenced and the enemy had at last begun to retreat. Men of the 2nd Division watched from Shell Hill the Russians retiring over the Tchernaya causeway, their Lighthouse Battery doing its best to cover their retreat.

As the last shots were being fired Captain Lowry, 47th, arrived on the field with a very small reinforcement from Balaklava.

The losses in the 2nd Division had been terribly heavy, out of 7,664 men collected on Mount Inkerman, 2,357 being killed and wounded; and every regimental commanding officer in the Division was a casualty.

In the 47th nineteen rank and file were killed, Lieut.-Colonel W. O'G. Haly, Ensign G. Waddilove, two sergeants and forty-three other ranks were wounded.

On the 13th November the 62nd Regiment arrived in the Crimea and

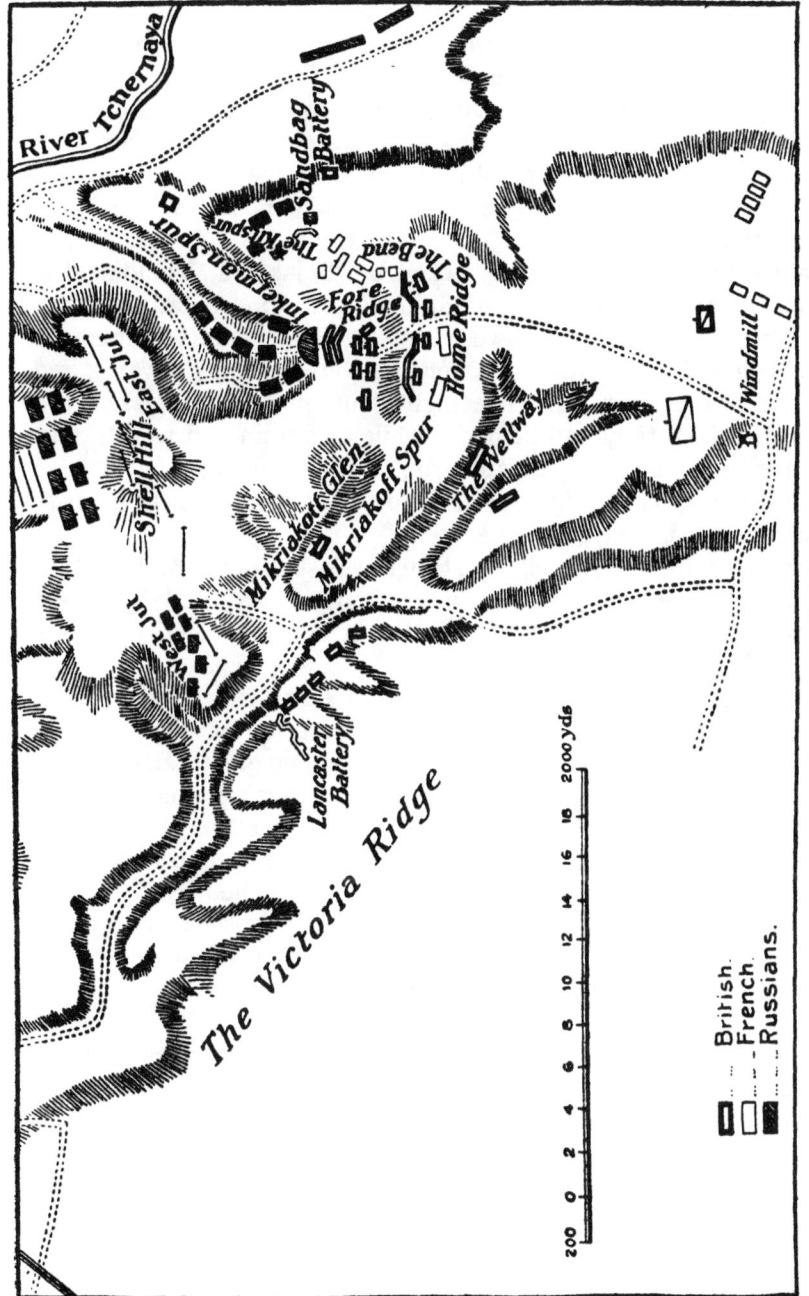

The Battle of Inkerman.

5th November, 1854.

joined the 1st Brigade of the 2nd Division; and on the following day a terrible tempest arose, the hospital marquees were almost at once blown down and it was not long before there were less than a dozen tents left standing; wagons were overturned and no man could stand against the storm at the height of its fury. An officer of the 47th says: " Our tents were lifted over our heads and the poles broken . . . the sick were obliged to wander about to find shelter where they could; many of them died a few days after."

Twenty-one British ships were wrecked off Balaklava, including the " Prince," laden with warm clothing of all kinds and stores greatly wanted, while the " Resolute " also went down with ten million rounds of ammunition. Snow followed the storm; the trenches were filled with water, and the men were generally on duty five nights out of six and wearing the same clothes in which they had landed; while on coming off trench duty the weary men had to go out again and grub up the roots of the brushwood for fuel with which to light a fire at which to cook their salt meat or roast their coffee berries—issued green.

In November, a draft, some eighty strong, was sent out from the Regimental Depot at Templemore under Ensign A. H. White, but these were nearly all recruits, and the majority had died, or been invalided, before six months were out.

Of the state of the British army during that first Crimean winter *The Times* correspondent wrote as follows: " The condition of our army was indeed miserable, pitiable, heart-rending. No boots, no greatcoats—officers in tatters and rabbit skins, men in bread bags and rags; no medicine, no shelter; toiling in mud and snow week after week, exposed in open trenches or in torn tents to the pitiless storms of a Crimean winter, fronted by a resolute and at times an enterprising enemy, and watched by the sleepless Cossack night and day from every ridge and hill top; flank and rear encamped on a plateau which was a vast black waste of sodden earth, where it was not covered with snow, dotted with little pools of foul water and seamed by brown-coloured streamlets strewn with carcasses of horses."

Reinforcements for the British army came out from home in small numbers and at irregular intervals, but the French were constantly receiving new units and more men, and by January, 1855, they had 78,000 men in camp, and took over more ground and provided a larger number of men for the actual siege operations. The losses in the trenches from the Russian fire were at this time not particularly heavy, and during some months after the close of the Battle of Inkerman, the 47th had only five men killed and nineteen wounded.

On the 6th January, 1855, it was announced that, as from the 6th of

THE CAMP OF THE 2ND DIVISION, CRIMEA.

January, 1855.

Messrs. P. & D. Colnaghi—By kind permission.

the preceding month, the establishment of the 47th Regiment was to be raised to a total of 2,218 of all ranks, contained in eight Service and eight Depot Companies, the number of each rank being approximately the same in each except so far as regards officers, the Service Companies had forty-three and the Depot Companies twenty-five only. Since, however, the numbers of the rank and file of the 47th were only 631 at the end of March, it is very clear that the reinforcements did not make up for the loss by wounds, sickness and death.

Early in April more guns and large supplies of ammunition were landed at Balaklava and brought up to the front; and by the 8th of the month something like five hundred allied guns were in position ready to open fire on the defences of Sebastopol. The bombardment opened on the 9th April and fire was kept up for ten days, much damage being done to the works and many casualties being caused among the defenders.

On the 11th March two companies from the Depot at Templemore had embarked at Cork in the " Great Britain " for conveyance to Malta, where was the advanced depot, or Provisional Battalion, composed of companies of all the Regiments of the 2nd Division. With the 47th Companies from Ireland were Captains G. W. Armit and T. Roper, Lieutenants E. Croker, J. A. Bloomfield, B. N. Garnier and R. P. Hawkes. These companies were quartered at Verdala, and on the 28th May Brevet Lieut.-Colonel Fordyce of the 47th was ordered to Malta for duty with this Provisional Battalion. In April and May nearly all the above-mentioned officers proceeded to the Crimea with drafts, and their arrival was no doubt especially welcome, for the 47th was at the time very short of officers: Captains H. M. Hamilton, W. Sankey and R. G. Ellison were employed on the staff, Captain B. W. Lowry and Lieutenant C. Finnerty were away at Scutari, while Lieutenant the Hon. B. M. Ward was also absent from the Regiment.

On the 8th May a Sardinian army had landed in the Crimea, joining hands with the British and French, and the Allied generals now decided to storm the enemy's advanced works and so confine him to his main line of defence. The works to be attacked consisted of the White Work on the north-east near the harbour, the Mamelon in front of the Malakoff, and the Quarries near the Redan. " The work known as the Quarries was situated at about 400 yards in front of the Redan, at a point where the gradual downward slope was broken by an abrupter dip, and it thus stood at what was comparatively a small eminence. The ground there had lately been occupied with heaps of stone and rubbish, but these had been replaced by a regular work, though retaining the old name."*

The fire from the batteries prior to the assault has been described as

* Hamley, *The War in the Crimea*, p. 248.

"tremendous beyond all precedent"; it continued throughout the 6th and 7th June and was remarkably effective.

The troops for the assault were furnished by the Light and 2nd Divisions, and numbered seven hundred in all, while included in this number were eight officers and three hundred men of the 47th commanded by Major J. Villiers; six hundred men were in support and the 62nd Regiment found the reserve, the whole being under the command of Colonel Shirley of the 88th Foot. At 6.30 p.m. on the 7th June the French columns under General Bosquet moved forward to the attack of the White Work and Mamelon, while on his left the British assailed the flanks of the Quarries in two columns, each two hundred strong, while three hundred more fell upon the collateral works. The enemy was swept out of the work by the first rush, but the troops pursued too far, the Russians counter-attacked and temporarily recovered the Quarries, but our men rallied and once more captured the ground.

The gallantry of the Regiment was most conspicuous on this occasion. Major Villiers was wounded early in the action, when Captain J. H. Lowndes took command, retaining it for some hours until, owing to loss of blood from a wound received earlier in the action, he was obliged to retire.

During the earlier part of the fighting Colour-Sergeant McDonald, of No. 7 Company, performed a very fine act; ammunition was running short, and although the ground between the advanced trench and the Quarries was quite open, the colour-sergeant volunteered to go and fetch a keg, bringing it in at great risk under a very heavy fire of grape, shell and musketry.

When darkness set in the firing slackened for a time, but about nine o'clock a body of Russians was seen to be advancing, the alarm was given, but after some firing the enemy retired, then coming on again and some hand-to-hand fighting took place. During that night some six attacks in all were made on the Quarries, and the most determined sortie by the enemy was made about 3 a.m. on the 8th when the whole ravine was lit up by the firing.

The gallant conduct during the action of Lance-Corporal Quinn of the Regiment is described as follows in the *United Service Magazine* for November 1856: "Suddenly Corporal Quinn uttered an exclamation, and, rushing out of the works which were not at that spot very strongly defended, our numbers being sadly thinned, I saw that, in less time than I take to describe the event, he had dashed into a group of five men, one of them an officer. Crash his musket-butt fell on the head of a luckless fellow, braining him as one cracks a nut. With a nimble turn of his strong wrist he drove his bayonet into the breast of a second, and while two others

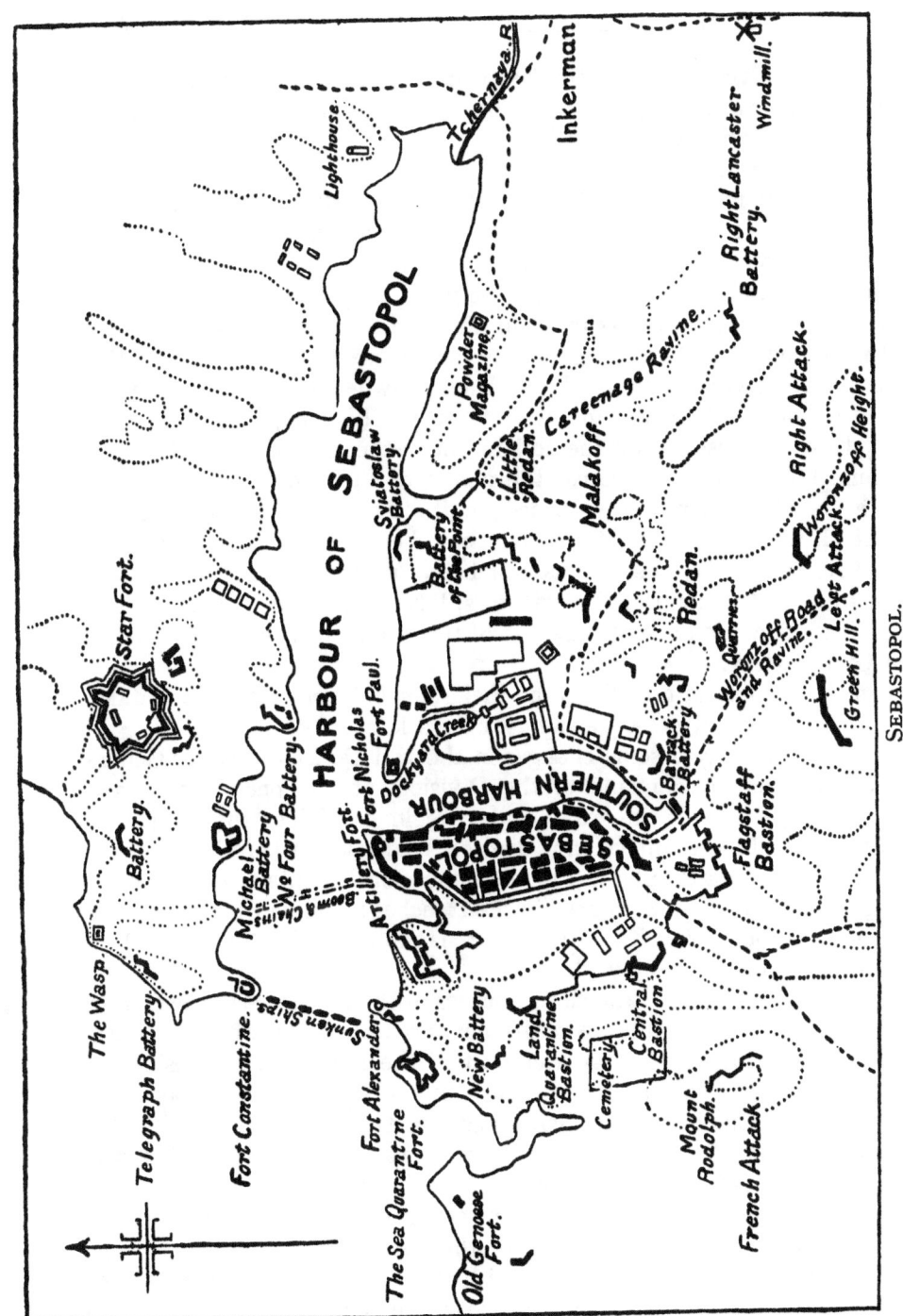

SEBASTOPOL.
1854–1855.

fled for their lives, he seized the last man by the collar, and, helping him a little with his bayonet-point, drove him into the Quarries and surrendered the Russian a prisoner to his officer, saying there were plenty more to be captured if we liked."

The sequel may be found in the *London Gazette* of the 3rd August, 1855, where we read: " 47th Foot. Sergeant Thomas Quinn to be Ensign without purchase. Dated 3rd August, 1855."

In this action the 47th had one sergeant and seventeen other ranks killed, four officers, two sergeants and fifty-seven non-commissioned officers and men wounded; the names of the officers are Major J. Villiers, Captains J. H. Lowndes and F. W. F. Hunter—who brought the Regiment out of action—and Lieutenant J. J. C. Irby. Eleven private soldiers of the 47th were missing after the action, but in the casualty rolls the words "Found killed" appear against the names of eight of the eleven.

The bombardment was reopened on the 17th June and on the 18th an attack was made upon the Redan, but the troops of the 2nd Division were held in reserve, and, the assault being unsuccessful, were not called upon to act. One man of the 47th was, however, killed by a round shot when lying down in line with the rest of the Regiment behind the Twenty-one Gun Battery.

On the evening of the 26th June Field-Marshal Lord Raglan was taken ill with cholera and passed away two days later.

In July there were some changes in the 2nd Division. Major-General Markham assumed command of the Division, and Colonel Windham of the 2nd Brigade, while the 3rd and 31st Regiments joined the Division.

In August Lieutenant Gaynor died on board ship where he had been sent for a change after illness; in the same month Captain T. Roper and Ensign A. C. Cattley were injured in the trenches; and on the 7th September Lieut.-Colonel W. O'G. Haly, Lieutenants J. M. Straton and O. G. De Lancey joined, or rejoined.

On the 8th September the closing scenes of the long siege opened, when the final combined assault upon the outworks of the great fortress was made. The 47th, with the greater part of the regiments composing the 2nd Division, was held in reserve and was not called upon to take part in the assault, but had three men killed and twenty-six wounded in the trenches; Major Rooke, of the 47th, who was acting as brigade-major to the 2nd Brigade, was severely wounded. The French attack on the Malakoff was successful, and that night the Russians evacuated the town and crossed over to the north side of the harbour.

Hostilities did not at once cease with this evacuation, but it was very evident that the end of the siege was near, the enemy blowing up certain of his defences and destroying his ships-of-war. On the 14th November there was a very serious explosion in the French artillery park, whereby much damage was done, and two sergeants and three men of the 47th were injured.

On the 6th December the establishment of the Regiment was as follows : one colonel, one lieut.-colonel, two majors, eight captains, sixteen lieutenants, eight ensigns, four staff, fifty-four sergeants, fifty corporals, twenty drummers and 950 privates.

During this second winter in the Crimea, the officers of the 47th gave a dinner to the officers of the 47th French Infantry Regiment, the ends of two huts being taken out and made to join each other in order to give the necessary room.

It was not until the 2nd April, 1856, that notification was received in the camp before Sebastopol of the signing of a treaty of peace between the warring nations, when preparations were at once made for the evacuation of the Crimea and the return of the British troops to England and other peace-time garrisons. The 47th embarked in the S.S. "Imperatrix" on the 27th May and landed at Malta on the 2nd June, when the officers were accommodated in the Auberge de Castile and the non-commissioned officers and men in the barracks in the Strada Torre.

On the 16th October, 1855, General Order No. 658 was published :—

"The Queen has been graciously pleased to command that in commemoration of the gallant conduct of the troops concerned, the words 'ALMA,' 'BALAKLAVA' and 'INKERMAN' be borne on the Regimental Colours of the Regiments specified in the accompanying list.

"Also that the several corps composing Her Majesty's Army in the Crimea on the 8th September, 1855, shall bear the inscription 'SEVASTOPOL' on the Regimental Standard, or Colour, as a memorial of the arduous and successful operations which have led to the reduction of that fortress.

"Regiments which have no Colours, or Standards, will bear those distinctions on their caps or helmet plates.

"Rifle Regiments will wear theirs on their breast plates and cap plates.

* * * * *

"47th Foot—'Alma'—'Inkerman' and 'Sevastopol.'"

In General Order No. 638 of the 13th December, 1854, the British Medal for the Crimean was authorized, with the three above-named clasps, with the addition of "Balaklava" for the Army and "Azoff" for the Navy.

The French, Sardinian and Turkish Governments also granted medals, but the last-named is the only one of which a general issue was made to the troops of the Allies.

CHAPTER X

1856-1881

HOME SERVICE AND CANADA
INTRODUCTION OF THE TERRITORIAL SYSTEM

BEFORE proceeding to recount the home service of the 47th on its return from the Crimean War, something should be said about the Depot of the Regiment.

The headquarters of the Depot seems to have remained stationary at Templemore during the greater part of the time that the remaining companies were away on active service in the field, but companies were occasionally sent away on detachment for periods of varying length, and on one occasion, in July, 1856, men from the Depot Companies of the various regiments at Templemore were ordered to Nenagh owing to some trouble with the Militia there quartered. In the disturbance which there took place the 47th had two men wounded.

The Depot Companies occupied quarters at Cashel and Fermoy, at this last-named station forming part of the 2nd Depot Battalion, commanded by Lieut.-Colonel Farren of the 47th. In August, 1857, the Depot was reduced from four to two companies.

We left the Service Companies of the Regiment at Malta on return from the Crimea, and they remained here until the 27th May, 1857, when they sailed for Gibraltar, arriving there on the 3rd June and being quartered first at Windmill Hill and then on the North Front. The 47th remained, however, only some six weeks at Gibraltar, for on the 18th August it embarked in H.M.S. "Conqueror," and sailed for Portsmouth, landing here on the 25th and being joined in the following March by a large draft from the Depot, due to the reduction in strength of the Depot above recorded. Two captains, four subalterns, ten sergeants, four drummers, ten corporals and 190 privates now joined regimental headquarters.

During the years 1857-58 Second Battalions were raised for some of the senior regiments of the British Army, and a large number of ten-year men of the 47th took their discharge and re-enlisted in some of these new

LIEUT.-COLONEL R. T. FARREN.

1855.

*General Sir Richard T. Farren, G.C.B.,
Colonel, The Loyal North Lancashire Regiment, 1885-1909.*

battalions, many going to the 2nd Battalion 6th Foot, to which Lieut.-Colonel Lowndes, late of the 47th, and a very popular officer, had recently exchanged. An officer of the 47th was at this time promoted into the new Second Battalion of the 22nd Regiment; this was Lieutenant O. G. De Lancey, who, on the voyage from Malta to Gibraltar, jumped overboard at night in the endeavour to save the life of Private Dempsey, who had fallen into the sea. Lieutenant De Lancey was in the water for an hour before he was picked up.

On the 8th July, 1858, the Regiment moved from Portsmouth to Aldershot, encamping during July on Cove Common and then moving in the second week of August into the Centre Block of the Permanent Barracks in the South Camp.

New Colours were presented to the 47th Regiment on the 19th November, 1858, by Major-General Sir James Yorke Scarlett, K.C.B., commanding the South-Western District, the Reverend G. R. Gleig, Chaplain to the Forces, conducting the service. The General Officer Commanding addressed the Regiment in very eulogistic terms, referring to the past services of the Corps in many fields. The old Colours are now in St. Mary's Church, Lancaster.

H.M. Queen Victoria, accompanied by H.R.H. the Prince Consort, visited Aldershot on the 30th November, 1858, and inspected the Division. The troops, who were in marching order, some thirteen thousand men of all arms, marched past Her Majesty in column of route near Frimley; the 47th Regiment being in the 3rd Brigade.

On the 20th August, 1859, the 47th, at a strength of thirty-five officers and 777 non-commissioned officers and men, proceeded to Shorncliffe, from where it provided a considerable detachment of seven officers and two hundred other ranks to Deptford; from Shorncliffe, the Regiment marched to Dover, arriving there in April, 1860, and occupying quarters in the Citadel and Shaft Barracks. During the musketry season of 1860–61, the 47th enjoyed the distinction of being the best shooting corps in the British Army, the figure of merit being 48·24, and the percentage of first-class shots, 47·00. No. 4, or Captain Bloomfield's Company, was the best shooting company, its figure of merit being 53·36. Much of the credit for the good shooting reputation of the 47th at this time is due to Lieutenant Newman, who held the appointment of musketry instructor from June, 1857, to June, 1863.

During these last years the Depot Companies of the 47th remained in Ireland, being quartered at, among other stations, Fermoy, Bandon, Cork and Athlone.

In April, 1861, the Regiment itself moved to Dublin where it was quartered in Ship Street Barracks ; but its stay in Ireland was of the very briefest, for on the 15th June it embarked at Kingstown, under the command of Colonel T. C. Kelly, C.B., in the S.S. " Golden Fleece," for Canada, the embarkation strength being thirty-five officers, forty-four sergeants, thirty-eight corporals, twenty-one drummers and 761 privates. Quebec was reached on the 2nd July, and on disembarking the Regiment was sent up the river in steamers to Montreal, where it arrived on the 5th July, when the companies were distributed as follows : six companies at Logan's Farm and the remaining four at St. Helen's Island, the whole being concentrated in the Quebec Gate Barracks in the City of Montreal by the end of August. Some months later detachments were furnished to St. Lamberts under Lieutenant King and to the Isle-aux-Noix under command of Major Villiers.

After a stay of some eighteen months in Montreal, the Regiment left and arrived at Kingston, Ontario, on the 27th May, 1863, one wing being quartered in the old Tête du Pont Barracks and in Fort Henry overlooking the lake : here the Regiment remained for just a year, leaving again at the end of May and proceeding, mainly by march route, to Hamilton, Crystal Palace, Shaver's Farm, Brantford, encamping here on the banks of the Grand River, and on by Burford, Woodstock and Putmanville to London which was reached on the 9th June and where the Regiment was put up in the Royal and Palace Barracks. Having completed a stay of three months in London, the Regiment marched back by the same route to Hamilton, and remained here from the 14th September, 1864, to April, 1865. It was then moved to Toronto and was quartered in the Parliament Buildings and in the Old Fort ; and it was while stationed here that trouble broke out on the Canadian-American frontier, necessitating the employment of the 47th in the restoration of peace and order.

" In 1865 the Fenians in the United States, constantly recruited by emigrants from Ireland and numbering many who had gained military experience during the Civil War, planned an invasion of Canada, under the delusion that they would have the sympathy, if not the open support, of the powers in Washington. Canada, realizing at once the weakness of her defensive forces, and urged on by the Governor-General, set to work to reorganize her militia. In May, 1866, the long-expected invasion by the Fenians took place,* and early on the morning of the 1st June their leader, one " General " O'Neill, crossed the Niagara River from Buffalo to Fort Erie with some twelve hundred men.

On the news reaching Toronto, Major-General Napier, who was then commanding in Canada West, dispatched a Volunteer Brigade from Toronto

* *Life of Lord Wolseley*, pp. 39-42.

and Hamilton to oppose the raiders, and the Volunteers came into action with the Fenians at Limestone Ridge on the 2nd June, but fell back after a smart skirmish. In the meantime Regular troops were being collected, and two hundred of the 47th under Major Lodder, with a field battery, and followed later by another one hundred and fifty of the Regiment under Brevet Lieut.-Colonel Villiers, were railed to the suspension bridge at Niagara Falls, which was considered a place where the invaders might attempt a crossing. Here a column was formed, composed of the above-mentioned troops, the headquarter companies of the 16th Foot and one thousand Volunteers, the whole under Colonel Peacock of the 16th. On the next day another body of troops was sent on—another field battery, more of the 16th, the 60th Rifles and five hundred Volunteers—all these under Colonel Lowry of the 47th who was to assume command on the Niagara Frontier.

Early on the 3rd June this force, numbering 3,300 men, reoccupied Fort Erie, the Fenians—excepting some fifty or sixty who were captured—effecting their escape or being arrested by the United States Gunboat "Michigan" which was patrolling the river. Another body of Fenians had assembled about Ogdensburg, opposite Prescott, on the frontier of Lower Canada; these were watched by a body of Volunteers, while a field force, included in which was the party of the 47th under Major Lodder, the whole under Colonel Pakenham, 30th Foot, was formed at Cornwall, sixty miles west of Montreal, as a precautionary measure. This force numbered nearly 2,400 men in all, and was divided into two bodies, one under Major Lodder. No invasion, however, took place at this point, though there was some skirmishing, and the Fenians were finally driven back across the frontier.

The Cornwall Field Force was now gradually reduced, and the various detachments of the 47th rejoined headquarters at Toronto on the 19th and 20th June and the 4th July. Then on the 16th the whole Regiment embarked in the S.S. "Grecian" and "Kingston" for Montreal where it arrived on the 17th, being then transhipped to the river steamer "Montreal" and conveyed via Quebec to Halifax, which was reached on the 25th. Here the 47th occupied quarters in the Wellington Barracks.

During the past year a change had been introduced in the designations of the companies of regiments: in Horse Guards Memorandum No. 343 of the 10th June, 1865, it was laid down that companies were to be known by letters instead of by numbers as heretofore—the titles of "Grenadier" and "Light" Companies had already been abolished some seven years earlier in an Order issued on the 29th January, 1858.

In 1867 the Snider breech-loading rifle was issued and was taken into use in the Regiment on the 9th September.

The 47th embarked at Halifax for Barbados on the 29th December, 1868, the headquarters and seven and a half companies under Colonel Lowry in the "Simoom," and the remainder under Major Fitzroy in the "Barracouta". Landing on the 6th January, 1869, headquarters and six companies were quartered at St. Ann's—the same barracks the Regiment had occupied twenty-eight years previously—when the rest of the 47th was disposed as follows : one and a half companies to St. Vincent under Captain Waddilove and two and a half to Trinidad under Lieut.-Colonel Villiers. The establishment of the Regiment was reduced from the 1st April, 1869, to 631 of all ranks.

This year the 47th returned home, embarking at Barbados in H.M.S. "Himalaya" on the 4th December, and, picking up the detachments at Trinidad and St. Vincent, finally disembarked at Kingstown on the 20th of the month, going on thence by rail to the Curragh. Here the Regiment remained until the 13th January, 1870, when it moved to Dublin and was there quartered in Richmond Barracks.

The following movements to the North of Ireland took place during this year in aid of the Civil Power: on the 30th June, "A" and "B" Companies, under command of Captain E. P. Newman, proceeded to Lurgan, and on the 1st July "F" and "K" Companies to Armagh, under Captain J. M. Straton. "K," under Captain H. Gem, was later sent to Cookstown, having been relieved at Armagh by "E" Company, under command of Captain F. G. Berkeley, and on the 9th Colonel Lowry was ordered to Portadown to take command of all the troops there assembled. Finally, on July 11th "D" and "I" Companies were sent to Dungannon under Lieut.-Colonel Villiers. All these detachments returned to Dublin between the 13th and 16th July.

The outbreak of the Franco-Prussian War of 1870 was not without its effect on the establishment of the British Army, and on the 26th August, the strength of the 47th was ordered to be raised from five hundred to seven hundred rank and file.

In the latter part of September the Regiment was called upon to furnish many detachments in the south-western part of Ireland, and companies were at different times and for varying periods sent to Clare, Nenagh, Gort, Clare Castle, Oughterard, Galway and Carrick-on-Suir.

Under the terms of a Royal Warrant dated the 20th July, 1871, the purchase of commissions in the Army was done away with, and the new regulations regarding the granting of commissions were published in General Order No. 89 of this year ; at the same time the ranks of Cornet and Ensign were abolished and all first commissions gazetted after the 26th August, 1871, were to the rank of Sub-Lieutenant. The last company sold in the

47th Regiment under the old Regulations was purchased by Lieutenant L. de F. Prevost *vice* Captain W. Fitz W. Smithwick for £1,500 : over regulation price.

On the 23rd September, 1871, the Regiment embarked for Liverpool, and on landing the Right Wing, with Headquarters, proceeded to Fleetwood and the Left Wing, under Major Waddilove, to Carlisle ; and from these stations the 47th was sent in the early autumn of 1873 to take part in manœuvres at Cannock Chase, an advanced form of military training which had only been introduced two years previously. The 47th was in the 2nd Brigade of the 1st Division with the 33rd and 35th Regiments and the 6th West York Militia. The manœuvres over, the Regiment was sent to Preston.

In the year 1873 a change of very considerable importance took place, when, resulting from the Reports of a Parliamentary Committee, which had been for some time past in session, on the subject of the " Organization of the various Military Forces of the Country," General Order No. 18 was issued on the 3rd March, 1873, under which a new scheme was introduced for the localization of the Army. A system of Brigade Depots in certain of the towns of the United Kingdom was set on foot, and the regiments of the Army were linked together, for the most part in pairs, for recruiting purposes, it being intended that the regiment on the home establishment should receive the recruits from the Depot, train them and provide drafts for the linked regiment abroad. Under the terms of this Order the 47th was to be linked with the 81st Regiment, the two forming the Preston Brigade Depot of No. 12 Sub-District. Then in General Order No. 22 of the same year certain battalions of the Auxiliary Forces were associated with the Regular Regiments of the Army, and the following units were now to compose the 12th Brigade Depot :—47th (Lancashire) Regiment ; 81st Loyal Lincoln Volunteers ; 3rd Royal Lancashire Militia ; 6th Administrative Battalion, Lancashire Rifle Volunteers ; 27th Lancashire Rifle Volunteer Corps.

The Depot Barracks at Preston were not at this time ready for occupation, and the Depot Companies of the 47th and 81st Regiments continued to move from one station to another with the headquarters of the first-named Regiment. It was not indeed until the month of June, 1877, that " I " and " K " Companies of the 47th and the Depot Companies of the 81st were separated from the Service Companies of the Regiment, leaving to form the 12th Brigade Depot at Preston. The Official Army List for October, 1877, gives for the first time the names of the following officers as composing the 12th Brigade Depot : Colonel R. W. Lowry, C.B., Major G. Waddilove, 47th, Captains G. V. Boyd, 47th, J. C. Bell, 47th, and G. B.

Bevan, 81st ; Lieutenants W. H. R. Gunner, 47th, R. K. Brereton, 81st, and N. D'E. Roberts, 81st ; Sub-Lieutenant H. G. Leonard, 47th ; Hon. Major J. Falls, 8th Regt., Acting Paymaster.

In the first week of July, 1874, the Regiment moved to Aldershot and occupied huts in " A," " B " and " C " Lines in the North Camp ; in December the Martini-Henry rifle was issued in place of the Snider, and in January, 1875, a new valise equipment replaced the old knapsack.

On the 1st July, 1876, the 47th left Aldershot by train for Portsmouth and there embarked in H.M.S. " Assistance " for Jersey ; disembarkation took place on the 8th when headquarters and six companies proceeded under the command of Major J. M. Straton to St. Peter's. " B " Company to Greve de Lecq and " C " Company to Rozel. The stay of the Regiment in Jersey was, however, of the shortest, for on the 8th June, 1877, it was re-embarked in the " Assistance " and sailed by way of Liverpool to Kingstown, arriving here on the 14th June, when three companies were dispatched to the Curragh—whence two companies were later detached to Castlebar—while headquarters proceeded to Athlone.

However short the Regiment's stay in Jersey may have been, it appears to have been long enough to establish an excellent reputation among the inhabitants of that Island, as may be seen by the following tribute which was sent to the 47th on its departure :—

" Resolved :

" That the admirable conduct of the soldiers of Her Majesty's 47th Regiment and of the Depot of Her Majesty's 81st Regiment during the time in which they have been on duty in this Island having been brought under the notice of the Assembly, this Assembly has decided, at this its first meeting since their departure, to express the great satisfaction they feel in common with the inhabitants at being able to testify to the friendly feelings which these Regiments have inspired, and to the exemplary behaviour of all ranks during their stay here.

(sd.) " W. L. D<small>E</small> G<small>RUCHY</small>,
" Constable of St. Helier's.

" *June* 21*st*, 1877."

While quartered at Athlone and the Curragh the Regiment furnished detachments to Sligo, Boyle and Westport, but in April, 1878, the whole Regiment was concentrated in Richmond Barracks, Dublin.

During the year 1878 Russia and Turkey were engaged in hostilities, and at one time it seemed by no means improbable that Great Britain might become embroiled, and that it might be necessary for her, as in 1854, to take up arms against Russia in alliance with Turkey. By a Royal Proclamation dated the 2nd April, the Army and Militia Reserves were called up, seven thousand Indian troops were ordered to Malta, and all the regiments on the home establishments were placed upon a war footing. The strength of the 47th Regiment was now fixed at the following : one colonel, one lieut.-colonel, one major, eight captains, eight lieutenants, eight second-lieutenants,* one adjutant, one quartermaster, fifty sergeants, forty corporals, sixteen drummers and 960 privates. Between the 1st April and the 6th May, 235 men of the First Class Army Reserve and 209 men of the 3rd Royal Lancashire Militia Reserve were posted to the Regiment for duty, making a total of 1,093 non-commissioned officers and men.

This was the first occasion upon which the Army and Militia Reserves appear to have been called out since the passing of the Reserve Force and Militia Reserve Force Acts in 1867 ; but when the Acts first became operative the First Class Army Reserve and the Militia Reserve numbered only 3,545 men in all, though these constituted the only force available for the first line for active service. In 1870, however, when the Army Enlistment Act was introduced, the strength of the Army Reserve was estimated at 23,000 men ; this number continued to increase, so that when on the 8th March, 1901, the Secretary of State for War moved the Army Estimates, he was able to say : " After thirty years Lord Cardwell's system, with but slight modification, gave us 80,000 Reservists, of whom 96 or 97 per cent. were found efficient, and has enabled us to keep an army of 150,000 Regulars in the field for fifteen months."

In June, 1878, the Army and Militia Reserves made a splendid response to the call and the number of absentees was practically negligible.

Before the end of July the efforts of diplomacy had brought into being the Congress of Berlin and the peace of Europe remained undisturbed ; then, in accordance with the terms of special Army Circular of the 20th July, 1878, all the Reservists were struck off the strength of the 47th Regiment from the 31st of that month, and were dispersed to their homes.

On the 1st August the number of non-commissioned officers and men to be now borne on the strength of the Regiment was reduced to 658 ; on the 1st January, 1879, the number of these was raised again to 718, and on the 1st May of the same year the number of sergeants, rank and file were once more increased to 840.

In July, 1878, the new pattern helmet was issued to the infantry of the Army in the place of the old shako.

On the 9th August of this year the headquarters went from Dublin to

* The rank of Second-Lieutenant was substituted for Sub-Lieutenant under Royal Warrant for December, 1876.

the Curragh, and during some two and a half months of the summer of 1879 " A " and " H " Companies garrisoned Spike Island in Queenstown Harbour under the command of Captain A. C. Yard, while early in 1880 " C " Company, under Captain C. V. Trotter, provided a detachment at Tuam.

At the end of October of this year the Regiment left the Curragh for Dublin, where the Headquarter Companies occupied Beggar's Bush Barracks, while three companies under Major Dudley North were quartered in Ship Street Barracks.

On leaving the Curragh Major-General C. C. Fraser, V.C., C.B., issued the following farewell order :—

> " Curragh Camp, *22nd October*, 1880.
> " Major-General Fraser regrets that he was unable personally to bid farewell to the 47th Regiment on leaving the Curragh Brigade ; but feels he cannot allow them to depart after a sojourn of upwards of three years without placing on record his opinion of the unvarying good conduct, general soldier-like bearing and ready compliance with orders of all ranks of the Regiment, which was so ably commanded by Colonel Fitzroy. Major-General Fraser feels confident that in whatever station the 47th Regiment may be quartered, it will continue to maintain under command of Lieut.-Colonel Straton the good old customs and that reputation for good conduct, proficiency in drill and field sports, in which it so excelled during its stay at the Curragh.
> " By Order,
> (sd.) " H. G. L. CRICHTON, Captain,
> " Brigade-Major."

In accordance with General Orders of the 1st June, 1880, a new-pattern forage cap was taken into wear, and the rank badges for officers, hitherto worn on the collar, were transferred to the shoulder-straps.

During the months that now followed many detachments were found from headquarters in Dublin—to Boyle, to Ballyshannon, to Pigeon House Fort and to Tullamore ; and during the same period there was more than one change in the establishment of the Regiment.

On the 1st April, 1881, it was directed that the establishment should stand at twenty-four officers, fifty sergeants, forty corporals and 910 privates ; but on the 14th and 18th May these numbers, of the lower ranks, were increased by drafts received from the 8th, 14th, 59th and 82nd Regiments, numbering in all 208, and bringing the strength of the 47th in private soldiers alone up to the large total of 977.

This now brings us up to the time when the 47th Regiment was to experience the greatest and most far-reaching change which had befallen it during its one hundred and forty years of Army life.

In the year 1877 a Committee, of which Colonel Stanley, Financial Secretary to the War Office, was president, expressed the opinion that the connection should be made closer between the Line Battalions of a Brigade and the Militia Battalions of a Sub-District ; and stated that "this could best be effected by their being treated as one Regiment, such regiment bearing a Territorial designation, the Line Battalions being the 1st and 2nd, the Militia Battalions being the 3rd and 4th, etc., of such Territorial Regiment, the Depot being common to all and being the last battalion of the series."

On the 23rd December, 1880, a small Committee of seven senior Army officers was appointed, with the Adjutant-General as chairman, to consider whether the proposals of Colonel Stanley's Committee should or should not be adopted ; and assuming they were adopted, to determine the following questions, as specially affecting regimental *esprit de corps* :—

1. The Territorial designation which the Regiment should bear, and whether it were desirable to readjust the combinations of the present linked battalions, having due regard to the extreme inconvenience likely to be caused by any alterations.

2. The Record of Victories on the Colours.

3. Arrangements for uniformity of clothing for the Territorial Regiments, including the Militia Battalions.

The Report of this Committee was published on the 25th February, 1881, and it was accompanied by an appendix showing the composition of the proposed Territorial Regiments ; it was adopted so far as concerned the general principles governing its proposals ; and on the 11th April, 1881, General Order No. 41 was published and—in view of its extreme importance—is here given practically in full.

"1. The following changes in the organization, titles and uniform of the Infantry of the Line and Militia having been approved, are promulgated for general information. Where not otherwise stated, they will come into effect on 1st July, 1881.

"2. The Infantry of the Line and Militia will in future be organized in Territorial Regiments, each of four battalions for England, Scotland and Wales, and of five battalions for Ireland ; the 1st and 2nd of these being Line Battalions and the remainder Militia. These regiments will bear a territorial designation corresponding to the localities with which they are connected, and the words ' Regimental District ' will in future be used in place of ' Sub-District ' hitherto employed.

"3. In those Regimental Districts where more than the requisite number of Militia Battalions at present exists, the supernumerary battalions will either be converted into Artillery or Engineers, or absorbed, according to circumstances. In those where only one exists, another will be found as soon as practicable. . . .

"8. All distinctions, mottoes, badges or devices, appearing hitherto in the Army List, or on the Colours, as worn by either of the Line Battalions of a Territorial Regiment, will in future be borne by both those Battalions. Battalions which have not hitherto borne a special device, will adopt a national badge, as follows :—

English Regiments	A Rose.
Scotch ,,	A Thistle.
Irish ,,	A Shamrock.
Welsh ,,	A Dragon.

"9. With the exceptions noted in para. 13* the uniform of all the Battalions of a Territorial Regiment will be the same. The title of the Regiment will be shown on the shoulder-strap.

"10. The facings, and the Officers' lace of Territorial Regiments will be the same for all Regiments belonging to the same Country (Royal and Rifle Regiments excepted), and will be as follows :
English and Welsh Regiments, Facings white, pattern of Lace, Rose.
Scotch Regiments, Facings yellow, pattern of Lace, Thistle.
Irish Regiments, Facings green, pattern of Lace, Shamrock.

"11. Royal Regiments will retain blue facings, wearing the national lace. The black line will be maintained in the lace of Territorial Regiments, any of whose battalions are now authorized to wear it. . . .

"14. The accompanying tables show the precedence, composition, title and uniform of the new Territorial Regiments. . . .

"16. Changes of facings and alterations in badges (for battalions in which these and the Officers' lace only are changed) will come into effect, both for the Line and the Militia as regards the men, on 1st July, 1881. Officers newly appointed to these battalions will at once provide themselves with uniform in accordance with these instructions and other Officers in them as they may require to replace that now in possession. . . .''

In the tables mentioned in para. 14 of the above-quoted General Order, the Title of the new Territorial Regiment of which the 47th was now to form part, is given as " The North Lancashire Regiment," having precedence as 45th and the composition of the Regiment being given as under :—

1st Bn.	47th Foot.
2nd ,,	81st Foot.
3rd ,,	3rd Royal Lancashire Militia.
4th ,,	3rd Royal Lancashire Militia.

* Refers to Scotch or Highland Regiments only.

The Headquarters of the Regimental District was to be at Preston: the uniform scarlet; facings white; pattern of lace, Rose.

In General Order No. 70, however, specially issued on the 30th June, 1881, it is laid down in para. 1 that certain changes had been sanctioned in the composition and titles of Territorial Regiments, as laid down in General Order No. 41, and in Appendix A, published with G.O. 70, we read that the title of the Regiment is now to be "The Loyal North Lancashire Regiment," the number of the Regimental District being 47.

The following are the names of the Officers who were serving in the 47th Regiment when its old number was done away with and its designation changed: Lieut.-General Sir W. S. R. Norcott, K.C.B., Colonel of the Regiment; Lieut.-Colonel J. M. Straton; Majors W. B. G. Cleather and F. G. Berkeley; Captains D. North (Brevet Major), A. C. B. Hall, V. R. Biscoe, W. L. Wreford, H. Cooper, A. C. Yard, W. H. R. Gunner, C. V. Trotter, C. E. Sawyer, S. Jackson, E. C. Morris and H. S. B. Hodgkinson (Adjutant); Lieutenants D. de Hoghton, D. A. G. Lascelles, A. J. Lees, H. R. Day, H. G. Leonard, N. A. K. Burne, H. A. Taylor (Instructor of Musketry), F. W. Jones, J. R. Fraser, J. B. W. Atkin and W. H. E. Murray; 2nd Lieutenants, H. F. Coleridge, G. A. Norcott, G. W. H. Le Feuvre and G. W. Dowell; Paymaster G. H. Moore-Lane; and Quartermaster J. Donnelly.

THE 81st REGIMENT OF FOOT

CHAPTER XI

1793–1803

THE RAISING OF THE 81st REGIMENT
THE WEST INDIES AND THE CAPE OF GOOD HOPE

BEFORE proceeding to recount the origin and the services of the Regiment, which, raised as the 81st Foot, became in course of time the 2nd Battalion The Loyal North Lancashire Regiment, something must very briefly be said about two other Regiments of the Line, which were raised under and for a very short period bore the number 81.

The first of these, known as the 81st Invalids, was raised by Colonel Alexander, Lord Lindores, on the 7th April, 1758, at Bristol and was mainly formed of veterans of the Flanders campaign. When first raised it was quartered in the Island of Guernsey and was later employed on garrison duty in Germany. After the peace of 1763 it was re-numbered the 71st Invalids, being finally disbanded in 1769. The colour of the facings of this regiment was green.

The second Regiment to be numbered 81st was raised at Stirling by Colonel the Hon. William Gordon of Fyvie, brother of the Earl of Aberdeen, under a Letter of Service issued in March, 1777, but the date of the commissions of all the officers first appointed is the 19th December, 1777. Very shortly after being raised the Regiment was sent to Ireland, but in 1782 it was brought over to Portsmouth with a view to its being embarked for India. The men had all, however, been enlisted either for three years only or for the duration of the war, and on their raising the very strongest objection to being shipped off to the Far East for an indefinite period, the embarkation orders were cancelled and the Regiment was sent back to Edinburgh, where it was disbanded in April, 1783.

The third Regiment raised as the 81st—now the 2nd Battalion The Loyal North Lancashire Regiment—came into being at the time of the outbreak of the War with Revolutionary France, the Government of which country had declared war against England in February, 1793. The British Army of that day was not only very weak in numbers, but the units of which it was composed were widely scattered, since of the eighty-one battalions which the Army at this date contained, there were no more than twenty-eight on home service. They were all of them, moreover, greatly below strength, the whole of the twenty-eight battalions not mustering more than fifteen thousand effective men, and in point of fact there was hardly a single battalion which could muster more than half its establishment.

It was now, somewhat belatedly and hurriedly, resolved to increase the British Army, and between August, 1793, and December, 1794, the total additions to the Regular Army amounted to no fewer than fourteen regiments of cavalry and seventy-four battalions of infantry; it must, however, be stated that some of these last do not appear to have ever been actually formed, while others were no more than recruiting regiments and existed for drafting purposes only.

The Letter of Service for the raising of the new 81st Regiment is as follows:—

"War Office,
"23rd September, 1793.

"SIR,—

"I am commanded to acquaint you that His Majesty approves of your raising a Regiment of Foot, without any allowance of Levy money, to be completed within three months upon the following terms, viz.:—

"The Corps is to consist of one company of Grenadiers, one of Light Infantry, and eight Battalion Companies. The Grenadier Company is to consist of one Captain, two Lieutenants, three Sergeants, three Corporals, two Drummers, two Fifers and fifty-seven Private men.

"The Light Infantry Company of one Captain, two Lieutenants, three Sergeants, three Corporals, two Drummers and fifty-seven Private men: and each Battalion Company of one Captain, one Lieutenant, one Ensign, three Sergeants, three Corporals, two Drummers and fifty-seven Private men; together with the Staff Officers, and with a Sergeant-Major and Quartermaster-Sergeant, exclusive of the Sergeants above specified. The Captain Lieutenant is, as usual, included in the number of Lieutenants above mentioned.

"The Corps is to have one Lieutenant-Colonel and one Major, each with a Company; and it is to be under your command, as Colonel with a company.

"The pay of Officers is to commence from the date of their commissions, and that of the Non-Commissioned Officers and Privates from the date of their attestations.

"His Majesty is pleased to leave to you the nomination of the Officers of the Regiment, but the Lieutenant-Colonel and Majors are to be taken from the list of Lieutenant-Colonels or Majors on half-pay, or the Major from the Captains on half-pay. Six of the Captains are to be taken from the half-pay, and the other Captain and Captain Lieutenant from the list of Captains or Captain Lieutenants on half-pay, or from Lieutenants on full pay. All the Lieutenants are to be taken from the half-pay. And the Gentlemen recommended to be Ensigns are not to be under sixteen years of age.

"No Officer, however, is to be taken from half-pay, who received the difference on going upon the half-pay, nor is any Officer coming from the half-pay to contribute any money towards the Levy; but he may be required to raise such a quota of men as may be agreed on between you and him.

"The person to be recommended for Quartermaster must not also be proposed for any other commission.

"In case the Corps shall be reduced after it has been established, the Officers will be entitled to half-pay.

"No man is to be enlisted above thirty-five years of age, nor under five feet five inches high. Well-made growing lads, between sixteen and eighteen years of age, may be taken at five feet four inches.

"The recruits are to be engaged without limitation as to the period or place of their service.

"The Non-Commissioned Officers and Privates are to be inspected by a General Officer, who will reject all such as are unfit for service, or not enlisted in conformity to this letter.

"In the execution of this, I take leave to assure you of every assistance which my office can afford.

"I have, etc.,

(sd.) "GEO. YONGE.

"To Colonel Albemarle Bertie,
  "1st Foot Guards."

The services and dates of commissions of this officer are as under:—
Ensign, 1st Foot Guards, 1.3.1762; lieut. and captain, 30.8.1769; captain and lieut.-colonel, 1.4.1776; colonel, 20.11.1782; third major, 12.3.1789; second major, 8.8.1792; colonel, 81st Foot, 23.9.1793; major-general, 12.10.1793; colonel, 9th Foot, 31.12.1794; lieut.-general, 1.1.1798; general, 25.9.1803; colonel, 77th Foot, 18.6.1804; colonel, 89th Foot, 23.3.1808; Died at Uffington House, near Stamford, 17.9.1818. He seems to have seen no active service in the field. Succeeded as Duke of Ancaster and Marquis of Lindsey, 9.2.1809.

MAJOR-GENERAL ALBEMARLE BERTIE.
Colonel
The 81st Regiment
1793—1794.

In the *Lincoln, Rutland and Stamford Mercury* for the 20th September, 1793, it is announced that "the following offers for raising corps have been accepted and their letters of service have been issued in the usual form, viz.: Lord Paget, Lord Eardley, Lieutenant Colonel de Burgh and Lieutenant Colonel Bertie." As the regiment raised by the first named of these four officers was numbered the 80th, Colonel Bertie's regiment would have been numbered 83rd instead of 81st, had each of the others raised a regiment in the order given; but Lord Eardley and Colonel de Burgh failed in their efforts, thus leaving Colonel Bertie's corps to become the 81st. It seems, however, that this Regiment was actually known as the 83rd for a short time, as appears from the following recruiting advertisement, printed in the above-named paper on the 25th October, 1793:—

"Old England for Ever.
"Honour and Glory.

"A large bounty will be given to all Loyal Lincolnshire Volunteers, or 83rd new-raised Regiment, commanded by the Right Hon. Major-General Albemarle Bertie, Colonel of The Lincolnshire Volunteers, and the Hon. Lieut. Colonel Lewes.
"Those Loyal Heroes, who, ambitious of gaining Glory in the Honorable Profession of Arms, have now an opportunity of entering a Regiment, where Honor and Happiness, will be sure to reward their noble exertions for their King and Country, and a liberal pension will soften the sorrows of declining life, and procure a more comfortable competence than can be acquired by many years of hard labour. Every Hero will be provided with genteel clothing, fit for a Gentleman Soldier.
"Boys, five feet four inches high, under twenty years of age, and men, five feet five, above that age to thirty-five, will be accepted.
"The present moment calls for the exertion of all good subjects for a short period, and it is believed will be very short indeed.
"Young men of abilities will be preferred to Sergeants and Corporals by applying to the Commanding Officers, Headquarters, Lincoln: or to Sergeant-Major Fawkner, Stamford.
"Bringers of good recruits will be liberally rewarded.

"God Save The King."

The new Regiment was raised at Lincoln under the title of the "Loyal Lincoln Volunteers," and the Militia of the County came forward as a body to serve in it.

The *London Gazette* of the 28th January, 1794, contains the following appointments of officers to the "81st Regiment of Foot":—

"Major-General Albemarle Bertie, from the 1st Foot Guards, to be Colonel.
"Major John Lewes, from the 64th Foot, to be Lieutenant-Colonel.
"Captain Boyd Manningham, from the 39th Foot, to be Major.

"*To be Captains of Companies*

"Captain Andrew Despard, from the half-pay of the late 79th Foot.
"Captain John Watling, from the half-pay of the late 79th Foot.
"Captain Andrew Bernard, from the half-pay of the 27th Foot.
"Captain Martin Eccles Lindsay, from the half-pay of the late 101st Foot.
"Lieutenant Richard Lewen Glyn, from an Independent Company.
"Lieutenant Robert MacFarlane, from the 59th Foot.
"Lieutenant William Tennant, from an Independent Company.

"*To be Captain Lieutenant*

"Lieutenant Henry Andrews, from Lieut.-General Campbell's Regiment.

"*To be Lieutenants*

"Lieutenant Daniel Watling, from the half-pay of the late 79th Foot.
"Ensign Guy Hughes, from the 47th Foot.
"Ensign Hugh Andrews, from an Independent Company.
"Ensign Andrew Gemmell, from an Independent Company.
"Ensign Francis Bowzer, from Major-General Balfour's Regiment.

"*To be Ensign*

"John Otto Beyer, Gent.

"*To be Adjutant*

"William Dalrymple, Gent.

"*To be Quartermaster*

"William Smith, Gent."

On first raising, the 81st was quartered at Lincoln and Gainsborough, but on the 23rd January, 1794, it marched by way of Chester to Liverpool where it embarked for Ireland and proceeded to the north. Its stay in Ireland was but a short one, for at the end of July the Regiment embarked at Belfast for Bristol, at which port it arrived on the 3rd August, marching a few days later, and in three divisions, to Windsor, Richmond and Hampton Court. Not here either was the Regiment to make more than the very briefest sojourn, for on the 27th September, 1794, it embarked at Southampton to take part in an expedition designed to operate against the French West Indian Islands.

Two years before an expedition, naval and military, had been sent out from England to attempt the capture of the French Windward Islands, and although at first our efforts had been successful, the arrival of large French reinforcements had caused the loss of all our earlier captures, our seamen and troops had suffered terribly from the climate, and there had been a very serious native rebellion instigated by emissaries from the French Directory. At the end of 1793 the British force in the West Indies was so seriously reduced that the British commander at Martinique had barely two thousand men available for the defence of nearly a dozen different islands.

Reinforcements, though repeatedly promised, were not sent, and it was not until early in 1794 that the British Cabinet, realizing how very serious was the state of affairs in these distant possessions, decided that an expeditionary force must be sent thither; it was not, however, until the autumn of this year that the commander was appointed and the troops detailed.

The commander's instructions were to sail direct to Barbados, deal first with the Islands of Guadaloupe and St. Lucia, and then consider the feasibility of an attack upon the Dutch Settlements of Surinam, Berbice and Demerara.

The force embarked in one hundred and fifty-eight transports, escorted by a squadron under Rear-Admiral Christian, and proceeded down Channel with a favourable breeze; it had not, however, sailed beyond Weymouth when the wind changed and became a furious gale. Some of the ships got safely into Weymouth and Portland, but seven of the transports were lost. When on the 3rd December the fleet put to sea again, it once more met a violent gale, and while some of the transports struggled on to Barbados, others put back again to English ports and others again were captured by French cruisers. The ships containing the 81st did not reach the original rendezvous off the Island of Jersey before the month of February, and it was the end of March before the transports with the Regiment on board arrived in Carlisle Bay, Barbados, to be met here by orders to sail on to the French Island of San Domingo, where a contest was being carried on between our troops and the French Republican forces.

The 81st arrived off the Mole, St. Nicholas, San Domingo, on the 6th April, 1795, and here the Regiment was obliged to remain inactive until

December, for the prevalent fever had so reduced the British garrison that offensive operations on any large scale were quite out of the question.

The climate of San Domingo at once began to play havoc with the Regiment, and by November it was so greatly reduced that it was formed into a composite battalion with the 32nd Foot, which had landed just after the 81st and had suffered in equal measure. This amalgamated battalion was commanded by Lieut.-Colonel Hamilton who had just joined the 81st, and the joint establishment was fixed as follows: one colonel, one lieutenant-colonel, two majors, seven captains, one captain lieutenant, twenty-one lieutenants, eight ensigns, one chaplain, one adjutant, one quartermaster, one surgeon, two surgeons' mates, fifty-two sergeants, fifty-four corporals, twenty drummers, two fifers and 950 privates.

In December this battalion was moved to Malabrie Heights to furnish the outposts, and remained here until June, 1796, when it took part in the attack upon Fort Bombarde, the possession of which seemed desirable for the greater security of Mole, St. Nicholas.

Bombarde was a strong quadrangular fort high up in the hills and some fifteen miles by road from Mole, St. Nicholas; it mounted cannon at the angles and was surrounded by a deep ditch, so that it was by no means an easy place to attack. It was reached from the Mole by two roads, the shorter of these running through a deep ravine, sandy and waterless. The longer road, by way of Jean Rabel, passed through more fertile country and crossed several streams.

On the morning of June 8th, 1796, Major-General Forbes assembled a small force to carry out the attack, and this body of troops consisted of detachments of the 13th Light Dragoons, the composite battalion of the 32nd and 81st, and detachments of two other regiments. The column paraded early and rations were served out and water-bottles filled, but the men were kept under arms for some time, and it was nine o'clock before they moved off, by which time many of them had emptied their water-bottles and consequently suffered terribly from thirst before Bombarde was arrived at. In the 32nd alone fourteen men are reported as having died of apoplexy before they had advanced two miles. A mile short of Bombarde the column came upon water, and the men, refreshed, pushed on towards their objective. The fort was captured with little loss, the garrison of three hundred whites laying down their arms on condition that they should be allowed to withdraw to the nearest republican territory.

"But the conquest proved to be of little value. Within a month it was surrounded and cut off by a large force of brigands, and Major-General Whyte, who was in command at the Mole, finding it impossible to keep open communications with it by land or (owing to the multitude of French privateers) by sea, contrived by skilful manœuvring to bring the whole of the garrison into the Mole, and abandoned Bombarde for ever. Meanwhile sickness raged with increasing fury among the troops. The garrison stationed by Forbes at the Mole numbered eighteen hundred, of whom in a single month thirty officers and five hundred men died."*

By this time it was clear to the authorities at home that so costly a campaign could not be prolonged, for during the years 1794, 1795 and 1796 some twenty-five thousand men had been lost to the army, mainly of course from the ravages of the climate; and during the two years that the 81st spent in the Island of San Domingo the Regiment lost by death two whole battalions on its original establishment, while the 32nd in one whole year lost thirty-two officers!

On the 19th March, 1797, the 81st—itself no more than a skeleton of a regiment—embarked in the armed transport "Calcutta" in company with all that was left of the 17th Dragoons and 62nd Regiment, sailing immediately for England. In the course of the voyage—on the 21st April—Major Drinkwater of the 62nd, who had been exercising marksmen in the "Tops," fell overboard, whereupon Sergeant Rowland of the 81st threw himself into a boat that was being towed astern, followed almost at once by a man of the 62nd and two seamen. The boat was immediately cut away and every effort made to save the officer, but it was blowing very hard at the time and Major Drinkwater was drowned.

On the 29th April the Regiment landed at Portsmouth and marched thence to Hilsea Barracks, where it remained until the 3rd May only, being sent from here to Chelmsford; at the end of August the 81st marched to Chatham from where, in September, it sailed for the Island of Guernsey, arriving here by the beginning of October.

During the six months that the 81st had been at home since its return from the West Indies, everything possible had been done to refill its attenuated ranks, to bring it up to establishment, and to secure suitable officers, so as to make the Regiment once more fit to take its place in the field during the troublous times which were in view. The task was none too easy, and especially difficult does it appear to have been to expedite the fitting out and re-equipment of the rank and file. In an inspection report dated the 2nd August, 1797, complaint is made that the Battalion "is deficient of Grenadiers' Corps and Pioneers' appointments," and it also states that "some of the Ensigns are much advanced in life"—a by no means uncommon complaint in those days!

Among the men enlisted at this period for the 81st was a curious character, one Robert Flockhart, who left behind him a biography, a copy of

* Fortescue, Vol. IV, Part I, pp. 472, 473.

which is in possession of the Regiment, and which throws an interesting light upon the Army of those days and the class of man who composed it. Flockhart joined the 81st very shortly after its arrival in England from San Domingo, having enlisted at Leith. From his own admission he had previously been rejected for enlistment into the Breadalbane Fencibles, and he is unflatteringly described as being " of a diminutive stature, only five feet three inches in height, of a shuffling gait, ill-hung in the limbs and with a curious cast of the eye ! " Of the draft with which he arrived to join the Regiment, then at Chatham, he gives the following account :—

" When we came to Chatham we were ordered into a barrack room ; there we met such characters as I had never seen nor heard of before. Nothing but swearing, drinking, quarrelling and fighting on every hand. I thought they were very wicked men, and I did not like to be obliged to live with such characters at first. The body of the 81st Regiment had come from the West Indies, sadly thinned by disease and the climate, and they filled it up with recruits and I was one of them. Our number being complete, we embarked for Guernsey. We filled two transports and the one I was in was six weeks in reaching her destination. . . . The Regiment was composed chiefly of Englishmen and Irishmen ; there were very few Scotchmen in it. Being a native of Scotland they made game of me when I spoke my own mother-tongue. On my passage to Guernsey a sergeant asked me to do something I did not like. Being a young soldier, I refused, on which, with a cane (commonly called a ratan) that he had in his hand he gave me such a beating as made my young head ache and left marks on my body for many days after. I took this very ill at the time and regarded it as hard usage, but afterwards I saw that it smartened me up, and I believe kept me from being flogged at the halberts.

" I never was flogged all the time I was in the Army, and that is what very few of the young soldiers could say. They were very strict and severe after we landed at Guernsey, so much so, indeed, that flogging was almost constantly going on every morning. Gin being cheap, undisciplined men made too free with it, and so got themselves often into scrapes, for which they were severely punished. It was no uncommon thing to see ten or twelve men flogged before breakfast. . . .

" We remained nearly twelve months at Guernsey, during which period we were almost constantly on drill or duty. We were expecting the French to land on the Island every night, and, in consequence, had provided beacons of dry whins on all the most conspicuous places around. A sentinel was stationed beside each beacon, and his orders were to fire it on the first alarm, so that the inhabitants might be prepared for the enemy. These preparations, however, proved unnecessary, as no landing was attempted."

In February, 1798, the officers of the Regiment got up among themselves a subscription in support of the expenses of the war then being carried on against France; and on this becoming known among the "other ranks," all voluntarily came forward and resolved to make an annual subscription until the end of the war. The following was the scale of the subscriptions :—

Sergeants, seven days' pay per annum; corporals, three days' pay; drummers and privates, two days' pay each—a substantial proof indeed of their splendid patriotism!

At the beginning of August of this year the 81st was ordered to prepare again for foreign service, and the establishment was now fixed at the following :—

One colonel, two lieutenant-colonels, two majors, seven captains, one captain lieutenant, twenty-one lieutenants, eight ensigns, one paymaster, one adjutant, one quartermaster, one surgeon, two assistant-surgeons, one sergeant-major, one quartermaster-sergeant, fifty sergeants, fifty corporals, twenty drummers, two fifers and 950 privates; employed on recruiting duty were one captain, two lieutenants, one ensign, eight sergeants and eight corporals.

Since in 1795 the British Government had captured and occupied the Cape of Good Hope, there had been periodic outbreaks of trouble and unrest, necessitating the presence there of a tolerably large garrison of British troops. But as the operations of the war with France grew ever more serious and the theatre of the war expanded, so also did the need for troops arise in India, and the Cape garrison had necessarily to be reduced; so that when, in the winter of 1798, an insurrection of a somewhat serious character broke out at Graaff Reinet in the Cape Colony, the troops there maintained were considered insufficient in number adequately to deal with it, and it became necessary to send out regiments from England.

The 81st Regiment, as has been said, was placed under orders for foreign service at the beginning of August, 1798, and being conveyed to Portsmouth about the middle of the month, it was embarked in the Indiamen "Thames" and "Ocean"; but it does not appear to have sailed until nearly the end of October, when, escorted by a 44-gun sloop, the 81st set out for the Cape of Good Hope, the 61st Regiment forming part of the same convoy. The 81st arrived in Table Bay on the 1st January, 1799, and took up its quarters in Cape Town.

Of the incidents of the voyage Private Flockhart, of the 81st, has something to tell :—

"We embarked in a large ship, formerly a 74-gun ship, but now cut down to a transport. Before she was out of sight of land she struck a rock and remained immovable. She then hoisted a flag of distress and fired signal guns to apprise the ships in the harbour of her situation; she was soon surrounded by boats and by their assistance once more got afloat. After this we met with no further mishaps till we reached Spithead in two days. When we arrived our Regiment was divided among different ships bound for the Cape of Good Hope. There was a large fleet of merchant ships (one hundred and six in number) that sailed with us, bound for different parts of the world. We had a 98-gun ship and two frigates for our convoy. During our passage from England to the Cape of Good Hope, out of about one hundred men, thirty died. They died very suddenly, some would be well in the morning, and be dead before night. When dead, the sailors would sew them up in a sack and throw them overboard immediately, because they said the disease of which they died was the plague. . . . We were three months on our passage from England to the Cape of Good Hope. We arrived in the month of January, 1799. . . . Numbers of our men died soon after we arrived and many more during the time we remained, for although the climate is healthy and the water good in Cape Town, yet the immoderate use of cheap wine and cheap fruit shortened men's days."

What Flockhart said about the sickness in the Regiment is borne out by the author of the *History of South Africa since September, 1795*,* who, writing of the trouble which arose in 1798, says : " The time seemed opportune for the purpose, as the garrison was then weaker than at any other period since the conquest. In the first and second weeks of January, 1799, the 61st and 81st Regiments had arrived at the Cape, but they were chiefly composed of boys, were only 1,500 strong between them, and a very large proportion of the rank and file were sick and unfit for duty. The 86th, a fine regiment of over 1,000 men, was under orders for India and left South Africa on the 19th February. It was evident to every one that the garrison was greatly weakened by the exchange, so much so that the English civil servants and merchants in the town volunteered to assist in keeping guard, and though only sixty-one in number, their services were accepted by the Government."

In January, 1799, a prominent Dutchman in the Graaff Reinet district had been arrested on a civil charge, but had almost immediately been rescued from custody by a party of malcontents. The matter was reported to the General Officer Commanding on the 16th February and on the following morning Brigadier-General Vandeleur left Cape Town to march to Graaff Reinet, taking with him two light guns, some eighty men of the

* Theal, Vol. I, p. 43.

8th Light Dragoons and the flank companies of the 61st and 81st Regiments; and on arriving in the Swellendam district found all the Dutch inhabitants in strong sympathy with the insurgents of Graaff Reinet. These did not, however, offer any really serious resistance to the troops; many came in and surrendered, and before the end of May the country, so far as the Dutch people inhabiting it were concerned, had been pacified.

While these events were taking place, however, the Colony was invaded by a powerful tribe known as the Xosas, who crossed the Fish River, spread all over what was known as the Zuurfeld, and were joined by nearly all the local clans. General Vandeleur does not appear to have anticipated any real trouble from the Xosas, and, having called in his various posts, marched towards Algoa Bay. Arrived at the Sunday River the column was suddenly attacked by the Kaffirs from an ambush, who poured in a shower of assegais, but did not expose themselves or continue the contest for any length of time.

On the 5th May a party of the Grenadier Company of the 81st—one sergeant, two corporals and twenty-five privates, under command of Lieutenant Chamney, had been sent to reconnoitre the country towards the coast, and General Vandeleur now fell back to the Bushman's River to enable the party to rejoin; but disaster overtook the officer and his men, and the account of what happened is given in a book published only five years later.*

"This officer had been detached towards the sea-coast and was returning to the camp on Bushman's River, when he was surprised among the thickets by a large party of Kaffirs, who attacked them hand to hand with the iron part of their Hassagais" (sic), "the wooden shaft being previously broken off. This young officer defended himself bravely till sixteen of his party were killed. The remaining four with a Dutch Boer, got into a waggon that accompanied the detachment and arrived safe at the Camp. Poor Chumney" (sic) "was on horseback and when the waggon set out had three Hassagais sticking in his body. Finding himself mortally wounded, and perceiving that the whole aim of the enemy was directed towards him, he made a sign to the waggon to drive off, and, turning his horse, he set off in a contrary direction, pursued by the whole body of Kaffirs; affording thus an opportunity for the small remains of his party to save their lives by flight."

(The name of this officer is spelled in various ways: in the regimental digest, the printed records of the 81st and in Theal's *History of South Africa*, it is given as Chamney; in Barrow's book above quoted from, the name

* Barrow, *An Account of Travels into the Interior of Southern Africa*, Vol, II, p. 130.

appears as Chumney; in the Annual Army Lists of the period as Chamnes; but the unfortunate officer's real name was Lieutenant John Chamney.)

Emboldened by this success the Kaffirs then attacked General Vandeleur's camp, only to be met with a heavy repulse, after which they were pursued across the Bushman's and Fish Rivers, losing most of their cattle in their flight. Being now completely discouraged, they sent in to sue for peace, offering to give up the instigators of the outbreak in exchange for the Kaffir prisoners in British hands, and to disperse to their houses. To these terms General Vandeleur agreed and the campaign then ended.

Several of the Kaffirs killed in this action were found to be wearing parts of the uniform of Lieutenant Chamney, and one of the prisoners reported that this officer was still alive when captured, but was killed by a Kaffir whose efforts to strip him he had resisted.

For a while the flank companies of the 61st and 81st lay encamped at Algoa Bay and there built a blockhouse, so commencing the formation of the settlement, which is now known as Port Elizabeth; on the 13th June the troops were re-embarked and rejoined their headquarters at the Castle, Cape Town. Here the 81st was quartered during the remainder of the time it was stationed at the Cape, except that the flank companies were again detached in April, 1802, with some of the 8th Light Dragoons and the 34th Foot, to Hillenbosch, where there was a threatening of trouble. Nothing came of this, however, and the troops were back again in Cape Town before the end of May.

On the 15th December, 1801, it had become known at the Cape of Good Hope that preliminaries of peace between Great Britain and the Continental Powers had been signed in London, and that the restoration of the Colony to the Batavian Republic was one of the conditions. The actual peace treaty was not, however, signed until the 27th March, 1802, at Amiens, and General Dundas soon after received orders to draft men from the 81st to complete the 22nd, 34th and 65th Regiments to their full establishments, and then to send these three regiments and the 8th Light Dragoons on to India, the remaining corps returning to England.

"Accordingly two ships were chartered to take home all the invalids, and they left early in December with 396 men, 36 women and 40 children. Several men-of-war, homeward bound from India, called at the Cape in December, and advantage was taken of them to send the 81st—then a skeleton regiment—and about 240 of the 91st to England."*

The 81st may then, indeed, have been described as a "skeleton Regiment," for it was "drafted" to the extent of between 600 and 700 men, most of whom went to the 22nd. About this Flockhart records: "Any

* Theal, Vol. I, pp. 95, 96.

man belonging to the two regiments that were ordered home was at liberty to volunteer into any of the three regiments that were going abroad and get two guineas of volunteer money. I think there were three days given for the volunteering. On the first day a great many of my comrades volunteered, and got their bounty money. As I lay on my bed I thought that, after all my sufferings and privations I was just as poor as when I left home. I resolved to volunteer into the 22nd Regiment the second day."

And here, then, we can take leave of Private Flockhart, who, when he left the Army, appears to have achieved notoriety as a street preacher in Edinburgh, in which capacity his vehemence in the cause of religion occasionally led him into such intemperance of speech as to bring him into conflict with the authorities !

In December some of the Batavian troops intended to garrison the Colony had arrived at the Cape, and on the 27th December the remains of the 81st were shipped on board H.M.S. "Victorious," "La Sybille," "Orpheus" and "Undine" and sailed for England on the 29th.

On the 11th January, 1803, the squadron anchored in James's Bay, St. Helena, where the "Victorious," which had sprung a leak, had to be hove to for repairs. While stopping at St. Helena, H.M.S. "Imogene" passed through bearing despatches from England dated the 17th October, directing General Dundas to delay the transfer of the Colony to the Dutch, but to avoid friction of any kind with the Batavian officials; and there seemed some likelihood that the ships conveying the 81st might be required to return to the Cape. However, when the repairs to the "Victorious" had been completed, the squadron again sailed homewards, but within a few days' sail of Land's End, a violent gale was met on the 7th March, which lasted for eight days, during which the "Victorious" again gave trouble, losing all her masts and making water faster than the pumps could cope with. She put in to the port of Lisbon, where she was left with the "Orpheus," while the two other vessels went on to England, sending back from there fresh transport for the troops waiting at Lisbon.

Finally the whole Regiment arrived at Portsmouth, where a large draft of recruits from Ireland was awaiting it.

Two unhappy events—unfortunately by no means rare in those days—occurred during the stay of the 81st at the Cape: on the 5th July, 1801, Lieut.-Colonel Brock being killed in a duel with Captain Menzies of the 22nd Regiment, while Lieutenant Mackay of the 91st was mortally wounded in another duel with Ensign Monteith of the 81st. Duelling continued in the Army for nearly half a century more, there being a very strong objection among men in authority, like the Lords of the Admiralty, the Duke of Wellington and others, to a suggestion put forward in 1843 as to the establishment of courts of honour, to the arbitrament of which officers should refer their differences. The matter was, however, later taken up by the Cabinet, with the result that in April, 1844, Article 98 was added to the Articles of War, ordaining that "every person who shall fight or promote a duel or take any steps thereto, or who shall not do his best to prevent a duel, shall, if an officer, be cashiered, or suffer such other penalty as a general court-martial may award."

In a duel the weapons most frequently used were either the pistol or rapier; the challenged usually having the choice.

In the eyes of the law a duel has always been regarded as an offence, and the sending of a challenge as a breach of the peace; while the killing of an opponent grounds a charge of manslaughter, or even murder, not only against the survivor, but also against the seconds.

The practice of thus satisfying wounded honour was not confined to any one section of the community.

CHAPTER XII

1803–1812

THE BATTLE OF MAIDA

IN the beginning of April, 1803, the Headquarters of the Regiment received orders to leave Portsmouth for Jersey, and embarked for this purpose on board the sloops of war H.M.S. "Aurora" and "Déterminée"; the latter, unfortunately, struck on a rock when entering St. Aubin's Bay, Jersey, and became a total wreck. The weather was luckily fine and the "Aurora" and other vessels were standing by, so that there was but little loss of life.

The 81st Regiment had been no more than a very few weeks in the Island of Jersey, when the likelihood of its employment on active service seemed far more than problematical, since on the 16th May of this year Great Britain declared war against France.

The Treaty of Amiens was actually little more than a truce, giving France a breathing space during which her ruler prepared for fresh conquests. Her boundaries had, consequent on events lately concluded, been extended to the east and north-east; Holland was subservient to her, while the greater part of Northern Italy was under her domination. Under the terms of the treaty her East and West Indian possessions were to be restored to her, and Napoleon was seriously considering how he should become supreme in the Mediterranean and eject the British from India.

The British Cabinet was not unobservant of events and of possibilities, and within three weeks of the signature of the Treaty of Amiens, it had brought in a bill to consolidate the militia laws and augment the Militia, the establishment of which force was now fixed at 72,000 men. A few days later a bill was introduced enabling the Country to accept the offers made by certain Yeomanry and Volunteer Corps to continue their service; while it was not long before new Army Estimates were framed, fixing the establishment at rather over 70,000 men for the United Kingdom, 25,000 for the Colonies, and 26,000 for India, the total of these, including 10,000 artillerymen, being over 132,000 men. Later again, in June, 1803, "the Additional Forces Act" became law, providing for an "Army of Reserve" of 50,000 men.

In the meantime Napoleon, recognizing England as his chief enemy and France being inferior at sea, designed to strike at her by land or through her commerce, and to further this latter object he devised his Continental System, whereby British merchandise was to be excluded from the ports of every country under French influence or protection, and he then proceeded to enforce this measure by occupying harbours or strategic points in the weaker states; in pursuit of this policy he ordered the seizure of the ports of Brindisi, Otranto and Taranto, and having effected this, he forced a treaty of neutrality on the Court of Naples.

Great Britain now aimed at a coalition, or at least a defensive alliance with Russia and Austria; but as time went on and the French grew more and more aggressive, the Cabinet of St. James's became very nervous about the Mediterranean garrison and Egypt, and at the same time had good grounds for the fear that the Court of Naples might hope to placate Napoleon and secure his favour by throwing open to him the Island of Sicily. This would have been a great blow to British interests, more particularly now that Spain had definitely thrown in her lot with France.

So when, in January, 1805, the French fleet broke out of Toulon on the cruise that finally led it to defeat and disaster at Trafalgar, the British Ministry decided to send more troops to the Mediterranean while there was yet time.

The original intention of those who created the Army of Reserve, previously alluded to, was that it should be formed into fifty Second Battalions to as many existing Regiments of the Line; as a consequence the 81st was now to have a Second Battalion, and this was raised at Plymouth, where the 81st, or 1st Battalion as it must now for some time be called, was also at the time stationed, having arrived from Jersey on the 1st October and being quartered in Mill Bay Barracks. The following Counties had between them raised for the Regiment some 1,800–1,900 men: Anglesea, Brecon, Carnarvon, Carmarthen, Cardigan, Denbigh, Flint, Glamorgan, Hereford, Monmouth, Montgomery, Merioneth, Pembroke and Radnor.

On the 30th January, 1804, the whole of the men for unlimited service —as distinct from those who had enlisted for limited and home service only—were enrolled in the 1st Battalion, and, under a General Order of the 8th March, all the senior officers of each rank were posted to the 1st Battalion, the officer corps of which was then composed of the following: one lieut.-colonel, two majors, ten captains, twelve lieutenants, eighteen ensigns, one paymaster, one adjutant, one quartermaster, one surgeon and two assistant-surgeons.

The Battalions were now to be separated, the 2nd Battalion embarking on the 27th November for Ireland, where for the present we may leave it, while the 1st Battalion remained some weeks longer at Plymouth, receiving on the 21st March, 1805, orders to hold itself in readiness for foreign service. Embarking in transports at Plymouth, these sailed on the 1st April for Portsmouth, where an expeditionary force was being fitted out under Lieut.-General Sir James Craig, whose orders were "to protect Sicily from the French with or without the consent of the King of Sicily"—instructions sufficiently comprehensive for any situation that might arise. The troops detailed consisted of the 20th Light Dragoons, the 1st Battalions of the 39th, 44th, 48th, 58th and 81st Regiments, the Royal Veteran Battalion and two Brigades of Artillery, each of five 6-pounders and two 9-inch howitzers. The force sailed from Portsmouth on the 17th April in thirty-seven transports, escorted by a small squadron of three ships-of-war under Rear-Admiral Knight.

When off Lisbon a frigate brought the news that a junction had been effected between the French and Spanish fleets, so that as these had passed the Straits of Gibraltar they might at any moment intercept Rear-Admiral Knight's small armada. Hearing this, the admiral at once sailed for the shelter of the Tagus, where he arrived on the 8th May, and on the following day the troops were brigaded in view of the possibility of their being obliged to be put ashore for action, and the 44th and 81st then composed the 2nd Brigade under Brig.-General Cole.

The protests of the French Ambassador and the representations of the Portuguese authorities obliged the ships to put to sea again after a stay of only two days, but off Cape St. Vincent Admiral Lord Nelson's fleet was met, when it was learnt that the Franco-Spanish naval force had sailed away westward and that the seas were clear of enemy craft.

Sailing on, Gibraltar was reached on the 13th May, and here the general uncertainty of the naval situation obliged the expeditionary force to remain until the 18th June, when the voyage was resumed, and, the 48th Foot and the Royal Veteran Battalion having been left behind, Malta was reached on the 20th July. Here the 1st Battalion 81st disembarked on the 23rd and occupied quarters in Fort Ricasoli.

At Malta Sir James Craig found despatches awaiting him from which he learnt that the Court of Naples had, for the moment, decided to throw in its lot with the Coalition—Great Britain, Russia and Austria—and that he was to co-operate with a Russian force under General Lascy in the endeavour to free the mainland of Northern Italy from French troops; this done, the combined force was to advance and join hands with the Austrian army on the Adige. After much delay, partly due to the double-dealing of the King of Naples, and partly to the inherent difficulty of arranging the details of a campaign with an ally whose headquarters—at Corfu

—were four hundred miles distant across the sea, the allied British and Russian troops landed at Naples on the 20th November, 1805. It was then discovered that the whole of the French troops had evacuated Neapolitan territory and gone north to engage the Russians in Venetia, so the allied army took up a position covering the northern frontier of the Kingdom, from Pescara, on the Adriatic, to Gaeta on the western coast, there remaining inactive.

The 1st Battalion 81st did not accompany the force as a battalion but remained all this time in Malta; the flank companies, however, joined a Grenadier and a Light Battalion which had been formed from the flank companies of the regiments composing the Malta garrison, and these battalions accompanied Sir James Craig to Naples, the Light Battalion under command of Lieut.-Colonel Kempt of the 81st.

On the 2nd December the crushing defeat sustained at Austerlitz by the Russian and Austrian armies, forced the rulers of those two countries to conclude a treaty with Napoleon; and under the terms of this, Russian troops, in whatever theatre of war, were bound to abstain from hostilities against the French. On the 7th January, 1806, the Russian commander was informed of this decision and prepared to retire to Corfu. Sir James Craig realized that with his small force of barely seven thousand men it was useless to attempt to hold the mainland, since the Neapolitan troops were of more than doubtful value and of uncertain loyalty; he therefore decided to abide by his original instructions and to secure the Island of Sicily against the French. News also now came in that some thirty-five thousand French soldiers were in full march southward and would reach the Neapolitan frontier in a few days; against so large a force as that General Craig could hope to effect nothing, so on the 19th January, 1806, he re-embarked his troops and sailed for Messina where he arrived on the 22nd, the King of Naples joining him within three weeks.

In February the flank companies of the 1st Battalion 81st rejoined their Battalion at Malta. But on the 4th April the Battalion embarked and sailed to join the force in Sicily; it arrived in Messina on the 12th and on landing was quartered at Carraba; the flank companies now returned to their respective Grenadier and Light Battalions.

Just about this time General Craig, who for some time had been ailing, was compelled to give up his command and sailed for England, so ill that he was not expected to reach it alive, and the command in the Mediterranean devolved upon Major-General Sir John Stuart. Two more regiments, the 78th and 89th, were now sent to reinforce the troops in Sicily, and by the end of May the British force, increased to some eight thousand men, lay with its left fortified at Milazzo and with outposts on its right extending towards Taormina.

During this summer the people of Calabria rose repeatedly in insurrection against the French invaders, in obedience to the agents sent among them by the Queen of Naples; and the very strong fortress of Gaeta was holding out stoutly against the French, for though blockaded by Massena on the land side, it was open from the sea, and the British admiral was able to throw into the place a much-needed supply of ammunition.

General Stuart now, without much encouragement from the admiral in these waters, decided on a descent upon Calabria, and having made all his preparations with the greatest secrecy,* on the night of the 25th June the embarkation commenced. The expeditionary force contained 5,531 officers and other ranks and was made up as follows:—

Advanced Corps under Colonel Kempt, 81st: the Light Companies of the 20th, 27th, 35th, 58th, 61st, 81st and of de Watteville's Regiment; Flankers, i.e. picked shots, of the 35th, two companies of Corsican Rangers, one company of Sicilians and two 4-pr.-guns.

1st Brigade under General Cole: 27th (8 companies), Grenadier Companies of the 20th, 27th, 35th, 58th, 81st and de Watteville's Regiment, and three 4-pr.-guns.

2nd Brigade under General Acland: 78th (10 companies), 81st (8 companies), and three 4-pr.-guns.

3rd Brigade under General Oswald: 58th and de Watteville's (each 8 companies). Eight companies of the 20th were detached to make a diversion at Reggio and were to rejoin later.

The 1st Battalion 35th and the 1st Battalion 61st contributed their flank companies only, the Battalion Companies remaining in Sicily; all the regiments were very weak in numbers, averaging less than 600 men apiece, the strength of the 1st Battalion 81st was 570 only. Of the regiments that sailed, Colonel Bunbury † remarks as follows: " The 1/27th was the only battalion of old soldiers; the flank companies of the 20th, 35th and 61st were also hard-biting fellows of old standing; but the 1/58th, 2/78th and 1/81st were young regiments." †

The force sailed on the 26th June, escorted by H.M.S. " Pompée," " Apollo " and two small frigates, and anchored in the Bay of St. Euphemia on the evening of the 30th. At dawn the next day the Light Battalion and the Corsican Rangers landed unopposed and occupied an old tower which stood on the shore below the village of St. Euphemia and which was known as the Tower of Malta. A belt of wood bordering the beach was then occupied, and, while the boats returned to the ships for more troops,

---

* Fortescue, Vol. V, p. 338, states that " not a soul had an idea of the object of the expedition except the General and two of his staff; and it must be said that this part of the proceedings was admirably managed."
† *Narrative of Military Transactions in the Mediterranean*, pp. 54, 55.

General Oswald, who was in command of this advanced party, pushed his men out cautiously towards St. Euphemia through the trees and scrub which spread along the front and on the right. Soon came the rattle of musketry from the wood and the skirmishers of the Corsican Rangers were driven in on their supports, having come in contact with three companies of a battalion of Poles from the French post of Monteleone.

General Oswald steadied his men and charged the enemy on both flanks, whereupon they fled with a loss of ten officers and eighty men, killed, wounded and prisoners. In this affair Sergeant O'Neal of the Light Company of the 81st distinguished himself by taking several prisoners single-handed. St. Euphemia was occupied, and the disembarkation proceeded rapidly, so that by the evening of the 1st July the whole force was ashore and holding a defensive position—the right on the Bay of St. Euphemia, the centre covered by the Tower of Malta, and the left towards St. Biaggio.

On the 2nd the Grenadier Battalion pushed on and seized Nicastro, five miles inland and astride the main road from Naples to Lower Calabria, and the landing of stores and ammunition was commenced, a task which, owing to heavy surf, occupied the whole of the 2nd and 3rd. "During these two days," writes Bunbury, "we were joined by about two hundred straggling Calabrese, provided for the most part with firearms; but they were ruffians of the lowest description."

On hearing of Sir John Stuart's departure from Messina, the French general, Reynier, began to move north from Reggio, where most of his troops were cantoned; and gathering together such of his men as were occupying outlying posts, he arrived on the night of the 2nd-3rd July at Maida, about nine and a half miles from St. Euphemia. On arrival here his force consisted of some 6,400 troops, of which 5,700 were infantry, and of the nine battalions containing them six were French, two were Polish and one was Swiss. There were also 300 cavalry and four guns, while it was rumoured that another division was marching to reinforce him.

On the morning of the 3rd July General Stuart learned that Reynier was encamped on the River Lamato close to the village of Maida, and, accompanied by a small escort of grenadiers, he went out on to the hills to examine the enemy's position, and decided that it must be turned by the left flank since the entire front was covered by the river, while the flanks, especially on the right, were protected by dense underwood. Stuart then rode back, quite unaware that his opponent, with a small cavalry escort, had been in the wood at the same time as himself, observing the British position, and had only missed him by a few minutes!

Sir John Stuart issued orders that evening for his troops to march the next morning at daybreak to attack the French position. Four companies of de Watteville's Regiment and four guns were detailed to hold the entrenchment on the beach, leaving something under 4,300 men of all ranks—the companies of the 20th Foot not yet having appeared—with three field and eight mountain guns, to form the attacking force.

The advance began at dawn on the 4th. Soon, as the troops trudged along the shingly beach and through the long, coarse grass of the salt marshes bordering the shore, the sun rose and beat down upon them, and the men—especially the Grenadier Battalion which had marched all night—became jaded by the time they had crossed the River Ippolito and had reached the Tower of Lamato. From this point a track ran inland towards Maida, along which some of the enemy's light cavalry fell back as the British approached, while the French army was seen to be filing by its right from the high ground where it had bivouacked, and moving down towards the upper part of the plain of Maida, where Stuart's army now stood.

The British advance along the shore had been made in two parallel columns and in the following order : Left or Inland Column : the advanced corps under Colonel Kempt of the 81st ; this was followed by Cole's brigade ; Acland led the inshore column with Oswald following him, and the three field-guns were with this column. As long as they moved along the actual shore line, the British Admiral "followed with the ' Apollo ' frigate and two smaller vessels to cover the flank of the marching columns with his fire, in case the French should come down and fight close to the water, intending to drive the British force actually into the sea." As the brigades disentangled themselves in succession from the marshes and copses of the foreshore, their direction was changed to the left, and the troops were deployed in battle formation to move upon the enemy ; this movement had the effect of removing the British column from the protection of the guns of the ships, which could no longer help when Stuart turned inland.

" The brigades now advanced in échelon, Kempt leading, then Acland, the late head of the inshore column, then Cole. Oswald, who was to form the reserve with his weak force of only eight hundred and fifty men, was placed behind the interval between Cole and Acland. The march of two miles from the beach towards the French camp was far more fatiguing than the first seven miles, for the Lamato spreads out into marshes at its estuary, there was no road, save a track followed by Kempt, and many of the battalions were ankle-deep in black slime."

At the same time the French were moving down the valley in a very similar formation, possibly owing to the greater distance which the flank battalions had to cover to reach their places of deployment. Sending out his cavalry and horse-artillery guns to cover his movement, Reynier came rushing down from his camp in three columns ; the southern one was to deal the main blow, the second was to form a support for the first or to continue its line northwards so as to form a centre for the army, while the third had to make a long sweep round to get into line. Reynier's right was his weak point, for it was out in the open plain and not covered, as was the left, by a wood. The result of the simultaneous advance of the three French columns, each with different distances to traverse, was that they, too, fell into an échelon of brigades, the left advanced, the southern column leading, the second some way to the right and rear, while the third column was some distance to the right and rear of the second. The cavalry and guns, already down in the low ground, were by this time far ahead of the remainder of Reynier's force.

"As our right drew near to the steep and woody bank on the left side of the Lamato, Colonel Kempt detached the Corsican Rangers across the stream to scour the thickets and secure him from ambuscades on his flank, sending at the same time the Light Company of the 20th as a support. Scarcely had the Corsicans entered the wood when they were met by a brisk fire, followed by the headlong charge of about two hundred French, and were driven in such confusion upon the 20th that this company was hard put to it to keep its ground. . . . The fire for some minutes was very sharp, and the parties were close to each other; but Kempt instantly detached Major Robertson across the stream with the flankers of the 35th, and matters were speedily righted. The French retreated in confusion; the Corsicans rallied and pursued them, and the men of the 20th and 35th rejoined the right of their brigade." *

While this action was proceeding on the right, Acland's brigade—containing the 78th and 81st—had closed up into the line and was now coming into contact with the enemy, the 42nd Regiment of French Infantry being directly in front and moving deliberately towards it; the sudden defeat of the battalion on its left by the troops under Kempt and their hurried retirement, seemed now to alarm the 42nd French Infantry for the safety of its flanks. At this critical moment it received two well-directed volleys from the 78th and 81st and turned and fell back, but being a veteran regiment and Acland's men not at once pursuing, it halted and took up a new position covering Reynier's exposed left flank.

"Acland, following the routed regiment for some way, soon came into contact with its supports, the three foreign battalions—900 Poles and 600 Swiss—a fresh force outnumbering him by 200 men. Here he had a second, but a very short fight to sustain—the Poles broke at the first shock, though Reynier himself had ridden up to them and was using all his efforts to keep them steady. Their rout was disgraceful—their casualty list shows only

* Bunbury, p. 57.

The Battle of Maida.
4th July, 1806.

one officer hit, but four taken prisoners unwounded; of the men, it would appear that nearly 250 were captured, nearly all without a wound. This was the work of the 81st, while the Highland Regiment at their side got engaged with the Swiss. This battalion was dressed in red, like all the other Swiss corps in the French Army. According to the Regimental History of the 78th, they were at first mistaken by the Scots for de Watteville's Swiss Regiment of the British force whose uniform was very similar. They were allowed to approach within a very short distance before the fighting began, and their first volley did the 78th much harm. But after ten minutes of very close fighting the Swiss gave back—though not in disorder—and fell off towards their right. Acland did not pursue them . . . and they rallied and re-formed. Acland was prevented from moving after them by the French cavalry . . . and his battalions, being much disordered by the two fights they had gone through, the Brigadier bade them form squares and kept them halted for some time under artillery fire by which they suffered some loss. When the French cavalry moved off, it was found that the battle on the left, no less than on the right, was over.

"Acland's brigade suffered, in its two successive victories over the 42nd and the three foreign battalions, a heavier loss than any other part of the British army. The 2/78th had eighty-five killed and wounded, the 1/81st eighty-four—together more than half the total loss at Maida, which only came to 327 casualties." *

By this time the battle had spread to General Cole's brigade on the extreme left. This had advanced somewhat slowly, supported by Oswald's brigade, but Reynier, seeing that the day was as good as lost in other parts of the field, ordered one of his brigades to prepare to act as a rearguard, and this the commander did with considerable skill. Placing two guns and two battalions in a defensive position across Cole's front, he detached the rest of his infantry with orders to make a wide counter-attack on the British left, moving through the scrub and bushes on the banks of the Ippolito River, while the cavalry offered a continued menace to any move that Cole might attempt. The left of the 27th Foot was thrown back to resist the counter-attack, while Oswald's brigade came up to fill the gap between Cole and Acland. The situation for Stuart's army was, however, none too good; ammunition was running short, the men were all greatly exhausted, and Cole was fighting more or less a detached and inadequately supported action.

Matters were at this critical stage when an aide-de-camp galloped up with the news that the naval squadron detached towards Reggio had returned, and that the 20th Foot, which had accompanied it, was actually

* Oman, *The Battle of Maida*, Journal of the R.A., Vol. XXXIV, pp. 556, 557.

MAIDA.

4th July, 1806.

From a contemporary Engraving.

disembarking at the mouth of the Lamato, directly behind the battle-field. The O.C. 20th, hearing the heavy firing, did not wait to complete his disembarkation, but hurried off across the marsh with such men as had landed; and on the way he fell in with Colonel Bunbury, the Q.M.G., who told him his intervention would prove most effective were he to pass behind Cole's line, and turn the French extreme right. This he did and opened a sudden and well-directed fire at fifty yards' range.

The effect was decisive. Surprised and wholly disconcerted by the appearance of a fresh antagonist from an unexpected quarter, Reynier gave the order for instant retreat, his battalions going off across the open plain to the east, covered by two squadrons of cavalry and four horse-artillery guns.

"If," writes Bunbury, "we had then a couple of hundred of good cavalry, we might probably have destroyed the enemy's army; but we could do little more with our jaded infantry. Our column continued to advance upon the enemy till he abandoned the plain of Maida and retreated rapidly up the valley (beneath the town of that name) through which runs the road to Catanzaro." The British infantry halted, utterly exhausted, near the Maida–Nicastro road. "By midday our soldiers were resting on their arms, gasping with heat and thirst, and watching through the dust, with disappointed eyes, the rapid retreat of the French column. Our ammunition was nearly spent; there was no water for the men, save for those on the right, and every step we might make in advance led us further away from our supplies of every sort."

The only pursuit was carried out by Kempt's troops who followed up as far as Maida, but being unsupported and without supplies or orders of any kind, Kempt brought his men back to camp during the night, leaving out a company of the 20th to keep touch with the enemy; Kempt only got in next morning, but the 20th Company followed up the French to within ten miles of Catanzaro, where Reynier finally rallied his routed host.

In the meantime General Stuart had issued orders for the return of his force to the beach for repose, food, water and ammunition; but on the next day the column marched to Maida, where "during forty-eight hours," so Bunbury complains, "our troops remained kicking their heels and eating grapes," while the General composed his despatch on the action.

Professor Oman gives the strength and losses of the British at Maida, and from his return it appears that on the date of that action, the 1st Battalion the 81st stood at a strength of thirty-three officers and 570 other ranks, to which number the flank companies have presumably to be added; and that the casualties in the eight battalion companies totalled nineteen men killed and two officers and sixty-three other ranks wounded; the two officers wounded were Captain P. Waterhouse and Lieutenant and Adjutant J. Ginger.

At the close of the battle General Sir John Stuart published an order to the troops under his command :—

"Plains of St. Euphemia, near Maida.
"*6th July*, 1806.

"Major-General Sir John Stuart finds himself incapable of expressing to the troops the sentiments excited in him by their brave and intrepid conduct in the late action of the 4th, in which they gained so signal a triumph over a boasting and insolent enemy. . . . The 78th and 81st Regiments, which formed the brigade of General Acland, shared the first and severest part of the action with the Light Infantry, whom they were ordered to support, and the gallantry and good conduct of the Brigadier-General in fulfilling this duty were most nobly seconded by the brave regiments under his orders. . . ."

On the evening of the 7th July Oswald's brigade was sent southward to Monteleone, where a small garrison of Polish troops at once surrendered, and Reynier's hospitals and magazines fell into British hands ; but the delay and the jealousies and the differences of the British commanders, naval and military, caused the move on Gaeta, the relief of which fortress was the main object of the operations, to be deferred until too late and the place fell on the 18th July—one of the chief strategic objects of the expedition being then lost.

On the 7th July General Stuart entered Monteleone, where he spent four days, and arrived at Palmi on the 14th. Here he heard of the fall of Tropea and Reggio, and also learnt that his naval colleague was laying siege to Scilla. Oswald was sent with his brigade to the last-named place, and the admiral then, leaving the prosecution of the siege to the soldiers, departed, too late, for Gaeta. Scilla surrendered on the 24th July and Cotrone four days later ; but news now coming to hand that Massena was collecting his forces to march into Calabria, Stuart re-embarked his troops for Sicily, leaving garrisons at Reggio and Scilla.

Colonel Bunbury thus sums up the results of the expedition : "The enemy had been driven out of Lower Calabria ; he had been defeated in fair fight under such circumstances as reversed the previous belief of the Italians and Sicilians, and taught them to consider the British soldiers to be superior to the French. This in itself was no trifling gain. All the stores and guns and boats which our enemy had been collecting with a view to his establishment in Calabria, and for the future invasion of Sicily, had fallen into our hands. Five hundred of the best of the enemy's troops had been slain in battle, and between two and three thousand more were prisoners. These results had been obtained with little loss of life on our part; and a confidence had revived in our officers and soldiers which increased in an immeasurable degree the moral strength of our little army."

On arrival back in Messina General Stuart found that General Fox had been sent out from home to assume command of the Mediterranean in his place, with Lieut.-General Sir John Moore as second-in-command.

By early in September the 1st Battalion 81st was back in Messina, occupying quarters in the Citadel.

In commemoration of the victory at Maida a gold medal was struck subsequently and conferred upon all the superior officers who were present. On the obverse is the laureated head of the Sovereign, left, inscribed "GEORGIUS TERTIUS REX"; the reverse has Britannia brandishing a spear with her right hand, and on her left hand and arm a shield charged with the crosses of the Union banner. A flying figure of Victory is crowning her with a wreath of laurel; behind Britannia is the triquetra, the ancient symbol of Sicily, and before is the legend "MAIDA, IVL. IV. MDCCCVI." The name and rank of the recipient were engraved round the edge. There was only one size of this medal, which was worn suspended from the buttonhole of the coat; the riband being crimson with blue edges; a gold buckle was attached. The issue was limited, and confined to the Commander of the Forces engaged, officers in command of brigades, battalions, or of corps equivalent to a battalion, or the officer who succeeded on the removal from the field of the original commander. Generally, no officer below the rank of major was considered eligible unless he succeeded to the command of a battalion during the period of the action. (See Illustration, page 202.) Amongst the recipients was Lieut.-Colonel J. Kempt.

When, under the General Order dated Horse Guards, 1st June, 1847, the Military General Service Medal was sanctioned with a clasp for Maida, there were only little more than one hundred survivors who received this clasp—seven officers, ten sergeants, four corporals, one drummer and ninety-five privates; the officers were Major W. Plenderleath, Captain W. C. Eustace, Lieutenants F. Edwards, E. K. Williams, J. D. de Carteret, G. Adams and J. Ginger.

Among the mess-plate of the 2nd Battalion, The Loyal North Lancashire Regiment, is something which dates from the Battle of Maida; this is the silver-mounted shell of a small tortoise, and the story of its acquisition is as follows: Separated from the rest of the force on the evening after the action, the Light Brigade found itself tired, hungry and wholly without supplies of any kind, on the hills between Maida and the seashore, and Colonel Kempt was more than thankful to make his supper off a tortoise, retaining the shell as a memento of the day. Some years afterwards that officer—then General Sir James Kempt—had the shell mounted in silver and made into a snuff-box and presented it to the Regiment of which on the 12th July, 1819, he was appointed full Colonel.

All through 1807 the Battalion led a comparatively uneventful life at Messina, but its strength was appreciably augmented by two large drafts which came out from the 2nd Battalion, one, one hundred and seventy-five strong, being sent out from home in January, followed in November by a second of seventy-five men.

In December the 1st Battalion was moved out from the Citadel into cantonments in support of the coast defence lines, from which the movements of the French were constantly watched on the further side of the Straits. Here the Battalion remained until June, 1808, when its quarters were shifted for a time into mountain villages, whence in September it was sent to Milazzo. It was while quartered here that the following order, dated Horse Guards, 20th July, 1808, was received:—

"The Commander-in-Chief directs it to be notified that in consequence of the state of preparation for immediate service in which the whole Army is at the present moment to be held, His Majesty has been graciously pleased to dispense with the use of queues until further orders. . . ."

Early in 1808 Lieut.-General Sir John Moore had been recalled from Sicily to take command of an expedition which was proceeding to Sweden, and Sir John Stuart then came back and resumed his old command. For some time Colonel Lowe had been holding the Island of Capri against the French with a few companies of Corsicans, and on the evening of the 7th October the 58th and 81st Regiments, together with the 4th Battalion King's German Legion, under command of Brig.-General Acland, were embarked at three hours' notice to go to the relief of Capri, in response to an urgent appeal for succour brought by a fast-sailing ship. Foul weather at sea caused the voyage to be protracted over fourteen days, and the force only arrived to find the white flag flying from the works. By the terms of the capitulation the garrison of Capri was permitted to return to Sicily, so all that remained to be done was to embark Colonel Lowe's men and carry them back to Milazzo.

This reverse was something of a moral victory for the French and did much to tarnish the glory of Maida.

Murat, who had recently been placed by Napoleon on the throne of Naples, now did all he could to keep Sir John Stuart immobilized in the north-east corner of the Island of Sicily; and one of the results of his efforts was that the 81st remained in Milazzo until May, 1809. By this

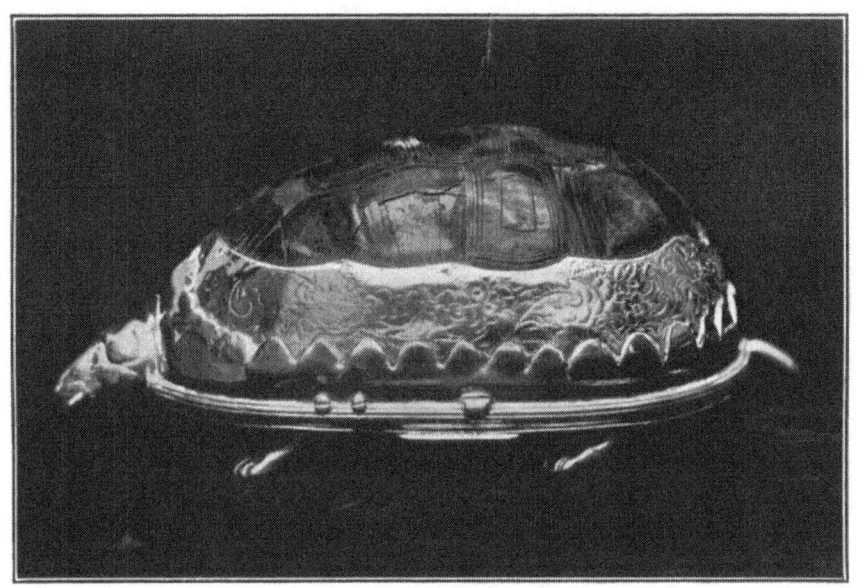

THE MAIDA TORTOISE.

time the Austrian Government had made a direct appeal to General Stuart to create some kind of a diversion on the coast of Italy, and he accordingly decided to make an attack on the Islands of Procida and Ischia on the north side of the Bay of Naples. To effect this he embarked some thirteen thousand troops and sailed on 11th June, picking up a Neapolitan squadron on his way to the objective. Six battalions remained behind in Sicily.

The expeditionary force was curiously divided, comprising an Advanced Corps, an Advanced Brigade, a Reserve Brigade, and four more brigades numbered from one to four; the 81st, 656 strong, was in the Advanced Corps, commanded by Brigadier Lumley, with the cavalry—20th Light Dragoons and Mounted Infantry, and the 1st Light Infantry Battalion.

Again was the weather unfavourable; calm and light winds prevailed, so that the fleet was thirteen days making the passage to the Bay of Naples, and the delay thus unavoidably caused, made General Stuart decide upon an immediate attack upon the Island of Ischia, despite the fact that the shore batteries appeared to be much stronger than had been anticipated. Two warships of the naval escort and a certain number of gunboats were told off to engage the shore batteries, and Lumley's Advanced Corps— 2,380 rank and file—was ordered to force a landing. The bombardment by the guns of the warships opened at dawn on the 24th and the boats pulled for the shore. The batteries could not keep down the fire of the naval guns, the defenders made little or no stand, and in a very short space of time the whole of the Island of Ischia was won, except the Castle, whither the French troops—except one hundred and eighty who were captured by the Advanced Corps—had hurriedly retired.

The Island of Procida was captured even more quickly, and all that now remained to be done was the reduction of the Castle of Ischia. Heavy guns were landed, the siege batteries opened, and on the 30th June the Castle surrendered, in all fifteen hundred men and a hundred guns being secured at a total loss of less than twenty men killed and wounded.

General Stuart was now at a loss how further usefully to employ his force; it was not strong enough to attack Naples, where Murat disposed of twenty-five thousand men, while the troops could not remain for any length of time in the Islands of Ischia and Procida as these were so wanting in natural resources that the army must be maintained by the fleet, which might be driven away by superior forces or stress of weather, when the garrison would be starved into surrender. Stuart then decided upon evacuation; and on the 26th July the 81st, having destroyed the coast batteries, left Ischia, the last corps to embark, and was back again in Milazzo on the 29th.

The Battalion was now, almost at once, embarked in three transports, and under the convoy of the " Delight," sloop-of-war, made demonstrations along the Caprian coast, but at the end of September it was disembarked at and quartered in Messina ; here it remained for two years, returning to Milazzo in November, 1811.

Early in 1812 the 1/81st was moved, with a division of British troops, to Palermo, for political rather than for military reasons, and while here was quartered in the Convent of St. Dominica.

In May an urgent letter was received in Palermo from the Duke of Wellington, pressing for a diversion upon the east coast of Spain, and it was decided to send thither a force of some 7,000 men under General Maitland. The force detailed contained the 20th Light Dragoons, the 1/10th, 1/58th, 1/81st—1,274 strong—two battalions of the King's German Legion, de Roll's, Dillon's and a Calabrian Regiment, and it left Palermo on the 6th June, the transports escorted by H.M.S. " Red Wing." Owing to adverse winds the armada was unable to pass the straits before the 28th, and then made for Minorca where there was further delay ; consequently it was the 9th August before the force arrived at Alicante in Murcia, and the 11th before it was disembarked, when the 1st Battalion 81st was brigaded with de Roll's and Dillon's Regiments in the 2nd Brigade, commanded by Colonel McKenzie, 81st, of the Division of Reserve.

CHAPTER XIII

1812–1817

OPERATIONS IN EASTERN SPAIN
CANADA. FRANCE

IN ordering the force from Sicily to the east coast of Spain it had been the design of Lord Wellington that General Maitland's arrival in these parts would so greatly add to the anxieties of General Suchet, that he would find himself unable to send any troops to the aid of either King Joseph or Marshal Marmont. Before, however, Maitland's force landed in Spain the Battle of Salamanca had been won, and at first sight it seemed that Maitland's force could be even more usefully employed than had originally been intended; the expedition started, however, too late and was far weaker than it had been meant to be. "The original idea," so Oman tells us, "was to have come ashore somewhere in the midst of the long coast-line south of the Ebro, between Tortosa and Valencia, with the object of breaking Suchet's line in the middle. But the news of Joseph O'Donnell's gratuitous disaster at Castalla, which obviously enabled the Marshal to use his whole army against a disembarking force, and the suggestion that Alicante itself might be in danger, induced Maitland in the end to order his whole armament to steer southward", to Alicante.

At Alicante, Maitland was joined by the 67th Foot, and had now some eight thousand British troops under his command, besides as many more Spaniards under Generals Roche and Whittingham; he was, however, very weak both in cavalry and artillery, while there was, moreover, great difficulty about transport and supplies.

At the end of a week the army was on the move and advanced towards Villena, a fortified town some twenty-five miles to the west of Alicante; but on arrival at Elda on the 17th August Maitland heard of the junction of King Joseph's army with the main body of the French further to the north in Valencia, and accordingly fell back on Alicante where the troops went into cantonments, the 81st at Palma, a few miles distant.

On the 25th August General Maitland's health obliged him to leave for England, and Major-General Mackenzie assumed command, until the arrival later of Major-General Clinton.

The allied force now lay for some weeks inactive about Alicante, while Suchet, finding himself uninterfered with, made several reconnaissances from the north and harried the outposts; and it was with the view of checking this enemy activity that it was decided to attempt to carry the Castle of Denia, the southernmost place in French possession, and on the coast some fifty miles distant from Alicante. To this end the left wing of the 81st, the Grenadier Company of de Roll's Regiment and a company of Marines, some six hundred men in all under the command of Major-General Donkin, were secretly embarked in H.M.S. "Fame" and "Cephalus": these landed near Denia on the morning of the 5th October, and, the Light Company of the 81st in the advance, drove in the French outposts, some of the attackers almost entering the castle with the fugitives. Several men of the Light Company were wounded actually in the ditch itself.

General Donkin now reconnoitred the place, and finding it too strong to be carried without artillery, the Light Company fell back on the main body, which was posted in a ravine, the whole force then retiring to some high ground. Here our troops were attacked by the enemy, who had collected a superior force, while news also came to hand that French reinforcements were on their way. Though the enemy attacks were covered by the fire of two guns, they were repeatedly driven back, but the French continued to harass our troops during their retreat to the beach. Here, fortunately, the British were covered by the guns of the warships and the re-embarkation was effected in good order.

The gallantry of Sergeant Patterson of the 81st was conspicuous on this occasion. He volunteered to carry the order of recall to the Light Company, then under the walls of the fort, accomplishing this task under a heavy fire; his conduct was highly commended by Major-General Donkin. The following are extracts from the Major-General's despatch dated H.M.S. "Fame," 6th October, 1812:—

"Major-General Donkin begs leave to express his approbation of the conduct of the troops during the operations on shore yesterday. The Light Infantry of the 81st Regiment, under the command of Captain Pearson, distinguished itself throughout, and particularly by its advance in pursuit of the enemy; but those gallant soldiers must learn to obey the sounds of the bugle, for, by advancing close under the walls of Denia, although the halt was repeatedly sounded to keep them under cover in the wood, they exposed themselves to be destroyed by the fire of troops whom they could not with all their bravery get at, as they were behind high walls. . . .

"Major-General Donkin feels much indebted to Major Waterhouse of the 81st Regiment for his assistance during the whole day, but particularly at the moment of embarkation which he covered in a manner that did him the highest credit. The good conduct of Lieuts. Kingsbury, Fenton, Fair and Gordon and Ensign Norlock,* of the 81st Regiment, was conspicuous on that occasion, as was the steadiness of the troops. . . .

"The re-embarkation of the detachment, it is to be recollected, was not a measure of necessity but of choice. With such gallant troops it is more than probable that the Castle of Denia might have been taken by assault, but defended as it was by at least four times the number of men expected to be there, the height of the walls became too serious an obstacle to encounter under the fire of so much musketry; and too many valuable soldiers whose services will be required for more important occasions, would have been lost in the attack. What the troops have done they have done with credit to themselves; what they have left unaccomplished was from choice and in conformity with the plain intentions with which they were embarked at Alicante; they were landed at Denia with a determination not to attempt the assault of the castle unless it could be carried with ease."

During the winter of 1812–13 the allied troops remained in and around Alicante, in the early part of 1813 a draft of six subaltern officers, three sergeants and seventy rank and file joining the 1st Battalion 81st from Jersey. Nothing of an offensive nature was attempted, and all of note that occurred was the arrival of a succession of fresh generals to take command. General William Clinton, who had arrived at the end of the previous October, was early in December superseded by Major-General Campbell, who came from Sicily, bringing with him a welcome reinforcement of four thousand troops, mostly Sicilians. Included in them, however, were two British battalions—the 1st Battalion 27th and a Grenadier Battalion made up of companies of regiments which had been left in Sicily. These brought the force under General Campbell's command up to approximately twenty-two thousand. The commander experienced the very greatest difficulty in organizing and supplying his army of five different nationalities, and in February, 1813, he was still not more than holding his ground, with his troops cantoned along a thirty-mile front on either side of Alicante. On the 25th February another change in the command took place, Lieut.-General Sir John Murray taking over from General Campbell. Of this appointment Oman tells us that "the unlucky man was quite unequal to the position, being singularly infirm of purpose and liable to lose his

* There is no "Ensign Norlock" to be found in any of the Army Lists, Monthly Returns, Description and Commission Books as belonging at this time to the 1st Battalion 81st. There is, however, an Ensign James Imlach, and it seems possible that the name may have been incorrectly transcribed in General Donkin's despatch here quoted from.

head at critical moments. It is surprising that Wellington, knowing his record, should have acquiesced in the appointment—perhaps he thought that here at least was a general who would take no risks, and have no dangerous inspirations of initiative." *

In addition to the troops under his immediate command Sir John Murray had also complete control over General Whittingham's Majorcan Division of some 4,500 men; while in the neighbourhood was a Spanish division under General Roche, which, though belonging theoretically to the army of Murcia, could at need be called upon to act with Murray's force. In addition, there lay within the borders of the Kingdom of Murcia an army under General Elio, which numbered some 30,000 men, but whose moral was of a low order.

In February, 1813, the line of occupation reached as far as Biar, Castalla and Xixona, all held by Whittingham's division, while Roche and the Anglo-Sicilians were mostly in second line at Elda, Monforte and Alicante.

Shortly after taking over command at Alicante, General Murray thus expressed the opinion he had formed of the very mixed force he was required to lead: " Of the nature of its composition your Lordship is well informed, and as, with the exception of the British and German details, nothing from every account can be worse, I anxiously hope that the expectations of His Majesty's Government will not be too sanguine "!

At this time Suchet, with a force little more than a third the size of Murray's, was endeavouring to hold a front of fifty miles from the foot of the Murcian Hills at Moxena to the mouth of the Xucar River, and at Alcoy, a town in a very productive upland valley, was a weak brigade of French troops.

Murray had early obtained accurate information as to the disposal and numbers of the French troops, and seeing the very exposed position of the brigade at Alcoy, he decided to make an attempt to cut it off by the concentric advance of four columns. Napier states that "one was to move on the left by Elda, to watch the Great Madrid road; one on the right composed of Spanish troops under Colonel Campbell, from Villa Joyosa, to get to Consentayna behind Alcoy; a third, under Lord Frederick Bentinck, issuing by Ibi, was to turn the French right; the fourth was to march from Xixona straight against Alcoy, and to pursue the remainder of Habert's division" (to which the brigade at Alcoy belonged) "which was behind the town."

Advancing on the 3rd March the allied force drove in the enemy outposts about Alcoy, and Murray then drew up a scheme whereby he proposed to surround and cut off the troops there stationed. The attack,

* *A History of the Peninsular War*, Vol. VI, pp. 275, 276.

which was to have taken place on the 7th, unfortunately miscarried, partly by reason of the late arrival of Whittingham's division, forming the right column, and partly because Murray did not support his advanced troops at the proper moment. Alcoy was, however, occupied, and during the next few days there was some skirmishing with the French outposts which were pushed further back; and on the 20th March the Anglo-Sicilian force was concentrated at Castalla, from which point it could, if necessary, support the divisions under Whittingham, Elio and Roche.

At this time it was rumoured that Suchet, strongly reinforced, was moving forward, and Murray, instead of advancing in full strength to meet his opponent, decided to try and harass his rearward communications and sent away some of his troops with instructions to make a diversion by landing north of the Xucar River. Just at this moment, however, two thousand of Murray's best troops were recalled to Sicily, and the allied force being thus appreciably weakened, Murray abandoned the enterprise, and decided to fall back again upon Alicante and stand strictly on the defensive. He did not, however, move at once but remained at Castalla, and his indecision was to cost him dearly.

By the night of the 11th April Suchet had concentrated a considerable force at Fuente de Higuera, and remaining here with the greater part of his troops so as to render Murray immobile, he sent cavalry and infantry in considerable strength to fall upon Elio's detachment at Yecla. Elio's men made a stout resistance but were defeated, losing heavily, and on the 12th the Castle of Villena also fell into French hands.

At this time the 1st Battalion 81st was in General Clinton's division, which also contained the 1st Battalion 10th, 1st Battalion 58th, de Roll's and Dillon's Regiments and the 2nd Italian Levy,* and the account of the fighting which took place on the 12th and 13th April between the armies of Murray and Suchet had better perhaps be given by extracts from the former general's despatch, since the accounts of these operations are but comparatively slightly touched upon in histories of the war, and these are not always in strict agreement.

General Murray's despatch, it may here be mentioned, was carried home by Captain C. G. D'Aguilar of the 81st, of whom the general wrote that "he eminently possesses every quality which we prize in the character of a soldier."

"On the 12th, about noon, Marshal Suchet began his attack on the advance of this army posted at Biar, under the command of Colonel Adam.

"Colonel Adam's orders were to fall back upon Castalla but to dispute the passage with the enemy, which he did with the utmost gallantry and

* See Oman, Vol. VI, p. 748.

skill for five hours, though attacked by a force infinitely superior to that which he commanded. The enemy's advance occupied the pass that evening, and Colonel Adam took up the ground in our position which had been allotted to him.

"On the 13th at noon, the enemy's columns of attack were formed, composed of three divisions of infantry, a corps of cavalry of about 1,600 men, and a formidable train of artillery. The position of the allied army was extensive. The left was posted on a strong range of hills, occupied by Major-General Whittingham's division of Spanish troops, and the advance of the allied army under Colonel Adam. This range of hills terminates at Castalla, which, and also the ground on the right, was occupied by Major-General Mackenzie's division, and the 58th Regiment from that of Lieut.-General Clinton. The remainder of the position was covered by a strong ravine, behind which Lieut.-General Clinton was stationed, supported by three battalions of General Roche's division, as a column of reserve. . . .

"The enemy necessarily advanced on the left of the position. The first movement he made was to pass a strong body of cavalry along the line, threatening our right, which was refused, . . . when this body of cavalry had passed nearly the half of our line of infantry, Marshal Suchet advanced his column to the foot of the hills, and certainly his troops, with a degree of gallantry that entitles them to the highest praise, stormed the whole line, which was not less than two and a half miles in extent. But gallantly as the attack was made, the defence of the heights was no less brilliant; at every point the enemy was repulsed—at many with the bayonet."

So far Murray's own brief account and it may be expanded as follows:—

While the move of the French cavalry was in progress, the French infantry advanced for a mile along the road, then deploying on a ridge running parallel to the allied left and some 1,400 yards from it, sent out a battalion of Voltigeurs to turn the allied left, a cloud of skirmishers moving against the whole line right up to Castalla. The French commander now sent forward five different columns of attack—three directed against the Spaniards on the left and the remaining two against Mackenzie's Anglo-German division in the centre. Owing to the broken nature of the ground the columns were only able to advance very slowly, and the three on the left were separated from the two others by a rocky spur which ran out at right angles to Murray's position.

All five columns appear to have reached the allied line, and for the moment the Spaniards were pressed back; they quickly rallied, however, and, counter-attacking with the bayonet, drove their assailants down the hill in confusion. By the middle of the afternoon every battalion which

Suchet had sent into action had been decisively defeated and with considerable loss, while the allies had suffered comparatively few casualties.

To quote again from General Murray's despatch :—

"Having united his shattered battalions with those which he kept in reserve, Marshal Suchet took up a position in the valley, but which it would not have been creditable to allow him to retain. I therefore decided on quitting mine; still, however, retaining the heights, and formed the allied army in his front, covering my right front with the cavalry, while the left rested on the hills. The army advanced in two lines to attack him, a considerable distance, but unfortunately Marshal Suchet did not choose to risk a second action with the defile in his rear. The line of the allies was scarcely formed, when he began his retreat, and we could effect nothing more than driving the French into the pass with defeat, which they had exultantly passed in the morning. The action terminated at dusk, with a distant but heavy cannonade."

Both Oman and Fortescue state, what Murray's despatch does not, that the only touch with the retreating French was maintained by Mackenzie, who, "contrary to Murray's intention," pushed forward with four battalions; and that he would probably have driven in Suchet's rearguard upon the disordered troops behind it, had Mackenzie not then received stringent orders from Murray to fall back and rejoin the main body. Fortescue implies * that the 1st Battalion 81st was one of these four battalions.

In this action the allied loss was some 670 officers and men killed and wounded, that of the French was nearly double; the 1st Battalion 81st was fortunate enough to escape without any casualties.

The French now retired through the Pass of Biar on Villena and thence by Fuente de Higuera and Onteniente on the Xucar River; while Murray, having on the 14th got in all his wounded, advanced on Alcoy, halted there for a few days and then marched back to Castalla, so as to be in a strong position and within easy reach of Alicante, while awaiting further instructions from the Commander-in-Chief.

These instructions were contained in two despatches to Murray dated the 14th and 16th April, and dealt with three main objects—"the possession of the open portion of the Kingdom of Valencia; the establishment of a place of arms; and the expulsion of the enemy from the Lower Ebro."

"Should Murray be able to embark not less than ten thousand infantry and artillery, he was directed to attack Tarragona with the largest force available, including the divisions of Whittingham and Roche. It was calculated that this operation would induce Suchet to weaken his army

* Vol. IX. Note to p. 45.

in Valencia to such an extent as to enable Elio and Del Parque to occupy a great part, if not the whole, of the open country. Thus, even should Murray fail at Tarragona, the first of the three objects would be gained and would be secured by Murray's return. If on the other hand Murray succeeded, the second object would be achieved and the attainment of the third would not be far distant." *

In his instructions to Murray, the Duke of Wellington imposed a condition which was to all intents and purposes to paralyse Murray's initiative; he said, " I shall forgive anything excepting that one of the corps should be beaten and dispersed "; and the result of such an order was to make a man like Murray resolve that he would not take even the smallest risk.

Prior to starting on this new expedition Murray completed his force to compose an army of fourteen thousand infantry, eight hundred cavalry, twenty-four field-guns and a battering train; he had now one more British battalion than before, the 2nd Battalion 67th having joined him from Carthagena. The other units had been re-distributed, and the 1st Battalion 81st was now in Major-General Mackenzie's division, which also contained the 1st Battalion 10th, 1st Battalion 27th, a combined battalion of de Roll's and Dillon's Regiments, and the 1st Italian Regiment; the two brigades of the division were under Brigadiers Warren and Prevost.

The force sailed from Alicante on the 31st May, escorted by three ships of the line and some smaller craft under Admiral Hallowell; and on the 2nd June entered Salou Bay, eight miles south of Tarragona, and before anchor was dropped Murray sent off two battalions to occupy the Pass of Balaguer, twenty miles west of Tarragona and on the direct road from Tortosa. This done, the remainder of the troops were landed and proceeded to invest the fortress of Tarragona.

After Marshal Suchet had captured the place two years previously, he had done little or nothing to repair the damage caused by its siege. " The outer enceinte had been left in a condition of ruin and only the Upper City on its high cliff was occupied. Its western front, where the breaches had been, was repaired, but the Lower City and its fortifications remained untouched. All that had been done was to patch up two isolated strong points, the so-called Fort Royal and Bastion of St. Carlos. These had been cut off from the mass of the ruins and closed in at the rear; each was armed with one gun. . . . These outlying posts, dangerously remote from the city above, were held by no more than a company each." † The place was defended by an entirely inadequate force of sixteen hundred men, under General Bertoletti.

* Butler, *Wellington's Operations in the Peninsula*, Vol. II, p. 643.
† Oman, Vol. VI, p. 593.

The weakness of the place and of the garrison was not appreciated by Murray, and several days were wasted in cannonading works which were later found to be unoccupied; and the infantry of the besieging force seems to have been held back in expectation of attacking posts afterwards discovered to have never been occupied, or long abandoned.

Six days were consumed in reducing or breaching San Felipe and Fort Royal; and now Murray began to grow anxious, for it was reported that two French forces were approaching, the one from the north and the other from the south, and on the 9th June came definite news that at least twenty thousand French were closing in upon Tarragona. In view of the instructions he had received from the Commander-in-Chief, Murray's position was undoubtedly one of some anxiety; but he now appears to have lost his head, for, after allowing the preparations for an assault to go forward until late on the 10th, he suddenly countermanded all orders, giving instructions for the immediate embarkation of guns, stores and troops, and the total abandonment of the siege operations. To such an extent did he give way to panic that he caused many guns to be abandoned in his haste to get afloat again. After much vacillation and many orders and counter-orders—General Clinton, at the subsequent trial by court-martial of General Murray, stated that he received seven different orders between dawn and 1.30 p.m.—he finally re-embarked his infantry on the 12th June, marching his cavalry and mobile artillery along the coast road to the Col de Balaguer, whither he sent the rest of his command by sea, thus incidentally abandoning his Spanish allies.

On the 17th June General Lord William Bentinck arrived from Sicily to take over command of the force, joining it at Balaguer, and at once assuming command. He then caused the fortifications about Balaguer to be destroyed, embarked his troops and returned to Alicante with the view of initiating further operations against the French in accordance with Lord Wellington's orders. The 1st Battalion 81st reached Alicante on the 24th June and was temporarily quartered at Palamos.

Early in July Lord William Bentinck projected certain operations against the French forces in Valencia; but before any action was taken the news of the victory at Vittoria changed the whole situation, and Marshal Suchet then determined to concentrate his troops in the northern province of the east coast. Leaving garrisons in certain places, the French fell back behind the line of the River Ebro, it being intended there to organize the force into a field army for employment between the Ebro and Barcelona. Lord William at once followed them into Catalonia, passing the Ebro at Amposta towards the end of July.

There was some attempt then made at a second investment of Tarragona, but within a few days Suchet came down in strength to the relief of the place, whereupon the operations were again abandoned and a retirement was made down the coast to Cambrills; Suchet then blew up the fortifications of Tarragona on the 18th August and fell back to the line of the Llobregat.

For a month the opposing armies lay watching each other on either side of the river, and during this time the 1st Battalion 81st, with the Reserve Division, remained stationed at Altafulla, some ten miles to the east of Tarragona. Early in September, however, reports became more and more insistent that the French armies were being steadily withdrawn from Spain, and in order to test the truth of these rumours, Bentinck sent an advanced body, composed almost wholly of Italians and Spaniards, to a position of observation at the Pass of Ordal, a strong post some ten miles in advance on the road to Barcelona, and consequently not far from the position occupied by Suchet. Here, on the night of the 12th, the post was attacked in overpowering strength and the garrison, after a very stout defence, driven out with heavy loss.

Marching on towards Villafranca, Suchet found the allied army drawn up in front of the town, and halted to await the coming of reinforcements; in view of the arrival of these Bentinck drew back to a stronger position between Villafranca and Arbos. During this retirement a rearguard action developed in which the 81st was employed in assisting to cover the retirement. The movement involved the passage of the bridge of Arbos, which was held by the Battalion until all had crossed and the bridge itself had been prepared for demolition.

Suchet now stayed his advance, finally retiring once more behind the Llobregat, while the allies fell back to Vendrell, retiring next day to Altafulla and finally to Tarragona.

In this day's fighting the Battalion had two men killed, five were wounded and six were missing.

The troops had barely arrived back in Tarragona when Lord William Bentinck received orders to return to Sicily, and he left on the 22nd September, when the command devolved upon Lieut.-General Clinton.

At the end of this month the troops went into cantonments, the 1st Battalion 81st occupying Valls until the end of October, when it was moved forward again to Vendrell, where it remained until January, 1814.

By this time the tragedy of the downfall of the Emperor Napoleon was moving rapidly and inevitably to its climax; and in the latter part of January some ten thousand of Marshal Suchet's best troops were recalled to aid the Emperor's falling fortunes in the final great struggle. Marshal Suchet himself took post at Gerona, holding Barcelona and other important strategic points in Northern Catalonia; early in February the allied army crossed the Llobregat, and Barcelona was shortly afterwards invested. In March still more of Suchet's troops were taken from him, so that he was unable to effect anything of importance; and he then destroyed most of the posts his men had been holding, and concentrated what remained of his force at Figueras, just in front of the French border.

It was now considered that the Spanish troops might reasonably be regarded as strong enough to deal with such of the French forces as still remained in Catalonia, whereupon the bulk of the British troops, including the 1st Battalion 81st, was ordered to the plain of Toulouse, where the final issue seemed to lie. A division of six battalions was accordingly formed at Tarragona under Lieut.-General Clinton, these being the 1st and 2nd Battalions 27th, 44th, 1st Battalion 58th, 1st Battalion 81st and 4th Battalion King's German Legion. These marched from the neighbourhood of Barcelona on the 14th April, and were probably overtaken on their march by the following appreciative message from the Duke of Wellington, a copy of his despatch to Earl Bathurst: it is dated "Toulouse, the 19th April, 1814," and runs as follows:—

"Upon the breaking up of this army I perform a most satisfactory duty in reporting to your Lordship my sense of the conduct and merit of Lieut.-General Clinton, and of the troops under his command, since they have been employed in the Peninsula.

"Circumstances have not enabled these troops to have so brilliant a share in the operations of the war as their brother officers and soldiers on this side of the Peninsula; but they have not been less usefully employed; their conduct when engaged with the enemy has always been meritorious; and I have every reason to be satisfied with the General Officer and with them."

Moving by Lerida, Saragossa, Tudela, Pampeluna, Tolosa and Irun to Biarritz, where the division arrived on the 4th May, the regiments, that had come north hoping to share in the final successes of the main army, learnt that the long-drawn-out war was over, that the Empire of Napoleon I had crumpled to the dust and that the monarchy had been re-established in France.

The 1st Battalion 81st was now formed in a brigade with the 27th and 58th Regiments, and, leaving Biarritz on the 22nd May, these marched by way of Bayonne to Bordeaux, where they arrived on the 26th, and here orders were almost at once received for the Battalion to be transferred to a brigade, containing also the 9th and 37th Regiments and commanded by Major-General Kempt, and which was then stationed at Blanquefort. To this place the Battalion marched on the 30th May and found that its new brigade was under orders to proceed at once to Canada for the purpose of reinforcing the troops in that country.

The struggle with the United States, which had declared war against Great Britain on the 18th June, 1812, and which the American Government had entered upon with the main object of gaining possession of Canada, had proceeded with varying success. Towards the end of 1813 the Americans could place one substantial gain to their credit—the destruction of a British fleet upon Lake Erie; but on the other hand we were in possession of the whole peninsula of Niagara and had captured the fort of that name on the American border. By this time the Americans appear to have given up any hope of effecting the conquest of Canada, and, for the campaign of 1814, three objects only were seriously considered—the re-capture of the Island of Michilimacinac at the entrance of Lake Michigan, the possession of which seriously interfered with American trade; the re-taking of Fort Niagara; and an attack upon Kingston.

General Sir George Prevost, who was commanding in Canada, had made earnest appeals to the Home Government for reinforcements, but many of those sent him, earlier in the operations, were of inferior quality, since the best troops were still needed in Spain. But when the Peninsular War came to an end, some of Wellington's brigades became available for service in other fields, and in all sixteen thousand men were despatched to Quebec.

"Their influence upon the operations on the Canadian frontier is not to be duly estimated by the actual fighting part which they were able to take in Canada, because . . . they were not made use of in Lower Canada to any full extent. They landed in July and August, 1814, some of the regiments being sent to the Niagara frontier, a brigade to Kingston, and the remainder encamped south of Montreal, between the St. Lawrence and the Richelieu."*

From the above it will not be anticipated that the 1st Battalion 81st was to take any specially active part in the concluding operations of the war with the United States; and all that can here be set down is a record of movements until the final return of the Battalion to England—and thence to France.

On the 4th June, 1814, the Battalion embarked in transports at Pouillac and dropped down the Gironde, leaving France on the 16th under escort of H.M.S. "Plantagenet," and reaching Quebec on the 8th August. From here the Battalion was at once sent on by detachments to Montreal, where it remained about a month under the command of Captain Downing, Lieut.-Colonel Farrer having been left behind sick at Quebec.

* Robinson, *Canada and Canadian Defences*, p. 76.

Whilst at Montreal the Battalion was inspected by Major-General Kempt on the 23rd August.

The Americans were at this time engaged in the blockade of Machilimacinac, and on the 8th September Captain Wardrop's company of the Battalion proceeded up the Ottawa River in canoes laden with stores for that place. The remaining companies of the Battalion began to move by divisions on the 10th September from Montreal to Coteau-de-Lai and Matilda, remaining at these stations until the 17th October, when the Battalion marched to rejoin its brigade at Kingston. Here all the troops were kept busily employed at the defences of the place, which had now become the arsenal for Lake Ontario.

The treaty of peace with the United States was signed on the 24th December, 1814, after negotiations which had lingered on since the 6th August; but it was not actually ratified until February, 1815, and was not finally announced to General Kempt's brigade at Kingston until the 1st March of this year. On the very day, however, that this news reached the army in Canada, Napoleon, having escaped from Elba, had landed in France, entered Paris on the 20th and proclaimed himself Emperor.

On his escape from Elba, Napoleon had landed at Cannes in Provence, and between that place and Paris quite an army had joined him on the road. This was scarcely to be wondered at, for these officers and soldiers had won fame under his command and gladly welcomed their former leader under whom they hoped, once again, to win fresh honours which might cancel the memory of the reverses and defeats sustained in the Peninsula and the South of France. Louis XVIII had fled from Paris to Ghent. Immediately Napoleon resumed his former dignity of Emperor of the French the Allied Powers determined not to acknowledge this assumption and resolved to deprive him of his sovereignty by again restoring the ancient dynasty. War was forthwith declared against the usurper.

The 1st Battalion 81st was now, in common with many other units, withdrawn from Canada, and left Kingston for Quebec in the middle of May, sailing on the 4th July, escorted by H.M.S. "Bulwark," and arriving at Portsmouth on the 28th July.

By the time of the arrival of the Battalion in England, the Battle of Waterloo had been fought, Napoleon had again been exiled, and the French monarchy had been restored; but an Army of Occupation was for some time to remain in France, and the Battalion was not disembarked, the transports sailing again on the 1st August. The 1st Battalion 81st landed at Ghent on the 3rd and proceeded at once to the neighbourhood of Paris, on arrival here being encamped near St. Denis and brigaded with the 9th, 57th and 90th Regiments under the command of Sir Thomas Bradford.

Towards the end of the year the Battalion was transferred to the 9th Brigade of the 3rd Division.

In December the Battalion was stationed at Compiègne, and from here, in January, 1816, it marched to Valenciennes, being moved on the 18th October to the plain of St. Denain, where, on the 22nd, it took part in a grand review of all the allied forces by H.R.H. the Dukes of Kent and Cumberland, returning thereafter to Valenciennes.

It had now been decided that the strength of the British contingent of the Army of Occupation might safely be reduced, and several units, the 1st Battalion 81st among them, were ordered home. Leaving Valenciennes on the 13th March, 1817, the Battalion reached Calais four days later, and on the 26th sailed for Cork, which was reached on the 4th April, the right wing remaining at Cork in garrison, while the left wing marched to Tralee.

We now return to the 2nd Battalion of the 81st Regiment; the narrative of the 1st Battalion being continued in Chapter XVI.

CHANGING QUARTERS.

1807.

CHAPTER XIV

THE 2ND BATTALION, 81ST REGIMENT

1804–1809

THE CORUNNA CAMPAIGN

WE left the 2nd Battalion 81st in Ireland, whither it had been sent very shortly after being raised in 1804, and for the next four years its record is little more than a chronicle of moves from one quarter in that island to another. Having landed at Cork at the end of November, 1804, the Battalion marched to Kinsale, where it remained until March, 1805, then moving back to Cork and from there to Athlone, being stationed there until September, 1806, when it proceeded to Galway.

On the 6th June, 1807, the Battalion was ordered to Dundalk, and while it was quartered there a great many men volunteered to it from the Dublin, King's County, South Devonshire and Montgomeryshire Militia; and on the 25th December of this year the establishment was raised, and then stood at forty-four sergeants, twenty-two drummers and eight hundred rank and file.

From Dundalk the 2nd Battalion 81st marched to Mullingar, thence in June, 1808, to the Curragh, and from there, in August, to Kinsale. It was while quartered here that the Battalion was placed under orders for active service to take part in the overseas expedition which was being organized, consequent upon the operations recently conducted with the object of freeing Spain and Portugal from the domination of Napoleon.

The campaign of Rolica and Vimiera was over, the agreement known as the Convention of Cintra had been signed, Portugal was temporarily freed from the enemy and her harbours were secured as bases for further operations. The three general officers who in turn had exercised command in Portugal, had all returned to England, and Sir John Moore was left in command of the British forces in Portugal—these, with the bodies of troops now assembling at Cork and Falmouth—being intended to make up an army of forty thousand men. Napoleon now made up his mind that the conduct of the forthcoming operations in the Peninsula should not be entrusted to any of his subordinate commanders, and on the 30th October, 1808, he left Paris to assume command of the army of two hundred and fifty thousand men which was being assembled behind the River Ebro.

The British Cabinet having carefully considered with its military advisers where and in what manner the army now being got together could best be employed, finally decided, on the 25th September, that our troops already in, or about to proceed to, Portugal should act in co-operation with the Spanish armies in the North of Spain; and it was left to the judgment of Sir John Moore, either to embark his troops now in the Peninsula and bring them round to Corunna by sea, or to march them from Lisbon to Valladolid, where it was thought that the concentration of the whole allied force could best be effected. Sir John Moore gives in his diary his reasons for adopting the latter alternative, saying that "the passage by sea is precarious, an embarcation unhinges, and when I get to Corunna I should still have to equip the army before I could stir, and in Galicia it might have been impossible to have found sufficient means of carriage."

On the 11th October, then, Moore's leading regiments left Lisbon, marching in four columns by four different roads; Moore himself quitted the capital on the 27th, leaving behind him a force of ninety thousand men under General Cradock.

The force which was to leave England under Sir David Baird was composed of some twelve thousand five hundred infantry, one thousand artillerymen and three regiments of cavalry, and all were ordered to concentrate and embark at Falmouth where transports were awaiting them. The 2nd Battalion 81st accordingly left Cork on the 9th September and embarked in the transports "Hermione," "Nancy," "Montevideo," "Volga," "Ann" and "Helen," and proceeded to Falmouth, where there was considerable delay, as no horses had yet arrived for the field artillery of the force and Sir David Baird refused to sail without them, though repeatedly pressed to do so by "higher authority."

The Battalion finally left Falmouth on the 9th October and after a favourable passage all the transports, excepting those containing the cavalry, anchored at Corunna on the 13th. Here General Baird's troubles began. He expected to find that all the necessary arrangements had been made for the reception and accommodation of his troops, but he was early informed by the local Junta that the arrival of his army was unlooked for, that the urgent need of the Province was money and arms, rather than troops, and, most serious of all, that the British regiments could not be allowed to land without the sanction of the Central Junta at Madrid. Ten precious days were consequently wasted while a courier was sent to

Madrid to obtain this permission, which was granted, but without either any sign of appreciation of the help about to be afforded by Great Britain, or any promise or suggestion of practical assistance on the part of the Spanish authorities. In fact, as General Baird wrote on the 24th October to Sir John Moore, "the Galician Government merely permits us to land here in the event of it being found impracticable to send us by sea to St. Andero; and directs that, if a disembarcation takes place, it shall be made in detachments of two or three hundred men each, which are to be successively pushed on into Castile, without waiting for the necessary equipment of mules and horses." To this extraordinary proposition Sir David Baird naturally objected in the strongest terms, with the result that, as he wrote, "it has been decided that we should be cantoned in the towns and villages on the two principal roads leading from this place towards Leon and Castile, until such time as the necessary equipment could be effected to enable us to take the field."

In consequence of the above delays it was nearly the end of October before the army commenced disembarkation, but on the 3rd November Baird was able to write to Moore announcing that "all the regiments of my division, with the exception of the 3rd Bn. 60th, are now on shore,"[*] and were already moving on Astorga, where Baird hoped that his advance would arrive by the 13th.

There had been many changes in the brigading of the force; according to a newspaper of the period, the 2nd Battalion 81st was initially posted to a brigade commanded by Brig.-General Slade which contained also the 3rd Battalion 1st Foot and the 2nd Battalion 23rd Fusiliers, and in this paper the number of the effective rank and file of the Battalion is given as 722. To this state there is a footnote to the effect that "the Brigade allotted to General Slade has since been put under the orders of General Manningham, the former having been ordered to Portsmouth to take the command of the cavalry embarking there." Hamilton, in his *History of The Grenadier Guards*, Vol. II, p. 380, gives the brigading of Baird's force after arrival at Falmouth, and according to him the 2nd Battalion 81st was then allotted to Major-General Mackenzie's brigade containing also the 51st, 59th, 60th and 76th Regiments. On arrival at Corunna other changes were made; the 3rd Battalion 60th was detailed to remain there; while in accordance with orders contained in a letter dated the 22nd October from Sir John Moore to General Baird, the 27th and 31st Regiments, which now, *pace* Hamilton, formed with the 3rd Battalion 1st and 1st Battalion 26th Manningham's brigade, were ordered down to Lisbon to take the place of two other regiments which Moore had drawn from that garrison;

---

[*] The 81st Digest of Service states the Battalion landed on the 7th November.

this left Manningham's brigade with two infantry battalions only, and the 2nd Battalion 81st appears then to have been transferred to it.

It may be gathered from Sir David Baird's correspondence of this period that by the 23rd November most of his infantry battalions had reached Astorga, but that he lacked cavalry to screen his movements, to procure information, and to enable him to test the truth of the many conflicting rumours then in circulation. On the 23rd November news came in of the rout of one Spanish army, and he was apprehensive of the fate which later overtook the other two. He had written to Moore asking his views as to the advisability of an advance from Astorga, and in reply Moore directed that if his cavalry were up by the 1st December, Baird should advance on Benevente. Baird then commenced to put everything in train, but within a very few hours came another letter from Moore, telling him of the disaster which had befallen the remaining Spanish armies, and stating that, seeing no prospect of further helping the Spaniards, he —Moore—proposed retiring on Portugal and defending that country as long as possible. Baird was now to fall back on Corunna and ship his army thence to Lisbon, where a junction would be effected with Moore's troops.

On the 30th November Sir David Baird had commenced the retrograde movement of his infantry, but on the 3rd December he himself was still at Astorga with all his cavalry and several of his infantry regiments.

It is impossible exactly to locate the position of the 2nd Battalion 81st at this stage of the operations; but from the pay-roll it appears that on the 26th November the Battalion was at Bembibre, so the brigade of which it formed part was evidently not up with the headquarters of the force when the order for the retirement was given out. Another clue to the location of the Battalion is contained in the diary of a cavalry officer in the Corunna Campaign (Captain Gordon, 15th Hussars), who mentions that on the 3rd December, when he was moving up to the front from the base with a detachment of cavalry to join the army, he breakfasted at Villafranca with some officers of the 81st, and he goes on to say that the camp rumour of the day credited Sir David with the intention of holding the very strong position there until the Spanish troops should be rallied, adding also that the town was full of troops. The retirement had, however, already gone beyond Villafranca, for Captain Gordon had met the 51st and 59th Regiments of Baird's 3rd Brigade on the march five miles on the Corunna side of the town on the 2nd December.

The Spanish commander, the Marquis de la Romana, was greatly disturbed at learning Sir John Moore's decision, and at hearing of Baird's consequent preparations for retiring from Astorga; and he wrote to the latter general officer imploring him to delay his retreat, and expressing his conviction of the ruinous consequences to the Spanish cause should the British troops be withdrawn. On receipt of this appeal, and sharing the opinion that the continuance of a British force at Astorga was essential to afford security to the Spanish army assembling at Leon, and to enable it to retire unmolested upon Galicia, Sir David Baird proceeded to take steps to halt his troops on their rearward march, pending any fresh instructions which might reach him from Sir John Moore. This decision was speedily justified. On the 5th December Moore wrote to Baird from Salamanca, ordering him to suspend his march till he heard from him again, and to make arrangements for returning to Astorga should that be necessary; this was immediately followed up by a second letter from Moore telling Baird to " put to the right about and return bag and baggage to Astorga," adding, " I mean to proceed bridle in hand, for if the bubble bursts and Madrid falls, we shall have a run for it." Later again Baird was ordered to send his cavalry at once to Zamora and to move the rest of his force to Benevente.

Meanwhile, Sir John Moore had heard of the fall of Madrid, but he adhered to his decision to move on Burgos and strike at the French flank; and on the 10th December he sent Baird orders to join him at Valladolid as soon after the 12th as possible, further movements to be governed by events. On the 14th, however, before the junction of the two forces had been effected and when Moore was at Alaejos, an intercepted despatch came to hand. This " was addressed by Berthier to Soult, dated the 10th December, and contained not only mention of Soult's own force—two divisions of infantry and four regiments of cavalry—but bade him at once seize Leon, Zamora and Benevente, and overrun the province of Leon. There was, said Berthier, nothing to stop him, for the British were in full retreat upon Lisbon, and therefore, as soon as Soult had verified the fact of the British retirement, he was to push forward rapidly. The Marshal then added the following summary of the French position at that moment. The advanced guard was at Talavera ready to move on Badajoz; Bessières was pursuing the beaten army of Castanos towards Valencia; the fifth corps under Mortier was moving to Saragoza; the head of the eighth corps under Junot had arrived at Vittoria, and the whole of it would probably concentrate at Burgos." *

Under these circumstances, for Moore to move on Burgos as he had intended, would have been to walk into a trap; but a stroke at Soult's corps, isolated and unsuspicious of the proximity of the British forces, seemed a sound and promising enterprise; and upon this course Moore at once decided, changing the direction of his movements accordingly.

* Fortescue, Vol. VI, pp. 326, 327.

He wrote to Baird, acquainting him of the altered situation and ordering him to join forces, indicating at the same time that the combined army was to live on the country and base itself on Corunna.

The concentration of the two bodies was effected on the 19th December at Valderas.

It may be presumed that the 2nd Battalion 81st retraced its steps at once from Villafranca to Valderas, and on the 20th December, at Mayorga, the force was reorganized as a single army, the Battalion remaining with the same regiments in the same brigade, but this last now forming part of the 1st Division, commanded by Sir David Baird in person.

The state dated the 19th December, 1808, gives the total strength of Moore's army on that day as 29,357 all ranks, a considerable drop since embarkation at Falmouth. The pay-rolls of the Battalion account for no more than three privates dead and six missing, so those unaccounted for were probably sick in hospital at Lugo and Astorga, or on command at Corunna and elsewhere. Of those with the Colours, they were, so Fortescue says, " in good health and order, their behaviour so far had been exemplary ; and their confidence in themselves was, if anything, rather too great."

Moving north-east from Mayorga on the 20th December, Sir David Baird's division occupied the town of Sahagun, after our cavalry had there completely routed a brigade of French cavalry ; and, having halted here for two days, the army was ready to make a night march to the Carrion, preparatory to attacking Soult at Saldana, assisted by ten thousand Spaniards under de la Romana. Soult's corps stood alone and isolated on the Carrion River, with a strength little more than half that of Moore's force and could be attacked with advantage, whether it advanced or remained stationary, and without fear of interference from the French in the south or east.

It was close upon midnight on the 23rd December, some of the troops had already gone forward and the others were waiting in column of route on the road, when an orderly came to General Baird conveying a message that the Commander-in-Chief desired to see him at once ; and it was not long before it was made known that the advance was to be abandoned and that the troops were to return to their quarters—the enemy was on the march northward from Madrid and Napoleon himself was well on the way to Benevente.

" The troops, who had long panted to meet the enemy, and who but an hour ago were full of life and confidence, suddenly appeared like men whose highest hopes were withered and their favourite expectations overthrown. Few gave vent to their feelings either by complaint or murmur ; but all retired to their quarters in a state of sullen silence. . . . We rose next morning perfectly ignorant, and, to a certain degree indifferent, as to the fate which awaited us." *

The message now to hand from de la Romana, and confirmed in almost every particular by the British Intelligence Service, contained a warning to Moore that practically every French corps in the Peninsula had been ordered to move on Leon, and that Napoleon himself had left Madrid with the object of cutting off the British from Galicia. Madrid was only some six marches distant from Mayorga, and as Napoleon had already completed two, if not indeed three, of these, the margin of time for Moore's army to cross the Esla and gain the high road to Corunna was already all too short. There was no time to be lost, nor indeed was any wasted. The dispositions for retreat were at once made out and issued to the different subordinate commanders, and on Christmas Day the retreat began.

"From the points occupied by the British army two principal roads lead on Astorga. That on the north, crossing the Esla by a bridge at Mansilla de los Mulos, and passing through Leon, but that was already occupied by de la Romana's division. . . . The southern line crosses the Esla by the bridge at Castro Gonzalo, about a league in front of Benevente, through which town it passes. It was along this latter road that Sir John Moore and the principal part of the army began to retreat; whilst Sir David Baird was directed with his division to take an intermediate direction by cross-roads, leading to Valencia de Don Juan, a town situated on the Esla, about equidistant from the bridge before mentioned, at which place the river is passable by a large ferry boat, and in a dry season at a ford in the neighbourhood." †

There being no personal record of the movements of the 2nd Battalion 81st in existence, we must follow these as best we can by tracing the progress of Baird's division during the three terrible weeks that now followed.

Marching in miserable weather by the most execrable roads, the division halted on Christmas night at some villages half-way between Sahagun and the Esla; and moving on again early on the 26th, the river was reached at Valencia de Don Juan in time to pass all the troops over considerably before nightfall, the crossing being accomplished partly by ferry and partly at the ford. But the rain which had recently been falling, had caused the Esla to rise greatly, and even while the troops were passing, it rose so rapidly that some men were drowned and the passage by the ford had to be abandoned. Happily the river now presented a serious natural obstacle to a pursuing enemy. The division occupied the town of Villa Marrian and some villages close to the Esla, strong posts were placed on

* Londonderry, *Narrative of the Peninsular War*, Vol. I, pp. 247, 248.
† Hook, *Life of Sir David Baird*, Vol. II, p. 302.

the banks, and General Baird at once wrote to de la Romana at Mansilla, urging the destruction of the bridge at that place.

Remaining halted here during the 27th and 28th to give time for the main body to effect a crossing at Benevente, the march was resumed on the 29th and Astorga was reached the same night; but this town was found to be crowded beyond its capacity by two British and one Spanish divisions, and by 4 a.m. on the 30th Baird's men were again on the march towards Manzanal, "a small village seated in the midst of stupendous mountains deeply covered with snow."

During the original advance Astorga had been made something of a depot, and all the camp equipage and baggage, which Baird's division had brought with it from Corunna, had been stored there; there was now, however, no means of removing it and the whole was ordered to be destroyed, and the Battalion, equally with the rest of the force, lost all its heavy baggage. There was very little food to be had, only a two-days' supply of bread being available, for nearly all the other supplies were at Villafranca, some fifty miles in rear, and with no transport to bring it on. Under the circumstances Moore abandoned all idea of holding the strong line of the Sierra de Lilleros and decided to pursue his way to the sea. Such food and stores as the men could carry were distributed amongst them, the remainder was burnt, and some four hundred British sick and wounded had to be left behind when the remainder of the troops marched on. The toilsome, uphill march, in falling snow, was completed by the afternoon of the 30th December, and at Manzanal some bullocks were procured and slaughtered, but there was no issue of fuel and the men attempted to cook a meal with wood torn from the miserable cabins of the peasantry. They sought such shelter as was obtainable under banks and hedgerows, but long before the meal had been cooked an order was received to continue the march to Bembibre; and by ten o'clock at night the weary column "was again in motion down the long descent which extends for eight miles from Manzanal to the village of Torre; a most trying and arduous service at that hour of the night, in that season of the year, and in the state of hunger and exhaustion in which our brave soldiers were.

"The division reached Bembibre just as the morning of the 31st December dawned. The place evidently could not afford shelter or cover to one-third of the men. . . . All the houses were closed; but the urgency of the case rendering the men deaf to refusals, they were speedily broken open; the wine-cellars were immediately invaded, and the exhausted state of the men rendering them more obnoxious to the effects of the liquor, those who drank most fell into a state of torpor, from which it was exceedingly difficult to rouse them when the march was again to be continued."

Many of these men had to be left behind—to the sabres of the French dragoons or the prison camps of the Peninsula.

The 2nd Battalion 81st seems to have lost but few men on this day, according to the pay-roll; but possibly some explanation of this may be found in the fact that Baird's division was the last to enter Bembibre and the first to leave it, for within less than ten hours of arrival it was on the road to Cacabellos, arriving here on the night of the 31st after having covered fifty miles in thirty-six hours.

From Cacabellos the retreat of the division was continued through Villafranca to Las Herrerias—eighteen miles; and on the 2nd January, 1809, the mountain of Pietra Fita was passed in a severe storm of wind and snow. Many of the women and children accompanying the army died of exposure, and some of the soldiers sank down under their trials. The snow on each side of the road was much higher than the points of the men's fixed bayonets, the road was frozen hard and slippery, the men's shoes were wholly worn out, and the gun-horses were constantly falling. Marching on through Nogales and Constantinhos, the division reached Lugo on the 5th January.

Napoleon had arrived at Astorga, where he met Soult, on the 1st January, but en route despatches had reached him from Paris, the contents of which were of a highly disturbing character. From them he learnt of hostile movements in Austria, disturbances in Turkey and conspiracies in Paris; he had, too, by this time realized that Moore's army was making good its retreat, and it seemed to him that the European situation appeared to call more urgently for his personal attention in his capital, than did the pursuit of an elusive British army amid the winter snows of the Galician mountains. He then handed over the conduct of the pursuit to Soult, drafted orders for the general conduct of the war in Spain, and returned to Valladolid, whence, after a very few days' stay, he made his way back to France. Soult, with an army of thirty thousand men, was to follow up the British, while Ney, with some seventeen thousand more, was to hold the province of Leon and give such support as he could afford.

The early departure of Baird's division from Cacabellos, caused the 2nd Battalion 81st to miss the rearguard action which there took place on the 3rd January. Having reached Lugo on the 5th January the Battalion had a couple of days in which to rest, and on the 7th the division marched out and occupied the left of the position which Sir John Moore now took up in front of Lugo, where he offered battle to his pursuer. The position, so Fortescue states, "was exceedingly strong. His right rested on the Minho, which was unfordable; his front was covered by a ravine and by innumerable enclosures which might serve as natural entrenchments; and only his left, which leaned upon rugged mountains, could be turned." The approach to the position was by a gentle, glacis-like slope, a mile in extent.

Soult had by this time concentrated three infantry and two cavalry divisions in front of the British, but his units were weakened by the hardships of the pursuit, and he does not at first seem to have realized that anything more than a strong rearguard was opposing him. He sought, therefore, to detain Moore by demonstrations till Ney's corps should close up. On the 7th, then, he did no more than feel the British position, bringing forward guns against the centre, making a feint against the right, and a more serious attack on the left, all of which were easily repulsed. On the 8th some French reinforcements came up, but Soult still considered himself too weak to make a serious attack; and as the day wore on, without any real sign of movement on the part of the enemy, Moore began to grow anxious, fearing the arrival of heavy French reinforcements, or some flank attack by Ney's corps.

"I can never," wrote Leith Hay, "look back to the scenes in front of Lugo, without a feeling of regret that the battle was not there fought, nor ever bring to recollection the gallant bearing of the troops under all their miseries, without admiration of the spirit that appeared to animate them, and must have led to certain victory."

During the 8th both armies observed one another, the British soldiers were all keyed up expectant of a battle, of the favourable result of which they had no doubt whatever; but Moore then resolved to resume his retreat, for he had but one day's bread left in Lugo, and if he took the offensive he would be unable to follow up any success. His resolve has the approval of Napier, who writes that "a defeat would have been ruin and victory useless."

At nightfall on the 8th the orders went round to continue the retirement, and, leaving the bivouac fires stoked up to burn for hours, the British army, bitterly disappointed, took the Corunna road once more. Though the withdrawal began at midnight, the difficult country, the dispersal of the troops and the pitch-dark, rain-sodden night made the collecting together of the different units a slow and troublesome process, so that it was getting on towards dawn before some of the battalions were clear of Lugo. Having crossed the Minho, seven miles north of the town, the bridge was blown up, thus effectively checking the French pursuit and contributing greatly to the safety of the retreat; those who would learn of the real horrors of the march that followed should study the account given in the *Narrative* of Lord Londonderry.

On the morning of the 9th the head of the column had reached Guitiriz, the tail of it straggling many miles in rear. A halt was called to enable the column to close up, but a terrible storm of wind and hail swept over the soaked and hungry soldiers, and these, seeking food and shelter, became scattered over the country-side and separated from their regiments. In this way Baird's division suffered severe losses, and several hours were occupied in getting the men together again.

Soon after dark the march was resumed, Betanzos, twenty miles on, being the destination—and during the whole morning of the 10th January the wreck of an army was trickling into the place. During this day something was done in the way of reorganization—one regiment—not the 2nd Battalion 81st be it noted—had marched into Betanzos at a strength of nine officers, three sergeants and three privates—and so well and so quickly did the British soldiers pull themselves together, that when on the 11th the army marched out of Betanzos, all ranks were " perfectly unlike what could have been expected to re-form from the *débris* of an army, which but the preceding day had exhibited an alarming state of demoralization and exhaustion."

The real hardships of the retreat ended at Betanzos; on the 11th the weather changed for the better and the sun shone out; and on the night of the 11th when the troops marched into Corunna, the men remaining with the Colours had regained their strength and spirits.

The retreat had almost throughout been admirably covered by Paget's division and the cavalry, with the result that though followed up closely by the French the pursuit had never been really pressed, the fact being that bridges had nearly everywhere been destroyed behind our rearguard, that the ranks of the French divisions were, like ours, thinned by fatigue and by straggling, and that Soult had throughout acted with great caution.

The few days' delay now vouchsafed to Moore were invaluable. He had brought his army to Corunna and he had regained his sea-communications, but his troubles and anxieties were by no means at an end. Originally he had intended to retire on Vigo and the transports had been ordered thither; but when the army arrived at Astorga, the opinions of the officers who had been sent to report on the respective advantages for embarkation of the two ports, Vigo and Corunna, were unanimously in favour of the latter. Moore had then to send urgent requests for the transports to be sent to Corunna and not to Vigo.

Unfortunately, contrary winds upset his calculations, and when, on arrival on the hills overlooking Corunna, he looked down upon the port, it was almost empty of shipping; but on the afternoon of the 14th the long-expected vessels ran into the harbour, and the embarkation of the sick and wounded, the cavalry and all the surplus guns was at once proceeded with.

"Something like 5,000 men had perished or been taken during the retreat; 3,500 had embarked at Vigo, so that about 15,000 men, all infantry save some 200 gunners, remained behind to oppose Soult. Considering all that they had gone through, they were now in very good trim; all the sick and weakly men had been sent off, those who remained in the ranks were all war-hardened veterans. Before the battle they had enjoyed four days of rest and good feeding in Corunna. Moreover, they had repaired their armament; there were in the arsenal many thousand stand of arms, newly arrived from England for the use of the Galician army. Moore made his men change their rusty and battered muskets for new ones, before ordering the store to be destroyed. He also distributed new cartridges, from an enormous stock found in the place. The town was, in fact, crammed with munitions of all sorts. Seeing that there would be no time to re-embark them, Moore utilized what he could, and destroyed the rest." *

The preliminary embarkation completed, there remained some 15,000 infantry and twelve guns to take part in the action which now seemed inevitable to cover the safe embarkation of the remainder of the British force; and on the 14th January General Baird's division was moved out to occupy its place in the position which Sir John Moore had selected.

To have occupied merely the fortifications of Corunna itself would have been impossible, since such a step would have allowed of the enemy approaching sufficiently close to have laid the whole harbour under fire. There was a choice of three other positions, but two of these, though actually stronger than that eventually taken up, were too extensive for the limited force available. The line finally decided upon was just a mile long and two miles in front of the town, the left resting on the estuary of the El Burgo River, and the right on the western slopes of Monte Mero, above the village of Elvina. Sir John Hope's division occupied the left of the line, and that of Sir David Baird the right, each with two brigades up in line and one in reserve. Manningham's brigade, with the 2nd Battalion 81st in the centre, formed the right centre. The weak point about the position was that west of Elvina the ground fell very rapidly into a wide valley, leading directly into Corunna, so that the right flank was open to a turning movement. Here, however, Moore had placed two divisions, that of Paget being posted at the village of Oza, a mile behind Elvina, while Fraser's occupied the heights of Santa Margarita, a half-mile to the west of Paget.

The British troops lay in their positions all through the 14th, Soult

* Oman, Vol. I, p. 582.

showing no anxiety to attack with the inferior force immediately at his command; two of his divisions were still in rear and Ney's corps was a week's march behind, so Soult had every reason to delay attacking, so long as his quarry could not escape him. He spent the 14th in passing his men and guns over the River Mero, but when, late on this day, he saw the transports in the harbour he realized that he must attack or lose his prey altogether. On the 15th one of his divisions joined him and many stragglers had come up, and during the morning the light troops of Mermet's and Merle's divisions advanced against the heights of Penasquedo and Palavea, occupied by the British outposts, and some fighting developed, the British advanced posts being withdrawn to the Monte Mero line.

The French now occupied the whole of the commanding ridge and there established some of their heavy guns; that night the two armies remained observing each other from the parallel ridges, some three-quarters of a mile apart.

From the position occupied by Soult he was unable to see the whole of the British position, nor to form any accurate opinion as to the strength in which it was held; he may well have thought that possibly much of Moore's infantry had already embarked, and he now decided to attack, pinning down the British left, driving in or turning the right, and then interposing his cavalry between the Monte Mero position and Corunna, thus, so he hoped, cutting off a large part of the British army and forcing its surrender. These dispositions took some time to effect, and it was after midday before any movement was discernible in the French lines.

Moore was in the meantime perfecting his embarkation arrangements, intending, should the enemy not attack, to put some of his troops aboard the transports in the afternoon, and the remainder under cover of darkness; but shortly after 2 p.m. he learnt that French columns, in great strength, were descending the slopes of the Penasquedo and moving on the village of Elvina.

The right of the British position, of which Elvina formed an advanced post, was held by Bentinck's brigade of Baird's division; on its left was Manningham's brigade, with Warde's brigade in reserve. Leith's brigade prolonged the line to the left, while that of Hill held the ground between Corunna and the sea, with Craufurd's brigade in reserve. Against this position Soult now sent twelve battalions with orders to carry Elvina and turn the British right; Merle, with thirteen battalions, was to fall upon the centre, while another division of ten battalions was to contain the left wing; the French cavalry was to work round the British right and cut in on their line of retreat.

Covered by a cloud of skirmishers the French advanced, and the heat of the action developed about Elvina; the British picquets were driven from the village, and the French cavalry, passing on, threatened to envelop the right flank; at this moment Sir David Baird was seriously wounded, being carried from the field. Sir John Moore was happily at hand, and he ordered up the two reserve divisions.

The musketry-fire of the British line was now telling on the enemy and causing confusion to his deployment, and two regiments then charging forward with the bayonet the French columns were repulsed; and for some time the issue hung in the balance, victory inclining at one time to the French and at another to the British. Sir John Moore was riding about the field from one hard-pressed regiment to another, when a round shot from the French battery on the Penasquedo ridge struck him on the left breast and shoulder, hurling him from his horse, the command of the army then devolving on Sir John Hope.

The fall of the commander, coming as it did so soon after that of Baird, deprived the right wing of a leader, but troops had come up from Paget's reserve division, and these counter-attacking forced the French back on to the defensive.

The second French attack upon Elvina had exhausted Mermet's last reserves, and to sustain the fight Merle sent forward some of his troops. These, to reach their objective, had to move across the right front of Manningham's brigade, and that general sent some of his men to take this column in flank, whereupon the 3rd Battalion 1st, and 2nd Battalion 81st became very closely engaged, and a furious combat resulted which endured for two hours. The pressure was then taken off the British right, but the 2nd Battalion 81st sustained a heavy loss, fourteen officers and one hundred and forty other ranks being killed and wounded.

The Battalion fired away all its ammunition in this encounter, so that it became necessary to relieve it in the firing-line by the 59th of General Leith's brigade, and he brought the relief in person and highly complimented the 2nd Battalion 81st on its gallant conduct.

Soon afterwards, as the dusk was beginning to fall, the French broke off the action in this part of the field, and fell back to the slopes of Palavea.

On the left, where the British were strongly posted, they were hardly attacked at all, and some regiments here stationed did not fire a shot until quite late in the afternoon; and the fire which had everywhere slackened about five, died away altogether at six. Hope then debated whether to wait in his position to attack or to be attacked, decided to embark the army, and at 9 p.m. that day the troops were withdrawn from Monte Mero, leaving only the picquets behind to feed the watch-fires. "At the close of the action," wrote Leith Hay, "there was not the same exhilarating

CORUNNA.

16th January, 1809.

From a contemporary Engraving.

feeling, the same excitement, that usually attends a victory. No pursuit, no trophies, nor any prisoners, at once to attest the services and the fortune of the army. . . . A stillness prevailed for hours. The repose of the camp was only interrupted by the formation of the troops at midnight, when the whole, with the exception of the picquets, marched towards the harbour."

To Sir John Moore, who was struck down on the field and, dying of his wounds, was buried in Corunna while the embarkation was taking place, General Sir John Hope paid the following fine tribute:—

"His career has been unfortunately too limited for his Country, but has been sufficient for his own fame. Beloved by the Army, honoured by his Sovereign, and respected by his enemy, he has terminated a life devoted to her service by a glorious death, leaving his name as a memorial, an example, and an incitement to those who shall follow him in the path of honour; and it is from his Country alone that his memory can receive the tribute which is its due."

In a report made on the action of the 16th January, Sir John Hope wrote:—

"On no occasion has the undaunted valour of British troops ever been more manifest. . . . The brunt of the action fell upon the 4th, 42nd, 50th and 81st Regiments, with part of the Brigade of Guards and the 26th Regiment"; while in a General Order circulated from H.M.S. "Audacious," off Corunna and dated 18th January, 1809, he wrote:— "Major-General Manningham,* with his brigade consisting of the Royals, the 26th and 81st Regiments, will also be pleased to accept his best thanks for their steady and gallant conduct during the action."

The French made little or no attempt to interfere with the embarkation which was safely completed on the afternoon of the 17th, the last of the ships leaving the harbour before sundown, and the whole fleet anchoring in the roads for the night. The 2nd Battalion 81st, like most other regiments, found itself split up among several transports, but thirty officers and 291 other ranks, with twenty-one women and one child, are shown in the log of H.M.S. "Victory" as rationed for the voyage: five officers and the remainder of the rank and file sailed in other craft: Oman gives the embarkation strength of the 2nd Battalion 81st as 478 all ranks.

Plymouth was reached on the 28th January and here the sick and wounded were put ashore, the remainder of the Battalion going on to Portsmouth and landing on the 2nd February. During this month other parties came ashore at different ports from various transports and seventeen from

---

* Major-General Manningham died on the 23rd August of this year from illness due to the hardship and exposure of the campaign.

H.M.S. "Rodney," and all were sent on to Lewes, where, by the middle of March, the surviving effectives finally assembled under Major Williams. Shortly after, the Battalion was moved to Bletchingley to refit, and here, in May, it was joined by a draft of two hundred and fifty volunteers, chiefly from the West Country and Irish Militia.

Before and during the retreat to Corunna the Battalion losses were one officer died and one missing, seven privates died, and two sergeants, one corporal, one drummer and one hundred and sixty privates are shown as "missing." In the battle itself the 2nd Battalion 81st had one officer, one sergeant, three corporals and twenty-two men killed, three officers, the sergeant-major, two sergeants, two corporals, and twelve men died of wounds; and ten officers, five sergeants and ninety-one other ranks were wounded.

The following officers took part with the Battalion in the Corunna Campaign: Majors W. Williams, wounded, H. Milling, wounded, and C. Crigan, died of wounds; Captains A. G. Downing, wounded, R. Digby, killed, N. Brown, H. Bowles, and R. Cole; Lieutenants J. Lutman, adjutant, wounded, A. McAlpine, S. Corbett, died, J. G. Hort, wounded, G. Pearson, wounded, L. Macartney, wounded, D. Fan, K. Montgomery, B. V. Derenzy, wounded, J. Sisson, A. S. Taylor, G. Jackson and T. L. Fenwick; Ensigns E. Lee, T. H. Hammer, died of wounds and buried at sea, R. Crofton, H. Biggam, T. Griffin, died of wounds, T. Manning, wounded, R. Pape, T. L. Serjeant, wounded, T. C. Wheate, A. Gordon, G. Smyth and R. Mostyn; Volunteer J. A. Lutman, Paymaster A. Thompson, Surgeon P. Schoole, Assistant-Surgeons J. Steele, missing, and H. Chislette.

For their services in the Peninsular War the two Battalions of the 81st Regiment were granted the Battle-Honours of "Maida," "Corunna" and "Peninsula," the first under Horse Guards letter of the 24th February, 1807, the second under a similar letter dated the 3rd March, 1812, and the last, which, for some obscure reason, was not allotted for the Corunna or pre-Corunna fighting, was granted under an Order dated the 18th April, 1815.

When in 1847 the Medal was granted for the wars of the end of the eighteenth and the beginning of the nineteenth century, eleven surviving officers, seven sergeants, two corporals, three drummers and seventy-four privates received the clasp "Corunna" to their medal; the officers were Captains N. Brown, R. Cole, and J. Lutman, Lieutenants G. Pearson, G. Jackson, J. Sisson, A. Thompson, J. G. Hort and B. V. Derenzy; Ensigns E. Morgan (?) and H. Biggam.

CHAPTER XV

THE 2ND BATTALION, 81ST REGIMENT

1809–1816

THE WALCHEREN EXPEDITION
BERGEN : SERVICE IN THE NETHERLANDS : BRUSSELS

IN the years 1803 and 1806 the British Government had seriously entertained the idea of sending a force to occupy the Island of Walcheren at the mouth of the River Scheldt, and in 1809 the idea was revived. "In this year Napoleon was making every effort to establish at Antwerp a commercial rival to London, and to avail himself of the naval resources which the possession of Holland and the Scheldt placed at his command, thus keeping the 'pistol presented at the breast of England' ready charged for any future contingencies. The English Government thought, by striking a blow in the Scheldt, to forestall Napoleon's hopes of maritime rivalry at the outset, and, further, to detain in Holland a portion of the forces the Emperor was at that time setting in motion against Austria.

"To effect these objects the English Government, in the summer of 1809, determined to send an expedition to the Scheldt, and on the 16th July Lieut.-General the Earl of Chatham, K.G., was appointed to the command of a land force destined to attack and destroy the naval forces and establishments at Flushing, Antwerp and Terneuse, and in the Island of Walcheren, and to render the river unnavigable for ships-of-war." *

The first notification received by the Army in the United Kingdom of any expedition of the kind being under contemplation, appears to be contained in a letter sent to the Commander-in-Chief by Lord Castlereagh dated the 8th May. In it the writer expressed the hope that "the Regiments of the Line may by this time have made considerable progress towards being again fit for service"; stated the season was advancing when their exertions might again be called; and asked for a return of all infantry battalions then in England, the effective strength of which was over six hundred men.

In reply to this letter a return was submitted on the 10th May, showing

* *British Minor Expeditions*, p. 57.

fifty-three battalions then in England, but the Government seems now to have experienced some difficulty in making up its mind as to the size of the force to be employed. In the first instance the Commander-in-Chief was asked to provide 25,000 infantry and 5,000 cavalry, with a reserve 10,000 strong, which was "to be disposable for any other service." Four weeks later Sir David Dundas was ordered to prepare an expeditionary force of 35,000 infantry and only 1,800 cavalry, and to hold it ready for immediate embarkation.

On the 4th July the 2nd Battalion 81st received orders to march to Portsmouth, there to embark on foreign service. The necessary preparations were somewhat hurriedly made, for the Paymaster's accounts show that only on the 11th July did he obtain a clearance permitting of his "writing off" the sum of £850 for replacement of necessaries "lost in the last campaign"; and on the same day it is noted that two officers —Captain Lutman and Lieutenant Hort—must be left behind as they were "insufficiently recovered from wounds received at Corunna" to proceed again on active service.

Marching to Portsmouth at a strength of forty sergeants, nineteen drummers and 638 other ranks, under command of Major Williams, the Battalion embarked on the 18th July in H.M.S. "Achilles," and at five o'clock on the morning of the 28th the fleet set sail for the mouth of the Scheldt.

"It was incomparably," writes Fortescue, "the greatest armament that had ever left the shores of England. The troops of all ranks numbered close upon 40,000, of which 25,000 were embarked upon men-of-war, and the remainder upon transports. In all, the infantry numbered about 33,000, the cavalry rather more than 2,000, and the artillery about 3,000. The whole were organized, nominally, in two wings and actually in six divisions, the cavalry being incorporated with the Light Infantry corps in each wing. The battalions varied greatly in strength, some of them barely exceeding 400 bayonets, while others reached 1,000," so that the 2nd Battalion 81st appears to have been somewhere about the average in numbers.

The Battalion was in the 1st Division commanded by Lieut.-General Sir J. Cradock, and in Major-General Graham's brigade, which contained also the 3rd Battalion 1st, and the 2nd Battalion 35th Regiments.

The following were the objectives of the six divisions composing the army under Lord Chatham: the 1st and the Reserve Divisions were to land on the Island of Schouwen on the north shore of the East Scheldt, capture the fort of Goes on South Beveland, and take in rear that of Borssele and other defences on the north bank of the Western Scheldt;

the 2nd Division was to seize the Island of Cadzand and the river batteries, so as to assist any advance on Antwerp; the 4th Division was to disembark on the south-west coast of the Island of Walcheren and capture Flushing; the 3rd and Light Divisions were to remain in their ships in the Downs until they should be sent for, but this would not be until the whole of the disembarkation had been completed and Flushing was contained, when Lord Chatham, with the rest of the army, was to push forward on Antwerp.

The 1st, 2nd and Reserve Divisions composed the Left Wing under Lieut.-General Sir Eyre Coote, the remainder formed the Right Wing, which was, however, broken up by two of its divisions remaining at the outset in the Downs, as already stated.

It will be seen that the scheme depended for its working out upon the success of a number of operations all undertaken simultaneously; the failure of any one would jeopardize the fruition of the main object—the capture of Antwerp; while any delay or lack of co-ordination would rob the attack of its essential factor of surprise. Further, information about the enemy was very meagre, so that on the whole the odds may be said to have been rather against the success of the expedition. The French were aware that our attack was to be made, but were not fully cognizant as to where and when it would fall; they were, however, quite prepared to concentrate their troops at any threatened point.

The fleet arrived off the mouth of the Scheldt during the night of the 28th July, but the wind, which had been fair during the passage, was now freshening to a gale, so that some of the smaller craft were wrecked, and by daylight on the 29th a heavy sea was beating on the shore. Any landing on the Island of Cadzand had to be postponed, while that on the western, or south-western, shore of Walcheren was pronounced impracticable. The anchorage of what was known as the Roompot was, however, surveyed by the naval commanders and found to be safe and of sufficient size to accommodate the whole fleet, so all the vessels were directed thither. Early on the afternoon of the 30th the whole fleet was at anchor off Zieriksee. "Foul weather had delayed the embarkation for full thirty-six hours, and had then diverted it to the quarter remotest from Flushing. From this point the principal lines of advance were blocked by the petty fort of Veere and by the town of Middelburg, which, though not coming within the description of a fortress, was enclosed by bastioned lines and by a ditch."

It was now discovered that by changing the landing places to certain points on the lee side of the islands, approachable from the Roompot, the Left Wing and the Reserve might be put ashore, despite the bad weather, in order to proceed with the tasks allotted to them. The troops, once landed, would have to cover a longer distance in order to arrive at their objectives, but this seemed preferable to waiting indefinitely on board ship for the weather to moderate. Unfortunately no such course could be taken in the case of Cadzand, the lee shore of which was covered with batteries, and the attack upon this island was necessarily postponed day after day.

Napoleon had early realized that a fortress like Flushing could not be reduced in a moment, and had taken steps for the fortification of the island and the reinforcement of its garrison. Thus Commodore Owen's ships, with the division under General Huntley, of the Right Wing, on board, tossed off the coast while reinforcements could be seen pouring into the place. The weather had slightly improved by the evening of the 1st August, but by this time, though the British were unaware of the fact, the French garrison numbered over six thousand men. The boats of the British fleet were insufficient to land more than seven hundred men at one time, a number, of course, wholly useless in view of the opposition to be expected, and no more boats could be supplied from the other ships of the fleet. The contemplated attack here was at first merely postponed and finally abandoned on the 3rd August, when the division was also sent into the Roompot anchorage to await further orders.

Thus the expedition failed to obtain possession of its most important objective, for without control of the Cadzand channel, the ships must wait for the fall of Flushing before they could enter the river for the attack upon Antwerp. This latter city was well known as a fortress of great strength; its garrison was none too strong, but it was tolerably certain that Flushing could hold out sufficiently long to enable reinforcements to reach Antwerp, for until Flushing fell, the British could not enter the Scheldt; thus the necessary respite was ensured when the attempt to land on Cadzand was given up.

Meanwhile, on the evening of the 30th July the Left Wing had at last managed to get ashore on the lee side of Walcheren and near the small fort of Veere; and it was close on 7 p.m. before five thousand men were landed, none of them fit for a long march, uncovered by cavalry, and all the worse after five days at least spent on board ship, much crowded and probably suffering in no small degree from sea-sickness.

There had been several eleventh-hour changes in the composition of brigades and divisions, and the 2nd Battalion 81st was now in Brigadier Browne's brigade, one of the first to land, and which contained also the 2nd Battalion 23rd, and the 1st Battalion 26th—the Battalion was at a strength of 644 all ranks.

The two brigades of the division—Browne's and Rottenburg's—landed

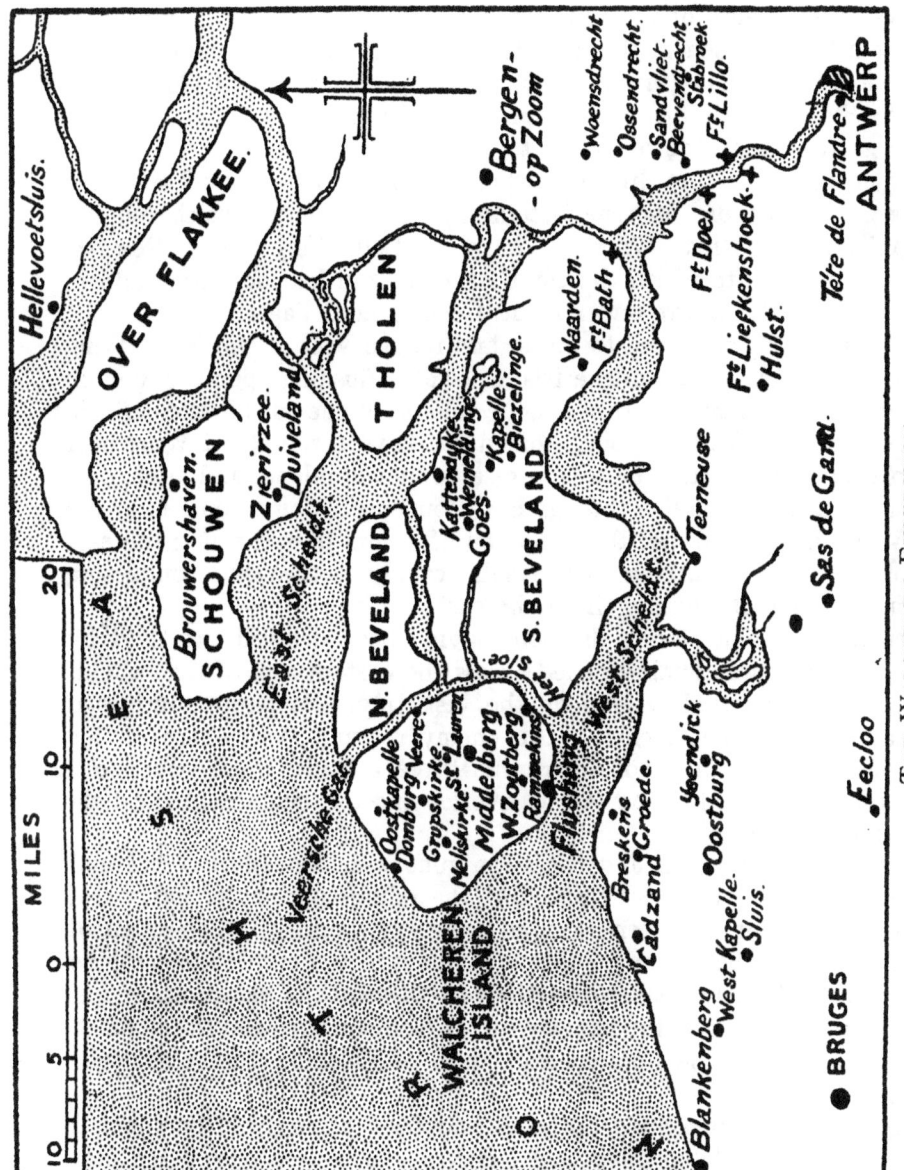

The Walcheren Expedition.
1809.

and made their way through the sand-dunes to the battery at Ten Haak, which was found abandoned, and the troops then advanced towards Veere to cover the landing of the remainder of the Wing. Late that night a surprise attack by General Picton's brigade upon Veere was repulsed, but that place was formally invested next morning at dawn, as it blocked the road to Flushing; it finally surrendered early on the 1st August, some of the garrison escaping by water to Flushing.

By noon on the 31st July the whole of the troops of the Left Wing had been put on shore, and the force now on the Island of Walcheren was reorganized in a Right Wing, a Centre, a Left Wing and a Reserve. Browne's brigade, to which the 1st Battalion 32nd had now been added, formed part of the Centre under Lieut.-General Lord Paget.

The Left Wing remained to invest and reduce Veere; the Right Wing moved by the south coast of the Island to take Flushing upon the western side; the Centre marched through the middle of the Island and, after a slight skirmish at West Zoutburg, joined hands with the Right Wing near that place; while, further east, the Reserve moved inland, and after some fighting, prolonged the line through East Zoutburg. Some hours later the Left Wing, having effected the reduction of Veere, moved round the east side of the Island, masking some small posts en route, thus completing the encirclement of Flushing from the east.

General Sir John Hope's division, having been delayed two days by squally weather, was finally ferried across the eastern arm of the Scheldt and landed on South Beveland on the 31st July. He swept southward and eastward without incident, the enemy retiring everywhere on his approach; and on the 2nd August his three brigades were strung out across the eastern end of the Island, overlooking the junction of the East and West Scheldt.

Flushing was invested and the siege guns were landed at Veere and dragged laboriously across the Island. The reinforcing of the fortress of Flushing could not, however, be interfered with, since the possession of Cadzand enabled the enemy to throw troops into the city, these slipping across in light draught boats under the very bows of the blockading ships, which were prevented by the heavy weather from anchoring in the channel. By the 6th August the reinforced garrison of Flushing numbered eight thousand men.

The erection of breaching batteries had been commenced on the 3rd August, and the 2nd Battalion 81st is said to have been one of the first battalions to break ground in the construction of the siege works. The garrison of the city had, however, been so strongly reinforced that on the 7th it made a determined sortie, directed against the Right Wing, and this was only beaten back after three hours' fighting, the garrison troops having suffered considerable loss.

"On the morrow Chatham at last saw his desire fulfilled, for the wind permitted the English flotilla to extend across to Cadzand and cut it off completely from Flushing. . . . Huntley's and Rosslyn's divisions moved to their places of disembarkation . . . and on the 9th these two divisions landed in South Beveland."*

Then on the 10th a different kind of attack developed—the French cut the sea-dykes, and the water slowly filtered into the trenches until the men were up to their knees in water and there was much sickness: "not a regiment is to be found but what has suffered considerably; nearly the whole of the 23rd Regiment," of Browne's brigade, "is in the hospitals. The sentinels are sometimes relieved twice instead of once, by reason of the sudden indisposition of the men. I confess that this increasing disease has alarmed me exceedingly. Men are frequently carried from the parade. The attack is sudden and violent; the prevalent diseases are the dysentery and the intermittent. They of course originate in the infected air and in the unwholesome water. . . . Our men are dying hourly and almost by the minute; and an order has just been given, doubtless from this frequency, that all burials shall be by night, and without candles or torches." †

It was not long before the land batteries were nearly completed, and on the 11th the weather permitted a squadron of battleships and another of frigates to move up the river to positions from which they could bombard the town. On this day the land batteries opened fire with fifty-one guns, while the warships also began to batter the fortifications, the bombardment continuing almost ceaselessly until the 14th, when the French guns had been practically silenced, and many serious fires had been started in the city. The same night General Picton's brigade carried one of the advanced works on the east face, and on the 15th the commander of the fortress capitulated; on the following day the defenders, to the number of 4,379 of all ranks, marched out under General Monnet and laid down their arms, being immediately embarked at Veere for England.

In the course of the whole of the operations so far conducted, the 2nd Battalion 81st had only lost one drummer and four rank and file killed, three officers—Captain P. C. Taylor, Lieutenant K. Montgomery and Assistant-Surgeon H. Chislette—and five other ranks wounded—most of these from gunshot.

On hearing of the arrival of the British force in the Scheldt, Napoleon

* Fortescue, Vol. VII, p. 78.
† *Letters from Flushing*, pp. 119, 120.

had at once realized the menace it implied, and had issued the most explicit orders for the defence of Antwerp; reinforcements had been despatched thither, and Bernadotte had been hurried off to assume command of the place; and while Lord Chatham remained inactive after Flushing had surrendered, the French had so re-armed the forts and posts on the river that these were now capable of offering a really serious resistance to any naval force moving up-stream. By the 24th August Antwerp was secured against a *coup de main*.

On the 19th August the 1st and 3rd Divisions, the cavalry and the heavy guns were sent by water to the vicinity of Fort Bath, at the south-eastern extremity of South Beveland—where was already the Reserve—Picton's and Browne's brigades being left to hold Walcheren. Browne's brigade was sent to Middelburg where it remained until early in September.

Almost from the arrival of the expeditionary force, the troops composing it had suffered from an especially bad type of malarial fever. The medical authorities of those days describe it as "a low fever, similar to jail fever, spreading with extraordinary rapidity and for which no remedy was known." The disease seems to have first shown itself among the troops in South Beveland and later attacked those in Walcheren. On the 22nd August the sick numbered 1,564; on the 24th nearly 2,000 men were down; on the 27th it was reported that the sick numbered 3,467 and that the total was increasing hourly; on the 1st September the number was more than 5,000; by the 3rd it had risen to 8,194; and on the 7th September the sick of Lord Chatham's army made a total of 10,948!

In *British Minor Expeditions*, p. 79, there is a "Return of the Sick and Wounded sent to England" between the 21st August and the 16th December, chiefly from Veere and Flushing, and this shows a total of 12,863!

On the 27th August Lord Chatham assembled a council-of-war at Fort Bath, where he had lately established his headquarters, and put the following questions to his subordinate commanders:—

1. Whether the siege of Antwerp should be proceeded with?
2. Whether any, and if so, what, minor operations be undertaken?

To these queries Lieut.-Generals Eyre Coote, Lord Rosslyn, Lord Huntley, Grosvenor, Hope, Lord Paget and Brownrigg gave the unanimous reply that the undertaking of the siege of Antwerp was impracticable, and that no possible advantage could result from attempting any minor operations of any description. Lord Chatham thereupon decided to strengthen the Island of Walcheren, which it was still proposed to hold, and to at once embark the remainder of the troops in readiness to return to England.

No time was lost in preparing for embarkation; on the 29th August the captured works of Flushing were demolished and the surrendered guns were put on board ship; on the 1st September the troops began to embark, and on the 7th the corps bound for England sailed away, leaving for the garrison of Walcheren some eighteen thousand men, of whom six thousand were sick. This garrison consisted of seven infantry brigades, of which Browne's was one, with some cavalry and artillery, under the command of Lieut.-General Coote.

Browne's brigade now had another battalion posted to it—the 2nd Battalion 84th—but this did not appreciably increase its strength, for at this time, *pace* Fortescue, the 2nd Battalion 23rd, "could not furnish a man for duty." The daily state of the 19th September shows 224 officers and 9,627 men sick out of the Walcheren garrison. The hospitals at Middelburg, Flushing, Veere, Arnemuiden, Zoutelande and Rammekens were crowded, and at Middelburg, where the 2nd Battalion 81st spent the greater part of their time, there were not sufficient beds to allow of each patient having one to himself. On the 23rd September General Coote wrote home stating that the 2nd Battalion 23rd was so reduced by the fever that he had ordered it home at once, and that the 2nd 81st was so sickly that it had been struck off duty. The fever continued to spread and medical comforts began to fail, and on the 29th September the Battalion had only forty men fit for duty.

On the 18th July, as already stated, the Battalion's embarking strength was 658 effective rank and file; by the 7th September this had been reduced to 468, while on the 29th it stood at no more than forty.

On the 26th October, from a return of the medical officers doing duty with the eighteen infantry battalions, out of a proper complement of fifty-four surgeons only twenty-three were fit for duty, and the average sick per regiment was four hundred.

The Government had now decided upon the evacuation of Walcheren, having somewhat belatedly come to agree with General Coote, who had written home at the end of September that "something must be done, or the British nation will lose the British army—far more valuable than the Island of Walcheren."

On the 4th November the officer then commanding on the Island—General Don—received orders to destroy the naval and other defences and to embark the garrison, and on the 9th December the ill-fated spot was finally left behind; the expedition had cost the country close upon one million of money and the lives of four thousand men, of whom only one hundred and six fell in action. The survivors of the 2nd Battalion 81st landed at Portsmouth from the "Fame" transport, on the 26th December and marched thence to Bletchingley, the station from which it had set out only five months previously; the disembarkation strength was seven officers and fifty-one other ranks!

The total casualties incurred by the Battalion amounted to one officer —Major E. D. Maurice—nineteen sergeants, eight drummers and 269 rank and file, and out of this loss of 297 all ranks, only four fell in action.

Recruiting must at this period have been unusually brisk, for so early as April, 1810—only four months after the return to England of the greatly depleted Battalion—it was able to send to the 1st Battalion a draft of four sergeants and two hundred and fifty-eight rank and file.

On the 12th June the Battalion marched to Bexhill, moving again five months later to Eastbourne, where, during the summer of 1811, it received nearly one hundred and fifty volunteers, chiefly from the Warwick, Dorset and Gloucestershire Militia. Then on the 3rd October it marched to Portsmouth and there embarked for Jersey in the "Sir Joseph Banks" transport. In Jersey the Battalion remained until again ordered to proceed to the Continent.

At the end of 1813 the British Government, having decided to assist the Dutch in their endeavour to throw off the French yoke and regain their national independence under the rule of the Prince of Orange, had sent to Holland an expeditionary force, under General Graham, of close upon nine thousand men, in order to support the movement. Graham's orders from the British Cabinet were to attempt the surprise of Antwerp, but the season was late, the weather was too severe for operations in the field, and Graham's force remained scattered in cantonments until early in 1814.

Combined operations were then set on foot by the allied Anglo-Dutch and Prussian forces, and there was some desultory fighting until the beginning of February, when the Prussian contingent was withdrawn and sent to France, and Graham, now finding himself too weak to attempt anything against Antwerp, retired towards his base at Willemstadt. Here in the middle of February he was joined by a regiment of cavalry and four battalions of infantry; among these last was the 2nd Battalion 81st which disembarked at Helvoetsluys at a strength of twenty-nine officers and 416 other ranks, and then marched to Brasschaet, near Antwerp. The newly-arrived battalions—4th Battalion 1st, 2nd Battalion 30th, 2nd Battalion 81st and 2nd Battalion 91st—were now formed into a brigade under Colonel Gore of the 33rd Foot, and they appear to have been for some time employed in throwing up defensive works and in assisting in the blockade of Antwerp, being so engaged for some six weeks. As a result the Battalion did not share in the attempt upon Bergen-op-Zoom, and was fortunately spared the fate which overtook some of the regiments which formed the storming column.

General Graham's army was now reorganized, and the 2nd Battalion 81st found itself, with battalions of the 30th, 52nd, 78th and 95th, in a Reserve Division under Major-General Mackenzie. Preparations were then made for the investment of Antwerp, the blockade of Bergen and for an attack on Fort Bath. But the abdication of Napoleon and the restoration of the Bourbons led to an armistice between the English and French commanders, and under the terms of the Convention of Paris of the 23rd April, 1814, Antwerp was occupied by British troops.

Graham's force, in which the 2nd Battalion 81st was included, was later joined by the greater part of the King's German Legion and by fifteen thousand Hanoverian Militia; and "these troops, which in August, 1814, were placed under the command of the Prince of Orange, were stationed in the Netherlands under an agreement with Austria, Russia and Prussia, to maintain the provisions of the Treaty of Paris, pending the final settlement of Europe by the Congress of Vienna "*—thus constituting something of the nature of an Army of Occupation.

In consequence of the escape of Napoleon from Elba in the early part of 1815, and the prospect of the immediate renewal of hostilities, the Prince of Orange issued orders for the allied army, of which at the time he was in command, to be prepared to take the field, and at the end of April the 2nd Battalion 81st marched to Brussels. On arrival here it was posted to the 10th Brigade, commanded by Major-General Sir John Lambert, in the 6th Division under Lieut.-General Sir L. Cole; in the 10th Brigade were also the First Battalions of the 4th, 27th and 40th Regiments; the Second Brigade in the Division was composed of Hanoverian troops. The three other regiments of the 10th Brigade had only very recently returned from America and had not yet got beyond Ghent.

On the 15th June the Battalion received orders to be ready to march for the front at 4 a.m. next day; but the other three battalions not having even yet arrived, the 2nd Battalion 81st was detailed to take over the guard and other duties in Brussels and also the charge of the military chest. On the afternoon of the 16th the arrival of the remaining units completed the 10th Brigade, but at the time the Battalion was on duty at the various hospitals and guards, and on the morning of the 17th it was informed that it could not be spared from Brussels. The Commanding Officer, Lieut.-Colonel Milling, earnestly entreated Major-General Lambert to allow the Battalion to accompany its brigade; but the hospitals were then filled

* Fortescue, Vol. X, p. 228.

with wounded and it was held that the Battalion must remain behind; it was thus debarred from sharing in the crowning victory of Waterloo.

It was detained in Brussels until the 15th July, during which time it had to do much escort duty, accompanying the French prisoners to Ghent, preparatory to embarkation for England, and also in attending at the hospitals which were crowded to excess with French and English sick and wounded.

On the 16th July the Battalion moved from Brussels to Neuilly near Paris, then to Montmartre, and later to Belleville, where Major R. C. Lang died on the 5th December.

In *The Battle of Waterloo*, published "by Authority" in 1817, the following names of officers are given as serving with the 2nd Battalion 81st in the Netherlands in 1815: Lieut.-Colonel H. Milling; Major P. Waterhouse; Captains P. C. Taylor, R. Pilkington, F. J. Edwards, G. Adams, J. Duval, R. Duff, C. French, G. Pearson, R. Hipkins, J. Sinclair, H. T. Hearn and T. Collard; Lieutenants F. D. Dundas, J. Sisson, adjutant, E. Lee, H. Biggam, W. Hyde, T. C. Wheat, F. Home, A. Napper, W. Jones, J. Mollan, J. Godwin, P. Chevers, T. M. Smith and J. S. O'Donnell; Ensigns W. Betteridge, C. Beale, R. Beadle, T. Whitley, C. Oakley, J. Brown, A. Donaghue, R. Hamilton, J. Cannon, T. Lawton, A. J. Pictet and S. R. Dickens; Paymaster C. H. Marshall, Quartermaster P. Baker, Surgeon P. Schooles, Assistant-Surgeons H. S. Moy and J. Stockdale.

With the coming of peace followed the usual reduction of the Army, and five officers and 362 non-commissioned officers and men were transferred from the Second to the First Battalion of the Regiment. On the 9th January, 1816, the remnant of the 2nd Battalion marched to Calais, embarking at once in two transports, and landing at Dover and Ramsgate about the 18th.

Final orders directing the disbandment of the Battalion were now received, and it marched by way of Battle to Bletchingley, where on the 24th March, after thirteen years of a very distinguished and stirring existence, the 2nd Battalion of the 81st Regiment was finally disbanded, all serviceable men being sent to the 1st Battalion, while three field-officers, seven captains, eleven lieutenants, five ensigns, one paymaster, one quartermaster, one surgeon and one assistant-surgeon—thirty officers in all—were placed on the half-pay list.

CHAPTER XVI

1817–1856

SERVICE IN IRELAND, NORTH AMERICA, BERMUDAS, IRELAND, GIBRALTAR, WEST INDIES, NORTH AMERICA AND IRELAND

FIRST TOUR OF INDIAN SERVICE

SHORTLY after the arrival of the 81st in Ireland, the following very gratifying letter was received from Lieut.-General Colville, under whose command the Regiment had so recently served:—

"No. 5 Berkeley Square,
"14*th April*, 1817.

" MY DEAR COLONEL,—
" Although my own removal from the staff of the army in France makes that of the 81st Regiment from the same day of the less consequence to me, I cannot deny myself the satisfaction of expressing my very high opinion of it; though its excellent composition and state of discipline when it joined the 3rd Division left very little to be wished for. Yet I must request you will have the goodness to express to the Officers, Non-Commissioned Officers and Soldiers of the Regiment my acknowledgments of the prompt adoption and correct performance of whatever I had occasion to recommend during the period I had the honour to have the Regiment under my command.
" I remain, dear Colonel,
" ever faithfully yours,
(sd.) " CHARLES COLVILLE.
" Colonel McKenzie, 81st Regiment."

About the end of October the Right Wing of the Regiment marched from Cork to Clonmel, and the Left Wing from Tralee to Youghal, furnishing detachments to the different posts about Cork Harbour; but on the 11th June, 1818, the 81st was sent to the North of Ireland, with headquarters at Inniskillen, two companies at Cavan, and detachments of varying strength at Pettigoe, Ballyshannon, and Manorhamilton, and in the counties of Cavan, Sligo, Donegal and Fermanagh. In these parts the 81st remained for two years, chiefly employed upon revenue duty, or in the protection of those engaged upon this work.

In July, 1820, the Regiment marched to Dublin, where it arrived in the beginning of August, and on the 5th September, 1821, it was ordered to Cork with a view to embarking for North America. Having arrived at the port of embarkation the officials of the Transport Board came to the conclusion that it was too late in the season to send a regiment to Canada, and the 81st accordingly remained during the following six months or more in garrison in Cork. In the beginning of April, 1822, two transports arrived in Cork Harbour, when the Left Wing of the Regiment embarked for Halifax, but one of these vessels sprung her main mast and had to put back for repairs. In the meantime a third transport had arrived at Cork and, the rest of the companies embarking in her, the two ships sailed from Cork on the 4th June, the whole Regiment reaching Halifax by the 4th July and being quartered in the South Barracks.

At this time a former commanding officer of the Regiment—General Sir James Kempt—was Governor of Nova Scotia.

On the 6th August the number of companies was reduced to eight.

On the 19th April, 1823, the Regiment, and the Army generally, sustained a severe loss in the death of Lieut.-Colonel Waterhouse, who had served with and had at different times commanded with great credit both battalions of the 81st. His funeral was attended by the whole garrison of Halifax, and General Kempt was present as chief mourner. In St. Paul's Church, Halifax, there is a monument to his memory erected by his brother officers.

During the years 1823–25 the companies of the Regiment were a good deal moved about, furnishing detachments at different times, and usually in relief of or by companies of the 52nd Regiment, at Prince Edward's Island, Annapolis, Windsor and in Newfoundland; the whole Regiment appears, however, to have been concentrated again in Halifax, when on the 14th June, 1826, new Colours were presented to the 81st by General Sir James Kempt, now Colonel of the Regiment.

At noon on this date the three regiments composing the garrison of Halifax—the 74th, the 81st and the 1st Battalion Rifle Brigade—drawn up in line, received the General with a salute, and having then formed three sides of a square and the religious part of the ceremony having been conducted by the Reverend T. Twinning, Chaplain to the Forces, Sir James Kempt then handed the new Colours to Mrs. Creagh, the wife of the commanding officer, saying to her, "the Colours of the 81st Regiment will come with peculiar propriety and grace from your hands, and I request you will do me the honour of presenting them."

LIEUT.-GENERAL SIR JAMES KEMPT, G.C.B., G.C.H.
Colonel,
The 81st Regiment,
1819–1829.

On Ensigns G. F. de Rottenburgh and J. B. Creagh moving forward to receive the Colours, Mrs. Creagh delivered the following address to the Regiment :—

"In having the flattering honour conferred upon me in presenting Colours to a Regiment in which my tenderest affections * and most friendly regards are centred, it is difficult for me to give expression to all the feelings, which a ceremony so imposing and so deeply interesting to my heart, excites. I cannot pray for more than that, while serving under these new banners, you may display the same ardour and invincible bravery, which so highly shone forth under your old Colours at Maida, when the 81st was so gloriously led to victory by its distinguished general. May Maida, Corunna and the other glory, commemorating inscriptions on your Colours, be always present to your minds, and, with the blessing of the Almighty ever lead and preserve you in the path of honour and virtue.

"Into your hands, my young friend, I present your King's Colour and into your hands, my beloved son, I give the Colour of your Regiment. When your Country requires their defence, I, even as a mother, can say they never should be abandoned but in death. And may you, while fighting under them, and during the whole of your military lives, endeavour to pursue the splendid career of your illustrious General; and may you like him be distinguished with the well-merited rewards of a Gracious Sovereign, and the thanks of a grateful Country."

The two Ensigns having received the Colours and having resumed their usual places with the Regiment, Colonel Creagh then said :—

"Those Colours which, by the distinguished favour of His Excellency Sir James Kempt, have just been presented to the 81st Regiment in a manner so truly gratifying to my feelings, shall, I can promise, never be sullied by the Corps I have the honour and happiness to command. And in the day of battle, I trust, they will ever wave triumphantly, as did our old Colours, when the path of victory was pointed out to the 81st by the General under whom we have now the good fortune to be placed."

The Colours were then trooped and the regiments marched past and moved off to their quarters.

On the 13th July Captains P. Pratt and R. H. Willcocks joined with a draft of two sergeants and fifty other ranks from the Depot of the Regiment, then at Winchester; and two days later the 81st received orders to hold itself in readiness to embark for New Brunswick, there to relieve the 52nd which was stationed at Fredericton and St. John's. The Regiment left in three parties, the first one—five officers and 151 other ranks—embarked

* There were at this time in the 81st Lieut.-Colonel A. Creagh, Lieutenant G. V. Creagh and Ensign J. B. Creagh.

in the "Boridina" under command of Major J. M. Wardrop on the 22nd, while the second party under Captain R. H. Willcocks—three officers and 178 non-commissioned officers and men—left in the "Frinsbury" on the 25th; the headquarters with Colonel A. Creagh—three officers and ninety-eight other ranks—did not leave Halifax until the 26th August.

The Regiment remained at Fredericton and St. John's until November, 1829, when it was sent to the Bermudas in relief of the 74th Highlanders, arriving there on the 8th and 9th December; and here it remained until November, 1831, when it sailed for home, arriving at Portsmouth at the end of December.

While the Regiment was in the West Indies Ensign Thomas died, but the 81st suffered an even greater loss—so far as mere numbers were concerned—earlier in its stay. On the 1st April, 1831, a party consisting of one sergeant, one drummer and thirty-three privates, the majority of them married men of the Regiment, who had obtained free discharges with gratuities for the purpose of settling in the provinces of Nova Scotia and St. John's, had left Bermuda, under charge of Ensign W. C. Liston of the 81st, in the "Billow." In May the melancholy intelligence reached the Regiment of the total wreck of this vessel off the coast of Nova Scotia, with the loss of every soul on board her.

On arrival in England the Depot companies joined the Regiment, which remained at Portsmouth until the 27th February, 1832, when it marched to Congleton in Cheshire, moving from here in May to Bolton-le-Moor. After a stay of only a few weeks here, the 81st marched to Manchester, and at the end of July embarked for Dublin, on arrival there being quartered in Richmond Barracks.

81ST REGIMENT OF FOOT (LOYAL LINCOLN VOLUNTEERS)

In the *London Gazette* of the 20th April, 1832, an announcement of a somewhat cryptic character appears; there is no allusion whatever to it in the Regimental Digest, nor in the short history of the Regiment published at Gibraltar in 1872; it runs as follows:—

> "His Majesty has been graciously pleased to approve of the 81st Regiment resuming the appellation of 'The Loyal Lincoln Volunteers,' in addition to its present numerical title."

During the four years of its stay in Ireland the Regiment seems to have been very frequently moved from one station to another; in September it marched to Templemore; in May, 1833, it proceeded to Birr, from where in October, 1834, it was sent back again to Dublin; from here in October, 1835, it proceeded to Kilkenny, and while quartered here a letter having been received announcing the early move of the 81st to Gibraltar, the companies were concentrated at Fermoy. This was left on the 21st May, 1836, when, the Depot companies having been sent away to Clare Castle, the Regiment embarked in the transport "Barrosa" at Cork on the 28th and sailed for Gibraltar. On arrival here on the 9th the troops were at first accommodated in the barracks at Rosia Bay, moving ten days later to the South Barracks.

In the year 1835, the Queen Regent of Spain, through her minister at the Court of St. James's, asked permission from the British Government to raise a force in England in support of her cause and that of her daughter Isabella, against their absolutist rival, Don Carlos. The request was granted, and a force of ten thousand men was raised and sent to Spain, under the name of "the British Legion." In command of this Legion went General Sir de Lacy Evans in whose division the 47th was to fight in the Crimean War.

The contest for the throne was still going on, when on the 20th November, 1836, a division of Don Carlos' army, under General Gomez, arrived at San Roque, a little town on the further side of the strip of neutral ground to the north of Gibraltar. The inhabitants of this place fled on the approach of Gomez's troops, and took refuge under the guns of the Rock. The 81st and other regiments of the garrison were called out, and supplied strong picquets on and about the neutral ground for so long as the Spanish force remained in the vicinity of Gibraltar; while an English brig of eighteen guns cannonaded the partisan troops and obliged them to fall back again into the interior of Spain.

The Depot companies appear to have remained on in Ireland, after the departure of the Service companies, until September, 1837, when they left Dublin in the S.S. "Messenger," en route to Carlisle. The ship anchored on the 19th of the month off Skimberness, but when the landing of the heavy baggage was in progress, one of the boats, carrying Captain J. Gilby of the 81st and a party of fatigue men, was carried by the strong current under the paddle-wheel of the steamship and capsized, and Captain Gilby was unfortunately drowned.

During the year 1838 the headquarters of the Regiment at Gibraltar had two changes of quarters, and furnished two guards-of-honour to different Royal personages; in May the companies moved into the Casemate Barracks, and in August they were transferred to the Town Range Barracks. On the 24th August, the 81st provided a guard-of-honour on the landing at Gibraltar of H.R.H. the Grand Duke of Austria; and on the 14th October the Regiment furnished a similar guard on the occasion of a visit to Gibraltar of H.M. Queen Adelaide, the Queen Dowager.

While the 81st was stationed in Gibraltar Ensign R. Lake died—on the 24th August.

On the 3rd August, 1839, orders were received for the Regiment to hold itself in readiness to proceed to the West Indies, and on the eve of its departure from Gibraltar, where it had been stationed for three years and a half, the following was published in garrison orders:—

"Gibraltar, *8th December*, 1839.

"The headquarters of the 81st Regiment being about to embark to-morrow, Lieutenant-General Sir Alexander Woodford cannot take leave of the Corps without expressing his approbation of the general good order and discipline which it has maintained within this garrison, and he feels assured that wherever it goes its course will be marked by the same creditable and correct performance of all its duties, which has characterized it here.

"The Lieutenant-General Commanding desires Major Willcocks and the 81st Regiment to be assured of his best wishes for their continued welfare and honour."

The Regiment, under command of Major R. H. Willcocks, K.H., embarked in two divisions, on the 9th and 21st December, 1839, in the "Atholl" and "Sapphire," and arrived at Barbados on the 20th and 25th January, 1840, proceeding, on landing, to St. Ann's.

In the summer of this year the Depot companies were moved back to Ireland.

On the 8th December, 1840, the 81st Regiment was presented with its third set of Colours at St. Ann's, Savanna, Barbados, by Lieut.-General John Maister, detachments of the 14th and 74th being also on parade. Three sides of a square were formed, the new Colours were brought on parade and placed upon a pile of drums, and the Colours having been consecrated by the Reverend T. Gill, the Lieutenant-General addressed the Regiment as follows:—

"Officers and Soldiers of the 81st Regiment!

"In addressing a very few words to you on the present interesting occasion, it is not with the idea that any observation of mine can add one iota to the feeling of soldierlike pride and of devotion to the service of your Sovereign and your Country that the inspiring sight of the Colours about to be entrusted to you must have called forth; but it is that I am unwilling to let the opportunity escape of expressing my gratification at the high honour conferred upon the individual who has been so flatteringly selected to present them to you, and of also declaring my thorough conviction that on all occasions and under every circumstance you will fully perform your duty under them, and that however much we have cause to admire the brilliant achievements of your predecessors, and of one still amongst you,* at Maida and Corunna and on the Peninsula as perpetuated on these Colours, or the brave and soldierlike conduct which distinguished their career in the Army of Spain, in America, and in fact wherever their services were required. I feel satisfied that the 81st Regiment of the present day will in every respect emulate them, and not only maintain the high reputation already won, but, when the occasion offers, add fresh memorials of their gallantry to those already described on those Colours.

"I can in truth assure you, 81st Regiment, that there is no regiment in Her Majesty's service in whom I should place more perfect confidence whenever the honour of the Sovereign or the interest of their Country may call upon them to act, either in front of an enemy, or in any situation in which they may be placed.

"Go where you will, however, or on whatever service employed, you will always carry with you my good opinion and most sincere wishes for your honour and prosperity."

The old Colours, borne by Lieutenants H. Renny and the Honourable R. A. G. Dalzell, were now marched to the front, and the new Colours were then handed to Lieutenant J. Powell and Ensign J. Oldright, by the wife of the Lieutenant-General, who made a few remarks to which the commanding officer, Lieut.-Colonel Sir Charles Chichester, made a brief reply and the ceremony then terminated in the usual manner.

During the remaining two years of the stay of the 81st in the West Indian Islands, it was a good deal moved about, during 1841 the companies being distributed between Trinidad, Grenada, Tobago and San Fernando, while in the following year the Regiment was split up among three separate garrisons in Antigua. It was while in Antigua that, in September, a notification was received that the 81st was to move to Canada when relieved at Antigua by the 77th Regiment. In November and December the companies began to concentrate preparatory to the move; but before leaving Antigua all ranks underwent a very unusual and alarming experience. On the morning of the 8th February, 1843, a most sudden and destructive earthquake occurred at Antigua, and within two minutes nearly all the buildings in the island had been thrown to the ground, with very great loss to public and private property, and nearly all the barracks were knocked down or destroyed. Had the earthquake happened during the night the loss of life must have been very great, but happily there were no casualties.

* The reference made here is to Quartermaster James Patterson, who served with the Regiment at Maida as a sergeant and who retired on half-pay in July, 1844, thus completing forty-six years' service with the 81st.

By the 26th February all the companies were concentrated in Barbados, and the Regiment left for Canada in two divisions at an interval of several weeks; but by the 7th August all had arrived at Quebec, when the strength was as follows: one field-officer, two captains, six subalterns, four staff and 502 non-commissioned officers and men. It will be noticed that the Regiment at this time was weak both in officers and other ranks, so that the arrival of a draft soon after reaching Quebec, of four officers and sixty-eight other ranks, must have been especially welcome.

During the time the Regiment was in the West Indies it lost two officers from fever—Lieutenant L. Guy at San Fernando on the 27th March, 1841, and Captain J. U. Jeffery at Tobago on the 1st July of the same year.

Almost immediately upon arrival in Canada the companies were much detached, in the first instance two being dispatched to Three Rivers and one to St. John's, Canada East; later the headquarters and three companies were moved from Quebec to St. John's, where they were joined by the two originally sent to Three Rivers. In May, 1845, there was a further move to London, Canada West, the corps remaining here until, in May, 1846, it was sent to Toronto, remaining here until, on the 7th March, 1847, notification was received that the Regiment was due to return to England as soon as the seas were clear of ice.

While stationed in Canada three officers of the 81st died: Captain F. S. Perry at St. John's, Canada East, on the 27th May, 1844, Ensign W. S. Splaine at Toronto on the 4th September, 1845, and—greatest loss of all—Lieut.-Colonel Sir Charles Chichester at Toronto on the 4th April, 1847.

During August, 1847, the Regiment was sent back to Quebec, and here on the 28th of that month the headquarters and four companies, under Lieut.-Colonel Willcocks, K.H., embarked in the transport "Blenheim" and reached Plymouth on the 28th September, when they took up quarters in the barracks in St. George's and Cumberland Squares in Devonport. The Left Wing did not leave Quebec until some weeks later —in the "Maria Soames"—finally reaching Devonport and joining the rest of the Regiment at the end of October. Here the Service and Depot companies were reunited after a severance of eleven years.

While the 81st was abroad, the Depot, since arrival in Ireland in the autumn of 1840, had been quartered at Fermoy, Kinsale, Kilkenny, Athlone, Clare Castle, Buttevant, Templemore, and again at Kinsale, from whence, in June, 1845, it was sent to Jersey. While stationed in the Island the officers and men of the Depot were heartily thanked by the civil authorities for their exertions in extinguishing a fire near St. Heliers; and in September, 1846, the Depot twice provided a guard-of-honour, under command of Major G. V. Creagh, on the occasion of the visit to Jersey of H.M. Queen Victoria and the Prince Consort.

Again in May, 1847, were the officers and other ranks of the 81st Depot thanked by the local authorities—this time for helping to restore order on the occasion of a disturbance among some workmen. On the return of the Regiment from foreign service, it was joined at Devonport, as already stated, by the Depot companies from Jersey.

At Devonport the 81st remained, furnishing detachments of some size to Maker Heights and Pendennis Castle, till the 1st May, 1848, when it began to leave this station in three divisions, the companies being distributed among Preston, Stockport, Halifax, Chester, Bradford and the Isle of Man, and the total strength at this time appearing to be twenty officers, thirty-three sergeants, twelve drummers and 536 rank and file.

In consequence of an expected Chartist outbreak in Liverpool, a sudden move of detachments of the Regiment was hurriedly carried out in August of this year; the headquarters was sent by rail from Preston to Liverpool and marched into camp at Everton, and Nos. 2, 4, 6, 8 and the Light Company were also all moved into Liverpool from the different small towns where they had supplied detachments; and when all were assembled at Liverpool, the Regiment joined a small brigade composed of three guns of a field battery and the 46th Regiment. The services of the troops were not, however, called for, and on the 29th September the brigade was dispersed, when the headquarters of the Regiment marched to Preston, Nos. 2, 4, and 8 Companies to Burnley, and the Light Company and No. 7 Company also to Preston.

These stations were, however, occupied only for a short period, for on the 7th December the Regiment moved from its several stations in the North-Western District, and was distributed as follows: the headquarters, the Grenadier and No. 6 Company at Hull, Nos. 3, 4, 5, 7 and 8 at Leeds, No. 1 at the Isle of Man, No. 2 at Bradford and the Light Company at Scarborough. In these several quarters the Regiment remained until the summer of 1850, when it was again moved—headquarters and eight companies to Berwick-on-Tweed, and Nos. 1 and 6 Companies to Tynemouth. During the stay of the 81st at Berwick it furnished a guard-of-honour for H.M. the Queen on the occasion of her opening a railway bridge in that town, the remaining companies assisting to line the route by which Her Majesty passed.

In November of this year the Regiment moved by way of Liverpool to Dublin, and on disembarking here the headquarters proceeded to Templemore, from where detachments were furnished to Cashel, Maryborough, Thurles and Fethard, the Regiment remaining in these stations until the

12th March, 1852, when it was sent by rail to Dublin and occupied the Linen Hall Barracks.

In November, 1852, Field-Marshal the Duke of Wellington died, and on the 13th a party consisting of three officers—Major H. Renny, Captain J. H. Stewart and Lieutenant J. Woods—one colour-sergeant, one corporal and six privates, proceeded to London to represent the Corps at the funeral.

In Dublin the Regiment remained until the 18th January, 1853, when it went by rail to Kilkenny, supplying a detachment of one company to each of the following towns—Carlow, Maryborough, Wexford and Thurles; but after a stay of little more than three months orders were received to prepare for departure on its first tour of Indian service; and leaving Kilkenny on the 17th May it arrived four days later at Fermoy. Here all preparations for departure were made, the Regiment was completed to the Indian establishment by volunteers from no fewer than twenty-four different battalions, amounting in all to 238 men, and on the 21st June it marched to Cork and embarked for India. The companies were distributed among six different ships—the "Southampton," "Europa," "Wellesley," "Collingwood," "Clifton" and "Alfred," sailed on different dates between the 28th June and the 10th August; and five of the vessels reached Calcutta between the 1st October and the 22nd December. The sixth ship, however, the "Alfred," met with misfortune on her voyage.

This vessel, having run short of water, put into Vizagapatam to refill her tanks, but shortly after leaving this port, she struck on a rock off Calingapatam on the evening of the 5th December. By great exertions the "Alfred" was got off again in about an hour and a half, and by keeping the pumps going incessantly she remained afloat until the morning, when she was able to make her way to Bimlipatam.

The following is a copy of the report sent to the A.A. General, Calcutta, by Captain C. J. Skerry, who was in charge of the sixty-two men of the 81st travelling in the "Alfred," and was also O.C. troops on board:—

"Bimlipatam, Western Department of Madras,
"7th December, 1853.

"SIR,—

"Following up the information that I hastily despatched to the Major of Brigade yesterday, I have the honour to offer you a detailed statement of the circumstances connected with the disembarkation of the troops under my command.

"After leaving Vizagapatam, into which place we had put for water, etc., we kept the land on the inner tack, and the ship struck on some shoal or bank about thirty miles from this, on the evening of the 5th instant.

I immediately assembled the men and spoke to them encouragingly, and set them to work at the capstan as soon as a small anchor was got out; and finding that the water was gaining on her, I put the men to work by watches at the pumps. I told them I was sure that if matters came to the worst they would behave like soldiers; and the endurance, courage and resolution shown by them, fully satisfied me and confirmed my confidence in them. The men worked incessantly, but still the water gained on us. The ship struck on the shoal about dusk, and we, most providentially, got her off in about one hour and a half afterwards.

"The captain of the ship now consulted with his officers, and decided on making for a place about eighty miles off; but on his asking my opinion, I urged him with all my address, to run for this place, fearing the contingency of the wind failing us or the pumps choking. The captain altered his previous determination, stood off shore during the night, and ran for this place in the morning. Notwithstanding the extraordinary exertions of everybody on board (for Captain Sneyd, Bengal Army, at my suggestion got up a relief for the pumps among the gentlemen passengers), the water still gained on us. We arrived here and anchored about 2 p.m. on the 6th, the men being quite worn out.

"Communicating with the Assistant-Adjutant-General of the District, and taking the advice of the principal gentleman here, Mr. Mackenzie, about accommodation, I determined to disembark my men as soon as the ladies, women and children and other passengers should be got off, and sufficient coolies got to work the pumps. The passengers having landed, I disembarked my men at once, while the boats were about the ship, as the boatmen here will not work all night. The men were all landed (except three), with their arms, ammunition and light baggage, between six and 10.30 p.m. The three men I retained; and Ensign Smith, H.M.'s 29th Regiment, also remained with me, as I feared to crowd the last boat that left the ship. I am happy to say that no accident took place—all landed safe.

"I cannot conclude my letter without doing justice to the officers and men who, on this trying occasion, behaved in the most exemplary manner. Ensign Smith, H.M.'s 29th Regiment, Ensign Wyniatt, H.M.'s 52nd Regiment, and Ensign Carter, H.M.'s 22nd Regiment, I cannot sufficiently thank; every wish of mine was carried out by them to my utmost satisfaction, and I cannot say more than that I think they are a credit to the Army.

"My Sergeants, Stokes and Sheppard, gave me the greatest help, the latter was particularly useful from his having been a sailor.

"I have seen the Adjutant-General of the District. We are housed and expect the Commissariat at once. I have allowed twenty volunteers to go out to the help of the ship, which is not in quite so hopeless a state as she was thought to be, for the pumps are gaining on the water in her; but the chances are very much against her being got round to Calcutta unless she is filled with coolies to work at the pumps, and has a steamer to tow her.

"I have, etc.,
(sd.) "CHARLES J. SKERRY, Captain,
"H.M. 81st Regiment.
"The A.A. General, Calcutta."

Captain Skerry's report of the occurrence was transmitted to England, and General Sir William Gomm, K.C.B., then Commander-in-Chief in India, received the following appreciative letter from the D.A.G. Horse Guards, dated the 18th February, 1854:—

"I have had the honour to receive and submit to the General Commanding-in-Chief your letter of the 4th ult., reporting that the 'Alfred,' troopship, having on board a detachment under the command of Captain Skerry, 81st Regiment, struck on a shoal off the Madras coast, and that the conduct of the troops on this occasion had met with the expression of your satisfaction.

"In reply I am directed to acquaint you that his Lordship has read your report with much satisfaction, containing as it does another instance of the discipline and fortitude of British troops under trying circumstances."

The troops disembarked from the "Alfred" remained at Bimlipatam until the 18th December, when they embarked in the S.S. "Hugh Lindsay" and resumed their journey to Calcutta. The remainder of the Regiment had, on arrival at Calcutta, been temporarily accommodated in Fort William; but between the 5th November and the 28th December they were sent off by river in steamers and flats to Allahabad, and marched from there to Meerut, when the whole was assembled by the 13th March, 1854. The strength of the 81st was now four field-officers, eleven captains, eighteen subalterns, seven staff, fifty-two sergeants, forty-five corporals, twenty drummers and 930 privates.

The officers with the Regiment appear to have been Lieut.-Colonel H. Renny; Majors J. H. Stewart, A. T. Allan and H. E. Sorell; Captains A. F. F. Boughey, J. A. Gildea, F. E. Sorell, J. B. Flanagan, C. E. Goodwin, R. B. Chichester, H. J. Liddell, J. Bourchier, J. Woods, C. J. Skerry and W. J. Browne; the eighteen subalterns appear to have been among the following twenty at that time on the strength of the headquarters of the Regiment, viz., Lieutenants F. S. de V. Lane, W. E. Todd, M. Hanley, G. Betts, C. Hunter, H. A. Chichester, S. S. Bristowe, R. G. Charlton,

THE COLOURS—THE 81st REGIMENT.

1854.

S. J. Lowe, G. W. M. Harmer, R. R. D. Lecky, R. Swift, E. F. Foster, J. Tweedie, G. F. Lamert, H. G. Somerset, J. Trent and W. M. Harnett; Ensigns C. J. Hughes and J. A. Deans; Paymaster W. F. Nixon, Lieutenant and Adjutant A. Wright, Quartermaster C. Correll, Surgeon A. T. Jackson, Assistant-Surgeons C. F. Stephenson, G. Auchinleck and D. S. Smith.

On the 24th January, 1854, while the Regiment was in camp at Allahabad, it suffered a great loss in the death of its commanding officer, Lieut.-Colonel H. Farrant.

New Colours were presented to the Regiment on the 1st July by its Colonel, Lieut.-General T. Evans, C.B.

The 81st remained quartered at Meerut until the 13th October, 1855, when it marched to Mian Mir, arriving on the 17th November and detaching one company to form the garrison at the fort in Lahore.

During the thirteen months between November, 1855, and December, 1856, the strength was swelled by three drafts which arrived from England, totalling seven subaltern officers and a hundred and five other ranks, and by the arrival of forty-three volunteers from the 18th, 22nd, 80th and 96th Regiments which were under orders for home; but the year 1856 was to prove a very sickly one for the Regiment. In the hot weather of this year cholera broke out in the cantonment of Mian Mir, and was especially severe from the 15th August to the 24th September, during which time the 81st loss amounted to one officer—Ensign R. W. O'Dell—ten sergeants, two drummers, and one hundred and sixteen privates, besides a number of women and children; earlier in the same year—on the 8th April—Major A. F. F. Boughey died at Amritsar when proceeding to England on leave. Consequently, when in May, 1857, the Great Mutiny broke out, the 81st Regiment can hardly have been at a greater strength than nine hundred bayonets.

CHAPTER XVII

1857–1858

THE INDIAN MUTINY
NORTH-WEST FRONTIER OPERATIONS

THE first four months of the year 1857 were passed quietly at Mian Mir by the 81st Regiment, and the only event of any importance —of really vital importance as the occurrences of this year were so shortly to prove—was the re-arming of the Regiment with the Enfield rifle, the general issue of which had commenced at home in 1855.

"The many wars in which during the last twenty years the Army in India had been engaged, had necessitated a very large increase in the numbers of the Native troops. Between 1838 and 1849, the period extending from just before the First Afghan War to the Battle of Gujerat, the Native Army had been augmented from 154,000 to 260,000 men, whilst the number of British troops serving in Bengal had remained almost stationary. After Gujerat the strength of the Native Army was rapidly reduced, until in 1856 its grand total stood at 230,000 men, of whom 40,000 were recruited from Oude, the majority being Brahmins, whose influence was paramount with all castes. Though annexations had now ended, the consequences remained; each new province or territory added to the Empire had involved a permanent increase in the number of our sepoys, and at the same time a diminution in that of their best English officers, who were drawn away from their regiments to fill civil appointments. Not only did the sepoys lose the officers who possessed their confidence, but of the British regiments serving in Bengal, the great majority were located in the new province," that is, in the Punjab. "In 1856, out of the whole British garrison then in India—only 45,000 men—16,000 were quartered west of Delhi, and thence to Calcutta, a densely populated stretch of country a thousand miles in extent, the number of British bayonets was under 3,000." *

At the commencement of 1857 there appear to have been only one regiment of British cavalry and ten battalions of British infantry stationed

---

* Thorburn, *The Punjab in Peace and War*, pp. 191, 192.

in the Punjab: the 81st was the only one quartered at the capital of the province, and there were no others nearer than Sealkote or Ferozepur, both some fifty miles distant as the crow flies. The only other European troops at Lahore were two troops of the East India Company's artillery, while the remainder of the garrison was wholly native—the 8th Cavalry, the 16th, the 26th and the 49th Native Infantry, all regiments which in the past had rendered admirable service in many Indian campaigns.

In the spring of this year India, on the surface, was quiet enough; there had been in recent years few signs of insubordination on the large scale of which Sir Charles Napier had made serious complaint when he was Commander-in-Chief, but signs and portents were not wanting that an explosion might at any moment occur; to meet such an eventuality few, if any, steps had anywhere been taken. Almost everywhere forts, arsenals, magazines and treasuries had been handed over to the charge of Indian troops, there was an almost total dearth of railway communication, and the British regiments were so widely scattered that combination was practically impossible. In the Bengal Army, years of maladministration, coupled with injudicious curtailment of the powers of commanding officers, had greatly weakened the bonds of discipline, and in many Indian regiments the men were restless and suspicious, and only waiting for some excuse to break out into open mutiny. Such an excuse was to be found —and exploited—in the greased cartridge used in the newly-issued Enfield rifle.

The statement was widely made that the grease used in the cartridge was prepared from the fat of cows and pigs—thus equally abhorrent to the Mohammedan and the Hindu; and in January and March serious outbreaks occurred, evilly-disposed persons having spread the report that the introduction of the new rifle and its cartridge was part and parcel of a deliberate scheme to forcibly convert the Indian soldiers to Christianity. Two down-country regiments were promptly disbanded, but the harm had already been done, the story spread, and before many weeks had elapsed the whole of Northern India was in a blaze.

Nor were leaders found wanting to head the movement, for at this time there were three men in particular who considered themselves to have been unjustly treated by the Government of India, and each of these represented powerful and troublesome factions. Those three men were, the old King of Delhi, the Nana Sahib of Bithur and the Nawab of Oudh.

The disbanding of two Indian regiments at Berhampur and Barrackpur did little to crush the mutinous spirit which was abroad, and on Sunday, 10th May, the Native regiments stationed at Meerut revolted, murdered their officers, and fled along the road to Delhi, where they demanded that the old King, Bahadur Shah, should place himself at the head of the movement.

In the Punjab matters had not appeared so serious and few can have anticipated the turn affairs were to take; "for the Punjab had just been blessed for the third time in succession with a bumper harvest, and the people were consequently in a very happy frame of mind; . . . in addition the Punjab's Indus frontier was garrisoned by the lately-raised provincial army, men heartily loyal and keen for active service in any part of the world." At Mian Mir the shadow of coming events had not been sufficient to prevent several officers of the 81st from proceeding on leave in the beginning of May, some to Kashmir and others to the hill-station of Murree; and preparations had been made for a ball to be held at Mian Mir on the 12th May.

The Lieutenant-Governor of the Punjab at this crisis was Sir John Lawrence, and in view of the reports coming from the lower provinces about the "greased cartridge" trouble, he had himself visited a musketry school recently established at Sealkote, and had satisfied himself that in the Punjab at any rate trouble was unlikely. He does not appear to have heard of the outbreak at Meerut before leaving Lahore for change of air in the Murree Hills, when there reached him on May 12th at Rawal Pindi "the fateful telegram from Delhi, which electrified the Punjab and altered his summer destination. 'The sepoys,' it ran, 'have come in from Meerut and are burning everything. Mr. Todd is dead and we hear several Europeans. We must shut up.' In other words the Indian Mutiny had broken out, and Delhi, the seat of the Mogul and the historic capital of India, was in the hands of the mutineers."*

Rumours of the Meerut trouble seem to have filtered through to Lahore by the 11th May, and early on the morning of the 12th a telegraphic message was received from Delhi: "We must leave office; all the bungalows are being burned by the sepoys from Meerut; they came in this morning; we hear that nine Europeans are killed." Shortly afterwards came another telegram: "Many native troops are in open mutiny; cantonments south of Mall burned; European troops under arms defending barracks; several European officers killed; electric telegraph wires cut."

Mr. Montgomery, the chief civilian official in Lahore, saw at once that matters were urgent and summoned a conference of the leading officials; and at the meeting he informed those present of secret information which had just reached him that the four native regiments in the cantonment at Mian Mir, only five miles distant, were prepared to throw in their lot with their brother-sepoys at Delhi. "A motion was brought forward and

---

* Bosworth Smith, *Life of Lord Lawrence*, Vol. I, p. 536.

unanimously agreed to by the Council, that it was desirable that the sepoy regiments should be at once deprived of their gun-caps and ammunition. But the Civil officers had no authority in such a matter, and so Montgomery and Macpherson rode over to Mian Mir to urge the necessity for action on the brigadier in command. General Corbett, who was old in years and service, was, at first, naturally taken aback at the boldness of the proposal, but in the course of the afternoon he made up his mind to go even further and to deprive his troops not merely of their ammunition but of their arms." He is said to have remarked : " If anything is to be done, I will draw their teeth at once, and take their muskets."

As profound secrecy was essential to the success of the proposed disarmament, the ball was not postponed, but a general parade was ordered for sunrise on the next morning.

When the ball broke up and the company departed, three companies of the 81st under Colonel M. Smith—who had lately come to the Regiment from the 24th Foot—were fallen in and marched off to the fort at Lahore, a very timely step, for on this day the relief of the native portion of the garrison was due, with the result that had any trouble then broken out, there would have been just twice as many native troops in the fort as was ordinarily the case. To the companies of the 81st in the barracks at Mian Mir orders were issued that ten men per company were to pass the remainder of the night fully dressed and armed.

At 4 a.m. on the 13th the remainder of the Regiment paraded, an extra allowance of ball ammunition was issued to every man and the packets were ordered to be "loosened"; there were naturally many surmises among the men as to the reason for so unusual an order, but the explanation given by one of the men of the 81st was considered wholly satisfying : " I suppose it's them niggers again " ! *

The sepoy regiments appeared on the parade ground, quite unconscious that anything unusual was in preparation, and a simple movement brought them face to face with the European soldiers, five companies only of the 81st and twelve guns. While they were there drawn up, a staff officer read out the orders of the Brigadier, praising the troops highly for their services in the past, but saying that since an evil spirit seemed to be abroad in the Indian Army, it had been considered wiser to save them from others —and it might be from themselves, by taking from them their arms. When the staff officer was concluding his address the five companies of the 81st fell back a few paces, disclosing " the guns which had hitherto been concealed behind them, and left the sepoy regiments to look down the twelve black throats of the cannon, which were already loaded with grape, while

* Cooper, *The Crisis in the Punjab*, p. 2.

the gunners stood by with port fires lighted. Just as the staff officer ceased to speak, the word of command, ' 81st, load ' ! rang clearly forth, and the penetrating voice of Colonel Renny was next heard to say, ' If you have to fire, men, fire with effect.'

"There was, it is said, a slight hesitation, but the ringing of the ramrods as the charges were rammed home, spoke eloquently in favour of obedience, and so some 2,000 muskets, and some 700 sabres soon lay piled on the ground. The extremity of the peril was now over, and the capital of the Punjab, with its 100,000 inhabitants, its cantonments, and its civil station was safe from the mutineers." *

Meanwhile, the wing of the Native Regiment in the fort found itself suddenly confronted by the three newly-arrived companies of the 81st, and on being ordered by Colonel Smith to "pile arms," they reluctantly complied and the men were then marched unarmed into Mian Mir.

It was now of the first importance that public confidence should be established and maintained in the neighbouring big cities, "and before the day so big with the destinies of the Punjab—and if of the Punjab, then of India—had come to an end, a company of the same valiant regiment, which, without the firing of a single gun, or the shedding of a single drop of blood, had disarmed seven times their number, was speeding away in native carts, which had been hastily collected, to Amritsar." Close to this town was the fort of Govindghar, and it was to turn out the native garrison of the 59th Bengal Infantry and occupy the fort that Captain H. A. Chichester's company of the 81st was sent thither from Mian Mir.

A contemporary writer † has thus described the arrival of Captain Chichester and his men : " About midnight, Mr. Macnaghten, Civil Service, hearing a great tramp as of coming rebels, mustered all his Sikh villagers, drew carts across the road—some villagers suggesting that the oxen and bullocks should remain, as the Hindus would not cut through them—and awaited the attack. The noise was that of forty *ekkas*, containing about eighty gallant soldiers under Captain Chichester of H.M.'s 81st, who, seeing the barrier dimly through the darkness, drew his revolver. The *dénouement* of the anticipated drama was gratifying to both sides. Next morning the rustic soldiery returned to their homes."

The other companies of the Regiment were fully occupied at Mian Mir in protecting the station and in watching the sepoys, who though nominally disarmed, were later discovered to have in their possession weapons of all kinds. It was also known that they were in the habit of holding secret meetings ; and from their general restlessness and the constant reports

---

* Bosworth Smith, Vol. II, p. 10.
† Cooper, *The Crisis in the Punjab*, published in 1858.

—many of them of course false—which were going about, unremitting vigilance was necessary. All ranks of the 81st were, consequently, kept fully accoutred day and night, ready for any emergency.

The lines of the 26th Native Infantry and of the 8th Light Cavalry were at a considerable distance from the barracks occupied by the 81st, and it being absolutely necessary that the movements of all the sepoys should be watched, Captain G. Betts' Company, and one of a recently-raised Sikh battalion, were posted near the left of the Native lines, while the remaining companies of the 81st kept a watch on the right. It was later learnt that a scheme for a general rising among the native regiments had been determined upon, and that lots had been drawn as to which regiment should take the lead; the lot had fallen on the 26th Native Infantry, backed by the 16th; and on the 30th July the 26th broke out into open mutiny, armed with such weapons as they had secreted.

The Sikh company opened fire upon the mutineers, and Captain Betts' Company followed suit, while the rest of the 81st moved out and deployed into line, with guns on the flanks. The guns opened fire on the lines of the 26th, when these broke and fled, pursued by the artillery and the 81st, a few stragglers being accounted for; a sand-storm then came on under cover of which the mutineers effected their escape.

Parties were now organized to pursue the men of the 26th, who, it was expected, would endeavour to escape to the south, and the Grenadier Company of the 81st under Captain C. J. Skerry and two horse-artillery guns, the whole under command of Major A. T. Allan of the Regiment, were detached to hold the bridge of boats over the Ravi near Lahore, in order to prevent the rebels from crossing at that point. The mutineers then attempted to pass elsewhere, but were foiled by the opposition of some police and armed Sikh villagers, who disposed of many of the number, the remainder crossing by various means to an island in mid-stream. The island was surrounded, a party landed and many rebels were killed and captured.

The lines of all the sepoy regiments at Mian Mir were now levelled to the ground, and the men were marched into a camp guarded by the 81st and gunners, and from here they were led away in batches to Mian Mir for trial by general court-martial, with the usual sentence—to suffer death by being blown from the mouth of a gun. In these very trying and exacting duties the 81st passed the greater part of the hot weather of this year of trial.

Early in September news was received of the death at Cawnpore from cholera on the 6th of this month of Captain W. Sheehy of the Regiment, who had been serving since the 6th July with Captain Barrow's Volunteer

Cavalry, and had taken part in the operations under Major-General Havelock.

During the weeks that had gone by, every man who could be spared from the Punjab had been sent to reinforce the army engaged in the siege of Delhi; and on the 15th September the welcome news was received at Lahore that the ancient fortress-capital had been successfully assaulted on the previous day, that the greater part of the city was in our hands and that the rebels were everywhere giving way.

No letters of any kind reached Lahore on the 16th September, and on inquiry being made into the reason for the failure of the mails, it was learnt that on the very day of the assault on Delhi, the wild tribes inhabiting the country between Lahore and Multan had risen in arms and that in numbers, amounting to many thousands, they were marching on Gugera, a town of some importance, situated on the left bank of the Ravi, and about midway between Multan and the capital. From information that came to hand it appeared that the insurgents intended to plunder and burn the town, "by order," so they stated, "of the King of Delhi," and they had stopped the mail, appropriated the horses and disarmed the local police.

The strength of the reliable military force in and about Lahore had been greatly reduced, and no man could well be spared, but it was realized that the matter was one of real urgency, and by twelve o'clock that night two hundred horsemen of a newly-raised Sikh regiment had started off, followed at 3 a.m. on the 17th by three guns, the Light Company of the 81st, under Captain J. Woods and Lieutenant J. A. Deans, a party of Punjab Police and some companies of a regiment of Sikh infantry, all under the command of Colonel Paton, D.Q.M. General. From Multan was sent a regiment of cavalry under Major Chamberlain.

The mounted men from Lahore covered the whole distance—eighty-three miles—in one march, and the rest of the force, some in country carts, following as best they could, arrived exactly one hour before Gugera was attacked—just in time, that is, to save it. They repelled the assailants, and next day, assuming the offensive, killed Ahmed Khan, the leader of the tribe mainly concerned, and his son, burned down the chief offending village and took many prisoners.

The rebels, disheartened at the loss of their leader, withdrew from the neighbourhood of Gugera and took the road to Multan, whither Colonel Paton moved his column on the 21st, scouring the country, searching the villages and obtaining all the information possible by means of spies. On the night of the 25th September, when nearing the town of Harappa, the sound of native drums was heard and it was surmised that the rebels were in considerable force; the night was, however, too dark to make any forward movement, and by the morning but few of the enemy were in sight. They were followed for some six miles, but could not be brought to action, and the troops fell back to where the baggage had been left.

The column had barely arrived when a messenger appeared with a note from Major Chamberlain, stating that he and his men were besieged in the serai at the village of Chichawutni, a small town, some forty miles from Multan, and were in need of help. The Lahore troops at once marched off to Chamberlain's relief and arrived early the next morning at Chichawutni, the rebels immediately bolting into the dense jungle, where the difficulty was not so much to defeat the enemy as to find him.

After halting here for a few days, the two columns separated, Chamberlain moving towards Multan, while Paton returned to the neighbourhood of Gugera, where for several days and nights the troops skirmished with the rebels. "In a country so impracticable and impenetrable, it was obvious that the struggle might be prolonged for months. The rebellion was never formidable in itself—for the rebels were, many of them, armed only with clubs and stones and pitchforks—but so long as the embers were smouldering, they might at any time be fanned into a flame which, spreading from *doab* to *doab*, might envelop the whole southern Punjab in a prairie-like conflagration. Hence the extreme anxiety of the Chief Commissioner, evidenced alike by his letters and his acts, to bring the struggle to an early termination. He called up contingents from Lahore, from Multan, from Leia, from Jhang and from Hissar, which soon began to close in on the districts occupied by the insurgents."* The different columns advanced from various points, and the rebels being driven into a corner, fought desperately for some time; but they soon submitted, when the chiefs surrendered to the Chief Commissioner—or Lieutenant-Governor, as since 1855 he had been styled—and their followers were allowed to disperse to their villages.

Order having been in large measure restored in the district, the troops marched to their various stations, the company of the 81st being back in Mian Mir in November; but that there was still considerable unrest in certain parts is proved by the fact that Lieutenant R. H. Neville of the Regiment was murdered by rebels from the Gugera district on the banks of the Sutlej near Mamuki, on the 22nd October, when on his way down the river going home on sick leave.

Before the end of the year a draft reached the Regiment at Mian Mir from England; it consisted of one corporal, one drummer, one hundred and eighty-six privates and six boys, and early in January, 1858, another small draft, only twenty-nine strong, joined from the Regimental Depot.

* Bosworth Smith, Vol. II, p. 237.

It must have been about this time that the 81st received orders to be ready to move up nearer to the North-West Frontier, and on the 10th February, the Right Wing under command of Major Allan, and at a strength of thirteen officers and 460 non-commissioned officers and men, left Mian Mir for Nowshera, where it arrived on the 7th March. The remainder of the Regiment was now daily expecting to move also, and on the 14th February Brigadier S. Corbett, C.B., commanding at Lahore, published the following farewell order:—

"On the approaching departure of H.M.'s 81st Regiment in course of relief, the Brigadier Commanding has much pleasure in tendering his thanks thus publicly to Colonel Renny and the officers for the cordial and ready support they have at all times afforded him since he has been in command of the station, and particularly during the late disastrous times.

"The Brigadier requests the Commanding Officer to express to the Non-commissioned Officers and Soldiers his admiration of the manner in which they have uniformly conducted themselves, and of the great steadiness and cheerfulness with which all their harassing and incessant duties have been borne during the last nine months, which is a most gratifying proof of the excellent spirit which animates this fine corps.

"In thus taking leave of the Regiment, the Brigadier begs to express his best wishes for their future welfare."

The Headquarters and Left Wing of the 81st left Mian Mir on the 18th February under Colonel Renny, the strength being nineteen officers and 513 non-commissioned officers and men, and marched to Attock, on the left bank of the Indus, where Nos. 6 and 8 Companies were left to garrison the fort; the remaining companies and Headquarters moved on by way of Nowshera to Peshawar, where, on the 2nd April, the two companies joined from Attock; and less than three weeks later the Headquarters and part of the Regiment stationed at Nowshera was called upon to take part in a punitive expedition in the Yusafzai country.

The clansmen,* occupying the British border from the Black Mountain to the Utman Khel territory, belong, with the exception of the Gaduns, to the important tribe of Yusafzai Pathans, of which other branches are the Hassanzais, Akazais and Chagarzais. They inhabit the division of that name in the Peshawar district, as well as independent territory beyond the border; at the present day the Yusafzais occupy the north-east portion of the Peshawar district and several strips of independent territory north and east of the Peshawar Valley, and also possess considerable settlements to the east of the Indus.

* Most of what follows about these tribesmen is taken from *From the Black Mountain to Waziristan*, Chap. III.

These tribesmen had given continual trouble during the days when the Sikhs ruled the Punjab, but they had been tolerably quiet throughout the first few years which followed upon the taking over of the province and the border by the British. Some small punitive expeditions were sent across the frontier in 1852 and 1853, but there was no more trouble in the Peshawar district until the year of the Mutiny, and it was then almost entirely due to the presence on the Yusafzai frontier of men known as the Hindustani Fanatics, religious adventurers, who had established themselves in colonies among the hills and valleys of this part of the border.

At this time the Yusafzai country was controlled by the fort at Mardan, near Nowshera, usually garrisoned by the Corps of Guides; but when this Corps was ordered to Delhi in May, 1857, its place at Mardan was taken by a detachment of the 55th Native Infantry, the remainder of which was at Nowshera. On the night of the 21st May news reached General Cotton at Peshawar that some of the Nowshera companies of the 55th had mutinied and had joined the others at Mardan. A column was at once sent off from Peshawar to disarm the 55th, but these broke and fled, and those who escaped the guns and sabres of the pursuing column crossed the border into the hills of Swat.

A small column was again sent out in August of this year, with the view of attacking and destroying the village of Narinji—on the border not far from Mardan—where some 650 desperadoes had collected; but though the village was completely destroyed and many of the besieged were killed—among them several of the mutineers of the 55th—the spirit of the tribesmen was by no means broken and attacks upon our people continued to be made.

On the 22nd April, 1858, a force was assembled on the left bank of the Kabul River opposite Nowshera; it numbered 4,877 all told, was commanded by Major-General Sir S. Cotton and was at first divided into two brigades under Lieut.-Colonel H. Renny and Major A. T. Allan, both of the 81st. Before, however, the force crossed the frontier it was divided into three columns.

Of the 81st fourteen officers and 305 other ranks were employed on this expedition, the officers being Lieut.-Colonel H. Renny, Major A. T. Allan, Captains W. M. Browne, V. Tonnochy (Brigade Major, 1st Brigade) and H. A. Chichester, Lieutenants W. Musgrave (adjutant), H. J. Faircloth, T. C. S. Speedy, W. Humphreys and H. H. Briscoe, Ensign W. H. M. Jackson, Surgeon G. Auchinleck, Assistant-Surgeon W. H. Corbett and Quartermaster C. Correll.

The force was almost wholly made up of small bodies from some ten different regiments of cavalry and infantry, and the only other British corps represented was the 98th Foot, 270 strong only; and when the division into three columns took place, 200 bayonets of the 81st joined No. 2 Column and 105 No. 3.

The force assembled at the frontier village of Salim Khan, which was made the base of operations, and the village of a prominent chief was burnt, when the following arrangements were made : No. 1 Column was to enter the country of the Khudu Khel, a tribe having settlements in the Mardan district, moving by the Darhan Pass ; No. 2 was to march directly upon Panjtar, the chief town of the Khudu Khel ; while No. 3 was to hold the camp at Salim Khan. No. 1 Column only met with any opposition and both returned to camp, having destroyed much tribal property.

General Cotton now determined to attack a stronghold of the enemy, known as Mangal Thana, situated on one of the main spurs of the Mahaban Mountain, and a place where much trouble had been hatched ; and on this occasion No. 1 Column was to act against Mangal Thana, No. 2 was to move to Panjtar in support, No. 3 remaining as before at Salim Khan. No opposition was met with by either column, Mangal Thana was found to be abandoned, and having bivouacked here on the night of the 29th–30th April, the fort was blown up and the column withdrew on the 30th to Salim Khan, arriving there on the 1st May.

The colony of the Hindustani Fanatics at a place called Sitana had now to be dealt with, and accordingly on the 2nd May the force marched to Khabal, about four miles from Sitana ; and on the 4th a force of five guns and 1,050 infantry was sent to the left bank of the Indus and advanced against the villages from the east, while the main column moved against them from the south, and tribal levies, acting with our troops, occupied the hills on the north. Approaching Lower Sitana, two regiments were detached to take the mountain in rear, while the position itself was attacked in front, the enemy being driven back with loss to a secondary position. Here, however, they were met by a regiment coming up in their rear, and were driven back on to the bayonets of the troops in front. Hand-to-hand fighting now ensued, many of the Hindustani Fanatics were killed or captured, and the position having been carried at all points and the enemy villages destroyed, the force retired closely followed up.

This was the first occasion upon which the Enfield rifle had been used against the tribesmen, and the effectiveness of its fire made a very great impression upon them.

That night the troops encamped on the Sitana plain by the Indus, and marched next day to Khabal. Here the representatives of the tribes, chiefly concerned in the recent troubles, came in, and agreed to expel and keep out from their lands the Hindustani Fanatics, and to resist any other tribe which might in the future attempt to harbour them.

The objects of the expedition having thus been gained, and the services of the troops being no longer required, the force commenced its return march to Nowshera, where it arrived about the middle of May.

In May and June two small drafts for the Regiment arrived at Karachi from the Depot, the one of eighteen men under Captain W. E. Todd, the other of ten only under Lieutenant R. Swift ; four other small reinforcements landed in India before the end of the year—twelve men on the 2nd October, thirty-four on the 30th under Captain F. A. Magrath and Ensigns H. Maturin and W. A. S. Menteth, ten under Ensign T. A. Kerans on the 6th November and sixteen more on the 16th December. In addition sixty-three men joined in the course of the year—volunteers from the 10th, 29th, 72nd, 78th and 84th Regiments which were under orders for home.

On the 11th November the 81st marched from Peshawar to Rawal Pindi, arriving at that station on the 20th, the marching in strength being two field-officers, five captains, eleven subalterns, four staff, forty-eight sergeants, forty-two corporals, twenty-one drummers and 778 privates.

The following tribute to the services of the 81st Regiment during the Indian Mutiny was paid by Sir John Lawrence, Chief Commissioner of the Punjab :—

" My dear Colonel Renny,—

" I have much pleasure in testifying to the great merits and valuable services of Her Majesty's 81st Regiment during the late Mutiny and insurrection. When the Mutiny broke out the 81st was the only British Regiment in the tract between the Ravee and Beas. This is (as is well known) the country of the flower of the Seikh race. After furnishing a sufficient garrison for the fort at Lahore, and providing for the safety of the European families at Meean Meer, no more than 226 men of the 81st were available on the memorable morning of the 13th May, 1857. On that occasion Brigadier S. Corbett, with his small body of British Infantry and eight guns of the Bengal Artillery, overawed and compelled three regiments of Native Infantry, and one Corps of Native Cavalry to ground their arms.

" Directly this had been accomplished, a company of the 81st were conveyed to Umritsur in carriages in one night, and occupied the strong fort of Govindghur.

" For several months the 81st was the only British corps available with which to hold Lahore and the surrounding country.

" When the Googaira disturbance broke out, one company of this Corps was with difficulty spared for employment in this affair, when it performed good service.

"During the whole period of the crisis the constancy, endurance and good discipline evinced by Her Majesty's 81st Regiment, were highly honourable to both officers and men. Could the Corps have been spared it would have been sent to Delhi, but this was impossible; on it devolved the less glorious, but more irksome and equally important task of guarding day and night against the dangers which threatened us on all sides.

(sd.) " JOHN LAWRENCE.
" Chief Commissioner, Punjaub.
" Camp Rewat,
" 15th November, 1858."

For their services during the Indian Mutiny the officers and other ranks of the Regiment were granted a Medal in General Order No. 363 of the 18th August, 1858, wherein the Governor-General of India announced that " Her Majesty had been graciously pleased to command that a Medal should be granted to the troops in the service of Her Majesty or of the Honourable East India Company employed in the suppression of the Mutiny in India."

Some years later—in General Order No. 71 of July, 1869—it was given out that " Her Majesty the Queen has been graciously pleased to command that a Medal shall be conferred on every surviving officer, non-commissioned officer and soldier who was present at any of the military operations which took place between the years 1849 and 1863 inclusive, on the North-West Frontier of India . . . with a clasp for the operations referred to." The list of services for which the Medal was granted is given in an Appendix to this Order, and they are sixteen in number, the 81st being awarded the clasp inscribed " North-West Frontier," "for the expedition to Sitana, 22nd April, 1858, commanded by Major-General Sir S. J. Cotton, K.C.B., Commanding Peshawar Division, to punish Mokurrub Khan, Chief of Punjtar and the Hindustani Fanatics of Sitana."

CHAPTER XVIII

1859–1881

HOME SERVICE, GIBRALTAR, INDIA
THE SECOND AFGHAN WAR
INTRODUCTION OF THE TERRITORIAL SYSTEM

THE 81st Regiment remained on in garrison at Rawal Pindi until the 23rd December, 1861, when it left that station for Jullundur, arriving there, under the command of Colonel M. Smith, at a strength of two field-officers, five captains, ten subalterns, five staff, forty-six sergeants, twenty-one drummers, forty-two corporals and 966 privates. After a stay here, however, of little less than a year, the Regiment was on the march again, its new station being Morar, which was reached on the 20th December, 1862.

Early in the following year there were signs that the Regiment's period of Indian service was drawing to a close, for on the 1st March, 1863, it gave close upon one hundred volunteers to the 107th Foot; and on the 9th June of the year following the official announcement was made from Simla that during the ensuing cold weather the 81st would, on relief by the 2nd Battalion 10th Foot from the Cape of Good Hope, proceed to the port of embarkation with a view of return to England. Upon this, volunteering to other corps remaining on in India proceeded apace, and in October the 81st gave no fewer than 212 volunteers to fifteen different infantry battalions on the Indian establishment. As during the year seventy-four invalids or time-expired men had been sent home, the Regiment was a somewhat attenuated battalion when the year 1865 opened.

On the 17th January, 1865, the Regiment being then under orders to leave Morar for Calcutta, Brig.-General H. Tombs, V.C., C.B., commanding the Gwalior District, issued the following farewell order :—

" In bidding farewell to the 81st Regiment, which has served for the last two years in the Gwalior District, the Brig.-General Commanding desires to place on record the soldierlike and orderly behaviour which has characterized its ranks. Conduct so orderly and so soldierlike as that of the 81st Regiment ensures its own reward ; and the Brig.-General has only to point out to the men that the good health they have enjoyed, the small mortality, infrequency of courts-martial, and the rareness of punishment, as the result of their good conduct.

"The Brig.-General will always remember, with infinite satisfaction, his connection, short though it has been, with this distinguished regiment; and he begs Major Gildea, his officers and men, to rest assured that they carry with them his best wishes for their future welfare, and for a safe and happy return to their native land."

Three days after—on the 20th January—the Regiment marched from Morar and reached Agra a week later; and from here on the 28th, it commenced to move by rail to Allahabad in detachments of one hundred men each day; headquarters, with the last detachment, arrived at Allahabad on the 3rd February. From Allahabad the 81st was sent on by wings and by train to Calcutta, where all were assembled by the 18th, just in time to take part in a review held there in honour of the Duke of Brabant, the eldest son of the King of the Belgians.

On the 23rd February, headquarters with "A," "D," "F," "G" and "H" Companies under the command of Major Gildea, embarked in the "Sultana," sailing the same day. The strength of the Regiment on board was one field-officer, three captains, three lieutenants, three ensigns, two staff, twenty-one sergeants, sixteen corporals, thirteen drummers, 245 privates, fourteen women and twenty-nine children.

The remaining companies embarked under command of Major Flanagan in the "Red Rose" on the 1st March, and this ship met almost at once with a mishap of a minor character, for in moving from her anchorage in the Hugli, she came in collision with another vessel, touched ground and damaged her anchor. As a result all had to be disembarked until repairs were effected, when, on the 3rd March, the companies re-embarked, sailed the same day, and reached Gosport safely on the 3rd July. From the "Red Rose" there disembarked eleven officers, 286 non-commissioned officers and men, eleven women and twenty-six children.

The "Sultana" proceeded safely on her voyage until about 8.30 p.m. on the 22nd March, when a terrific cyclone was encountered in the Indian Ocean; this increased in intensity until midnight, and continued to rage for many hours afterwards with unabated fury. The storm was accompanied by almost incessant flashes of lightning and deafening peals of thunder, while the darkness between the flashes was most profound. Every sail was torn away and blown to shreds, one boat was wrecked by the wind and two others were carried away by the high sea, while masts and yards gave way and went over the side. The sea rushed down the hatches and carried away everything on the lower decks, and all must have thought that their last hour had come, but everybody, men and women, behaved with heroic fortitude.

Those on watch on deck had a very perilous time of it, but all were ready to try and carry out the orders received and to do what they could to help the sailors; but at one time an unusually heavy sea struck the rudder, rendering the vessel unmanageable.

About 3 a.m. on the 23rd the storm suddenly ceased, the wind dropped, and it was hoped that all danger was passed; but at the end of half an hour the wind again broke out with renewed violence. When day dawned those on board could see and take stock of all the havoc which had been made, and realize the helpless condition in which the ship lay. The hurricane continued to rage until the morning of the 24th March, when its fury abated to a heavy gale. At great peril to all so engaged, the wreckage was as far as possible cleared away, and the rudder was again brought under control. A foresail was bent and on the 27th the course was set for Mauritius —about two thousand miles distant—in order there to repair damages.

The "Sultana" arrived at Mauritius on the 13th April, when Major Gildea made the following report to Major-General Johnson, the G.O.C. :—

"Sir,—

"I have the honour to report for the information of the Major-General Commanding that the headquarters of the 81st Regiment on passage from India to England, under my command, on the 22nd March encountered a cyclone in Lat. 11·30 S. Long. 85·05 E. about 9 p.m.; and at three o'clock the following morning the ship, having lost all sail, set and furled, together with her upper spars, fore-top-mast, and main and mizen top-gallant masts, also three boats and her rudder broken from its bands, was quite at the mercy of the hurricane which lasted the following night, and continued to blow a heavy gale until the morning of the 24th when the wreck was cleared away, the rudder repaired, and the ship was put before the wind with what sail could be set, steering for the Mauritius; the commander of the ship having agreed with me in the necessity of making for the Mauritius to repair damages.

"It gives me great satisfaction to report that during the whole time the hurricane lasted and after, this portion of the Regiment fully bore out the character they have obtained in India for discipline and good conduct. The exertion of all was most praiseworthy.

"The watches on deck did their duty, and those battened below from the night of the 22nd to the morning of the 24th in a stifling atmosphere, endured their trying position without a murmur, many women and children being of the number.

"I was greatly rejoiced to find that, notwithstanding those awful nights, the exertions of the men at the pumps showed that the ship had not sustained any serious damage to the hull, and it was with a thankful heart to Providence that I saw an end to our immediate perils.

"I think it but right to say that the commander of the 'Sultana,' with his officers, did everything that could be done in such a trying situation.

"Owing to the difficulty of getting up fresh spars, sails, etc., and the lightness of the winds, we did not reach this island until the 13th inst.

"I regret to report that owing to the sea water, and things breaking loose between decks, the arms, accoutrements and clothing of the Regiment have been seriously damaged in this disaster; but on the other hand it gives me the greatest pleasure to report that I have not lost a man in consequence.

"I have the honour to be, Sir,
"Your obedient Servant,
(sd.) "J. A. GILDEA, Major,
"Commanding, 81st Regiment."

This report having been forwarded to Army Headquarters in England, the following very complimentary letter was awaiting the 81st Regiment on its arrival at Portsmouth :—

"With reference to the enclosed report from the General Officer at the Mauritius of the conduct of the 81st Regiment on board the 'Sultana,' I have the honour to signify to you, with a view to the same being made known to the 81st Regiment, that the perusal of the said report has afforded the Field-Marshal Commanding the highest gratification—under the trying circumstances of that Corps during the passage home from India."

The Headquarter Wing in the "Sultana" disembarked from that vessel at Port Louis on the 17th April, and camped in the barrack square while the necessary repairs to the ship were being carried out, the officers and men being very hospitably treated during their stay by all ranks of the 2nd Battalion 24th Foot there quartered. The companies remained at Mauritius doing garrison duty until the 24th May, when they re-embarked in the "Sultana" and, sailing the next day, had a tolerably fair run for the remainder of the homeward journey, finally landing at Gosport on the 11th August—five months and seventeen days since leaving Calcutta! The Service and Depot Companies of the Regiment were now all united at the Clarence Barracks, Gosport.

On the 12th October, all the troops in the command were paraded and reviewed by H.R.H. the Duke of Cambridge, Field-Marshal, Commanding-in-Chief, and in the remarks he made at the conclusion of the parade, H.R.H. said that " he began his service with the 81st Regiment at Gibraltar; it had a high reputation at that time, and he was glad to find that it maintained that reputation still."

The Regiment, it will be remembered, spent something over three years at Gibraltar between the years 1836 and 1839, a time when H.R.H. was at the very outset of his military career, and when it had been decided upon that Gibraltar was " a station where he could best acquire the first preliminaries to learning the duties of a soldier, viz. a knowledge of drill and discipline," * when the 33rd, 46th and 81st Regiments formed part of the garrison.

The Regiment left Gosport on the 20th March, 1866, and proceeded to Aldershot, where, however, it remained only a few months, leaving again in the following February, when the Headquarter Wing under Major J. B. Flanagan was sent to Chester Castle, five companies under Major J. Bourchier to Weedon, while one company commanded by Major J. Woods proceeded to Liverpool; the wing at Weedon was joined a few days later by the headquarter companies from Chester.

Within a very few months the Regiment was on the move again, being sent by rail, towards the latter part of August, 1867, to Liverpool, where it embarked for Ireland. Landing at Dublin, it was sent down at once to Cork by rail, furnishing on first arrival detachments, varying in size from one to three companies, to Skibbereen, Bandon, Youghal and Kinsale.

In Ireland the Regiment remained until the 28th February, 1870, detachments being frequently moved from one small garrison to another, while parties were as often dispatched to different places where trouble was expected—usually at election time—to serve, if needed, in aid of the civil power. For its services on such occasions the 81st was more than once commended by Lord Strathnairn, Commanding the Forces in Ireland, as also by the resident magistrates of the various districts visited.

Sailing from Queenstown in the " Tamar," troopship, on the 28th February, the Regiment arrived at Gibraltar for a second tour of service, on the 7th March, being at first somewhat dispersed, but by May was concentrated in the barracks at Buena Vista. The disembarkation strength was thirty officers, thirty-nine sergeants, thirty corporals, seventeen drummers, 525 privates, sixty-six women and eighty-seven children. The officers with the Regiment were: Lieut.-Colonel J. A. Gildea; Majors R. B. Chichester and J. Bourchier; Captains J. Woods, C. J. Skerry, G. Betts, G. B. Bevan, W. H. Warren and H. J. Faircloth; Lieutenants W. H. M. Jackson, J. de M. Armstrong, G. A. Wilson, W. C. Mathews,

* Willoughby-Verner, *Military Life of H.R.H. The Duke of Cambridge*, Vol. I, p. 15.

M. S. Wynne, F. E. Lindoe, H. Walpole and the Hon. H. Arbuthnot; Ensigns N. D'E. Roberts, H. W. Prior, F. Ryley, H. C. B. Farrant, B. A. Satterthwaite, F. H. Wheler, C. E. Sawyer and J. W. Flood; Major W. F. Nixon (Paymaster), Lieutenant and Adjutant R. K. Brereton, Quartermaster T. Rogers, Surgeon J. Wood and Assistant-Surgeon J. S. Duncan.

In April the Depot Companies moved from Templemore to Colchester, and were there attached to the 27th Regiment; in May, 1871, they were again moved—this time to Aldershot.

The 81st Regiment had only been home from India for something less than nine years, four of which had been spent at Gibraltar, when, on the 2nd May, 1874, orders were received directing the Regiment to be held in readiness to embark again for India. At the same time it was decreed that the establishment, from the date of embarkation, was to stand at thirty officers and 886 non-commissioned officers and men.

In July the Depot Companies were attached at Aldershot to the 47th Regiment, and on the 4th October the Service Companies left Gibraltar in the troopship "Euphrates," and, reaching Bombay on the 31st after— for the 81st Regiment—the somewhat unusual experience of a calm voyage, proceeded at once by train to Deolali. A very few days were spent here, and then the journey up-country was made by rail and in two parties, the first party arriving at Jullundur on the 12th November and the second party three days later.

On leaving Gibraltar the following order was published:—

"H.E. Sir Frederick W. Williams, Bart., Governor and Commander-in-Chief to the Forces, cannot permit the 81st to quit his command, without recording in orders the very high opinion he entertains of the Regiment, an opinion most fully borne out by the records of the various staff officers.

"During the long period the 81st Regiment has been quartered in this Fortress their good conduct, both as soldiers and civilians, merits unqualified approbation, and H.E. requests Lieut.-Colonel Chichester, Commanding 81st, will accept and convey to the Officers, Non-Commissioned Officers and Privates under his command, his best wishes for the welfare of the 81st (Loyal Lincoln Volunteers) Regiment."

At the end of 1877 the Regiment left Jullundur for Peshawar, where it was concentrated by the 1st December.

During the winter of 1877–78 operations of a punitive character were carried out against the Jowaki Afridis, a branch of the Adam Khel section of the tribe inhabiting the hilly country between Peshawar and Kohat, and who had been in the habit of receiving a government allowance for keeping open the road between those two towns by way of the Kohat Pass. In July of this year the Jawakis began to give trouble and adopted a hostile attitude, cutting the telegraph wires, raiding villages within our border and attacking parties moving along the road ; while the tribal *jirgas* refused to come in when called upon to answer for these outrages. An expedition into their country was then decided upon and a considerable force, moving from different points, was employed in the operations which became necessary. Only two British infantry regiments accompanied the force, the 51st and the 4th Battalion Rifle Brigade, but towards the close of the expedition it became necessary temporarily to relieve a detachment of the latter corps, which was in occupation of the Sarghasha Pass, leading to the Bori Valley.

For the purpose of this relief the 81st Regiment was called upon to find a detachment, and on the 15th February a party of two hundred bayonets, chiefly from " E " and " G " Companies, was sent to hold the Pass ; the detachment rejoined headquarters at Peshawar on the 28th February. The following officers accompanied the party : Captains W. H. Warren (in command) and G. A. Wilson, Lieutenants W. S. Morrice, S. Jackson, E. C. Morris and H. Crosbie.

This proved to be something of the nature of an introduction or prelude to the very much larger operations beyond the North-West Frontier, in which the Regiment was now about to be engaged.

Since the spring of the year 1876, when Lord Lytton had taken over the Viceroyalty of India, Russia had considerably extended her empire in an easterly direction. The Russian Governor of Turkestan had more than once made overtures to Sher Ali, the Amir of Afghanistan, whose relations with the Indian Government had never been so cordial as were those of his father and predecessor, the Amir Dost Muhammad, and of late Sher Ali had become almost hostile. In 1878 intelligence reached India that the Amir had admitted and favourably received a mission sent to Afghanistan from Russia, although he had previously refused to receive a similar deputation which the Viceroy had proposed sending to Kabul.

It seemed necessary for the maintenance of British prestige, or *izzat*, that we should insist upon the reception on equal terms of a British Envoy ; but on General Chamberlain, who had been appointed to the charge of the British Mission, arriving with an escort at Fort Ali Masjid on the 21st September, 1878, he was turned back by the Amir's local representative.

Some weeks before this our relations with Afghanistan seemed to have reached so unsatisfactory a stage that the Viceroy called upon the Commander-in-Chief, General Sir F. Haines, to formulate a plan of campaign. In his reply, dated the 10th August, the latter had suggested " that a demonstration should be made early in the operations of an advance by the Khyber, by encamping out a certain proportion of the Peshawar troops, making arrangements with the Khyberis for their passage through the pass, and negotiating at Jalalabad and elsewhere for supplies for twenty thousand men, so as to prevent, as long as possible, the ultimate object of our movements being accurately conjectured."

On the 3rd October the 2nd Battalion 9th Foot and two companies of the 7th Bengal Infantry marched from Peshawar and encamped at Hari-Singh-Ka-Burj, five miles from the mouth of the Khyber Pass. The next day the fort at Jamrud was occupied by thirty Indian cavalry, two hundred Indian infantry and fifty sappers, while on the 5th October the camp at Hari-Singh-Ka-Burj was reinforced by the arrival of five guns and detachments from one British and four Indian regiments.

The British regiment was the 81st, which sent " C," " E " and " G " Companies under Captain Faircloth, and these were joined on the 9th by " A," " B " and " H " Companies, Colonel Chichester now assuming command of the whole.

A suggestion had been put forward for the surprise of Fort Ali Masjid, but at the time it was considered that the force available on the spot was insufficient for the enterprise, and the early arrival of strong reinforcements of Afghan troops at the Fort necessitated the abandonment of the idea. The 81st companies were then withdrawn to a camp in the neighbourhood, where they arrived on the 28th October. On the 2nd November an ultimatum was forwarded to the Amir, demanding an apology and the acceptance of a permanent British Mission at Kabul; but no reply having been received within the period of grace allowed, war was declared against the Amir on the 21st of the month.

Four columns were detailed for the advance into Afghanistan, and by the 15th November the 81st was back at Peshawar, having been told off to the 3rd Brigade of the 1st Division of the Peshawar Valley Field Force. The Peshawar Valley Field Force was commanded by Lieut.-General Sir S. Browne, and contained two divisions, of which the 1st was to capture Ali Masjid, advance through the Khyber and occupy Jalalabad; while the 2nd Division was to hold the Peshawar Valley and act as a support to the 1st Division. The 3rd Infantry Brigade was commanded by Colonel F. E. Appleyard, C.B., and contained the 81st, the 14th Sikhs and the 27th Punjab Infantry; Colonel W. B. Browne of the Regiment was posted to the command of the 4th (Reserve) Infantry Brigade.

On the 21st November the 81st crossed the frontier with its brigade and the advance upon Ali Masjid commenced.

"The key to the Khyber was the strong position of Ali Masjid, and against it were to be directed the first operations of the force. . . .

" The Fort of Ali Masjid stands on a detached hill some 450 feet in

ALI MASJID.

21st November, 1878.

The Illustrated London News.—By kind permission.

height which rises precipitously from the right bank of the Khyber River about six miles from the pass and nine miles from the fort of Jamrud. It formed the centre of the Afghan position, of which the right rested on a ridge connected with lofty hills to the north. Due east from this ridge, and making with it an angle of 45°, ran a line of entrenchments broken by three peaks, each of which commands the fort. Between the eastern peak and Ali Masjid, distant from the latter about 500 yards, there is a deep gorge. Immediately opposite the fort, across the river, extending eastward from a cliff above the left bank, ran a sort of covered way with entrenchments for some 600 yards along the precipitous face of one of the spurs of the Rhotas Mountain. In the fort itself were eight guns; two more were placed on a cliff about forty or fifty yards below, and another a few feet above the stream. Along the breastworks of the ridge on the right were eight pieces of artillery; three were placed on the cliff above the left bank, on the right of the covered way, while two mountain guns were in position on commanding points of the same entrenchment. The Afghan garrison was estimated at three thousand seven hundred men.

"The pass at Ali Masjid is very narrow, and the approach from the south was completely commanded by the guns of the Afghan entrenchments. But the weakness of the position lies in the height of the neighbouring ground. To the east, north and north-east it is over-topped by the spurs and cliffs of the Rhotas and neighbouring hills. The scheme of attack therefore arranged by Sir S. Browne aimed at the establishment of his troops on these commanding points." *

The plan of operations for the capture of the Fort of Ali Masjid was as follows: the 1st and 2nd Brigades were to work their way to the rear of the fort, one brigade moving by way of the heights to the north, where the fort could be commanded; while the other was to make a wide detour behind the Rhotas Hills to the north of the fort, eventually coming out near the village of Katta Kushtia, thence commanding the exit from the defile by which it was expected that the evicted garrison of the fort would probably retreat. With the rest of his division the commander proposed making a frontal attack upon the enemy position.

The 1st and 2nd Brigades moved out on the night of the 20th November, it being hoped that they would arrive at their appointed positions by 1 p.m. on the 21st.

The remainder, the 3rd and 4th Brigades, together with the Cavalry, left Jamrud at 7 a.m. on the 21st, the 4th Brigade bringing up the rear. Two hundred and fifty men of the 81st, under Captain Faircloth, formed part of the advance guard, the remainder following at the head of the main column, which moved about half a mile in rear.

* *Official Account of the Second Afghan War*, pp. 18, 19.

"The advance guard pushed on by the Shadi Bagiar road into the Khyber Pass, and from a point a little short of Mackeson's Bridge a detachment of two hundred men of the 81st Regiment and of the 14th Sikhs, with the Mountain Battery, was dispatched up the bed of a ravine on the right, with the object of reaching the high ground beyond, so as to have the command of the Shahgai Heights in case any opposition should be offered at that point.

"Mackeson's Bridge was reached at 9.30 a.m. and from near there, at 10 a.m. the first shot was fired by a detachment of the 81st Regiment against a picquet of the enemy's cavalry, which was seen on the low hills above the bridge, and which retired slowly as the column advanced." *
(See Illustration and Map.)

In the *Daily News* of the 23rd December of this year, Mr. Archibald Forbes, the well-known war correspondent, thus described this incident: "The skirmishers crowned a low ridge, from the top of which the Afghan picquet was visible, distant perhaps a thousand paces. It had deployed, and the men had sent their horses to the rear behind cover. At 10 o'clock our Sikhs and the 81st detachment opened fire against the straggling party of the Afghans. There was some response—nothing to speak of; and the Afghan people quickly fell back, when the bugles sounded 'cease firing' and the skirmishing advance was continued."

At 11 a.m. the head of the advance guard of the main column arrived on the Shahgai Heights and shortly afterwards a battery of artillery, together with three 40-pounders, took up their positions on the ridge, opening fire on the Fort of Ali Masjid and the surrounding hills, at an approximate range of 2,800 yards; these guns continued in action until nightfall. Throughout the afternoon the cavalry remained under cover of the Shahgai Heights in support of the field and heavy batteries.

About 2.30 p.m., under orders from General Browne, Lieutenant Morrice went with " H " Company to clear a slope to the right which was believed to be occupied by some of the enemy; while the remaining three companies of the Left Half-Battalion—that with the main column—then advanced down a ravine, and, crossing the Khyber stream, finally crowned a ridge on the British left. " E " Company, under Lieutenant Wheler, was now detached as escort to the Mountain Battery, and " A " Company, commanded by Lieutenant Walpole, joined the Left Half-Battalion.

" A," " F " and " G " Companies under Colonel Chichester were now directed, with the 14th Sikhs and 27th Punjab Infantry, to form a left attack, which was to work round under cover of a spur towards the right of the line of the Afghan entrenchments, and endeavour to seize the heights

* *Official Account*, p. 27.

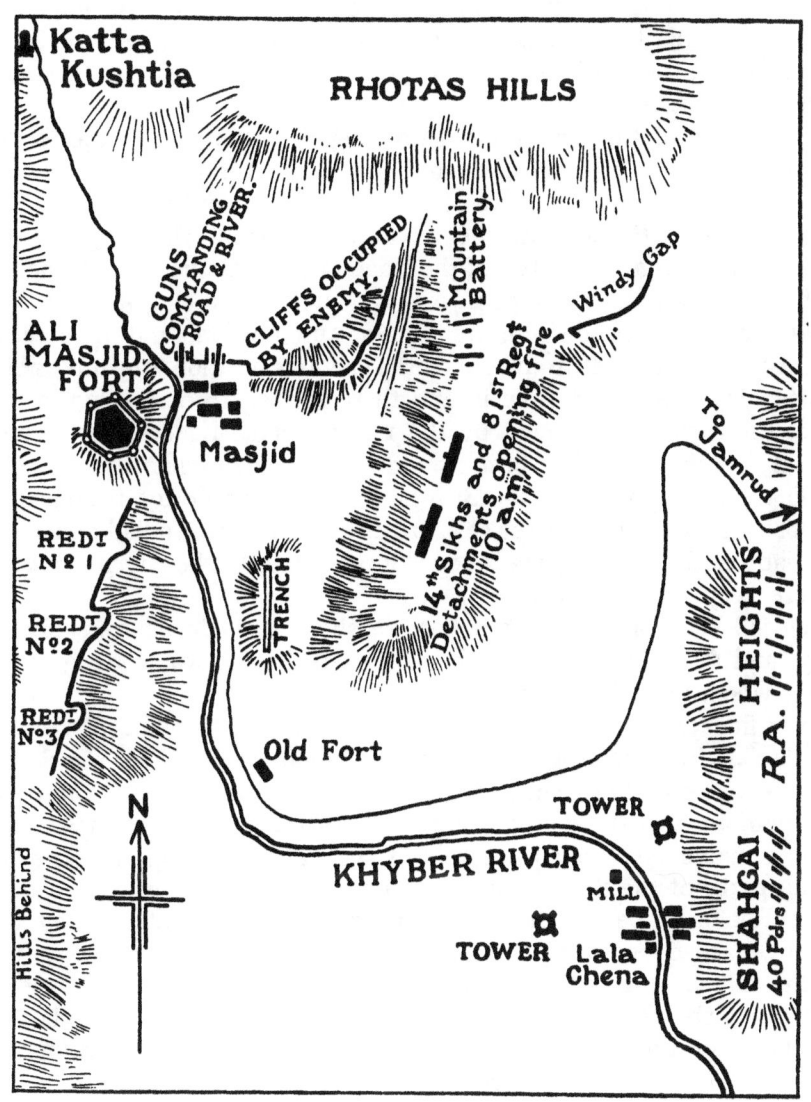

ALI MASJID.

21st November, 1878.

From a Sketch by an Officer, The 81st Regiment.

forming the key of the enemy position; the Sikhs were to lead, supported by the 27th, while the 81st companies formed the reserve. At the same time portions of the 4th Brigade were to make a right attack on the ridge in front of Shahgai.

The advance of the left attack—3rd Brigade—was made under cover of the outer slopes of the ridges, which did not, however, prevent the enemy from keeping up a continuous fire of round shot and musketry against the British advance. By 4 p.m. the advance troops of the brigade had approached the gorge at the top of the ridge in occupation of the Afghans; here the covering artillery came into action, but at the end of two hours the battery had expended all its limber ammunition, and it became apparent that any assault from here on the enemy's position was impossible. Moreover, day was now closing in and there seemed to be no sign of the effect of the turning movement by the 1st and 2nd Brigades, the ground traversed by them having been found to be extraordinarily difficult. Accordingly at 5 p.m. General Browne gave the order for retirement; but before this order reached the O.C. 3rd Brigade, his two Indian regiments had already pushed well up the steep slopes leading to the Afghan *sangars* and were very actively engaged.

They fell back on the order at last reaching them to do so, suffering heavily, and meeting as they fell back the 81st which was coming up in support, when all withdrew together.

Of this final phase of the action, the *Official Account* states that, " Colonel Maunsell, C.R.E., observing the loss to the troops involved by the determined resistance of the enemy, ordered up three companies of the 81st, part to reinforce their Regiment which was acting as a reserve to the attack, and the remainder to hold the gorge of the valley in support. The reinforcing party of the 81st did not succeed in reaching the advanced part of their Regiment before the retirement commenced; but as they fell back they reached a convenient position to repel any advance of the enemy along the valley." Here the companies of the 81st were joined by some of the 51st, which were posted under cover of the hill above, while the remnants of the 14th Sikhs and 27th Punjab Infantry were placed in support of the 51st and 81st Regiments.

Two companies of the 81st spent the night of the 21st–22nd on the ridge in advance of the Shahgai Heights, the rest of the Regiment being with the 3rd Brigade on the left rear.

During the night dispositions were made for the renewal next morning of the left attack, and at daybreak the Fort of Ali Masjid was shelled. No reply was elicited, and it was now discovered that the menace of the turning movement had proved effective, the fort was found to have been abandoned under cover of darkness, while the garrison had fled by way of the Bazar Valley to Pesh Bolak, harried and looted on their way by the local tribesmen.

The following are the names of the officers of the 81st Regiment who were present in the action of the 21st November: Colonel R. B. Chichester, Captains H. J. Faircloth, acting second-in-command, W. H. M. Jackson, "F" Company, G. A. Wilson, "G" Company, M. S. Wynne, "D" Company, and F. E. Lindoe, "B" Company; Lieutenants H. Walpole, "A" Company, B. A. Satterthwaite, "C" Company, F. H. Wheler, "E" Company, W. S. Morrice, "H" Company, H. Crosbie and P. Palmes; 2nd Lieutenants F. R. Borrow and P. R. S. Churchward; Paymaster C. H. Hignett, Lieutenant and Adjutant H. C. B. Farrant, Quartermaster M. Hanlon and Surgeon-Major J. Martin.

During the 22nd the Regiment remained in bivouac under the Fort at Ali Masjid, marched next day four and a half miles to Katta Kushtia, and advanced on the 25th to Landi Kotal, where it was ordered to remain for the present. The greater part of the 3rd Brigade garrisoned Landi Khana, while the 4th held Ali Masjid, the bulk of Sir S. Browne's force proceeding on through the Khyber Pass to Dakka, which was reached on the 24th November, and here it remained halted for some weeks. Upon the 4th, and to some extent upon the 3rd Brigade, devolved the very heavy and exacting duty of safeguarding the pass between Shahgai and Katta Kushtia, the defile being infested by predatory and enterprising tribesmen, where raids of all kinds were of daily—and nightly—occurrence, necessitating the frequent sending out of small punitive bodies of troops.

From Dakka on the 27th November Lieut.-General Sir S. Browne issued the following divisional order: "The Lieutenant-General Commanding has much pleasure in publishing the following telegram received last evening from H.E. the Viceroy and Governor-General: 'The Secretary-of-State sends you congratulations on successful operations against Ali Masjid; I desire to add my most cordial ones on brilliant success which attended your operations against Amir's troops in the Khyber.' Lieut.-General Sir Sam Browne in announcing the expression of satisfaction of the Government at the success of the capture of Ali Masjid, begs to tender his thanks to the officers and men of the force he has the honour to command for the good work they have done. He assures them he most fully appreciates the cheerfulness and soldierlike spirit with which they have borne the roughing on the hillside, and the Lieutenant-General will not fail to bring to the notice of His Excellency the Commander-in-Chief his approval and satisfaction of their good service."

From the 24th to the 29th November there was constant firing into the camp at Ali Masjid by the tribesmen of the neighbourhood, who assembled in considerable numbers on the adjoining heights. On the night of the 27th there was an organized attack upon the camp and the outlying picquets, and it was considered advisable to send reinforcements to Ali Masjid from the garrisons further up the pass.

In consequence of the above, "C," "D" and "F" Companies of the 81st were suddenly ordered back to Ali Masjid under the command of Captain Jackson, followed next day by the remainder of the Regiment; on arrival, the companies camped on the Shahgai Heights and remained there until the 26th December. While in this neighbourhood the Regiment was ordered out, with two mountain guns, on the 30th November, in an attempt to overtake and cut off a body of Afridis, who had attacked a convoy coming from Jamrud, and exchanged shots with the enemy, who was, however, too elusive, and too well acquainted with the ground, to permit himself to be overtaken.

During the early part of December the following officers joined the service companies: Captain W. C. Mathews, Lieutenants S. Jackson and C. Davidson.

At the end of the first week in December the brigades were redistributed, a new one being formed from the Sikhs and the Guides Infantry, while the 4th was amalgamated with the 3rd and remained at Ali Masjid and Shahgai, the troops at which places became part of Major-General F. Maude's division: Brigadier-General W. B. Browne, 81st, who had been up to this in command of the 4th Brigade, was directed to proceed to Peshawar and there to await further orders.

On the 1st January, 1879, three subaltern officers joined the Regiment, these were Lieutenant F. Ryley, 2nd Lieutenants A. C. H. Thomas and J. H. Young.

During the past weeks there had been much sickness among the troops composing the Peshawar Valley Field Force, the 14th Sikhs had suffered so greatly from pneumonia that the regiment had been sent down from the front, and by the beginning of 1879 the 81st was also greatly reduced by sickness, the numbers for duty having fallen below four hundred men. The Regiment was now also ordered to be sent down, and leaving on the 9th January, it marched by way of Peshawar to Rawal Pindi, where it arrived on the 24th.

The Regiment had only left the force rather over four months, when, on the 26th May, a treaty was signed by the Amir and by Major Cavagnari, representing the Government of India, by means of which it was hoped and believed that all the objects for the securing of which we had gone to war had been obtained. The orders were now issued for the withdrawal of our troops to begin and the return march to India then commenced. On the ratification of the treaty Major Cavagnari remained on in Kabul as British Envoy, accompanied by a small escort, and for some time everything seemed to go well. On or about the first week in August, however, the attitude of the Afghans became distinctly hostile, and on the 1st September an attack, in overwhelming numbers, was made upon the Residency, and Major Cavagnari and his escort were slain almost to a man.

Hostilities were at once resumed, a large force being once again mobilized and ordered to the frontier, and the 81st Regiment was at first warned for active service; it was, however, found to be still in a very sickly state, and the order to mobilize was consequently almost immediately countermanded.

On the 27th November the Regiment left Rawal Pindi for Jubbulpore, but on arrival at Mian Mir on the march it was first ordered to stand fast; later it was directed to retrace its steps and proceed to Ferozepore, there to take the place of the 1st Battalion 18th Foot, which had been ordered to the front. Moving by half-battalions, the Left Wing under Captain Warren, and the Headquarter Wing under Colonel Chichester, the two arrived at Ferozepore on the 2nd and 5th January, 1880, respectively.

In the *London Gazette* of the 7th June, 1881, the following appeared :—

" The Queen has been graciously pleased to permit the following Regiments to bear the words, specified below, upon their Standards, Colours or appointments, respectively, in commemoration of their gallant behaviour during the recent campaigns in Afghanistan :—

* * * * *

" 81st (Loyal Lincoln Volunteers) Regiment, ' ALI MASJID,' ' AFGHANISTAN 1878-79.' "

* * * * *

Under General Order No. 30 of the 19th March, 1881, all who had served in the Regiment in the first stage of the Afghan War, were awarded the Afghan War Medal with clasp inscribed " Ali Masjid."

The Royal Warrant of the 25th June, 1881, was followed by General Order No. 41 of this year detailing the very drastic changes in Army Organization, full particulars of which have been given in Chapter X of this History; it will be enough therefore to say here that, under those instructions, the title of the 81st Regiment was changed to that of the 2nd Battalion, The Loyal North Lancashire Regiment.

CHAPTER XIX

THE 3RD ROYAL LANCASHIRE MILITIA

1797-1881

LIKE the 1st and 2nd Battalions of the Regiment, what is now the 3rd Battalion came into existence in the eighteenth century. In 1797 it was raised under the Supplementary Act of that year as the second of five Supplementary Regiments of Militia for the County of Lancashire. It consisted of ten companies under the command of Colonel Sir Henry Hoghton, Bt., of Walton Hall, and in its first year of service it carried out four trainings, each of twenty-eight days.

The officers serving were as follows: Colonel Sir Henry Hoghton, Bt., Lieut.-Colonel Robert Fletcher; Major J. Sedgwick; Captains Fazackerly, Heath, Lowe, Barbauld, Eyres, Lewis Barton; Captain and Lieutenant Abraham Scott; Lieutenants Hardy, Turner, Robinson, Selby, Hopton, Parker, Stewart, Johnson, Lees, Morton, Bowden; Ensigns Scott Galbraith, Nixon, Akenside, Taylor; Adjutant Abraham Scott; Quartermaster Selby; Surgeon J. T. Robinson.

In 1798 the Regiment was embodied under the King's Warrant dated 25th February, and assembled at Lancaster on the 8th March following. On the 25th of the same month it marched to Sunderland "in the Bishopric of Durham," where it remained until November, 1801, when it returned to Lancashire and was disembodied at Preston on the 24th April, 1802.

Its establishment on first embodiment was as follows: 1 colonel and captain, 1 lieut.-colonel and captain, 1 major and captain, 7 captains, 1 captain adjutant, 11 lieutenants, 8 ensigns, 1 adjutant, 1 quartermaster, 1 surgeon, 1 serjeant-major, 1 quartermaster-serjeant, 30 serjeants, 30 corporals, 22 drummers, 610 privates.

"*N.B.*—The paymaster and surgeon's mate not being borne on the establishment of Militia Corps, are not distinguished in the above state, but the usual pay and allowance will be granted them; as also the allowance for the quartermaster's clerk."

While at Sunderland its name and status were changed. In 1800 it became the 3rd Battalion The Royal Lancashire Militia, two regiments having been added to the County of Lancashire which, prior to the augmentation, had only one Regiment of Militia. Simultaneously its establishment was raised to twelve companies.

In 1799 a General Order was issued which profoundly affected the whole of the Militia for more than a century to come and led ultimately to its undoing in 1907. It reads as follows:—

"H.R.H. The Commander-in-Chief directs it to be declared to the Militia forces at large that an Act of Parliament has passed with a view to enable His Majesty to provide for the vigorous prosecution of the war, in which among the provisions it is enacted that it shall be lawful for one-fourth of the Private Men of the Embodied Militia, to enter as Volunteers into such of His Majesty's Regular Regiments of Infantry as His Majesty shall by any Order under His Royal Sign Manual think proper to appoint."

Here follows a list of the appointed Regular Regiments open to such recruiting.

"The Commander-in-Chief," the General Order continues, "is well acquainted with the spirit that universally pervades every part of His Majesty's Forces, and from the frequent opportunities he has had of observing the zeal and honourable exertions which hath particularly characterized the Militia during this War, His Royal Highness entertains no doubt that many will embrace this opportunity of extending their services, and of adding fresh lustre to the British Arms, by aiding the efforts of our Allies, sharing their glory, and by improving their late successes, of contributing with them to secure the first object of His Majesty's paternal anxiety, a speedy restoration to Peace, on terms secure and honourable to the Country."

The terms offered to Militiamen to transfer were as follows: Engagement for five years or the duration of the war and for six months after the expiration thereof; not to be liable for service out of Europe, nor to be drafted from the Regiment they originally elected for; standard of height 5 ft. 4 in. and to be free from bodily infirmities; a bounty of ten guineas.

At the time this order was issued the Militia was raised under the supervision of the Lords-Lieutenant, by ballot, paid substitutes being recognized. Hitherto the transfer of Militiamen to the Line had been expressly prohibited. But the change indicated in the above General Order having once been made, it is only natural that the military authorities should use every possible endeavour to induce Militiamen to volunteer for overseas service. Later on, Militia officers were offered Regular commissions if they would bring sixty men with them. Later again eighty Militiamen with a proportion of officers were allowed to engage as a company, with an assurance that they should continue to serve together as a company.

There is no mention in the records of the 3rd Battalion of the numbers it gave to the Line between 1800 and 1815, but doubtless the total was considerable, for during that period more than one hundred thousand Militia-men voluntarily engaged for overseas service, and it has been stated with a good deal of truth that the Peninsular War was carried on on the Militia Regiments of England.*

On the rupture of the Peace of Amiens in 1803, the 3rd Battalion of the Royal Lancashire Militia was again embodied. It assembled at Preston on the 4th April and marched thence on the 21st May to Chelmsford, where it arrived on the 9th June. In September it moved to Landguard Fort; in November it proceeded to Ipswich New Barracks, and thence to Woodbridge.

One hundred and eleven years later the 3rd Battalion of the Loyal North Lancashire Regiment at Felixstowe was defending the same part that the 3rd Royal Lancashire Militia at Landguard Fort defended in 1803.

In May, 1804, the Regiment marched to Portsmouth, where it remained for a year. Here it was inspected by H.R.H. The Duke of Clarence. In May, 1805, it moved in four divisions to the Western Command, where it lay for three or four months at Woodbury Down Camp under Lord Lennox, afterwards the Duke of Richmond. In September it took part in field manœuvres. The operating force was composed of the following Militia Regiments:—

Worcester
N. Devon } Right Wing :—Lieut.-General Lennox.

Bedford
3rd Lancashire } Left Wing :—Major-General Cowell.

This force was opposed by the Volunteers and Yeomanry of the County of Devon. On the first day, the 16th September, after a long march opposed in every direction, the force found its camping-ground at Hall Down, near Chudleigh, occupied by the enemy "assembled in great numbers," who were, however, disposed of "after various movements, and finally by a charge in line with the two brigades." The manœuvres continued till the 21st. On the 18th " a fatiguing day's journey" is recorded, "the weather being intolerably hot and a distance of upwards of twenty-two miles having been covered." The casualties appear to have been considerable.

On October 21st (Trafalgar Day) the Regiment marched to Plymouth, where it spent the next eighteen months. In May, 1807, it marched viâ Kingsbridge and Berry Head to Bristol, and thence in November to Gos-

---

* While the 3rd Battalion was at Bristol in 1807, it is recorded that the whole front rank of the Grenadier Company volunteered for overseas service and went to the 29th Regiment of Foot. This statement appears in a poem by Sergeant W. Mallett of the Regiment which relates its movements and stations from 1803 till 1816.

A copy of this poem has recently been presented to the Regimental Museum by Lieut.-Colonel Sir Vivian Henderson, M.C., M.P.

port and its neighbourhood, where it remained till 1810, when it marched viâ Horsham and Rye * to Dover and was there quartered in the Citadel. While at Gosport it was "taught the use of field pieces, and also did duty on board ship over prisoners-of-war."

In 1812 it moved to Canterbury and Chatham and in July, 1813, it marched in three divisions to Bristol, where it embarked for Ireland on the 12th August "at five o'clock in the morning." Owing to contrary winds the transports had to shelter first in Tenby Bay and later in Milford Haven, and it was the 27th before the Regiment reached Dublin and disembarked. In Ireland it remained till nearly the end of 1815. During most of this time it was stationed in Dublin, with a brief interval in 1815 at Drogheda.

On the 2nd December, 1815, the Regiment arrived at Liverpool, where it was billeted on the inhabitants. On the 22nd December an order was received from the Secretary-at-War directing that the recruiting of the Regiment by beat of drum should be discontinued forthwith, and on the 24th all recruiting parties were called in. On the 27th and 28th the Regiment marched in two divisions to Preston, where on the 2nd January, 1816, it received the Lord-Lieutenant's order for disembodiment, which was effected on the 10th January.

The concluding lines of Sergeant Mallett's poem give a vivid picture of the return of the Regiment to Preston. They run as follows :—

> The day now came when we to Preston drew,
> To meet their friends, behold how each one flew;
> When fathers, uncles, mothers, wives and cousins,
> Now crowd the streets, acquaintances by dozens,
> The eager hand stretch forth to catch the grasp,
> While fathers now their wives and babes did clasp.
> Along the streets thus move the welcome throng,
> With cheers and shouts, to welcome us along;
> The new-rear'd steeple too its flags display,
> Whilst peals on peals were rung throughout the day.
> Thus welcom'd in—('tis but a just reflection)
> Our thanks are due for such a kind reception.
> Our toils now o'er, and we from war retreated,
> We chair'd our colonel, and our work completed.
> Thus close the scenes, and may we ever sing
> Success to Preston, and "Long live the King."

On disembodiment the following officers were serving with the Regiment: Colonel Wilson Braddyll; Lieut.-Colonel J. Sedgwick; Major T.

* From Rye to Hythe the Regiment proceeded in flat-bottomed boats up the New Military Canal (Mallett's poem).

Braddyll; Captains Tomkinson, Peach, Whalley, Smith, Bigland, Hansbrow, Dearden; Lieutenants Holland, Hardey, Cooper, Fielding, Mahony, Hallworth, Wheatley, Meeds, Farrar, Newsham, Scott, Adjutant J. Robinson, Quartermaster W. Tipson, Surgeon J. J. Kennett.

Except for one year from April, 1802, to April, 1803, the Regiment, since it was raised in 1797, had been almost constantly under arms, and in reading this account of the services of a Lancashire Militia Regiment, one gains some idea of the part the Militia of England played during the long struggle with Napoleon.

During this long period of embodiment various orders received and sundry episodes of historical interest are worth recording. Thus in February, 1800, the Commander-in-Chief sent a most positive order that the practice of wearing powder in the hair was forthwith to be discontinued, "agreeable to His Majesty's Command."

In the same year it was ordered that "the use of hats is to be entirely abolished throughout the whole of the Infantry of the Army," a cap being worn instead. Detailed instructions were issued regarding the use of numbers, badges and tufts on the caps.

On many occasions permission was given for a proportion of men, not exceeding one-third of the regimental strength, to be given leave to assist the farmers in the neighbourhood to get in their harvest. This privilege seems to have been abused in some instances, as in 1801 the Adjutant-General stated in a General Order that "some Soldiers . . . have so far forgot what was due from them to their Country as to take advantage of the pressure of Hands, and have exacted a most exorbitant price for their Labour." In future the price of such military labour was to be determined locally by the principal magistrates.

In December, 1800, all Colours were ordered to be sent to the Tower for the purpose of being altered owing to the Union of the Kingdoms of Great Britain and Ireland.

In 1802 the use of epaulettes and shoulder-knots was discontinued for N.C.O.s, chevrons placed on the right arm being substituted—four bars for sergeant-major or quartermaster-sergeant; three bars for all other sergeants; two bars for corporals.

In 1813 the Regiment was informed that "H.R.H. The Prince Regent has been pleased, in the name and on behalf of His Majesty, to approve of the 3rd Royal Lancashire Militia being in future styled 'The 3rd, or Prince Regent's Own, Regiment of Royal Lancashire Militia.'" In 1831 this title was changed to "The Duke of Lancaster's Own Regiment of Militia," a title retained until the formation of the Loyal North Lancashire Regiment in 1881.

Between 1816 and 1855 there are few events of importance to record. In 1816 new Colours were received. In 1818 Colonel W. G. Braddyll, who had been the Colonel of the Regiment since 1803, when he succeeded Sir Henry Hoghton, died when on his way to London to attend Queen Charlotte's funeral. He was succeeded by Sir Thomas Hesketh, Bt., of Rufford Hall, who remained in command till 1842. In 1825 Ensign J. Wilson Patten, afterwards Lord Winmarleigh, received his first commission in the Regiment, and in 1842 he succeeded Sir T. Hesketh as the Colonel Commandant of the Regiment and remained in command till 1872, when he became the first Hon. Colonel of the Regiment. He died in 1892; thus his connection with the Regiment extended over sixty-seven years. Probably a record!

During the years 1817–54, the Regiment assembled for training, usually at Preston, for twenty-eight days, occasionally for twenty-one days only. Its average strength during these years was about 650 all ranks. In 1825 it is stated that "the progress which the men made in the new system of tactics, recently introduced into the Army, by the Adjutant-General, Sir Henry Torrens, was most satisfactory to the Colonel and the Corps of Officers." Further we are told: "The Battalion was perfected in the new manual and platoon exercises, and in most other parts of the fire-lock exercise with the exception of the oblique firings. It practised breaking into open column—marching past in slow and quick time—wheeling into line—doubling into close columns—deploying into line—wheeling in close columns both from the halt and on the march—advancing and retiring in line—forming open columns from line—echelon change of position forward—square four deep from line—square two deep to the front from line—solid square from close columns—the square from quarter distance column—grand division squares from open column—street firing—retiring by threes and forming line to the original front, etc., etc., all of which movements were performed in strict conformity with the new system."

In 1827 the coatee was issued instead of the jacket, and the colour of the trousers was changed from grey to Oxford mixture. Boots were supplied instead of shoes and gaiters. Four years later, however, we are told that "the dress of the men was a red or white jacket, duck trowsers, and a blue forage cap. The officers wore the blue surtout, regulation forage cap, sword, sash and waistbelt, and duck trowsers on all occasions."

In 1853 new Colours were presented to the Regiment by Miss Wilson Patten, the daughter of the Colonel.

In 1854 the Crimean War began and the 3rd Royal Lancashire Militia readily offered its services for garrison duty overseas. On December 27th it was embodied and remained billeted in Preston till the 29th June, 1855, when the headquarters and eight companies embarked in the "Lord Raglan" transport at Liverpool for Gibraltar, where they disembarked on the 16th July. Four companies remained at Preston and formed the Depot of the Regiment.

In January Colonel Wilson Patten was obliged to return to England and the Governor of Gibraltar marked the occasion by issuing a Garrison Order of a most complimentary nature both to the Colonel and the Regiment. This Order was later communicated to the Army by Viscount Hardinge, the Commander-in-Chief, with the following remarks : " The valuable services of Colonel Wilson Patten and the zeal and exertion he has evinced in bringing his Regiment to its present high state of discipline and efficiency have been on other occasions most favourably brought to the notice of the Field-Marshal Commanding-in-Chief and his Lordship feels he can in no way better mark his approval than by thus promulgating Lieut.-General Sir James Ferguson's order so creditable to Colonel Patten and the Militia Service."

Peace with Russia having been proclaimed, the services of the Regiment were no longer required at Gibraltar, and on the 7th June, 1856, it embarked in the S.S. "Great Britain" for Liverpool, where it arrived on the 14th and proceeded by rail to Preston on the 16th. It was disembodied on the 7th July. Before it left Gibraltar, the Governor issued a long farewell order, of which the following sentence is an extract :—

"To the Regiments of Militia, His Excellency desires to bear testimony that they have come forward and volunteered their services at a most trying period, that their attention in learning their duties has been most assiduous, that their bearing has been soldierlike, and in a word that they have deserved well of their Country."

On the 3rd June, 1856, a communication from the Horse Guards directed the word "Mediterranean" to be borne on the Colours.

In 1860 a distinctive badge was approved by H.M. the Queen as follows :—

"Lion, Crown, and Red Rose all in gold on Forage Cap."

During the sixties, the usual period of training was for twenty-seven days—recruits thirty-five days in addition, increased later to forty-one days and later again to sixty-nine days. The strength became so abnormal —in 1863 over 1,200 of all ranks were present at training—that in 1864 an establishment of 25 officers, 45 sergeants, 12 drummers and 800 rank and file was laid down. For many years to come, however, the numbers present at training were considerably in excess of this establishment.

In 1870 the Regiment was supplied with the Snider breech-loading rifle.

In 1872, in consequence of the stir caused by the events of the Franco-

Prussian War, it was decided to hold manœuvres on an extensive scale, and the Regiment was detailed to form part of the Southern Army Corps, commanded by Lieut.-General Sir John Michel. It assembled at Preston on the 5th August and proceeded by train on the 16th to Blandford, where it was brigaded with the 7th Royal Fusiliers and the 23rd Royal Welsh Fusiliers under Major-General Sir E. Greathed. The manœuvres of corps against corps lasted from the 3rd to the 10th September, and after some strenuous marching and much fighting the Regiment returned to Preston on the 13th. Shortly afterwards the Duke of Cambridge published General Greathed's report together with his own remarks on " the soldierlike bearing and general good behaviour and discipline of the Regiment." General Greathed's report runs as follows : " I found the men stout-hearted fellows who bear fatigue to which they are quite unaccustomed with good spirit and always get well together at the end of a long day's march. I do not think one of them has ever fallen out except from sheer necessity and there have been very few stragglers. The Regiment marches past remarkably well and is in every point effective in the field. The conduct of the men in camp has been excellent."

The following officers took part in these manœuvres : Colonel Matthias in command, Lieut.-Colonel Feilden, Major Crosse, Captains Silvester, Sheals, Story, Hargreaves, Birch, Bird, Leese, Hicks, Miller, Walmesley; Lieutenants Butler-Bowden, Crothers, Gilden, Taylor, Harrison, De Hoghton ; Captain and Adjutant Percy Lake, Quartermaster Hewett and Surgeon Allen.

A year later, under the Warrant for the Reorganization of the Army, dated 22nd February, 1873, the Regiment was affiliated to the 47th and 81st Regiments. Thus began one of Mr. Cardwell's many reforms which came to full fruition in 1881.

The first practical outcome of the affiliation scheme was seen three years later, when, in 1876, Captain Berkeley, 47th Regiment, became the Adjutant of the Regiment; this appointment he held for five years.

In July, 1879, the Regiment was divided into two battalions, and two years later Colours were presented to the 4th Battalion, commanded by Lieut.-Colonel Silvester, by Lady Mary Crosse, wife of the Colonel of the Regiment.

On July 1st, 1881, the history of the 3rd Royal Lancashire Militia was ended ; the two battalions which bore its name and inherited its proud traditions then became the 3rd and 4th (Militia) Battalions of the Loyal North Lancashire, and henceforward their history is closely interwoven with that of the history of the Regiment of which they were now to form a constituent part.

No Militia Regiment ever had a finer record of service than the 3rd Royal Lancashire Militia; it is a record of which North Lancashire may well feel proud; it is a record which adds lustre to the prestige of the Loyal Regiment; it is a long record of unselfish and devoted service to King and Country which should prove a constant source of inspiration to the Force, which, constitutionally and in the affection of the people, has now replaced the old territorial Militia of England.

The following Officers appear in the Army List of July 1881, as serving with the 1st and 2nd Battalions, 3rd Royal Lancashire Militia :—

Hon. Colonel: Rt. Hon. J. W. Lord Winmarleigh, A.D.C. to H.M. The Queen. Lieut.-Colonels: T. R. Crosse, F. Silvester. Majors: T. M. Sandys, C. Birch. Captains: P. Sheals, C. H. Bird, W. A. Hicks, J. Walmesley, J. Munn, J. J. Harris, H. G. Wright, A. E. Da Costa, W. B. Baker, R. G. Chambres, L. Bonhote. Lieutenants: H. Higgins, J. H. W. Pedder, R. Dames, W. H. Goodair, H. B. Lowndes, C. R. Day, P. R. W. Wetherall, H. G. S. Young, R. P. Horsbrugh, S. D. Graham, C. A. W. Osmond, A. W. Biddell. 2nd Lieutenants: R. F. J. Feilden, J. C. Aitken, F. J. P. Gibson, C. J. C. Mee, H. E. Taylor, E. W. Dawes. Paymaster: Captain W. A. Hicks. Adjutant: Captain E. R. S. Richardson, (64th Foot). Quartermasters: J. Hewett and J. A. Furlong. Medical Officer: Surgeon-Major R. Allen.

THE LOYAL NORTH LANCASHIRE REGIMENT
CHAPTER XX

THE 1st BATTALION
THE LOYAL NORTH LANCASHIRE REGIMENT

1881-1899

HOME SERVICE, GIBRALTAR, INDIA, ZHOB, CEYLON, SOUTH AFRICA
THE OPENING OF THE SOUTH AFRICAN WAR

ONE of the first of the outward and visible signs of the amalgamation of the 47th and 81st into one Regiment was to be noted on the 26th September of this year—1881, when a draft, 282 strong of all ranks, proceeded to Queenstown for embarkation in H.M. Troopship "Jumna" to join the 2nd Battalion at Ferozepore in India. Lieutenants P. Palmes and R. E. Grimston accompanied this draft.

On the 30th January, 1882, the 1st Battalion—strength 1,079 rank and file—left Ireland in H.M.S. "Assistance," reached Portsmouth on the 3rd February, and, going on by train to Aldershot, occupied quarters in the West Infantry Barracks, being included in the 2nd Infantry Brigade, commanded by Major-General Willis, C.B.

On the 1st June the regimental number was worn on parade for the last time.

The stay of the Battalion at Aldershot was to be an unusually short one, for on the 6th July a telegram was received directing the Battalion to embark at Portsmouth on the 8th for Gibraltar; accordingly it left the West Infantry Barracks at eight on the morning of the 8th and proceeded in two special trains to Portsmouth, where, in company with the 2nd Battalion The Essex Regiment, it was put on board the "Malabar," sailing the same day and reaching Gibraltar on the evening of the 13th. The embarking strength was as follows : twenty-eight officers, two warrant officers, forty-eight sergeants, sixteen drummers and 800 rank and file. The Battalion was under the command of Lieut.-Colonel Straton, and on landing the headquarters were accommodated in the Grand Casemate Barracks, with a detachment at the North Front and another, later, at Catalan Bay.

In accordance with the terms of an Army Circular dated the 21st May, 1883, the establishment of the Battalion was to be altered as follows: viz., two lieut.-colonels, three majors, five captains, twelve lieutenants, one adjutant, one quartermaster, six warrant officers, forty-three sergeants, sixteen drummers, forty corporals and 910 privates.

On the afternoon of the 15th January, 1884, the Battalion sailed for Bombay in the "Serapis" at a strength of twenty-eight officers and 878 other ranks, a draft from the 2nd Battalion, sixty-seven strong, joining immediately prior to embarkation; the following were the officers who embarked with the Battalion for its second tour of Indian service: Lieut.-Colonel J. M. Straton; Majors D. North, A. C. B. Hall and A. C. Yard; Captains W. H. R. Gunner, C. E. Sawyer, E. C. Morris, H. S. B. Hodgkinson, adjutant, D. de Hoghton and E. Lindesay; Lieutenants H. G. Leonard, F. W. Jones, J. R. Fraser, W. H. E. Murray, H. F. Coleridge, G. A. Norcott, G. W. Dowell, C. J. Daniel, G. J. C. Hall, H. M. S. O'Brien, G. A. Brownrigg, A. A., M. M. Faulkner, J. N. Newall and F. J. Fowler; Quartermaster J. Donnelly and Staff-Paymaster G. H. Moore-Lane.

Touching at Malta, Port Said and Suez, the "Serapis" reached Bombay late on the afternoon of the 7th February, and, landing at 3 p.m. next day, the Battalion proceeded in two special trains to Poona, arriving there on the 8th and occupying the standing camp in the Wanowrie Lines. Leaving a wing of the Battalion behind at Poona under Major D. North, the headquarters and the remaining companies—"A," "B," "C" and "H" with the Bands and Drums—left Poona again on the 15th February and proceeded by train to Ahmednagar.

From the outbreak of the Second Afghan War in 1878 the attitude of the rulers of Zhob, a mountainous country situated in the north-east corner of Baluchistan, had caused serious anxiety to the Indian Government, the more that one Shah Jahan, in whose hands rested almost the whole power, was known to be hostile to the British, and likely to give trouble on our lines of communications should opportunity offer.

"The termination of the Afghan War brought the district of Thal Chotiali under our rule in accordance with the terms of the Gandamak Treaty with the Amir Ayub Khan. But as this part of the country was only separated from the Bori Valley by a low range of hills, Shah Jahan and his Bori friends found it easy to harass the district by outrages on employés of the Government. . . . It was felt that the frontier could never be safe, and the railway and other works never free from danger, until Shah Jahan was finally settled with and hostages taken from him for his and for the Boriwals' future good behaviour. The matter was referred to Government and sanction obtained to the despatch of a military expedition into Zhob against Shah Jahan. . . . In April, 1884, orders were issued for the movement of troops into the Zhob Valley. At that time the difficulties of procuring food and carriage in the country through which the troops would have to pass were such that it was decided to postpone the expedition until the autumn."*

The force eventually detailed contained ten guns, 561 sabres and 4,220 bayonets, was commanded by Brig.-General Sir O. V. Tanner, K.C.B., and included in it were the 1st Bn. The Worcestershire Regiment, the 2nd Bn. The North Staffordshire Regiment and a wing of the 1st Bn. The Loyal North Lancashire Regiment. The 2nd Bn. The North Staffordshire Regiment at this time formed part of the garrison of Quetta, and it was probably with the idea of not appreciably reducing the number of British troops maintained at that station, that the whole of the 1st Bn. The Loyal North Lancashire Regiment was moved up to this part of the Frontier.

The Battalion—in two wings—left Ahmednagar and Poona on the 22nd September, 1884, and both parties arrived at Bombay early the following morning. Here, on the 23rd, Headquarters, the Band, Drums and "C," "D," "E" and "F" Companies, under Lieut.-Colonel F. G. Berkeley, embarked in the "Clive," and on arrival at Karachi on the 26th these proceeded by train to Rindli and marched the remaining eighty-six miles to Quetta, arriving here on the 7th October and being quartered in the New Barracks, then only in course of erection and hardly completed.

The remaining companies, under Major D. North, left Bombay on the same day in the "Canning," also disembarked at Karachi on the 26th, and were sent on at once by train as far as the Nari Gorge, from where they marched for Thal Chotiali, a distance of one hundred and six miles, arriving there on the morning of the 10th October. The heat during the daytime was excessive and marching was carried out only by night.

The strength of the wing was nine officers and 346 non-commissioned officers and men.

The wing of the Battalion remained throughout the ensuing operations at Thal Chotiali, but the remaining regiments of the expeditionary force saw little if any fighting, for negotiations with the neighbouring chiefs were almost at once opened, and, though more than once broken off, all the local headmen finally submitted, and by the middle of November it was decided that the objects of the expedition had been satisfactorily accomplished and that the troops might now be withdrawn to British

* *Frontier and Overseas Expeditions from India*, Vol. III, p. 191.

territory; by the 22nd November all arrangements for the return march of the troops were completed, and in his final despatch Brig.-General Sir O. V. Tanner brought to the notice of Government the admirable conduct of the troops during the expedition.

The P.M.O. of the Force having recommended that the wing be retained at Thal Chotiali for a time, as the barracks at Quetta were not yet quite ready for occupation and the season was an unhealthy one, Major North and the wing under his command did not march until the 29th December when it moved by way of Gamboli to Sibi, where it was met by the Transport Officer, Lieutenant Coleridge and four hundred mules. At Sibi there was a halt for three weeks caused by the extreme severity of the weather in the Bolan Pass, and then, marching on, the wing joined headquarters in Quetta on the 18th February, 1885.

During the remaining months of this year and the greater part of 1886, the Battalion furnished many detachments and fatigue parties for employment on the new frontier road; but during the first week in November, 1886, the Battalion was sent by train in two parties to Karachi, on arrival there boarding the I.S.N.S. "Nuddea" and sailing to Bombay, where the ship arrived on the 13th. The same night the Battalion went on by train to Mhow, detaching "B" Company, under Major Tidy, en route, to Fort Asirgarh, and Mhow being reached on the 17th. On the 18th "D" Company, under Captain de Hoghton, marched on detachment to Indore.

There are no events of outstanding importance to be recorded of the remainder of the three years' stay of the Battalion at Mhow; this came to an end early in 1890, for on the 4th January the companies were all moved out into camp on One Tree Hill, pending their starting on the march to Kamptee, where the Battalion was to exchange stations with the 2nd Battalion Middlesex Regiment. When the march commenced on the 10th January the Battalion was at the following strength : twenty-two officers, two warrant officers, thirty-three sergeants, fifteen drummers, thirty-six corporals and 692 privates. The officers were : Lieut.-Colonel A. C. B. Hall ; Majors H. Cooper and S. Jackson ; Captains H. S. B. Hodgkinson, E. Lindesay, F. R. Borrow, D.S.O., and H. F. Coleridge ; Lieutenants H. M. S. O'Brien, F. C. L. Logan, R. L. Stable, adjutant, W. F. Elletson and G. C. Knight ; 2nd Lieutenants C. E. Thornton, F. A. Jacques, A. Hay, L. H. Marriott, C. E. A. Jourdain, G. H. Wylde-Browne, T. H. O'Brien and F. W. Hawks ; Hon. Captain C. Sandes, paymaster, and Lieutenant and Quartermaster W. Standring.

The march was a long one, of some 325 miles, and about midway the 2nd Middlesex Regiment was met and transport was exchanged. At the last of the many halting places a small detachment under Lieutenant H. M. S. O'Brien was dropped to occupy Seetabuldi Fort near Nagpore and the Battalion finally reached Kamptee on the 20th February and settled down for a two-years' stay at this station.

On the 5th November, 1891, a detachment of the Battalion on its way to rejoin headquarters was concerned in a very serious railway accident whereby several men were killed and others injured. The train was one of twenty-three carriages drawn by two engines, and among the passengers carried by it was General Sir George Greaves, the Commander-in-Chief of the Bombay Army, and members of his staff.

The accident occurred about 6.30 a.m. on the 5th November about three miles from Nagpore and was due to the breaking of the tyre of a wheel of one of the two engines; seventeen carriages were derailed, and twelve of these were dragged down a steep embankment, only the breaking of the couplings preventing the remaining carriages from following. Of this accident Sir George Greaves wrote: "My carriage was the first that did not fall over the embankment, though it hung over in a dangerous manner. However, I got out unhurt and looked out for the soldiers to see if they had escaped. Alas! they had not. . . . Several British and Native soldiers were killed and over thirty British and four Native soldiers were injured. . . . The drivers of both the engines, the two firemen and the guard were all killed on the spot. I had a wonderful escape, and realized it when I got out of the carriage and saw it suspended over the parapet with the wrecked carriages down below." *

Of the detachment of the Loyal North Lancashire Regiment twelve private soldiers were killed on the spot or died later of their injuries, while one sergeant and eight private soldiers were injured, and of these nine, six had to be discharged from the Army.

The following was published in Battalion Orders: "The Officer Commanding has been desired by H.E. the Commander-in-Chief, Bombay Army, to express his and his staff's deepest sympathy with the Battalion in the loss it has sustained in the accident on the 5th instant, and also how pleased H.E. was with the conduct and plucky behaviour of all ranks under very trying circumstances."

The Governor of Bombay, Lord Harris, telegraphed as follows: " Much distressed at loss of life and heavy casualties. All sympathy with the Regiment and the families of deceased and sufferers."

Then on the 16th the Commanding Officer received, through the Adjutant-General, Bombay Army, the following telegram from General Sir F. Roberts, Commander-in-Chief in India, dated the 9th November

* *Memoirs of General Sir George Greaves*, p. 210.

from "Camp Gomal Pass. I have just heard of the very serious railway accident near Nagpore and am indeed grieved that twelve soldiers were killed and twenty-five wounded. Please let the Regiment know."

During the winter months 1891–92, two considerable drafts joined the 1st Battalion of the Regiment from the 2nd, the one of 85 non-commissioned officers and men, under charge of 2nd Lieutenant Godfrey, the other, 171 strong, brought out by Lieutenant F. H. O'Brien.

On the 1st January, 1893, the Battalion, less one company remaining in Poona and the small detachment at Seetabuldi, proceeded by rail to Ahmednagar, where it took part in manœuvres, which lasted just under four weeks and during which a draft from home, 174 strong, under Captain Churchward and 2nd Lieutenant Codrington, joined the service companies. At the conclusion of the operations the Battalion marched to Kirkee and trained thence to Colaba, Bombay, relieving here the 2nd Bn. The King's Own Yorkshire Light Infantry : " A " and " B " Companies, under Majors Tidy and Purdon respectively, were detached to Deolali.

Very shortly after arrival at Bombay the Lee-Metford magazine rifle was issued to the Battalion.

During the hot weather of this year serious conflicts broke out between the Hindus and the Mohammedans in different parts of India, and in the Bombay Presidency a disturbance took place at a village in the vicinity of the famous shrine of Somnath. This was followed by a rumour which spread among the Hindus that the Mohammedans were intending to make a general slaughter of cows, while a counter-rumour arose among the Mussulmans that the Hindus proposed attacking all the Mohammedan butchers' shops. On the 11th August the pent-up fires burst into flame, the Mohammedans attacking a Hindu temple and coming into conflict with the police stationed to protect it. Disturbances followed in other parts of the native town, several mosques and temples were destroyed, and it was at last found necessary to call out the troops. In the afternoon the Battalion received sudden and urgent orders to proceed at once to the native city to assist in the restoration of order, and was on duty continuously until 11 a.m. on the 13th, when it was relieved by the 2nd Lancashire Fusiliers from Poona, but the Battalion continued to be employed in preserving the peace off and on until the 18th September.

That these riots were of a very serious character is proved by the fact that 4,000 copies of an incendiary pamphlet were seized by the authorities, while over 1,500 prisoners were brought before the magistrates on various charges connected with the riots ; the number of deaths resulting from the outbreak was officially given as 76.

The following District Orders were published in regard to the behaviour of the troops :—

"The Brigadier-General Commanding takes this opportunity to thank Officers, Non-commissioned Officers and Men of the Royal Navy, Military Forces and Volunteer Forces for the cheerful and efficient manner in which they have invariably performed, during the last three weeks, the very arduous duties thrown on them in connection with the suppressing of the late riots.

"It is due to the firm and temperate spirit shown by the Naval, Military and Volunteer Forces, aided as they were by the untiring energy and devotion of the Police, that the disturbances were so soon got under. The Brigadier-General cannot speak too highly of the conduct of the troops, and of their general demeanour towards the Natives of the City during the above-mentioned period.

"The Brigadier-General Commanding has much pleasure in publishing the following Government Resolution, referring to the part taken by the Military Forces, Regular and Volunteer, in the suppression of the riots in Bombay in August last.

"'Military Department No. 2097, Bombay Castle, November 1st, 1893. Resolution of Government in the Judicial Department, No. 6736, dated 26th October, 1893.

"'Conveying the thanks of Government to the various officials and persons who rendered service during the recent riots in Bombay, and requesting this Department to communicate the same to General Budgeon and the Officers and Men of the Military Forces, Regular and Volunteer, under his command for the excellent discipline maintained and the temper and moderation displayed.'

"The Brigadier-General Commanding further notifies that the receipt from Government of so favourable a comment upon the conduct of the troops is highly gratifying to H.E. The Commander-in-Chief."

During the remainder of the stay of the Battalion in Bombay, detachments were furnished to Deolali, Khandalla and Ahmedabad, but in December, 1894, all these were called in and by the end of the year the whole Battalion was concentrated at Poona. Here, however, the 1st Battalion The Loyal North Lancashire Regiment was to remain little more than a year, for on the 18th and 19th February, 1896, it left again for Bombay, where it embarked in the H.T. "Pavonia," leaving on the 20th for Ceylon. Arriving here five days later, the headquarters remained in Colombo, while "B" and "G" Companies went to Trincomali and "D" Company to Kandy. In Ceylon a draft from England—181 all ranks— was awaiting the arrival of the Battalion ; it was accompanied by Captains

W. H. E. Murray and R. R. Feilden, 2nd Lieutenants C. de Putron and R. E. Berkeley.

The following officers landed in Ceylon with the Battalion : Lieut.-Colonel A. G. Tidy ; Majors S. Jackson and H. G. Purdon ; Captains P. R. S. Churchward, G. L. Parker and C. E. A. Jourdain ; Lieutenants G. H. Wylde-Brown, T. H. O'Brien, J. G. Lowndes, H. A. Robinson, F. J. Bowen, A. R. Wallace, C. H. M. Bingham, F. R. R. Greene and F. W. Woodward ; 2nd Lieutenant K. Z. P. Macaulay ; Captain and Adjutant G. C. Knight and Lieutenant and Quartermaster H. J. Gill.

In November another draft came out from the Second Battalion, it was 232 strong and was accompanied by Captain R. L. Stable and 2nd Lieutenant A. W. Hewett.

During the stay of the Battalion in Ceylon it lost two officers by death, Lieutenant F. R. R. Greene on the 10th October, 1897, and Major H. G. Leonard on the 4th June, 1898.

On the 1st June, 1898, Major R. G. Kekewich was promoted to command the 1st Battalion The Loyal North Lancashire Regiment from the Royal Inniskilling Fusiliers ; and when on the 11th February, 1899, the Battalion left Ceylon for a new station in another continent, it fell to this officer to proceed thither in command. The Battalion embarked on the above date in the H.T. " Avoca," speeded on its way by the following farewell message from the Ceylon Government :—

" SIR,—

" I am directed by the Governor, who is absent in the east end of the Island, to request that you will, with the permission of the General Officer Commanding the troops, communicate to the Officer Commanding the 1st Battalion The Loyal North Lancashire Regiment, His Excellency's acknowledgment of the general good conduct of the men of the Regiment which is about to be relieved after three years' service in Ceylon.

" The Inspector General of Police has reported the behaviour of the men in Colombo, the headquarters, to be excellent, and I am to express the Governor's thanks for such service and His Excellency's appreciation of the good leading and discipline of the Officers of the Regiment which has brought about such a favourable result.

" I am, Sir,
" Your obedient Servant,
(sd.) " H. L. CRAWFORD,
" for Colonial Secretary.

" To the D.A.A. General, Ceylon."

The "Avoca" sailed from Ceylon to South Africa, and on the 9th March, 1899, the Battalion disembarked at Cape Town; the following officers accompanied the Battalion from Ceylon: Lieut.-Colonel R. G. Kekewich; Majors J. R. Fraser and W. H. E. Murray; Captains M. A. Humphrys, C. E. A. Jourdain, G. H. Wylde-Browne and T. H. O'Brien; Lieutenants F. J. Bowen, A. R. Wallace and C. H. M. Bingham; 2nd Lieutenants R. B. Flint, W. R. Clifford, C. C. Wood, A. W. Hewett and A. Mc C. Webster; Lieutenant and Adjutant A. C. Lowndes and Lieutenant and Quartermaster H. J. Gill.

Immediately on arrival steps were taken towards the formation of a Mounted Infantry Company, from men of all companies having experience of horse management and practised in riding, and the officers selected for this company were Captain Wylde-Browne, 2nd Lieutenants Clifford and Wood; the strength of the company was fixed at five sergeants and one hundred and twelve rank and file, and it was at once sent to Wynberg, where it was later joined by "C" Company under Lieutenant Wallace. "B" Company—Captain O'Brien's—proceeded now on detachment to Simonstown.

For more than a year prior to the arrival of the Battalion at Cape Town, a correspondence had been going on between the Government of the South African Republic and the Colonial Secretary in London upon the existence, or non-existence, of the Suzerainty. This question was far from even approaching a settlement when there arose the very vital matter of the wrongs of the Uitlanders; and Sir Alfred Milner, the British Commissioner in South Africa, early realized how widely the two governments differed in their views, and that the danger of war between Great Britain and the South African Republic was daily drawing nearer. During the summer of 1899 these differences led, in the first place, to a situation of extreme tension, and finally to the outbreak of war. President Kruger's claim that the Transvaal be considered a Sovereign State, was rejected in September by the British Government, and upon this, the President and his government had incontinently refused every one of the counter-proposals which our Cabinet had earlier advanced. The Government in London now realized that the outbreak of war at an early date was by no means impossible and that the Imperial garrison in South Africa was dangerously weak * in face of the warlike, and indeed threatening attitude of the Transvaalers, and the uncertainty of the action of the Government of the Free State. Reinforcements were therefore sent to South Africa from Europe, and five

---

* In the middle of September the only Regular troops in Cape Colony were three and a half battalions of infantry, two companies of Royal Engineers and two companies of Royal Garrison Artillery.

thousand British troops were ordered from India to Natal, these all arriving in the country before the end of September. That month had hardly come to an end before the Government of the Free State made it abundantly clear that, in the event of war arising between the United Kingdom and the Transvaal, its whole weight would be thrown on the side of the Sister-State. On the 9th October a proclamation was issued in Great Britain and Ireland calling out the Army Reserves ; and on the same date President Kruger presented an ultimatum to our representative, demanding a reply thereto within forty-eight hours. Her Majesty's Government refused so much as to discuss this ultimatum, and consequently on the 11th October the Governments of the Transvaal and of the Orange Free State declared war upon Great Britain, and sent their armed forces across our border from both north and west.

At the moment when war was declared the British forces in Cape Colony, Natal and Rhodesia numbered 27,054 men, and already on the 7th October orders had been issued at home for the mobilization of a Cavalry Division, an Army Corps of three Infantry Divisions and eight battalions of Lines-of-Communication troops.

Long before there was any thought of war, the isolated position of Kimberley and the probability of an attack upon it in the possible event of war with the Boer Republics, had made it a source of anxiety to the military authorities at Cape Town, the more that it was an important place on the lines of communication with Mafeking, and, through Mafeking, to the north. In 1896 a staff officer had been sent from Cape Town to Kimberley to report upon its defences, and he had very strongly urged the increasing of the strength of the local volunteer corps, the formation of certain artillery units, and the addition of a small nucleus of Regulars to its permanent garrison. These last could not at the time be spared and practically no action was at the time taken.

In July, 1899, several Special Service Officers were sent to South Africa from England, and one of these—Captain O'Meara, R.E.—joined a staff officer already at Kimberley, with the object of concerting defence measures. Then early in September two thousand Lee-Metford rifles and a certain amount of ammunition was dispatched from Cape Town to Kimberley, and it being considered desirable that a senior officer of the Regular Army should be sent thither to report confidentially on the local situation, Colonel R. G. Kekewich, Loyal North Lancashire Regiment, was selected to proceed to Kimberley and inquire into the arrangements made for the protection of that town, and of the communications to Mafeking in the north and to Orange River Station in the south.

Colonel Kekewich reached Kimberley on the 13th September, when the two staff officers explained the general situation; from their information it was clear that Boer mobilization had already begun across the frontier, and that Kimberley was seriously threatened; work upon the defences had not yet begun; there were no Regulars in the place and the local Volunteers numbered 540 only. "To protect the 300 miles of railway between Mafeking and the Orange River there were only the Volunteers at Kimberley, some half-dozen small posts of Cape Police, and a single company of sixty-one Volunteers at Vryburg.

"Kekewich at once telegraphed to Headquarters to represent the urgent need for reinforcements, and on the 20th September the following troops reached him from Cape Town:—

	Officers	Men
"23rd Company, R.G.A. (with six 2·5-in. R.M.L. guns on mountain carriages)	3	90
"7th Company, R.E.	1	50
"Headquarters and four Companies, 1st Loyal North Lancashire Regiment	9	413
"Detachment Army Service Corps	1	5
"Detachment R.A.M.C.	1	5
"Total.	15	563 "*

This wing of the Battalion—"A," "B" "G" and "H" Companies—left Cape Town by train on the night of the 18th September at a strength of four hundred non-commissioned officers and men, followed next day by the transport under Lieutenant Woodward; and arriving on the 21st, was camped on the open ground between the Reservoir and the town. The following officers accompanied the wing: Major Murray; Captain O'Brien; Lieutenants Wallace, Bingham, de Putron and Webster; 2nd Lieutenants Hewett and Fletcher; Lieutenant and Adjutant Lowndes and Lieutenant and Quartermaster Gill. On the 27th Lieutenant W. R. Clifford arrived with twenty-two men of a Mounted Infantry Section.†

The services of this wing in the defence of Kimberley will now be recorded, those of the other wing of the Battalion being related later; but it may usefully be stated that "C," "D," "E" and "F" Companies proceeded by train on the night of 19th to Orange River Station and on arrival on the 21st at once began to put the place in a state of defence; with this wing went Major Coleridge, Captain Jourdain, Lieutenants Bowen and

---

* *Official History of the War in South Africa*, Vol. II, pp. 44, 45.
† It will be noticed that these figures, taken from the Regimental Digest, do not altogether agree with those given in the *Official History of the War*.

Flint and 2nd Lieutenant Wells. A portion of the Mounted Infantry Company accompanied this wing under Captain Wylde-Browne and Lieutenant Wood.

Captain Feilden remained behind in the Main Barracks, Cape Town, in charge of the Base Company.

CHAPTER XXI

1899-1900

THE SOUTH AFRICAN WAR
THE DEFENCE OF KIMBERLEY
BELMONT : GRASPAN : MAGERSFONTEIN

"THE town of Kimberley lies between its two principal diamond mines, the 'Kimberley' and the 'De Beers.' The original settlement, the smaller township of Beaconsfield, is a thousand yards south-east of the present town. A mile and a half further to the south-east the little Boer village of Wesselton stands upon the lake known as 'Du Toit's Pan.' There are two other mines, 'Du Toit's Pan' and 'Bultfontein,' between Wesselton and Beaconsfield. The 'Premier Mine,' projects into the plain a mile due east of 'Du Toit's Pan.' North-east of Kimberley the monotony of the veldt is broken by plantations of eucalyptus trees surrounding the village of Kenilworth. To the south-west of Kimberley lies the main reservoir, which in normal times draws its supply of water by pipes from the Vaal at Riverton, nearly eighteen miles away. The terrain encircling the two towns, Kimberley and Kenilworth, is on the whole favourable to defence. To the eastward a plain, unbroken save by the heaps of débris from the mines, stretches to a dark range of low kopjes on the Free State side of the frontier line. To the north the ground slopes gradually towards the valley of the Vaal River, the fall being crossed, some six miles out, by the wooded ridge of Dronfield. To the west of the town, separated from it by a shallow valley, rises Carter's Ridge, a wave of ground from which, at a range of 4,000 yards, artillery fire could be brought to bear on the town itself. Southward the country rises and falls in almost imperceptible undulations until the commanding position of Wimbledon is reached, some six miles distant.

"The heaps of débris much aided the defence. Built up by the accumulations of the tailings of the mines, they formed a series of large mounds some sixty to seventy feet high, skirting the towns on the north, east and south. In front of these mounds a network of barbed-wire fences effectually obstructed all approach except by the roads, while the electric searchlights, installed by the De Beers Company, were available for military use. A few, however, of the débris heaps, such as those of the Premier Mine to the south-east, and those of the Kamfer's Dam Mines to the north-west, were of doubtful advantage to the defence, as their occupation would cause undue extension, while, if not held, they would be dangerous." *

The Volunteers in Kimberley had been called out directly the military situation had assumed a threatening aspect, but when embodied these only numbered twenty-three officers and 517 other ranks, a force wholly inadequate for the defence of the town even after the arrival of the reinforcements of Regulars on the 20th September. On the 30th, however, the enlistment of a Town Guard was taken in hand, and within a week more than 1,100 men had been enrolled, officers appointed and non-commissioned officers of the Regular troops had been detailed for purposes of drill and instruction.

As the movement of the Burgher forces of the Free State, reported to be taking place opposite the Griqualand West frontier of the Cape Colony, indicated that an attack on Kimberley might be made without warning at an early date, the construction of certain important portions of the Kimberley defence works was commenced on the 18th September, and by the 7th October this was so far advanced that the town was practically secure against anything like a *coup de main*. "The Kimberley defences consisted of a series of redoubts with open gorges, which completely encircled the whole town and included the Kimberley and De Beers mines. A part of the front of this *enceinte* was protected by barbed wire and abattis, and efforts were made to restrict egress or ingress to points on certain roads at which movable barriers had been erected. A series of advanced works to the south-east guarded Beaconsfield; Kenilworth formed a salient projecting northward; the Premier Mine was held as a detached post. An isolated redoubt on the southern road near Van Druyten's Farm, and another to the westward of the town covering Otto's Kopje Mine, completed the defences." The actual perimeter was about ten miles, or fourteen if the Kenilworth and Beaconsfield salients were included. To each redoubt a permanent garrison of fifty men was assigned.

The number of people within the lines of investment was about 48,000, white and coloured, and included 12,000 women and 10,000 children.

President Kruger's ultimatum to the British Government expired on the 11th October and next day the Boers crossed the frontier and destroyed the railway line near Kraaipan, capturing an armoured train which was conveying two guns to Mafeking, and breaking all telegraphic communication to north and south.

* *Official History*, Vol. II, pp. 41, 42.

KIMBERLEY.

7th October, 1899.

At 3 a.m. on the 15th October Colonel Kekewich sent out an armoured train from Kimberley under the command of 2nd Lieutenant A. Mc C. Webster, of the Battalion, with orders to proceed southwards and locate the spot where the Kimberley telegraph line had been destroyed. On reaching Spytfontein Railway Station the train was fired upon by enemy guns posted on the rocky kopjes south-east of the station. Their fire was returned by our machine-guns, but as the Boers had three guns in position, 2nd Lieutenant Webster wisely decided to withdraw, and, taking the station-master, his family and some gangers on board the train, he steamed back to Kimberley without having suffered any damage or loss.

At noon on the 15th October Colonel Kekewich proclaimed martial-law in Kimberley and assumed supreme control of the civil population.

By this date the 1st Battalion The Loyal North Lancashire Regiment was distributed as follows:—

Captain O'Brien, with "B" Company—seventy-five non-commissioned officers and men—two guns under Lieutenant Rynd, Royal Artillery, and the Town Guard, held the Premier Mine.

Lieutenant Wallace, with "G" Company—seventy-eight non-commissioned officers and men—held the Sanatorium.

Major Fraser was placed in charge of the Beaconsfield Town Guard, a body numbering some twenty-two officers and five hundred other ranks.

Major (Local Lieut.-Colonel) Murray, with headquarters and "A" and "H" Companies, formed the reserve, and was encamped in the Gardens in the centre of the Town.

The various Police detachments in the country round Kimberley now began to fall back before the advance of the Boers, and by the 22nd October the greater number of them had arrived safely in Kimberley.

The want of mounted troops to operate against the enemy surrounding Kimberley had been much felt during the early days of the investment, and in response to Colonel Kekewich's representations sanction had been given for the raising of an irregular mounted corps. By the generous financial assistance of the Rt. Hon. C. J. Rhodes, who had reached Kimberley just before the Boer ultimatum expired, the Kimberley Light Horse, some five hundred strong, was rapidly raised and horsed; the command was assumed by Major Scott-Turner of the Black Watch, and Lieutenant (Local Captain) Clifford, of the Battalion, was appointed adjutant, later taking command of a squadron of the Corps. Until, however, the Kimberley Light Horse had proved itself, the whole of the patrol work about the neighbourhood of the town had to be carried out by Lieutenant Clifford and his section of the Battalion Mounted Infantry.

The rapid increase in the numbers and mobility of the mounted troops in Kimberley which now took place, made it possible to send out reconnoitring parties in every direction and at frequent intervals. On the 24th October a reconnoitring party of the mounted troops started out early in the morning in the direction of Riverton Road, north of Kimberley, with orders to destroy the local pumping station and ascertain the strength of the enemy there reported. The armoured train was sent in support. On reaching Dronfield Siding, six miles out, the party came in collision with a body of the enemy, estimated at eight hundred, near Macfarlane's Siding, and it became necessary to reinforce the mounted men with guns and infantry.

"A" and "H" Companies of the Battalion, under Major Murray, were sent off from Kimberley by train, the guns moving by road, and on arriving near Macfarlane's Siding, it was found that the Boers were holding Dronfield Ridge, of which it was believed that our mounted men were in possession; the train accordingly steamed back some little way with Major Murray's command, the men then detraining and lining a ditch beside the railway line. It was now seen that the guns were in action, and that the enemy was concentrating a very heavy and accurate rifle-fire on the gun detachments.

"A" Company, under command of Lieutenant Bingham, accompanied by Major Murray and Lieutenant Lowndes, advanced against Dronfield Ridge, and, on topping it, was met by a heavy fire from the enemy concealed in the long grass only 150 yards distant. At the same time our mounted troops advancing against the Boer right, were equally held up by riflemen behind a stone wall, by whose fire our mounted men were enfiladed. "H" Company, with Lieutenants Woodward, de Putron and Hewett, now came up in support and the enemy was driven off, the ridge was cleared and considerable execution done to the Boer led-horses in the valley behind the ridge. The action then terminated and the Kimberley party withdrew, having had three men killed and nineteen officers and other ranks wounded.

Of the Battalion, Lieutenants J. G. Lowndes and C. H. M. Bingham and two privates were wounded.

The retreating enemy left a considerable quantity of ammunition behind him. During the next few days the enemy drew nearer to the town and attempted several raids, with the object of driving off the cattle upon which the defence depended for its food supply; and then about midday on the 4th November Commandant Wessels, of the Free State Forces, sent in a demand for the surrender of the Town, but this was of course ignored. On the 6th, with the possible object of showing that Wessel's time-limit had expired, the enemy opened shell-fire on the defences

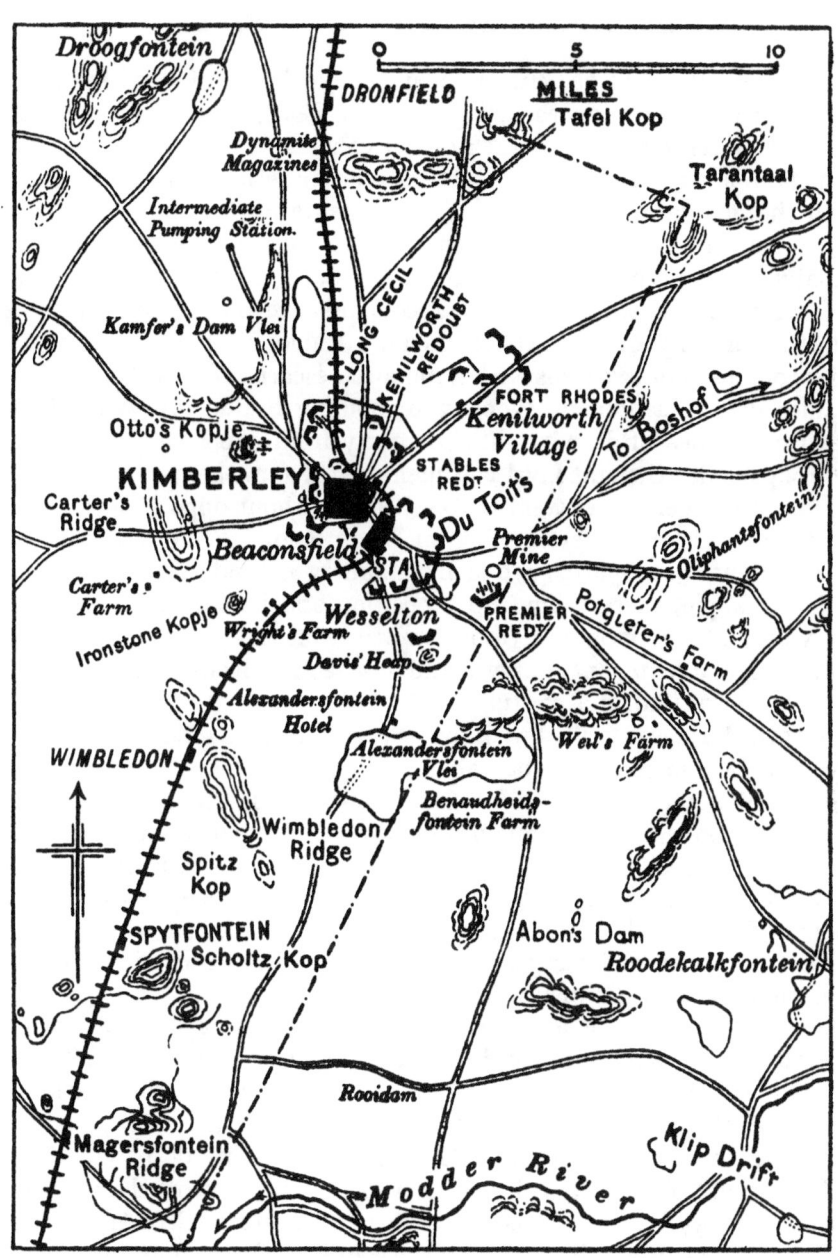

KIMBERLEY.

1899.

of the Premier Mine, but the first regular bombardment of Kimberley did not open until 5.30 a.m. on the 7th, when the Boers shelled the defences between the Reservoir and the Sanatorium, continuing throughout the next day, but no one was injured and practically no material damage was done.

With the general object of keeping the enemy on the move and constantly in fear of an attack from an unexpected quarter, Colonel Kekewich continually sent out his mounted men. On the 25th November, for instance, the mounted troops made a reconnaissance on a tolerably large scale in the direction of the forts on Carter's Ridge, a force under Colonel Chamier composed of two guns with a mounted escort and "A" and "H" Companies under Lieutenant Woodward, holding the enemy west of the town, with the idea of drawing off the enemy from opposing the advance of the troops under General Lord Methuen. At 4 a.m. the mounted troops had succeeded in getting beyond Otto's Kopje without opposition, Colonel Chamier's guns shortly after opening on Black Kopje, 4,000 yards west of our defences at 2,000 yards, while his infantry extended and advanced towards the kopje, there taking up a position and holding the enemy by steady volleys. Our mounted troops now advanced against the forts on Carter's Ridge, Lieutenant Clifford and his section leading, and a Boer picquet was surprised and captured.

One of the forts was rushed with the bayonet, nine wounded and twenty-four unwounded prisoners being taken.

On reaching the high ground a Boer laager was seen below and fire was opened upon it; but as ammunition was running short and the enemy appeared to be receiving reinforcements, it was decided to retire and the force was soon back in Kimberley. The Battalion had one man wounded. Lieutenant Clifford won great praise for the way in which he moved about under a heavy fire, collecting ammunition from the dead and wounded and distributing it to the men in the firing-line.

There was a reconnaissance of a similar character on the 28th when all the companies were employed; on this occasion Major Scott-Turner was killed and Lieutenant Clifford was wounded, while the Battalion had a sergeant and a private killed.

Of these operations Colonel Kekewich wrote in his despatch of the 15th February, 1900: "It will be observed that portions of the mounted corps were employed on every occasion. The work which fell on the detachment of the Loyal North Lancashire Regiment, Cape Police, Diamond Fields Horse and Kimberley Light Horse was in consequence very arduous; not only did the corps mentioned respond cheerfully, but nothing can exceed the bravery and dash with which these troops attacked the enemy on several occasions in his entrenched positions."

MAJOR-GENERAL R. G. KEKEWICH, C.B.

About this time Lieutenants Woodward and de Putron were appointed respectively signalling and assistant-signalling officer, and it was under arrangements made by them that searchlight communication was established by night with Modder River about the 3rd December. This signalling was wholly carried out by men of the Loyal North Lancashire Regiment, Sergeant Herbert being in charge.

Vegetables and meat were now running very short, and milk for the hospitals was scarce, so many cows having been captured by the Boers early in the siege; on the 20th December all food stocks were taken over by the Supply Committee and everybody was put upon a fixed scale of rations.

Messages were now reaching the garrison from Lord Methuen, and on the 5th December Colonel Kekewich was informed that, on the arrival of the relief column, the garrison of Kimberley would be strengthened by the other wing of the Loyal North Lancashire Regiment and four naval guns. On the 11th, however, a brief message came in from Lord Methuen saying his advance was checked, and on the 17th definite news of the ill-success of the action at Magersfontein arrived, though it was not until the 26th December that it was made clear to Colonel Kekewich that the operations for the relief of Kimberley were indefinitely postponed.

At Christmas a message was received from Her Majesty the Queen and was greatly appreciated: " I wish you and all My brave soldiers a happy Christmas. God protect and bless you all."

On the 2nd January, 1900, the meat ration was reduced to a quarter of a pound, and by the middle of the month the issue of horse-flesh had commenced; soup-kitchens were also established and 8,000 pints were daily distributed.

By this time the defenders were in possession of a locally-made piece of ordnance—a 28-pounder rifled gun, which made an effective reply to the cannons of the besiegers: but on the 7th February the enemy had brought up a 96-pounder which opened from Kamfersdam, four miles from the centre of the town, and which was directed not so much against the defence but against the populated part of the town. Eighteen men of the Battalion, under Lieutenant Wallace, used to go out overnight and remain out until dark, occupying trenches within 1,800 yards of the big Boer gun; these did excellent execution, one of their chief victims being one Leon, the head Boer gun-layer.

The fire of the big Boer gun proved a sore trial to the civilian population of Kimberley, and on the 10th February a local newspaper contained an article urging immediate relief, while it even seemed as though some of the Kimberley people were actually in favour of surrender should a relief force not at once arrive in the neighbourhood. Colonel Kekewich sent a summary of all these hysterical views to Field-Marshal Lord Roberts, and the result was that on the afternoon of the 10th February the Chief of the Staff communicated to the lieutenant-general commanding the cavalry division the Commander-in-Chief's anxiety as to the position at Kimberley, and informed him that the cavalry must relieve the town at all costs. On the morning of the 11th the movement began, the cavalry marching on Ramdam, followed by a mounted infantry brigade and the 7th Infantry Division.

On the night of the 13th Major Fraser of the Battalion, having been informed that Alexandersfontein, some three miles to the south, had been vacated by the enemy, dashed out with some of his Town Guard and seized the place, killing and wounding about half a dozen of the enemy and capturing a certain amount of grain. At midday on the 14th Captain O'Brien and Lieutenant Hewett moved out with " B " and " A " Companies and relieved the Town Guard, the enemy in the neighbourhood opening a very steady and continuous fire in the endeavour to drive our men out : in this, however, they were unsuccessful.

Then at 2.30 p.m. on the 15th a body of horsemen was seen to be approaching from the direction of Jacobsdal, and, on heliographic communication being established, this force turned out to be the advance of General French's Cavalry Division. The news soon spread abroad and the townspeople were nearly mad with delight, and all the heaps of mine débris were crowded with spectators watching the cavalry coming in and the Boers clearing off.

At 6 in the evening " A " and " H " Companies fell in under Major Murray and marched off towards Kamfersdam in the hope of preventing the withdrawal of the big Boer gun, but the Boers had somehow managed to get it away. These two companies remained out till the next day covering the left flank of the cavalry which went north early in the morning as far as Riverton Road, clearing away the enemy who fought a stubborn rearguard action all day, to cover the retreat of their wagons.

On the morning of the 17th General French left Kimberley with the cavalry, having received instructions during the night to head off General Cronje, who had retired from Spytfontein in an easterly direction ; and on the 22nd the 9th Brigade arrived from the Modder River, and the wing rejoined the Headquarters of the Battalion.

We left the wing of the Battalion when it had just arrived under command of Major Jackson at Orange River Station on the 21st September, 1899, on the Headquarters and remaining four companies proceeding to Kimberley.

On detraining at Orange River Station the troops were at once set to work putting the place in a thorough state of defence, "C" and "F" Companies taking over the Bridge Section, the other two companies joining them on the 11th October.

Captain Jourdain was now appointed acting adjutant of the wing and Lieutenant Flint acting quartermaster, and on the 14th October Major Churchward joined from England and took over command of "E" Company.

Orange River Station was, with Kimberley, De Aar, Naauwpoort and Stormberg, one of a series of military posts encircling the western and southern frontiers of the Free State, and these immediately prior to the outbreak of war, had each been garrisoned by a half-battalion of Regular infantry, a company of mounted infantry and two 9-pounder guns; as the situation developed, more troops were gradually moved up to these posts, and by early in November the wing of the Loyal North Lancashire Regiment had been joined at Orange River Station by the 1st Northumberland Fusiliers, the 2nd Northamptonshire and the 2nd King's Own Yorkshire Light Infantry.

On the 12th November Lord Methuen arrived from Cape Town at Orange River Station with orders from General Buller to assume charge of all troops at that place and at De Aar, with the object of marching on Kimberley as rapidly as possible. Including the troops at De Aar and Orange River Station, then about to be formed into the 9th Brigade, he was to have also at his disposal the 1st Infantry Brigade, the Highland Brigade, a Brigade Division R.F.A., divisional troops and other details.

Before Lord Methuen's arrival at Orange River Station, the troops there had been engaged in reconnoitring and on the 10th November "D" and "E" Companies of the Battalion—five officers and 158 men—left for the north by train at 5.45 a.m., "C" and "F" Companies following in the afternoon, and these took up a position to cover the mounted troops. A few miles to the east of Belmont several hundred Boers with field-guns were encountered and a skirmish ensued, in which there were several casualties, Lieutenant C. C. Wood of the Battalion being mortally wounded, while two men of the Battalion Mounted Infantry were also hit.

On the 13th November Lord Methuen inspected the wing and expressed himself as very pleased at the absence of crime, the fitness of all ranks, and the amount of hard work all had done while at Orange River Station; on the 15th Captain F. C. L. Logan and 2nd Lieutenant L. R. D'Arcy joined from England—2nd Lieutenant R. C. Wiltshire had already reported his arrival on first appointment a few weeks earlier.

The 9th Infantry Brigade was now formed under Major-General R. S. R.

Fetherstonhaugh and the wing—strength eleven officers and 353 non-commissioned officers and men—joined it on the 20th November, the other battalions composing it being the 1st Northumberland Fusiliers, the 2nd Northamptonshire and the 2nd King's Own Yorkshre Light Infantry. The 9th Brigade, with the Guards Brigade and a Naval Brigade, constituted the 1st Division, of which the mounted troops were furnished by the 9th Lancers, the New South Wales Lancers, Rimington's Guides, and three M.I. Companies, one of these being from the wing of the Loyal North Lancashire Regiment. "Behind the 1st Division, the Highland Brigade, under Major-General Wauchope, guarded the railway up to the Orange River and overawed the disaffected element among the inhabitants along the line of communication. In the neighbourhood of Colesberg, Lieut.-General French, with a mixed force of all arms, was engaged in stemming the tide of invasion from the Free State, and by incessantly occupying the attention of the commandos opposed to him, prevented their massing against Lord Methuen's right flank as he advanced towards Kimberley." *

The country to be traversed by the force under Lord Methuen's immediate command did not appear to offer any serious military difficulties; it was a plain for the most part, dotted here and there with isolated kopjes, and there seemed to be three places at most where the 4,000–5,000 Boers available to oppose the 8,000 men whom Lord Methuen commanded, might make any really effective stand—these were at Belmont, at Rooilaagte, between Enslin and Graspan, and at Magersfontein. The British commander's plan was to advance along the line of the railway, thus enabling him to reduce his field transport, keep in close touch with his base and bring forward reinforcements or supplies as these might be needed.

The task of checking Lord Methuen's advance was, pending the arrival of General Cronje, in the hands of Prinsloo, the Orange Free State Commandant, and he was to be supported if necessary by a Transvaal contingent under De la Rey. Prinsloo's headquarters were at Jacobsdal, some ten miles east of Modder River railway bridge.

The greater part of the Division marched off from Orange River Station early on the morning of the 21st November, but the Loyal North Lancashire wing did not start until some twenty-four hours or more later, being in charge of the divisional baggage, and joined the remainder of its Division near Thomas's Farm, a mile and a half south-west of Belmont Station, to the east of which the enemy was found to be in strength among the hills, the wing coming up just as the action had opened.

"The position in which the Boers awaited Methuen's attack was a mass of hilly country to the east of Belmont Station, rising to a height of

* *Official History*, Vol. I, pp. 215, 216.

100–200 feet and roughly triangular in its general outline, the point facing north, while the base, some three miles wide, deeply indented by a spur of the veldt, was seamed by a great forked donga running up into the centre of the position. In the western half of this bunch of kopjes two points rose most conspicuously and steeply from the veldt, one a broad-topped hill to which the name of Table Mountain was given by the troops, and the other—Gun Hill, an irregularly-shaped crest a mile or more in length, forming the south-western corner of the complex. The eastern half, on which the generic name of Mont Blanc was bestowed, was an almost continuous mass of high ground, only broken by a nek about two-thirds of the way down." * Lord Methuen's plan was to attack Table Mountain with the 9th Brigade, while the Guards Brigade seized Gun Hill and the high ground beyond; these heights once captured, the 9th Brigade was then to sweep round, clearing Table Mountain, and, pivoted on the Guards, was to carry the rear of the Boer position on Table Mountain. To minimize loss as much as possible this operation was to be carried out as a night attack, so timed that the troops should be established on the position just before daybreak.

The troops left their bivouacs soon after 2 a.m. on the 23rd November, the Guards Brigade on the right and the 9th Brigade on the left, and the battle developed in general agreement with Lord Methuen's plans, though rather more slowly than the General had anticipated. The resistance offered by the defenders of Table Mountain and Gun Hill was very stubborn, but the defence gradually weakened and the enemy retreated in all haste to the valley, pursued by long-range volleys from the British troops who had now gained the high ground, and followed by our cavalry and mounted infantry. It was not until 6.30 a.m. that the companies of the wing arrived near the scene of action, when " E " Company relieved a company of the Coldstream Guards on a kopje south-east of Thompson's Farm, with orders to prevent the enemy from breaking back that way; the remaining companies remained in the low ground, and when by ten o'clock all fighting was over, the wing assisted in the clearing of the ground and in bringing in the wounded, and was also placed in charge of all the captured Boers.

" Eleven miles north of Belmont Station the road and railway leading to Kimberley enter a network of kopjes, which dominate the line until the plain through which the Modder River flows is reached. Those rough outcrops of rock and boulders from the plains of the open veldt have been arranged by nature in clusters of small hills, the most southern group being so shaped as to form a natural redoubt astride of the railway, midway between Graspan and Enslin, thus barring any advance from the

* "*The Times*" *History of the War*, Vol. II, p. 325.

south along the line. The larger portion of the Boer force, defeated at Belmont, had fallen back under Prinsloo, on the 23rd November, across the Free State border to Ramdam, about thirteen miles east of Enslin Station. De la Rey, however, whose command had taken but little part in that action, halted his men at Graspan and occupied the excellent position which this redoubt offered for a further stand. That same evening the Transvaal general sent an urgent message to his Free State colleague, imploring him to return to the railway line, and in compliance with this request Prinsloo on the following day left Commandant van der Merwe with eight hundred men at Ramdam, and moved to Graspan with the rest of his men." *

The infantry remained in camp during the early part of the day following the action, but the armoured train and the mounted infantry were sent forward to reconnoitre, and on their return reported that the hills about Graspan appeared to be held by a Boer force of some five hundred men with two guns. Early in the afternoon General Lord Methuen sent the whole of his mounted men in advance, covering the front for three miles on either side of the railway line, while the rest of the division marched about seven miles to Swinkpan—a small vlei surrounded by steep kopjes —arriving here after dark.

From the reports which he had received as to the strength of the enemy force in his front, Lord Methuen judged that he should be able to capture the position with one infantry brigade and his mounted troops, and he proposed to employ the 9th Brigade, which had suffered less loss than the other at Belmont. He therefore moved out about 4 a.m. on the 25th from Swinkpan, the wing of the Loyal North Lancashire Regiment bringing up the rear of the column ; and it was very soon seen that the enemy position was one of considerable natural strength, consisting of a range of low hills over two miles long, sinking in the middle to a mass of heaped boulders, and rising at the eastern end into a steep conical hill. At each end the line of kopjes was drawn sharply back at a right angle, falling on one side towards Rooilaagte Farm, at the other to the railway.

The mounted men were in front moving so as to turn either flank of the enemy position, and the two field batteries were kept at first with the main body of the 9th Brigade ; as the Boer position was neared, however, the guns were ordered forward to engage the enemy on the hills to the east of the railway line, and one of these batteries was then escorted by the Loyal North Lancashire. Our guns opened fire immediately, and soon after a party of Boers, about two hundred strong and some two miles distant, was seen retiring in a south-easterly direction, then halting and

* *Official History*, Vol. I, p. 229.

taking up a position on a high kopje to the south from which a heavy fire was opened on our mounted men, causing them to fall back. Our guns were now advanced, "C" and "F" Companies moving as escort, with "D" and "E" in support, all in very extended order.

Lord Methuen, who was close to the guns, now ordered Major Churchward to advance with "C" and "F" Companies and endeavour to capture the two kopjes on the right of the range of hills held by the Boers; the companies accordingly moved forward under a heavy fire, mainly directed against the Naval Brigade, who, being in somewhat close order, suffered heavily. "E" Company, hearing the heavy fire in front, advanced to assist the firing-line, and in topping the rise saw the Naval Brigade and "C" and "F" Companies advancing under some difficulties, so opened long-range volleys over the heads of the others, thus assisting them in getting to the foot of the hill attacked, where was dead ground. All now fixed bayonets and commenced to scale the hill, the key of the enemy position was seized and the Boers under De la Rey and Prinsloo fell back to the north, pursued by long-range volleys from the infantry only, for by the time the guns could be brought on to the high ground the fugitives were practically out of range.

The loss suffered by the companies in this action was slight, by reason no doubt of the wide extensions adopted, and amounted only to one man killed and twenty men wounded.

Two men—Privates Johnson, "E" Company, and Turner, "C" Company, were specially brought to notice for gallant conduct during the attack.

Driven now from two positions, the Boers fell back to Jacobsdal, where De la Rey used such influence as he possessed to induce the burghers to make a third attempt to stay Lord Methuen's advance; and a new position was selected at the junction of the Modder and Riet Rivers, presenting quite different characteristics to the positions at Belmont and Graspan. It was now decided " to fight from the bed of a river, surrounded on every side by a level plain, destitute of cover, over the surface of which the burghers could pour a continuous and grazing fire upon the British from the time they first came within range, up to the very moment of their final charge. . . . The Riet and the Modder together formed not only a gigantic moat across the approaches to Kimberley from the south and south-east, but a covered way by which its defenders could move unseen to any part of the position." *

Early on the morning of the 27th November the Division marched to Wittekop, six miles to the south of the Modder River Bridge, and while the bulk of the force remained in camp, the mounted troops reconnoitred to the front, but were held up by the fire of the Boers about the bridge.

* *Official History*, Vol. I, p. 244.

Lord Methuen's intention was to mask the Modder bridge by a reconnaissance in force, while he marched to Jacobsdal and thence by Brown's Drift, across the Modder to Abon's Dam, sixteen miles north-east of Jacobsdal, so turning the position at Spytfontein where he believed the Boers meant to make a stand. He did not know that a ford existed at Bosman's Drift, and looked upon Modder Village as no more than an advanced post. He was, moreover, wholly unaware that well-concealed entrenchments had been thrown up along the left bank of the Riet River, that shelter trenches had been dug on the northern bank, that the local farms had been prepared for defence, the houses in the villages loopholed, and that at several points behind the Riet River epaulements for guns had been thrown up and pompoms concealed in the undergrowth.

The infantry marched off at 5.30 a.m. on the 28th, the Guards with orders to attack the left of the Boer position, while the 9th Brigade crossed the railway and extended to the left. The companies of the Battalion, which at the outset had formed the advance guard to the Division, were now detached on the extreme left flank. The advance began in successive rushes across a perfectly open plain and when about one thousand yards from the river the wing came under a very heavy fire from the front and right from the enemy on both banks of the stream. "C" and "F" Companies were in front and "D" and "E" in support, and "C" Company, having reached the ridge overlooking the river, was there exposed to a devastating fire and had to fall back under cover, where "E" Company lined up on its left. With some difficulty the Boer firing-line was at last located about seven or eight hundred yards away in an entrenched position on the further side of the river and volley firing was resorted to. After lying for some two hours in this very exposed position, it became evident that the four companies of the wing were confronted by the whole of the enemy right flank, and that no advance was feasible unless this flank could be turned. Captain Jourdain was sent to the Chief Staff Officer to ask for guns; two were sent and on these opening fire the Boers commenced to retire and the wing to advance.

Major Churchward led the way with "C" Company, followed by details of other corps, and having crossed the river the wing formed up under cover and awaited orders. When those came, they were to the effect that the companies were to fall back across the river again, and this was done; but later the wing re-crossed, threw out outposts and bivouacked for the night, all expecting to have to renew the action on the following morning; but when day broke it was found that the enemy had abandoned the position during the night and retired, taking all his guns with him.

In this action the wing of the Loyal North Lancashire Regiment had two sergeants and one private killed, Lieutenant Flint and fourteen men wounded. Corporal Hodgson and Private Caddick were brought to notice for gallant conduct in assisting wounded men under heavy fire.

During the afternoon of this day the Division crossed the Riet River and was concentrated on the further bank, and here the Division remained until the 10th December. There was a good deal to be done; men and horses needed rest; reinforcements and supplies had to be brought up from the base; the railway line had to be repaired; while the Modder River Station itself had to be placed in a state of defence for the garrison it was proposed to leave there when the advance should be resumed.

The Boer leaders had by this time made up their minds that they would not make their next stand at Spytfontein, as had initially been intended, but on the heights of Magersfontein, and the entrenching of a position nearly nine miles in length had been put in hand. The centre of the line to be held was occupied by Magersfontein Hill, a rocky eminence rising precipitously and dominating the plain, six miles in width, stretching thence to Modder River bridge. From this hill the Boer line extended five miles north-west to Langeberg Farm along the foot of a series of kopjes, while from the south-east of Magersfontein Hill a low ridge, three miles long, ran southward to Moss Drift on the Modder. The ground rose gradually from the river to the Boer position, it was covered by low scrub and crossed by high wire fences, while on the plain were two knolls—one intended by Lord Methuen to be his headquarters in the coming action, while the other was to be an artillery position.

The enemy had been considerably reinforced, the number of the defenders of the position being variously given as from four thousand to seven thousand; the Boers had in position five field-guns and five pompoms.

By the 10th December the British force had also received certain reinforcements, and by this date Lord Methuen had something like fifteen thousand men under his immediate command, while other troops had also been brought up to hold or strengthen his lines of communication.

In Lord Methuen's orders for the attack on Magersfontein Ridge it is stated that "it is the intention of the G.O.C. to hold the enemy on the north, and to deliver an attack on the southern end of Magersfontein Ridge," and to this end the following dispositions were made: the force was divided into three columns, and one of these, while the bombardment of the main Boer position was in progress, was to move forward from the Modder River towards the southern end of Magersfontein Hill; a second column was to co-operate with No. 1, making a diversion against the ridge along the railway; while the third, from a position west of the railway, was to co-operate with the artillery engaged in the bombardment.

The camp on the Modder River was to be held by the wing of the Loyal North Lancashire, by some details of other corps and by part of the Naval Brigade with four 12-pounder guns. Since the wing was thus prevented from taking any prominent part in the action, the operations of this day, known as the Battle of Magersfontein, may thus be epitomized ; the attack on the key of the enemy's position, on the success of which Lord Methuen's later combinations depended, failed, the brigade engaged falling back with heavy loss and being temporarily unavailable for further employment ; the Guards Brigade was fully occupied in holding the right of the British line ; and no other troops were available for reinforcing any portion of the much-pressed line. Withdrawal from immediate contact with the enemy was imperative and by the afternoon the whole division was re-assembled at Modder River Station.

With this action ended the march of Lord Methuen's division to the relief of Kimberley; for on returning to the camp at Modder River orders were found to have arrived from General Buller directing Lord Methuen, unless he felt confident of the success of another attack, to fall back on Orange River. This retrograde movement was first postponed and finally countermanded, and the Division remained at the Modder River camp until the 16th February, 1900, by which date Field-Marshal Lord Roberts had arrived in South Africa and assumed command of all the forces there assembled, and was engaged in transferring to the neighbourhood of Modder River the army with which he proposed to manœuvre the Boers out of the Magersfontein position, to relieve Kimberley and to march on Bloemfontein.

On the days immediately following the Battle of Magersfontein the wing was several times sent out to make demonstrations towards the Boer position, coming under enemy shell-fire, but happily incurring no loss.

On the 19th and 20th December the companies were inspected by Lord Methuen who was very complimentary, saying on the first occasion, " this is the smartest half-battalion I have got," and on the second " this half-battalion has retained its smartness and is always quick at turning out."

" D " and " F " Companies, under Major Coleridge, marched to Klokfontein on the 21st December and were joined here by " C " and " E," under Major Jackson, three weeks later ; in the meantime a draft from home, 134 strong, came out under Captain J. H. Ansley and 2nd Lieutenant E. G. Case. At this time there was a good deal of sickness in the wing, attributable to the bad drinking water which had to be sent up in trucks from Modder River to Klokfontein, and many men and six officers—Majors Churchward and Coleridge, Lieutenants Bowen, Flint, Wells and Fitzpatrick—were all down with a bad type of fever. Captain Jourdain now took over command of the Battalion Mounted Infantry Company at Belmont from Captain Wylde-Browne.

On 17th February, 1900, Lord Methuen was placed in command of the troops on the railway between Kimberley and the Orange Free State, and two days later he left for Kimberley, taking with him the 9th Brigade, now commanded by Major-General Douglas, and his divisional troops; and on the early morning of the 22nd February Kimberley was reached and the four companies of the wing of the 1st Loyal North Lancashire Regiment rejoined the headquarters of their Battalion.

CHAPTER XXII

1900

OPERATIONS IN THE WESTERN TRANSVAAL

WHEN Lord Roberts arrived at Bloemfontein, Lord Methuen's force was the only one left on the western line; south of Mafeking. The infantry at Kimberley consisted wholly of the 9th Brigade, which, as eventually constituted, contained the 1st Northumberland Fusiliers, 1st Loyal North Lancashire, 2nd Northamptonshire and the 3rd South Wales Borderers. Towards the end of March, another brigade had been told off to join the 1st Division, mainly composed of Militia Battalions, but these only began to arrive in Cape Town during this month, and it was quite the beginning of May before Lord Methuen's new division was in every way complete.

During March there was a good deal of sickness in Kimberley, the number of sick in hospital on the 22nd of the month being as high as 597, of which 234 were enteric cases.

At this time there was little opportunity of effecting anything beyond the collection of supplies and the preparation of transport, while the railway was repaired towards Fourteen Streams; still, small expeditions were sent out from Kimberley to the north, north-east and north-west, and early in March the 9th Brigade moved out to and camped at Dronfield.

It was here that a reinforcement joined the Battalion, one composed of officers and men whose employment on active service in the field marked a wholly new departure from the old-time methods for the replacement of casualties; and of the inception and conduct of these methods some description must now be given. When war with the Dutch Republics seemed inevitable, offers to raise companies and battalions of Volunteers for field service were made to the military authorities, and these were renewed more than once during the first weeks of hostilities. These offers were, however, invariably declined, on the grounds that no Volunteers could possibly be needed until the Militia Reserve was exhausted, and that there was no immediate prospect of this; the fact apparently being that neither the Cabinet nor the War Office had contemplated the necessity for the need of anything of the nature of "emergency troops." On the 18th

December, however, the Government sanctioned the volunteering of a limited number of Militia Battalions for service abroad or embodiment at home; and also the formation of "a strong force" of volunteers from the Yeomanry, with a contingent of carefully selected officers, non-commissioned officers and men of Rifle Volunteer Corps for service in South Africa. These last were to form "Service Companies," each of a strength of four officers and one hundred and ten other ranks, and were to be attached to Regular Battalions at the front to make up for such companies of these as had been converted into Mounted Infantry.

By the end of April, 1900, some sixty-eight of these Service Companies had arrived in South Africa, while during the three years that the war lasted over 16,500 Volunteers went from home to South Africa in those companies.

The 1st Volunteer Company to join the Regular Battalion arrived while it was quartered at Dronfield, and was accompanied by Captain B. Musgrave and Lieutenant G. Hesketh, of the 2nd Volunteer Battalion of the Regiment, and Lieutenant F. W. Foley, of the 1st Volunteer Battalion.

On March 28th Lord Roberts ordered the 1st Division to concentrate at Boshof, which had been occupied on the 11th, and on the 4th April the concentration there was duly effected; here Colonel Kekewich rejoined the Battalion and reassumed command.

On the 5th April Lord Methuen's mounted men had a very successful action against a comparatively small body of Boers, under a French soldier of fortune, the Count de Villebois Mareuil, who, quite unaware of the recent large increase to the Boshof garrison, had approached the town with the intention of effecting a surprise attack. The enemy was completely outnumbered, and the majority, realizing in time the hopeless nature of the fight, made their escape, but a good many were killed or wounded or made prisoners; their leader was killed, and he was buried with full military honours in Boshof, the Battalion providing the escort and firing-party, and Lord Methuen attending the funeral in person.

The special interest in the fight arose from the fact that the new Yeomanry were for the first time in action and did their work well.

Two days later Lord Methuen, leaving a small garrison of a Militia Battalion at Boshof, pushed off to Zwartkopjefontein, fourteen miles to the north-east, but on arrival here he was ordered to make no further advance since General Rundle's division, which was to support him, could not arrive for some time. While remaining at Zwartkopjefontein two small bodies were sent out to scour the surrounding country and some skirmishing ensued; and when on the 20th the column, acting under orders from Lord

Roberts, fell back again on Boshof, the rearguard, of which the Volunteer Company formed part, was somewhat harassed by the enemy, and one man, of " H " Company of the Battalion, was wounded.

All hands were now set to work to put Boshof in a good state of defence, but enteric fever had broken out and claimed many victims, five officers —Captains O'Brien and Musgrave, Lieutenants Wallace, Hewett and de Putron, being all admitted to hospital.

By this time a further reinforcement had reached the Battalion, a draft, mainly composed of reservists, having come out from home with Captain H. A. Robinson, Lieutenants W. H. Creak, R. E. Berkeley and 2nd Lieutenant R. J. Smyly.

On the 14th May Lord Methuen, having left a garrison in Boshof, marched off and arrived on the 19th at Hoopstad, whence it had originally been intended that he should move on Reitzburg and Parys; but on arrival at Hoopstad he found orders awaiting him to divert his march on Kroonstad, as there was a rumour that the enemy was preparing for an attack on that important depôt town. Marching again on the 25th in two columns, the infantry under General Douglas in the first, and Lord Methuen following with the mounted men, the troops arrived at Kroonstad on the 28th and 29th, having en route collected some seventy rifles and destroyed 12,000 rounds of enemy ammunition.

It had been intended to march from Kroonstad on Heilbron where it was understood that the garrison was in difficulties, and the column had gone as far as Klipfontein on the 30th May when it was learnt that Heilbron was safe; but almost immediately afterwards news came in that a party of Yeomanry, five hundred strong, had been manœuvred into something of a trap on the Valsch River, near Lindley, where it was very hard pressed. On hearing this Lord Methuen at once left for Lindley with his mounted men and guns. The remainder of the column followed on the 31st, and, marching by Doornkopfontein, Quaggafontein and Paardeplatz, arrived at Lindley early on the morning of the 2nd June, only to find that the Yeomanry had surrendered on the previous day; the mounted troops of Lord Methuen's force had engaged the retreating Boers in a running fight, but these had managed to get away, taking their prisoners with them.

In the following Divisional Order dated Lindley, 2nd June, Lieut.-General Lord Methuen expressed his appreciation of the efforts made by all :—

" The Lieut.-General Commanding shares with his Division the feeling of deep regret at having been unable to relieve the Regiment of Irish Yeomanry, under the command of Colonel B. E. Spragge, before it was captured by the enemy. Colonel Spragge stated he could hold out till

Saturday (2nd) but had to surrender on Thursday at midday on account of the enemy having been largely reinforced with men and guns.

"The Division made a splendid effort, the Yeomanry, four batteries R.F.A. with pompoms, having engaged the enemy for five hours at the end of the forced march and the infantry having marched forty-four miles in fifty-one hours.

"The Lieut.-General thanks the Division for the work performed."

On the 3rd June the 20th Brigade, under Major-General Paget, joined Lord Methuen at Lindley, and on June 5th, in consequence of a telegram from Lord Roberts saying that supplies were urgently needed by the garrison of Heilbron, Lord Methuen started thither, taking with him a convoy, the Yeomanry and the 9th Brigade, leaving the 20th Brigade behind at Lindley. During the march a number of Boers hung on the heels of the column, the mounted troops, supported by the Battalion, engaging the enemy, but there was no serious fighting and Heilbron was reached on June 7th.

Intelligence now coming in of the very successful raids recently made upon the railway line by General de Wet, and Lord Methuen having been ordered to try and drive away the marauders, he left Heilbron on the 9th, taking with him the Yeomanry and the 9th Brigade—less the 2nd Northamptonshire which remained behind—some Scouts and the 2nd Royal Highlanders, and reached Vredefort Road on the railway on the 10th.

On the following morning a southward movement was begun, Colonel Spens, who had lately arrived, with two battalions and some mounted men, marching on the western side of the line, while Lord Methuen followed on the eastern, against de Wet's men who were holding the kopjes overlooking the Rhenoster River. The Battalion formed for attack, "C," "D," "E" and "F" Companies forming the firing-line, the remainder the supports and reserve, "F" Company being on the extreme left on the railway; the Black Watch was on the right of the Battalion; "D" Company of the Battalion, under Captain Logan, led the attack. The fire of our guns was very effective, and after no more than a pretence at resistance the enemy fell back westward. A few prisoners were taken and the railway line was found to have been very much damaged, while the Rhenoster River bridge had been blown up.

The infantry had no casualties.

Leaving Colonel Spens and his men here, Lord Methuen marched away southwards, having heard that Kroonstad had been occupied by the enemy, but this rumour was almost at once contradicted, and Lord Methuen then moved to Honing Spruit.

On the 14th the Lieut.-General inspected the Battalion transport and complimented all concerned on the excellent condition of the mules ; and on the same day Captain Ansley was sent into Kroonstad suffering from fever.

On the 15th June the column marched from Honing Spruit, leaving there " A " and " H " Companies under Majors Murray and Fraser, and arrived next day near Kopje Station, where the 9th Brigade remained, while Lord Methuen with the rest of his force left for Heilbron. While the Battalion was at Kopje Station, twenty men of a Volunteer Company joined under Lieutenant E. Stowell of the 1st Volunteer Battalion, and news came in from Honing Spruit that Lieutenant R. J. Smyly, who was detached with " H " Company, had been slightly wounded.

" Lord Roberts now planned to bring the Orange River Colony into a state of subjection. In a telegram sent from Pretoria on June 17th to Lord Methuen, Sir L. Rundle, Lord Kitchener, Clements, Sir H. Colvile, MacDonald, Sir H. Hunter and C. E. Knox, he made known the measures which he now proposed to take to ensure the security of the railway, and to establish order in the north-eastern districts of the Orange River Colony. Lord Roberts' intentions were to provide adequate garrisons for the principal towns and vulnerable points on the railway, and to organize four flying columns to be constantly on the move through the various districts in which the burghers were still in arms. These columns were to be commanded by the following generals : Ian Hamilton, Lord Methuen, Clements and MacDonald, and were to be based on Heidelberg, Rhenoster River, Senekal and Heilbron respectively. All movements were to be completed by 23rd June.

" Lord Methuen's column (Rhenoster River) : two battalions of Yeomanry, two batteries R.F.A., two Vickers-Maxims, two 5-in. Howitzers, 1st Northumberland Fusiliers, 1st Loyal North Lancashire and 2nd Northamptonshire Regiments." * A few days later these instructions were somewhat modified.

During the next few days the Battalion was constantly employed, usually by wings, in escorting convoys to the different places where garrisons had been established ; but early in July it became apparent that the Boers, in increasing strength, were working round Lord Roberts' left flank with the intention of threatening his left rear. Serious enemy incursions had been made into the Western Transvaal, and to the British commander it seemed of the first importance that our forces about Rustenburg and Krugersdorp should be substantially strengthened. On June 12th, then, Lord Methuen was ordered to proceed to Krugersdorp with a division now very much reduced in number, containing as it did only a small body of mounted men and 2,400 rifles.

* *Official History*, Vol. III, pp. 134, 135.

The Battalion entrained at Kroonstad on the 15th July, the men in open trucks, and arrived at Krugersdorp two days later.

On the 18th the Division, and the troops forming the garrison of Krugersdorp, moved out in two columns towards Hekpoort, a district which had now become of importance as General De la Rey had lately been there stirring up and commandeering the farmers. The Battalion was in the right column under Major-General Douglas, the left column was under the command of Major-General Smith-Dorrien, and the following account of the events that now followed is abridged from his *Memories of Forty Years' Service* :—

"The right column marched six miles, the left four and a half and encamped on Riet Spruit, about three miles apart. The left column thus made a wide turning movement to the left and occupied the heights in the neighbourhood of Doornbosch, then, swinging to its right, covered the advance of General Douglas' force on to the range looking down on Hekpoort. The Boers made a feeble show of resistance. The whole force looked down on the rugged country round Hekpoort, distant some two miles ; then, swinging its right round, cleared some two hundred Boers off the heights about Zeekoehoek, and camped at Vaalbank, at the mouth of the Zeekoehoek gorge."

The troops passed over ridge after ridge of mountainous country, and drove away the Boers holding it with but small loss. Nearing Olifant's Nek the opposition became stronger, the Boers holding their ground to give time for their convoy to get away through the defile.

The nek at last secured, two companies of the Battalion remained to hold it, while the rest of the force marched through and camped two miles to the north.

It had been intended that the column should remain for some days in this neighbourhood, pursuing and dispersing the commandos operating to the north-east of Rustenburg ; but it was now learnt that De la Rey had again raided the line of railway, cutting the line and capturing a train near Bank Station between Krugersdorp and Potchefstroom, and the force under Lord Methuen was at once ordered back to the line of rail. On the 23rd July the column moved south, leaving the Battalion to garrison Olifant's Nek with twenty-five mounted men and two mountain guns, the whole under command of Colonel R. G. Kekewich ; the Rustenburg district, in which Olifant's Nek was included, being under the command of Major-General Baden-Powell.

Of the Battalion three and a half companies were disposed on the defence works, in the improvement of which all worked very hard, the remaining companies being kept in reserve ; but on the 25th "D" and "E" Companies marched into Rustenburg to form part of the garrison there, and were followed on the 1st August by " A " and " H " under Major Jackson, thus leaving at Olifant's Nek " B," " C," " F " and " G " and the Volunteer Company.

Helio communication was early established and regularly maintained with Rustenburg, and on the 6th August a message was received at the nek, directing the remainder of the Battalion to vacate the position and join that night a column under General Ian Hamilton which had just arrived at Rustenburg from Pretoria; General Hamilton's orders were to the following effect: " You will occupy and hold Commando Nek, leaving there a suitable force as garrison to entrench themselves. . . . As soon as you are in touch with Baden-Powell you should arrange to evacuate Rustenburg and Olifant's Nek, withdrawing the battalion at Olifant's Nek *via* Hilspoort and the south side of the Magaliesberg, if this can be conveniently arranged."

In the force commanded by General Hamilton was a mounted body under Brigadier-General B. T. Mahon, included in which was the Battalion Company of Mounted Infantry.

The Battalion on leaving Olifant's Nek joined General Hamilton's column at Elandsfontein, where, Rustenburg having also been evacuated, the four companies which had been there under Major Jackson, now rejoined the Battalion.

On the morning of the 11th August General Hamilton's whole force moved on, the Battalion taking the place in Brigadier-General Cunningham's brigade of the Border Regiment which was left to hold Commando Nek. On this day the column marched thirteen miles to Bultfontein, and on the 12th fourteen miles to Zeekoehoek, the Boers sniping en route at the flank and rear guards. Of the remaining events of the chase of De Wet, so far as concerns the share in it of General Hamilton's men, the *Official History* relates that :—

" On August 13th his (General Hamilton's) cavalry were sent forward, carrying three days' supplies, to endeavour to gain touch with De Wet. They moved so slowly that the infantry closed up on them before 8.30 a.m. when they were again pushed on. When they finally halted at Hartebeestfontein, De Wet, in the act of crossing the Witwatersrand and Hamilton's line of advance, was going into laager at Vlakfontein, eighteen miles from the cavalry bivouac. Many of his men had already passed over Olifant's Nek; the rest followed next morning, and the chase was over."

The Battalion remained some ten days longer with General Hamilton's column, moving about the country beyond the Magaliesberg, and doing

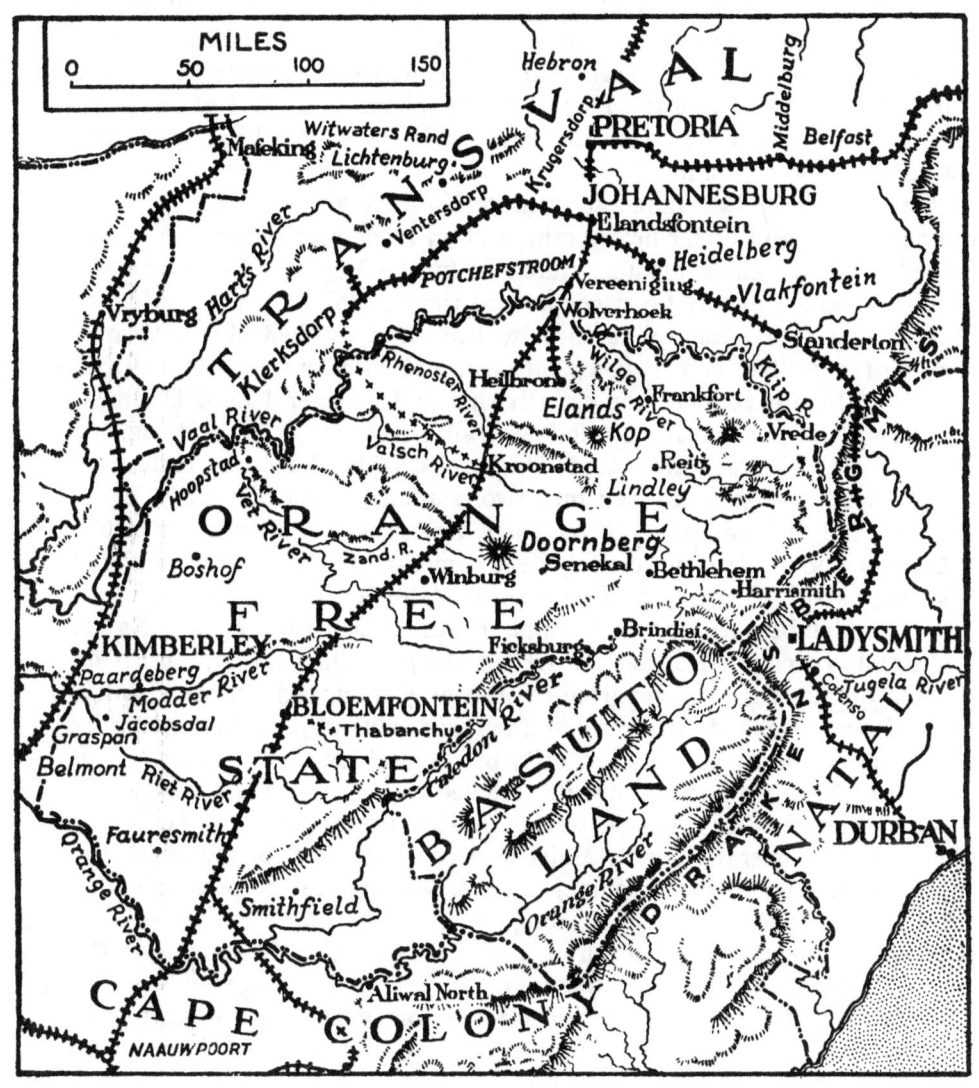

South Africa.

1899–1902.

much convoy duty, often on half and even quarter rations ; and on the 25th August a halt was called at Pienaar's River Bridge, where, in the course of the afternoon, orders were received for the Battalion to entrain at once for Pretoria. The Transvaal capital was reached late that night and on the following day the Battalion was joined by a draft of one hundred and fifty reservists under Lieutenants Bingham and Fitzpatrick and 2nd Lieutenant Wiltshire.

On the 27th the Battalion left again for Kimberley en route for Mafeking in open trucks and under heavy rain, and on reaching the town they had helped to defend, the companies were met by the Mayor and were to have been entertained by the townspeople had time permitted ; the Battalion, however, left again almost at once by train and reached Mafeking at 3 p.m. on the 1st September, going into camp four miles to the east of the town, and here it rejoined the 1st Division under General Lord Methuen.

During the week that now followed all were very busy refitting, for the men were in rags after their long trekking in the bush-veldt.

The force was now divided into two columns of approximately equal strength and each composed of the three arms, the Battalion being in No. 1 Column under Lord Methuen's direct command ; and, having provided a strong garrison for the local defence of Mafeking, the column marched off on September 8th, No. 1 Column towards Lichtenburg, and No. 2, under Major-General Douglas, to Otto's Hoop. While on the march on the 9th the presence was reported of an enemy commando in the vicinity, and this was attacked, driven off and pursued, several prisoners, a number of wagons and a considerable quantity of ammunition being captured.

"Lord Methuen had meanwhile received orders from the Commander-in-Chief that the 1st Division was to hasten to the relief of Schweizer Reneke, in co-operation with Major-General Settle. This township, the most considerable of the Bloemhof district, was reported to be surrounded by a body of the enemy 2,400 strong, with a large number of guns. . . . The two columns marched southward with all speed." On arriving in the neighbourhood of the place it was found to be in little danger, being very elaborately fortified, while the Boer force was very much weaker than had been reported ; this commando was easily dispersed and from it was captured a Maxim, one of the guns lost at Colenso, several prisoners, twenty-six wagons, 800 cattle, 4,000 sheep and 20,000 rounds of ammunition, while several Boers were killed during the pursuit.

From here the column started off again in an easterly direction, but on the march " Lord Methuen received orders to take his whole force to Rustenburg, as Mr. Steyn " (late President of the Free State) " had left the Eastern Transvaal, and was on his way back to the Orange River

Colony. Marching northwards on parallel roads both columns captured a few prisoners, and would have taken more had not parties of Boers avoided capture only by being disguised in British uniforms. On September 28th Douglas' column had a slight bout with the enemy. The rest of the march to the Magaliesberg *via* Rietfontein, was without incident," and on the 8th October, having passed the previous day through Olifant's Nek, the whole force arrived at and encamped at Rustenburg.

It was now evident that several independent bodies of Boers were moving about this part of the country, and the columns under Generals Paget and Lord Methuen were ordered so to operate as to prevent any reunion of these different enemy forces—Lord Methuen, moving out from Rustenburg, was to drive De la Rey's commando westward and to ravage the country towards Zeerust. As the passes through the Magaliesberg were all held by our troops and we had also columns north and south of the range, the Boers could move only by the west of the mountain, and the westward routes from Rustenburg by the Magato and Boschhoek Neks were thus of great importance.

"On October 9th Lord Methuen endeavoured by moving over Boschhoek Nek and sending Douglas through Magato Nek, to attack De la Rey from north and south. That leader, with seven hundred men and several guns, was reported to be holding a position from Tweerivier to Wysfontein, with his main laager at Bulhoek, about fifteen miles north-west of Magato Nek. Lord Methuen's column moved directly upon Bulhoek. . . . The enemy's column could not be discovered and the northern column, annoyed only by skirmishers, marched to Lindley's Poort. The southern column came upon a party of about a hundred Boers near the Selous River; these retired to the south-west as the country favoured the enemy's tactics, both columns marched by the same road, and Douglas, crossing Magato Nek, turned northwards by Waterval, and joined Lord Methuen near Lindley's Poort. . . .

"Reports were now received that De la Rey was moving on Roodeval, west of Lindley's Poort, but finding that both columns were marching together, the enemy dared not attack. When, however, Lord Methuen reached Nooitgedacht on the Little Marico River, his camp was shelled by a Creusot gun, which killed four men and wounded six."

According to the Battalion account, this took place about 9 a.m. on the 17th October, when camp had just been reached and the men were in their bivouacs, and the gun opened on the camp from a kopje on the left flank, the very first shell fired falling in the Battalion lines, killing one man and mortally wounding another. One of our batteries at once got ready for action, but was unable to locate the Boer gun until it had fired some ten rounds and done more execution, the Battalion, though withdrawn to the cover of a spruit, having six more men hit by shell splinters.

Zeerust was reached on the 18th, and here Lord Methuen inspected and bade good-bye to the Volunteer Companies of the Brigade which were under orders to return home; and here a re-arrangement of the columns was made—the 1st Northumberland Fusiliers and half the 1st Battalion The Loyal North Lancashire joining Lord Methuen, while the other half of the Loyal North Lancashire and the 2nd Northamptonshire went to Major-General Douglas; "C," "D," "E" and "F" Companies under Colonel Kekewich were with General Douglas, the remaining companies under Major Jackson with Lord Methuen.

On the 19th Lord Methuen's column moved towards Buffelshoek, when the enemy at once closed in on Zeerust and occupied some kopjes to the south-east of the town. The other column, which had not proceeded far, now attempted to work round the enemy's left flank so as to prevent his retreat, but the Boers rapidly fell back to high ground near Quarriefontein, where for some time they held up the pursuit by our mounted men. These being reinforced by infantry and guns, the enemy gave ground, and, leaving some troops to hold the position, Lord Methuen moved on with the rest of the column to Buffelshoek.

Hearing of the presence of a Boer force in the neighbourhood, a combined movement of both columns took place on October 24th. Lord Methuen proposed to hold the enemy in his position on the Kruis River, while the Zeerust force moved out and forced him back. Attacked in front and their flanks turned, the Boers hurriedly retired towards Kaffir's Kraal, harassed by our guns and pursued by our mounted men, who inflicted several casualties and captured many prisoners and much sheep and cattle.

Lord Methuen and General Douglas then returned to Jacobsdal and Zeerust respectively, Douglas being ordered to move on Mabalstad.

On the 27th October, when in camp at Buffelshoek, the detachment with Lord Methuen was joined by a draft from the 2nd Battalion under Captain M. A. Humphrys, and while "A" and "H" Companies remained in temporary garrison at Buffelshoek, "B" and "G" Companies left on the 1st November for Zeerust, there to strengthen the garrison. The Buffelshoek companies were largely employed on escort duty in the Jacobsdal, Lichtenburg, Mafeking and Otto's Hoop districts; and when towards the end of November Lord Methuen moved out to clear the country about Lichtenburg, he found it necessary to leave a strong garrison in that town, included in which was one company of the Loyal North Lancashire

Regiment.* At the end of December " A " and " H " Companies moved, as a temporary measure, into Mafeking.

Major-General Douglas' column, with " E " and " F " Companies of the Regiment, under Colonel Kekewich, arrived at Mabalstad on the 5th November, the march being conducted in heavy rain and under much sniping from the Boers on the right of the road. Many reports now coming in from various sources of an impending invasion of Cape Colony, several British columns were ordered to converge on Elands River, and General Douglas was directed to move as rapidly as possible on Klerksdorp. Marching by Ventersdorp across a waterless desert, General Douglas collected abundance of supplies and stock with but little opposition, but when approaching Klerksdorp on the 16th the column came under the fire of Boer guns and pompoms from a high and isolated hill. Klerksdorp was now garrisoned by three companies of the Coldstream Guards, who arrived on the 25th, by " E " and " F " Companies of the Battalion, two guns and about eighty mounted men, while Colonel Kekewich was appointed commandant, with Major Coleridge as Assistant Provost-Marshal and Lieutenant Woodward as Station Staff Officer. The remainder of General Douglas' column then marched to Potchefstroom, taking with it all the captures made.

General French was now in chief command of the different columns operating in this part of the Transvaal, and by the end of December he had drawn a line of columns from Olifant's Nek through Ventersdorp to Klerksdorp, thus checking the unrest in this portion of the country.

On the 25th December, Colonel Kekewich assumed command of General Douglas' column, that officer having been invalided to England; and when on the 26th the column moved, Colonel Kekewich took with it the two companies of his Regiment, which were attached to the wing of the 2nd Somersetshire Light Infantry. The various columns now marched towards Ventersdorp, which it was decided to hold, and the two companies of the Loyal North Lancashire were told off to form the garrison with two companies of the Sherwood Foresters; all at once turned to place the town in a sound state of defence.

We must now return to Zeerust where events of a somewhat momentous character were transpiring.

On the 2nd November the garrison of Zeerust was told off to its defence posts and the companies of the Battalion were stationed as follows : " B " Company on South Kopje, " G " Company half on the West Kopje and half in the gaol, while " C " and " D " Companies occupied Signal Kopje

* So stated in the *Official History*, Vol. III, p. 514, but there is no mention of this in the Battalion Digest.

and found all the duties in the town; the officers present with the wing were Major Churchward, Captains Logan and Wylde-Browne, Lieutenants Bingham, Webster and Fitzpatrick and 2nd Lieutenant Wiltshire.

Towards the end of the month there were rumours of a Boer attack upon the town, and on the 27th the garrison was augmented by the arrival of four companies of the Northumberland Fusiliers, two guns and a squadron of Imperial Yeomanry; but as no attack took place or was even threatened, the garrison reverted to the normal, the above-named units leaving Zeerust and joining Lord Methuen's column. At this time Captain Logan proceeded to Cape Town, 2nd Lieutenant Wiltshire was sent sick to Mafeking, and Lieutenant Bingham took over the duties of Station Staff Officer *vice* Captain Logan. Twenty-three men, details, came in and joined the companies.

On the 24th December Lieutenant Wallace arrived in charge of a convoy and took over command of " C " Company, and at this time the defence works were occupied as follows: " B " Company on South Kopje, " C " Company at the gaol, " D " at West Kopje and " G " at Signal Kopje.

Two days later there was something of the nature of a smart skirmish, when " G " Company went out towards Botha's Farm as escort to a convoy, and a sharp rifle-fire was opened upon the company by a party of some forty Boers occupying a position at Maricopoort. The Yeomanry were at once sent out in support and occupied a covering position, while twelve men of " C " Company cleared the heights held by some of the enemy.

The next day some firing was heard from the direction of Kaffir's Kraal, and an attack being expected, the alarm gun was fired about nine o'clock in the evening and all stood to arms; the alarm, however, was a false one.

Some twelve men of the wing in Zeerust were now mounted on spare horses and formed into a Mounted Infantry Section; a town guard was formed on the 29th December; and on the following day telegraphic communication was found to have been cut and the town from this date was to all intents and purposes besieged.

CHAPTER XXIII

1901–1902

OPERATIONS IN THE WESTERN TRANSVAAL
THE END OF THE WAR
THE MOUNTED INFANTRY COMPANY

FOR the garrison of Zeerust the year 1901 was ushered in with very heavy rain-storms, whereby the trenches were completely flooded, and some of the posts were for a time isolated from one another. On the 6th January intelligence was brought in that the enemy was advancing in force on the town and the trenches were at once manned, all remaining on the *qui vive* during the night. At 5 a.m. on the 7th January the Boers opened fire on a Cossack post which was moving out to occupy its usual day position on Gun Kopje, wounding two of the Yeomanry, while at the same time a heavy fire was delivered upon " G " Company on West Kopje, and here also two men were wounded. The mounted men too, who were moving out on the usual reconnoitring patrol, came under enemy fire and were obliged to retire back into the town.

Fire now became general on all sides and was especially heavy about the gaol and West Kopje. About 9.30 a.m. however, the fire slackened, and a white flag was sent in, presumably from Commandant Beyers, demanding the surrender of the town, and stating that, failing compliance, Zeerust would be bombarded. As, however, the demand was unsigned, Major Churchward, the commandant of Zeerust, refused to recognize it, but in view of a possible bombardment all women and children were moved for greater safety into the Dutch Church in the town.

During the course of the morning the fire of the enemy increased in intensity and was impartially distributed against all points of the defence, but two of our guns opened upon the Boer riflemen from the ridge above the gaol and silenced them; finally, about dusk the fire slackened and then at last the enemy withdrew, despite the fact that the Boer fire had not met with any very serious response, due to the need for the garrison to conserve their ammunition.

Of the Loyal North Lancashire detachment three men were slightly wounded.

On the 8th an unfortunate accident occurred, Lieutenant Bingham, while visiting the sentries, being fired on by mistake by one of his own men; he was shot through the left arm which had to be amputated, Lieutenant Wallace then taking over from him the duties of Station Staff Officer of the town. On the 13th, however, this last-named officer was killed while attempting to lay a lyddite mine, the ignition of which he had himself invented. A corporal of artillery was also killed and several men were struck by the stones thrown up by the explosion.

About this time Major Churchward found it necessary to send out a formal protest to the Boer Commandant against the misuse of a flag of truce.

On the 29th January news was received of the death of Her Majesty Queen Victoria, and on the following day all the available troops attended a memorial service.

Orders had by this time been issued to commence the erection of blockhouses and this work was seriously taken in hand, and proceeded as rapidly as the somewhat reduced state of the garrison permitted; there was at this time a good deal of sickness, among both men and animals, and horses and mules were now dying so fast of lung-sickness that the Mounted Infantry Section of the Battalion had perforce to be disbanded.

On the 17th February Lieutenant Bingham, being pronounced convalescent from his wound, was sent in an ambulance to Mafeking; but he was stopped by an enemy party and sent back again into Zeerust; he was, however, successfully evacuated about a month later, when he proceeded to England.

The presence of a Boer laager on the Kruis River having been reported, "C" Company with a gun went out and, taking up a position on Gun Kopje, opened fire on the position of the laager, causing its hurried withdrawal. From this onward there were constant "alarms and excursions," rumours of impending attacks on the town and of the presence of enemy parties in the neighbourhood; all this kept the garrison constantly on the alert, entailing a ceaseless activity in order to impress upon an enterprising enemy that the troops were not to be taken by surprise.

On the 4th March a raiding party moved out from Zeerust, comprising sixteen men of the Loyal North Lancashire under Sergeant Watts and thirty of the Yeomanry, intending to surprise a Boer patrol and raid certain farms, whence it was hoped to obtain stock and supplies; Captain Robinson with thirty men, and Sergeant Ennis with sixteen more, also took up positions in the hope of preventing the escape of the patrol, but dogs on the farms gave the alarm and the Boers got away, losing one man killed, but several cows, calves, goats and donkeys were captured and brought into the town. Usually when armed parties left the town on patrol, few if any Boers showed themselves, but unarmed parties almost invariably ran up against small but active bodies of the enemy. Thus on the 18th the garrison chaplain left Zeerust for Mafeking with the mails, but at once fell among Boers who captured the mails, apparently leaving the chaplain to pursue his lonely way to his destination. The Yeomanry went out next day, supported by a half-company of the Battalion, and came across the empty mail-bags. The Yeomanry retired, whereupon a party of some thirty Boers attempted to cut off their retreat, but were scattered by the rifle-fire of the infantry and by a gun which opened on them from Signal Kopje.

On the 21st Major Churchward made a reconnaissance in force directed on some neighbouring farms, and on this occasion good work was done by Corporal Lewis of the Battalion and a small party with him, who accounted for several of the enemy, one of his men being slightly wounded.

It had for some time past been hoped, and even expected, that Lord Methuen's column would be back at Zeerust before long, but on the 27th April a message was received from that commander stating that he must not be expected for some time, and that the reserves of provisions in the town must be made to last as long as possible; at this time anything of the nature of luxuries was running very short, there was no tobacco to be had and the men were smoking tea-leaves. The arrival of a convoy on the 22nd May was therefore especially welcome, and the fact that the empty convoy returned unmolested to Mafeking seemed to show that the Boer pressure on Zeerust was now beginning to relax.

We may now relate what "A" and "H" Companies had been doing since we left them at Buffelshoek early in November, 1900.

At the end of December these two companies marched into Mafeking in charge of a return convoy, and while "A" Company remained here with Major Murray, "H" Company, with Captain Humphrys and Lieutenant Mace, was on the 3rd January, 1901, railed down to Vryburg, there to join Lord Methuen, who after much manœuvring and marching had arrived at that town on the last day of the year. The column left Vryburg again on the 7th January, and, meeting with but trifling opposition though a certain amount of harmless sniping, Taungs was reached on the 13th. From Taungs Lord Methuen garrisoned and provisioned Kuruman, ninety-eight miles south-west of Vryburg, and parties were sent out to clear the country.

On the 30th "A" Company joined the column from Mafeking.

Owing to the departure of the column from the Krugersdorp command and the disturbed state of the country south of that place, Lord Kitchener decided to call Lord Methuen eastward, and on the 5th February the column marched from Taungs—"A" and "H" Companies, under Major Murray, accompanying it—had a slight engagement at Schweizer Reneke, and on the 13th the force arrived at Wolmaranstad. Marching on, Lord Methuen learnt on the 15th that a large Boer laager was at Brakpan, north-west of Klerksdorp, comparatively weakly guarded, and that a strong Boer force was lying in wait for him at Hartebeestfontein, on the direct Klerksdorp road. He decided to attack the laager first, and marching at midnight on the 17th he captured the whole laager by noon next day, taking several prisoners and a number of wagons.

He then marched on Hartebeestfontein, and here is the Battalion's story of the action that followed:

"A little in front of Hartebeestfontein, in the poort, fifteen hundred Boers had taken up a practically impregnable position. The columns had to descend from a plateau to lower ground and to wind its way through a rocky ravine, on the sides of which was an invisible enemy. The firing was at a range of from 500–1,000 yards and the Boers were contesting every yard of the ground, shelling the column with a 7-pounder Creusot gun. The Imperial Yeomanry attacked the Boers on the right of the road, drove them out and held the position. Another party of Yeomanry and Bushmen attacked the enemy left, but the advance here was checked by very heavy fire, and by 9 a.m. little if any material progress had been made.

"Lord Methuen now directed Major Murray to bring up his two companies, which up to this had been with the ox-convoy, and these had to advance across the open exposed to fire. Though several men were hit, the forward movement was not stayed, and moving forward as though on parade, the position indicated to the companies was reached, and from here they poured in so heavy and accurate a fire that it was not long before the Boers were everywhere falling back."

In his telegram of the 21st February Lord Kitchener mentions the Loyal North Lancashire Regiment as having "greatly distinguished themselves," but in this action the Regiment had two officers—Lieutenants A. W. Hewett and W. H. Creak—and four non-commissioned officers and men killed and eight were wounded.

Lord Methuen highly complimented the detachment on its good work and presented "A" and "H" Companies with a Boer flag.

By this spirited action the road to Klerksdorp was opened and on February 19th the column marched in with a large quantity of captured stock and forage.

On the 24th Major Murray was admitted to hospital and the command of the detachment was assumed by Captain Humphrys.

Lord Methuen was not, however, to remain any length of time about Klerksdorp, for after operating for a few days with another column under Colonel Benson in the triangle Klerksdorp–Potchefstroom–Ventersdorp, he marched off to withdraw the garrison of Hoopstad, moving by Wolmaranstad, south of which, on March 6th, he found a commando between him and Commando Drift where he had intended to cross the Vaal. The river, moreover, was in flood, so the column marched down to Fourteen Streams, where it crossed and arrived at Warrenton on the 15th. Here the detachment of the Loyal North Lancashire relieved a battalion of the Royal Dublin Fusiliers, Militia, remaining as its garrison until the 28th, on which day the column left for Hoopstad, withdrawing the garrison and then retiring to the neighbourhood of Warrenton.

Towards the end of April Lord Methuen was directed to transfer his force to Mafeking for service against De la Rey in the Lichtenburg district, and on the 1st May the greater part of the column, and Captain Humphrys' two companies with it, was railed to Mafeking, marching thence to Lichtenburg, where it arrived on the 3rd.

From here during the greater part of May the companies were mainly engaged in convoy work, and on one of these occasions " A " Company was on rearguard to a convoy when it was suddenly attacked in heavy bush, and one man was hit. The accompanying Yeomanry were driven in, but the company took up a position behind a dam, and, some guns coming up, fought a rearguard action into Brakpan.

On the 13th May Major Murray was discharged from hospital and resumed command of the detachment. To Mafeking the companies returned on the 1st June, but on the 3rd they left for Zeerust with a convoy, arriving there on the 6th June.

We now resume the account of the doings of Battalion headquarters with " E " and " F " Companies.

At the beginning of the year 1901 four columns, of which Colonel Kekewich's was one, were in the immediate neighbourhood of Ventersdorp under the orders of Major-General Babington, the approximate strength of Colonel Kekewich's force being seven hundred mounted men, two hundred and eighty infantry, five guns and two machine-guns. The two companies of the Regiment, however, now formed part of the garrison of Ventersdorp, while the mounted portion of the column operated about the district; but on the 11th January Colonel Kekewich was sent sick to hospital at Johannesburg and his column was then broken up.

Of the work of the companies of the Loyal North Lancashire Regiment during the following twelve months that the war still endured, it is impossible to give any really consecutive account, since the companies were dispersed in many different towns and posts, engaged in convoy duty from one place to another ; while occasionally those employed on garrison duty would be relieved at comparatively short notice to take the place of companies of their own or of other regiments, which were considered to have been over-long on trek and to be in need of a rest. It is possible, therefore, that the recital that follows may appear somewhat involved.

On the 21st January Major Jackson came into Ventersdorp with a convoy and remained on, taking over command of the headquarters of the Battalion in that town. During February the usual work went on—convoys being sent out, defence posts established or strengthened, and wood-cutting parties were constantly engaged ; and all the time every precaution had to be taken against enemy attack, for many Boers were known to be hovering about the neighbourhood, since there was an abundance of supplies of all kinds in the district. On the 6th March Major Jackson left for England on retirement and Captain Ansley came to command headquarters in his place. Colonel Kekewich was now in charge of the Potchefstroom district.

On the 28th April the headquarters of the Battalion left Mafeking for Potchefstroom, where Major Palmes took over command, and here it remained until the 23rd May, when it left again with a full convoy intended for Ventersdorp, where at this time was "F" Company with Lieutenants Wells and Howard. The Potchefstroom and Ventersdorp convoys were arranged to meet half-way when the Ventersdorp escort would take over the full convoy, the Potchefstroom escort then returning with the empty wagons. The mounted men with the Ventersdorp party were rather raw Yeomanry just out from home, and when the two escorts parted on handing over their wagons, Lieutenant Wells of the Battalion was ordered to move with the advanced screen of Yeomen in order to guide them.

The Imperial Yeomanry found the advance, flank and rear screens, supported by thirty men of "F" Company, while twenty more men of the Royal Welsh Fusiliers provided an escort for the guns. Approaching Kaalfontein the left front and flank of the screen suddenly came under a heavy fire at close range, and the Yeomanry fell back through their infantry support and took up a position in rear. Lieutenant Wells and his men now charged forward and occupied a ridge, upon which was also a party of the enemy and heavy fire was opened. The convoy, massed on the road below, was soon surrounded by the Boers who fired into it from all sides.

Some of "F" Company, under Sergeant Barrowman, were holding a position between Lieutenant Wells' party and the convoy ; the infantry of the rearguard was in position on a small kopje behind the wagons ; while the gun with the escort was firing on the enemy with case shot.

A BLOCKHOUSE IN THE WESTERN TRANSVAAL.

1901.

A gun was now heard firing from the direction of Witpoortje, and from this it seemed clear that the Potchefstroom party was returning to the assistance of their Ventersdorp comrades.

Corporal Waterhouse and two men of the Battalion were sent out to reconnoitre, but coming under fire from concealed Boers at a hundred yards' range, one of the men was killed while the corporal was wounded in two places. The enemy now set fire to the grass to windward of the convoy and things were looking black, when mounted men were seen approaching from the direction of Witpoortje, and these being followed by the infantry of the Potchefstroom convoy-escort, the enemy drew off, and each party then proceeded on its way. The Potchefstroom one was unmolested, but the one returning to Ventersdorp had some severe fighting before it got in. A third man of the Battalion was wounded, and Corporal Waterhouse, Privates Gaskell, Wyatt, Gallagher and Brown were all brought to notice for gallant conduct this day.

On the 8th July 2nd Lieutenants A. S. G. Cattell and W. D. Hill joined on appointment from the South Lancashire Militia.

From this time onward the headquarters of the Battalion remained quartered at Mafeking, serving as a sort of depot for the companies detached with Lord Methuen's column and in garrison at Zeerust.

On the 20th July Captain W. R. Lloyd and Lieutenant L. K. D'Arcy joined headquarters from England; and when a few days later Lord Methuen's column was divided into two bodies, the one under the General himself and the other under Colonel von Donop, Captain Lloyd was told off to command "C" and "D" Companies with Colonel von Donop, while Captain Robinson was in charge of "B" and "G" with the main column; these companies were, however, employed on convoy duty practically throughout, visiting Taungs, Schweizer Reneke, Lichtenburg, Ventersdorp, the Lead Mines and Otto's Hoop. Such fighting as there was was chiefly carried out by the mounted troops with the columns, but during July the companies marched some four hundred miles and on at least one occasion the convoys they were escorting were attacked. This kind of work went on for many weeks and the companies were constantly sent to garrison different towns, those which had been sitting still taking their places in mobile columns.

On the 6th October a draft of fifty-seven rank and file joined from England, while two days later 2nd Lieutenants W. H. H. Paul and W. R. Goodwin were sent with fifty men to join the garrison at Lobatsi, not far from Otto's Hoop; by this time 2nd Lieutenant Mace had been sent into Pretoria to join the Mounted Infantry.

On the 16th another party of fifty men was sent to Lobatsi, where

Captain Robinson was now in command. On the 16th November Captain Robinson and 2nd Lieutenant Goodwin with fifty men were withdrawn to Mafeking, the rest staying at Lobatsi with 2nd Lieutenant Paul.

There was a very determined attack made by some one hundred and fifty Boers on one of the blockhouses held by the Battalion on the Pitsani line on the 28th November at dawn. The blockhouse was garrisoned by nine men only of "B" Company under command of Sergeant Waring, and all behaved with the most determined gallantry and devotion. The attackers called on the garrison to surrender, but this demand was refused, and the enemy fire was mainly directed from a ganger's hut; but as Sergeant Waring and his men knew that the hut was also occupied by women and children, their fire could not be directed upon it. The attack was, however, evantually beaten off with loss to the enemy, but of the garrison of the blockhouse the sergeant and two men were wounded, while nearly all of the others suffered injuries of a minor character.

On hearing of this affair Lord Methuen caused the following message to be forwarded: "Please compliment the sergeant and garrison of the blockhouse on its excellent defence. I expect nothing but what is of the best from the 1st Battalion The Loyal North Lancashire Regiment."

At the beginning of January, 1902, "A," "C," "D," "E" and "F" Companies were with the column at Vryburg; but on the 12th the four last-named companies left for Lichtenburg, where later on, in addition to ordinary garrison duties, the companies were holding some ten blockhouses on the Lichtenburg–Klerksdorp line. When at the end of February Colonel von Donop's column met with something of a reverse and three of his guns fell into the hands of the Boers, orders were issued that all blockhouses were to have trenches dug round them for occupation in case of fire being opened on them from these captured guns.

On the 28th February orders were received for reinforcements to be sent to Vryburg to join the infantry units, which were there operating with Lord Methuen's column; 2nd Lieutenants Paul and Wallis were at once dispatched thither with a hundred men, mostly of "B" and "G" Companies: with this party also went Lieutenant Fitzpatrick, who was required to take up the appointment of A.D.C. to Lord Methuen.

A portion of the Battalion was now to be involved in an unfortunate affair and for the first time in this long-drawn-out campaign, some of its officers and men found themselves forced to surrender.

On the 2nd March Lord Methuen marched out of Vryburg with a column commanded by Major Paris and which was made up as follows:

5th Battalion Imperial Yeomanry	.	.	.	184 Men
86th Company	,,	,,	. . .	110 ,,

Cape Police	233 Men
Cullinan's Horse	64 ,,
B.S.A. Police	24 ,,
Diamond Fields Horse	92 ,,
Dennison's Scouts	58 ,,
Ashburne's Light Horse	126 ,,
4th Battery R.F.A.	2 Guns
38th ,, ,,	2 ,,
Vickers-Maxims	2 ,,
1st Bn. Northumberland Fusiliers	200 Men
1st Bn. Loyal North Lancashire Regiment	100 ,,

It will be seen from the above how very heterogeneous was the composition of the column, more particularly as regards the mounted portion of it.

Marching by Grootpan, Barberspan and Leeuwspruit, the column reached Tweebosch, on the Little Hart's River, on the evening of the 6th March but little molested by the enemy, but finding a good deal of difficulty in regard to the water supply. It was known that a small commando under van Zyl was in the neighbourhood, but it was regarded as too weak in numbers to be really formidable. At 3 a.m. on the 7th the column was again set in motion, marching northward towards Leeuwkuil: but as the enemy was to the south, the rear was the more vulnerable part of the force and the transport therefore preceded the rest of the column. The mule transport went on first, followed by the ox-wagons, both escorted by a squadron of Cape Police, a company of Imperial Yeomanry, two guns, a Vickers-Maxim, and detachments of the Northumberland Fusiliers and Loyal North Lancashire Regiment. Behind these, and starting off an hour later, was the remainder of the column.

The force marched for two hours before it began to get light, and during the whole time it was being shadowed by two thousand men under De la Rey, who had under his orders some of the best of the lesser men among the Boer leaders. "Enveloping the British rearguard under cover of the gloom, at break of day—5 a.m.—the commandos suddenly opened so terrible a fire from three sides that, with scarcely a pretence at resistance, the untrained, undisciplined irregulars broke and fled before the guns of the 38th Battery and the Vickers-Maxim, which were sent to their assistance, could come into action. The burghers were upon them at once, riding in five lines and firing from the saddle and galloping forward among them in a confused mass bore down upon the front and flanks of the mounted supports which had been moving with the guns to reinforce the now shattered screen in rear. . . . Soon the guns remained isolated in the midst of the enemy . . . but until every man had fallen the guns were served with care." *

The loss of the guns left the column completely open to attack, while the fire of the enemy caused the wagon-teams to stampede, adding terribly to the confusion. The enemy was now firing from three sides; but Lord Methuen directed Major Paris to rally as many of the mounted men as he could collect at a kraal on some rising ground a mile distant, while he himself, with the infantry and guns, stood by and endeavoured to protect what remained of the convoy.

"For two hours the devoted troops around him kept off their inevitable fate. Surrounded at point-blank range by a force of marksmen five times their number, their only prospect was to show how soldiers may perish. The two guns of the 4th Battery were fought as nobly as those of the 38th had been . . . the gunners remained at their work until all were down. The men of the Northumberland Fusiliers showed that even constant misfortune could not lower their spirit. The Loyal North Lancashire vied with the Fusiliers. Lord Methuen himself was the central figure of his forlorn hope until his horse was killed and he himself fell with a fractured thigh. Soon after the fighting here ceased. . . . Thus, after five hours from its first surprise, Lord Methuen's column was completely destroyed. Three-quarters of the personnel were killed, wounded or taken prisoner."

The column lost sixty-eight officers and men killed and one hundred and thirty-two of all ranks wounded, and of these three men killed and five wounded belonged to the detachment of the Loyal North Lancashire Regiment.

The 2nd Volunteer Company sent out from home, which had been some time in South Africa, but had never joined the Battalion in the field, having been employed on the lines-of-communication, now sent a half-company to the headquarters at Mafeking under Lieutenant T. P. Phethean, of the 2nd Volunteer Battalion, while Captain W. Swindlehurst, of the 1st Volunteer Battalion, who had come out in command of this company, was seconded for transport duties in Mafeking. The remaining half-company was sent to Kuruman, there to form part of the garrison, and never joined the Battalion.

From this date onwards Mafeking was now for some time practically denuded of troops, since every available man was employed in the construction of a line of blockhouses along the thirty-five miles of road between Mafeking and Lichtenburg—very hard work which had, moreover, to be carried out as rapidly as possible, lest it might be interfered with by the enemy before completion; the line of blockhouses was ready and garrisoned by the end of the first week in April.

* *Official History*, Vol. IV, p. 418.

The infantry of the Mafeking garrison was constantly out now on convoy duty, and on one occasion when a " drive " was taking place, part of the Battalion reinforced different blockhouse lines ; there were also frequent reliefs of the garrisons of neighbouring posts, while men were constantly employed on armoured trains.

By the middle of May there was a decided lull in the operations, for peace conferences had now begun to take place : but the authorities at home were evidently " taking no chances " since, on the 19th May, a draft arrived from England for the Battalion under Major G. A. Norcott and 2nd Lieutenant L. T. Allason ; then at last on the 1st June the news was received that peace had been signed on the previous day.

On the 3rd June Captain Ansley, three non-commissioned officers and seven men, who had been selected to represent the Battalion at the Coronation of King Edward VII, left for Cape Town and sailed for England in the S.S. " Bavarian " ; the troops began to be gradually withdrawn from the blockhouse lines ; and on the 19th the 3rd Volunteer Company, which had never joined and had been quartered at Maritsani, left for Cape Town en route for England.

The reservists with the Battalion now began to leave, a party of one hundred departing on the 27th July under Lieutenant F. H. E. Torbett ; this was followed by a second party of the same strength on the 6th July under Major Coleridge ; on the 30th Lieutenant Trefusis and 2nd Lieutenant Woodman went off to Cape Town with one hundred more ; Captain Flint proceeded home with another hundred reservists on the 13th August ; another fifty left with Captain Robinson on the 20th ; and finally on the 21st Captain Wylde-Browne railed for Cape Town en route to England with twenty time-expired men.

By this time nearly every detachment had come in from all outlying garrisons, and the greater part of the Battalion—joined by men who had been away with mounted infantry—was concentrated in Mafeking. Here on the 7th September orders were received directing the Battalion to be in Cape Town by the 14th ready for embarkation for England. An advance party was at once sent off, and on the 11th the Battalion left Mafeking by special train and on arrival at Cape Town on the 14th, went into camp at Green Point Depot Camp. On the 17th, played out by the band of the Royal Fusiliers, it marched to the docks and embarked in the " Carisbrooke Castle."

One hundred non-commissioned officers and men remained behind with Major Pine-Coffin, Lieutenants Helme and Colley, awaiting an opportunity to proceed to join the 2nd Battalion of the Regiment at Gibraltar ; the remainder—twenty officers and five hundred other ranks—sailed for England the same afternoon. The following officers left South Africa with the 1st Battalion : Lieut.-Colonel P. Palmes ; Majors G. A. Norcott and G. A. Faulder ; Captains M. A. Humphrys, R. R. Feilden, C. E. A. Jourdain, W. R. Lloyd, G. H. Wylde-Browne, T. H. O'Brien, F. J. Braithwaite, F. W. Woodward, adjutant, and E. C. Halton ; Lieutenants G. T. Body, A. McC. Webster, L. K. D'Arcy, R. T. C. Mace and W. R. Goodwin ; 2nd Lieutenant W. D. Hill, and Captain and Quartermaster H. J. Gill.

The Battalion disembarked at Southampton on the 4th October, being met on arrival by Major-General Berkeley, Colonel Kekewich and other officers, and proceeded at once by train to Devonport, where it was accorded a civic reception, and then marched to Raglan Barracks, which had been prepared for occupation by a draft of one hundred and thirty men under Captain A. J. Carter, D.S.O., Lieutenants Fitzpatrick and Case.

For their services during this war the troops engaged were awarded two Medals known respectively as the " Queen's Medal " and the " King's Medal." No order for the issue of the earlier of these was issued during the lifetime of Her Majesty Queen Victoria, though an Army Order on the subject was drafted and actually printed, being dated the 5th August, 1900, but it was never promulgated. In Army Order No. 94 of 1901, His Majesty King Edward confirmed the order which Her late Majesty had intended to issue ; and in succeeding Orders of this year—Nos. 124, 145, 180 and 195—the scope of its distribution was widened, and finally in Army Order No. 232 of 1902, King Edward caused the award of the second Medal to be announced.

The Queen's Medal has twenty-six clasps, the King's Medal but two, and this last was given only to those actually serving in South Africa on or after the 1st January, 1902, and who had completed eighteen months' war service on that date.

The Honours for the campaign were announced in a Special Army Order dated the 21st December, 1904, which ran as follows :

" His Majesty The King has been graciously pleased to approve of the following corps of the Regular and Auxiliary Forces being permitted, in recognition of services rendered during the South African War, 1899–1902, to bear upon their Colours, or appointments, the words specified in each case :—

* * * * *

" The Loyal North Lancashire Regiment.
" South Africa, 1899–1902,
" The Defence of Kimberley."

The Mounted Infantry Company
1900–1902

On the 6th February, 1900, at Richmond, the Mounted Infantry Company of the Battalion was taken over from Captain Wylde-Browne by Captain Jourdain, and was then incorporated in the 3rd Battalion Mounted Infantry commanded by Lieut.-Colonel T. D. Pilcher. On the evening of this day the Mounted Infantry Battalion marched in a westerly direction with a force under Colonel Broadwood, the strength of the Company on this day—including thirty-six men of the 2nd Battalion Northamptonshire Regiment—being two officers, 101 other ranks and 114 horses. The only officer at the time with the Company, besides Captain Jourdain, was Lieutenant Buckley, Northamptonshire Regiment, but within a week 2nd Lieutenant Darwall joined for duty—also of the Northamptonshire.

On the 11th the force arrived at Belmont, from where on the same evening, the Mounted Infantry, leaving all baggage behind, marched as escort to two hundred wagons of supplies for Lord Roberts' force which was then at Ramdam; and having handed over the wagons on the 12th the escort left again the same evening and bivouacked for the night at de Kiel's Drift on the Riet River, where were now assembled the three brigades of the Cavalry Division under General French. On the 14th, when the Division moved on towards the Modder River, the Mounted Infantry Company of the Battalion was separated from Colonel Pilcher's command and remained behind for a short time.

On the day that the Cavalry Division marched northward Captain Jourdain and his men were sent to Blaubosch Pan to repair the telegraph line which had been destroyed in places, and consequently had to march all night to overtake the main mounted column, coming up with it at Wegdrai at 2 a.m. on the 15th. In the afternoon a half-company was sent off to the assistance of a large convoy of supplies for the main army which had been attacked by the enemy in very considerable strength near Waterval Drift on the Riet River. On nearing the spot, it was learnt that, under orders from Lord Roberts, the wagons had been abandoned to the Boers, into whose hands thus fell about 176 wagons containing over 70,000 rations of preserved meat, 180,000 rations of breadstuff and groceries, nearly 39,000 grain rations, eight wagon-loads of medical comforts, with all the ox-teams and some 500 slaughter cattle. The blow was a very serious one and might very easily have impeded Lord Roberts' plan of campaign.

On the 16th February Captain Jourdain's company was attached to the 7th Division—General Tucker—and, marching by day and night, arrived at 4 a.m. on the 18th near Paardeberg and took up a position on the hills south-west of the Boer laager, the battle opening a few hours later. The Company was not, however, actively engaged until the next day, when it was sent, in company with some of the New South Wales Mounted Infantry, to work round a hill which the enemy was occupying. Here the Company came under fire and two men and several horses were hit ; but, reinforcements now arriving, the Boers were driven from the position, and the Company held it during that night with others of our troops.

The M.I. Company of the 1st Battalion of the Regiment does not appear to have taken any further part in this decisive action, for on the 20th it was withdrawn to camp, and during the next few days was employed on escort duty with guns and prisoners, not returning to Paardeberg until the 26th, the eve of Cronje's surrender ; the Company then marched to Koodoosrand and rejoined the 3rd Mounted Infantry.

On the 3rd March Lieutenant S. A. M. Orr, 2nd Lancers, Hyderabad Contingent, Indian Army, was attached to the Company for duty.

On the 6th the Mounted Infantry was redistributed into four brigades, and the 3rd Regiment M.I. was now in the 1st Brigade, which also contained the 1st Regiment M.I., Roberts' Horse, the New Zealand M.I., Rimington's Guides, the Tasmanian M.I. and the New South Wales Lancers, the Brigade being under the command of Lieut.-Colonel E. A. H. Alderson ; on this day the 1st M.I. Brigade was with General French's division at Osfontein. Leaving here at 3 a.m. on the 7th the Company covered twenty-five miles and then came into action, with the remaining units of its brigade, about Middelpunt Farm, and was under a heavy fire during most of the day in what is known as the action of Poplar Grove. Three days later —on the 10th—it was engaged in the action of Driefontein, which opened the way for the occupation of the capital of the Orange Free State ; for in this engagement the severe punishment which the Boers had received spread panic throughout the commandos, described by De Wet as " a disorderly crowd of terrified men blindly flying before the enemy." *

Marching now by way of Doorndam and Ventersvlei, the Company camped outside Bloemfontein on the 13th, the horses by this time greatly done up and the Company only eighty-one strong, all ranks ; on the 16th it was joined by two subaltern officers, Lieutenants C. R. J. Mowatt, Northamptonshire Regiment, and F. A. Brown, Royal Munster Fusiliers. On the 18th it marched to Bosman's Kop where the Company was reorganized, the Loyal North Lancashire men forming Nos. 1 and 2 Sections and the men of the Northamptonshire Regiment composing Nos. 3 and 4.

* *Three Years' War*, p. 70.

Marching on, the 3rd Regiment M.I. arrived on the 20th March at Thabanchu, and next day left as part of a small force under Lieut.-Colonel Pilcher with orders to occupy Leeuw River Mills, and on arrival here a strong position was taken up and entrenched. "From information gathered that day, Colonel Pilcher reported that General Grobelaar was at Ladybrand, that the enemy's main body was on the way to Clocolan, and that a detachment, apparently a flank guard, was at Modder Poort. This message was received at Thabanchu shortly before midnight on the 21st March. Communications by telegraph and signal were opened with Bloemfontein on the 21st, and on the 22nd with Pilcher's force. During the next four days Lieut.-Colonel Pilcher strengthened the ground he occupied, and reconnoitred actively in all directions. On March 26th, having strong reasons for wishing to arrest the Landrost of Ladybrand, and having been led to believe that the task would not be difficult, he marched with a hundred men"—including twenty-five of the Company under Captain Jourdain—" and a Maxim, upon the village which is eighteen miles from the Mills, and about forty miles from Thabanchu. When he drew near to Ladybrand, he posted half his men and the Maxim in reserve, and entered it with the remainder. He was received with open arms by the inhabitants. He then arrested the landrost and a field cornet, and had just obtained with some difficulty a conveyance in which to transport them, when he was told that about a thousand men were rapidly approaching. He succeeded in carrying off his prisoners and in withdrawing safely, pursued by the fire of the Boers and of the inhabitants, who had now exchanged the white flag, with which they had originally welcomed him, for rifles. His retreat was covered by the Maxim gun. The Boers did not pursue, and Lieut.-Colonel Pilcher reached the Mills that evening, with the loss of one man wounded and a sergeant and four men missing." *

On the 30th the 3rd Regiment M.I. again formed part of General Broadwood's force, only some 1,700 strong inclusive of Colonel Pilcher's command, 835 all told, and formed the eastern flank guard of Lord Roberts' army. Towards midday on this date Broadwood learnt that from 3,000–4,000 Boers were on the march from Ladybrand, while reports came in from natives that another force from the north was approaching the left flank. "All preparations were made to meet attack and to evacuate Thabanchu if necessary, and General Broadwood telegraphed to Bloemfontein that if there were any likelihood of his flank being turned, he would be compelled to retire to the Waterworks, twenty-three miles east of Bloemfontein and on the left bank of the Modder River, where he would be in open country and close to support.

* *Official History*, Vol. II, pp. 262, 263.

"At about 3.30 a.m. on the 31st March General Broadwood's main body arrived at the Modder, crossed it by the Waterworks drift and bivouacked, the 3rd M.I. having formed the rearguard throughout the march. Broadwood's troops, tired with the long night-march, had hardly begun to stir in their bivouac, when first musketry and then a heavy shell-fire opened upon them from the east of the Modder. The enemy's guns were posted upon the kopjes, which from the north overhang the road from Thabanchu to the Waterworks, over which the column had marched but three or four hours earlier. . . . Broadwood now decided to withdraw to Bosman's Kop."

The 3rd Mounted Infantry, however, stayed in position on the flank until the Boers got round the left, when our mounted men fell back, followed up by the enemy, occupying one position after another until at noon Bosman's Kop was reached. But in the meantime the convoy and guns had been ambushed and captured. "By successive companies Rimington's Guides and the 1st and 3rd M.I. Battalions gradually fell back towards the positions further south, which were being held by Alderson's second line. . . . As each company retired behind the next, the Boers advanced in rushes up to within a hundred yards, only to be stopped by the fire of the company that remained to face them. There was no confusion and no undue haste, where all seemed to have a noble emulation to save a comrade or to retrieve the day from utter disaster. . . . The Boers pursued right up to the drift; then, after a final skirmish with the 3rd M.I. left to hold it, they returned to gather up their spoils."*

The force engaged had 138 killed and wounded and 430 taken prisoner, while seven guns and eighty-three laden supply wagons fell into the hands of the enemy. In the Company of the 1st Battalion Loyal North Lancashire Regiment one man was killed, two officers—Lieutenants Brown and Darwell—were wounded and twenty men were missing.

In his report on this affair General Broadwood wrote that "the action of 'Q' Battery, the Company of Durham Light Infantry, and of Lieut.-Colonel Pilcher's Regiment of Mounted Infantry was specially worthy of notice"; while, writing to Colonel Alderson, he said: "Will you please let all know how much I appreciate the work done by your Brigade to-day, it was splendid; if any unit should be mentioned it would be the 3rd M.I."

In a camp some few miles out of Bloemfontein the mounted troops were refitted, and the strength of the Battalion Company was now four officers and eighty-two other ranks.

For some little time now the 3rd M.I. was a good deal moved about

---

* "*Times*" *History*, Vol. IV, p. 43.

the country in the neighbourhood of Bloemfontein, often coming under fire, but happily incurring no casualties; and during this time the Company was strengthened by the arrival of Lieutenant Clifford and of the men who had been employed under him on mounted infantry duty.

On the 5th May the 3rd M.I. was engaged with the enemy on the Vet River, when the New South Wales Lancers did excellent work under Captain Knight of the Regiment; and again a few days later near Velgelegen —but indeed there was desultory fighting in all parts of the country at this time. About the middle of the month the Company was again reorganized, three of the sections being now formed from the Regiment and one only from the Northamptonshire.

A large force of Mounted Infantry was at this time marching, under command of Colonel Ian Hamilton, with General French, and the 3rd M.I. was included in this body, which was operating in the Transvaal, and there was some fighting about Florida, where Lieutenant Clifford distinguished himself by making several captures, one of his prisoners being a German officer. The remainder of this year appears to have been spent in continuous trekking about the eastern and south-eastern Transvaal.

Having moved to Belfast on the 2nd January, 1901, the Company was in time to take part in the defence of that place; and then, having received a draft of forty-one men, it marched away with a mounted brigade under the command of Colonel Henry. There was some skirmishing about Wonderfontein, and then near Carolina, on the 27th January, the Company was called upon to assist the rearguard which had been attacked by the enemy in thick mist and rain; for gallantry on this day Lance-Corporals Fletcher and Woodhouse were specially brought to notice. There was renewed fighting on the next day, when one man was killed, Lieutenant K. Z. P. Macaulay was mortally wounded and two men were hit. The 3rd Mounted Infantry, and the Company with it, took part with Major-General Smith-Dorrien's column in its sweep to the Swaziland Border.

In May the M.I. joined a new column under Lieut.-Colonel Douglas, and, during part of the operations that followed, Captain Jourdain was in command of the 3rd M.I. The column went north across the Crocodile River and in some fighting on the 13th June two men of No. 1 Section were killed.

On the 19th, near Lydenburg, Major Faulder of the 2nd Battalion of the Regiment joined the 3rd M.I.

Early in July the Company was split up and distributed in several detachments as follows: at Machadodorp, 2nd Lieutenant Wallace and twenty-three men; at Belfast, Captain Jourdain and twenty-two men; at Wonderfontein, Sergeant Hellers and seventeen men; at Pan, Lieutenant Blake-White and twenty-four men, and elsewhere eight non-commissioned officers and men. In these posts the Company remained until the 20th October, employed mainly on escort duty. On this date the 3rd M.I. joined at Driefontein a column commanded by Colonel Benson, the Company being now under the command of Lieutenant Blake-White, *vice* Captain Jourdain admitted to hospital, but having now another subaltern officer in Lieutenant Mace who had recently joined for duty from the 1st Battalion.

Colonel Benson's column, containing some 2,000 men, four guns and two pompoms, was made up as follows:

501 of the 3rd M.I. under Major Ansley.
462 of the 25th M.I. under Major Eustace.
434 of the 2nd Scottish Horse under Major Murray.
650 of the 2nd Bn. The Buffs under Major Daughlish.

The column had been provisioned so as to be independent of supply depots, and there consequently marched with it 250 vehicles, of which 120 were ox-wagons.

At first everything went well, thirty-seven Boers were captured on the 22nd, but on the succeeding days there was constant skirmishing, and on the evening of the 29th Colonel Benson halted his troops at Zwakfontein, fifteen miles west by north of Bethel.

The column left camp at 5 a.m. on the 30th and marched in a north-westerly direction on Bakenlaagte, where it was intended to halt. The ox-convoy moved first, escorted by two companies of the 25th M.I., one and a half companies of the Buffs and two guns; with the mule-wagons was the remainder of the column, the 3rd and 25th M.I. providing the advanced and flank guards, while the rearguard consisted of one hundred and eighty men of the 3rd M.I. (Yorkshire Light Infantry, Loyal North Lancashire and Royal Dublin Fusiliers), a company of the Buffs and one pompom under Major Ansley.

Directly the march began the enemy began to press the rearguard, while harassing also, but in a lesser degree, the front and flanks. At 9 a.m. a difficult drift caused considerable delay and widened the interval between the rearguard and the troops in front; and at this time the rearguard was thus disposed: the North Lancashire Company formed the rear screen, the Dublin Fusiliers supplied small flanking parties, while the Yorkshire L.I. Company and the pompoms kept about one thousand yards ahead of the rear screen, covering its advance with fire.

It was not long before the Boer pressure became overpowering, and Major Ansley gave the order to abandon the bogged wagons and fall back to a ridge in rear. In the very hard fighting which ensued, the various

MOUNTED INFANTRY.

1902.

portions of Colonel Benson's force were greatly separated; some were overcome by superior numbers and were shot down or made prisoners. Of the 3rd M.I. the heaviest loss fell upon the Yorkshire L.I. Company, the North Lancashire getting off with one man killed and one wounded. The 3rd M.I. fell back on the camp which was hurriedly entrenched and the enemy was held off until dusk, when, satisfied and exhausted by their success, the Boers came no further, and had all disappeared by the next morning.

On the 1st November a relief column came up under Colonels Barter and de Lisle, and on the 4th Benson's force fell back to the railway line at Brugspruit to refit.

Brigadier-General Alderson paraded the 3rd M.I. on the 5th and, speaking of the fight, said, " If it had not been for the 3rd M.I. the whole camp would have been taken, from what I can make out."

The rest of the year was spent by the 3rd M.I. in the Carolina district attached to a column under Colonel Colin Mackenzie, chiefly engaged in convoy work. Early in December Captain Jourdain rejoined and took over command of the Company again, and he was in command during the " drives " which were the main feature of the operations of the early months of the year 1902. On the 15th May the 3rd M.I. reached the railway at Vlakfontein, having two days before received orders not to resume the offensive in view of the peace conference then sitting at Vereeniging.

On the 18th May the 3rd M.I. was transferred to Colonel Wing's column, and marched to join it at Greylingstad; on June 1st the news of the signing of peace was received in camp; on the 3rd Private Kaywood left for England to represent the 1st Battalion at the Coronation; and on the 4th the column marched for Pretoria, where it arrived on the 9th—the strength of the Company being four officers, 75 men and 107 horses.

On the 12th August the Company left the 3rd Mounted Infantry and entrained for Mafeking, where four days later it arrived and rejoined the Battalion, the Mounted Infantry Company being then disbanded and the non-commissioned officers and men dispersed among the other companies.

CHAPTER XXIV

1902-1914

HOME SERVICE

THE OUTBREAK OF THE GREAT WAR

ON the arrival of the Battalion in England it was joined by the Band and details from the 1st Provisional Battalion * at Shorncliffe, and with these came Captain Carter, D.S.O., Lieutenants Fitzpatrick and Case.

On the 31st March, 1903, Lieut.-General Sir W. Butler, commanding the Western District, presented all ranks of the Battalion with the South African War Medals.

This year there were some very extended manœuvres in which the Battalion took part, marching from Devonport on the 13th July, and encamping at Windmill Hill Camp, on Salisbury Plain, where, with the 2nd Bn. Royal Warwickshire, 2nd Bn. Duke of Cornwall's L.I., 1st Bn. The Border Regiment and 1st Bn. King's Shropshire L.I., it formed the 12th Infantry Brigade, under the command of Colonel Lomax, in the 6th Division. The Battalion took part in Brigade, Divisional and Army Corps manœuvres and was not back in Devonport again until the 20th September.

At the beginning of the next year, the Battalion was placed under orders to proceed to Ireland, and on the 31st March, 1904, Major J. H. Ansley, Lieutenant R. Howard-Vyse and twenty non-commissioned officers and men proceeded to Kinsale to take over barracks. The remainder of the Battalion followed on the morning of the 4th April, marching to Millbay Dock and embarking there in the S.S. "Dunera." She sailed the same evening and Queenstown was reached at midday on the 5th, and from here the Battalion proceeded by train to Kinsale, on arrival there relieving the 2nd Bn. Royal Munster Fusiliers, which left for Gibraltar.

* As the War in South Africa progressed there remained in England very few units of cavalry and infantry which could have been used for home defence. It was therefore decided to form reserve squadrons and infantry details into provisional units, and, in all, eight Provisional Regiments of Cavalry and fifteen Provisional Battalions of Infantry were raised, remaining in existence until the War ended.

On the 10th May sixty men of " B " Company were sent on detachment to Fort Carlisle, Cork Harbour, under Lieutenant A. McC. Webster; and on the 6th July fifty-eight men of " C " Company went to Fort Camden under Captain W. R. Lloyd.

In the autumn of this year—on the 6th October—there was unveiled at Preston the South African War Memorial raised to the memory of all those of the Regiment who had lost their lives between 1899 and 1902. The Memorial takes the form of a granite obelisk twenty-five feet in height, and recorded on it are the names of seven Officers and one hundred and seventeen Non-commissioned Officers and Men. The Memorial was unveiled by Major-General R. G. Kekewich, C.B., and speeches were made by Colonel Satterthwaite, commanding the Regimental District, and by the Mayor of Preston, to whose safe keeping the Memorial was entrusted. The Band and Drums of the 1st Battalion attended, and the following officers of the Loyal North Lancashire Regiment were present: Colonel P. Palmes, C.B.; Majors H. F. Coleridge, D.S.O., G. W. Dowell and J. H. Ansley; Captains R. R. Feilden, C. E. A. Jourdain, D.S.O., adjutant, W. R. Lloyd, R. R. Bowlby, T. McG. Bridges and F. W. Woodward, D.S.O.; Lieutenants F. H. E. Torbett, A. McC. Webster, E. R. Fitzpatrick, R. Howard-Vyse and L. T. Allason.

On the 28th February, 1905, " A " and " D " Companies, made up to a strength of one hundred and sixty non-commissioned officers and men, left by march route for detachment duty at Spike Island, Cork Harbour, under Major G. A. Norcott and Captain W. R. Lloyd.

By the terms of Army Order No. 107 of the 1st June, 1905, the establishment of a Line Battalion on home service was fixed as under: one lieut.-colonel, three majors, six captains, eight lieutenants, four 2nd lieutenants, one adjutant, one quartermaster, one sergeant-major, one bandmaster, one quartermaster-sergeant, one colour-sergeant instructor-of-musketry, one orderly-room-sergeant, one orderly-room-clerk, one sergeant-drummer, one pioneer-sergeant, one sergeant-cook, eight colour-sergeants, twenty-four sergeants, forty corporals, sixteen drummers and 710 privates.

On the 18th November of this year the Battalion experienced a great loss in the death, after a comparatively short illness, of Quartermaster and Honorary Major H. J. Gill. This officer had enlisted in the Regiment in December, 1870, so that he had served in the 1st Battalion, The Loyal North Lancashire Regiment, as private, non-commissioned officer, warrant officer and commissioned officer for more than thirty-four years.

Major Gill was succeeded as quartermaster by Quartermaster and Honorary Lieutenant J. H. Hiland, of the Royal Garrison Regiment.

In July, 1906, the short Lee-Enfield rifle, Mark II, was issued to the Battalion.

By Army Order No. 287 of 1906, the establishment of an Infantry Battalion serving at home was fixed at twenty-four officers, thirty-nine warrant officers and sergeants, forty corporals, sixteen drummers and 680 privates.

The news had now spread that the Battalion was shortly to leave Kinsale, and the following copy of a resolution passed at a meeting of the Urban District Council of Kinsale was forwarded to the Commanding Officer :—

"That we, the Magistrates of Kinsale Petty Sessions District having heard, with regret, of the approaching change of quarters of the 1st Battalion The Loyal North Lancashire Regiment from Kinsale to the Curragh, desire to place on record our appreciation of the excellent manner in which the men of the Regiment have behaved during their stay at Kinsale.

"And we direct that a copy of this Resolution be forwarded to Lieutenant-Colonel Coleridge, D.S.O.
(sd.) " RICHARD FORDE,
" Clerk of Petty Sessions."

On the 21st November, the Battalion, at a strength of seventeen officers, three warrant officers and three hundred and seventy-four other ranks, with twenty-eight women and fifty children, left Kinsale by train for the Curragh, where the Battalion occupied Beresford Barracks in relief of the 1st Bn. The East Lancashire Regiment : it was now in the 14th Infantry Brigade under Brigadier-General A. W. Thorneycroft, of the 7th Division, commanded by Major-General Sir H. Plumer, and the other units of the 14th Brigade were the 4th Bn. Royal Fusiliers, 1st Bn. East Lancashire Regiment, and the 1st Bn. The Black Watch.

There is nothing specially important to record as happening during 1907, but the outstanding event of 1908 was when in June the Battalion was visited at the Curragh by Colonel Harris, C.M.G., V.D., of Kimberley, accompanied by Captain Humphrys, adjutant of the Kimberley Regiment, when, on behalf of the citizens of Kimberley and Beaconsfield, Colonel Harris presented both the officers' and the sergeants' messes with silver models of the "Honoured Dead Memorial" erected in Kimberley to the memory of those who fell during the siege of that town, 1899–1900.

The Battalion had now served in Ireland—at Kinsale and the Curragh —for the comparatively long period of seven years, when, in September, 1909, it was placed under orders to return to England ; and on its departure from the Curragh the following farewell order was issued by the Brigadier :—

"The 14th Infantry Brigade is about to lose the 1st Bn. The Black Watch and the 1st Bn. The Loyal North Lancashire Regiment.

"In a few weeks the Brigadier-General will have completed the four years of his command, and he therefore takes the opportunity, before the departure of the two Battalions, of expressing his high appreciation of the unswerving spirit and loyalty with which the duties assigned to them have been carried out.

"Without co-operation, no organization can become efficient, and the Brigadier-General feels that his task of command has been rendered easier and most instructive to himself by the ready response which he has had on all occasions from the distinguished Battalions which he has had the honour to command.

"In bidding them farewell, he is assured that they will render a good account of themselves wherever they may be, both in the fields of war or sport, and all ranks may be certain that he will take a deep interest in their future achievements."

On the 24th September the Battalion, strength seventeen officers and 790 other ranks, and under the command of Brevet-Colonel H. F. Coleridge, D.S.O., left the Curragh Camp from the Race Course Siding, and, played out by the bands of the 18th Hussars, the Essex and Royal Berkshire Regiments, left for North Wall, where it embarked in the S.S. "Hibernia," arriving at Holyhead the same night. From here two trains conveyed the Battalion to Tidworth, on arrival at which place in the early hours of the 25th September, it marched to Bhurtpore Barracks.

In October, 1909, a detachment of the Regiment, composed of a colour-sergeant and twenty men under Captain G. T. Body, was sent out on an experimental march with the object of testing the quantity and variety of food necessary for active service, the march being carried out under War Office instructions and medical supervision, and a battalion being made up from different units of the 7th Infantry Brigade. The march was over the uninhabited part of the Wiltshire downs, the men lived under canvas, and were only allowed those rations they would receive on active service. Dr. Haldane, the civilian doctor accompanying the troops, spoke very flatteringly of the way the work was organized and carried out, of the interest the men took in it, and of "the cheery way the men stuck to their job" in very inclement weather.

On the 20th May, 1910, the Battalion, strength nineteen officers and 632 other ranks, under command of Major R. W. Thompson, D.S.O., proceeded by special train to London to take part with the 7th Brigade in the ceremonies connected with the funeral of His late Majesty King Edward VII. The troops camped for the night in Kensington Gardens, and next day assisted to line a portion of the route along which the procession passed, returning to Tidworth at the end of the proceedings.

" During the autumn of 1910, a general election was in sight, and South Wales was disturbed by a miners' strike, which had commenced early in September. During the first week of November the question arose of sending troops to South Wales in consequence of the spread of the strike throughout the Rhondda and Aberdare valleys, and the threatening attitude of the miners. . . . The use of troops under such conditions had not been fortunate in the past, and the Government, especially in view of the approaching general election, were anxious that untoward incidents should not occur." *

It was eventually decided to send some troops, both cavalry and infantry, and on the 8th November a detachment of the Loyal North Lancashire— three officers and one hundred other ranks under the command of Captain T. McG. Bridges—left Tidworth for the coal district, and arrived at Aberaman, near Aberdare, Glamorganshire on the following day, remaining here ready to turn out at short notice. This detachment was followed on the 22nd by a second of much the same strength under Captain H. L. Helme, which was sent to Newport. The troops were, however, very rarely brought into collision with the populace, and both detachments rejoined Battalion headquarters early in January, 1911.

The following letter from Major-General C. N. F. Macready, C.B., commanding the troops in the strike area, South Wales, was received by the Commanding Officer regarding the behaviour of those employed on this the most disagreeable of all duties for soldiers :—

"While under my command they"—the troops employed—"have been models of good behaviour and cheerfulness and I know they have created a very good impression in the district."

On the 21st June, 1911, the Battalion—twenty-two officers and 560 other ranks—proceeded to London with the rest of its brigade for duties in connection with the Coronation of Their Majesties King George V and Queen Mary ; camp was again formed in Kensington Gardens, and on the 22nd and 23rd the Battalion assisted to line the streets, returning to Tidworth in the evening.

The following officers, warrant officers and private were later awarded the Coronation Medal : Lieut.-Colonel G. C. Knight, Major W. R. Lloyd, Captain and Quartermaster J. H. Hiland, Sergeant-Major A. Hills, Bandmaster G. Frayling and Private P. Molloy.

* Macready, *Annals of an Active Life*, Vol. I, p. 136.

Later on in the year there was a recrudescence of labour trouble, strikes occurring amongst the miners, dockers, railwaymen and others, and the troops had again to be called out and sent to the areas where there appeared to be any chance of outbreaks against the law. On the 22nd July the whole Battalion—531 of all ranks under the command of Lieut.-Colonel G. C. Knight—left Tidworth for Bristol in company with the 18th Hussars, both units being accommodated in Horfield Barracks. Three days later the Left-Half Battalion—279 all ranks under Major W. R. Lloyd—was sent from Bristol to Pontypridd, South Wales, whence on the following day " F " Company under command of Captain A. Burrows went on to Llwynypia in the Rhondda Valley, regarded as the area where most trouble was likely to occur. Then on the 27th the wing which had been sent in the first instance to Bristol, joined the Left Wing at Pontypridd, from where on the same day " G " Company left with Captain E. R. Fitzpatrick for Gilfach Goch, where rioting was also anticipated.

The situation temporarily became easier and on the 31st July the Headquarter Wing returned to Tidworth, and on the 14th August left again with the 7th Infantry Brigade for the ordinary summer training near Hungerford. The Brigade had, however, barely arrived, when it was ordered back again to Tidworth by reason of renewed labour unrest; the railwaymen were now joining the rest of the strikers, twelve hundred goods porters in Liverpool having struck work, while similar discontent was perceptible on almost all the other great railway systems in the country. The Headquarter Wing of The Loyal North Lancashire Regiment was now dispatched, with the 2nd Lancashire Fusiliers, by special train to Swindon, being joined there at Coate Camp by the 11th Hussars and The Gloucestershire Regiment; and in the meantime " F " Company from Llwynypia, " E " and " H " from Pontypridd and " G " from Gilfach Goch, had all been hurried off to Cardiff, while on the 21st August the Headquarter Wing left Swindon for Bristol, the Lord Mayor of which town having asked for reinforcements of troops.

The Right Wing returned to Tidworth on the 25th August, but the Left Wing did not rejoin headquarters until the middle of September.

In the meantime the G.O.C. Southern Command had caused the following Special Army Order, dated 21st August, to be circulated to the troops:—

" The Secretary of State for War has received the following gracious message from His Majesty The King for communication to the troops employed in the disturbed areas: ' I desire to express to the Officers, Non-Commissioned Officers and Men my appreciation of the manner in which they have performed a very difficult duty, and of the forbearance and self-restraint shown by all ranks.' "

Early in September it was announced in Command Order that the Battalion would move to Aldershot at the end of the month, and on the 27th it left Tidworth in two trains, and on arrival at Aldershot was accommodated in Tournay Barracks, Marlborough Lines, there joining the 2nd Infantry Brigade of the 1st Division, the latter commanded by Major-General H. S. Lomax, and the Brigade by Brigadier-General T. L. N. Morland. This was a somewhat scattered brigade, the 1st Bn. Loyal North Lancashire being the only battalion quartered in Aldershot itself, of the remaining three, two—the 2nd Bn. Yorkshire and 1st Bn. Dorsetshire Regiments—being stationed at Blackdown, while the 1st Bn. East Lancashire Regiment was at Woking.

On the 16th May, 1912, His Majesty The King presented new Colours to the 1st Bn. The Loyal North Lancashire Regiment, on which occasion the Battalion, with the 2nd Bn. Scots Guards and the 1st Bn. Dorsetshire Regiment, was drawn up in line of quarter-columns on the Queen's Parade. Their Majesties The King and Queen were received with a Royal Salute, after which the King inspected the three Battalions. The two flank battalions then wheeled inwards, forming a hollow square, the drums were piled in the centre and the new Colours were uncased and placed on the drums, the consecration service which followed being conducted by the Rt. Rev. Bishop J. Taylor-Smith, Chaplain to the Forces, assisted by the Rev. B. W. Stothert, the Rev. R. E. V. Hanson, and the Rev. T. M. Simms.

The Colour parties now took post and, taking charge of the Colours, advanced in turn to His Majesty, who, receiving the King's Colour from Major W. R. Lloyd, presented it to Lieutenant L. T. Allason, and the Regimental Colour from Major A. Burrows, handed it to Lieutenant S. T. Lucey.

His Majesty, accompanied by the Queen, now advanced to the centre of the square and made the following address to the Battalion :—

"Lieut.-Colonel Knight, Officers, Non-Commissioned Officers and Men of the 1st Battalion The Loyal North Lancashire Regiment.

"The presentation of new Colours is a memorable event in the history of a Regiment and one in which I am always glad to take part. It is especially interesting that the Colours of these three Battalions tell us that the Regiments to which they belong have been together in four identical campaigns, while two of them have seen service together on six different occasions.

"There is much to be learnt from the Colours. They are a Regiment's historical record and from them the young soldier should be taught the story of past deeds, thus handing down the glorious regimental traditions, while ever instilling into him a strong sense of duty to his King and Country.

"Though no longer carried into action the Colours are still the pivot round which the whole life of a Regiment moves. For they are a sacred symbol of its honour and prestige, to uphold which is a precious trust shared by all ranks, and whether in peace or war I feel sure that you will display the same proud strenuous effort to uphold your Colours untarnished as in those days gone by when lives were cheerfully and readily given in carrying and keeping them in the forefront of the battle; and if ever the time should come that you should be called upon to fight for your Country's cause, I know that you, and those who come after you, will add fresh lustre to the Colours which I have now entrusted to your keeping.

"You have a proud record, extending over more than a hundred and fifty years, and your Colours remind us that the Regiment has seen service in Europe, Asia, Africa and America. You first gained distinction as a battalion of Wolfe's Brigade in the attack upon Louisburg, and in the following year you served under the same General in the historic action on the Heights of Abraham.

"During the next fifty years you experienced hard though unrewarded work in North and South America; but you have inherited a noble tradition from the Peninsula, the Crimea and South Africa.

"In 'Tarifa' you have an honour which is shared by few, and in the 'Defence of Kimberley' you have another which is all your own and shared by none.

"Continue to maintain your grand traditions and strive to emulate the deeds of the past."

The new Colours now took post, and the old Colours, carried by Lieutenant G. H. Goldie and 2nd Lieutenant H. R. Loomes, were marched to the rear, the Band playing "Auld Lang Syne" and the Brigade presenting arms. The Brigade then marched past Their Majesties in column of double-companies, the old Colours, cased, following in rear, borne by Colour-Sergeants H. Herbert and H. Hatwell.

The old Colours, presented, also at Aldershot, in 1858, were laid up in Preston Parish Church.

The following order was published at the conclusion of the visit of H.M. King George V to Aldershot :—

"H.M. The King has commanded the General Officer Commanding-in-Chief to convey to all ranks of the Aldershot Command, His Majesty's appreciation of the state of the troops, and of the operations which He saw carried out. His Majesty was particularly struck by the fine military bearing and discipline of the troops, the intelligent keenness displayed by all Officers and Men, and the sound system of training obtaining in the units of the Command.

"His Majesty also expressed the pleasure which both He and The Queen felt at being again with His troops at Aldershot. His Majesty further commanded the General Officer Commanding-in-Chief to convey to all ranks serving in the Aldershot Command his satisfaction with all that he had seen, both in barracks and in the field."

In September of that year the Battalion took part in the Army Manœuvres held in the Eastern Counties; and on the 1st October, 1913, the new organization of an infantry battalion, in four, instead of as heretofore in eight companies, was introduced under Special Army Order No. 323 of the 16th September of this year.

Only once again, before the epoch-making events of 1914 commenced, was the Battalion to take part in anything of the nature of ceremonial, and this was on on the 12th May of this year, when, at a strength of twenty-nine officers and 481 non-commissioned officers and men, it proceeded to London by train and lined the streets along the Mall and Pall Mall in honour of the visit to this country of Their Majesties The King and Queen of Denmark. Within little more than two months nearly all the nations of Europe were at war.

The following is an epitome of the events which led up to the Great War: on the 28th June the heir to the throne of Austria-Hungary was murdered at Serajevo in Bosnia, and on the 23rd July, after much correspondence, the Cabinet of Vienna presented an ultimatum to the Government of Serbia. Two days later Austria declared war on Serbia, and on the 31st Russia ordered the mobilization of her forces. On the 1st August Germany declared war on Russia and on the 3rd against France, having already on the previous day presented demands to the Belgian Government which virtually amounted to a declaration of war. On the 2nd August German troops crossed the French and Polish frontiers, and on the 4th the armed forces of Germany entered Belgium; on the same day Great Britain declared war on Germany.

On the 5th and 6th August Cabinet meetings were held in London, attended by, among others, Lord Kitchener, who had just taken over the post of War Minister, and Field-Marshal Sir John French, C.-in-C. designate of our Expeditionary Force, and the following decisions were come to:

    1. That one Cavalry Division and four Infantry Divisions should at the outset be sent to France.
    2. That the force should be organized in three Army Corps.
    3. That on arrival in France the British Divisions should be concentrated in the region Le Cateau-Avesnes.

It is probable that the British Army was never before so well prepared and so ready for war on the continental scale as it was in the autumn of 1914. The South African War of 1899–1902 had shown us in a strong light all our defects of training, organization and armament : and during the years of peace which had followed its close the military authorities had gone seriously to work to remove, or repair, the more outstanding of our deficiencies. An Army Council was set up, a General Staff was organized, an Expeditionary Force was established, the Yeomanry became the second line of Cavalry, the Volunteer Force was set upon a really workmanlike footing, while the Militia, under a new name, resumed its ancient position as a draft-producing body for the Regular Army.

Military training had been brought up to date and mobilization on a large scale had frequently been practised, so that "in every respect the Expeditionary Force of 1914 was incomparably the best-trained, best-organized and best-equipped British Army that ever went forth to war. Except in the matter of co-operation between aeroplanes and artillery and the use of machine-guns, its training would stand comparison in all respects with that of the Germans. Where it fell short of our enemies was first and foremost in numbers, so that, though not ' contemptible ' it was almost negligible in comparison with continental armies even of the smaller states."*

The order for mobilization was issued from the War Office at 4.40 p.m. on the 4th August.

* Official History of the War, *France and Flanders*, Vol. I, pp. 10, 11.

CHAPTER XXV

THE 2ND BATTALION
THE LOYAL NORTH LANCASHIRE REGIMENT
1881–1914

HOME SERVICE, MALTA, THE WAR IN SOUTH AFRICA
THE WORK OF THE BATTALION MOUNTED INFANTRY, CYPRUS, CRETE, GIBRALTAR, SOUTH AFRICA, MAURITIUS AND INDIA
THE OUTBREAK OF THE GREAT WAR

ON the 4th November, 1881, the 2nd Battalion of the newly-amalgamated Regiment commenced the move from Ferozepore to Allahabad, the journey being accomplished by road as far as Ludhiana, and thence by rail in two parties, the last of these arriving at Allahabad on the 15th November; ten days later a detachment of sixty-seven non-commissioned officers and men was sent to Fort Chunar under command of Captain Farrant.

There is nothing of special importance to record during the two years that the Battalion remained in garrison at what was to prove its last station during this tour of Indian service, for it left Allahabad for Bombay on the 27th October, 1883, and, embarking in the "Euphrates" troopship, on the 10th November, arrived at Portsmouth on the 5th of the following month. On disembarking the Battalion occupied the Clarence Barracks.

The officers who landed from India with the Regiment were: Lieut.-Colonels G. B. Bevan and G. A. Wilson; Majors F. E. Lindoe, H. Walpole, N. D'E. Roberts and F. Ryley; Captains H. C. B. Farrant, B. A. Satter-thwaite, J. Davidson (adjutant), H. Crosbie and P. Palmes; Lieutenants J. R. Borrow, P. R. S. Churchward, A. C. H. Thomas, E. Davies, R. S. L. Wynell-Mayow, C. M. Brunker, G. A. Faulder, R. E. Blakey and E. G. Costobadie; Captain and Quartermaster M. Hanlon and Paymaster C. H. Hignett.

On the departure of the Battalion from Allahabad the following valedictory order was issued by Major-General Sir H. Macpherson, V.C., K.C.B., K.C.S.I., Commanding the Division:—

"The Major-General Commanding greatly regrets that circumstances prevented his being able to say farewell in person at Allahabad to Lieut.-Colonel Bevan and the 2nd Battalion Loyal North Lancashire Regiment, but he begs to assure them that he parts with the Battalion from his Command with a feeling that he is losing a well-commanded and admirably-conducted body of men. Their bearing during the period of their stay in Allahabad has been exemplary, and Sir Herbert Macpherson feels that he re-echoes the feelings of the society of Allahabad in deploring the departure of a Regiment that they had got to know so well.

"He wishes them God-speed and a happy meeting with their friends at home."

The Battalion had not been in England more than eighteen months, when it seemed possible that its services might be needed in a war against a European Power. At the end of 1884 the attitude of Russia, and the advance which, in defiance of her many peaceful protestations, Russia had made towards the Indian frontier, especially in the direction of Afghanistan, had revived mistrust in Muscovite good faith and had caused serious uneasiness to the Indian Government, by which the Amir had been guaranteed protection and assistance against foreign aggression from any quarter.

In view of nullifying the danger of collision it was arranged that Great Britain and Russia should each send a mission to effect a delimitation of the western border of Afghanistan. The British Commissioner reached the place of meeting at the appointed time, but the Russian representative delayed his coming on various pretexts, while the Russian forces in the vicinity pushed eastward, finally taking up a strong position on the Herat road, some miles beyond the limits previously occupied by Russia. The Czar's representative had not made his appearance by the middle of January, 1885, and the Russian troops continued their advance, until, on the 30th March, they came into collision with the Amir's men posted at Penjdeh on the Kushk River, defeating them with great loss and capturing guns and stores of all kinds. The British Government now made ready for war, the Premier asked for a vote of five millions, and the Army Reserve and Militia Reserve were called out, the numbers available under this demand being about 40,000 of the former and 30,000 of the latter category. In India two Army Corps, each of 25,000 men, with a reserve of 10,000, were mobilized, and reinforcements to the number of 10,000 British troops were asked for from England.

Under the operation of Special Army Circular of the 20th April, 1885, one hundred and eighty-nine Reservists of the Regiment were recalled to the Colours and joined the 2nd Battalion at Portsmouth, remaining with it until in October demobilization took place.

On the 11th September the Battalion, strength twenty officers, 464 non-commissioned officers and men, thirty-two women and forty-two children, left Portsmouth and proceeded by sea to Pembroke Dock, disembarking there on the 14th. Here the Battalion remained quartered until the 5th August, 1887, when it left for Jersey, and on arrival there was distributed as under:—

Headquarters with "B," "F" and "G" Companies to Fort Regent, "A" Company to Rezel, "D" Company to Grêve de Lecq, "C," "E" and "H" Companies to St. Peter's.

On the 22nd June, 1888, the Battalion experienced the loss of a promising young officer in Lieutenant R. E. Blakey, who was unfortunately drowned.

On the 7th January, 1890, the Battalion moved from Jersey in the troopship "Assistance" to Ireland, and, disembarking at Kingstown, proceeded by rail to Dublin; from here the headquarters were sent on to Enniskillen, being there quartered in the Main and Castle Barracks, while detachments were sent to Londonderry and Dunfanaghy; the detachment stationed at the last-named town was on more than one occasion during its stay employed on eviction duty in aid of the civil power. In August, however, this company—"E"—was withdrawn and rejoined headquarters at Enniskillen, while "B" Company proceeded on detachment to Belturbet.

In January, 1893, the Battalion was placed under orders to proceed to Mullingar, when the Commanding Officer was presented by the local authorities of Enniskillen with a resolution "expressing on behalf of the inhabitants the great regret all felt at the approaching departure of the Battalion, and testifying to the good conduct and orderly behaviour of all ranks while there quartered, which had earned for them the high opinion of all classes; and conveying to the Commanding Officer, Officers, Non-Commissioned Officers and Men of the Battalion their warm appreciation of their courteous demeanour and friendly attitude towards the inhabitants."

The Battalion—only nine officers and four hundred other ranks—left Enniskillen for Mullingar on the 2nd February, and from here furnished a detachment to Sligo. This summer the Battalion spent at the Curragh Camp, returning to Mullingar in September, and this procedure was followed during each summer that the Battalion remained in Ireland.

In the winter of 1895, however, the stay of the Battalion in Ireland was terminated, and on the 14th November—strength twenty officers and eight hundred other ranks—it left for Preston, detachments being furnished from there to Fleetwood and the Isle of Man. On the 4th May, 1897, a move was made from Preston to Aldershot, where the Battalion formed part of the 2nd Infantry Brigade, commanded by Major-General W. O. Barnard.

During the summer of this year " the Diamond Jubilee " of Her Majesty Queen Victoria was celebrated, and on the 22nd June the Battalion, at a strength of eighteen officers, two warrant officers, thirty-four sergeants, sixteen drummers and five hundred other ranks, proceeded to London, under the command of Lieut.-Colonel B. A. Satterthwaite to take part.

At the end of the year 1898 the stay of the Battalion at Aldershot came to an end, and on the 5th November it proceeded to Dover : after rather less than a year in this new station, however, orders were received that a further move would be made to Malta at an early date, and on the morning of the 20th September, 1899, the companies were railed from Dover to Southampton. Here the Battalion embarked in the S.S. " Jelunga," the embarking strength being twenty-six officers, two warrant officers and seven hundred and four non-commissioned officers and men, with thirty-three women and thirty-three children. The officers who left England with the Battalion were : Lieut.-Colonel B. A. Satterthwaite ; Majors J. Davidson, P. Palmes and A. C. H. Thomas ; Captains G. A. Norcott, R. S. L. Wynell-Mayow, G. W. Dowell, G. A. Faulder, and J. E. Pine-Coffin ; Lieutenants E. S. Smith, F. J. Braithwaite, A. Burrows, T. McG. Bridges, C. J. Newton and E. C. Halton ; 2nd Lieutenants J. G. Fairlie, F. H. E. Torbett, G. T. Body, F. W. Greenhill, H. F. B. Ryley and J. S. F. Chamberlain ; Captain and Adjutant W. R. Lloyd and Lieutenant and Quartermaster W. Bentley.

On disembarking at Malta the Battalion was stationed at Pembroke Camp.

By this time the War in South Africa had broken out and many arrangements of a more or less novel and temporary character had to be made to meet the various calls upon the Army in general, and upon individual corps and regiments in particular.

At home a Provisional Battalion of the Regiment was formed with its headquarters at Shorncliffe, and this was composed at the outset of 120 non-commissioned officers and men under Captains J. H. Ansley and F. C. L. Logan. No sooner had war been declared against the Dutch Republics than General Sir Francis Grenfell, Governor and Commander-in-Chief in Malta, who, in his early days, had seen much service in South Africa, was convinced that every available mounted man would be needed in that country, and he suggested to the War Office that he should be authorized to start a training school for Mounted Infantry in the Island. The necessary sanction was accorded, and towards the end of December, 1899, the Mounted Infantry School was there formed.

This seems an appropriate place to break off the general narrative of the service of the 2nd Battalion of the Regiment, and to give some account of the work of the Mounted Infantry Company and sections during the War in South Africa, in the years 1899–1902, while the Battalion remained on in Malta, providing drafts of seasoned soldiers to reinforce the 1st Battalion, and trained mounted infantry men to keep up the companies sent to South Africa.

About the middle of February, 1900, orders were received for No. 1 Malta M.I. Company to sail in the " Pavonia," and this left Malta on the 20th, the Company being under the command of Captain J. E. Pine-Coffin of the Battalion, while its sections were made up as under :—

One and a half sections of the Battalion under Captain J. E. Pine-Coffin and Lieutenant F. J. Braithwaite.

One section of the Royal Warwickshire Regiment under Lieutenant C. G. M. Blomfield.

One section of the Lancashire Fusiliers under Lieutenant W. J. Woodcock.

Half a section of the 2nd Bn. The Sherwood Foresters under Lieutenant H. K. Attfield.

The total strength of the Company was fifty-six men.

Cape Town was reached on the 20th March and the Company received orders to proceed by rail to Aliwal North and join the Colonial Division there being formed under Brigadier-General Brabant ; the move was made at the end of a week, spent in issuing clothing and saddlery. The name—" Malta Mounted Infantry "—appears to have given rise to an impression that the personnel of Captain Pine-Coffin's command was wholly composed of Maltese, so much so that on the Company joining General Brabant's Division, that officer expressed his regret that the only languages he could speak with any fluency were English and Dutch !

On the 14th April the M.I. Company marched off from Aliwal North with the Colonial Division to effect the relief of Wepener, at that time strenuously besieged by a strong Boer force under De Wet. Zastron was reached on the 15th and the column then moved on to Rouxville, where it was joined by a force under Major-General Hart, the two combined now numbering rather over four thousand rifles. Advancing again on the 19th there was considerable fighting on the 22nd at Bushman's Kop, where a Boer force had been placed in the hope of delaying the advance of the relieving column ; but after a certain amount of skirmishing, in which the enemy was manœuvred out of his positions by wide turning movements, combined with direct attacks covered by artillery fire, Wepener was reached on the afternoon of the 25th, De Wet having retreated northwards that morning. In these operations one man of the Company was wounded.

Captain Pine-Coffin's Company now joined General Hart's brigade and moved on Smithfield, the garrison of which place at once surrendered, and the troops then marched on to Bethulie, which was reached on the 5th May and from here the M.I. Company was sent by train to Bloemfontein. Here fresh remounts were drawn, and, after a two-days' rest, the Company was attached to a column proceeding to join the main army under Lord Roberts, and at Zand River, where it arrived on the 19th, a position was held for some time and the Company had several skirmishes with the enemy, especially later on, about Senekal and Winburg and north of Kroonstad in the Orange River Colony. Then again, south of Kroonstad, the Boers had held up a train, and on arrival at the scene the Company came into action against the enemy rearguard, inflicting considerable loss upon it and taking many surrenders. To the O.C. column Lord Roberts telegraphed: " Please convey to Captain Pine-Coffin my thanks for his very well-managed affair ; also to the men under his command."

The Company was now broken up into sections and dispersed along the line of railway, headquarters with one section being at Ventersburg Road and the Battalion portion of the Company being at Rietspruit ; on this duty the Company remained for the best part of six months.

It was not until the 14th October that the Company had any further serious engagement. It was then that on the receipt of information that a force of some one hundred Boers was holding a kopje, at a place called Cyphergat, near the railway line south of Kroonstad, that the Company was ordered out and successfully engaged the enemy, taking several prisoners. The M.I. body, some one hundred and fifty strong with a pompom and a Maxim, was then retiring to Ventersburg Road, when the enemy was seen coming on from both flanks in superior numbers, and the Company suffered several casualties, Lieutenant Attfield and four men being killed and several wounded. For their services Lance-Sergeant Gowan, Corporal Peacock and Private Daw were brought to notice, receiving the D.C.M.

In January, 1901, the Mounted Infantry was reorganized, and a section, which had come out under Lieutenant E. C. Halton, from the Battalion with the 2nd Malta M.I. Company, was amalgamated with No. 1 Company, which now formed part of the 9th Battalion M.I. under Captain Pine-Coffin. By the end of March the 9th Battalion was fitted with transport and was employed for some days in clearing the country about Ventersburg Road. At first there was a good deal of opposition, but this gradually decreased. In June larger operations were undertaken, and in July Captain

Pine-Coffin's Column, to which other troops had been assigned, made the largest " bag " of any of the columns engaged in similar work. In August this Column took part in a sweeping movement on a very large scale from Kimberley along the Vaal to Vereenigen, thence to the Modder River and back again to Kimberley; large quantities of wagons and supplies were captured, though but few prisoners were taken.

The Column, and the Battalion M.I. Company with it, was later returned to the Kroonstad district, where, except for a very few brief periods, it remained until the end of the War, doing much night marching and covering a great extent of country. Towards the end of 1901 Captain Pine-Coffin was invalided home, and the 9th M.I. was sent south of the Vaal River to help a small column which was in difficulties; later it was dispatched to cover the building of the Bothaville and Lindley lines of blockhouses, and met with a good deal of opposition. Finally it took part in the last of the De Wet hunts, when it marched for over forty-eight hours on a half-day's supplies; on one occasion the Company claimed to have marched one hundred and ten miles in twenty-four hours.

In August, 1902, the 9th Mounted Infantry was brought into Bloemfontein and broken up, officers and men returning to the battalions of their respective regiments then serving in South Africa.

The following officers of the 2nd Battalion The Loyal North Lancashire Regiment also served with M.I. Companies in the Boer War: Captain G. W. Dowell, Lieutenants G. T. Body, T. McG. Bridges, F. H. E. Torbett, H. P. Magill, G. R. Trefusis, and A. W. Colley, and 2nd Lieutenant H. L. Helme.

We now return to the doings of the Service Companies at Malta.

On the 13th September, 1900, a detachment, one hundred strong, of " C " and " G " Companies, was sent to the Island of Cyprus, in relief of a company of the 3rd Battalion Lancashire Fusiliers, Major G. A. Norcott being in command and accompanied by Lieutenant G. T. Body and 2nd Lieutenant H. F. B. Ryley. Six months later—on the 22nd February—headquarters and the remaining six companies, strength fifteen officers and 542 non-commissioned officers and men, left Malta for Candia in Crete, arriving there on the 27th. There being no accommodation in Candia for married families, these were sent to England, while a detachment remained in Malta under the command of Lieutenant F. W. Greenhill.

On the departure of the Battalion from Malta the following General Order was published:—

" His Excellency the Commander-in-Chief cannot allow the 2nd Loyal

North Lancashire Regiment to leave Malta for service in Crete without placing on record the steady conduct and soldierlike bearing of the Battalion on all occasions.

"His Excellency has noticed the great interest taken by all officers and men in the tactical field days."

The Battalion remained in the Islands of Crete and Cyprus until the 7th May, 1902, when it moved to Gibraltar, and was present on parade when, in April, 1903, His Majesty The King landed at the fortress and saw all the troops on parade : His Majesty graciously informed the Commanding Officer of the Battalion that "He was much pleased with the fine appearance the Battalion presented on parade on Saturday the 11th April, 1903."

On the 11th April, 1904, the Battalion made another and a very much longer move, leaving on that day for Cape Town en route to Pretoria, moving at a strength of twenty-four officers and 966 other ranks, with thirty-one wives and sixty children ; Cape Town was reached on the 29th April and by the 3rd May the whole had settled down in the barracks on Roberts' Heights. Shortly after arrival "C" Company—five officers and 147 other ranks—was sent to Ladybrand to form the M.I. Company of the Battalion, joining there the 2nd M.I. Regiment ; the officers with the Company were Captain H. A. Robinson, Lieutenant J. F. Allen, 2nd Lieutenants R. E. Crane, R. H. Logan and J. P. D. Underwood.

Under Special Army Order dated the 12th May, 1905, the establishment of the Battalion was now to stand at twenty-eight officers, two warrant officers, forty-six staff sergeants and sergeants, sixteen drummers, forty corporals and 726 privates.

On the 4th October, 1906, the Battalion moved by rail from Pretoria to Standerton, and about a year later—on the 19th October, 1907—it embarked at Durban for conveyance to Mauritius, the embarking strength being twenty officers, two warrant officers and 623 non-commissioned officers and men, with thirty-seven wives and seventy-nine children. Port Louis was reached on the 25th of the month, when the Battalion was sent on by rail to Vacois, where it was to be quartered.

The stay of the 2nd Battalion The North Lancashire Regiment in the Island of Mauritius was a comparatively uneventful one until the year 1909, when it was presented with new Colours by H.E. Sir C. Boyle, Governor and Commander-in-Chief. On this occasion the Battalion was formed up on the Polo Ground and the consecration ceremony was carried out by the Right Reverend the Bishop of Mauritius, at the conclusion of which the Governor addressed the officers and men.

The Battalion was now to move further east, and on the 29th November of this year it embarked in the R.I.M.S. "Dufferin" for conveyance to Bombay, on arrival here going on by rail to Poona, where all were settled by the middle of December. The Battalion was somewhat weak in numbers on reaching India, only fourteen officers and 669 other ranks disembarking; for during its stay in Mauritius there had been much sickness, and 173 non-commissioned officers and men had died or been invalided.

During four and a half months of the year 1910—1st May to 31st July and 15th September to 31st October—the Battalion furnished a detachment of six officers and 368 non-commissioned officers and men at Kirkee to supply guards over the arsenal at that place.

In the year following, Their Majesties The King and Queen paid a visit to India, and the Battalion moved into Bombay on Royal escort duty on the 15th November, 1911, returning to Poona on the 13th January, 1912. On the 3rd December the Battalion furnished a guard-of-honour of one hundred rank and file with the King's Colour, under the command of Captain R. E. Berkeley; this was mounted at the Apollo Bunder on the landing of Their Majesties from H.M.S. "Medina." His Majesty inspected the guard and congratulated Captain Berkeley on its smart appearance: later he presented signed portraits of himself and Her Majesty The Queen to Lieut.-Colonel J. H. Ansley, expressing a wish that they should be hung in the Officers' Mess.

The following officers and other ranks of the Battalion were awarded Durbar Medals in connection with the above duties: Major C. E. A. Jourdain, D.S.O., Captains R. E. Berkeley and J. F. Allen, Lieutenant and Adjutant C. V. M. Bell, Lieutenant and Quartermaster E. C. Mudge, No. 3461, Sergeant Drummer J. Brunnen, No. 5019, Colour-Sergeant M. Hampson, No. 3792, Sergeant E. McGarry and No. 5745, Private J. Bellingham.

On the 10th November, 1913, the Battalion left Poona for Belgaum under the command of Major C. E. A. Jourdain—strength fourteen officers and 791 other ranks, and arrived at this station on the 29th; two days later it went on by train to Bangalore and on arrival was accommodated in Baird Barracks, and it was still here when in the summer of 1914 the Great War broke out.

On receipt of the orders for mobilization, those officers who were on leave in India were instantly recalled by telegram, each man was medically examined, the horses and mules underwent a searching veterinary inspection, clothing and boots were fitted, arms, equipment and ammunition were drawn, and all the necessary stores required for active service in the field were issued. Thanks to the completeness with which the various relative orders and documents had been kept and prepared the work proceeded with the utmost smoothness throughout, and the Battalion was ready and awaiting marching orders well within the allotted time.

The Quarterly Indian Army List for October, 1914, shows the distribution of the officers of the 2nd Battalion The North Lancashire Regiment on that date: Lieut.-Colonel C. E. A. Jourdain, D.S.O., in command; Majors W. D. Sanderson, H. A. Robinson, F. J. Braithwaite and T. McG. Bridges; Captains E. C. Halton, R. E. Berkeley, R. B. Flint, J. G. Fairlie (Depot), H. F. B. Ryley (Depot), G. R. Trefusis and R. G. Stokes; Lieutenants R. H. Logan, C. V. M. Bell (adjutant), D. P. J. Collas, C. J. de V. l'Anson, F. G. Wynne (Depot), P. A. Edwards, G. P. Atkinson, J. F. B. Watson, W. H. Anderson and C. G. Dickson; 2nd Lieutenants S. V. Einem-Hickson, B. H. Withers, R. L. C. Keays, M. E. Leeb, G. G. R. Williams and G. C. Kingsley (not joined); Hon. Lieutenant and Quartermaster R. L. Rowley.

CHAPTER XXVI

THE 3RD BATTALION
THE LOYAL NORTH LANCASHIRE REGIMENT
1881–1914
THE MILITIA
HOME SERVICE, MALTA, SOUTH AFRICA
THE SPECIAL RESERVE

THE two battalions composing the 3rd and 4th Battalions of the Regiment continued to follow the usual routine of trainings and inspections during the years that immediately followed upon their definite inclusion in the Regiment.

On the 7th April, 1882, the Martini-Henry rifle was served out, replacing the old Snider, and on the 16th November, 1887, the new valise equipment was issued.

On the 11th July, 1892, the death occurred of Lord Winmarleigh, who had been connected with the Regiment for over sixty-seven years, had commanded it from 1842 to 1872, and had been Honorary Colonel from the latter date until his death. He was succeeded as Honorary Colonel by Colonel T. R. Crosse.

During the drill season of 1893 the 16th Militia Brigade was assembled for training as a complete unit, for the first time, under the new mobilization scheme, when the following were called out: the 3rd and 4th Bns. The Royal Lancaster Regiment, the 3rd and 4th Bns. The Lancashire Fusiliers, the 3rd Bn. The East Lancashire Regiment, and the 3rd and 4th Bns. The Loyal North Lancashire Regiment, the whole under the command of Colonel F. G. Berkeley, commanding 47th Regimental District.

In April and June, 1894, the Martini-Henry rifles on charge of the two battalions were withdrawn into store and the Lee-Metford (magazine) rifle was issued in their place.

For some years prior to 1896 the reports of the Inspecting General Officers had remarked on the low strength of the two battalions, which were nearly always below establishment, though both appear to have regularly sent a considerable number of men to the Regular Army. The difficulty experienced in the maintenance of the authorized establishment

FIELD-MARSHAL EARL ROBERTS,
V.C., K.G., K.P., G.C.B., O.M., G.C.S.I. G.C.I.E., V.D.

Honorary Colonel, 3rd Battalion.
1898–1914.

was, no doubt, responsible for the decision come to in February, 1896, for the amalgamation of the two six-company battalions into one battalion of ten companies, a change which came into effect on the 1st April of that year, when the 3rd and 4th Battalions The Loyal North Lancashire Regiment were designated the 3rd Battalion.

The establishment was now to be one lieut.-colonel, two majors, ten captains, ten lieutenants, five 2nd lieutenants, one adjutant, one quartermaster, three warrant-officers, forty-one sergeants, forty corporals, ten drummers and one thousand privates.

The following officers were on the strength of the Battalion on the date when the new regulation came into force : Hon. Colonel, Colonel T. R. Crosse ; Lieut.-Colonel T. M. Sandys ; Majors L. Bonhote and J. H. W. Pedder ; Captains A. E. Da Costa, T. Cowper, R. G. Chambres, W. Harrison, P. Ormrod, S. Bibbins Allen, P. W. Harrison and H. A. P. Soppitt ; Lieutenants A. H. Turner, C. H. Orpen, W. C. Salmon, P. Strahan, D. C. Percy-Smith and H. V. Lockwood ; 2nd Lieutenants E. G. Case, W. G. P. Miller, T. Edwards-Moss, A. G. Cowan and B. R. Lambert ; Captain and Adjutant H. G. Leonard and Captain and Quartermaster J. A. Furlong.

In the following year—1897—was celebrated the Centenary of the raising of the Regiment, and this happily coincided with the celebration of the Diamond Jubilee of Her Majesty Queen Victoria.

On the 1st January, 1898, the Battalion was singularly honoured by the appointment of Field-Marshal Lord Roberts, V.C., K.P., G.C.B., G.C.S.I., G.C.I.E., to the Honorary Colonelcy.

In an earlier chapter of this History a full account has been given of the circumstances under which war broke out in South Africa in the autumn of 1899, and of the effect which the opening of hostilities with the Dutch Republics had upon the regiments of the Regular Army, and upon the non-commissioned officers and men of the Regular and Militia Reserve.

" The Royal Proclamation, authorizing the embodiment of the Militia, was dated October 26, 1899 ; the first order issued in pursuance of this proclamation was dated November 3rd, and ordered the embodiment of thirty-five battalions and five companies of the Militia Medical Staff Corps. The latter were embodied at once, but before the infantry were embodied the Nicholson's Nek disaster had occurred and three more battalions were added. These thirty-eight battalions were called out between December 4th and 13th. Eight more battalions were embodied on the departure of the 5th and 6th Divisions respectively, the first coming out in the middle of December, and the last in the beginning of January, 1900. After this, units had not only to be embodied to take the place of line units as they left the Country, but also to replace Militia units as they embarked.

One regiment of artillery and twenty battalions of infantry were called out between the end of January and the beginning of March, and the whole of the remainder of the Militia was embodied during the first half of May." *

The 3rd Battalion was embodied at Preston on the 13th December, 1899, at a strength of twenty-nine officers and 892 non-commissioned officers and men, and on the same day proceeded by wings to Shorncliffe and Lydd. Previous to embodiment the Battalion had been afforded by the Secretary of State for War the opportunity of volunteering for service in the Mediterranean, in relief of the regular garrison of those stations; the response had been especially gratifying, and drew a letter of warm approval from Lord Roberts, of which the following is an extract: " The Battalion has responded so well to the call for foreign service; it is most patriotic of all officers, non-commissioned officers and men, and I am very proud of being the Honorary Colonel of a Battalion the members of which take such a sensible and patriotic view of what the Militia ought to do when a great war is going on."

Agreeably to this response, the Battalion was now ordered to Malta, and on the 12th January, 1900, it embarked in the " Maritana," the strength being twenty-eight officers and 888 other ranks; on arrival at Malta on the 27th it landed and was quartered in Fort Manoel. The following were the officers who accompanied the Battalion on this its second tour of foreign service: Lieut.-Colonel L. Bonhote; Majors J. H. W. Pedder and T. Cowper; Captains A. E. Da Costa, R. G. Chambres, W. Harrison, P. W. Harrison, H. A. P. Soppitt, W. G. P. Miller, T. Edwards-Moss and C. E. Earle; Lieutenants E. P. Ormrod, C. B. Wallis, J. E. Massy, J. F. Allen and H. M. Dillon; 2nd Lieutenants H. A. B. Salmond, J. A. G. Marshall, A. de M. Bellairs, P. F. Gell, H. G. Stafford, J. C. Wilson, W. B. Anderson, W. Leslie, P. M. Brooke-Hitching and G. Pilcher; Captain and Adjutant R. L. Stable and Lieutenant and Quartermaster J. Kelly.

On the 17th May a draft of sixty-five recruits joined the Battalion from Preston, and on the 26th July the whole of the officers and nine hundred of the other ranks offered to serve in China in relief of regular troops, drawing a fine tribute from H.E. the Governor of Malta and a letter of thanks from the Secretary of State for War.

During August and September Captain J. G. W. Tetley, 2nd Lieutenants D. R. H. Jackson and J. S. Gaskell and ninety-seven men joined from home.

At last the Battalion's many offers of service were accepted, for on the 2nd March, 1901, it embarked for South Africa in the S.S. " Formosa," the embarking strength being eighteen officers and 805 other ranks; the officers were Majors J. H. W. Pedder, in command, and T. Cowper; Cap-

* "*Times*" *History of the War in South Africa*, Vol. VI, pp. 263, 264.

tains A. E. Da Costa, R. G. Chambres, H. A. P. Soppitt, W. G. P. Miller, C. E. Earle and C. P. Wallis; Lieutenants E. P. Ormrod, A. de M. Bellairs, W. B. Anderson, J. C. Wilson and G. Pilcher; 2nd Lieutenants J. S. Gaskell, D. R. H. Jackson, G. N. Mackie; Captain and Adjutant R. L. Stable and Lieutenant and Quartermaster J. Kelly. Lieutenant J. A. G. Marshall had already left for South Africa in January with fifty men to join Mounted Infantry in that country; Captain W. Harrison and Lieutenant H. Stafford joined the Battalion later; and the following officers who were posted at a subsequent date joined in South Africa: 2nd Lieutenants R. E. Crane, J. McG. Greig, G. C. Morris, W. L. Kerans, N. C. Phillips, H. D. MacCall, S. W. Price, C. Fletcher and S. E. Armitage.

On the departure from Malta of the Battalion the following farewell order was issued by the Governor and Commander-in-Chief:—

"The Commander-in-Chief in bidding good-bye to the 3rd Loyal North Lancashire Regiment desires to express his entire satisfaction at the result of the inspection he made yesterday. Associated as the Commander-in-Chief has been with Militia in the past, among the many militia battalions he has inspected, he has never seen a finer or more efficient battalion than the 3rd Loyal North Lancashire Regiment.

"The Battalion while at Malta has been conspicuous for good conduct and soldierlike behaviour, and the Commander-in-Chief has particularly noted the interest taken by officers and men in the tactical field days. Although the training of the soldier is a difficult task in Malta owing to the restricted manœuvring area, still he feels sure that the lessons learnt here in peace-time will be useful to officers and men when on active service.

"The patriotic spirit shown by the fact that every man of the Battalion volunteered to serve his King and Country in South Africa is worthy of all praise, and will be ever remembered in the history of the Regiment.

"While regretting that Colonel Bonhote is not able to lead in the field the Battalion which he has so ably commanded in quarters, the Commander-in-Chief has full confidence that under the command of Major Pedder the high reputation of the Loyal North Lancashire Regiment will be kept up and enhanced by this Battalion, and in this full assurance he wishes the Battalion good-bye."

The Battalion landed in South Africa on the 30th March, 1901, and the headquarters were stationed at Port Elizabeth, while three companies were at once sent on detachment—"A" Company to Barkley Bridge, "F" to Cradock and "K" to Aberdeen; and the following is an epitome of the services of the Battalion during the something less than twelve months which it remained in South Africa.

The Battalion was almost wholly employed on the lines-of-communication and furnished many detachments to places in the neighbourhood of and also at considerable distances from Port Elizabeth ; but owing to the nature of the operations to which the army in South Africa was committed at this stage of the war, it had but few opportunities of active service against the enemy in the field.

The following is, however, an account of operations in which part of the Battalion was engaged : On one occasion a patrol under command of Lieut.-Colonel Salmond, commandant of Stormberg, composed of Major Cowper, Lieutenant Mackie and seventeen M.I. of the Battalion detachment, rode twenty-five miles and bivouacked on the nek north-east of Tafel Kop, with the object of surprising any enemy patrol which might attempt to come through. About 4.30 in the morning of the following day four mounted men of the enemy rode towards the pass, then turning and riding back ; but these were fired on and one man was wounded and captured. While bringing in the wounded man the Boers opened fire from a hill on the north-east side of the pass, and a strong body of the enemy then appeared and, gradually working round the left flank, cut off the only line of retreat for Major Cowper's party. Some of the M.I. rode by singly, but one man of the Battalion was killed and two were wounded. The enemy, continuing to advance, gradually seized a hill commanding the position occupied by the British party and Colonel Salmond ordered the retirement. The party became broken up, and Major Cowper, Lieutenant Mackie and three men were captured by the enemy.

All the party of the Battalion behaved with exceptional coolness, and Lieutenant Mackie won especial praise for the way he handled his men and for his efforts to bring away one of the wounded.

On the 8th February, 1902, the Battalion was ordered to concentrate at Port Elizabeth in view of embarking for England, and, sailing in the S.S. "Gaika," reached Southampton on the 14th March, proceeding at once to Preston, where on the following day it was disembodied.

For its services during the years 1899–1902 the Battalion was granted the Honours "Mediterranean 1900–1901" and "South Africa, 1901–1902"; it lost during the war three non-commissioned officers and men, and Lieut.-Colonel J. H. W. Pedder, Captain and Adjutant R. L. Stable and Sergeant-Major R. Rowley were mentioned in despatches.

The Special Reserve

There is nothing of special importance to be chronicled during the six years immediately following upon the return of the Battalion from South Africa. At the end of the year 1907 a very drastic change was effected, whereby, under an Army Order dated the 23rd December of that year, the whole of the Militia was converted into the Special Reserve, the conversion to date from the day following the completion of the annual training of 1908.

The following is a general outline of the conditions of this Army Order:
"The provision of a Third Battalion to each pair of Regular Battalions of the Line was intended to form an integral portion of the Cardwell system. In every war which has occurred since that time the want of a Reserve Battalion was felt in proportion to the magnitude of the operations, and arrangements, such as provisional battalions, had to be improvised on such occasions; but no such temporary arrangement could fulfil the heavy and important functions which devolved on these battalions on mobilization or other times of stress.

"To meet this want, to each pair of Regular Battalions of a Regiment a Reserve Battalion, composed of special reservists, was now to be added. Besides these Third Battalions there were also to be twenty-seven (extra) Reserve Battalions, also composed of special reservists. Reserve Battalions were to be known by a number and the name of certain Regiments of the Line to which they were to be affiliated.

"Then—of the one hundred and twenty-four infantry Militia Battalions on the existing establishment, seventy-four will become Reserve Battalions to the sixty-nine infantry regiments (148 battalions), and twenty-seven will become extra Reserve Battalions, while twenty-three remaining Militia Battalions, of which fifteen were localized in Great Britain and eight in Ireland, will be disbanded.

"These Reserve Battalions, organized in eight companies, will be trained annually as battalions under their own officers.

"On mobilization being ordered the Reserve Battalions will move into vacant infantry barracks, the depots continuing to receive all recruits, clothing them and then sending them on to the Reserve Battalions to be trained. The Reserve Battalions—other than the twenty-seven extra Reserve Battalions—will take over the immature and unfit from the Line Battalions, and provide trained drafts to replace casualties. Later on, as men sent home wounded or invalided become fit for home service, they will be received into these Reserve Battalions.

"The establishment of Regular officers and non-commissioned officers in the Third Reserve Battalions is fixed on a scale which will allow of their being used as training centres for the officers and non-commissioned officers of the Territorial Force; thus they will become in the fullest sense training battalions. The periods of training for infantry battalions are—recruits, six months' drill on enlistment; trained men, fifteen days' training and six days' musketry. All men joining the Special Reserve become Army reservists, and therefore subject to the same conditions of service and liabilities, including discipline, under the Army Act as Regular reservists. When called out for training or on mobilization they become in all respects soldiers of the Regular Army."

The reasons which led to the Militia being converted into a Special Reserve are of historic interest, and are only vaguely hinted at in the Army Order referred to above. As mentioned in that order, the provision of a draft-finding battalion for each pair of Regular Battalions was a cardinal feature of the Report of the Localization Committee of 1875 of which Major-General Sir Garnet Wolseley was a member. The bulk of the Militia Battalions were designated for this purpose, as became evident by the changes promulgated in 1881. The institution of a Militia Reserve also formed part of the scheme. This Reserve consisted of a considerable proportion of the N.C.O.s and older militiamen who accepted an annual bounty and so became liable to be drafted into the Line in the event of mobilization.

During the South African War, in its earlier stages, the Militia Reserve was largely drawn on to complete drafts for the Regular Battalions at the front, and many Militia Battalions were then "bled white," to use the expressive phrase of representative Militia officers. Later these same battalions were asked to volunteer for service in South Africa which, to their credit, they readily consented to do.

When the war was over, those who spoke for the Militia service made strong representations to the Government regarding the unfairness of this dual duty of draft-finding and acting as Service Battalions, and it was then decided to relieve the Militia of finding drafts, thus enabling them to make themselves efficient as combatant units, which was their ambition.

So matters stood when Mr. Haldane became the Secretary of State for War and, after due consideration, he decided to organize the Home Army in two lines, an Expeditionary Force, with draft-producing machinery, in the first line and a Territorial Force in the second. It at once became apparent that there was no room, or money, for an independent Militia force, and the alternative to be faced was whether the old Constitutional Force should resume draft-finding as its normal rôle or should become the foundation on which the Territorial Force should be built. Those who spoke for the Militia resolutely rejected both alternatives, and accordingly the Government was left to decide the matter. The final decision was come to at Lord Derby's seat in Lancashire, where a large gathering of Militia commanding officers unanimously agreed that the Militia with its old ideas of independence must be sacrificed for the public good and new draft-finding machinery substituted for it. Thus the Special Reserve came into being and nobly it played its part throughout the Great War, as will be seen later.

Every officer on the strength of the 3rd Battalion elected to serve in the Special Reserve under the above-quoted conditions, while as regards the "other ranks," out of 595 who attended the training, 405 elected to join the Special Reserve, 85 to remain on as militiamen, while 105 took their discharge.

On the 23rd May, 1914, the Battalion assembled for the usual annual training and proceeded to Conway where this was carried out, returning to Preston on the 18th June. Within a very few days the events which led to the outbreak of the Great War had taken place, and on the 4th August orders were received for mobilization.

At the time of the declaration of war, the undermentioned, as stated in the Army List, of August 1914, were the Officers of the 3rd, Special Reserve, Battalion :—

Hon. Colonel : Field-Marshal Earl Roberts. Lieut.-Colonel : T. Cowper-Essex. Majors : P. W. Harrison, R. R. Bowlby. Captains : A. H. W. Saunders-Knox-Gore, J. G. Fairlie, H. F. B. Ryley, E. C. Miller, M. C. C. Harrison, F. W. Greenhill, R. E. Crane, G. W. Hay, G. Loch. Lieutenants : S. T. Lucey, J. H. Miller, F. G. Wynne, R. C. Mason, J. G. W. Hyndson. Adjutant : Captain F. H. E. Torbett. Quartermaster : Lieutenant E. C. Mudge.

CHAPTER XXVII *

THE 4TH BATTALION
THE LOYAL NORTH LANCASHIRE REGIMENT

1746–1815, 1859–1914

THERE were volunteers, of a military kind, stationed at, or belonging to, Preston, in 1746. Probably, they were raised at the time of the Rebellion, in 1745, for protective purposes, or immediately after the rebels had left the town, in their retreat northward, by way of precaution against future contingencies of a threatening character. In 1746 a notice, of which the following is a copy, was issued :—" Preston, 10th April, 1746. This is to inform the public, that Tuesday, the 15th day of April, being his Royal Highness the Duke of Cumberland's birthday, the morning is to be usher'd in with ringing of bells, and in the afternoon the Mayor, Aldermen, Common Council, and Gentlemen of the Corporation, together with several Companies displaying their respective Colours, attended by the Gentlemen Volunteers, will walk the streets ; after the Procession, the Volunteers are to be drawn up in the Market-place, before a grand bonfire, in order to receive information against the Elcobites, Perthites, Kilmarnockites, Jacobites, and all other rebellious persons, against the present government : such as are convicted are to be burnt, in order to make a final end of them ; so that we and our posterity may live in true felicity for ever. ' God Save King George. Amen.' " This is the earliest reference to " Volunteers " at Preston of which there is any record.

At the end of the eighteenth century the imperialistic tendencies of the French Government, especially after Napoleon's rise to power, caused grave anxiety in these islands. Measures of defence were quickly inaugurated. Lancashire, on whose western coast a " landing " was apprehended, roused herself to a vigorous attitude of defence. Preston, as one of the principal towns in the shire, was in the fore rank of preparation.

In March, 1797, a meeting of the inhabitants was held in the Town Hall for the purpose of increasing the armed forces of the kingdom, with the immediate result that a body of one hundred and ten men was raised to serve as the Royal Preston Volunteers ; the gentlemen nominated for

* Much of the information in this chapter is taken from Hewitson's *History of Preston*.

commissions were Nicholas Grimshaw, Captain George Bolton, Captain Joseph Seaton Aspden, William Cross, Francis Chadwick, and Richard Pedder, Lieutenants.

The force was divided into two companies—a Grenadier and a Light Infantry. The uniform of the Grenadiers was to be a scarlet coat with blue facings, and lined with white shalloon, but the turned laps with white kersemere: a blue wing edged with a little gold fringe on each shoulder, and a yellow button with the letters R.P.V. embossed thereon: white kersemere waistcoat single-breasted, light mixed pantaloons edged in the seams with scarlet and black cloth gaiters: a black velvet stock: a smart cocked hat with a black cockade and black feather. The uniform of the other company was a scarlet jacket with blue facings: the wings as also the waistcoat, pantaloons, gaiters and stock, the same as the other company: the hat round, small in the rim, and turned up on the left side, with a handsome black cockade and green feather.

In the June following rules and regulations were agreed to; some of these are interesting as showing the kind of discipline which was enforced, as for example: "When the line is formed and the word 'attention' given the persons in the ranks are to stand steady without speaking or laughing until the command 'stand-at-ease,' under the penalty of sixpence."

"Every officer, non-commissioned officer, or private, appearing upon parade or in the field in liquor, shall forfeit for each offence, if an officer ten shillings, if a non-commissioned officer or private five shillings."

"All fines be collected by the non-commissioned officers of each company immediately if the defaulters are present."

"Each officer to pay one shilling and each private threepence weekly ... for the wages of the band of music belonging to the Corps."

The force was managed by a committee of the townsmen, on which only two were members of the Corps.

To this committee Captain Grimshaw reported that Robert Nickson seldom attended drill and wished to resign, upon which it was resolved that unless he paid a fine of ten guineas the committee would order a court-martial to be held.

Mrs. Nabb and Miss Shawe were requested to collect subscriptions for a pair of Colours, which were duly purchased and presented.

It is recorded, in the proceedings of the Corporation of Preston, under date April 20th, 1797, "that the inhabitants of the town and neighbourhood of Preston having entered into an association and subscription, with the approbation of the King, for raising a Volunteer Corps of Infantry, for the internal defence of the town of Preston and the neighbourhood for five miles circumjacent, and to extend their services to the North-West

Military District, in case of actual invasion or imminent danger thereof, it is agreed and ordered that the sum of £50 be subscribed by Mr. Mayor on account of this Corporation towards defraying the expense of the said Corps": and the treasurer was ordered to "pay the same out of the Corporation funds in the same proportion as other subscriptions are paid for the like purpose." This Corps was the "Royal Preston Volunteers," and Nicholas Grimshaw, Esq.,* had command of it. In the same year a rival Corps, called the "Loyal Preston Volunteers," was formed in the town, and this was under the command of Mr. John Watson. On the 14th of May, 1798, the Corporation subscribed twenty-five guineas to the funds of the Royal Volunteers. Both Corps met with popular encouragement; and the spirit of volunteering ran so high in the town that a "Rifle Corps" was afterwards formed, under Mr. Ogle.

Not only was Preston active in the Volunteer cause, but Lancashire, as a whole, seems to have been much in earnest in the matter. It has been calculated that, in 1804, there were 14,856 Volunteers in this County, viz. 586 Cavalry, 13,710 Infantry, and 560 Artillery. No other County, except Devon, had so large a number of Volunteers enrolled within its boundaries. In the summer of 1804 the Preston Volunteers, commanded by Lieut.-Colonel Grimshaw, were at Lancaster for about a week; and while there they were brigaded with the Lancaster Volunteers. In May, 1805, the same Corps of Preston Volunteers were on duty at Lancaster for twenty days. In 1807 the different Corps at Preston were inspected by Colonel Webber, and pronounced to be "fit for any service his Majesty might honour them with."

In June, 1808, the Preston Volunteers were on duty, for fourteen days, at Blackpool; and on the 24th of the following month these same Volunteers, with Lieut.-Colonel Grimshaw at their head, also the "Rifle Corps," in charge of Captain William Brade, unanimously offered their services to, and were amalgamated into, the "Local Militia." The great bulk of the Volunteers, at this time, were working men; and, as working hours were very long, they had to use Sunday very considerably for volunteering purposes: they cleaned their muskets and accoutrements in the forenoon of that day, were drilled in the Market-place in the afternoon, and in summer time (during Sunday) marched down to the Marsh for exercise, etc.

The Local Militia, properly designated the Amounderness Local Militia, were up for a month's training, in 1809, under Lieut.-Colonel Grimshaw, and the muster was equal to one thousand rank and file. Volunteer-Militia Regiments of this character were formed in several parts; indeed,

---

* A portrait of Nicholas Grimshaw in the uniform of the Volunteers is in the Preston Art Gallery.

in 1809, their establishment appears to have been general in the Country.

Near the end of 1813, the officers of the Amounderness Local Militia " volunteered their services to any part of the kingdom, if required." In 1815, when Napoleon was vanquished, the old Volunteer-Militia lost their mission, and, in due course of time, were disbanded. The Colours of the Amounderness force were deposited in Preston Parish Church, and there they hung over the chancel arch till 1853 when, on the rebuilding of that edifice, they passed into the possession of the Grimshaw family.

In 1859 there was talk of a possible French invasion of England generated by the bellicose bombast of certain Gallic politicians and officers. The Country was thoroughly aroused. Civilians of all orders, professional and commercial gentlemen, office and shop men, artisans and operatives, began to ask for rifles. This was known as " The Volunteer Movement." On the 30th of May, 1859, a meeting convened by the Mayor, in compliance with a communication from Colonel Wilson Patten, the Vice-Lieutenant of the County, was held in Preston Town Hall, to consider the Volunteer question. Various local gentlemen attended, and, on the motion of Mr. John Cooper, seconded by Mr. E. Pedder, it was resolved—" That it is desirable to establish a Volunteer Rifle Corps for the Borough of Preston and the neighbourhood." Afterwards, it was decided to form two Corps, 11th and 12th, the name thereof being the " Eleventh Lancashire." On the 29th of October, 1859, the first enrolment of members took place, at the Militia storehouse, or depot, near the gaol; and about this time a general subscription was embarked on, to raise funds on behalf of the movement.

The first assembly for drill took place on the evening of November 23rd, in the same year, in the area of the Corn Exchange, which was for some time used for that purpose. On the 8th of December following, there was a large public meeting in the Corn Exchange, to raise additional money for the development of the Corps. Financial aid was also obtained from another source. When the Local Militia, commanded by Lieut.-Colonel Grimshaw, ceased duty, in 1815, there had been a balance in connection with the officers' mess fund, which was subsequently invested, part being put in the Consols and part in one of the banks. This fund was, in 1859 or 1860, given to the local Rifle Volunteer Corps, and a connection between the Volunteers of 1859 and their predecessors of the Napoleonic period is thus clearly established.

About the middle of December, 1859, both the Preston Corps had their full complement of members, the 12th being the stronger of the two. On first formation, Henry Newsham Pedder, Esq., had command of the 11th Corps, and with him, as ensigns, were Mr. James Catterall and Hugh Dawson. The 12th Corps was commanded by William Henry Goodair, Esq., the officers under him being Mr. Thomas Goodair (lieutenant) and Mr. Robert L. Ascroft (ensign). Mr. Robert Clarke was the paymaster. After the establishment of the Corps, certain companies, formed in contiguous country districts, joined them. For the storage of arms, premises in Fox Street were obtained. Afterwards, a large house, on the southern side of Fishergate, was used for depot purposes. Later on the depot was removed to the north side of Lord Street; the drill ground being at the rear of the borough Police Station, and on the 1st of December, 1882, the Militia storehouse (at the south-eastern side of the gaol) was taken possession of, as the depot, this building being still occupied by the Corps.

For about a year after the formation of the Corps, the practice ground for shooting was in Brockholes; subsequently for about five years a portion of Hutton Marsh was used for this purpose; then some ground above Longridge was obtained, and there rifle practice, as well as the annual competition for prizes, took place.

In 1883 the 11th Lancashire Volunteers became the "1st Volunteer Battalion, Loyal North Lancashire Regiment." At the time the change was made the strength of the Corps was as follows: three field-officers, seven captains, four subalterns, 51 sergeants, 16 buglers, 42 corporals, 701 privates; total, 824. Of this total the Chorley wing of the Battalion comprised one field-officer, three captains, one subaltern, one chaplain, 15 sergeants, 6 buglers, 15 corporals, and 198 privates; and the Leyland company, one captain, one chaplain, five sergeants, one bugler, four corporals, and 41 men; so the actual number belonging to Preston was 536. The Right Hon. the Earl of Lathom was the hon. colonel of the Corps; W. H. Goodair, Esq., was the lieutenant-colonel; he having been continuously associated with the Corps since 1859. The general roll of the officers was as follows: majors, R. Duckett and P. Widdows; captains, P. W. Mackarel, A. C. Widdows, W. E. M. Tomlinson (one of the parliamentary representatives of Preston), J. P. Goodair, F. J. Lightoller, J. Lawrence, and J. O. Pilkington; lieutenants, W. Sudell, G. Tobin, J. B. F. Whiteside, and J. Carter; quartermaster, Alderman E. Garlick (the Mayor of the Town); surgeon, J. B. Hodgson; hon. chaplains, Rev. J. Stock, M.A., and Rev. T. R. Baldwin, M.A. The adjutant was Captain S. Jackson, of the North Lancashire Regiment. He had succeeded, in October, 1881, Colonel Charles Denison Pedder, Captain Stephen having been Colonel Pedder's predecessor.

When in the early autumn of 1899 war broke out with the Dutch Republics in South Africa, offers to raise companies and battalions for service at the seat of war were made to the military authorities, and the result of these patriotic offers has been stated in the chapters dealing with the services of the 1st Battalion of the Regiment in the South African War, wherein also are described the doings of the Volunteer Service Companies when they joined and became an integral part of that Battalion.

The First Volunteer Service Company was formed in January, 1900, at Fulwood Barracks, Preston, and was composed of one officer—Lieutenant F. W. Foley—and fifty-nine men from the 1st Volunteer Battalion and two officers—Captain B. Musgrave and Lieutenant G. Hesketh—and the remaining non-commissioned officers and men from the 2nd Volunteer Battalion, Captain Musgrave being in command.

After a brief period of training at home the Company left England in February, part in the S.S. "Mexican" and the remainder in the S.S. "Assaye," which transports also carried the Volunteer Service Companies of several other regiments. Disembarkation took place at Cape Town on the 15th March, and after spending some few days in the Main Barracks, the Company marched for Dronfield where the 1st Battalion was all together for the first time since arrival in the country. Very soon after the Company marched off with the 1st Battalion, covering not far short of 1,500 miles during the next five months. At Dronfield all were glad to meet Major Coleridge, who was then temporarily commanding the Battalion, and who in his time had been adjutant of the 1st Volunteer Battalion.

On joining, the Company retained its individuality and became "I" Company, 1st Battalion.

At Boshof about the 23rd April Captain Musgrave went sick with enteric fever and was invalided home, the command of the Company devolving upon Lieutenant Hesketh.

The Company was engaged in the action near Schwartzkopfontein, where the well-known Boer leader, the Frenchman de Villebois Mareuil was killed, and was buried with all military honours by the Battalion; and thereafter the Company had some very strenuous marching to Lindley and on to Heilbron.

About the 18th June a draft of twenty men furnished by both Volunteer Battalions joined the Company, but Lieutenant E. Stowell, of the 1st Volunteer Battalion, who had come out from England in command of the party, did not arrive with it, having been detached for other duties en route; he eventually joined up at Mafeking on the 2nd September.

On the 19th October the Company was inspected by Lord Methuen and shortly afterwards proceeded to De Aar where the next four or five months were spent, Lieutenant Foley commanding the Company during the temporary absence of Lieutenant Hesketh, sick in hospital, and being himself soon afterwards relieved by Captain Musgrave who had rejoined from home. While at De Aar the Company was frequently employed on armoured trains.

During this time a Second Volunteer Service Company had been raised to take the place of the First, each Volunteer Battalion providing half the required non-commissioned officers and men, with Captain W. Swindlehurst, 1st Volunteer Battalion, in command, and Lieutenants T. P. Phethean and C. K. Potter, both of the 2nd Volunteer Battalion. This Company sailed for Cape Town on the 16th March and arrived on the 18th April. The first Company then sailed for England on the 27th April in the S.S. "Montrose" at a strength of fifty all ranks, the remainder of the original party having been either invalided to England or left behind sick: two men had died during the operations in which the Company had taken part.

In consequence of the prevalence of plague at Cape Town the Company was not permitted to land there, but was transhipped to the S.S. "Idaho" and disembarked at Port Elizabeth, proceeding thence by rail to De Aar and on to Deelfontein; but in June it was sent back to De Aar, where it was temporarily attached to the 3rd Battalion Grenadier Guards. The left half-company was sent off with a column taking supplies to Kenhardt and Upington in the Orange River Colony, a march of some seven hundred miles through a desert-like country; the enemy was met with about Prieska and Kenhardt and gave some trouble, though no actual encounter took place. On return to De Aar the Company was attached to the 3rd Battalion The Queen's Regiment, shortly afterwards moving to the Modder River area for duty on the blockhouse line, the right half-company being on the north of the river up to Spytfontein, the left half-company holding the south of the Modder as far as Honey Nest Kloof.

In January, 1902, the Company proceeded to the Vryburg area, the left half company joining the column under Major Paris, which had been detailed to effect the relief of Kuruman, being engaged in action about Zwartfontein. The column was sniped by the Boers all the way to Kuruman, on arrival at which place the half company was used to reinforce the garrison; here it remained beleaguered and on half-rations until the declaration of peace. The rest of the company joined the column under Lord Methuen and was consequently involved in his defeat by General De la Rey near Lichtenburg.

On the declaration of peace the Second Volunteer Company rejoined the 1st Battalion in Mafeking, and left for Cape Town on the 10th July, 1902, sailing thence for home in the S.S. "Fort Salisbury" on the 16th, finally arriving at Southampton in the first week in August and being at once sent on to Preston for disembodiment.

Yet a Third Volunteer Service Company was raised and on the 14th March, 1902, this left Southampton in the S.S. "Greek" and arrived at Cape Town on the 7th April. The personnel of the Company was furnished in equal parts by the 1st and 2nd Volunteer Battalions of the Regiment, while the officers were Captain E. Stowell of the 1st and Lieutenants C. R. Shaw and L. A. Dobson of the 2nd Volunteer Battalion.

Immediately on disembarkation the Company was sent up to Mafeking where it took over part of the Maretsani–Polfontein blockhouse line, one which the Boers under Botha and Viljoen made several attempts to force. In May the Company took part in one of the last of the big "drives," which resulted in the capture of some 450 prisoners. On peace being declared the Company was relieved and returned to Cape Town, where on the 25th June it embarked for home in the S.S. "Walmer Castle." England was reached on the 12th July and Bolton in the early hours of the 13th, the Company being officially disbanded on the 29th of that month.

In recognition of their services, both the 1st and 2nd Volunteer Battalions of the Regiment were awarded the battle honour "SOUTH AFRICA, 1900-02."

THE TERRITORIAL FORCE

The next event of outstanding importance in the history of the 1st Volunteer Battalion, as indeed of the Volunteer Force generally, was the formation of the Territorial Force.

Under the Territorial and Reserve Force Act of 1907, the 1st and 2nd Volunteer Battalions of the Regiment ceased to be known by these numbers and designations and became the 4th and 5th Battalions of The Loyal North Lancashire Regiment, and as such they appear for the first time in the Army List for August, 1908. The function of the Territorial Force, as the Second Line was now to be termed, was twofold—to provide support and expansion for the Regular Army. It was no longer to be composed of dispersed units, but of all arms and services forming integral parts of a division in their proper proportion. There were to be fourteen infantry divisions, each containing three brigades of four battalions. Each battalion was of uniform establishment and consisted of eight companies or 1,009 all ranks.

The 4th and 5th Battalions The Loyal North Lancashire Regiment formed part of the West Lancashire Division, the first commander of which was Major-General E. C. Bethune, who at the time when the Great War commenced occupied the post of Director-General of the Territorial Force.

In Section XIII of the Territorial and Reserve Forces Act it was laid down that "no part of the Territorial Force shall be carried or ordered to go out of the United Kingdom"; so it is clear that primarily the Force was intended for home defence only. The general scheme of Army re-organization under which the Territorial Force was formed, provided for six months' training, should war break out, prior to its dispatch on active service. It had, however, confidently—and as it turned out, rightly—been expected that, should anything of the nature of a national emergency arise, a large percentage of all ranks of the Force would volunteer for active service abroad. As a matter of fact, it was open to all members of the Territorial Force to accept such an Imperial Obligation; but when war broke out in August, 1914, the percentage eligible for such service was comparatively small.

On the outbreak of the Great War Lieut.-Colonel H. L. Beckwith was the commanding officer, whilst Captain C. C. Norman, Royal Welsh Fusiliers, and Major H. J. Whitehead were adjutant and quartermaster, respectively.

The Rt. Hon. the Earl of Derby, K.G., G.C.B., G.C.V.O., T.D., is honorary colonel of both Territorial Battalions of the Regiment, having been gazetted to the 4th Battalion on the 18th June, 1909, and to the 5th Battalion on the 18th May, 1899.

THE EARL OF DERBY, K.G., G.C.B., G.C.V.O., T.D.
Honorary Colonel, 4th and 5th Territorial Battalions.

CHAPTER XXVIII

THE 5TH BATTALION
THE LOYAL NORTH LANCASHIRE REGIMENT

1794-1816, 1859-1914

IN 1859 the position of affairs on the Continent was serious. Public opinion was much perturbed owing to the increasing strength of Continental navies and the supposed weakness of our own Navy and coast defences. Matters came to a head when certain French colonels issued an aggressive letter, urging retaliation against England for supposed insults to the Emperor, Napoleon III, and the British press strongly advocated the formation of Volunteer Corps. On the 25th May, 1859, General Peel, the Secretary of State for War, issued a circular authorizing the formation of such Corps and, as will be explained later, Bolton readily responded. The 27th Lancashire Rifle Volunteers, now the 5th Battalion, The Loyal Regiment, then came into existence.

Volunteering in Bolton was nothing new, and the existing regiment is a worthy descendant of other similar military forces raised in the past in the town and its neighbourhood. Thus in 1513 Sir E. Stanley raised bowmen at Bolton to fight at Flodden Field, and it was to the " Bolton lads " who distinguished themselves in this fight that the following inscription on the walls of the Parish Church in 1701 had reference :—

> " The bolt shot well, I ween,
> From Arablist * of Yew Tree Green," etc.

Again at the time of the Spanish Armada, Sharples of Sharples and other Lancashire gentlemen raised a corps of bowmen for the defence of the Country.

During the wars with the French Revolutionary Government and later with Napoleon, Bolton's effort was noteworthy and well sustained. In 1793 the gentlemen of the town and neighbourhood raised one hundred and sixty Marines at their own expense, and on the 11th April this body marched to Chatham under Captain Hindle.

In the following year the Loyal Bolton Volunteer Infantry was formed.

* Arbalist, i.e. crossbow.

This corps consisted at first of two companies to which two were added in 1798. The officers at this time were Lieut.-Colonel Peter Rasbotham; Major R. Fletcher; Captains P. Hewitt, J. Ridgeway, R. Ainsworth and T. Ainsworth; Lieutenants W. Gray, J. Pearson, J. Williams; Ensigns S. Heelis, J. Gardner, H. Horrocks and R. Bolton; Adjutant J. Warr; Chaplain T. Bancroft. Among the N.C.O.s and the rank and file occur many names still well known in Bolton and in the 5th Battalion, The Loyal Regiment.

In May, 1802, on the conclusion of the Peace of Amiens, the Loyal Bolton Volunteer Corps was disbanded and its Colours were deposited in the Parish Church.

Besides the Infantry corps, two troops of Bolton Light Horse Volunteers were raised in 1798 under the command of Major Pilkington, and they remained in existence till 5th April, 1816, when they were disbanded.

On the resumption of the war with Napoleon in 1803, Bolton was called on for a fresh military effort, and a new Regiment of Volunteers, 1,019 strong, consisting of ten companies under Lieut.-Colonel R. Fletcher, was raised without difficulty. In 1808 this regiment, then of twelve companies amounting to 1,423 men, volunteered into the Local Militia for the Division of Bolton.

In 1813 it is recorded that " the regiment set an example to all the other local militia regiments in the kingdom, for in a patriotic spirit it volunteered to take the duties of the old militia in any part of Great Britain, according to the bill then pending in Parliament brought in by Lord Viscount Castlereagh."

Early in 1814 the Bolton Volunteers took their share in the defence of the Country by going on garrison duty for six weeks to Manchester, where they gained high praise from the military authorities for their soldierly behaviour and good discipline.

Soon after the general peace of 1815 the corps was disbanded, but the officers and part of the staff were still liable to be called upon. Colonel Ralph Fletcher, who had been the heart and the soul of the volunteer movement since 1794, was still in command in 1815. The Colours of the Bolton Local Militia are now in the Parish Church.

The volunteer spirit, so marked during the early years of the nineteenth century, remained dormant in Bolton during more than forty years of peaceful security at home. It only needed the call which came in 1859 to give it renewed life. The gentlemen mainly concerned with the formation of the Bolton branch of the 27th Lancashire Rifle Volunteers were Arthur Bailey, Esq., and James Watkins, Esq. The last-named was a lineal descendant of both Colonel Fletcher and Major Watkins who served so long with the Bolton Volunteers at the beginning of the century. Both Bailey and Watkins served for many years with the 27th Lancashire Rifle Volunteers, which the former gentleman eventually commanded.

On the 13th July, 1859, at the instigation of Mr. Bailey, a meeting was held at the Town Hall in Little Bolton at which John Fletcher, Esq., took the chair. It was then decided to enrol one or more Volunteer Rifle Companies of one hundred men each for Bolton and its neighbourhood; to raise a subscription to defray the necessary expenses attending the formation of such corps; to provide arms, accoutrements and uniform for such persons as might be willing to join but were unable to meet the expense; and lastly to form a committee with Major Pilsworth as chairman and Messrs. Bailey and Watkins as its hon. secretaries, to give effect to the meeting's resolutions.

An advertisement was inserted in the local newspapers in the following terms :—

"It is particularly requested that persons of all classes, of good character, who are desirous of joining in the present movement to form a Volunteer Corps in Bolton . . . will at once communicate their names, addresses and occupations to Mr. Bailey, 14 Wood St., Bolton. By order of the Committee."

A further meeting, attended by many of those who had volunteered, was held on October 12th, when it was decided that members of the Corps should provide their own rifles, as the Government would only supply twenty-five per cent. of the number required. The short rifle was agreed on, as most volunteer regiments had adopted it. Members were to drill five hours per week, Saturday's drill to count as three. Fines were to be imposed for non-attendance, and an entrance fee of 5s. was fixed, election being by ballot.

On the 15th November the Corps was officially established, and next day thirty-three members were sworn in at the Town Hall and took the oath of allegiance to Her Majesty. It was announced that Mr. Hardcastle had offered land by the riverside at Bradshaw as a shooting range and, as the place was very suitable, though only giving 300 yards' range, it was accepted. The rent was to be £5 a year which Mr. Hardcastle proposed to remit as a prize for the best shot.

The names of the original thirty-three members of the 27th Lancashire Rifle Volunteers are as follows :—

Regtl. No.	Regtl. No.
1. A. Bailey	3. C. F. Ainsworth
2. J. H. Knowles	4. S. Crowther

Regtl. No.		Regtl. No.	
5.	J. Bayley	20.	W. Wilson
6.	C. Bayley	21.	J. Pendlebury
7.	F. S. Nicholson	22.	A. Greg
8.	J. C. Ormrod	23.	L. Wild
9.	T. Wilkinson	24.	T. Winder
10.	J. Holt	25.	R. Hughes
11.	F. Greenhalgh	26.	R. Horridge
12.	W. Watkins	27.	J. W. Taylor
13.	J. Thwaites	28.	J. Wrigley
14.	W. E. Brown	29.	C. Crook
15.	R. Settle	30.	J. M. Parker
16.	W. H. Pendlebury	31.	J. Slater
17.	R. Knott	32.	J. E. Bayley
18.	T. F. Wallwork	33.	T. Ratcliffe
19.	C. Holt		

On the 24th November it was decided "that the uniform of the Corps should consist of a light grey tunic, to be made of the same colour and shade as the uniform of the Manchester and Bury Volunteers, undressed cloth with invisible green facings; the skirt to be 16 inches in length, with bronze buttons; black enamelled belts, with bronze mountings. Trousers of the same colour, shade and cloth as the tunic, to be formed slightly in the peg top shape. Caps to be of the same colour, shade and cloth as the tunic."

During the succeeding months the Corps prospered, and a proposal to equip sixty men who should pay £1 10s. and an annual subscription of a guinea produced more members. A second and third company resulted, the latter being raised in Deane by Mr. J. Broughton Edge. Later a fourth company was raised from Farnworth and Kearsley. The Bolton companies drilled in the Cattle Market and in Lum's Factory. Sergeant Regan was the drill instructor.

In April, 1860, the formation of the Corps was authoritatively recognized, though November 15th is accepted as the official birthday of the Bolton Battalion. The official letter runs as follows:—

"London,
6th April, 1860.

"SIR,—

"I have the honour to inform you that Her Majesty has been graciously pleased to approve and accept the service of a company of Rifle Volunteers at Bolton under the Act 44 of Geo. III. C. 54. This company has been incorporated with the 27th Lancashire Rifle Volunteers, the maximum establishment of which will consist of

1 Major | 4 Ensigns
4 Captains | 1 Adjutant
4 Lieutenants | 1 Surgeon.

400 Men of All Ranks, divided into 4 Companies.

"I am, Sir, your obedient servant,

"SEFTON.

"A. Bailey, Esq., Captain, Commanding 27th L.R.V."

It was a rule of the Corps that on the last Sunday in March, June, September and December in each year the Regiment should attend morning service at the Parish Church.

The headquarters of the Corps was in 1860 at a house rented in Crook Street, and in 1861 it was moved to 25 Bridge Street. It was not till 1863 that the present headquarters in Fletcher Street were purchased from the Poor-Law Guardians and Overseers of Great Bolton, for £1,800. In May, 1861, a long rifle range was acquired on Kearsley Moor. In later years it had to be closed owing to new works and buildings springing up in the neighbourhood.

In the latter part of 1860 the Regiment was augmented by two new companies, and drill was held under the New Market. Again in January, 1863, two additional companies were raised, one being in the Halliwell district. It was not till the 2nd February, 1876, that the ninth and tenth companies at Hindley were added to the 27th Lancashire Rifle Volunteers. These had formerly belonged to the 82nd Lancashire Rifle Volunteers.

On the 11th August, 1860, the original four companies of the Corps took part in a review at Newton, which was attended by eight thousand Volunteers from all the principal towns of Lancashire. The Bolton Corps was in the Second Brigade, commanded by Lieut.-Colonel Lightfoot, C.B. Staff work appears to have been faulty. "Owing to arrangements," it is recorded, "the Regiment could not leave the ground till 11.30 p.m., and consequently did not reach home till 1.30 a.m. on Sunday morning." The men, it may be observed, were all drenched to the skin.

In 1861 the officers and staff of the 27th Lancashire Rifle Volunteers were as follows :—

Staff. Lieut.-Colonel W. Gray, M.P., Captain and Adjutant E. L. Frances, Paymaster Arthur Greg, Surgeon Robert Settle, M.D., Hon. Chaplain, Rev. H. Powell (Vicar of Bolton).

No. 1 Company. Captain Arthur Bailey, Lieutenant J. Cross Ormrod, Ensign James Watkins.

No. 2 Company. Captain J. Bridson, Lieutenant J. Knowles.
No. 3 Company. Captain Kearsley, Lieutenant Edge, Ensign Caldwell.
No. 4 Company. Captain W. Whittam, Lieutenant Y. Whittam, Ensign Haffeley.
No. 5 Company. Captain J. Gorton, Lieutenant W. Wallwork.
No. 6 Company. Captain T. Hesketh, Lieutenant Higson, Ensign C. Bayley.

As is customary with all new movements, the question of funds soon became pressing. Heavy expenses were incurred at the Kearsley range, and proper barracks and a drill ground were needed. Moreover, the subscription for privates had been reduced to 8s. a year. It was determined, therefore, to hold a bazaar in the Temperance Hall on the 23rd April, 1862. On this day the Regiment assembled in the Borough Court and, accompanied by the Mayor, marched to the Hall via Nelson Square, Bradshawgate, Deansgate, Knowsley Street and Bath Street. It halted in front of the Hall. It testifies to the public interest taken in the Corps that a sum of £2,640 was taken at the bazaar. Out of this sum, £2,000 was applied in purchasing and outfitting the present barracks. A loan on the security of the property was found to be necessary, while the officers of the Regiment guaranteed £1,000 in addition.

The early events of the Volunteer movement in Bolton, doubtless repeated in many other towns of England, have been given in some detail, as they demonstrate the difficulties that attended the movement at the beginning and the fine spirit and enthusiasm which overcame all initial obstacles. Little perhaps did the pioneers of 1860 foresee the ultimate outcome of their efforts. The fourteen Territorial Divisions, complete in all arms and services, which answered the Country's call in August, 1914, were the product of their patriotic endeavour. The descendants of those men may well feel proud of their achievement.

From 1862 onwards steady progress was made. The events recorded relate chiefly to reviews, field-days, inspections and public celebrations in which the Regiment took part. Thus in August, 1862, there was an inspection, with some volley firing, and sports at Lever Hall, Lieut.-Colonel Gray's residence; in September the Guild Review at Preston and the inauguration of the Crompton Statue; in October a review of nearly four thousand troops in Heaton Park, when General Sir George Wetherall, K.C.B., K.H., took the salute; later, further reviews at Newton and in Knowsley Park, the latter promoted by the Earl of Derby.

In February, 1863, the Regiment adopted scarlet uniform with green facings, and in November of the same year a second major was added to the establishment, Captain A. Bailey, who had done so much for the Corps in the early days, being then promoted. Later, he became the commanding officer.

In 1867 the Regiment held its first encampment at Lytham from June 13th to 17th. The Bolton Volunteers were one of the first regiments to institute encampments which subsequently became so prominent a feature in the Volunteer movement. For many years the Regiment continued to go under canvas at Lytham, and it was not till 1885 that a change was made to Rhyl. On one occasion the Regiment under Colonel Bailey took part in autumn manœuvres at Cannock Chase.

In June, 1873, the 27th Lancashire Rifle Volunteers gained unstinted praise from the London press by reason of its fine appearance (new uniforms and accoutrements!) on the occasion of the visit of T.R.H. the Prince and Princess of Wales to Bolton to open the Town Hall. "The display and deportment of the men," so it was reported, "would have done credit to a Line Regiment."

On the 2nd September, 1880, by order of the Secretary of State for War, the title of the 27th Lancashire Rifle Volunteers was changed to 14th (late 27th) Lancashire Rifle Volunteers. On the 15th November of the same year the Regiment attained its majority, when the junior officers entertained at dinner the original members of the Corps. They were Lieut.-Colonel Bailey, Major T. Hesketh, Major J. Cross-Ormrod, Surgeon Settle, Captain Fell, Captain James Watkins, Lieutenant and Paymaster A. Greg, and Canon Powell, the Honorary Chaplain. The first seven were still serving with the Regiment, and they were the only seven members remaining of the original sixty-five enrolled in the year 1859.

On the 1st February, 1883, it was decreed by General Order that the 11th and 14th Lancashire Rifle Volunteers would in future be designated the 1st and 2nd Volunteer Battalions of the Loyal North Lancashire Regiment.

The story of the 27th Lancashire Rifle Volunteers (to give it the title by which the Bolton Regiment was known for so many years) thus came to an end. Henceforth its history becomes part and parcel of the history of the distinguished Regiment of which it became an integral portion. That history is dealt with in subsequent chapters.

This chapter which deals with Bolton's Regiment from 1859 till 1883 cannot be closed without once more drawing attention to the many patriotic men, civilians as well as Volunteers, who devoted their time, their means and their talents to placing their town in a foremost position, by promoting and sustaining during many years the voluntary military spirit which was and remains one of England's proudest possessions. No other country can show anything like it. It is to men like Rasbotham (1794–1802), Fletcher (1794–1816), Pilkington (1798–1816), Gray, Bailey, Watkins and the other pioneers of 1859, and the Officers, N.C.O.s and the rank and file of the 27th Lancashire Rifle Volunteers, who without pecuniary reward worked hard to uphold the honour of their town—to all these Bolton owes a deep debt of gratitude.

They, and all those men and women in and round Bolton who in various ways supported their patriotic endeavour, deserved well of their Town and Country.

When the 14th Lancashire Rifle Volunteers became the 2nd Volunteer Battalion of the Loyal North Lancashire Regiment, the headquarters of the Corps were still situated at the old Workhouse in Fletcher Street, Bolton. The rifle range was at Bradshaw, but it extended to no more than 300 yards, and this, though well enough for the limited range of the old Snider rifle, was rightly pronounced to be unsafe when the Martini-Henry rifle was taken into use. In 1900 a very fine four-section range was opened at Entwistle, four and a half miles from Bolton, admitting of rifle practice up to 800 yards.

In May, 1897, the Battalion sent a detachment of one officer, one sergeant, one bugler and twenty men to take part in the celebration in London of the Diamond Jubilee of Her Majesty Queen Victoria. The detachment was stationed on Westminster Bridge. This was one of the very last occasions on which the Battalion paraded with the Martini-Henry rifle.

During the South African War of 1899–1902, the Battalion sent out six officers and 172 men in Volunteer Service Companies, formed in close co-operation with the 1st Volunteer Battalion, and the services of these will be found fully recorded in the chapters which treat of this Battalion and of the 1st Regular Battalion of the Regiment.

The Territorial Force

When in 1908 the Territorial Force was formed under the circumstances and conditions described in Chapter XXVII the 2nd Volunteer Battalion became the 5th Battalion The Loyal North Lancashire Regiment, and formed part of the West Lancashire Division, the first divisional camp being held at Caerwys in 1909, when twelve thousand men attended, forming a complete division, with the proper proportion of cavalry, artillery, Royal Engineers and Army Service Corps.

In May, 1914, the 5th Battalion was 750 strong and the Commanding Officer organized a review of all arms in Bolton, composed of units of the East and West Lancashire Divisions: great enthusiasm was shown and as a result 200 recruits were raised for the 5th Battalion alone. By August of this year over 950 non-commissioned officers and men had fired their annual course of musketry, and had thus increased enormously their efficiency as soldiers when shortly afterwards the Great War broke out.

INDEX

A

Additional Forces Act, 69, 187, 188
Afghanistan (1878), 278–284, 285
  Ali Masjid Fort, 278–284
  Battle-honours, awarded, 285
  Dakka, advance on, 283
  Medal awarded, 285
Aldershot, at, 161, 166, 275, 276, 295, 362–365, 368–369
Alma, Battle of, 142–147
American War of Independence (1773–1777), 41–65
  Boston, quartered in, 41–43, 48, 49
  Bunker's Hill, Battle of, 43–48
  Champlain, Lake, 53–57
  Concord, stores burnt, 42
  Lexington, affair at, 42–43
  Saratoga, surrender at, 62–65
  Skenesborough, advance on, 57
  Stillwater, action at, 60, 64
  Ticonderoga Fort, 53–59, 64, 65
Amherst, Gen. J., 18–24, 39–41
Ansley, Lieut.-Col. J. H., 322, 342, 347, 354, 374
Auchmuty, Gen. Sir S., 71–79
Ava, expedition to (1825–1826), 128–134

B

Backhouse, Lieut.-Col., 69–74
Bahamas, service in, 68
Baird, Gen. Sir D., 69–70, 218–230
Barbados, at, 137, 164, 177, 250
Battle-honours, awarded, xxiv, 35, 115, 134, 159, 232, 285, 348, 380, 391
Bell, Lieut. C. V. M., 374, 375
Beresford, Maj.-Gen., 70–73
Berkeley, Capt. R. E., 302, 326, 374, 375
Bermudas, in garrison at, 248
Bertie, Albemarle, Maj.-Gen., 174–176
Bombay, 117–126
Brabant, Duke of, reviewed by, 272
Browne, Lieut.-Gen. Sir S., 278–283
Brussels, guard duty, 243, 244

Buenos Ayres, attack on, 70, 74–79
Bunker's Hill, Battle of, 43–48
Burgoyne, Gen. J., 42, 51–65
Burma War (1825–1826), 128–134
  Ava, advance on, 133
  Battle-honour awarded, 134
  Donubyu, attacked, 130–131
  Hlaing River, 130
  Malun, armistice at, 133
  Medal awarded, 134
  Napadi Hills, 132
  Nawin River, 132
  Operations, early, 128
  Prome, occupied, 131–132
  Rangoon, at, 128, 133
  Sarawa, halt at, 130, 131
  Situation, political, 126–127
  Syriam, action at, 130
  Toungoo, to, 131
  Yandabo, peace signed, 133
  Yuadit, arrival at, 130

C

Cadiz, blockade of, 82
Calabria, 191, 198
Calcutta, stationed at, 127, 133, 134
Cambridge, H.R.H. Duke of, inspection by, 274–275
Cameron, Volunteer, 28
Canada, 25–40, 162–163, 214–215, 252
Cape of Good Hope, 69, 70, 79, 81, 117, 181–185
Capri, capitulation of, 200
Carleton, Lieut.-Gen. Sir G., 47–54, 67
Cavagnari, Major, 284–285
Ceylon, 301–303
Chamney, Lieut. J., death of, 183
Chelmsford, re-formed at, 116
Chichester, Lieut.-Col. Sir C., death of, 252
Colours, presented, 161, 246–247, 250, 257, 362, 373
Companies, flank, abolished, 163
  numbered, 163
Company, four, organization, 364

INDEX

Cope, Gen. Sir J., 4–12
Corfu, in garrison at, 138
Corunna Campaign, the (1808–1809), 217–232
County title, the, 67, 170, 175, 248
Craufurd, Brig.-Gen. R., 73–78
Crete, occupation of, 372–373
Crimean War (1854–1856), 139–159
    Alma, Battle of, 142–147
    Balaklava, Battle of, 148
    Battle-honours, awarded, 159
    Bulganak River, crossed, 142
    Cause, nominal, of, 139–140
    Departure from, 159
    Inkerman, Battle of, 149–153
    Landing, the, 142
    Medals awarded, 159
    Peace, treaty of, 159
    Sebastopol, siege of, 155–158
    Storm, the, 154
    Winter, conditions, in, 154
    Varna, at, 140
    Victoria Cross, awarded, 151
Cyprus, detachment, 372–373

D

Depots, Brigade, system, 165
Deptford, duty at, 161
Derby, Earl of, Colonel, 392
District, Regimental, 171
Dover, march to, 161
Duelling, fatal, 185–186

E

Edinburgh Castle, 4–12
Edward VII, H.M. King:
    Coronation, 347, 355
    Funeral, 360
    Inspection, by, 373
Elba, escape of Napoleon, 116, 215, 243
Elizabeth, Port, founded, 184
Elrington, Col. R. G., 74, 122–137
Ensign, rank, abolished, 164, 167
Evans, Lieut.-Gen. T., 257
Expeditionary, British, Force (1914), 365

F

Farmer, Capt. M., 69
Farrant, Lieut.-Col. H., death of, 257
Farren, Lieut.-Col. R., 139, 140, 152, 160
Fenians, the, 162–163
Flockhart, Pte. R., 179–185

G

Gates, Gen. H., 59
George V, H.M. King:
    Colours, presents, 362–363
    Coronation, 360
    guard-of-honour to, 374
    India, visit to, 374
    message from, 361
    portraits, presents, 374
Ghent, landed at, 215
Gibraltar, 81, 82, 136, 160, 249–250, 275, 276, 292, 295, 347, 393
Good Hope, Cape, 69, 70, 79, 81, 117, 181–185
Graham, Lieut.-Gen. T., 82–108, 234, 242
Great War, outbreak of, 364, 374, 388, 392, 400
Guernsey, embarkation for, 179
Gujerat, expedition to, 121

H

Hale, Lieut.-Col. J., 17, 23, 32, 34
Halifax, quartered in, 14, 50, 68, 163–164, 246–248
Haly, Lieut.-Col. W. O'G., 138–152, 158
Headquarters, Regimental District, 171
Hoghton, Col. Sir H., 286, 291

I

Independence, American, War of, 41–65
India, 79, 116, 117–124, 126, 133–134, 254–272, 276–285, 296–301, 366–367, 374
Indian Mutiny (1857), 257–266
    Amritsar, detachment, 262, 269
    Delhi, siege of, 262, 269
    Lahore, detachment, 263, 269
    Medal, awarded, 270
    Mian Mir, at, 257–266
    Mutineers disarmed, 262, 269
    Yusafzais, operations against, 266–267
Inkerman, Battle of, 149–153
Ireland, service in, 13–14, 40, 136, 138, 139, 160–162, 164, 166–168, 176, 188, 216, 217, 245–246, 248–250, 252–254, 275, 295, 356–359, 368
Ischia, Island of, 201

J

Jacobite Rebellion, outbreak of, 4
Jersey, 166, 187–188, 205, 242, 252–253, 368
Jourdain, Lieut.-Col. C. E. A., 298–305, 320, 323, 348–355, 357, 374, 375
Jowaki Afridis, operations against, 276–277

INDEX

K

Kekewich, Maj.-Gen. R. G., 302–313, 325, 329, 334, 335, 341, 342, 348, 357
Kempt, Lieut.-Gen. Sir J., 190–200, 213, 215, 246, 247
Kimberley, Defence of, 304–314, 363
  presentation from citizens, 358
Knight, Lieut.-Col. G. C., 298, 302, 353, 360, 361, 362

L

"Lancashire," title, 66–67
Lascelles, Col. P., 3–13, 26–32, 47
"Lincoln," title, 175, 248
Linked Battalions, 165
Liverpool, march to, 116
Logan, Lieut. R. H., 373, 375
Loudoun, Earl of, 17–18
Louisburg, siege of, 14, 18–25
  battle-honour awarded, 35
Lumley, Brig.-Gen., 71–78

M

McDermond, Pte. J., awarded Victoria Cross, 151
McDonald, Col.-Sergt., bravery of, 156
Madras, arrival at, 79, 117
Maida, Battle of (1806), 192–199, 202, 232
  Battle-honour awarded, 232
  Casualties, 196, 197, 198
  Medal, Gold, for, 199, 202
  St. Euphemia, landing at, 191
  Tortoise, the, 199–200
Mallett, Sergt., poem, 289
Malta, at, 136, 138, 139, 159, 160, 189, 190, 369–373, 378–379
March, experimental, 359
Mauritius, at, 273–274, 373–374
Medals, 115, 134, 159, 232, 270, 285, 348, 374
Milazzo, at, 200–202
Militia, the, 66, 81, 175, 286–294, 376–380, 380–383
  Affiliated, 293
  Amalgamation of battalions, 377
  Battalions, two, 293
  Cardwell, system, introduced, 293
  Centenary, celebration, 377
  Colonels, 291, 377, 378
  Colours, the, 290, 291, 292, 293
  Equipment, valise, 376
  Gibraltar, in garrison at, 292

Militia, the—*continued*
  Honours, awarded, 292, 380
  Malta, in garrison at, 378–379
  Raised, 286
  Reserve, Special, the, 380–383
  Rifles, 292, 376
  South Africa, service in, 378–380
  Title, 286, 290, 293
  Uniform, 290–292
Molesworth, Major, killed in action, 125
Monckton, Col. Hon. R., 15–36
Monte Video, storming of, 70–74, 79
Montreal, advance on, 39–40, 52
Moore, Lieut.-Gen. Sir J., 199, 200, 217–231
Mordaunt, Col. J., 2–4
Musketry, distinction in, 161

N

Navanagar, expedition, 120
Nesbitt, Brig.-Gen., 47, 52, 53
Netherlands, service in, 242–244
Neuilly, in garrison at, 244
Nive, Battle of, 112
Norcott, Gen. Sir W. S. R., 35, 171
Nova Scotia, 14–25, 50, 68, 163–164, 246–248
Numbered, regiment, 4, 14

O

O'Donoghue, Lieut.-Col. J. W., 91, 130–134
Officers, the first, 2–3, 176, 186, 394
O'Neal, Sergt., bravery of, 192

P

Pack, Col., 73–78, 96, 100
Palermo, at, 202
Patterson, Sergt. J., commended, 204, 251
Peninsula, the, War in (1808–1814), 81–116, 202–213, 217–232
  Adour, River, passage of, 114
  Barrosa, Battle of, 83–84
  Battle-honours, awarded, 115, 232
  Bidassoa, River, crossed, 108–110
  Cadiz, siege of, 92
  Corunna Campaign, 217–232
  Hostilities, cessation of, 115, 213
  Medal awarded, 115, 232
  Nive, Battle of, 112
  Nivelle, Battle of, 110–111
  Pyrenees, the, 104
  St. Pierre, 114
  St. Sebastian, siege of, 103–108

Peninsula, the, War in (1808–1814)—*continued*
  Spain, Eastern, operations in, 202–213
    Alicante, 202–211
    Barcelona, invested, 213
    Biarritz, move to, 213
    Denia, Castle of, 204–205
    Tarragona, 85, 209–212
  Tarifa, defence of, 82, 86–92
  Truxillo, arrival at, 92
  Vittoria, Battle of, 97–102
Persian Gulf, expeditions, 117–120, 124–126
Pindari War, the, 121–123
Poona, stationed at, 120, 126, 127, 374
Prestonpans, Battle of, 7–10
Provisional Battalions, 356, 369
Purchase, abolition of, 164

Q

Quebec, 18, 26–35, 36, 40, 50, 52
Queues, dispensed with, 200
Quinn, Lce.-Cpl., gallantry of, 156–158

R

Railway accident, fatal, 299
Raising of Regiments, 1–3, 172–176
Rebellion of 1745, 4–12
Regiments:
  8th Light Dragoons, 183, 184
  9th Light Dragoons, 76
  10th Dragoons, 2
  12th Dragoons, 2
  13th Dragoons, 5, 7, 8, 10
  13th Light Dragoons, 178
  14th Dragoons, 7, 10
  17th Dragoons, 179
  20th Light Dragoons, 74, 189, 201, 202
  21st Light Dragoons, 74
  4th Dragoon Guards, 2
  6th Dragoon Guards, 76
  9th Lancers, 316
  11th Hussars, 361
  14th Hussars, 13
  15th Hussars, 220
  18th Hussars, 359, 361
  Kimberley Light Horse, 309, 312
  New South Wales Lancers, 316, 350, 353
  New South Wales M. I., 350
  New Zealand M.I., 350
  Tasmanian M.I., 350
  1st Foot, 13, 18, 20, 128, 219, 230, 234, 242
  3rd Foot, 158
  4th Foot, 42, 49, 94, 106, 110, 231, 243
  5th Foot, 44, 46, 76, 78

Regiments—*continued*
  6th Foot, 7, 161
  7th Foot, 293
  8th Foot, 50, 166, 168
  9th Foot, 52–60, 82, 110, 139, 213, 215, 278
  10th Foot, 42, 202, 207, 210, 269, 271
  11th Foot, 86, 88
  13th Foot, 118, 132, 133
  14th Foot, 168, 250
  15th Foot, 18, 20, 27–39
  16th Foot, 163
  17th Foot, 18–23
  18th Foot, 2, 48, 257, 285
  20th Foot, 54, 59, 60, 191–197
  21st Foot, 53, 54, 60
  22nd Foot, 18–25, 161, 184, 185, 255, 257
  23rd Foot, 42, 144, 219, 236–241, 293
  24th Foot, 52, 54, 60, 261, 274
  26th Foot, 219, 231, 236
  27th Foot, 176, 191, 196, 205, 210, 213, 219, 243
  28th Foot, 18–26, 31–38, 82, 83
  29th Foot, 14, 51, 54, 255, 269, 288
  30th Foot, 13, 82, 94, 140, 141, 146, 151, 163, 242, 243
  31st Foot, 52–54, 158, 219
  32nd Foot, 178, 179, 238
  33rd Foot, 165, 242, 275
  34th Foot, 54, 184
  35th Foot, 18–24, 31, 38, 39, 165, 191, 194, 234
  36th Foot, 76, 78
  37th Foot, 213
  38th Foot, 44, 50, 70–78, 128–133
  39th Foot, 176, 189
  40th Foot, 16–25, 49, 74, 243
  41st Foot, 128–151
  42nd Foot, 14, 231
  43rd Foot, 28, 31, 32, 38, 44, 49
  44th Foot, 5, 7, 49, 94, 189, 213
  45th Foot, 14–25, 59, 74–79, 133
  46th Foot, 5, 7, 253, 275
  47th Foot, 1–171, 176, 276, 293
    2nd Bn., 69, 81–116
  48th Foot, 18, 20, 31–39, 189
  49th Foot, 13, 49, 138–152
  50th Foot, 231
  51st Foot, 219, 220, 277, 282
  52nd Foot, 44–49, 243, 247, 255
  53rd Foot, 53, 54, 57, 64
  54th Foot, 69
  55th Foot, 138–141, 146, 150
  57th Foot, 215
  58th Foot, 18, 20, 31–39, 189, 191, 200–208, 213

INDEX

Regiments—*continued*
  59th Foot, 48, 92, 106, 110, 168, 176, 219, 220, 230
  60th Foot, 18-31, 37-39, 59, 163, 219
  61st Foot, 181-191
  62nd Foot, 53, 54, 60, 139, 152, 156, 179
  63rd Foot, 18, 49
  64th Foot, 176, 294
  65th Foot, 118-126, 184
  67th Foot, 83, 203, 210
  68th Foot, 139
  71st Foot, 69-73
  72nd Foot, 269
  74th Foot, 246-250
  76th Foot, 219
  77th Foot, 152, 174, 251
  78th Foot, 190-198, 243, 269
  79th Foot, 176
  80th Foot, 257
  81st Foot, 165, 166, 170, 172-285, 295
    2nd Bn., 188, 217-244
  82nd Foot, 86, 88, 90, 168
  84th Foot, 241, 269
  86th Foot, 182
  87th Foot, 76-93, 133
  88th Foot, 76-79, 152, 156
  89th Foot, 130, 133, 174, 190
  90th Foot, 215
  91st Foot, 184, 185, 242
  95th Foot, 140-151
  96th Foot, 48, 257
  98th Foot, 268
  100th Foot, 48
  101st Foot, 176
  107th Foot, 69, 271
  3rd Royal Lancashire Militia, 165, 167, 170, 286-294
  Berkshire, R., 359
  Black Watch, 309, 312, 327, 358, 359
  Border, 356
  Coldstream Guards, 83, 84, 317, 335
  Cornwall L.I., 356
  Dorsetshire, 362
  Dublin Fusiliers, R., 354
  Durham L.I., 352
  Essex, 295, 359
  Fusiliers, R., 347, 358
  Gloucestershire, 361
  Grenadier Guards, 92, 174, 176, 390
  Inniskilling Fusiliers, R., 302
  Kent, E., 354
  Lancashire, E., 358, 362, 376
  Lancashire, Loyal N.: :
    1st Bn., 295-365
    2nd Bn., 366-375

Regiments—*continued*
  Lancashire, Loyal N.—*continued*
    3rd Bn., 376-383
    4th Bn., 391-392
    5th Bn., 400
  Lancashire, S., 343
  Lancashire Fusiliers, 300, 361, 370, 372, 376
  Lancaster, R., K.O., 376
  Middlesex, 298
  Munster Fusiliers, R., 350, 356
  Northamptonshire, 315, 316, 324-328, **334**, 349-353
  Northumberland Fusiliers, 315, 316, 324-336, 345, 346
  Rifle Brigade, 72-93, 243, 246, 277
  Scots Guards, 2, 362
  Sherwood Foresters, 335, 370
  Shropshire, L.I., K., 356
  Somersetshire, L.I., 335
  Staffordshire, N., 297
  Surrey, R.W., 390
  Wales, S., Borderers, 324
  Warwickshire, R., 356, 370
  Welsh Fusiliers, R., 342, 392
  Worcestershire, 297
  Yorkshire, 362
  Yorkshire, L.I., K.O., 300, 315, 316, 354, 355
Renny, Lieut.-Col. H., 251-269
Reserve, Special, the, 380-383
Rifles :
  Enfield, 258, 259, 268
  Lee-Enfield, 358
  Lee-Metford, 300, 376
  Martini-Henry, 166, 376, 400
  Snider, 163, 376, 400
Roberts, F.M. Lord, 299, 377, 378, 383
Russia, Emperor of, inspection by, 137-138
Ryan, Mr. W., case of, 81

S

San Domingo, 177-179
St. Denis, encamped at, 215
St. Foy, action at, 38
St. Sebastian, siege of, 103-108
Sebastopol, siege of, 155-158
Shorncliffe, at, 161, 356, 369
Sicily, embarkation for, 190
Skerrett, Col., 85-94
South Africa (1889-1902), 303-355, 356, 357, 370-372, 388-391, 400
  Arrival in, 303
  Bakenlaagte, action near, 354
  Battle-honours, awarded, 348, 391

South Africa (1889-1902)—*continued*
  Belfast, move to, 353
  Belmont, Battle of, 315-317
  Bethulie reached, 371
  Blockhouses, 338, 344-347, 372
  Bloemfontein, 322, 324, 350-353, 371, 372
  Boshof, concentration at, 325
  Bosman's Kop, action at, 352
  Carolina, rear-guard, 353
  Crocodile River, 353
  Cyphergat, casualties, 371
  Driefontein, action at, 350
  Dronfield, camp, 324
  Florida, fighting near, 353
  Graspan, Battle of, 318-319
  Hartebeestfontein, at, 340
  Heilbron, arrival at, 327
  Home, return, 347-348
  Kaalfontein, affair at, 342-343
  Kimberley, defence of, 304-314, 363
  Klerksdorp, 335, 340, 341
  Kroonstad, 326, 371, 372
  Krugersdorp, entrained for, 329
  Ladybrand, withdrawal from, 351
  Lichtenburg, district, 332, 334, 341-346
  Lindley, at, 327
  Machadodorp, detachment, 353
  Mafeking, 332-347
  Magaliesberg, the, 330-333
  Magersfontein, Battle, 313, 321-322
  Medals, awarded, 348
    presented, 356
  Memorial, War, unveiled, 357
  Modder River, 319-320
  Mounted Infantry, 303-306, 309, 323, 330, 336, 338, 343, 349-355, 370-372
  Olifant's Nek, held, 329-330
  Orange River Station, 305, 314, 315
  Paardeberg, laager, 350
  Peace, signed, 347, 355
  Poplar Grove, 350
  Potchefstroom, convoy, 342, 343
  Pretoria, arrival at, 332
  Rhenoster River, 327
  Riet River, crossed, 321
  Rustenburg, occupied, 330
  Senekal, skirmishes at, 371
  Situation, political, 303-304
  Smithfield, surrender of, 371
  Swaziland Border, the, 353
  Thabanchu, at, 351
  Tweebosch, disaster, 344-346
  United, the Battalion, 314, 323
  Ventersburg Road, 371
  Ventersdorp, around, 335, 341-343

South Africa (1889-1902) :—*continued*
  Vet River, engagement, 353
  Vlakfontein, reached, 355
  Volunteer Service Companies, 325, 328, 330, 334, 346, 347, 388-391, 400
  Vryburg, column from, 344
  War, declaration of, 304
  Waterval Drift, 349
  Wepener, relief of, 370
  Winburg, near, 371
  Zand River, crossing, 371
  Zeerust, at, 333-341
South Africa (1904), 373
Spain, Eastern, operations in (1812-1814), 202-213
Special Reserve, the, 380-383
Straton, Lieut.-Col. J. M., 158, 164-168, 171, 295, 296
Strike duty, 360, 361
Stuart, Maj.-Gen. Sir J., 190-201
Subscriptions, voluntary, 181
"Sultana," voyage of the, 272-274

T

Tarifa, defence of, 82, 86-92
Territorial Force, the, 391-392, 400
Territorial system, initiated, 66-67
Territorial system, introduced, 169-171, 285
Territorial title, 66-67, 170, 175, 248
Ticonderoga, Fort, 53-59, 64, 65
Tidworth, at, 359-362
Tortoise, snuff-box, 199-200

U

Underwood, Lieut. J. P. D., 373
Uniform, 167-171, 295

V

Valenciennes, march to, 216
Victoria, H.M. Queen :
  death of, 338
  guard-of-honour to, 253
  inspected by, 161
  Jubilee, Diamond, 369, 377, 400
  message from, 313
Victoria Cross awarded to Pte. J. McDermond, 151
"Victory," H.M.S., embarked in, 231
Vigo, Sir J. Moore's decision, 227-228
Villebois, de, Mareuil, funeral, 325, 389
Vittoria, Battle of, 97-102

INDEX

Vizagapatam, off, the troopship "Alfred," 254–256
Volunteers, the, 384–391, 393–400
  1st Battalion, 388–391
  2nd Battalion, 399–400
  Bolton, the, 393–399
  Colours, the, 385, 387, 394
  Officers, first, 385, 394, 396–399
  Preston, the, 384–386
  South Africa (1900–1902), service in, 325, 328, 330, 334, 346, 347, 388–391, 400
    Battle-honour awarded, 391
    First Service Company, 325–330, 334, 389, 391
    Second Service Company, 346, 390, 391
    Third Service Company, 347, 391
  Uniform, 385, 395, 396, 398, 399

W

Walcheren expedition (1809), 233–242
  Cadzand, Island of, 235–239
  casualties, regimental, 239, 242
  dykes, sea, cutting of, 239
  evacuation, decided upon, 241
  Flushing, invested, 238
  landing, difficulties of, 236
  Middelburg, at, 240
  Scheldt, arrival of fleet, 235, 239
  sickness of troops, 239–241
  situation, political, 233
  strength of Battalion, 234, 242
  Veere, attack on, 238
  Zoutburg, skirmish at, 238
War :
  Afghan, Second, 278–285
  American Independence, 41–65
  Buenos Ayres, attack on, 70, 74–79
  Burma, First, 128–134
  Canada, operations against Fenians, 162–163
  Crimean, 139–159
  Great, outbreak of, 364, 374, 383, 392, 400
  India, North-West Frontier, 266–270
  Indian Mutiny, 257–266
  Louisburg, siege of, 14, 18–25
  Maida, Battle of, 192–199, 202, 232
  Monte Video, storming of, 70–74, 79

War—*continued*
  Netherlands, service in, 242–244
  Peninsular, 81–116, 202–213, 217–232
  Persian Gulf, expeditions, 117–120, 124–126
  Pindari, 121–123
  Prestonpans, Battle of, 7–10
  Quebec, 26–35
  Rebellion, 1745, Jacobite, 4–12
  South African, 303–357, 370–372, 388–391, 400
  Walcheren, expedition, 233–242
  Waterloo, campaign, 244
Waterhouse, Lieut.-Col., death of, 246
Waterloo, Battle of, 244
  Brussels, guard duty at, 243–244
Wellington, Duke of, funeral, 138, 254
Wells, Lieut. J. B., 306, 322, 342
West Indies, 137, 164, 177–179, 250–252
  Antigua, 137, 251
  Barbados, 137, 164, 177, 250
  Grenada, 251
  San Domingo, 177–179
  St. Kitts, 137
  St. Vincent, 164
  Tobago, 251–252
  Trinidad, 164, 251
Whitelocke, Lieut.-Gen., 73–80
Wight, Isle of, stationed, 135–136
Wilson-Patten, Ensign J., 291–292, 387
Winmarleigh, Col. Lord, 291, 294, 376
Wolfe, Gen. J., 20–34
  death of, 34
Wynyard's Marines, 1

X

Xixona, occupied, 206
Xosas, the, ambushed by, 183
Xucar River, 207–209

Y

Yorke Scarlett, Maj.-Gen. Sir J., 161
Yusafzais, operations against, 266–267

Z

Zhob Valley, the, 296–298

Printed in Great Britain by
Butler & Tanner Ltd.,
Frome and London

www.ingramcontent.com/pod-product-compliance
Lightning Source LLC
Chambersburg PA
CBHW060333010526
44117CB00017B/2813